Anonymous

Transactions and Proceedings of the second International Library Conference

Held in London, July 13-16, 1897

Anonymous

Transactions and Proceedings of the second International Library Conference
Held in London, July 13-16, 1897

ISBN/EAN: 9783337188986

Printed in Europe, USA, Canada, Australia, Japan

Cover: Foto ©ninafisch / pixelio.de

More available books at **www.hansebooks.com**

TRANSACTIONS AND PROCEEDINGS
OF
THE SECOND INTERNATIONAL LIBRARY CONFERENCE

TRANSACTIONS AND PROCEEDING

OF THE

SECOND INTERNATIONAL

LIBRARY CONFERENCE

HELD IN LONDON

JULY 13-16, 1897

LONDON
PRINTED FOR MEMBERS OF THE CONFERENCE
1898

PREFACE.

AT the meeting of the Library Association held at Aberdeen in 1893, a resolution was carried, inviting the American Library Association to cross the Atlantic. Much friendly correspondence followed in the course of the next two or three years, and at one time it was hoped that a joint conference of the two Associations might be arranged. At the annual meeting of the Library Association at Buxton in 1896, congratulatory telegrams were exchanged between the two bodies, and finally a great number of American visitors promised to come to London in 1897. The idea of a joint meeting developed into the larger scheme of an International Conference, which it was thought would appropriately mark a date just twenty years after the first International Conference of Librarians in 1877.

A representative Organising Committee was formed, of which a complete list will be found on page 210. The work of making the arrangements for the Conference was divided up among the following committees:—Papers and Discussions (*Chairman*, Dr. Richard Garnett, C.B., LL.D.; *Secretary*, Mr. J. D. Brown), Reception Committee (*Chairman*, Mr. Charles Welch; *Secretary*, Mr. E. M. Borrajo), Exhibition Committee (*Chairman*, Mr. Herbert Jones; *Secretary*, Mr. Thomas Mason), Finance Committee (*Chairman*, Mr. Henry R. Tedder, Honorary Treasurer of the Conference; *Secretary*, Mr. J. W. Knapman). The Honorary Secretary-General of the Conference was Mr. J. Y. W. MacAlister.

The Organising Committee were fortunate in securing Sir John Lubbock as President. A very large number of Vice-Presidents, including distinguished names in science, literature, and art, men of mark of all kinds, and librarians from all countries, added the support of their names. Invitations were issued to the ministers of public instruction of Europe and all the great libraries of the world to send delegates; and no less than fourteen Governments and 313 libraries were represented at the Conference. The total roll of members amounted to 641. About forty of these had attended the first Conference in 1877, whose membership extended to 217 names. The Corporation of the City of London kindly offered a meeting-place in their Council Chamber, and permitted an exhibition of library appliances to be held in the great hall itself. The subjects discussed extended to all departments of library economy. The papers numbered forty-six, and covered important subjects like History and Evolution of Libraries, Libraries and Public Culture, Training of Librarians, Cataloguing and Classification, Choice of Books, Helps to Readers, Library Committees, Library Buildings, Bibliography, and History of Printing. Some departments were very fully treated: for instance, the Progress of Libraries in the British Empire and the United States, the Training of Librarians, Library Co-operation, State Library Associations in the United States, and Library Committees. Special attention was paid to Bibliography.

v

A reference has been made to the members attending the first International Conference in 1877, and a word may be added to indicate the progress since that time. The zeal and enthusiasm shown twenty years before were in no way slackened. The proceedings of the Conference of 1897 showed a further development of professional feeling, an increased fellowship, a higher tone as regards the duties and qualifications of librarians, a more earnest desire to serve the public, and a determination to bring the best books to the very homes of the people and even to young children.

The Conference was in every way a great success. The meetings were well attended, and the quality of the papers and discussions may be seen in the present volume. Every quarter of the world sent representatives—Austria, Belgium, Denmark, France, Germany, Hungary, Italy, Japan, Sweden. Representatives from the libraries and the Governments of the British Colonies, and about seventy visitors from the United States, greatly added to the success of the gathering. While quite international in its character, the Conference was remarkable as showing the advance which has been made in Great Britain and the United States during the last twenty years. This has been largely due to the work of the two Associations. The Conference was an undertaking separate from both bodies, but was planned and carried out by members of the Library Association of the United Kingdom, with the active co-operation of the American Library Association. The English Association having received from the Queen the rarely-bestowed honour of a charter of incorporation, British librarians may now claim to be recognised by the State as belonging to the organised and professional classes. The advantages of this charter to the library profession throughout the empire cannot fail to be great.

The business of the Conference lasted four days—July 13 to 16, 1897. The papers and discussions form the present volume, which also includes an account of the social pleasures of the Conference, a brief catalogue of the exhibition, a financial statement from the Treasurer, a geographical classification of the libraries represented, and a list of the members.

The duty of editing this volume was confided by the Organising Committee to—

    J. D. BROWN, *Secretary of the Papers Committee.*
    RICHARD GARNETT, *Chairman of the Papers Committee.*
    J. Y. W. MACALISTER, *Secretary-General.*
    HENRY R. TEDDER, *Treasurer.*

CONTENTS.

	PAGE
PREFACE	v
INAUGURAL ADDRESS. By the President, the Right Hon. Sir John Lubbock, Bart., M.P., F.R.S.	1
INTRODUCTION OF EUROPEAN PRINTING INTO THE EAST. By Richard Garnett, Keeper of the Printed Books, British Museum	5
SOME TENDENCIES OF MODERN LIBRARIANSHIP. By J. Y. W. MacAlister, Librarian of the Royal Medical and Chirurgical Society, London	9
THE EVOLUTION OF THE PUBLIC LIBRARY. By H. R. Tedder, Secretary and Librarian, The Athenæum, London	13
RELATION OF THE STATE TO THE PUBLIC LIBRARY. By Melvil Dewey, Director of the New York State Library, Albany, U.S.A.	19
LIBRARY AUTHORITIES, THEIR POWERS AND DUTIES, ETC. By Herbert Jones, Librarian, Public Libraries, Kensington, London	23
THE DUTIES OF LIBRARY COMMITTEES. By Harry Rawson, President of the Library Association	27
TRAINING OF LIBRARIANS. By Charles Welch, Librarian, Corporation Library, Guildhall, London	31
SPECIAL TRAINING FOR LIBRARY WORK. By Hannah P. James, Librarian, Osterhout Free Library, Wilkes-Barré, Pa., U.S.A.	34
FEMALE LIBRARY ASSISTANTS AND COMPETITIVE EXAMINATION. By E. R. N. Mathews, Librarian, Public Libraries, Bristol	40
HINDRANCES TO THE TRAINING OF LIBRARIANS. By J. J. Ogle, Librarian, Public Library, Bootle	44
BOOKS AND TEXT-BOOKS: THE LIBRARY AS A FACTOR IN EDUCATION. By F. M. Crunden, Librarian, Public Library, St. Louis, U.S.A.	46
NATIONAL BIOGRAPHY AND NATIONAL BIBLIOGRAPHY. By Sidney Lee, Editor of the "Dictionary of National Biography"	55
THE RELATIONS OF BIBLIOGRAPHY AND CATALOGUING. By Alfred W. Pollard, Hon. Secretary of the Bibliographical Society	63
THE ALPHABETICAL AND CLASSIFIED FORMS OF CATALOGUES COMPARED. By F. T. Barrett, Librarian, Mitchell Library, Glasgow	67

CONTENTS

	PAGE
ON THE AIDS LENT BY PUBLIC BODIES TO THE ART OF PRINTING IN THE EARLY DAYS OF TYPOGRAPHY. By C. Dziatzko, University Library, Göttingen, Germany	72
FREEDOM IN PUBLIC LIBRARIES. By Wm. H. Brett, President of the American Library Association	79
THE EXPANSIVE CLASSIFICATION. By Charles A. Cutter, Librarian, Forbes Library, Northampton, Mass., U.S.A.	84
CLASSIFICATION IN PUBLIC LIBRARIES. By A. W. Robertson, Librarian, Public Library, Aberdeen	89
LIBRARY WORK IN NEW SOUTH WALES. By H. C. L. Anderson, Librarian, Public Library of New South Wales, Sydney	93
THE HISTORY AND CATALOGUING OF THE NATIONAL ART LIBRARY. By W. H. J. Weale, Librarian, National Art Library, South Kensington Museum, London	97
REMINISCENCES OF LIBRARY WORK IN LIVERPOOL DURING FORTY YEARS. By P. Cowell, Librarian, Public Libraries, Liverpool	99
PUBLIC LIBRARY ARCHITECTURE FROM THE LIBRARIAN'S STANDPOINT. By F. J. Burgoyne, Librarian, Public Libraries, Lambeth, London	103
LIBRARY ARCHITECTURE FROM THE ARCHITECT'S STANDPOINT. By Beresford Pite, F.R.I.B.A., London	106
BOOKS THAT CHILDREN LIKE. By Caroline M. Hewins, Librarian, Public Library, Hartford, Conn., U.S.A.	111
OUR YOUNGEST READERS. By J. C. Dana, Public Library, Denver, Colorado, U.S.A.	118
THE ORGANISATION OF CO-OPERATIVE WORK AMONG PUBLIC LIBRARIES. By J. N. Larned, late Librarian, Buffalo Library, Buffalo, N.Y., U.S.A.	120
CO-OPERATION IN A CATALOGUE OF PERIODICAL PUBLICATIONS. By H. H. Langton, Librarian, University of Toronto, Canada	122
PRINTED CARD-CATALOGUES. By C. W. Andrews, Librarian, John Crerar Library, Chicago, U.S.A.	126
LOCAL LIBRARY ASSOCIATIONS IN THE UNITED STATES. By Herbert Putnam, Librarian, Public Library, Boston, Mass., U.S.A.	129
THE PUBLIC LIBRARIES OF THE NORTHERN STATES OF EUROPE. By A. S. Steenberg, Horsens, Denmark	135
AN INDICATOR-CATALOGUE CHARGING SYSTEM. By Jacob Schwartz, Librarian, Free Library of the General Society of Mechanics, etc., New York, U.S.A.	142
A HINT IN CATALOGUING. By F. Blake Crofton, Librarian, Legislative Library, Halifax, Nova Scotia	146
THEORETICAL AND PRACTICAL BIBLIOGRAPHY. By E. A. Petherick, London	148
BIBLIOGRAPHICAL ENDEAVOURS IN AMERICA. By R. R. Bowker, Publisher, New York, U.S.A.	150
DESCRIPTION OF IMPORTANT LIBRARIES IN MONTREAL, ETC. By C. H. Gould, Librarian, McGill University, Montreal, Canada	154
LIBRARIES THE PRIMARY FACTOR IN HUMAN EVOLUTION. By E. C. Richardson, Librarian, Princeton University, New Jersey, U.S.A.	158

CONTENTS

	PAGE
COUNTING AND TIME-RECORDING. By John Thorburn, Librarian, Geological Survey of Canada, Ottawa	160
THE APPRAISAL OF LITERATURE. By George Iles, New York, U.S.A.	166
LIBRARY WORK IN JAMAICA. By Frank Cundall, Librarian, Institute of Jamaica, Kingston, Jamaica	173
EDUCATION AND LIBRARIES OF THE CAPE OF GOOD HOPE. By H. C. V. Leibbrandt, Keeper of the Archives of the Cape of Good Hope, etc.	179
REGISTRATION OF COLONIAL PUBLICATIONS. By J. R. G. Adams, Public Library of South Australia, Adelaide	194
LIBRARY OF THE UNIVERSITY OF SYDNEY. By H. E. Barff	197
PUBLIC LIBRARIES IN NEW ZEALAND. By Thomas W. Rowe	199
AUCKLAND FREE PUBLIC LIBRARY. By Edward Shillington	201
LIBRARY FACILITIES OF SCIENTIFIC INVESTIGATORS IN MELBOURNE. By E. F. J. Love	204
THE AUSTRALIAN MUSEUM LIBRARY. By Sutherland Sinclair	207
GENERAL PROGRAMME	209
PROCEEDINGS AND DISCUSSIONS OF THE CONFERENCE	227
BRIEF ACCOUNT OF THE SOCIAL PROCEEDINGS. By E. M. Borrajo	251
CATALOGUE OF THE EXHIBITION OF LIBRARY APPLIANCES HELD IN THE GUILDHALL	255
LIST OF (641) MEMBERS OF THE CONFERENCE	259
LIST OF (313) LIBRARIES AND (14) GOVERNMENTS REPRESENTED	273
FINANCIAL STATEMENT. By Henry R. Tedder	277
INDEX. By Miss E. Hetherington	281

INAUGURAL ADDRESS.

IFE is a succession of surprises, and I am full of astonishment at finding myself President of this Congress.

However, I will not waste any time in making excuses.

Besides, I am sure that you will wish me at once to thank the Lord Mayor for his kindly welcome and for all he has done to promote the success of the Conference.

The Library Association is to be congratulated at meeting in the Guildhall. One of my predecessors, speaking in the far north, indeed remarked that, while no doubt possessing many attractions, "Meetings in London, I may say for the information of our northern friends, labour under a serious defect as compared with Aberdeen and other more favoured places—a deficiency in the accessories of sight-seeing and hospitality."

I confess I was surprised that anyone should describe London as devoid of objects of interest; and certainly no one who looks at our programme could complain of any want of hospitality.

We meet indeed under favourable auspices, and I fully hope you will have a good meeting.

The existence of this Congress is an indirect result of an Act passed by a private Member of Parliament, Mr. Ewart, in the year 1850.

We often hear arguments in favour of leaving the time of the House of Commons mainly to Government, on the ground that comparatively little legislative work has been accomplished by private members.

No doubt Government pass most of the contentious political Bills, but, having regard to the time at their disposal, in social measures private members have certainly done good service.

The Public Libraries Act is a striking example. It has been adopted by some three hundred and fifty places containing nearly half our people. Moreover, the progress has been remarkable. It was passed in 1850, and soon adopted by several places. From 1857 to 1866 it was adopted by fifteen localities, from 1867 to 1876 by forty-five, from 1877 to 1886 by sixty-two, from 1887 to 1896 by no less than 190!

In London the recent progress has been even more remarkable. From 1850 to 1866 only one public library was established, and Westminster has the honour of taking the lead; from 1867 to 1876 not one, from 1876 to 1886 only two, from 1887 to 1896 no less than thirty-two.

These libraries now contain 5,000,000 volumes; the annual issues amount to 27,000,000, and the attendances to 60,000,000.

Five millions of volumes sounds enormous, but after all, in proportion to the population, it is not large.

Passing to the Colonies, Australia has 844 public libraries, with 1,400,000 volumes; New Zealand 298, with 330,000; South Africa about 100, with 300,000. In Canada the public libraries contain over 1,500,000 volumes.

The United States possessed in 1890 1686 public libraries, containing 13,800,000 volumes.

In 1891 the United States had, according to the Government statistics, 3804 public and school libraries, containing 26,896,537 vols.; in 1896, according to the last official statistics, it had 4026 libraries and 33,051,872 vols.

These numbers, however, are hardly comparable with ours. They include in some cases college and law libraries. Moreover, we have many public libraries which are not included in the above numbers. The British Museum alone contains 2,000,000 volumes.

Those who doubt the advantage of public libraries generally base their argument on the assertion that an immense preponderance of the books read are novels. But there is one consideration with reference to this which they seem to overlook. Suppose that 50, 60, or even 70 per cent. of the books read are novels. Still, it must be remembered that a book of poems, and even more a work of science, will take much longer to read than a novel. We all run through a novel in a few hours; a work of science takes days, or even weeks; so that, even taking the facts as stated, the time devoted to books of fiction would be much less than to solid works.

Moreover, many novels are not only amusing and refreshing, but also instructive. A great critic (Mr. H. D. Traill) has recently told us that the average novel had much improved; the "workmanship is so respectable, and in some cases so excellent, that the reviewer has absolutely to read them through before he can pronounce judgment."

We are, however, all agreed that, useful as public libraries are, they are not so useful as they might be.

There is indeed the preliminary question, "What is a book?" The Chancellor of the Exchequer has told us that he used to think he knew, but that the *Postal Guide* devotes two pages and a half of close print to a definition; and after reading them he found he was quite mistaken and could not understand what a "book" really is, so that the definition must be even more difficult than finance or bimetallism.

No doubt the wise choice of books is becoming more and more difficult. This has been slowly dawning on us. We are becoming more and more in need of lists and indexes.

The National Home Reading Union has done and is doing excellent service in assisting our countrymen and countrywomen to what to read, and how to read.

Moreover, the question is not only what to read, but where to find it. We not only want books to be in existence, but get-at-able.

A recent writer has referred to the treasures of ancient lore in Egyptian papyri, which are now scattered in large numbers through the museums of Europe,

where, for want of catalogues and descriptions, they lie well-nigh as profoundly buried as if they were in their original tombs. Many authors bury their own creations by misleading titles, or by bringing together incongruous subjects, which lead to unfortunate results, like other ill-assorted marriages.

A friend of mine recently mentioned a remarkable case in point.

"In the year 1850, Dr. Mitchell, the Director of the Observatory of Cincinnati, which was then the only astronomical observatory in the United States, brought out a perfectly beautiful book, and it came over here for sale in the ordinary way. It was called *The Planetary and Stellar Worlds*. A wise friend of mine afterwards happened to see the publisher of the book, who complained bitterly about it, and told him that he had not sold a single copy. My friend said, 'Well, you have killed the book by its title. Why not call it *The Orbs of Heaven*'?" That was acted upon, and I am told that six thousand copies were sold in a month.

The result of bringing together incongruous subjects is also unfortunate, and may be compared to the custom said to have formerly existed in Mexico, of chaining together the criminal and witness to await the trial, with the result that when the day arrived neither of them were forthcoming.

Mr. Campbell, of the British Museum, in his interesting work on Bibliography, has well said that "we continue to build libraries and to accumulate books, but we have not paid sufficient attention to making books still more accessible for research. Our attention has been too exclusively concentrated on collections in particular libraries, to the neglect of the great annual national collection pouring from the press."

He mentions, as offering special difficulties, the publications issued by Governments and by scientific societies.

As regards Governments, I believe that our own has set a good example. In saying this I do not rely on any English authority, which might be prejudiced. I may quote an American writer (E. H. Walworth) in an article on "The Value of National Archives," who has paid us the compliment of stating that "Perhaps no nation has been more careful than England in the preservation of her archives, and perhaps no nation has been more careless in this direction than the United States."

This is, however, no longer true of the United States Government, which now issues excellent monthly catalogues. India also has for some time taken much pains to make her publications as available as possible.

The Royal Colonial Institute has recently taken an important step in adopting and forwarding to every Colonial Government a resolution "that the Colonial Governments be respectfully invited to issue—through the medium of their Government Gazettes or otherwise—registers containing entries of all publications within given periods, and also all other locally published works, with their full titles, so as to furnish for general information complete records of the literature of each colony." To judge from the replies that have been received, some at anyrate of our colonies are doing little justice to their own publications.

Turning to the scientific societies, our own Royal Society has accomplished a great and most useful work in its catalogue of scientific papers, contained in nine thick quarto volumes. These have been—and here I speak from personal experience—extremely useful. The Society is, moreover, organising a catalogue which aims at completeness, and is intended to contain the titles of scientific publications, whether appearing in periodicals or independently. In such a catalogue the titles of scientific publications should be arranged not only according to authors' names but also according to subject-matter, the text of each paper, and not the title only, being consulted for the latter purpose. And the value of the catalogue would be greatly enhanced by a rapid periodical issue, and by publication in such a form that the portion which pertains to any particular branch of science might be obtained separately.

It is needless to say that the preparation and publication of such a complete catalogue is far beyond the power and means of any single society.

Led by the above considerations, the President and Council of the Royal Society have appointed a committee to inquire into and report upon the feasibility of such a catalogue being compiled through international co-operation.

There is one other catalogue to which I should like to refer to and to express my gratitude, namely, the Classified Index of the London Library. Here are given the names of the principal authors who have written on each subject; and the assistance there given to the student is invaluable.

To every true lover of books it is sad to see our countrymen and countrywomen neglecting the great masterpieces of science and literature, and wasting their time over "books that are no books," merely because they are new—in many cases, to use Ruskin's words, "fresh from the fount of folly."

But, ladies and gentlemen, I feel myself intruding on subjects with which you are much more competent to deal.

There is, however, one point of view in which I yield to no one present, and that is the love for and gratitude to books.

"Through the walls of time and sight
Doors they are to the Infinite."

Sir G. Grey, when Governor of the Cape, was anxious to obtain some remarkable manuscripts from N.E. Africa.

Some years after, an old Arab gentleman, Mohamed Naser Eben, boarded an English man-of-war at Mombasa, and delivered a packet addressed to Sir George, and containing some manuscripts for which he declined any payment, which he spoke of as "full of golden leaves," and with the following letter :—

"DEAR FRIEND,—If we see a garden surrounded by a wall, and its gate is locked, I do not think we can judge as rightly about its fruits—whether they are sweet and delicious or not—except we enter into it and taste its different varieties. So it is with books: unless you understand and read them with care, you cannot realise their beauty and sweetness."

Ascham, in *The Schoolmaster*, tells a touching story of his last visit to Lady Jane Grey. He found her sitting in an oriel window reading Plato's beautiful account of the death of Socrates. Her father and mother were hunting in the park, the hounds were in full cry, and their voices came in through the open window. He expressed his surprise that she had not joined them. But, said she, "I wist that all their pleasure in the park is but a shadow to that I find in Plato."

I assure you that we in the city are not so immersed in business but what we can many of us re-echo the words of an old English song—

> "Oh for a book and a shadie nooke,
> Eyther in doore or out;
> With the grene leaves whispering overhead,
> Or the street cryes all about;
> Where I may rende all my ease,
> Both of the newe and old;
> For a jollie goode booke whereon to look,
> Is better to me than gold."

Gentlemen, we welcome you here in the old City of London. We hope you will have a pleasant meeting, and are sure that we shall benefit by your deliberations.

We thank you for your valuable assistance in the search for what we want, and for your wise guidance in our choice, and congratulate you on your noble privilege of presiding over these stores of concentrated interest and delight.

Sir John Lubbock.

INTRODUCTION OF EUROPEAN PRINTING INTO THE EAST.

PEAKING to-night as President of the Bibliographical Society, I have found it necessary to select some point of bibliography as the subject of my discourse. The subjects which profitably occupy the ordinary meetings of the Society would not be appropriate to a numerous and various assemblage like the present. Now that Internationalism and Imperialism are in the air, and that the thoughts of the Queen's home-bred subjects have perforce been carried far beyond the precincts of their native isles, I have deemed that interest might be felt in a brief retrospect of the first steps by which the most intellectually valuable of all the arts was transplanted from Europe to the other quarters of the Old World. American typography I leave to our visitors, better qualified to treat it. I prefer no claim to originality, but rather rest the utility of my paper upon the advantage of bringing to one focus a number of facts hitherto scattered through a number of books, and by consequence but partially known.

I have often thought that our reunion with our Aryan brethren of Hindostan, when, after millenniums of separation, we Europeans returned to them in the character of travellers, merchants, and missionaries, may be compared to the meeting of Jacob and Esau. As of old, the younger brother had been the more prosperous. We brought them gifts more precious than any we could receive from them, and among these was the art of printing. But it was out of our power to bestow such a boon upon the more numerous yellow race, for it already possessed it. China, and Korea too, had been acquainted with printing for centuries, and not merely with block printing, but with movable types. These, however, were rarely employed, in consequence, I imagine, of the great extent and complexity of the Chinese alphabet, or rather syllabarium; and it no more entered into the head of a Chinese to print a foreign language than it occurred to a Greek of the Roman Empire to translate a Latin book. Amazing consequences would have followed if China would but have reformed her alphabet and communicated her art to her neighbours. Had it but found its way to Constantinople by the tenth century, we should have preserved most of that lost classical literature for which, with much to encourage and much to dispirit, we are now sifting the dust of Egyptian catacombs. It does indeed appear from recent discoveries among the papyri of Archduke Rainier that the Saracens of Egypt had grasped the principle of block printing in the tenth century, probably from intercourse with China. But this does but increase the wonder that they should have merely struck off a few insignificant documents and carried the idea no further.

Even when at length the art of printing became known in Europe, its progress was for some time marvellously slow. For several years its practice was confined to a single city, and this would probably have continued still longer but for civil dissensions, which drove the printers abroad. We need not be surprised, then, that it should have been a hundred and six years after Gutenberg before any book proceeded from a European press upon the continent of Asia; or, if we date from the voyage of Vasco da Gama, now exactly four hundred years ago, we shall see that sixty-four years, or two generations, elapsed before the Portuguese conquerors gave a printing press to India. There was probably but little need for typography either in the military or the civil service; but in process of time another interest asserted

5

itself—the missionary. We shall find that the larger number of Spanish and Portuguese books printed abroad, whether in America or the East, were designed for the conversion and instruction of the natives.

This was not, however, precisely the case with the first book printed in India, or printed by Europeans in any part of the Old World outside of Europe, although it was a religious book, *The Spiritual Compendium of the Christian Life*, by Gaspar de Leão, first Archbishop of Goa; Goa, 1561. The author had come out as Archbishop in 1560, and this book appears to be either the full or the abridged sermons preached by him in the visitation of his diocese in that year. It is much to be hoped that a book so memorable for the circumstances of its publication may be still extant; but Silva, in his Portuguese Bibliographical Dictionary, does not, as he usually does when he can, intimate the existence of a copy in the National Library of Lisbon or elsewhere; nor does Martim Antonio Fernandes allude to the existence of it, or any other of Archbishop Leão's writings at Goa, in the sermon which he preached on the occasion of the translation of his remains in 1864. Archbishop Leão printed two other books at Goa—a tract against the Jews, and another against the Mahometans; but these were posterior to the second Goa book, a copy of which is in the British Museum—the *Dialogues on Indian Simples and Drugs*, by Garcia da Horta, printed at Goa in 1563. This is a work of great merit, said to contain the first account of Asiatic cholera. It is also remarkable as the first book in which any production of Camoens was given to the world; for, although the Lusian bard had written much, he had published nothing previous to the appearance of a complimentary copy of verses to da Horta, prefixed to this book. The Museum is, no doubt, indebted for its copy of this very rare work to its founder, Sir Hans Sloane, for whom it would have much interest. A Latin translation went through many editions, and the original was reprinted in 1872.

Thirteen books are enumerated by Ribeiro dos Sanctos as having been published at Goa up to 1655, and there were probably others of a merely ephemeral character. The most interesting are a *Life of St. Peter* in Marathi, by Estevão da Cruz, 1634—if not a translation, perhaps the first book, other than a catechism, written by a European in an Indian vernacular; and the record of the proclamation of John IV. in 1641, when Portugal recovered her independence. This book, which is in the British Museum, indicates the lowest stage of typographical debasement, but is interesting from its patriotic feeling.

Two Tamil books are said to have been printed by the Jesuits in 1577 and 1598 respectively, at Ambalakata, a place on the Malabar coast, probably now ruined, or known by some other name.

Before leaving India, I may mention a remarkable circumstance, not, so far as I know, hitherto recorded in typographical history. It appears from that marvellously interesting book, too soon interrupted, Mr. Saintsbury's *Calendar of the Papers of the East India Company*, that in 1624 the Shah of Persia "having an earnest desire to bring into his country the art of printing," was "very importunate" with the agents of the Company at Ispahan, "to write for men skilful in the science, whom he promises to maintain at his own charge." It does not appear that the Company, who were then meditating the relinquishment of their Persian branch as unprofitable, took any steps to fulfil the Shah's wishes, and of course the casting of Oriental types in Persia, or their transport thither, would have been very difficult undertakings. But the desire to endow Persia with a printing press nevertheless reflects the highest honour upon the Shah, who was no less famous a person than Abbas the Great.

From India we pass to China; and here an important discovery has been made of late years. It has until very lately been universally believed that the first book printed by Europeans in China was by Eduardus de Sande, *De Missione legatorum Japonensium ad Romanam Curiam*, Macao, 1590. My friend, Señor José T. Medina, the Hercules and Lynceus of South American bibliographers, has, however, found from the book itself that this cannot be the case, for the writer of the preliminary address, Alexander Valignanus, states that he has himself previously published at the same place a book by Joannes Bonifacius, *De honesta puerorum institutione*. This must have appeared in 1589, if not sooner, and is undoubtedly the first book printed by Europeans in China. Unfortunately it cannot be produced, for it is not to be found. A copy may still be lurking in some ancient library, and great will be his merit who brings it to light. It may be mentioned that although the book *De Missione* principally relates to Europe, and was compiled under the fiction of imaginary conversations with the Japanese ambassadors (who really had visited Europe and returned) for the information of the Japanese pupils of the Jesuits, one chapter is an account of China for the benefit of European readers. It is full of interest; and although its particulars have long become common property, it would be well worth translating as a contemporary account. Sande's book, it is needless to state, is of exceeding rarity. It may be seen in a show-case in the King's Library at the British Museum, side by side with the very oldest South American books.

European publications in China since 1590 are numerous, and have been enumerated by that distinguished Sinologue, M. Henri Cordier, in his epoch-making bibliography. Time, however, compels me to pass to Japan, where the subject has received most important illustration from the labours of the present English minister to that country, Sir Ernest Mason Satow. Sir Ernest found examples of the use of movable types in Japan about 1598, and endeavoured to ascertain whether the art had been imported from Korea, where, as I have already stated, it existed at a much earlier period, or whether it was taught to the Japanese by the Jesuit missionaries. The point remains undecided; but Sir Ernest's researches have acquainted him with fourteen books printed by the missionaries between 1591 and 1605—some in Latin, some in Japanese, some in both languages. Some are religious in character, others philological. One, exceptionally, is a translation into Japanese of *Æsop's Fables*, thus curiously restored to the East, whence they originally came. Sir Ernest, himself a Japanese scholar, has given a minute account of all, with the aid of numerous facsimiles. All, of course, are of the greatest rarity, and chiefly to be found in the public libraries of London, Paris, Lisbon, Oxford, Leyden, and Rome, or in the collection of the Earl of Crawford. Sir Ernest Satow mentions, in an appendix, others which have been stated to exist, but have not been recovered. Some of these, it is probable, were merely manuscripts. It may be added that the engraved frontispieces of these books, engraved by natives under European direction, evince much talent, and that the same is the case with similar work subsequently executed in South America and the Philippines.

The extirpation of Christianity in Japan destroyed European printing in that country; but books relating to Japan, chiefly acts of Japanese martyrs, continued for some time to be produced at Manila, the capital of the Philippines. The history of Manila printing is thoroughly investigated in the classical work of Señor Medina, whom I have already named as the discoverer of the real beginning of printing at Macao. It seems probable that the art was directly imported into Manila from the latter city. Two books—one in Spanish and Tagala, the other in Chinese—appear as printed in 1593, then follows a gap of nine years, after which publications begin to be tolerably frequent, and altogether a hundred and twelve are enumerated up to the end of the seventeenth century. A large proportion are in the vernacular languages. It is remarkable that the Caxton of the Philippines was a Chinese convert, whose celestial origin is disguised under the name of Juan de Vera. This fact is only known by the testimony of a Dominican, since it is another remarkable circumstance and peculiar to the Philippines, that for a very long time the name of no private individual appears as that of a printer, the imprint being always that of some religious or educational institution.

One other important city in the Eastern Archipelago possessed printing at an early date. This was Batavia. The Museum possesses treaties with native princes printed there in 1668, and these were probably not the first. A printed book also is referred to the same year.

Now, like Scipio, we must carry the war into Africa. As might be expected in the Dark Continent, the appearance of the first African printed book is a matter of some obscurity; not that the statements respecting time and place and authorship are not precise, but because it has hitherto been impossible to verify them. Nicolas Antonio, in his *Bibliotheca Hispanica*, distinctly mentions *Theses rethoricæ, varia eruditione refertæ*, by Antonio Macedo, a celebrated Portuguese Jesuit, who is said to have had a hand in the conversion of Queen Christina of Sweden, as printed at Funchal in Madeira in 1637. I cannot find that this book has ever come to light, or that any other early production of the

Funchal press has been recorded, though one would think that such must have existed. I need not say that the first African book would be a treasure almost rivalling the volume with which Mexico initiated American typography in 1539, or the Goa and Macao books whose probable disappearance we have been lamenting. There is room for error; Antonio hardly appears to have himself seen the book. But, on the other hand, there may well be copies in the possession of persons to whom the imprint Funchal suggests nothing. A Macao or Manila book at once announces itself as something extraordinary by the peculiarity of its paper, but a book printed at Madeira would probably be indistinguishable in general appearance from contemporary productions on the Portuguese mainland, whose appearance at the period was fully in keeping with the then fallen fortunes of the nation. If, therefore, the book ever existed, I shall not despair of its being found, most probably at Lisbon, Funchal, or Rome. If its existence is mythical, the first African printed book would probably be the Catechism or Baptism in the Angola language by Francisco Pacconio, executed at Loanda, the capital of the Portuguese settlements on the West Coast, said to have been printed in 1641, but perhaps only sent out from Lisbon. If actually printed at Loanda, it would be the first book printed on the African mainland, and hence of the highest bibliographical interest. But it may have been confounded with a similar Catechism by the same author, published at Lisbon in 1642. Books were printed at Santa Cruz de Tenerife at least as early as 1754. Port Louis, the capital of Mauritius, followed soon afterwards. Apart from official documents, the first book printed in South Africa is G. F. Grand's *Memoirs of a Gentleman*, Cape Town, 1814, exhibited at the British Museum. To prevent misunderstanding, it may be remarked that the honour due to the first African book has been claimed for a narrative of the capture of the island of Terceira by the Marquis de Santa Cruz in 1583, but it is clear that the date Angra, the capital of the island, is not an imprint, but refers merely to the place where the despatch was written, and that it was printed in Spain.

I am not quite sure whether Australia properly belongs to my subject, but two circumstances of especial interest induce me to include it. One is that the first Australian publication, the official *Sydney Gazette* of 1803, is, I understand, at present a visitor to England in the custody of Mr. Anderson, librarian of the public library at Sydney, who contemplates reproducing it. The other is that what is believed to be the first Australian book, as distinguished from a newspaper or official notification, has been very recently acquired by the British Museum. It is a narrative of the crimes and death of William Howe, the last and worst of the bushrangers of Tasmania, and was printed at Hobart Town in 1817. It was noticed by the *Quarterly Review* so long ago as 1819, when it was prophesied that Australian bibliographers would one day fight for it as fiercely as English collectors contend for Caxton's *Reynard the Fox*. If they do, they must fight with the Sydney Public Library, which, I am informed, has three copies. There is also a copy in the Bodleian.

The subject of the beginning of printing by Europeans in Asia and Africa is one which must gain in interest as printing itself extends. Typography in these countries is as yet but in its infancy, for it has not laid hold of the mass of the people. It seems evident that the cumbrous Oriental alphabets must eventually give way to the simplicity of Roman type, and then one great bar to the intercommunication of ideas among Oriental nations will have ceased to exist. It may be that they will go a step further, and employ a single language for the purposes of general intercourse. So far as we can see at present, this language can hardly be any other than English. Should this come to pass, Lord Beaconsfield's celebrated saying, "England is a great Asiatic power," will prove true in a deeper and wider sense than he intended, and we shall look back with augmented veneration to the labours of the zealous and disinterested men who paved the way for European culture by first bringing the European printing press to the far East.

RICHARD GARNETT.

SOME TENDENCIES OF MODERN LIBRARIANSHIP.

EFORE this Conference is over, we shall have enough of mutual congratulation and of trumpet blowing to hearten us for another twenty years of unappreciated labour, and therefore it will not hurt us much if, before the multitude of smooth things we are to hear, we are reminded of some of the rough things that may be said.

When we compare things as they are now with the conditions existing sixty years ago, we have indeed much to be thankful for.

Even twenty years ago it would have been impossible to have organised such a meeting of library folks as are gathered here under the hospitable roof of the mother of cities. The Conference of 1877 was, for its time, a brilliant success, but it demanded an enormous exercise of energy and dogged hard work on the part of the able men who promoted it—whereas this Conference has organised itself. Our difficulty has been not to get enough together to make a respectable meeting, but to cope with the unexpected numbers that have upset the calculations of even a month ago.

This is a significant fact that speaks for itself, and which, therefore, I need not enlarge upon.

With a few brilliant exceptions of the type of Panizzi, combining sound scholarship with business capacity and organising power,—which are the three essentials of good librarianship,—the average librarian of sixty years ago was one of two kinds, both of them utterly unfitted for present-day needs.

The best was a scholar,—narrow, probably, and pedantic, but still a scholar,—generally of the type that absorbs and gives nothing back. If such a man failed to succeed in one of the learned professions, it was thought to be not only kind to him but to the institution to instal him as a librarian—and in some quiet haven of refuge he would spend the remainder of his days, happy in his surroundings, which he regarded as specially designed for his comfort, and keenly resented the impertinence of any rash reader who dared to suggest that he too had his rights.

It was an extravagant way of endowing a learned failure, and a pension list as long as that of our American cousins would have been sounder economy in the long-run.

The other type is still familiar to many of us: the superior servant past his work but fond of reading, or the old sergeant who had charge of the regimental library, consisting of fifty odd novels and an old army list,—these are still occasionally provided for at the expense of a long-suffering community by the selfish so-called generosity of their friends, who possess local influence.

Only the day before yesterday, on the Calais boat, I was introduced to a world-famed military officer, who, when he understood I had some connection with the L.A., exclaimed, "Why, you're just the man I want! I have been rather anxious about my man of late, old Atkins; you see the old boy with a stoop sheltering behind the funnel. Poor old beggar! quite past his work, but as faithful as a dog; and it has just occurred to me that if you could shove him into some snug library in the country—nice mild climate, etc.—I'd be awfully grateful to you. His one fault is a fondness for reading, and so a library would be just the thing," and so on.

I am too busy just now to look for a place for Atkins, but shall be glad to give his address to any committee man present.

About fifty years ago the movement, which was to change all this, began to be felt.

The people, beginning to feel the effects of the repeal of the Corn Laws, Free Trade, and other ameliorative legislation, finding the struggle for existence a little easier, and that they could enjoy occasional leisure, began to think that they had a right to ask the State to do something more than merely protect life and property; and the earliest library legislation was initiated. It is significant that in the beginning libraries were sought for as means of *recreation*, and the Bills expressly set this forth.

The first libraries were wanted by readers who, having leisure, wanted to *read*, and knew what they wanted.

The occupation of the old type was gone, and the librarian of the earliest public libraries must be a smart business man, with a faculty for organisation, and if mechanical, so much the better. He must arrange his books in such a way that the reader knowing his book should get it in the shortest possible time—and that was all. He need not be a scholar—indeed a scholar had a poor chance, as possibly regarding himself as superior to his masters; and dictation or advice from a *mere librarian* would be resented.

But so great a movement once begun could not stand still, and even the central idea is undergoing a change.

Two things have happened which have combined to change the old library idea. Free and universal education has produced a generation that has learned to read, but has no knowledge of what it should read, and stands waiting for guidance.

Their fathers also have learned that in the public libraries which were created for their recreation they possess a potent teaching agency, which, if wisely used, may, for every son or daughter of the people, realise Carlyle's great ideal of a public library.

They therefore demand three things of their libraries:—

1. That we shall provide wholesome literature for the young, and guide them in their choice.

2. That we shall provide for their elders books both to recreate and to instruct, and that we shall so arrange our catalogues and our libraries that the time of the reader who knows his wants shall be saved, and that he may instantly find what he wants.

3. That we shall, from the stores of our personal knowledge, be able to give to every man that asketh the information he wants, or unerringly to direct him to it.

I believe we can honestly boast that the first two demands are complied with, and on the whole admirably; but can we boast that we satisfy the third demand?

I am afraid not. Why?

When the practical and business-like librarian was first called for, as I have shown, scholarship was not wanted. If it was there (as we know it was, and is—in many places), good and well; but the librarian was given to understand that it was not much appreciated. If he could unostentatiously put it into his catalogues it was welcome, but he must not obtrude it elsewhere. And so it has gradually come to be ignored and almost repudiated, and a librarian who wants to distinguish himself is driven to mechanical inventions, designed to save either the time of himself or his readers.

My critics will tell you that the more time-saving apparatus is used the more time the librarian will have to cultivate his intellect and discourse with his readers on the beauties of Browning or of Byron. But is the time saved by mechanism used in this excellent way? I am afraid not. The taste for such things grows on what it feeds, and the librarian who has invented an appliance for supplying his readers with the books (they would rather not have) by means of an automatic ticket-in-the-slot machine will not be happy, or spend any time in reading Browning, until he has invented one which will, by the touching of a button, shoot the book into the reader's home, and so save for the busy librarian the time lost in opening the library door. Master craftsmen tell us that an excess of time-saving machinery and consequent specialisation of labour deadens the intellects of the workers. Bookbinders tell us that the old craftsman, who through all the stages of stripping, folding, sewing, forwarding, covering, and tooling, finished the entire book, was a more intelligent person than the present-day worker, who does only one of these things.

And so I think we should do well to rest content for a while with our present mechanical achievements, and devote the time thus saved to the polishing up of our own intellectual armoury—in too many cases grown rusty for want of use. If a new machine comes to be wanted very badly, it will be produced; but let us wait for an imperative demand, instead of cogitating how we can, by clipping off the corner of a card, or sticking in a new pin, or even by calling an old spade an agricultural implement, secure fame for ourselves as original inventors.

Akin to mechanicalism, and though loftier in aim almost equally dangerous, is the exaggerated value attached by many to co-operative work. It is no exaggeration to say that the ideal of some librarians is that all cataloguing should be done by a central co-operative board, and that there should be prepared by co-operative labour one gigantic universal catalogue on cards, one gigantic universal index of knowledge, also on cards, and that these cards should be bought at so much per gross by every library according to its stock.

If this could be realised, your catalogue and index would overwhelm you by their unwieldy immensity; the references to John Smith alone, and his achievements in the regions of theology or of crime, would fill the British Museum, and would make it necessary to found a college of John Smith specialism. But it would have another and more deadly effect upon ourselves.

With such a central bureau of bibliology available, a score of consulting experts in library economy could organise and supervise all the libraries in the British Empire in five years, and thereafter committees would find a staff of junior clerks at twenty shillings a week, each quite adequate for all the work of the library. And where should we be?

Another tendency, which was at first wholly good, but now goes too far among a large class of libraries.

As I have pointed out, recreation was a distinct if not a leading object with the early promoters of the movement, and, in consequence, some libraries may have contained an over-proportion of light literature. As the instruction idea gained strength in the minds of the people, this predominance of fiction became a grievance. The tendency of some people being always towards exaggeration, the instruction idea has become with them a sort of religion; and this, like all new religions, has found plenty of new-made priests.

These priests are the librarians who, to please their co-religionists, lose no opportunity of crying out against the deadly thing, fiction.

Here and there I have no doubt there is a librarian the narrowness of whose skull or whose bringing up allows him to be sincere in this, but for the most part I fear it is canting humbug.

Every wholly sane person loves good fiction, and no just person will deny to the poorer public library reader the refreshment and recreation which he himself obtains from this source.

Let us be honest with our public, and assert that the recreation side of our libraries in these days of overstrain and hurry is one of the most important and valuable. Let us not try to cook our fiction issues; let them appear honestly, and remind critics that if they are large the need for them was large, and that you were proud and thankful you were able to supply the need.

One more tendency and I have done. If what I am now going to say be rightly understood, I have nothing to fear; but if my remarks are interpreted narrowly and from a selfish and local point of view, I shall not escape calumny.

All of us would like to see librarianship raised and developed into a profession.

Some of us are fond of calling it so now, but it isn't.

In which of the professions are its members trained and chosen as we are?

The first generation of modern librarians had to be procured ready-made as it were, and it is wonderful what they have achieved; but for the next what are we doing?

The learned professions (to be regarded as one of which is our aspiration) are recruited by men who, after enjoying a liberal education, deliberately, from their own bent or by the advice of their friends, choose a profession, and then begin a special course of training lasting about five years.

Our present plan is to take boys of tender age and merely rudimentary education, whose circumstances compel them to earn something. There is no question with them of choosing librarianship; they want a berth, and scan the advertisements; and whether it be a shop or a library is a matter of indifference if a few shillings can be earned immediately.

One out of a hundred of such boys is perhaps a born librarian—he breathes the atmosphere of books, loves them for their own sake, and with great labour and self-denial he educates himself, and in time becomes a great librarian; and straightway people declare that his method is the only true way to make a librarian. One of the greatest physicians of this century began his career in a druggist's shop, and we all know the history of the distinguished jurist who was proclaimed by the laureate of the Savoy "a good judge too."

But we do not find the learned professions agreed that the training of these gentlemen is the ideal one. Whether we like it or not, as libraries assume their proper place in the national system of education, our masters will demand that librarians shall be scholarly as well as practical; and it would be well for us to lead this tendency rather than to be dragged after it or left out in the cold.

My last word will, I hope, destroy for ever a text which has proved a great comfort to many a so-called practical librarian when pricked by conscience or reproached by the looks or words of disappointed inquirers.

Mark Pattison is quoted more frequently at meetings of librarians than any other author. He wrote in one of his least lucid moments, "The librarian who reads is lost," but until this moment I believe poor Pattison has never been rightly understood. The *s* at the end of *read* was a printer's error. I am certain that Pattison had in mind the great scholars of the past, and lamented their disappearance. He meant to say that the learned librarian of the past had vanished—was lost—perhaps for ever.

Let us find him again.

J. Y. W. MACALISTER.

THE EVOLUTION OF THE PUBLIC LIBRARY.

N that division of Mr. Herbert Spencer's system of synthetic philosophy — *The Principles of Sociology*, now happily completed — there are no more interesting chapters than those devoted to professional institutions, in which the illustrious thinker deals with the physician and surgeon, the dancer and musician, orator and poet, actor and dramatist, biographer, historian and man of letters, man of science and philosopher, judge and lawyer, teacher, architect, sculptor and painter. With his usual logical force, Mr. Spencer shows how each profession has a common origin, and starts from the ruler or priest. In his opinion (§ 722), "No group of institutions illustrates with greater clearness the process of social evolution; and none shows more undeniably how social evolution conforms to the law of evolution at large. The germs out of which the professional agencies arise, forming at first a part of the regulative agency, differentiate from it at the same time that they differentiate from one another; and, while severally being rendered more multiform by the rise of sub-divisions, severally become more coherent within themselves and more definitely marked off. The process parallels completely that by which the parts of an individual organism pass from their initial state of simplicity to their ultimate state of complexity."

It is with the library as an institution and only incidentally with the librarian that I propose to deal, but the same process of development and differentiation will be discerned. Nothing but the most cursory glance at the general history of the subject can be offered, as my object is merely to indicate how a question deeply interesting to us all may be studied in relation to that "multiform and brilliant philosophy of the universe which has taken so deep hold of the science and literature of our time" (Sir J. W. Dawson's *Modern Ideas of Evolution*, 1891. Preface). In obedience to the general law already referred to, we find that the earliest use of inscribed or written signs was to record religious or political transactions, and that the earliest libraries were temples, and the earliest librarians priests. Such collections find a counterpart in modern times among State and governmental archives. At Athens, the State documents were kept in the Temple of the Mother of the Gods. The repository was called the Archeion, and corresponded with the Tabularium at Rome and elsewhere, where the *tabulæ publicæ* were preserved. From an early date the records of the censors and of finance were kept in the treasury of the Temple of Saturn. The annals of the most ancient civilisations known to us—the Accadian, the Assyrian, and the Egyptian — tell of ancient libraries, and even of their classifications, their catalogues, and their librarians. Here and there we hear of libraries like that of Assur-bani-pal and of Rameses I., to which our definition of public might be attached, but, as a rule, those ancient collections, whether of clay tablets, or of inscribed stones, or of papyrus rolls, were essentially of an ecclesiastical or administrative and historical character. Coming to a later period and a more cultivated people, we find public libraries at an early period in Greece. Aulus Gellius is the authority for the statement that Pisistratus was the first to collect books on a large scale in the sixth century B.C., while, in the opinion of Strabo, Aristotle was the first person to collect a library, and it was to him that the Ptolemies owed their taste for book collecting. It would be safe to say that libraries began to multiply through all the cities of Hellas between 500 and 300 B.C., especially private ones, and that the monarchs of the new Greek kingdoms, Egyptian, Syrian, Minor Asian, and elsewhere, simply transferred the practice to their capitals. Each centre of intellectual activity was a nursery of libraries. The scholars and men of science, attracted to Alexandria by the Ptolemies, required books as a necessary part of their equipment, and the public libraries of that city were the most important of the ancient world. Under Ptolemy Philadelphus those institutions were properly organised and arranged in separate buildings. We have the names of the chief librarians at Alexandria during a hundred years, and the first attempts at bibliography were catalogues of their libraries. Ptolemy ordered class-lists to be prepared both of the tragedies and of the comedies in his collections. The librarian Callimachus drew up a catalogue of the principal books, arranged in a hundred and twenty classes. The doleful story of the destruction of the libraries, whether by the Romans, the Saracens, or the Christians, needs only a passing reference.

The kings of Pergamus rivalled the Ptolemies in their encouragement of arts and literature, and collected and endowed great public libraries. We learn from Suidas, that in 221 B.C. Antiochus the Great made the poet and grammarian, Euphorion of Chalcis, his librarian. Most Greek towns seem to have been in possession of libraries by the second and first centuries B.C.

It was not until the last century of the Republic that we hear of libraries at Rome. As might be expected among a military people, the first libraries at Rome were part of the spoils of war, although the collections which fell into the hands of Scipio on the sacking of Carthage (146 B.C.) were only thought worthy of bestowal on the petty African kings. Æmilius Paulus (a rude warrior, who carried the library of the last Macedonian king to Rome), Sulla, and Lucullus, were book collectors not unwilling that others should enjoy their treasures. One of Cæsar's many projects was the endowment of public libraries at Rome. Varro was to collect and arrange the books. He wrote a work on libraries, of which, unfortunately, only a few words remain. Either he or Asinius Pollio was the first to ornament a library with the statues and busts of learned men. To Pollio is due the credit of having first erected a really public library from the spoils of the Illyrian campaign. Augustus founded two famous public libraries, the Octavian and the Palatine. Tiberius, Vespasian, and Domitian deserve our regard as founders of public libraries. The most famous and important of these Imperial foundations was, however, the Ulpian Library, first established in the Forum of Trajan, and afterwards removed to the baths of Diocletian. The great provincial cities possessed their libraries.

It is interesting to inquire what the libraries of the Romans were like. We know that an eastern aspect was usually chosen. The books or rolls were arranged upon the shelves of presses placed against the walls, with additional cases in the middle. In the middle of the eighteenth century a private library was excavated at Herculaneum, containing 1756 MSS. on shelves about six feet high, running round a small room, with a separate central press. The presses in the larger libraries were numbered, and often made of rare woods and richly decorated. A good idea of the general appearance of a Roman public library may be derived from the library of the Vatican, fitted up by Pope Sixtus V., in 1588, with presses, busts, and antique vases.

As the libraries in Rome increased, the librarian, who was usually a slave or a freedman, became a recognised public officer. At first the librarian was generally a man occupied with other duties. The librarian of Augustus was also his physician. Besides special custodians, there was usually one general director of public libraries under the empire.

We have reached a culminating stage in the evolution of libraries. Christian literature, probably for the first time, found a place in a public library when Constantine removed the seat of empire to the Bosphorus. Among his successors, Julian and Theodosius are specially to be honoured as adding to the Imperial collections. We now enter a new era. Concurrently with the spread of Christianity, the formation of libraries became a part of the organisation of the Church. When the Church of Jerusalem was founded in the third century, Bishop Alexander added a collection of books. The most important of these ecclesiastical libraries was that of Cæsarea. We know that Bishop Augustine bequeathed his collection to the Church at Hippo. Other libraries are recorded at Cirta, at Constantinople, and at Rome. The library of St. Peter's at Rome was close to the north limb of the transept. The library founded at Rome by Pope Damasus at the end of the fourth century was housed in the basilica of St. Laurence at Rome. Most of these libraries were probably within the walls of the churches, and largely consisted of MSS. of the sacred writings, liturgical books, and works of devotion. They also contained the *Gesta Martyrum* and *matricula pauperum*, and copies of official correspondence. Many of the basilicas had the apse subdivided into three smaller hemicycles, one of which contained the sacred books (Lanciani, *Ancient Rome*, tr. p. 187). The influence of the Church was hostile to the study of the masterpieces of the ancient world, but not to such an extent as to destroy them. In fact, they continued to be studied for their educational value, and few monastic libraries were without some volumes of the older classics. For centuries after the fall of the Western Empire pure literature at Constantinople fell into evil times; but to trace the fortunes of letters and learning for this period does not belong to our scope. We must not forget Photius and his catalogue of the remains of old Greek literature. There are allusions to libraries in the writings of the Fathers and other early writers, but the real origin of libraries in the Christian world—one may even go so far as to say the real origin of the modern library—began with the Rule of St. Benedict early in the sixth century. In the forty-eighth chapter the monks are ordered to borrow a book apiece from the library and to read it through.

Whenever a Benedictine house arose, books were multiplied and a library established, and as the successive religious orders came into existence there followed an ever-increasing care for books, for their accumulation and safe-keeping. The Cluniacs had a special officer to take charge, and there was provision for what we should call an annual stocktaking. The Carthusians and the Cistercians were the first to allow books to be borrowed by persons outside the convent. This step towards the free library idea was followed by the Augustinians and the Premonstratensians. By the end of the eleventh century it was common for the Benedictines to possess a lending as well as a reference library. The Augustinian rule prescribed the exact kind of book press that was to be used. The Mendicant Friars found books so necessary, that at last, Richard de Bury tells us (with pardonable exaggeration), their libraries excelled all others. There was no special library apartment in the primitive Benedictine house. After books became too numerous to be kept in the church, their first resting-place, they were probably preserved in *armaria*, or chests in the cloister; from *armarium* we have *armarius*, the Benedictine librarian.

No monastic bookcase at present exists in this country, but there is a doubtful example at Bayeux. The *Customs* of the Augustinian priory at Barnwell, written towards the end of the thirteenth century, provide for the lining of the presses "with wood, that the damp of the walls may not moisten or stain the books." The presses had also to be partitioned off, both horizontally and vertically, to prevent the books rubbing one against the other. The volumes were probably placed horizontally on the shelves. In the treasury or spendiment were two classes of books — one accessible to the monks at large, others more securely preserved. A press near the infirmary contained books used by the reader in the refectory (Dom Gasquet, "Mediæval Monastic Libraries," in *The Old English Bible*, 1897, p. 10).

Sometimes there were recesses in the walls of the cloisters, fitted with shelves and closed by a door. In the Cistercian houses these recesses developed into a small windowless room. At Clairvaux, Kirkstall, Fountains, Tintern, Netley, and elsewhere, this small chamber was placed between the chapter-house and the transept of the church. At Meaux in Holderness the books were lodged on shelves against the walls, and even over the doorway, of such a chamber. A great number of the catalogues of the monastic libraries still exist. Many are classified and give shelf marks, each book being marked with the case, shelf, and number, as in modern practice.

By the end of the fifteenth century the larger monasteries were the possessors of many hundreds of volumes, which had to be placed somewhat at random throughout the building. It thus became necessary to devote a particular room for the general custody of the books in addition to the cloister collection, and we find libraries now being specially built at Canterbury, Durham, Citeaux, Clairvaux, and other places. These libraries gradually became less exclusively restricted for use by the monks alone. Learned strangers were admitted, and thus we see a shadowing of the public library of our own day. From early times students were permitted to borrow books from the library of the Benedictine house of St.-Germain-des-Prés at Paris, of which a later foundation owned in 1513 a noble library, erected over the south walk of the cloister. This was greatly enlarged in the seventeenth and eighteenth centuries, and made very accessible to the outside world.

We do not know exactly how these later monastic libraries were fitted up. Mr. J. Willis Clark, whose interesting Rede Lecture on *Libraries in the Mediæval and Renaissance Periods* (Camb. 1894, 12mo, p. 32) is the chief source of information on the subject, is of opinion "that a close analogy may be traced in the fittings of monastic libraries and those of college libraries." The colleges certainly borrowed their library methods from the earlier community. They had an annual giving out and inspection of what might be styled the lending library books, as was the general monastic practice. At the same time the origin of the reference library is to be discovered in the books kept in the library chamber, fastened with chains, for the common use of the Fellows. By the fifteenth century the libraries of all monastic and collegiate bodies were very much alike in arrangement. There was the separate room, with the books placed on their sides on desks or lecterns, and fastened by chains to a horizontal bar above. An example may be seen at Cesena in North Italy, as well as in the Laurentian Library at Florence, designed by Michael Angelo. The Sorbonne Library was similarly fitted up. This system was only suitable to a small collection. As the books accumulated, it became necessary to arrange them in one or two shelves above the desk.

The library of Merton College has been little altered, and is a good illustration of the "type of a mediæval collegiate or monastic library. It is a long narrow room, as all mediæval libraries were, with equidistant windows, and the bookcases stand at right angles to the walls in the spaces between each pair of windows, in front of which is the seat for the reader" (*ib.* p. 41).

In the chaining system usually to be found in this country one end of the chain was attached to the edge of the board, while the other ran along a bar set in front of the shelf on which the volume stood. The fore-edges, not the backs, faced the reader. The bar was kept in place by a system of double locking. Sometimes the seat and the book shelf were combined in one piece of furniture. As books increased, it became necessary to interpose low cases between the high cases, as at St. John's, Cambridge, completed in 1628. Later on, the seat, being no longer necessary, was replaced by a step, as in one of the apartments of the University Library at Cambridge, fitted up after 1649. In the same room may be seen a specimen of the shelf list, which was always placed at the end of each case. The first example of books placed against the walls is to be found in the Escurial Library, erected in 1584. Here is no evidence of chaining, but the fore-edges, and not the backs, are turned outwards, and the desk is represented by a shelf all round the room. The same system was borrowed by Sir Christopher Wren at Trinity College Library in 1695, probably from the Bibliothèque Mazarine at Paris. Although the chains had disappeared as appliances in these new libraries, they continued to be used and to be ordered in bequests in England down to the early part of the eighteenth century. In those old libraries, revolving desks, sometimes elevated by a screw, were common. Richard de Bury refers to a piece of furniture which contained books under a sloping desk, on which the student wrote or read. Sometimes a kind of triple desk for array of books was used.

The cathedral libraries of England were all fashioned after the same system. We have a striking example at Westminster. Of late formation, it shows all the old methods: books against the walls and on cases jutting into the room; the shelf for the chained volumes with slot for the chains to drop; the shelf is hinged to allow access to volumes underneath. The shelf catalogue at the end of each case is represented by the merest survival—an ornamental tablet.

At the end of the seventeenth century we find the form of the public library fixed, as it were, throughout Europe.

I have dwelt somewhat at length on the material aspect of the monastic and collegiate library, first, because it is a form which still survives, and secondly, because it is the remote ancestor of the modern public library The seventeenth century saw the foundation of many famous libraries which still flourish, of which the Bodleian and the Mazarine are monuments of private beneficence. Royal collections grew into great national institutions for the use of scholars. The great universities throughout Europe prided themselves on the possession of large and well-ordered libraries. Law libraries are examples of early specialisation. The library system has again reached a culminating point of development, but it is still merely a part of the apparatus of the professional scholar. The modern type of the popular library cannot be found, except in a few sporadic cases, at a date earlier than the middle of the eighteenth century. The booksellers' libraries, like that of Allan Ramsay at Edinburgh in 1726, were already spread in all large towns. Franklin established the Philadelphia Library Company, "mother of all the subscription libraries in North America," in 1732. Circulating libraries at this time flourish in London, while proprietary libraries are founded at Liverpool, Birmingham, Leeds, and elsewhere. The ecclesiastical basis may again be observed in the French provincial libraries, most of which were founded at the end of the eighteenth century, from the spoils of the monastic collections at the time of the Revolution.

The free library movement in England was, at the outset, educational. Ewart's first Bill, which enabled ratepayers to tax themselves for the establishment of free libraries, was an offshoot of the exertions on behalf of primary and secondary education, which have formed so striking a feature of civilisation in the present century, and which have achieved so much within the last fifty years. The Mechanics' Institutions, which were originally intended as centres of technical instruction, gave a stimulus to the movement. The rapid growth of the rate-supported libraries—institutions peculiar to these islands—is remarkable. Nowhere has library activity been more marked than in London, which ten years ago possessed only one free public library. Here the foundation of libraries has followed the work of the School Board. These libraries have lost their primary educational and didactic features, and have become an active force in introducing and maintaining a love of literature and healthy reading in the very homes of the people, while they offer every facility for the pursuit of severer studies. Within the same period the State and town libraries of the United States have also greatly increased in number, and have reached a very high standard of proficiency, while in no other country have private individuals so abundantly contributed to library endowments. France, Germany, Austria, Italy, Belgium, and other continental countries have similar institutions.

A few words may be devoted to the librarian. We found him in the earliest times a priest or teacher. When books increased, their proper care demanded a special official, and with the further development of libraries came the librarian as we find him at Athens, Rome, and Alexandria. Again, in the Middle Ages, a priest (who is also the cantor in the monastery) is the first librarian. From the fifteenth to the seventeenth century he is a scholar, like Magliabecchi. The French and German writers on library economy in the eighteenth century trained a race of patient bibliographers, and in the nineteenth century we find such splendid examples of the scholar and professional man as Panizzi and Watts. The librarian should not forget what he owes to such writers as Ebert, Petzholdt, Peignot, Namur, and Edwards; for the Library Associations of America and the United Kingdom, both founded about the same time twenty years ago, did not invent the professional librarian, although they may be said to have given him for the first time a formal status. It is not necessary for me to dwell upon the useful work of the two associations, but I may point out how they have followed the same law of differentiation. At the commencement, our homogeneous Library Association occupied the whole field of librarianship, including bibliography. While it has not narrowed its range of activity, it has already given birth to many separate organisations, such as the Bibliographical Society, the Index Society, the Museums Association, the Ex-Libris Society, the Midland, the Mersey District, and other library associations; the Society of Public Librarians, and the Library Assistants' Association. In the United States there are also many town library clubs and State associations, offsprings of the parent society.

The public library is now universally recognised as the real university of the unattached student, and there is every reason to believe that its usefulness will be still further increased. The distinctive feature of the modern system is the facility with which books may be borrowed for home reading. The practice of lending books will probably be still further developed, and may extend to most or to many libraries now exclusively of a reference type. Special collections will probably be endowed for use away from the library. We may conclude that the public spirit which directs these institutions, whether State-supported, rate-supported, or privately endowed, will extend in the direction of liberality as regards the requirements, I will even say the exigencies, of readers. There will be still greater efficiency of organisation, an increase of all mechanical aids and appliances, and especially as regards every kind of catalogue and book-list. Open access to the shelves is a problem of the very near future.

Finally, as to the librarian. I think the public librarian may claim that the qualities which should particularly distinguish him—the large public spirit, the faculty for business and administration, the professional ardour—have permeated the whole sphere of librarianship. It is a subject for congratulation that women find an increasing place among us. Professional skill, based upon systematic training, is now recognised as absolutely indispensable. The librarian of the future, while he will be expected to be a scholar and bibliographer, must add to those general qualifications a thoroughly practical knowledge of all the details of technical librarianship.

My endeavour has been to present to you, however imperfectly, a phase of the history of libraries as a chapter in the history of sociological development, and, in conclusion, I desire to express the conviction that the spirit of the public library in its great work of moral and intellectual improvement, and as an alleviator of some of the sorrows incident to man, is best expressed in the well-known words said to have been inscribed over the door of his library by Rameses I.—for each public library should be "The dispensary of the soul." And may I be permitted once more to remind you, my fellow-librarians, of your remote origin, and at the same time to hope that you will always remember that you are priests of literature.

HENRY R. TEDDER.

RELATION OF THE STATE TO THE PUBLIC LIBRARY.

E have been listening to an admirable account of the development of the library movement from earliest times to the present day, and I venture to believe that when the history of the age in which we live is written, and is looked back upon by those who shall come after, it will be known distinctively as the "Library Age."

Libraries of one sort or another have existed from the beginning of human history, and we are now well into the fifth century since the invention of printing; so that it would seem as if there had been abundant time for library development. But so great an institution as the modern library is of slow growth. It has taken a thousand years to develop our school system from university down to kindergarten. The public library is much more rapidly going through corresponding stages in order to come to its own. The original library was a reservoir, getting in and keeping safely, a storehouse for posterity. That was and is a great function, for which I have profound respect. Then, after many centuries, came another library epoch, for which we all feel still greater respect. The cistern was made a fountain; giving out was seen to be more important than getting in. The library is no longer merely a passive receptacle, but becomes an aggressive educational force in every community. The reservoir will not become a stagnant pool, for, in its branches and deliveries, the public library has mains and pipes laid through every street, and reaching almost to the door of every householder. And we live now not in the age of the reservoir, but in the age of the fountain. In our zeal and admiration, however, we are apt to forget that there is yet another and even more important stage to reach. In my own city, some time ago, we spent half a million dollars in providing an ample supply of water. But we found that we had really opened convenient communication with the cemetery by water, for the quality of the new and abundant beverage was such that our death-rate steadily rose. The burning question became qualitative, not quantitative, and we are now spending our money on efficient filtration. Of course no library intends to circulate injurious books, but equally no town intends to distribute harmful water. We are concerned more with the results than with the intention. The mortality tables make plain the physical defect, but alas! science has as yet devised no instruments delicate enough to record the greater danger to the individual and the State from poison in the great current, which has come to be a mighty flood, of modern reading matter. The most hopeful, and perhaps the only practicable, method of guarding against this serious danger is through the public library, which must now in the last days of this eventful century recognise the gravity of the new responsibility which it cannot shirk. Before another audience I might dwell at length on what this problem of selection means, but the representative librarians of the world will understand my claim that, wonderful as was the development from the cistern to the fountain, its importance is overshadowed by this great question of excluding the pernicious, which I sum up in the word filtration. This is the great problem of the modern library, and its solution must depend largely on the State.

It is often said that the modern periodicals and newspapers are our greatest danger; but this, of course, is true only of the sensational and other objectionable types. I yield to none in my high appreciation of what the best kind of newspaper may do in its capacity as the strongest ally of the public library and of the public school. I am confident that early in the next century such journals will be recognised as a distinct part of our educational machinery, but I am equally clear that the worst journals, conducted merely as money-making enterprises, and catering to the worst instead of to the best elements of both society and individuals, are the most potent factors for evil, and the greatest enemy which the ideal librarian has to combat in carrying forward his best work. They leave their habitual readers with neither time nor taste for anything above their own low plane. The mind will inevitably rise or fall to the level of its habitual reading, and we apostles and missionaries of the book have no more disheartening outlook than on the readers whose literary atmosphere is limited to the modern sensational newspapers. But the apologists for such reading say that the history of their own times is of more importance to them than any other history: should they not, therefore, become as familiar as possible with it? But when a man, on account of "pressure of business," never looks inside any good book, yet has time to read everything in the newspapers, he is—well, specialising too much in "history." How many men and women there are, who, from year's end to year's end, read nothing but the so-called history of their own times, and who can tell you nothing better than which dog won the last fight! It is a good thing to know the history of our own times; so is a pinch of salt a good thing on one's breakfast potato, but it is not necessary to drink a barrel of sea water each morning in order to get it.

It is highly desirable that I should know the geology and topography of my own State, but I can learn all that is worth knowing without creeping on hands and knees with nose close to the ground over the barnyards and dump heaps of our commonwealth, under the vain delusion that I am exhaustively studying its geology. We must join this battle squarely. The eternal conflict of good and the best with bad and the worst is on. The librarian must be the librarian militant before he can be the librarian triumphant. At the end of another century, when a conference like this is held, our descendants will look back with wonder to find that we have so long been satisfied to leave the control of the all-pervading, all-influencing newspaper in the hands of people who have behind them no motive better than the "almighty dollar." The solution of our difficulties lies in recognition by the State that public libraries are not only good things, but that they are an absolutely necessary part of our educational system. We started with the university, but found that we had to put under it the college. Then we went a step further, and had the academy and high school to prepare for the college; the primary and grammar schools to prepare for the high school; and now we have the kindergarten under the primary school. I am not giving a chronology, but simply pointing out that during these centuries educators have constantly been facing the question of adequate provision for meeting completely the public wants. We have at last reached step by step from the university to the nursery, and have provided a series of schools covering the entire field. Yet, with all this, we have not attained the full system of education that we ought to attain, and every thoughtful person is now asking, "What next?"

Huxley has well said that a system of education which in the early years trains boys and girls to read and then makes no provision for what they shall read during all the rest of their lives, would be as senseless as to teach our children the expert use of the knife, fork, and spoon, and then make no provision for their daily food. The whole history of education has been a series of broadening conceptions. I can recall no case in which the ideal has narrowed, but step by step we have come to a general recognition that education is for poor as well as rich, for plebeian as well as prince, for black and white, for native and foreigner, for brilliant or backward, for women as well as men, for deaf, dumb, and blind, and all defectives and delinquents, who in the old conception were left without the pale. It is almost within our memory that we have come to substantial agreement that the State owes an elementary education to every boy and girl born within its limits, not alone as a right to the child, but as a matter of safety and practical wisdom on the part of the State; and this broader conception is followed closely by a second and still broader one, that every boy and girl is entitled not only to an elementary, but to something also of higher education. I have met no competent student of this subject who dares deny that hereafter the State must recognise that education is not alone for the young, for limited courses, in schools which take all the time of their pupils, but that it must regard adults as well; and not alone for short courses, but all through life—not in our recognised teaching institutions alone, but in that study outside of office or working hours that may be carried on at home. I may sum it up in the one sentence, "Higher education, for adults, at home, through life."

In this home education, which must hereafter be recognised side by side with school education, the library is the great central agent round which study clubs, reading circles, extension teaching, museums, and the other allied agencies must cluster. A statesman solicitous for the future welfare of his country will find his most fruitful field in protecting and guiding the reading of the people. It is what a man reads that shapes his future, which depends, not at once upon the rostrum and the pulpit, but on the book and the newspaper. In education we recognise that the supreme end is the building of character, but many of us have never thought clearly how directly this character-building rests upon the public library. It is reading that begets reflection, reflection begets motive, motive begets action, and action begets habit, and habit begets character; and who here dares question this, that it is not the air nor the water, nor yet the "roast beef of Old England," not its history nor traditions nor laws nor geographic location, but *character*, that has made the Anglo-Saxons, England and her daughters across the seas, the most wonderful people of the earth. It is not brawn, but brain. The dogs and horses might have the physical qualities, but it is the mind and soul, and those elements of true greatness which can best be instilled into a people through the reading of good and great books, that have made a race of which we are justly all so proud. One of the wisest of Frenchmen said of the Franco-Prussian War, when the needle-gun was suggested as the explanation of German victory, "No; it was not the needle-gun, nor the German soldier who held it, nor yet the German schoolmaster who trained the soldier, but it was the German university that made the schoolmaster."

"Knowledge is power," and it is knowledge that has made England and America great. Think of the men who read the poorest newspapers, but know nothing of our best books. Can the State afford to make other things free, and not make free true and useful knowledge as preserved in books? Can the State recognise the necessity for free schools, and fail to provide free access to the best reading in all realms of knowledge?

"Free as air" was the old-time strongest expression. Then men learned how absolutely essential to physical well-being was abundance of water, and our language records in its favourite expression, "free as water," the meaning of the untold millions that civilisation has spent to supply all people freely with this essential. We are learning the greater lesson about the necessity of free knowledge more slowly, because intellectual and spiritual things are not so readily discerned by our mortal eyes, and it takes more time to read even those messages that God has written very large for those who have eyes to see; but the time is not far distant, mark my words, when our speech will again record the general acceptance of a great truth in the common phrase, as "free as knowledge." We should make the public understand the relation of the school system to the library system; that the library is not merely a collection of books, or a storehouse, but an aggressive and active source of education, side by side with the free schools. If the issue came—but, thank God, it never will—between giving up either the library or the free school, I am not sure that I would not choose for the welfare of the country the public library rather than the school. This may sound strange from one who has given his life to education, but I believe that even without our schools nearly every boy and girl would somehow learn to read; and when I soberly consider the influence on lives and characters and on the State, it seems probable that, infinitely valuable as is the work of our free schools, it would be exceeded by what could be done by a system of free public libraries, reaching every boy and girl and man and woman in the community, and so administered as to provide each freely from childhood to the grave with the best reading in every field of interest and activity.

The State, whatever it may or may not do, should recognise the library as being as essential to public welfare as is the school, and it should give it as careful protection from dangers without and within as it gives to institutions like banks and insurance companies. The State should protect the library against unjust laws, improper interference, or pernicious influence of any kind from without. It should guard it also against misconduct, incapacity, or neglect on the part of its trustees, officers, or employees. Beside the direct appropriations for its support, it should grant the most liberal powers for holding property given by individuals for the public benefit, and, above all, should grant entire exemption from taxation. To tax a free public library for doing its beneficent work is theorising gone mad. It is as absurd as for a missionary to refuse admission to his preaching, or for the manager of a theatre in which a fire has just started to shut out every fireman till he had presented the conventional coupon for a reserved seat. The example first set by my own State (New York) in the statute which I had the honour of drawing ought to be followed universally. We created a public libraries department, to devote its entire attention to advancing the best interests of public libraries. It would take the entire morning to sketch to you the various forms of beneficent work which we have found practicable. We help to establish new libraries, reorganise old ones, revise methods, select books, lend single books or entire libraries, grant books or money up to $200 yearly to any library raising an equal sum from local sources, and, by means of correspondence, personal inspection, and steady work in a dozen directions, help every community to get the greatest practical good from the labour and money given to its free library. We have now about five hundred travelling libraries moving about in all parts of the State. The public library is rapidly becoming universal. For the Government not to recognise it in its own organisation is as absurd as it would be to have a standing army and no war department, or schools dotted all about the State and no department of education. Time forbids more than the mere naming of what is needed, but the first great step in summing up the relation of the State to public libraries is the establishment of a public libraries department, in charge of a strong man who appreciates the almost limitless opportunities for usefulness which this new field affords.

Our discussions this morning took such a turn that you could almost hear behind them, like the recurring motive of one of Wagner's operas, the question, "Who shall be greatest among librarians?" In our State Library School I give each year a course of five lectures on the qualifications of a librarian, and point out under a half-hundred different heads the things we should demand in an ideal librarian; but when we have covered the whole field of scholarship and technical knowledge and training, we must confess that overshadowing all are the qualities of the man. To my thinking, a great librarian must have a clear head, a strong hand, and, above all, a great heart. He must have a head as clear as the master in diplomacy; a hand as strong as he who quells the raging mob, or leads great armies on to victory; and a heart as great as he who, to save others, will, if need be, lay down his life. Such shall be greatest among librarians; and, when I look into the future, I am inclined to think that most of the men who will achieve this greatness will be women.

It is well to hold up high ideals, but it would be a sad mistake to underrate the services of the noble men and women who in some, perhaps many, respects fall far short of the standards we lay down, and yet who have done, and are doing well, much of the world's best work. Let us dwell on what has been well done, not on what has been omitted or on what might have been done by other men in other circumstances.

I remember, some twenty-five years ago, reading in George Eliot's *Romola* these words, which we should remember when thinking of any great librarian who of necessity fails in some respects to meet all our ideals "It was the fashion of old, when an ox was led out for sacrifice to Jupiter, to chalk the dark spots and give the offering a false show of unblemished whiteness. Let us fling away the chalk, and boldly say the victim was spotted; but it was not therefore in vain that his mighty heart was laid on the altar of men's highest hopes."

MELVIL DEWEY.

LIBRARY AUTHORITIES, THEIR POWERS AND DUTIES, AS THEY ARE AND AS THEY SHOULD BE.

THE subject upon which I propose to speak to you to-day may not be one of great historical interest, such as that which Mr. Tedder has just dealt with; nor, on the other hand, one of a critical character, such as that which Mr. MacAlister has spoken of; nor, in the third place, does it aspire to the wide philosophical ground into which Mr. Dewey so boldly led you to-day. While I may not aspire to occupy any of these important positions, I will endeavour to speak to you about what I consider — and I think you will agree with me — to be one of the most important matters that can engage the attention of those who are practically concerned with public library administration. It may be that some men will think more of the visible details of their houses than they do of the foundations upon which they rest. But if so, surely such men are not to be commended for their common-sense, and will not expect to find much support in their houses in the future. I am afraid that, to a great extent, too much attention has been devoted to what may be called the ornamentation of the library house in which we live and move and have our being, and not sufficient to the foundation on which the edifice rests. The foundation upon which the public library must stand is acknowledged to be that public library authority which has all the administration in its hands. The public library of this country was of slow and irregular growth, and, as is the case with all institutions in our land, the work of legislation has been carried out bit by bit, spasmodically, by many men, without collaboration, and in the usual happy-go-lucky style which characterises our parliamentary procedure, with, no doubt, beneficial results on the whole, but serving, and indeed not intended to do other than serve, a transitory phase of the existence of libraries in England. The time, I think, has come when the question of the public library authority in this country should be put on a more logical, uniform, and, I venture to think, a more liberal basis. When the Acts were first passed, the authority was for cities and boroughs a committee of the local authority, and for parishes a board of commissioners, the commissioners being appointed by vestries. Thus we had, at the very inception, two utterly different classes of public library authorities placed in power, and who have since that time carried on the work. But not only that: in their powers, duties, responsibilities, and methods of procedure, the two classes of authorities varied in many directions, especially as to the means with which they were endowed for carrying on their work. This may be shown to you, familiar as you must be with its details, by recapitulating a few points, by which it will be seen that the library authorities were allowed all sorts of latitude in one direction, while, at the same time, they were severely limited in the other direction. We find the library authority may, if it be of a city or borough, consist of any number of persons; if of a parish, it must not exceed nine in number. So it is found in one city to consist of thirteen men, of whom four are honorary members. In another case twenty-nine is the number of the board, with no honorary members. In another twenty-three form the committee, and in a similar there are forty-one councillors and twenty non-councillors, making *sixty-one*

in all! for a borough with a library rate of about £1300. In a very similar district the number is seven. In yet another the library authority is an open vestry, consisting of about some hundreds of members. One district with a library rate of little over £1000 has a library committee of thirty-five men. Another with an income of nearly £12,000 has a committee of twelve men. This is not to be surprised at; the fact is, the legislation that governed the matter was so inconsequent and careless that no uniformity was probable. Some local boards, you will find from their reports, take the trouble to appoint men of light and leading, who may not be of their own body; others do not, and you have the councillor or vestryman, and nothing but the councillor or vestryman. Some committees keep minutes, as commissioners are bound under the Acts to do, and submit them to the local authority; others keep minutes, but submit them to nobody but themselves; and in some cases the librarian is clerk to the board; in others he is not, and attends no meeting of his own body, and obtains all his instructions second-hand through a non-library officer. Some committees and commissioners have separate banking accounts; others have not. Some draw their own cheques without intervention of the local board; others do not. Some can purchase books and carry on the various details of their library, without constant criticism of the larger local body at each board meeting; others cannot buy a coal-scuttle but it is subjected to the criticism of a large council or vestry, who have nothing better to do than to debate such matters of detail. Some meet fortnightly, some monthly, others whenever they think fit. I have not found out that some of them do not meet at all, but I should not be at all surprised if such were the case. I do, as a matter of fact, know one case which came before the Library Association this year, where the local authority only met twice a year, and then left everything to one or two members of the library committee to carry out with a free hand. You see, therefore, that there is little uniformity of action amongst the public library authorities, or, if there be any uniformity, it is got at by the common-sense of those boards, and not by any aid that legislation has given them. You will find also that the library committees have various methods of carrying on their work. When we come to the question of library commissioners, we find that the Act is much more formal, elaborate, and business-like, formulating provisions for the guidance of those boards as to their number, election, term of office, of resignation, re-election, and the like. They are limited in number, being not less than three nor more than nine. They are a body corporate, with a common seal. They have a large amount of liberty, influence, and power in carrying on their work. In fact, they are masters in their own house, which the library committee is not, and cannot be, unless by leave, not of the people, but of the superior local authority of which they merely form a part. You find that only very few local boards have delegated their powers to the library committee, as the Library Act allows, so that the committee may carry on its work properly and without unnecessary criticism or interference. When the case of transfer of library authority arose in many places, I asked questions on this point this year of some twenty librarians, and found to my surprise that this clause was hardly acted on at all. There is no doubt whatever that, in forming a body like library commissioners, the Legislature had been proceeding on the right lines, although it may not have gone far enough, and it would be well for us if they had continued on that line instead of departing from it as they have lately done. It was intended that the public library authorities were to carry out the behests of the people as regards those institutions, so it was most uncalled for that another body, no matter how important, should be put over them in their own district, and as to their own peculiar library work. Moreover, the Library Act said that the people adopting it should only incur the liability of the amount of rate legally fixed. Then why should it be necessary to go to another body, and year after year ask them formally to sanction what the voters of the district have already ordered by their votes shall be done? I say that this is an injudicious and needless limitation of library power. Neither as regards the method of obtaining the sanction of this local authority can we find any uniformity. One board requires the most minute statement of proposed expenditure from their library committee; another votes the amount of the rate, practically without inquiry. All this being so, you will see that the tendency of public library legislation has been twofold: it has tended to restrict the powers of one class of library authority and to amplify those of another. After the passing of the Public Library Act under which we now work, the public library commissioners were found to have fairly ample powers in their hands, and it was understood that those powers should be, if anything, extended, certainly not limited nor interfered with, much less done away with as regards some library authorities But no sooner was that understood in the library world than, for no possible reason and entirely uncalled for by anyone connected with library work, a clause was put into the Local Government Board Act of 1894, which, I say without fear of contradiction, marked the most retrograde step taken during the present generation in public library law, and which practically undoes the library advance of many years. Here we have a clause which gives certain local boards power to apply to the Government and have the public library authority of the parish transferred to themselves, for no cause shown. If that transfer be sanctioned by the Government, the commissioners thereby cease to exist, and their powers, no matter how well they may have been executed, are taken away and vested in another body, which may or may not be friendly to the carrying on of the libraries, and which may or may not have any time to properly see to the work, and which was never elected to do the work. It may be said that the tendency of modern legislation is that there shall be one body, and a responsible body, which shall have the control of all local matters. My answer is that this may be so as to general matters of public economy, but that it does not hold, and was never meant to apply to special cases and peculiar work, such as library administration essentially is; and anyone going on that general theory loses sight of the most important part of the matter—that is, Are we likely to have libraries better administered by a small and picked body of members, duly elected and specially selected for their fitness and appointed for a fair length of time, and retiring regularly by sections, or by a larger body, elected partly every year and engaged in all sorts of other matters, and who have not time to devote to the careful, special, and minute administration of the most skilled character, which public library work more than any other demands? I think the answer will be that the smaller body will be more likely to carry out the work efficiently than the other that has to attend to all sorts of other work and changing duties. I have said that no cause has been shown why these special boards that have carried on their work so well should be done away with, no cause as regards economy or administration has been alleged. Public control for the smaller boards such as commissioners is ample. Commissioners cannot levy their rate or collect it; the vestries do this. The commissioners cannot alter the incidence of the rate. They cannot expend their rate without the sanction of the vestries, a statement of which is submitted every year or half-year. The library board cannot borrow any money without the sanction of the vestry. It is obvious, therefore, that no question of economy can arise from the transfer of the commissioners' powers to a local board such as a vestry or council. Moreover, experience shows that, in any case in which the general local board has absorbed the library authority, additional expense has been the result. This must come out of the rate for the library or out of the other rates. If from the library rate, then the small sum available for carrying on these institutions is reduced by needless official expense; if out of the local rates, then the ratepayers have a new and uncalled-for library expense put upon them. So far, then, as economy is concerned, the unnecessary character of the Local Government Board Act change is evident. Now as regards efficiency. There is a universal concensus of opinion amongst those experienced in the administration of libraries that it is better to have a special and absolute authority, such as a board of commissioners, than a larger and less authoritative one, such as a committee of some larger body. It may be noted that continuity of policy is more probable under a body of special commissioners than under a committee. The former will, as a rule, be men who wish to devote their whole time to library work. In the case of a committee, there may be members whose time is much occupied by all sorts of other committee work, and who would not have the same time, even if they wished, to devote to the library. The question for library legislation for the future, I think, is, Should not more effort be devoted to the endeavour to secure a uniform library authority throughout the country? Let the public library authority be directly elected by the ratepayers of each district, parish, borough, etc. Let them be strictly limited in number, so many members *pro rata* for the population. Let them retire by one-third of their number yearly, as is the case now with commissioners. Let them be absolute as regards all matters of library administration, subject only to this, that they keep their expenses within the amount sanctioned by the voters in adopting the Library Act; and as regards loans, subject only to the sanction of the Local Government Board. Let it be necessary and required that their chief officer or librarian be also in every case a responsible clerk or secretary to the board. In too many cases it happens that the chief librarian is not the clerk and executive officer of the library board. I regard this as lamentable, inconvenient, and as tending to lower the status of librarians, that there should be any library office the executive power of which does not rest solely in, or subordinate to, the hands of the chief librarian. I would have this board elected by public vote, at the same time and in the same manner as the ordinary elections for the local council or board or vestry for the locality are carried on, the expenses to be borne out of the general rate. I would have a central Government control, more indeed of an advising than a curtailing character, from some department of the State, whose advice and supervision might tend to direct the energies of the libraries of this country in one steady direction, economising their strength, directing it more in a national and less in an aimless manner, and tending to make the public libraries more than they are now, a great department of State education. If you go upon these lines which I have foreshadowed, you are more likely to get a body of men who, having these great powers and responsibilities placed on them, will devote themselves systematically to the work, than would be the case with bodies which vary from year to year, and who look upon the library as a small and too often an irksome and even unnecessary encumbrance of their public work.

If the public libraries of the future are to be constituted on some uniform basis, the ordinary local board must have only the most *nominal* control over the library authority, and that solely as regards loans. The advance of our public libraries in England, I believe, will necessitate some such course being adopted, so that they be placed upon some more solid and sure foundation than that on which they now rest. Such legislation as I have briefly and imperfectly suggested will be the means of solidifying, unifying, and, I will add, of simplifying the duties and powers of the library authorities in England; and if this Conference only succeeds in drawing attention to this need, it will have done a most important work, and the country will have reason to thank you for having dealt with the matter to-day.

HERBERT JONES.

THE DUTIES OF LIBRARY COMMITTEES.

HATEVER qualification I may have to address you is derived from a long official connection with the public free libraries of Manchester. They were the first in England to be founded on the "Libraries and Museums Act" of Mr. William Ewart, of 1850, and were established in September 1852. It is interesting to know that, almost simultaneously, a movement in the direction of public free libraries took place in America; and since that time nowhere has the accumulation of books been so rapid as in the States, and nowhere has the economy and management of these invaluable institutions been carried to greater perfection or supported with a more munificent generosity. The coincidence of date is striking. It is possible enough that the sagacious author of our Public Libraries Act anticipated the American project. It is also conceivable that he obtained from the States a suggestion of his admirable measure. If so, he added another to the innumerable "*notions*," which have laid us under so many obligations to our esteemed cousins and friends on the other side of the Atlantic, which we will agree to regard, not as *dividing* us from them, but rather as *uniting* us in the bonds of a common brotherhood of confidence and affection.

At the opening of the first Manchester public free library the reference department contained 15,744 vols.; it has now 107,449. The lending library numbered 7195; our lending branches now contain 159,065. Instead of one lending library, we have now eleven, and four reading-rooms besides. Our annual circulation of books to the homes of the people is about a million, and the number used in the reference room is 419,949. Notwithstanding this extensive use of our literary possessions, our losses from missing or spoiled books are absolutely trifling, and may reach, perhaps, forty shillings a year. On our staff is the considerable number of eighty-four women librarians and assistants. I can speak with perfect confidence of their suitability in these capacities, and we employ probably more of them than are engaged in all the other libraries of the like kind in Great Britain. Their services in the reading-rooms set apart for boys are especially valuable, exercising a restraining influence over the lads, and conducing to quietness, order, and decorum.

In the engagement of officers and assistants, three main considerations present themselves to committees and other managers. First, the working hours should not be unreasonably prolonged; the salaries should be framed in a spirit of friendly liberality; and the younger members especially should be afforded opportunities for increasing their educational fitness and promoting their further culture. For this latter purpose, the English Library Association has for several years provided a summer school for literary and technical instruction, which has proved highly successful. Hitherto it has been available chiefly for London and the South; but plans are under consideration for supplying these valuable agencies to Lancashire and the North. Is it needful to say that entire confidence should be cultivated between committees and their officers, and that their intercourse should be accompanied by the courtesies which obtain amongst gentlemen?

Unlike some other library committees, the Manchester committee is composed entirely of members of the City Council. There are, undoubtedly, cases where it is found expedient to add a certain proportion of non-official persons, selected for their qualifications as experts in particular branches of literature; and much advantage may thence accrue. But whether it be from a trustworthy confidence in our own powers, or an overweening conceit about them, we have never called in any such extraneous aid.

Now, no more important duty devolves upon library committees than the selection and purchase of books. In the reference department, efforts should be made to fill up every special class with the best and newest publications. Old and obsolete copies should be periodically weeded out. This is especially important in various departments of physical science, as, for example, in chemistry and geology. Good editions of the standard poets, dramatists, and novelists are indispensable; but most of the modern novels may be relegated to the lending libraries. Their interest is often of a fleeting character; and every few years they may be removed, to give place to others, whose lives also may be brief, if not troubled. In this part of a committee's labours no little discretion is required. Whilst avoiding a too rigid or puritanic judgment, it often becomes a duty to decline works the moral tendency of which is at least doubtful. Perhaps one of the most conspicuous of the services rendered by public free as compared with many of the circulating libraries they have largely superseded, has been the exclusion of unwholesome literature from their shelves. Literary quality is not the sole requirement of a new story—however it may be for a time the rage. So numerous are our youthful readers, that parents and guardians may justifiably demand that nothing detrimental to morals shall be placed in their hands.

The extent to which theological works should be purchased sometimes excites a difference of opinion. Of course the great classics in divinity should be found in every good reference library. But modern controversial discussions may generally be left to those who find in them some irresistible attraction. When, however, they proceed from universally recognised authorities, they may be admitted, provided that no partiality be shown to any particular church or school. It may be remembered also that, as in physical science so in theology, a little revision is desirable now-a-days, and some advance towards present standards!

Although the preparation of lists and the recommendation of specific works pertain primarily to the office of the chief librarian, the final responsibility, in all cases, devolves upon the committee. The class of readers to be catered for, and the available means for purchases, must both be kept in view. A seaport or a commercial town may require some books that would be of comparatively little service in a cathedral city. A recommendation book should be available to readers who may wish to direct the attention of the committee to particular works. Many booksellers are willing to send in once a month a selection of the newest issues, on the principle of "sale or return," and at reductions from the publishing price so considerable that some tender official consciences scruple to accept them. Still, in dealing with public money, as we have nothing to "sell in the dearest," we are, I think, bound to "buy in the cheapest market."

Hints as to desirable books may be obtained from an inspection of *The Publisher's Circular*, *The Bookseller*, from other lists, and from reviews. The latter are not to be implicitly relied upon, but their critiques are often very useful. When exceedingly expensive works are recommended, it is desirable to ascertain whether copies have been or are being purchased for neighbouring libraries, so as to avoid needless duplication. In the case of such as deal with peculiarly technical subjects, we have consulted local authorities on the staff of The Owens College, whose kindly services are never sought in vain. Whether or not it be expedient to attend public sales of books is a question worthy of attention, but it is difficult to lay down any rule thereupon.

So far as to *books*. What about the ever-increasing flood of *periodicals* and *newspapers* for the reading-rooms? How to make a judicious selection from amongst them, so that, whilst instructive and entertaining, they shall also answer to every variety of opinion and taste? Again, which shall be preserved for binding, and which shall end their brief existence in the paper-maker's vat? These are points of no little difficulty, and demand the serious attention of committees. Obviously, as to newspapers, the leading organs of the chief political parties must be provided. Now, I am inclined to attach peculiar value to the educational influences exerted by the perusal of opposing party papers. Surely we are all too much in the habit of reading those only which harmonise with our own opinions—thus contracting our mental range, and probably intensifying our prejudices. But let a man study some burning question of the hour in, say, the columns of *The Times*, and then on the same subject consult *The Daily News*, and he will derive a valuable illustration of the truth that there are two sides to most things. It should also provide him with an argument against the infallibility of human judgments, and a lesson in the virtues of toleration. With regard to periodicals, the same remarks will, in a measure, apply. Among reviews, *The Quarterly* and *The Edinburgh* remain, like a couple of grand old battle ships of the line, surrounded with a swarm of petty steamers and fussy ferry-boats. They should still be preserved as storehouses of information and discussion on topics of permanent importance, and as examples of deliberate and stately composition. The Conservative organ on the one hand, and the Whig "buff and blue" on the other, are equally indispensable. In the discretion of committees, such additional monthly and weekly magazines will be secured as seem best adapted for their readers. In the case of soiled periodicals and books which must occasionally be discarded, appreciable service may be done by selecting those least damaged for use by the inmates of workhouses and hospitals.

There is hardly any duty more incumbent on committees than the provision of ample and suitable furniture and other appliances. The lighting, heating, and ventilation of the various rooms must also be sedulously regarded. Not only are the health and comfort of the staff thus promoted, but much will be effected in the preservation of the books. The use of gas as an illuminant should be abandoned, and the electric light take its place. It has, however, to be remembered that, whenever this change is made, a demand will arise for some additional artificial warming apparatus—the difference in the temperature of a room between the one light and the other amounting to many degrees.

No chief librarian should be entirely immersed in the details of his office. He should be at liberty to supply useful clues to sources of information generally, and especially to render assistance to inventors and specialists. He should, indeed, be a centre of literary life and activities in his locality. He can perform no higher office than that of the friend and consultant of students and inquirers.

I think it is obvious that, in the near future, the connection already begun between free libraries and technical schools is destined to become closer, and their influence on each other more considerable. Notification should be publicly made of recently acquired books on technical subjects, so that teachers and pupils alike may learn where to look for the most recent additions to knowledge in their particular departments.

Within the last few years much increased facilities have been afforded to borrowers. Formerly, in Manchester, a guarantee against loss or damage was required from two responsible householders. Now one only is asked for, and non-ratepayers may borrow on their own surety. No harm has resulted from these relaxations of the old rule, whilst the number of readers has largely increased. I may add that we never levy fines of any kind.

Now, as he would lamentably fall short of "the whole duty of man" who should restrict his attention to merely personal concerns, so every library committee should cultivate relations of amity and goodwill with every other. Excellent service may be done to the common cause by the exchange of information, the communication of experience, the explanation of success, the discussion of failure. The establishment of new libraries, the extension of their usefulness, the improvement of library legislation,—all are proper subjects of interest to committees and managers. In these and many other directions valuable contributions have been made by the Library Association of the United Kingdom, established in 1877. It was, indeed, the offspring of the First International Library Conference. Unity is strength; and hence changes have been successfully accomplished, to effect which separate effort would have been powerless. As an illustration, may I quote the defeat of a recent attempt by the English Revenue Office to extend the income tax to public free libraries; and this in spite of the indefensible restriction of the wretched penny in the pound, against which I have always protested and shall still protest. But, supported by pecuniary contributions from most of the important libraries, the committee managing those at Manchester resisted this new imposition. Defeated in one court, they carried their case to a second, a third, and a fourth, up to the highest tribunal in the land. Ultimately they succeeded. Not only their own, but every other public free library was thus protected from the threatened danger. It was a happy combination of forces, crowned with a brilliant victory.

Mr. President, many years ago it was my happy privilege to hear a marvellous series of speeches in my native city, which led to the abolition of the Corn Laws. We had "the unadorned eloquence" of Richard Cobden, and the fervid rhetoric of the "great orator of the Saxon race"—John Bright. On one occasion Mr. Cobden closed his speech with this remark, "Mr. Chairman, I have said my say. I never perorate." I don't think I can now do better than humbly follow so excellent an example.

HARRY RAWSON.

TRAINING OF LIBRARIANS.

HE subject is a very wide one, and might well form the subject of a whole treatise of cyclopædic extent, as it is from one point of view co-extensive with librarianship, and varies with the ever-differing standard which public opinion for the time being sets up as the ideal of what it expects from the librarian. In years gone by the librarian was master of the situation, being a keeper of the books in a very literal sense of those words; and in some old-world libraries this tradition lingers to the present day, the claims of the public on the library being almost resented, or entertained only on sufferance. Modern opinion and practice have deposed the librarian from this autocracy, and the tendency in recent years has been to select a librarian with special qualifications for administering the library whose management he is required to undertake. For instance, in scientific or other special libraries, a disposition may be seen to regard as a main or even sole qualification an extensive knowledge of the special subject with which the library treats; and again, in a popular rate-supported library, preference is frequently given to a candidate whose sole qualification is practical experience.

It is even possible that, with the present tendency to over-estimate the importance of the practical side of a librarian's qualifications, the librarian of the near future may be chosen with main regard to purely physical qualities and pre-eminence in muscular activity. It seems desirable, therefore, on such an occasion as the present, when it is possible to reach the public ear, that the importance of a wide and liberal educational training as an indispensable part of a librarian's qualifications, though it be a thrice-told tale, should be kept prominently in view. This purely intellectual side of the librarian's training can, however, only claim a secondary place.

I propose to consider my subject in three divisions, following what I conceive to be the order of their relative value and importance.

1st. The library as a training school.
2nd. The general education and culture supplied by self-training or by a college and university career.
3rd. The bibliographical training to be acquired in the book mart.

Each of these three great schools of librarianship may claim its triumphs and point to a long series of distinguished alumni.

It will no doubt be admitted that the ideal training for a librarian would be a combination of these three schools, and, by the very nature of his duties, the practising librarian is continually receiving a professional, intellectual, and bibliographical training.

The immediate object of this paper, and all that is possible in the short summary which I propose to lay before you, is to discuss the preliminary training of the librarian—his proper equipment for starting in his career. Opinion will doubtless be agreed that he should possess a liberal education as a foundation for all subsequent attainments.

If it were necessary to choose between the three courses of education which I have mentioned, there could be no hesitation in selecting the training of the library as far superior to any other educational course. It is conceivable that the art of swimming may be acquired on dry land, and that the soldier may be trained to the duties of his profession in mimic warfare; but the water is the only natural school for the swimmer, and campaigns make the soldier. So it is equally indisputable that no librarian can be properly trained without that insight into the duties of his profession which can only be gained by actual practice in each department.

There can be no doubt, in the second place, that the elevating influences of college life are highly desirable; and if this course can be crowned with a university qualification, the possession of a degree will be of great advantage to the librarian in many ways. The problem to be faced is how these purely intellectual qualifications are to be secured without the loss of the practical training which we have just considered.

The third school of librarianship—that of the book mart—is also of great importance, and the addition of a regular apprenticeship (no mere amateur study), by which two or three years can be devoted by the young librarian to this valuable means of gaining sound bibliographical knowledge, would be of the greatest value to him in his professional career.

There are certain subsidiary aids which it may be convenient to mention here, the principal of these being the attendance at schools of library economy, the study of library literature, and, perhaps more important than all, visits to other libraries and a study of their systems. I do not wish to undervalue any of these, more particularly the library school, which I am convinced is very helpful to librarians, both young and old; but I venture to think it is easy to attach too much importance to the systematic training, whether extending over weeks or years, which is received by the student in a large dose, and has a tendency, like systems of training in other professions, to give an artificial qualification without the sound experience that can only be gained by actual employment in the library. This systematic training, it seems to me, is wholly out of place at the beginning of the young librarian's career, but can come in most usefully at a later stage.

It is a trite saying that the librarian's training is never complete, and no one is more conscious of his ignorance and other defects than the conscientious librarian. As he becomes more expert in the technique of his profession, he will be the more anxious to educate the moral side of his professional faculties. For instance, a true sympathy for readers can best be gained by the librarian who tries to put himself in their position. He will never fully understand the best means of searching out authorities until he has himself become fairly practised, in some form or another, of literary search; and I venture to give a high place to literary work, undertaken, of course, in a moderate degree, as a subsidiary aid to the librarian's professional training.

To sum up, I fear that I have done little more than state what I conceive to be the great problem in the librarian's early education, namely, how to combine the university and purely bibliographical training with the practical training of the library itself.

An ideal system would be to combine these three methods of education,—to place a well-educated lad as an assistant in the library at the age of, say, fifteen, giving him at the same time facilities for keeping up his education; after four years in the library to send him to the university for his degree, with which might well be combined the training of the library school. After taking his degree, should the individual be so fortunate as to get a couple of years' experience of the book trade, he would probably be fitted, as far as training could fit him, for the post of assistant librarian, with a good chance of a distinguished career.

No doubt such a scheme is hopeless of realisation. It could not be attempted without Government aid, and such a uniform system of administration in libraries as would make it possible for librarians and assistants to be transferred from one library to another without loss of official seniority or the claims attaching to length of service.

It is pardonable, perhaps, for everyone to have his ideal, and this I venture to put before you as my ideal of what the training of the librarian should be. Meanwhile, we must look the matter practically in the face, and the great question that confronts all effort for raising the standard of the librarian's qualifications is the poor recompense which is at the present day considered as an equivalent for his services. In this country at anyrate, whatever may be the case in America, the public idea of the value of the librarian's work does not justify fathers in giving their sons an expensive education as a qualification for a librarian's post. It is only to the influence which assemblies such as this can bring to bear upon public opinion that we may hope for a change for the better. The public mind is slow to be convinced, but we must wait for the realisation of our hopes till the time when our masters, the public, will recognise that the efficiency of a public library and its value to the general welfare in chief measure depend upon the character and qualifications of the librarian to whom has been entrusted its custody and administration.

CHARLES WELCH.

SPECIAL TRAINING FOR LIBRARY WORK.

PECIAL training for special work is becoming an acknowledged necessity in every walk of life. Scientific training for scientific work is universally demanded. The opportunities for such training are multiplying, owing to the demand. The methods of half a century ago are no longer tenable. The technical schools of all kinds are the outgrowth of the scientific spirit of the age, which is not content to look at one side of a question only, but requires all the light possible upon it, and from every obtainable source.

Philosophy, religion, sociology, the arts, and history, as well as science, are feeling the breath of this inspiration to scientific research and methods; and what wonder is it, then, that the profession so intimately connected with one source of supply for all this study and research should awake to the necessity of more scientific methods of organisation and administration within its own borders?

When we reflect upon the change that has come over the conduct of libraries within the last half-century, we can see what an immense sociological influence has been at work to effect this development. The books in chains at Hereford Cathedral are typical of the administrative chains which were thrown around the free use of most libraries until a comparatively recent date.

Then the ruling principle was, how to keep, how to preserve; while now it is not alone how to preserve, but how to diffuse in the wisest and most effective manner.

The problems of to-day in connection with our public libraries are not only, How shall we obtain a collection of books best suited to the wants of the community in which we live? but, How shall we best organise and administer this collection?

The rapid increase of public libraries in America (there are fully 5000 of them now) has made the answer to these problems of vital importance, and in 1883 Mr. Melvil Dewey, then librarian of Columbia College Library, submitted a proposition to the trustees of the college, looking to the establishment of a school for the training of librarians. Among other arguments, he stated that, "In the past few years the work of a librarian has come to be regarded as a distinct profession, affording opportunities of usefulness in the educational field inferior to no other, and requiring superior abilities to discharge its duties well. There is a growing call for trained librarians animated by the modern library spirit. . . . Recognising the importance of this new profession, and the increasing number of those who wish to enter it, we are confronted by the fact that there is absolutely nowhere any provision made for instruction in either the art or science of the librarian's business. . . Young men and women of good parts, from whom the best work might fairly be expected, seek in vain for any opportunity to fit themselves as librarians. It is simply impossible for the large libraries to give special attention to the training of help for other institutions. Each employee must devote himself to the one part of the work that falls to his share, so that he can know little of the rest except what he may learn by accidental and partial absorption of its methods. There is a constantly increasing demand for such trained librarians and cataloguers, and there is no place where such can be trained. The few really great librarians have been mainly self-made, and have attained their eminence by literally feeling their way through long years of darkness."

Mr. Dewey's proposition was referred to the library committee of Columbia College, which reported unanimously the following year in favour of "establishing a school for the instruction of persons desiring to qualify themselves to take charge of libraries, or for cataloguing, or library or bibliographical work."

Owing to the erection of a new library building at Columbia, the school did not open until January 1887. The announcement of a three months' course in library economy had been made, and the number of students limited to ten. In response to urgent requests, this limit was raised gradually to twenty. At the middle of the term the class petitioned for a fourth month, and at its end a majority of the class had decided to take a two years' course which was then offered, while some asked for a third term of advanced work. In the second year the term was extended from four to seven months of solid work, and now it covers nine months.

In the spring of 1889 Mr. Dewey was elected State librarian at Albany, and the school was removed to that place. In 1891 the school, having been carefully examined in its working and results by the Board of Regents of the State of New York, it was unanimously accepted by them as an integral part of their great educational system, and was designated the New York State Library School, with power to hold regents' examinations and to confer degrees, to receive endowments and appoint fellowships and scholarships.

In the year 1883, the same year in which Mr. Dewey presented his plans to the trustees of Columbia College, he had also explained them at length to the Buffalo meeting of the A.L.A., and received its hearty endorsement, two eminent librarians only dissenting and favouring the old apprenticeship system. But, at the meeting of the Association in 1887, one of these dissenters offered the following resolution: "That this Association has observed with pleasure and gratification the first year's workings of the school of library economy at Columbia College, and that it regards the work there initiated as of great power for the future." Since 1883 the Association had kept in touch with the school by progress reports, and in 1889 it was resolved that, "With a desire to aid in securing the greatest efficiency of the library school, the library association appoints a committee of three as a committee of correspondence with the authorities of the school. Said committee is hereby instructed to inquire in what way they can be of service in promoting the objects for which the school is conducted, and to render such service to the extent of their power."

Thus it will be seen that the library school is not only a part of the university of the State of New York, but is officially recognised by the A.L.A., and has a vital connection with it.

From the first the aim of the school has been to fit its members for advanced positions in the different departments of library work.

To this end the entrance examinations are severe. College graduates are preferred, and admitted without examination, provided they have covered the prescribed ground. Other applicants must have taken a high-school course, or its equivalent in two years of college work; but the college-trained pupil is preferred, as having already acquired a capacity for persistent intellectual work, as well as a general fund of knowledge on many subjects. The examinations are in literature, history, general information, first-year French and German, and either Latin or Italian. An ability to read these languages readily is required. The work of the school is manifold, but all with a practical end in view. "Practical training rather than mere information is the end sought, and any method that promises to make more efficient librarians is tried."

The course of study for the junior year covers elementary cataloguing, elementary bibliography, accession department work, elementary dictionary cataloguing, elementary classification, shelf department work, loan systems, bookbinding, reading seminars, library language lessons, scope and founding of libraries, government and service of libraries, regulations for readers, library buildings, literary methods and bookmaking, library bookkeeping, and acquaintance with the specimens of the Bibliothecal Museum, which includes the collections made by the A.L.A., Columbia College, and whatever was added to it at the World's Fair exhibit. Students are also required to make personal collections of library blanks and equipments as far as possible, and arrange them systematically in albums for future reference.

The "senior year is designed to qualify students for more important and better-paid positions. The method is largely comparative, and students are systematically trained, not in a single good way for doing each thing, as in the junior year, but in knowledge of various systems, and specially of the principles that should determine which should be selected, or what modifications should be made in adapting any method to local requirements. Students who are specialising are allowed, as far as practicable, to do more of their work in the State library in the department chosen."

The course of study is a development of the junior course, and includes advanced bibliography, comprising reading-lists on different subjects, *e.g.* "A complete list of books and articles on the housing of the poor," "A select list for a travel club on Italian art, architecture, and antiquities"; reference work, with lectures and quizzes; advanced cataloguing, a comparative study of catalogue codes, advanced dictionary cataloguing and classification, history, and the origin of libraries. An original bibliography and a thesis must be prepared by each graduating student. All through the course lectures are given by visiting librarians who are specialists in some given department, and also by prominent educators, booksellers, printers, binders, and advocates of various systems and theories of library science.

"Problems presenting difficulties liable to be met with in all departments, *e.g.* cataloguing, indexing, aiding readers, hunting down hard questions by a skilful use of bibliographic apparatus, are given; and the novice faces many puzzling questions of after-experience, and learns their method of solution, without the mortification and expense of mistakes in real administration." Seminars are held frequently, in which all library questions are discussed, short papers read, and free expression of opinion encouraged. Practical work in the State library is done by each pupil, under the supervision of the teachers. The juniors devote one hour daily for sixteen weeks, and four hours daily for the rest of the year; while the seniors give two hours daily for forty weeks to the actual work of the library, thus enabling them to put in practice the lessons they have learned. The students are also encouraged to assist in various outside benevolent and other libraries, for the benefit of the experience gained. That the students may be brought in touch with other libraries more fully, the course requires a visit during the Easter vacation to the leading libraries of New York and Boston on alternate years. This study of comparative methods is very valuable, and impresses the fact upon them that there are many admirable ways of doing the same thing, and that individuality of method is to be looked for and respected. Peculiar points in the administration of these libraries are specified in advance, and reports by the students are required on their return, followed by free discussions. "Students are thus taught how to get most quickly and systematically from other libraries the lessons they have to teach. With similar preparation, there are visits under guidance to representative houses, where can be learned to the best advantage so much as a librarian needs to know about publishing, printing, binding, illustrating, bookselling, book auctions, second-hand book stores, and other allied business. Comparative study of all material and methods is one of the strong points of the school, and the students have fairly placed before them all methods approved in successful library administration, and are taught to select or combine from various plans what is best adapted to any circumstances in which they may be placed." The library school possesses especial advantages in being so intimately connected with the State library, which contains over 250,000 volumes, many manuscripts, and a large collection of pamphlets. It is also the headquarters of several hundred travelling libraries, which are constantly being sent out to villages, schools, study clubs, and extension centres throughout the State. Thus it is evident that every department of library work has been treated in a thorough and practical way. The student has been taught how to select, classify, catalogue, identify, and distribute his books in the most scientific and liberal manner. He knows the mechanism of the book, and can judge of its printing and its binding; he has also been taught that deeper lesson, how to find the hidden stores of wisdom within the book, not only for his own sake, but for the benefit of others; and if he has imbibed the true modern library spirit, he will realise that this is the chief reason why he is a librarian. The missionary spirit of the library school is one of its striking characteristics.

Thus equipped, theoretically and practically, with a knowledge of the beginnings of library administration, each student, according to his ability, is enabled to make more rapid progress towards the desired goal than would otherwise have been possible. He has an ideal of library work, the accomplishment of which will depend largely on his own personality.

This question of personality enters so vitally into the possibilities of his future work, that the directors of the school have wisely determined to grant hereafter the second year's course to those only who have shown decided qualifications for the profession. Librarians, as well as poets, are "born, not made," and though one may be able "to speak with the tongues of men and of angels, and understand all mysteries and all knowledge," yet, if he has not the peculiar qualities that go to the making of a true librarian, it will profit him nothing so far as really successful work is concerned. We have dwelt somewhat at length upon the course of study in the library school, in order to show what care is taken to prepare the pupils as thoroughly as possible for any question or emergency that may arise, not only by the most painstaking instruction, but by actual practice and the fullest discussion of all library methods. But it must not be supposed that at the end of the two years' course these library school graduates are expected or advised to assume responsible positions at once. At least a year of work in a subordinate position in some library is recommended, where everyday working with the public can be had and the two years of study can be tested by actual experience. After one or two years of such apprenticeship, the rise of the able student is rapid and assured. While the library school guarantees employment to none of its graduates, yet it is constantly looked to to supply some of the most responsible and important positions in State, college, public, and other libraries, as chiefs, as cataloguers, or assistants.

The high standard of requirements of the library school practically excluded many who, while unable to meet them, were yet fitted by nature and education to do admirable work as assistants or as heads of smaller libraries, and, with experience, to advance to more important positions. To meet this want, in 1890 a library training class was opened at the Pratt Institute, Brooklyn, under the direction of graduates of the library school. Miss Mary Wright Plummer (class of '88 library school), the librarian of the Institute, is also the director of the class. Examinations, while not as exacting as those of the parent school, yet require the equivalent of a good high-school course to ensure success, and whenever possible a personal interview with the applicant is requested. The examination covers general history, general literature, and current events. A one year's course of nine months was offered at the beginning, which covered the ground as thoroughly as possible in that time. Six months were devoted to study of theory, and the last three required twenty-four hours a week of practical work in the library. In 1896 a second year's course was opened to those who could pass the requisite examinations and had the necessary personal qualifications, and who wished more extended and thorough preparation for their work. This course is not wholly an extension of the first-year work, but rather a development of another phase—the historical and bibliographical, advanced cataloguing and bibliography, library administration and history of libraries, ancient and modern literature, history of books and printing, binders and binding, engraving, etc., and Italian. German is taken in the first year's course. Collections of books such as are requisite for this kind of work, including MSS., incunabula, etc., are rare in the United States; and this school is fortunate in being near, and privileged to use the fine collections of, the Lenox and Astor Libraries in New York. The final examinations on this second-year work are conducted by specialists outside of the school, who also mark the papers. Admirable work has been accomplished in the Pratt Institute class, and its graduates have filled with acceptance many places as assistants, and not infrequently as head librarians. The Institute offers the great advantage of a public library of 56,000 volumes, with a circulation of 300,000 yearly; and its nearness to the great libraries of New York City tends to broaden the student's idea of his chosen profession, and to quicken his enthusiasm from a sociological point of view.

In 1892 the "Drexel Institute of Art, Science, and Industry" of Philadelphia established a training class, under the direction of Miss Alice B. Kroeger, librarian, a graduate of the library school, class of '91, and with other graduates as assistants. While following the lead of the Pratt Institute class, the examinations have not been as severe, or the course as extensive. Instruction is in the form of talks or lectures, with practical work under supervision, and includes the technical and the literary or bibliographical work. A course in the history of English literature, studies in modern European authors, reference work, and bibliography is given, and also lectures are had by specialists in various departments of knowledge. This school has furnished many assistants to the Philadelphia libraries as well as to some other places, and graduates conscientious painstaking workers.

The next year, 1893, saw the establishment of another high-grade training class at the Armour Institute, Chicago, under the direction of Miss Katharine L. Sharpe, B.L.S., of class '92 of the library school. Within a few weeks this class has been removed to the beautiful new library of the University of Illinois, and has taken the name of the Illinois State Library School. There will hereafter be no examinations of candidates, as all must have matriculated at the university and have taken a two years' course. Freshmen and sophomores who register for the library course will take reference work and general lectures in connection with their college studies. The two years' technical work will rank as junior and senior, and will be given only to those who have received credit for the two years' college work. " Future purpose will also be considered, and physical condition and personal qualifications as well. . . . The intellectual life of a community must not consciously be put into the hands of a librarian who lacks gentleness, sympathy, tact, and public interest, however well qualified she may be in other respects."

Here a four years' course is provided, looking to a systematic and thorough training in library science from every standpoint—intellectual, technical, and practical. The practical side will be learned in the library of the university, which numbers 30,000 volumes, and is increasing rapidly every year. The Maine State College instituted a course in library economy in 1894, in which technical instruction, supplemented by lectures, is given.

Still another style of training class was developed at Los Angeles, California, where classes were organised to supply civil service instruction to applicants for library positions, and from their ranks to furnish assistants.

Classes are limited to six. Examinations are conducted by a committee of the board of directors, and designed to determine the previous education and adaptability of the candidates. Terms are divided into courses, six months each, three hours daily. Each student, under the direction of the assistant librarian, serves as under-study to the heads of the various departments of the library. Lessons in comparative methods are given in each department, which are followed by a term of general application. No promise of permanent employment is given to any of the students, but members of the library staff are added only from the training class.

In 1893 the Denver (Colorado) Public Library instituted a training class similar to that at Los Angeles. They receive but one class of six pupils, and desire that they should have received a high-school diploma. This is not an absolute requirement, however. Applicants must appear in person, and undergo a written and oral examination. They are admitted in the order of their standing. Practical instruction in technical work is given all through the course, and students give five hours daily for nine months to the work. Those most successful are taken on the staff as occasion requires.

To reach a class which none of the above-mentioned schools are adapted to assist, a number of summer schools have been opened. That at Amherst College was started in 1891, and is conducted by Mr. William I. Fletcher, well known in connection with Poole's *Index*. In five weeks of five days each and four hours a day, he exhibits, by lectures and by practical work of the pupil under his direction, the entire ground of library economy. This course is designed for beginners who wish to get some idea of library methods, and for librarians of small libraries who feel the need of special information, which they have been unable hitherto to obtain. The class of '96 numbered thirty-six.

The University of Wisconsin Summer School, opened in 1895, gives six weeks' teaching of the technical work of the library. In 1896 twenty-seven pupils were in attendance; all but four had previous experience. The New York State Summer School was open only during the summer of 1896. The moving of the school to different quarters in the Capitol will prevent their holding a session this season, but another year it will be resumed.

A very able comparative report on the four library schools was made by the committee of the American Library Association last summer—Professor J. N. Larned, chairman. He notes the greater proportion of technical instruction given in the library school at Albany than elsewhere, and predicts that the time now taken for the study of literature in the other schools will eventually be devoted to technical work, and more thorough and broader preparation be required in entrance examinations. That not only a previous familiarity with belles-lettres will be demanded, but also with the literature of science, of philosophy, of religion, of history, of biography, of politics and social economy, in which more than half the problems of library science and the difficulties of library service arise.

That the policy of the library schools will in the future, as in the past, be ever open to all wise and practical methods tending to a fuller and richer preparation for their chosen work is assured, for their watchword is ever " Forward ! " They are alive, and must progress to live.

The number of students in the New York State School in the ten years of its existence has been 246, and these have filled 529 positions. Pratt Institute has had in six years 142 students, Drexel Institute in four years 81 students, and Armour Institute in three years 41 students.

I have used throughout this paper the masculine form of the personal pronoun in speaking of the library student, referring thereby to mankind in general according to common usage, and the recognised principle that the greater includes the less. In this particular instance, however, the less so outnumbers the greater that it would have been almost entirely correct to use the feminine form, for over 99 per cent. of the students and graduates have been women. There is something in the profession that appeals strongly to them, and their ability to fill some of the most important positions has been proved by their successful management of State libraries, college libraries, large city libraries, and hundreds of smaller ones. The skilful direction of the library schools is in the hands of women, prominent among whom is Miss Mary S. Cutler, whose rare ability and intelligent enthusiasm have impressed themselves so strongly upon many of her pupils. Happily, however, the question of sex in library science seems not to be recognised, and, apart from occasional local prejudice or reason in favour of either man or woman, library positions are bestowed according to ability, and not according to sex.

Character, intelligence, executive ability, and a thorough training are the factors that count, and these are the qualities which the training schools are striving by their methods of education and elimination to furnish.

There is no limit to the possibilities of library extension in America. The library and the school have clasped hands, and before many years have elapsed the public library will be everywhere recognised as a part of the educational system of the country, the free university for all, and trained librarians will be deemed as indispensable for the one as trained teachers are for the other.

In the broad, judicious, enthusiastic training of the library schools lies our hope of the future.

HANNAH P. JAMES.

FEMALE LIBRARY ASSISTANTS AND COMPETITIVE EXAMINATION.

HY should not the public libraries of our large towns and districts employ female library assistants?" has been a topic frequently discoursed upon. Can public library work be regarded as a desirable occupation for young ladies? for the young woman (to use the more respectable designation) of education and social position, who may be indifferent to marriage, and may have no preference for any other profession? for those who would hesitate to seek a situation in shop, factory, or warehouse? for those, again, who may lack the necessary talent for public life in the musical or dramatic professions, or for whom the prosaic duties of governess would have little attraction? To the question raised, the Bristol Library authorities have long given practical answer in the affirmative.

From the time of the adoption, in 1874, of the Public Library Act at Bristol, young women of education and respectable parentage have been selected for the public library service. The example was no doubt offered by the earlier experience of the Manchester public libraries, which I believe were the first to engage female library assistants. In a paper read by Mr. Alderman Baker at the Manchester meeting of the Library Association in 1879, "On the employment of young women as assistants in public free libraries," what was then thought to be a new departure was referred to by Mr. Baker in the following words: "Neither the chance of promotion to better positions in the reference library nor to appointments as branch librarians, combined with a reasonable increase of wages, were sufficient to keep the young men in the service of the committee, while the frequent vacancies which occurred caused much trouble and inconvenience in the maintenance of that order and efficiency which are essential to the carrying out successfully of the work of the libraries." At that time the subject of woman—her rights, duties, and employment, particularly her exclusion from certain trades and professions—was attracting the attention of thoughtful people. The claims of the woman librarian were, however, not generally taken up very enthusiastically, and the new departure was then followed in few public libraries. Many library committees and librarians, on the contrary, were very much averse to the female library assistant, preferring rather to "bear those ills they had than to fly to others they knew not of." With the years that have intervened, we find the aspect of things considerably changed. The progress which women have made during the last decade or two in advanced instruction, and their growing importance as representatives and disseminators of that instruction, are among the notable features of our time. With the advance of education everywhere has been the successful operation of the Public Libraries Acts. The formation of the Library Association, with its examination tests, the Summer School, and the Library Assistants' Association, have all followed in sequence. These, together with the many other increasing facilities which to-day are in reach of the student, assuredly indicate that the position of the library assistant of either sex has greatly improved within the last twenty years.

With a view of increasing the efficiency of the library staff at Bristol (which comprises between forty and fifty women librarians and assistants), and for the purpose of making some improvements in its organisation, it was last year suggested that information might be obtained as to the employment of females in other places, and as far as possible also the opinions of the public librarians of some of the towns who employ them, viz. :—

Aberdeen, Battersea, Birmingham, Blackpool, Bradford, Chelsea, Clerkenwell, Derby, Edinburgh, Liverpool, Manchester, Nottingham, Oldham, Paisley, St. Helens, and Salford.

The following questions were asked and courteously responded to in each instance :—

How many women assistants have you?
Are any in charge of branch libraries?
Do you limit the age for admission to the staff?
When a vacancy occurs, do you throw it open to candidates by competition? If so, have you any form of examination?
What qualifications do you lay down as essential for young women candidates?
Are they appointed by the committee or librarian?
What salary do your female assistants usually commence with?
What is the highest salary paid to your female assistant or branch librarian?
Have you in force any scale of promotion and increase of salary? Are they advanced by capacity and merit, or length of service only?
What are their hours of duty?

It was felt that, for the better regulation of the staff at Bristol, it would be well that every assistant employed in the libraries should have her relative position on the staff assigned; that, in fact, a distinction should be made between the grade of a "junior assistant," entering the library service as a beginner to place herself in training for the work, and that of a "senior," who may have acquired experience and attained some degree of proficiency in librarianship beyond the mere initiative routine of giving out books. While recognising the truth of the adage that "learning is preferable to beauty," it was deemed inevitable that promotion should be contingent solely on ability and experience. It was then decided—

That the staff in future be graded as follows :—
(a) Junior assistant.
(b) Senior assistant.
(c) Branch sub-librarian.
(d) Branch librarian.

That for all future appointments in the libraries candidates between the ages of fifteen and eighteen only should be eligible for appointment.

That they would be expected to submit to a competitive elementary examination, to show their possible fitness for library work.

A medical certificate to be produced by the candidate at the time required.

At the first examination of candidates at Bristol, twenty-two young women presented themselves. The questions given were of a purely elementary character, as the following subjects that were then taken will show: Handwriting and dictation (orthography), arithmetic, geography, history, and English literature. The results on the whole were satisfactory. A few exceptions, however, were remarkable, to quote the following extracts from some of the papers :—

Name the first of the Tudor kings?
"George the First."
Mention in your opinion the best complete History of England for students?
"That written by Goldsmith."
Who was Jeremy Taylor? State if he is known as poet, historian, or theologian.
"Jeremy Taylor was a poet."
Under what countries would you place the following towns: Copenhagen, Madras, Quebec, Calais?
"Copenhagen in *Spain*, Madras in *Italy*, Quebec in *Africa*, Calais in *England*."

Another answer given was perhaps a slight improvement to the last question, while it suggests a prudent desire to avoid if possible any complexity in respect to "*subject-heading*" or "*cross-entry*."

"I should place Copenhagen under *Copenhagen*, Madras under *Madras*, Quebec under *Quebec*, and Calais under *Calais*."
Name the author of the "Idylls of the King"?
"Rider Haggard."

Who wrote the *Mill on the Floss*?
"Robert Southey."
Who is the author of *Modern Painters*?
"Mark Twain."

The adoption of the examination scheme at Bristol has, moreover, considerably relieved the pressure of candidates who formerly were constantly applying for employment in overwhelming numbers—young women from various grades of the community; ladies of uncertain age, desiring a genteel occupation and "thinking how much they would like to be in a library"; a few suffering from disappointment or bereavement; numberless letters, requiring an answer, from the clergy and Nonconformist ministers and others, requesting a position for their friends or relatives; daughters of parents "who had been ratepayers for upwards of so many years," etc. One application was received from a young woman armed with credentials from a lady of title, in whose service *she had been employed as cook*, the young person being very highly recommended on account of her "fondness for reading."

"To describe women," says Diderot, "the pen should be dipped in the humid colours of the rainbow, and the paper dried with the dust gathered from the wings of a butterfly." In much more prosaic language opinions have been freely expressed on the subject of women librarians and assistants by those in authority. The majority of these, it may be said, have been distinctly in favour of the gentler sex.

We are to-day everywhere being reminded of the fact that women are now practically on an equality with men, and that the legal subordination of one sex to the other is a thing of the past. In the words of Mr. Hall Caine, "There is next to nothing that a woman may not be and do now in England. She may be a guardian of the poor, a churchwarden or sexton, a medical officer of workhouse, or a member of the School Board. She may practise medicine and take academic degrees. She may go to law and maintain an action against her own husband, and he has even lost his ancient legal right of beating her." This being so, it is only equitable and right that she should take her chance with her fellows, *in a fair field and no favour*, in the librarian's vocation, which is one that, I hope I may be permitted to say, she is eminently fitted to adorn.

At the Paris meeting of the Library Association in 1892 a paper was read by Miss James on "Women Librarians." Another paper by the same lady was given at the Aberdeen meeting in 1893 on "American Women as Librarians." Miss Richardson, of the St. Helens Public Library, has also dealt with the subject in her paper on "Librarianship as a Profession for Women," which appeared in vol. vi. of the *Library*. Under the title of "The American Library School," Miss Petherbridge contributed a paper also, which she read at the Cardiff meeting in 1895. The absence of a national training school in England has been referred to by each of these ladies. Miss James, in speaking of American women as librarians, has contrasted England with America as follows: "Not every woman before being employed in a library is able to go through the admirable course of training provided by the New York State Library School at Albany, but those who have graduated there are much sought after by library commissioners and librarians, and are reasonably sure of getting a post worth having; in other words, the supply does not at present equal the demand." We learned at the same time, however, that many women there were trained as assistants in public libraries as in England, and these, by dint of thoroughness and perseverance, become as efficient as those graduating from the library school. I believe that it is the general opinion of English librarians that the best training school is the public library itself, where the knowledge gained by experience is practical rather than theoretical in effect. It is now beginning to be understood that it is very difficult, if not impossible, for either man or woman to satisfactorily take up the work of a librarian without definite and distinctive training. The days are past when candidates for responsible positions might be selected from the ranks of retired army officers, schoolmasters, or tradesmen. In the near future, it is probable no library appointment, even for a junior position, will be made without the provisional test of his or her knowledge and abilities. To eliminate unsuitable candidates, who are usually forthcoming in overwhelming numbers, and to successfully prepare the way for higher training, no simpler methods suggest themselves to me than the following, which I here submit to the better judgment of my colleagues:—

1. For junior assistants, admit only those who have successfully passed an examination, the subjects for which might be left to the library management; and in the case of senior assistants, only those who have graduated in library work elsewhere.
2. Recognise promotions from grade to grade upon a fixed scale, in respect to position and salary, such promotions to be earned by capacity and merit only.

The scheme recently adopted at Bristol has proved highly satisfactory in results; the female staff of the libraries having been re-organised upon these lines. All the district libraries of the city are served by (*a*) branch librarian, (*b*) branch sub-librarian, (*c*) senior assistants; and (*d*) junior assistants, each one taking up her work with an intelligent appreciation of the duties of the various departments.

Objections to women librarians have often been made on the score of their physical unfitness and the uncertainty of their health. In common fairness, I would like to say that such has not been our experience at Bristol. Very rarely indeed does absence from duty occur on the plea of indisposition, while at all times and seasons they have proved themselves equal to the strain which is inseparable from the daily routine of a large public library.

The absence of what may be termed the "business faculty" has often been thought to be a defect in the mental organisation of the woman librarian. Some have gone so far as to say that, with clearly defined rule, plain method and example to guide them, all is well; but, left to their own resources, there is danger of failure, owing perhaps to the lack of that imagination and originality which is needful sometimes in all administrative work. This may or may not be true. No one is perfect. All librarians of the opposite sex are not invariably what may be termed "good business men," while few, I venture to think, are gifted with that inventive genius which usually brings prestige to the librarian, and maybe in some cases even a considerable increase of income. Many women of education show a marked ability as cataloguers, and take to that important branch of library work almost as instinctively as ducks to water; while those who have been placed in charge of public reading-rooms in thickly populated districts have been able to successfully maintain the necessary order and discipline without anxiety or friction. It must be said, however, that in many instances they have yet to acquire that *savoir faire* which is really indispensable in dealing with the public.

Upon the point of economy something might also be said in favour of the woman. Her personal expenses and worldly responsibilities being so much lighter than are a man's, a lower rate of remuneration is, as a matter of course, usually assigned to her. The question, however, now before us is not one of finance, but rather how far the female library assistant adapts herself to the conditions of public library service to-day, and by her presence and work promotes its true development. Nothing succeeds like success, and indications are not wanting that the field for women librarians is now fairly opened, and that their work is being appreciated and is likely to grow in popular estimation. Man is ever ready to serve woman, to be her knight-errant as in days of old. Without, however, cherishing any mad desire to behold in the "glorified spinster" of to-day the sole public librarian of the future, let us meet her in a spirit of hearty comradeship and sympathy, for the good of the cause and the honour of our profession.

E. R. NORRIS MATHEWS.

HINDRANCES TO THE TRAINING OF EFFICIENT LIBRARIANS.

THE character of the esteem in which the free library movement is held in any part of the United Kingdom depends much on the impressions of leading inhabitants received from intercourse with librarians and visits to existing public libraries. A well-trained, courteous, and zealous librarian causes all who come in contact with him to carry away an opinion favourable to the library movement—an opinion which a different experience may afterwards reverse. It is desirable, therefore, that this Conference consider the nature of any obstacles tending to prejudice the people against free libraries through the production of inefficient librarians.

That such officials do even yet exist may be taken for granted. Men who regard the advocacy of the educational uses of a library as a fad, who cannot talk sensibly for a quarter of an hour on any literary theme outside that of current fiction, who never go to any conference of co-workers because they do not see the use, and who serve out books as they might have served out bacon, if fate had been more kind to their public, are not yet extinct; nor will they become so until a general agreement is arrived at regarding the qualities to be insisted upon in library assistants, and until opportunities of adequate training are brought well within the reach of all who enter the state of pupilage in a library.

It is hard to say how many assistants in training are at the present moment attached to the staffs of our free public libraries. In Great Britain and Ireland there are now more than 330 library authorities recognised by British law. One hundred and sixty-five of these, in places with a minimum population of 10,000, possess 309 lending libraries, and, say, 120 reference libraries. An average of five assistants to two libraries gives nearly 1100, to which number at least 200 must be added for uncounted places. Thus there can hardly be fewer than 1300 persons in training for librarianship in the free public libraries of this country.

Out of such a number, very many can never attain to the emoluments and dignity of a librarian-in-chief. To these clearly the public owes a duty, viz. to make the lot of the assistant librarian in itself an end worthy of the dedication of a life's energies. With a rapidly growing body of the users of libraries, and under present legal limitations of income, this cannot be.

But why? Let us particularise. The hindrances to the adequate training of library assistants in Britain are—

1. Deficient general education in the candidates for training.
2. Insufficient leisure for needed study.
3. Insufficient supply of technical literature in the libraries.
4. Lack of financial incentive to ambition.

The first-named cause of failure is too painfully obvious to every experienced librarian in this country, and will continue to plague him until librarianship offers a better chance of a comfortable livelihood.

As to leisure for study, no agreement seems to exist regarding the number of hours during which a pupil assistant should be employed. Certain it is that eight hours a day are greatly exceeded in many libraries. Bristol sets a good example by limiting the week's duty to forty-four hours.

A librarian's working books are woefully represented in the libraries of some considerable towns. Surely an office or staff library should be included in every public library, and the staff allowed the freest access to select bibliographies, special catalogues, dictionaries of literature, and other well-known works. The cause of the deficiency in some cases is the reluctance of the committee of managers to sanction the purchase of an expensive book, unless someone outside the staff has asked for it.

In approaching the last-named hindrance—the want of the prospect of a good livelihood in the practice of the profession of a librarian—we come to the main cause of trouble. During the period of pupilage, library assistants, speaking generally, are not too badly paid, but what shall be said of the trained assistant's remuneration? Advertisements for such at a salary of from £65 to £80 are not infrequent in England. Indeed, a librarian-in-chief is asked to face the upbuilding and organisation of a large town library for an annual salary oftener nearer one hundred than two hundred pounds.

In 1878 Mr. Robert Harrison advocated £250 as a minimum salary for a competent librarian. Are his views yet accepted? With few exceptions, that salary is only yet within the sphere of reasonable hope for public librarians in British towns below 100,000 inhabitants. Is this due to the deficiencies of the librarians themselves? Certainly not in scores of instances, for no craft or profession has called forth more generous and enthusiastic service than ours. Many bodies of commissioners and committees of public libraries would gladly reform the existing evil but for the statutory limit of one penny in the pound to the library rate. The crux of the difficulty is *here*.

In thus presenting the matter I speak not as an aggrieved party, for I have the good fortune to serve a considerate committee. The fear of a charge of trades-unionism has long kept librarians silent; but this matter is in reality one of public importance and affects educational progress. A school-board rate of 6d. or 1s. is willingly paid to teach our youth to read. Shall an additional twopence be grudged to turn that reading talent into right and safe channels, where it may work for the public welfare and economy?

One final word: let it not be thought that the British public library assistants of to-day are all uneducated or indifferent. I have reason to know that the devotion and enthusiasm of the men who attended the International Congress of twenty years ago are being worthily emulated by many of the younger generation, who are now beginning to gather the fruit of our predecessors' labours.

J. J. OGLE.

BOOKS AND TEXT-BOOKS: THE LIBRARY AS A FACTOR IN EDUCATION.

OME ten years ago it was my good fortune to spend a month's vacation in the company of one of the most distinguished members of our profession in America. In the course of one of our many discussions, the subject of success in life came up, and he sprang upon me the question, What constitutes success? I replied that success in life consists in making the most of one's self. I had never before formulated a definition, and I have not since been able to improve on that which occurred to me on the instant.

Tested by this definition, how many men have achieved success—how many have realised their highest possibilities, physical, mental and moral? It was thus our conversation ran; and I mentioned, as one who had seemingly brought to fullest fruition a rich natural endowment, a man who had found his recreation, amid the cares of statesmanship, in work that would have given him distinction as a scholar,—that man whom Americans, free from the animosities engendered by party strife, regard not only as the greatest Englishman of his time, but as to-day "the foremost man of all this world."

We referred to Darwin and Lowell and other men who seem to have made the most of high talents and exceptional opportunities. Another notable example of a successful life—a man who has won distinction in the fields of finance, letters, science, and statesmanship—is the gentleman who honours us by presiding over the deliberations of this International Conference. And yet the question arises, as it did in the conversation referred to, whether even Mr. Gladstone and Sir John Lubbock, in the wisdom of later years, could not point out defects in their early education which have hindered still higher achievement or, in some degree, lessened life's fruitage and enjoyment. While I have thought I should like to ask this question of some man whose career marks to the world the highest success, I disclaim any thought of using this opportunity to extort a confession from our honoured chairman; and I make these remarks merely as an introduction to my theme.

Obviously, that success which involves distinction, even local distinction, can come to but few. But success is a relative term. What would be great success for one man ought to be regarded as lamentable failure for another, and *vice versâ*. And, tested by this standard of possibilities realised or unrealised, life for the vast mass of mankind is a dismal failure.

This is not the place for a discussion of the relative potency of heredity and environment. All will admit that education plays a large part, if not the larger part, in determining career. On education, therefore, depends the progress of the race. If an approximately perfect system of education could be adopted and all the children in the world could be brought under its influence, a millenium's progress would be marked in a generation. Education, then, is the most important concern of man. As Jules Simon says, "Le peuple qui a les meilleures écoles est le premier peuple : s'il ne l'est pas aujourd'hui il le sera demain." Or, in the words of Wendell Phillips, "Education is the only interest worthy the deep, controlling anxiety of the thoughtful man."

In deciding on the best means to an

end, the first thing is to determine exactly the end sought.

In that famous book which has been a delight to tens of thousands of readers of all ages, and a beneficent influence in the lives of two generations of English and American boys, Squire Brown sums up his conclusion as to the objects for which Tom is sent to school in these words: "If he'll turn out a brave, helpful, truth-telling Englishman, and a gentleman and a Christian, that's all I want."

Herbert Spencer says, "To prepare us for complete living is the function which education has to discharge." Or, in other words, "Complete living is the end to be achieved."

Complete living is the highest possible development of all the human faculties, physical, mental, and moral: it is success in life. Here, then, is the desired end. Now, what are the means adopted to accomplish this end?

Let me premise that my criticisms are directed to the common school education of my own country, though I assume they apply in some degree to the school systems of other countries. And it is the education received by the masses of the people that makes the progress of the nation. A nation is like a railway train, which can go no faster than its hindmost car.

In the *Deutsche Rundschau* for March, Dr. Rein, of Jena, begins an interesting article entitled "Schulbildung und Volkserziehung," by quoting with approval (and taking as a sort of text) this expression of a well-known political economist: "The fundamental cause of all social danger lies not in the contrast of wealth, but of education and culture. All social reform must begin at this point. It must uplift the life, the moral character, the knowledge and opportunities of the lower classes."[1]

What, then, are our schools doing to make "complete living" a possible thing for the masses, a thing desired by them, a thing of which they have any conception? Can any such conception or desire come from text-books? And in how many schools still are text-books the only books known? In the grammar school to which I went until I was nearly ready for the high school, none but the prescribed readers, arithmetics, geographies, etc., were allowed. Other books were occasionally smuggled in; but reading them was a more hazardous, because a more absorbing, pastime than playing pins. Sooner or later the culprit was sure to be caught and thrashed, while the book was seized as contraband. Proving incorrigible in this particular, I was allowed during my last term to spend the last half-hour each day in reading; and having possessed myself of a copy of Sargent's *Standard Speaker*, which I had previously been reading on the sly, I daily feasted my mind, kindled my imagination and nourished my soul with poetry and eloquence, with beautiful images and noble thoughts. It was a scrappy diet, composed of tit-bits appearing under such general headings as "Moral and Didactic," "Martial and Popular," "Senatorial," "Narrative and Lyrical," and ending with a dessert of "Comic and Satirical."

To change the figure, this book was to me an Aladdin's lamp, a Fortunatus' cap that wafted me to distant countries and carried me back into past centuries. Now I sat in the Roman Senate and heard Cicero's denunciation of Catiline or the noble self-renunciation of Regulus; or I stood with the crowd in the streets of Rome and listened to the calm statement of Brutus and the artful and impassioned appeal of Mark Antony; or I went further back in Roman history and saw how Horatius kept the bridge—

"Alone stood brave Horatius,
But constant still in mind;
Thrice thirty thousand foes before
And the broad flood behind."

I had but to turn a few pages to enter the British Parliament and feel the spell of Burke's eloquence or the thrill of Chatham's appeal for justice to the American Colonies. Again, my heart went out in sympathy to Emmet as he stood a condemned man, asking only the charity of the world's silence; and, though I did not understand what it was all about, I was moved by the beauty and tenderness of Curran's appeal to Lord Avonmore, closing with the lines which I then committed to memory and have never forgotten, referring to those "attic nights" which they could "remember without any

---

[1] "The elements of general culture ought to be accessible without effort to every member of the community. A nation is bound to provide for its children the possibility of becoming good citizens."

other regret than that they can never more return; for

> 'We spent them not in toys or lust or wine,
> But search of deep philosophy,
> Wit, eloquence and poesy;
> Arts which I loved, for they, my friend,
> were thine.'"

"But," the school-keeper may say, "this was not education. Very innocent amusement, and kept you out of mischief; but it didn't teach you anything. You'd better have been studying the arithmetic lesson that you failed in the next day."

Why, my dear sir, those poems and speeches were worth more to me than all the arithmetical knowledge of Zerah Colburn. Man cannot live on numbers. Compared to my school text-books this volume was as bread to bran, as ambrosia to bitter aloes. It did not, to be sure, teach me arithmetic; but it did much to teach me the English language—its spelling and grammar and rhetoric. And as President Eliot says, "The highest education can do no more than impart to the pupil an accurate and refined use of the mother tongue."

It also taught me history—real history, not dates and names. I learned from the speeches of Pitt and Wilkes and Barré, what my school history failed to teach me,—that Lord North's ministry was not the English nation, that all Englishmen were not blind to the injustice inflicted on the American Colonies. But more than this, I learned patriotism, love of liberty, regard for justice, admiration for manly courage and unselfish devotion to duty. If this book did not teach me arithmetic, it helped me to endure that study and other school burdens, and encouraged me to try to master any task set me, by impressing on me, through an exhortation of Sydney Smith, that nothing is to be gained without effort, that genius itself is powerless without labour. Was not this worth more than the rule for finding the greatest common divisor?

I may say, then, that during this period the most valuable part of my acquirement at school was what I got myself surreptitiously, or by special favour, against the rules of the school. The book I have referred to furnished a daily repast that was palatable and wholesome, though there was rather too much variety and spice about it. It was like picking the plums out of the pudding. Fortunately, I found more solid fare at home. But if the school curriculum had been properly arranged, if reading had been encouraged instead of forbidden, then, instead of mere extracts, I should have read, with the greater interest that comes of understanding and the growth and discipline that are gained by unity and continuity of thought, the whole of the "Iliad" and "Marmion" and "The Lady of the Lake," and a dozen good histories, perhaps a play or two of Shakespeare—for I remember, long before I reached the dignity of the *Fifth Reader*, listening with rapt attention to the platform scene wretchedly read by the "first class"—certainly Lamb's *Tales*, which I did not come across till two years later.

Actual experience often makes a point clearer than abstract argument; therefore, with due apology, I venture to continue with another chapter—a contrasting experience—from my own school life.

Just before entering the high school I went to another grammar school, presided over by a young man whose views and methods were diametrically opposed to those of my former teacher. He encouraged his pupils to read, and to write and debate about what they had read. Every Friday evening he invited some of us to his room, and read to us from the "Biglow Papers," or "Hiawatha," or "Evangeline," or other literature, prose or poetry, which served at once as a delight and an inspiration. Occasionally he tried on us a portion of an essay by Emerson, or something else that was then supplying his own mental growth. From these, too, we derived much enjoyment and profit, though the thought was only partially comprehended. That last term in the grammar school was the turning-point in my life: to those Friday evenings I owe the pleasure and honour of appearing to-day before this distinguished gathering.

Did our school studies suffer by the time given to other books? No; our school carried off the honours in the examinations for the high school, and members of our class kept the lead all through the high school course. We learned reading and spelling and grammar in the only way they can be learned—by familiarity with the English language. Books of travel gave interest to our geography lessons: the dry bones of our text-book on United States history had here and there been clothed with flesh and given somewhat the aspect of a living reality through our reading of "Last of the Mohicans," "Green Mountain Boys," and "Grandfather's Chair." In short, our text-books became interesting, because we had acquired from other books a desire for knowledge as the source of power and pleasure. Sir John Lubbock once said (I cannot now recall where or when, but I have repeated it so often that I might omit the quotation marks if the author were not near at hand, and if, moreover, I did not always want to add the weight of his name to the wisdom of his words):—

"The important thing is not so much that every child should be taught, as that every child should wish to learn. A boy who leaves school knowing much but hating his lessons, will soon have forgotten almost all he ever learned; while another who had acquired a thirst for knowledge, even if he had learned little, would soon teach himself more than the first ever knew."

To resume my narrative: this grammar-school principal, as the natural result of the success of his methods, was shortly promoted to the principalship of the high school; and the last two years of my course there were under his direct influence. My four years at the high school were thoroughly satisfactory; but the subsequent college course was, instead of an advance, a retrogression—a reversion to the old, dry, text-book, recitation methods of our early years. The case was, of course, much worse because of our consciousness of the evil and because of the greater value of our time. Moreover, the period for the differentiation of studies had arrived; and we were all compelled to follow the same prescribed course, I chafing under the compulsory waste of time on chemistry, the general principles of which—all I cared to know—I had previously learned; while one of my classmates, who had chemistry in view as his life pursuit, was cursing Greek—in which he found plenty of company, though it was not because, like him, we wanted more chemistry. In the high school we studied Homer and Virgil as literature: the Greek we read in college was treated as collections of sentences and words to be dissected for rules and derivations; and it was much the same with the Latin. If I could go over my college course again, I would give the hour a day that for two years I devoted to grubbing for dead Greek roots to the sowing of living seeds of thought that would yield a rich harvest in after-years. I am not opposing the study of Greek itself, though I think the number very small to whom it is now a profitable occupation; I am condemning the narrow text-book method of education.

The most **letter-perfect student I ever knew stood at the head of my class in** college: **the only** brilliant man **we had** stood at the foot. The former knew the text-books thoroughly, but nothing else, and his life has been an utter failure: the latter would not interrupt his reading of Hegel or Comte to find out what Sir William Hamilton had to say on the subject of the day's lesson; and, though he could not give in order the chapters and headings of Whately's Rhetoric, he had already absorbed its substance in an extended course of reading in English and German classics.

But I am not greatly concerned about college men: they are few, and they ought to be able to take care of themselves. College methods, too, have been pretty generally reformed in the last twenty-five years. The elective system **is about** universal, and **the seminar** plan is followed in all progressive institutions. My plea is for the great masses, who do not, who cannot, under present conditions, go beyond the grammar school—most of whom, indeed, fall far short of completing even this elementary course.

When upon graduating I took **charge of** a grammar school, I determined **to follow,** so far as I could, the methods **of the** master whom I considered, and **still** consider, an ideal teacher. In the outset I had it understood by the graduating class, which I personally instructed, that if the reading lesson was well prepared the first four days in the week, I would read to them on Friday. They complied with the condition and accomplished more in the four days than they would otherwise have done in five; and I believe the Friday reading hour was as profitable as any other two. They were always glad to meet me on Saturday mornings. One of the Saturday readings was Poe's "Gold-bug." For several weeks afterwards the whole class was eagerly occupied in inventing and deciphering cryptographs; and I believe that from this they got at least as good mental **exercise** as from their arithmetic. They **did not, meantime, neglect** their arithmetic; indeed they took greater interest in all their studies, for they began to see the connection of these with the realities of life. The extension of this method throughout the school was opposed by my assistants, who had become accustomed to the well-worn ruts of routine; but eventually they saw that real books did not clash with textbooks, but assisted them; and those teachers who most encouraged their pupils to read, made the best showing at examinations.

Higher education is more and more accepting the dictum of Carlyle, that "the true university is a collection of books." Now, what is wanted is a system of secondary and primary instruction that shall regard all children as candidates for this university and proceed at once to prepare them for it. This preparation cannot begin too soon. The child learning his letters, as well as the young man in college, should be taught that his textbooks are merely tools, keys to unlock the doors to the temple of knowledge—the library. The most important function of the school is to awaken curiosity and to point the way to its gratification through books. Dr. William T. Harris, United States Commissioner of Education, says, "What there is good in our American system, points towards this preparation of the pupil for independent study of the book by himself. It points towards acquiring the ability of self-education by means of the library."

It was Franklin's theory that a child should be taught nothing till he desires to learn it. This maxim put into practice would form the basis of an ideal education. According to any rational system, the highest office of the teacher is to incite and guide, not to goad and criticise. President Eliot says, "American teaching in schools and colleges has been chiefly driving and judging; it ought to be leading and inspiring." The first thing is to awaken interest. This is not difficult to do: the novelty and the infinite variety of the world about him make the child eager to learn. This desire should be quickened and fed, not deadened and crushed by setting him at dull tasks that seem to bring him no result and to have no relation to the things he wants to know. He wants knowledge itself, not the tools and symbols of knowledge. These, of course, he must acquire; but he should be shown the use of them as he goes along; he should never be allowed to lose sight of the end they are meant to subserve. How absurd to give a child that universal tool of knowledge, reading, and never show him how, or encourage him, to use it! It should be applied from the beginning, and used to open up to his eager mind the realm of knowledge in every direction. In the May number of the *American Journal of Sociology*, Professor Albion W. Small says, "It is a misconstruction of reality to think and accordingly to act as though one kind of knowledge belongs to one age and another to another. The whole vast mystery of life, in all its processes and conditions, confronts the child as really as it does the sage. It is the business of the educator to help the child interpret the part by the whole. Education from the beginning should be an initiation into science, language, philosophy, art, and political action in the largest sense. When we shall have adopted a thoroughly rational pedagogy, the child will begin to learn everything the moment he begins to learn anything. Am I demanding a pedagogy which presupposes one philosopher as teacher and another as pupil? Certainly. Every teacher ought to be a philosopher. Every child already is one until conventionality spoils him. More than that, he is a scientist, poet, and artist in embryo, and would mature in all these characters if we did not stunt him with our bungling."

Therefore, from the first, open up the world of books, which is nothing less than the accumulated thought and experience of the race from the beginning of its history. This may be done even before the child can read, and it will serve as the greatest possible incentive to him to learn to read. It will be found, too, that he can discriminate between that which has literary merit and a mere sequence of sentences written to accompany a picture. A four-year-old will show marked preference for "John Gilpin" or "The Night before Christmas" over the inanities that make up the text of the ordinary reading-book. I have known more than one four-year-old to whom the reading before bedtime was the greatest enjoyment of the day. One of them is now ten years old. Last summer at the age of nine he read "Ivanhoe," "Talisman," and "Quentin Durward." He had previously read Bulfinch's "Age of Chivalry" and "Age of Charlemagne," and other books of similar character. He has also read Bryant's translation of the "Iliad," a prose translation of the "Odyssey," Malory's "King Arthur," and several other versions of the Arthurian legends; Prescott's "Peru and Mexico," Macaulay's "Lays," Longfellow's "Hiawatha" and "Miles Standish," the Jungle Books, and other books too numerous to mention. This reading has not been done at the sacrifice of his lessons or his play, and has indeed added to the zest and profit of both. His parents feel that, if he were never to receive another day's schooling, his education is better begun and more sure of being continued—that he is better prepared for success in life than if he had gone to school to the age of sixteen or nineteen, but had nothing but text-books put into his hands. In other words, three years of instruction under the stimulus and inspiration of good literature is worth more than twelve years of the text-book grind. "The liking for a good book is of vastly more consequence to youth and manhood than a knowledge of the equation of payments or adverbial elements of the third form."

I have no idea what this boy is going to be; but whether it be a librarian, a lawyer, a doctor, an engineer, or a merchant, I know that he is making the very best preparation for his future work. Whatever occupation he may follow, he will find no greater aid than a knowledge of the English language, which he is thus unconsciously acquiring. Rev. Dr. Parkhurst says, "The first and pretty nearly the last thing that the public schools ought to do for the average child is to teach him to read, speak, and write the English language intelligently. This will afford him no end of mental discipline, and will at the same time put into his hand the key to every door that he may need to swing further on."

Just before I left home I was discussing this subject with a teacher of wide experience, formerly principal of a large high school, now a publisher of text-books. He entirely agreed with my views as to the supreme value of literature in early education and the waste of time over routine studies, especially arithmetic. He concluded with this striking statement: he said he would take a boy whose mind had been developed by familiarity with the best literature, but who had never had an arithmetic in his hand or received an hour's set instruction — who, in short, knew nothing but what he would inevitably pick up—and he would guarantee to teach that boy in six weeks all the arithmetic that he would need to know and as much as he would have learned in eight years of the ordinary text-book instruction, which, he added, tends as much to deaden as to develop. "It must never be forgotten," says Sully, "that all through life forced attention to what is wholly uninteresting is not only wearing, but certain to be ineffectual and unproductive." "The most pitiful sight in the world," says the late Edward Thring, "is the slow, good boy laboriously kneading himself into stupidity."

"The primary end of education," says Professor Mackenzie, "is rather to develop intelligence and power than to communicate particular kinds of information and skill."[1]

While, as I have said, the development of all the faculties begins at once, and the desire for knowledge should in some measure be gratified simultaneously in every direction, to certain ages properly belongs the special activity of certain mental powers. The imagination is supreme in childhood. Speaking of the importance of developing this in early education, Sully says, "The habitual narration of stories . . . is an essential ingredient in the rudimentary stages of education. The child that has been well drilled at home in following stories will, other things being equal, be the better learner at school. The early nurture of the imagination by means of good, wholesome food has much to do with determining the degree of imaginative power and, through this, of the range of intellect ultimately reached."

Memory also is particularly active in childhood. In his *Theory and Practice of Teaching*, Thring says, "The child has memory in childhood, reasoning power in manhood, as his main life functions. . . . Nature prescribes, accordingly, that the main business of the young is to collect material. . . . This determines the first great axiom . . . of early teaching: open fairyland. Endeavour to delight, interest, fascinate the child by judiciously supplying melodious sounds, splendid imagery, touching narratives, noble adventure, noble endurance, noble sufferings. There is a

[1] *An Introduction to Social Philosophy.* To this may be added this sentence in the same vein: "In general, the teacher must aim at imparting such knowledge as will be useful in nearly all kinds of circumstances, such as will supply a key to a great variety of things, and, above all, such as will stimulate interest and develop character."

fearful theory born and bred in the quagmires of Marsh-dunce-land, that nothing is learning unless it is disagreeable, or worth having unless it is difficult. Thus the high beauty of the Waverley novels, the winsome charm of ballads, the music of lyric poetry, the glorious metrical romances of Scott, the holy organ tones of immortal song, are not considered to be training because they delight. But the world is large enough to tire the strongest. The more difficulties are removed, the farther the wayfarer can get. There is no fear that a too easy progress will ever do away with the need of labour.

Herbert Spencer expresses the same idea briefly in this sentence: "The method of culture must be one productive of an intrinsically happy activity — an activity not happy in virtue of extrinsic rewards, but in virtue of its own healthfulness." With the adoption of such a method, "the schoolhouse" will be, as Mr. Wotton, the friend of Roger Ascham, said it "should be, the house of play and pleasure and not of fear and bondage." The school, however, can never realise this ideal, it can never yield to the pupil that highest happiness which consists in "the exercise of unforced and unimpeded energy," it can never prepare the future man or woman for "complete living" so long as it puts none but text-books into the hands of boys and girls, so long as it fails to adopt as its cardinal maxim that its first and most important office is to stimulate the child's natural thirst for knowledge, so long as it fails to prepare the child for self-education through books, so long as it neglects the vitalising, inspiring, uplifting, ennobling power of literature.

In his preface to that admirable series, the "Heart of Oak" books, Professor Charles Eliot Norton says, "Poetry is one of the most efficient means of education of the moral sentiment, as well as of the intelligence. It is the best source of culture. A man may know all science and yet remain uneducated. But let him truly possess himself of the work of any one of the great poets, and, no matter what else he may fail to know, he is not without education."

The inadequacy of our educational systems arises, it seems to me, from three causes: first, from our failure to recognise practically, though we accept theoretically, the solidarity of the nation; second, from the narrow view of education as merely a preparation for making a living; third, from disregard of the obvious fact that since the vast majority of our children leave school at thirteen years of age, their schooling should provide for their continued development by starting them early in the path of self-culture. The public library has made this self-education easy if the desire for it exists. During our late campaign for a public library building in St. Louis, a Catholic priest, in the course of an exhortation to his congregation to vote for the tax, said:—

"Most of the people finish their schooling at the age of fourteen to sixteen. The public library enables them, if they have acquired at all the love of books, to add to and in many cases fairly complete their education. *If they have not acquired this love of books, it speaks badly for the system of schooling which they did have until their fourteenth or sixteenth year. The best test of a system of education is whether it creates and continues in those receiving it a taste for books and reading.*"

But the most potent and all-pervading source of educational weakness is limiting education to mere preparation for industrial pursuits. I accept in the main Spencer's "rational order of subordination" in education, but I hold that preparation in all these divisions should go on simultaneously, and that they can be made to do so through co-operation of school and library. Moreover, the whole includes the part; the higher aim will not fail of the lower mark. If children are in their earliest years brought into intimate contact with the higher life of the race, if they become familiar with the best thoughts of the greatest men of all ages, they will hardly fail of the plainest duties of life; they will hardly lack the ability and the will to make a living. In the words of Charles Dudley Warner, "Real literature is the best open door to the development of the mind and to knowledge of all sorts. The shortest road to the practical education so much insisted on in these days, begins in [thus] awakening the faculties."

What we want, what education should aim to create, is not mechanics or farmers or engineers or merchants, but *men*. This should be kept in view even in professional schools. An eminent civil engineer said to Professor Atkinson, "Do not train your young men into *mere engineers*. I can hire plenty of professional knowledge at any time, but what

I cannot find is the *men* I want to do professional work."

"With respect to the training of specialised abilities, the first requirement is to ensure their specialisation in the right direction. For this purpose it is important that everyone should be provided, as near the outset as possible, with a broad survey of life as a whole, in order that he may be able to choose as wisely as possible the particular line in which his own tastes and capacities lead him. This fact furnishes us with an additional argument for limiting the earlier parts of education to what is most universally applicable rather than to what is most immediately useful for practical purposes."[1]

If their early education is properly directed, advanced students will, before the age of preparation for their special work, have acquired an acquaintance with literature and a love for reading that they will never lose; and, other things being equal, they will be better students and more successful men, even in the narrower sense of professional success. For inspiration is better than instruction; a *desire* for knowledge is worth more than any knowledge that can be acquired in school or college; and it is written, "Man shall not live by bread alone." As that noble American, George William Curtis, once said, "The highest gift of education is not the mastery of sciences, but noble living, generous character, the spiritual delight that comes from familiarity with the loftiest ideals of the human mind, the spiritual power that saves each generation from the intoxication of its own success."

My plea is for the great mass of children who have little or no home training and but few years of schooling. Whether they remain at school four or six or eight or ten years, I would have those years made years of pleasure: I would give them a taste of the highest joys of human life—"the purest and most perfect pleasures that God has prepared for His creatures." However little they might learn, I would awaken and stimulate in them that divine thirst for knowledge that will impel them ever onward and upward through life. I would lead the child to the library, and tell him that here are gathered the most precious, the only indestructible treasures in the world—the accumulation of all time; that they are his—that he may help himself to whatever will yield him the greatest profit and enjoyment. Then, whether he leave school at ten or twelve or fourteen, it will be to become a life student in the People's University, the public library, in which he will find an infinite variety of elective courses adapted to every age, taste, and capacity.

Our school systems have been indifferently reformed; but the public library makes it possible to reform them altogether. Let text-books be made merely an introduction to real books: let the child from the first be brought into familiar contact with the highest thoughts and aspirations of the race: arouse in him "historic consciousness": awaken in him purer desires than those of the flesh, nobler ambitions than the acquirement of wealth and the enjoyment of luxury: place before him those ideals pronounced worthiest by the consensus of mankind. He will thus learn that his activity and usefulness, and his consequent happiness, depend in this world largely on the health and vigour of his body; that his body is the temple of the living soul, and that it must be kept clean and pure—a fit habitation for an immortal spirit. He will realise that he is the heir of all the ages, and that it is his duty to transmit that heritage, duly enriched, to succeeding generations; that, above all, it is his sacred obligation to give to those he has brought into the world the best possible training—mental, moral, and physical—and that the performance of this duty begins prior to fatherhood. He will know that, as he profits by the labours of countless millions in all parts of the world, he owes to his fellow-men a reciprocal service, and especially to those with whom he is bound by ties of a common nationality. And his reading of history will teach him that we owe the

---

[1] "In a complete education there seems to be three main stages. In the first place, there is that training which is necessary to produce a human being at all. In the second place, there is the training which is necessary to enable the man to become the particular individual into which he is by nature fitted to develop. In the third place, there is the training by which he is enabled to bring his own individuality into harmonious relationship with the rest of his world. In other words, we have first to acquire intelligence, then abilities, then wisdom.

"In spite of the authority of Dogberry, it is scarcely true that 'reading and writing come by nature'; but it is in the main true that those kinds of knowledge and ability which are immediately applicable to the affairs of life, are readily acquired by anyone whose intelligence has been fairly well developed. Hence it is on the whole safe to 'take care of the beautiful' and let 'the useful take care of itself.' There is not much fear that the common will be neglected. It is more important that we should be taught to rise above the commonplace, by which, as Goethe tells us, we are all in danger of being limited."—*An Introduction to Social Philosophy*, by Professor John S. Mackenzie, p. 410 *et seq.*

liberty and security that we now enjoy to a process of development which is far from complete, and that his views and his acts constitute contributing factors, however minute, in this infinite progress. All this will come to him as the natural result of a desire for knowledge and a taste for reading acquired in childhood; and having all this, there can be no doubt of his ability to render services that will secure for him the means of physical subsistence. The whole includes the part, the higher life the lower.

By thus placing the child in his earliest years under the tutorship, and securing for him through life the guidance and companionship, of the wisest, greatest, and best of mankind, you will develop his soul, you will furnish his mind with high ideals; you will lead him to "complete living"; you will enable him to secure success in life; you will make him "a brave, helpful, truth-telling Englishman, and a gentleman and a Christian."

"Let, then, lesson-books and lesson-hearers depart, and reading-books and teachers come in."

FRED'K. M. CRUNDEN.

NATIONAL BIOGRAPHY AND NATIONAL BIBLIOGRAPHY.

 HOPE I may take for granted that the librarians who are attending this Conference are acquainted with the *Dictionary of National Biography*. I had an opportunity of setting forth, in a lecture which I delivered last year at the Royal Institution, the general principles which determined the Dictionary's form and methods. The publisher of the Dictionary, Mr. George Smith, to whose enterprise and public spirit the work is due, and who honours us by his presence here to-day, has presented copies of this lecture to members of the Conference, and I understand that it is now in your hands.

I need not traverse ground that is, or will be, familiar to you (for I hope that you will find time to read my lecture), but I believe that I shall make my immediate purpose plainer if I devote a very few words to the Dictionary's aims and scope. In general terms, the Dictionary may be defined as a biographical census of all dwellers in the British dominions who have achieved anything that is likely to be deemed by their successors worthy of commemoration. No field of human energy lies outside our scope. We do not even overlook those who by evil deeds have left any permanent impression upon the nation's history, or have permanently excited the nation's imagination. Our business is not panegyric. We have to record with accuracy, sobriety, and impartiality every achievement of Englishman, Scotchman, Irishman, Welshman, or Colonist—and, as in Acts of Parliament, I intend the word "man" to denote "woman" as well—respecting whom information may be sought, now or hereafter, either by the student or the general reader.

I hope the visitors of other countries will forgive me for confining my survey of both national ·biography and national bibliography to the experiments made in both directions in this country alone, but I hope that I may say something that may be of service to other countries if our visitors will be good enough to substitute for the words "British Empire" the words "United States of America," or one or other of the great nations of Europe which are here represented.

The most notable feature in our methods of execution is our effort to give our authority for every fact we record. To each of our articles we append, in justification of our statements, a list of books or manuscripts, sometimes with critical comments on their credibility, which are intended to serve those who may afterwards follow in our footsteps. We also introduce *into the text of our articles* full references to sources of information respecting particular facts which are either matters of controversy or have hitherto escaped the notice of inquirers. The value of our articles, I venture to think, often largely depends upon the completeness of the critical apparatus which our bibliographical references supply.

The *Life of Shakespeare* would be practically useless did we not carefully determine step by step the authenticity of each of the traditions which have accumulated about his name. If any will do me the honour of examining that Life in the Dictionary, they will, I think, recognise that I have in effect attempted on a modest scale a bibliography of Shakespeariana arranged in the order in which the student of Shakespearian biography is likely to find it convenient to approach the books.

My bibliography is far from complete; the catalogues of the British Museum Library, with its 3680 entries, the Barton collection in the Boston Public Library, with its 2500 entries, and the Birmingham

Public Library, with 9640 volumes, supply far longer lists of Shakespeariana. But, following the example of Mr. H. R. Tedder, the honorary treasurer of this Conference, who added a bibliographical appendix to the article "Shakespeare" in the last edition of the *Encyclopædia Britannica*, I have endeavoured to observe some logical principle of classification which the larger library catalogues do not attempt.

Important books bearing upon critical incidents in Shakespeare's career are enumerated at the close of the paragraphs dealing with those incidents. The accounts of the poaching affray at Charlecote, of the travels of acting companies in which Shakespeare is often alleged to have taken part, of the publication and significance of the Sonnets, of the arguments for and against Shakespeare's responsibility for plays of dubious authorship, of the authenticity of the portraits, of the growth of Shakespeare's reputation at home and abroad,—my remarks on these subjects are fortified by a mention of the publications where opinions of value which other writers hold on such topics may best be studied.

At the close I give a chronological list of all original works which attempt a general biography, from Fuller's Worthies of 1662, in which the earliest attempt at a biography of Shakespeare was made, to Mr. Fleay's recent *Biographical Chronicle of the English Drama*, a short list of histories of Stratford-on-Avon, of concordances, and of notable collections of general criticism. I conclude with a brief bibliography of the Bacon-Shakespeare controversy, which I bring as far as Mr. Donnelly's *Cryptogram*.

I feel it somewhat presumptuous in me to suggest any change in the methods of cataloguing adopted by librarians; but I venture to suggest, merely in the capacity of a student of catalogues of Shakespeariana, that when cataloguing their "Shakespeariana" they might not find it unprofitable, at anyrate, to consider the principle of classification which the Dictionary seeks to exemplify. It will at least compare favourably with the common arrangement, which brings into immediately consecutive order such items as a forgotten elocution master's Shakespearian readings, Mr. W. H. Smith's lame argument in favour of the Baconian hypothesis, some early eighteenth-century anonymous remarks on Hamlet, an obscure historical play on Shakespeare's early days by a recent writer, illustrated editions of Shakespeare's songs, a collection of songs sung at the Stratford Jubilee organised by Garrick, an anonymous article in the *Westminster Review* on the Sonnets, and Spalding's valuable essay on the authorship of the *Two Noble Kinsmen*.

Of course there is no other author whose work has evoked so large a literature. Shakespeare consequently occupies an exceptional position in catalogues and elsewhere. But there are a good many authors about whom much interesting and valuable critical or biographical literature has collected—for example: Sir Walter Scott, Milton, Dryden, Sir Walter Raleigh, Dr. Johnson, Alexander Pope, and Charles Dickens.

A principle of classification under the general heading of the author's name, of titles of books dealing with his biography and criticism, similar to that adopted in the Dictionary, would, I believe, increase the value of library catalogues for students and readers of our great authors.

Take the comparatively simple case of Sir Walter Scott, ample materials for whose biography are found in comparatively few books. After lists of his separate publications in order of dates of the chief collected editions of his works, you would set down Lockhart's *Life*, followed by the recently published *Journals and Familiar Letters*, and the chief volumes of reminiscences, like those of James Hogg, R. P. Gillies, and Washington Irving's *Abbotsford*.

In the more difficult case of Sir Walter Raleigh, an enumeration of his literary works is succeeded in the Dictionary by brief critical notices of as many as ten modern general lives, while many monographs are noticed dealing exclusively with separate episodes of his career—his adventures in Ireland, his relations with North American exploration, his expedition to Guiana, and his literary efforts. Detailed references are also given to the accounts of his political career appearing in the chief political histories of the time, and to papers issued by the Devonshire Archæological Association on his family history and position in local society.

In the case of less eminent personages, there is no opportunity of observing any elaborate principles of classification in the enumeration of our sources of knowledge. All that is possible is to mention as a rule in chronological sequence the chief articles or memoirs previously published. But where, as often happens, the subject of the biography has devoted himself to developing some mechanical or scientific invention or some profitable train of thought in religion, philosophy, economics, or the natural sciences, it is desirable to tabulate among our authorities the books where the history of the topic has been already dealt with, so as to enable the reader to realise the character and extent of the advance made by the subject of the biography. In the case of eminent horologists or watchmakers like Thomas Mudge or Daniel Quare, we supply in our bibliographical appendices many references to the literature of horology. Our article on William Murdoch, the inventor of coal-gas lighting, or Patrick Miller, the projector of steam navigation, supplies at least the rudiments of bibliography of both those engaging topics. Our articles on the city poets—Thomas Middleton, Munday, Jordan, and Elkanah Settle—suggest the places where full light is shed on the genesis and development of the Lord Mayor's Show—a pageant which, in the days when it was officially illustrated by poems, came closer to the domain of literature than it does now that it is shorn of literary ornament. If anyone seeks to investigate the byways of religious life, he has only to turn to the article on founders of sects like Muggleton, Sandeman, or Ann Lee, the originator of the Society of Shakers, and study both the articles and their bibliographical appendices.

The literature of great events in history, like the struggle for Welsh independence, the growth of Welsh and English Methodism, the emigration of the Pilgrim Fathers, the Jacobite rebellions, the Irish outbreak of 1798, and practically every incident that has stirred the nation,—the literature recording such events is briefly catalogued under the names of the effective actors.

I could give the names of hundreds of men whose memoirs in the Dictionary supply the titles of books throwing light on dark places in the suppression of the Indian Mutiny. Take, again, our accounts of those who took part in the first Afghan War of 1842, which opened with the massacre of Kabul and the retreat and massacre of the British army through the Khyber Pass, and ended with the triumph of our armies at Jellalabad and Gandamak. I hope if you examine our biographies of MacNaghten, Burnes, Brydon,

Pollock, Nott, and Sale, that you will not find omitted any book that illustrates any important aspect of that disaster and its ultimate reparation. The same may be said of our references to a single incident in the Crimean War—the charge of the Light Brigade—as anyone can test for himself by examining our articles on Lord Cardigan or Raglan, and, above all, our article on a less eminent soldier, a knowledge of whose career is more or less needful to a full understanding of that fatality—our article on Captain Nolan, who was sent by Lord Raglan with the order that resulted in the charge.

Detailed accounts of epochs of literary history could be equally well worked out from the books enumerated under the names of Dr. Johnson and his disciples or of Byron and his friends, while interesting phases of literary or artistic society could, I believe, be recovered by similar examination of the memoirs by Mrs. Elizabeth Montagu and members of her bluestocking circle, or of Allan Ramsay, the Edinburgh barber-poet.

The Dictionary's list of authorities thus contains much that is material for the preparation of a subject-catalogue of literature. A subject-catalogue is obviously of high importance in developing the utility of public libraries. A perfect librarian—that is, one who combines with his other functions a capacity to guide his readers to the books where the subject they seek to study may be best and most exhaustively studied—should be himself a walking subject-catalogue. I daresay they often are. But many a perfect librarian, and many an assistant librarian who is on the road to becoming a perfect librarian, might, I believe, find his journey facilitated were he to use the Dictionary as the groundwork or substitute or supplement for a subject-catalogue. Of course I know there are many admirable subject-catalogues in existence. There are Mr. Fortescue's subject-catalogues of recent acquisition at the British Museum, of which all I need say is that they are so useful that I deeply regret that they do not cover chronologically more extended ground. There are indexes of wider scope, like that to Mr. Sonnenschein's bibliographics, which, serving the single purpose of subject-catalogues, are perhaps so arranged as to be easier of consultation than the Dictionary, which serves a great many other purposes. The Dictionary is, moreover, practically limited to the achievement of the **English-speaking** subjects of the British **Empire**, although we tabulate works **by foreign writers** throwing light on such achievement.

After making these qualifications, **and** allowing that **the** Dictionary treats **all** topics almost exclusively in their historical **aspect, I think** our bibliographical references **will** facilitate minute investigation, in pure historical research at anyrate, more efficiently than almost any existing subject-catalogue.

I notice, **for example, that in Mr.** Sonnenschein's *Best Books*, **under the** heading "**British Campaigns in Afghanistan,**" he notes only three volumes which are likely to aid students of that subject, whereas the Dictionary records nearly twenty. **When the work is** completed, it might **perhaps be possible to** devise an index **which should make the** uses of the Dictionary **more obvious in** this relation. Such an index **would in** effect be an index **to** British history **in** all its aspects —political, naval, military, literary, artistic, religious, legal, and social; but, even in the absence of such an aid, I do not think I have over-estimated the service that the Dictionary renders in sagacious hands to those who stand in need of a minute subject-catalogue.

The making of subject-catalogues is a subsidiary branch of the science of bibliography. In its essence, bibliography is the science of describing books as books in contradistinction to books as literature. To the bibliographer **the** contents or subject-matter of a book are **by** no means of first importance. **His** attention is mainly concentrated **on such** external material details **as the** title-page, the date of publication, **the place** of publication, the **printer's name, the** character of the **type, the number and** often the linear measure **of the** pages. The biographer need **not** concern himself with the whole **of** these details, but whenever he writes **the life of one** who has written books he **has to trench** on much that lies within the **bibliographer's** province. The **life** of an **author, that is to say,** such **portions of his life as are** worthy of commemoration, centres about the composition and publication of books, and, **in** a large record like the *Dictionary of National Biography*, which owes its efficiency to conciseness of treatment in its component parts, a small author's life must often resolve itself into **a catalogue** of the books he has com**posed and** published. In such a case a biographer, **for** all practical purposes, has to play **the** part of bibliographer. But the biographer ought always to remember that he is treating books **as** acts and **deeds**; for him they are parts **of** his hero's life. He has to bestow his chief attention on such of the books as are most closely interwoven with the author's intellectual development or material progress. In dealing with the life of Thomas Scott, the Calvinistic minister of the Church of England, whose commentaries on the Bible intensified the country's piety, as Cardinal **Newman** admitted in his *Apologia* from personal experience, our writer mainly dwells on the facts connected with **Scott's** composition of his voluminous **edition of** the Bible. The technicalities **that are** essential to the bibliographer's description of that or any other publication, **the** biographer **is** not merely permitted, **he is** bound, to **ignore.** Despite the enforced absence of technicalities, a work planned on the scale of the *Dictionary of National Biography* ought in the result to offer an exhaustive catalogue under authors' names of the titles of all books that have exerted influence of any moment on any section of the nation. If we who have contributed to the Dictionary have done our **work** aright, the Dictionary should supply **a** full account of the literary effort of the British Empire.

I am not of opinion that everything that is printed should find mention in a work like the Dictionary, or even in any work specially devoted to national bibliography, if national bibliography is to serve practical ends. The principle of selection, if effective completeness is **sought,** must be generously **conceived, and of course it** must not **be limited by** personal or sectional **prejudices. Discretion** must be given free **play. Literature** that serves in any degree **an** explicable purpose from any point **of** view, either æsthetic or historical or scientific, or even anthropological, is our quarry, and the bio-bibliographer **must** exercise his judgment in excluding or including each book as each one comes under his notice.

In dealing with only one class of printed **matter** have I deemed it desirable in my **own** experience to enunciate a hard-and-fast rule. Some years ago I laid down **for** my contributors the regulation that **"no sermons** or religious tracts should **be included in a list of an author's** publications unless of a very early date or possessing very special interest." I am not disposed to dispute the practical wisdom of this regulation. Sermons and religious tracts should always be spoken of respectfully. But national biography only deals with the distinctive features of a man's career,—with the features which distinguish one man's career from those of other men's careers. The composition of sermons and religious tracts forms part of their author's daily or weekly official duties. When we state that a man is a minister of religion, it goes without saying that he preaches a sermon fifty or more times a year. It is no uncommon practice in the seventeenth and eighteenth centuries for popular preachers to print five or six sermons annually—each under a different title—of inordinate length. Often the titles of all the published sermons of one preacher would fill many of our columns, and the space so occupied would in no way aid us in realising our aim of recording the distinctive achievements of our heroes, except in special cases, such as I will define in a minute or two. The national biographer adequately does his duty if he merely mentions the number in figures of those of his hero's discourses that enjoyed the honour of publication. The conscientious biographer may deem it needful to print all the titles at length, but I am not sure that such conscientiousness will even win the gratitude of librarians. I know it would excite the spleen of readers of a national biography.

By sermons or religious tracts of special interest I mean those which deeply affect large sections of the nation and leave an impress on the nation's history. The two sermons of Henry Sacheverell, the High Church parson, which led to his impeachment by the House of Commons in Queen Anne's reign and seemed at one time likely to produce a popular revolution, are the leading facts in the preacher's career, and all the information we can collect about them is pertinent to biography.

Keble's discourse on National Apostacy, preached at Oxford in 1833, which Newman always "considered the start of the Oxford movement," stands on the same footing; while Newman's Tract No. 90 is a good illustration of a religious tract answering my definition of one "possessing very special interest."

Collections of sermons published in one or more volumes, a mode of publication in itself proof that the preacher enjoyed an unusual measure of estimation, we invariably note.

The rules that apply to separate sermons apply equally well to all controversial literature that fails to become classical. Modern pamphlets, especially on passing phases of politics, hardly deserve, as a rule, more bibliographical attention than leading articles in the daily newspapers. But wherever a pamphlet can be shown to influence public policy, as in the case of Burke's tracts on the French Revolution or Mr. Gladstone's tracts on the Eastern question of twenty years ago, it must be accorded almost as much attention as a play of Shakespeare in Shakespeare's biography or a novel of Sir Walter Scott's in Scott's biography.

Thus, despite all limitations and the absence of the technicalities that belong to purely scientific bibliography, the memoirs of writers of books in a work like the Dictionary ought to satisfy the reasonable demands of intelligent readers, modest book-collectors of the more robust type, and directors of moderate-sized public libraries. In the case of early writers, say down to the end of Queen Mary's reign, all of whose books are rare and inaccessible, our aim has been not merely to mention all that are known to be extant, with an indication of the place where a copy may now be consulted, but the names of works which, although not now known to be extant, are known from trustworthy evidence to have been at some former time in existence. A lost book may possibly be recovered. There are many old libraries the contents of which are still as imperfectly known as was the library of Sir Charles Isham at Lamport Hall thirty years ago, when some of the richest extant treasures of Elizabethan literature were brought to light there for the first time for some two centuries and a half. We desire to give what aid we can in the establishing of the identity of newly-discovered literary treasures.

This may sound like a counsel of perfection, and this aim of ours may not always have been reached; but it was, and is, one of our aims. From the opening of Elizabeth's reign to the outbreak of the Civil Wars, some ninety-four years later, we have endeavoured to note in similar detail the publication and, wherever we could, the hitherto unprinted writings of all who achieved, or deserved to achieve, a genuine reputation in that great period of literary activity. During the Civil Wars we have endeavoured to allot to the authors we commemorate the more influential of those political and religious pamphlets in which the contemporary questions at issue were almost as hotly debated as on the field of battle. Thomason's great collection of seventeenth-century tracts in the British Museum has been overhauled by our writers, who have stripped many a malignant pamphleteer of his veil of anonymity. During the later periods we have consciously excluded very little apart from sermons and religious tracts. But we have not deemed it necessary to set forth in full the titles of every contribution to forgotten controversies, whether theological or otherwise. We have omitted, too, persons of whom nothing is known except that their names figure on the title-page of a single unimportant volume, and we have treated somewhat cavalierly poetasters and novelists of the last and present century whose reputation, always slender, may be treated as dead and buried and past the hope of resurrection. None the less we have cast our net very wide, and, for the sake of our own reputation and our pretensions to completeness, I have no personal wish that those writers whom we have omitted should, metaphorically speaking, come to life again.

National bibliography, I am aware, has been three or four times attempted independently and on a generous scale.

For the literature of Great Britain and Ireland there exists at present four notable experiments in national bibliography. At the beginning of the century Robert Watt, a poor surgeon of Paisley, sacrificed twenty years of arduous labour in compiling his *Bibliotheca Britannica*, an elaborate catalogue mainly of British literature, though a few foreign works are included, arranged in two indexes—one of authors' names, the other of the titles of books. The history of the publication is not encouraging to those who propose to follow in the same footsteps. Hardly any publication encountered a longer series of disasters. The author died when the printing of the MS. had just begun. His two sons, John and James, undertook to see it through the press, and one of them, John, died while most of the sheets were yet in proof. A portion of the MS. was then burnt by burglars, but the surviving son, James, repaired the damage, and, having seen the whole in type, sold the copies and all his rights in them to the Edinburgh publishers, Archibald Constable & Co., Sir Walter Scott's partners. James Watt received in payment bills of the nominal value of £2000, but when the bills fell due they were dishonoured. Neither the author nor his family thus received a single penny in exchange for their self-denying industry, and some years later Watt's last surviving daughter died in a Glasgow workhouse. Such was the reward accorded to the first endeavour to provide the nation with a national bibliography. It is seventy-three years ago since the last part of Watt's *Bibliotheca* was published. I believe public opinion in this country would not tolerate a repetition of the tragedy, at anyrate in all its gloomy episodes. The fact that Watt's *Bibliotheca* now fetches from £6 to £8 when it figures in public sales, is proof that it has at length achieved public estimation. Watt's performance is in no way critical. His index of authors was really little more than a magnified bookseller's catalogue, and his predilection for science led him, not always wisely, to supply in separate entries the titles of all papers contributed to transactions of scientific societies, thus greatly extending the bulk of the volume with hardly an equivalent advantage to the student.

The next effort in national bibliography was made by William Thomas Lowndes, who, in his *Bibliographer's Manual*, first published in 1834, endeavoured to arrange the titles of books (under authors' names) with some regard to their intrinsic interest. Lowndes mentions less than half the publications noticed by Watt, but, as in Watt's case, his labours brought him neither fame nor money. He finally became cataloguer to Henry George Bohn, the well-known bookseller and publisher, who, after Lowndes' death, revised, improved, and republished his manual. Lowndes, after many years of abject poverty, lost his reason, and died in 1843.

The third great attempt at a bibliography of English literature was made in America, and it is to the credit of that great country that its history involves no distressing incident, like those which accompanied the efforts of Watt and Lowndes. Allibone's ample *Dictionary of English Literature* was projected in 1850, and the last proof-sheets were read by the author on the last day of 1870.

The work was published by Messrs. Lippincott of Philadelphia, in three large volumes, and a supplement in two volumes, almost equally large, appeared in 1891. Living authors are included as well as the dead, and to all books of importance there are appended illustrative quotations from critical reviews. Although Allibone's book is open to criticism—a good many titles are included which could be spared, a good many books are noted which the compiler had not personally examined; there are very conspicuous inequalities of treatment on almost every other page, and many blunders—yet the work is an invaluable book of reference, as every librarian will acknowledge.

The fourth great experiment in national bibliography is the printed British Museum Catalogue, which is a permanent memorial of the skill, knowledge, and industry of Dr. Garnett, the keeper of printed books, and his staff. As befits the catalogue of a great national collection, its leading object is necessarily to render the books in the British Museum library easy of access to readers. It, of course, mentions no book that is not in that collection, and therefore makes no claim to be an exhaustive index to literature. Foreign books and the books of living authors that are on the shelves of the library are, of course, included. Dr. Garnett will forgive me if I say that his catalogue is not at all points perfect, but its defects are inconsiderable when compared with its general efficiency.

To all these works, and especially to the British Museum Catalogue, the *Dictionary of National Biography* owes very much. But I believe that the bibliography it supplies will compare favourably with any of them. I have taken at random the names of four authors whose works are likely to be frequently consulted by students or general readers, and I have compared the accounts given of them by the Dictionary with those given of them by the earlier experimenters in national bibliography. I take first Nicholas Breton, a voluminous and attractive Elizabethan writer in both prose and verse, whom no student of the period can afford to neglect: Watt mentions sixteen of his publications, Lowndes fifty-one, but of these seven at least are wrongly ascribed to him; Allibone gives no list, but merely refers his reader to Lowndes' account; the British Museum Catalogue gives twenty-nine, the Dictionary forty-four. In the case of the poet Andrew Marvell, Watt mentions eight works, Allibone and Lowndes each five, the British Museum Catalogue fourteen, including some doubtful entries, the Dictionary sixteen, of which five are shown to be dubious. Of Fielding's works—novels and plays—Watt enumerates twenty-three, Lowndes only four, Allibone thirty-one, the British Museum Catalogue thirty-six, the Dictionary forty-one. In the case of a more modern writer like Thomas Love Peacock, who flourished after Watt and Lowndes had ended their labours, Allibone mentions twelve publications, the British Museum Catalogue sixteen, the Dictionary eighteen. Thus, to sum up in the case of these four authors, we find that Watt only deals with forty-seven of their books, Lowndes with sixty, Allibone with thirty-nine, and the British Museum Catalogue with ninety-five, while the Dictionary records a total of 119. I do not wish to attach undue importance to these statistics, but I believe the figures roughly indicate the degree of completeness subsisting among these five elaborate endeavours to form a national bibliography.

I am aware that the bibliography of the Dictionary has been occasionally criticised from two mutually contradictory points of view. It has been objected that, in a work having so many other objects, we pay more attention to bibliography than it deserves; while I have heard it hinted, on the other hand, that here and there we have paid too little attention to bibliography. With regard to the second point, if we have inadvertently sinned against our established rules of inclusion or exclusion in one or two of our 30,000 articles, we may hope to supply the defects. Critics holding the first view have asserted that men and women who write books figure more numerously in our pages than any other class of the community, and our predilection for authors has been explained on the homeopathic principle that the compilers of the Dictionary, being themselves men and women of letters, prefer to deal with the practisers of their own craft rather than the practisers of another. I do not think this criticism, which has always been expressed in the friendliest terms, is quite justifiable. As I have said, whenever we commemorate a man who happens to have written a book, we record the fact. But not all the men, the titles of whose publications we record, prove, when their articles are carefully read, to be, like most of the contributors to the Dictionary, professional authors. Physicians, surgeons, soldiers, sailors, artists, actors, lawyers, occasionally write books, but they can very rarely be classed among professional authors; and if this qualification be allowed, I do not think that the professional authors who figure in the Dictionary are greatly in excess of the representatives of other professions. Even if the criticism were justifiable, I do not think the result is one which librarians are likely to deplore.

I could conceive a national bibliography which should be independent of national biography, that should satisfy at all points the desires of the technical bibliographer, and should prove a far more exhaustive catalogue of titles than the Dictionary could within its limits supply. But when one considers the organisation requisite for so herculean a labour, the vast expense it would entail, and the improbability that the general public, which regards bibliography as something of a dismal science, would bestow upon the enterprise much effective favour, I doubt the possibilities of its realisation. Librarians are the persons to take such a scheme in hand, but remembrance of the fate of Watt and Lowndes will not, I fear, evoke among them much enthusiasm for the suggestion. At anyrate, while they are hesitating to come forward, they may be expected to study our Dictionary with some enthusiasm, and to express gratitude to Mr. George Smith, the initiator and proprietor of the Dictionary, and to Mr. Leslie Stephen, my predecessor as editor, who defined the scope of the work, for having relieved them of the pressing necessity for sacrificing their lives and fortunes at the altar of national bibliography.

SIDNEY LEE.

THE RELATIONS OF BIBLIOGRAPHY AND CATALOGUING.

VERY great improvement brings with it its small dangers and **temptations**, and the **trifling** dangers of which I am about to speak—for as yet they are little more—may perhaps be regarded as arising out of the inestimable advantage of printed catalogues. So long as a catalogue remains in manuscript, no one is likely to spend his time in foisting upon it bibliographical refinements, whether of arrangement or of description. But as soon as it comes to be prepared for press, the compiler is sorely tempted to bethink him of the existence of other librarians into whose hands it will fall, and of other catalogues with which it may be compared; and **a** spirit of rivalry may spring up, quite healthy in itself, which **may** possibly lead our cataloguer at least **some** inches astray from his proper business. Even in the breast of such a fly **on** the wheel as the writer of this paper, **a** wild desire at times arises that, in this point or that, the British Museum should "go one better" than the Bibliothèque Nationale; and it is at such moments, when they occur **to** more responsible persons, that the interests of readers, who care very little for the minutiæ which we think important—who, **in** fact, **only want to** get their books as quickly **as possible**—are in danger of suffering. **For, if we are** honest, we must confess that **what** readers **do** want from us, in ninety-nine cases out of a hundred, is just this and **no** more—to help them to get their **books** quickly; and that as we are bound in honour to be librarians first (for business), and bibliographers afterwards (mainly for pleasure), any system which compels **a reader** to look **in two** places instead of **one, any system** which compels him to **read a page of a** catalogue instead of **a single entry,** any system which demands of him the special knowledge which it is so easy for us to pick up in the course of our work, but for which he may have no opportunities or **no** appetite, is really, from the point **of** view of librarianship, fundamentally wrong.

To take some trifling examples first, I hope we shall all agree in condemning the pedants who want to enter the works of Ouida (despite her protests) under her birth-name, La Ramée, or those of Max O'Rell under Blouet, or those of George Eliot under Evans, or Lewes, or Cross.[1] It is said, of course, that the **real names** of these writers **are an open secret,** or not a secret at all. **But if it is our** business to know these **facts it is not the** business of our readers, **and to send them** from one end of the **catalogue to another, in** order that **we may air our knowledge, is** surely unwarrantable.

I wish I **were equally sure of** carrying this Conference **with me in my own** preference **for** the alphabetical **system of** arranging a subject-catalogue **over** the most beautiful of those logical classifications, which demand that a reader shall take exactly the same view as the librarian of that very debatable subject, the classification of knowledge, or else that he shall **refer to** the catalogue at least twice for every subject required. It seems to me so obviously better, if I want a book on Miracles, or on Miracle Plays, or on Missions, or on the Mississippi, to be able to find it at once under these headings, with no other help than a knowledge of the alphabet, that I sincerely hope that I am

---

[1] I hope it will be observed that the instances given are examples not of ordinary pseudonyms, but of pseudonyms which, for literary purposes, have entirely superseded the real name. Whatever rule is adopted in other cases, I think there can be no doubt that these should be adopted as headings, in preference to the private names for which they have been substituted.

right in thinking that Mr. Barrett's paper, which is to follow mine, is intended specially to deal with this question, and that I may learn from him, more clearly than I have been able to do from others, what there is to be said on the other side. But you will gather from what I have already said that I think we ought to rule out of court any arguments based on the Eternal Fitness of Things, or on the Educational Value to our readers of exhibiting to them all the departments of knowledge in the beauty of their interdependence, or even on the advantage to ourselves of a system which will force us to face such a fact as that we possess no work on the philology of the South Sea Islands. I think that a librarian ought to be able to take stock of his possessions without forcing on his readers a special form of catalogue for the purpose, and I would rather leave the educational side of the question in the hands of experts like Mr. Herbert Spencer and his critics. But, as I have said, I hope to learn a great deal from Mr. Barrett's paper, and I have no desire to trench further on his subject.

I pass on, therefore, to another section of my argument—the difference between a bibliography and a catalogue in the entries of the different works of a single author. In a bibliography I think all bibliographers will agree that the true arrangement of the works of an author is that which follows in chronological sequence the dates of publication of the first editions. It is only by such a chronological arrangement that we can pass in review the author's literary career, note the subjects or kinds of composition which attracted him from year to year, and (if we care for such trifles) the different printers and publishers with whom he dealt, and the material form (type, paper, and binding) with which his books were invested. No other arrangement, it is agreed, can show all this so well as the chronological, and we must all hope that it may be more and more generally followed in bibliographies. But how irritating it would become if it were applied to catalogues, and what mistakes from overlooking rare issues the hard-pressed cataloguer would be likely to make! Except, indeed, in the case of complete collections, the special advantages of the chronological system would almost disappear. A chronological arrangement by the dates of the earliest editions which happen to be in the library would be absolutely misleading, and a chronological arrangement of the second or later issues according to the dates of the absent first editions would be partly bewildering and wholly unsatisfactory. Moreover, the chronological arrangement, as soon as it is regarded not as an exposition of facts to be studied, but as a means of indicating what books are in a given library, breaks down altogether. For it requires everyone using a catalogue, either to read through the whole of a heading or to carry in his memory the dates of the first publication of all the author's works—dates which we librarians can ascertain, more or less accurately, from works of reference, when preparing a special catalogue, but which it would be absurd to expect the average reader to remember.

I approach next the thorniest part of my subject—the cataloguing of books interesting on account of their printers; and here I tremble lest I should find myself treading on the corns of some of my most valued friends. But, in the first place, I would respectfully protest against any treatment of the books of the fifteenth or sixteenth century which ignores the paramount rights of their authors. The fifteenth century was not a great age of literary originality, but it is the meeting ground of Mediævalism and the New Learning. It is extremely interesting to note what books were in the greatest demand when the press was first established—and there are many of these books which students still want to read, and of which there are few or no modern editions available. Thus, even for the fifteenth century, we shall all agree that, before the compilation of any special catalogue of any kind, these incunabula ought to be entered, at least in the general catalogue, in the same way and according to the same rules as to the selection of headings as any other books. But for the sixteenth and seventeenth centuries we may go further. As decade after decade passes, the literary interest of the books published, more especially in our own country, grows stronger every year, and the typographical interest declines. It is only reasonable, therefore, that special catalogues for this period should be provided for the students and collectors interested in the history of literature, before the students and collectors interested in the history of printing can expect to be catered for. For this reason I cannot help regarding any proposal that the "General Catalogue of English

Books printed before 1640," about which we so often talk, or any contribution to it, should be arranged according to towns and printers, instead of by authors, as, literally, a most preposterous plan. That we should look for the main entries of the works of Shakespeare under Eld, and Sims, and Jaggard, and Roberts, and Field, and F. G., and W. W., and the rest of the piratical publishers and third-rate printers of the day, is to me so monstrous a proposal that it seems strange that it can ever have been entertained. Nobody buys or studies Shakespeare quartos, or the works of Sydney and Spenser, for the sake of Eld and Sims and their compeers. The people who want accurate collations of these early editions want them to make sure that their own copies are perfect (or that someone else's isn't), not to study the typographical eccentricities of inferior presses. The interest of these books is purely literary, and not in the least typographical; and to give the place of honour to the printers and relegate the authors to an index, is surely an outrage upon literature.

Special catalogues of incunabula issued as supplements to the general author-catalogue of a library raise some interesting points of their own. Even here I am old-fashioned enough to think that we shall do well in the first instance to follow Hain in adopting the arrangement by authors, supplementing it, of course, by the indexes of printers and places for which his *Repertorium* had to wait too long. When the exhaustive bibliography of fifteenth-century presses is brought out, the arrangement of the main entries by places and printers will, of course, be right, because only by this arrangement can the bibliography throw the light on the history of printing, which will be the reason for its compilation. But in a catalogue of a particular collection, intended for the use of readers in a library, this arrangement has many disadvantages. Suppose, for instance, I have an edition, without place, date, or name of printer — and such editions are only too common — of some popular work which was often reprinted, and I want to compare it with a perfect copy and find out who printed it. If the catalogue is arranged by authors, all the editions of the same work will be together, and from the collations I can identify the duplicate of my copy at once. But if the catalogue is arranged by printers I have to refer to the index of authors, and look perhaps at ten entries in different parts of the catalogue, before I can find to what press the learned librarian has assigned it. In other words, in order to find the book, I have to acquire, by a clumsy process of exhaustion, the very information of which I am in search, and which a single entry might suffice to give me. If, moreover, the catalogue is arranged by countries, towns, and printers, according to the date at which printing was introduced into the country, and in that country into a particular town, and in that town was first used by a particular printer, to find my way about that catalogue I have not only to carry in my head the whole history of printing in its minutest details, but I have also to know what view the compiler of the catalogue happens to take on a number of disputed points of chronology as to which fresh evidence may any day come to light. A bibliographer has a right to use this method, though the great Panzer was content to stop far short of it; but in a catalogue it seems to me unjustifiable, and I would apply the same censure to an apparently simple system by which all the entries are arranged in a single chronological series. This system has lately found favour in France, but it is a purely bibliographical method, not at all suited for library work. In the French catalogue of which I am thinking, the dates assigned to many undated books — that is, the dates which rule their arrangement — are ludicrously wrong; and we must all rejoice that Mademoiselle Pellechet, despite her far greater knowledge, has adopted the modest and serviceable arrangement by authors in her catalogue of the incunabula in all the public libraries in France, of which the first volume has just appeared. It is a great work this catalogue of Mademoiselle Pellechet's, — in my judgment the greatest contribution to the history of printing since the *Repertorium* of Hain, — and I hope that there are many members of this Conference who will take pleasure in the fact that it is to the unflagging enthusiasm of a woman-librarian that we shall owe it.

I come now to the two points at which the librarian's work necessarily becomes bibliographical. If a library possesses two editions of the same work we are bound in some way to show how they differ; and if there is any peculiarity by which the library copy of a book is distinguished, even if (alas!) it be only by imperfection, from other copies, that also may commendably be stated. But here also we must be on our guard against sudden attacks of zeal. It is so easy, gentlemen, to make a catalogue, even a respectable catalogue, tell lies, and the victim of those lies is too often one of those lazy bibliographers for whose delivery from temptation I am especially concerned. If we have ten books in black letter, and we state the fact about nine of them and don't state it about the tenth, we make our catalogue say, as loudly as it can, that that tenth book is *not* in black letter. If we abridge ten titles, and in nine cases use some mark of omission where words have been left out and use no such mark in the tenth, our catalogue asserts glibly that that title is complete. It is the same with capital letters, the same with old spelling, the same with contractions and a dozen other points. If we have leisure to attend to these minutiæ uniformly, by all means let us do so; but if we have not leisure to do it uniformly let us leave it alone, and content ourselves with some less exacting method of transcription, or else—a plan which might perhaps be adopted—let us put an asterisk or some other mark against the titles whose absolute minute accuracy we can guarantee, so that they may be distinguished from the workaday entries we make in our less bibliographical moods. It is the lack of some such rule as this which is responsible for no small share of the errors in average bibliographies. Our blunders, it is true, ought not to have this effect, for the bibliographer ought to verify his facts for himself. But the bibliographer who takes nothing at second-hand is almost as rare as the phœnix, and we ought not to lead the weaker brethren astray if we can help it.

To sum up, then: let us keep clearly in our minds the fact that the aims and ideals of the bibliographer and the cataloguer are by no means the same. As librarians, let us think of our readers and not of our hobbies, and let us ride our hobbies manfully in our leisure hours. The duplication of bibliographical work in great libraries is at present enormous. If we could combine together to produce better and more complete bibliographies, we should not have to go over the same ground with such wearisome iteration. We should probably, also, be in less danger of forgetting that a librarian with bibliographical tastes, when he visits another library and inspects its catalogues, is not quite a typical reader.

ALFRED W. POLLARD.

THE ALPHABETICAL AND CLASSIFIED FORMS OF CATALOGUES COMPARED.

HE subject to which I invite the attention of the Conference for a short time is not perhaps among the most important of those which arise in the administration of public libraries. It is, however, one which very intimately affects the convenience of the users of libraries, and is therefore one very worthy of the consideration of a representative meeting such as this. I am free to confess that I had long regarded this question as one which was settled almost by common consent in favour of the alphabetical form of catalogue, and it was with interest therefore that I observed the recent revival of the classified form, and followed the controversy which has appeared in *The Library* and elsewhere, although I have not had the privilege of reading the paper which Mr. Doubleday contributed to a recent meeting of the Association. The case for the classified catalogue has been presented with much interest, energy, and ingenuity, but it is to be regretted that the discussion has been conducted in part with a quite unnecessary use of what is by a polite fiction called "strong" language. When Dr. Erasmus Darwin a hundred years ago published his poem "The Loves of the Plants," he was satirised in *The Anti-Jacobin* in a parody entitled "The Loves of the Triangles." There is perhaps some danger that, as an emotional absurdity, the "Loves of the Triangles" may be furnished with a pendant in the shape of "The Animosities of the Catalogues." The subject is quite unsuited in itself for the employment of heated language, but there is possibly a suggestion of the cause of this warmth in a remark of one of the advocates of the classified catalogue, when he was speaking of what he considers the stereotyped or even fossilised condition of dictionary cataloguing, and, by way of contrast, stated that the class-list was as yet hardly out of the gaseous state or stage. If this be so, it is not wonderful that it has developed a somewhat high temperature. High temperatures, however, are not conducive to cool consideration. We shall be more likely to be led to a right conclusion if, without in any way abating the earnestness of our search, we can conduct it without arousing undue feeling.

The question is, "Of the two forms of catalogues, classified or alphabetical, which on the whole is the better suited to public library use?" and it is here applied only to complete catalogues, not to supplements to catalogues or lists of additions. At the outset I may be permitted to express a regret that no better name has yet been suggested for the kind of catalogue which we call the dictionary catalogue. The descriptive word "dictionary" implies no more than that the entries in the catalogue follow each other in the order of the alphabet, and it is equally applicable to all catalogues which follow that order. It does not at all indicate the characteristic features of the form of catalogue referred to, namely, that it contains mention of the books in the library under the names of their authors, under their subjects, and under their titles when these are significant, with references which unite related headings into a systematic whole. I have failed in my endeavour to find a dictionary word which will adequately fit the dictionary catalogue; and I venture to submit that the best name is that which to all librarians will at once suggest what is meant, namely, the Cutter catalogue. It is no doubt true that this form of catalogue did not originate with Mr. Cutter, but it will always be associated with his name in virtue of the service he rendered in codifying the rules for its compilation—a service which will be partially acknowledged by the use of this name. By a classified catalogue is here meant one in which the entries follow each other in an order coincident with the relations existing between the subjects with which the books deal, according to one or other of the many schemes of classification which have been devised from the time of Lord Bacon or earlier down to our own days.

A very interesting attempt was made by the late Mr. Noyes to combine the two principles in his catalogue of the Brooklyn Library. That is a work which can only be mentioned with sincere respect for its many valuable features, but I do not think that this special feature (for instance, placing the whole of the theological entries under the heading "Biblical, Religious, and Ecclesiastical Literature," and inserting the mass in the alphabetical arrangement under that heading) is one which can be mentioned for commendation or imitation.

In considering this question of classified or alphabetical catalogues I do not propose to have in view any one of the many existing classifications, but merely the principle of classed as against alphabetical sequence. Nevertheless, it must be said that the conflicts and contrarieties of classification, illustrated in the fact that the group of books which comes last of all in the "expansive" scheme forms the vanguard in the "decimal" scheme, have an important bearing on our question. The order of the letters of the alphabet is settled and is universally known. There is no present prospect of that becoming true of the order and sequence of classes of books.

The object we all aim at, of course, is the production of that form of catalogue which will render the greatest service to the public or to the constituency of the library in the way of guiding them by the shortest and simplest route to whatever information they desire at the moment of their reference, and generally to the fullest command of the resources of the library. The catalogue which best does that is the best catalogue. In searching for this we are not tied by any other consideration than that of expediency. There is no question of ethics or of principle involved.

It is desirable to say this, because it has been suggested that there is some impropriety, something innately wrong, in arranging titles in any other than an order more or less following the relations of the subjects of the books entered.

It is desirable, in passing, to inquire in what way the question is affected by the size and character of the library for which the catalogue is required. My own work has been almost wholly in the service of two reference libraries, each of them of considerable size. I have no doubt that my view of this question is affected by that circumstance, and I recognise that it is quite possible that in libraries of smaller extent, and in lending libraries, considerations will emerge which do not appear in the work of a large reference library; and in any case it may be taken that the various considerations will be present in different proportions. But with due allowance on this score it will, I think, be found that in all except very small libraries the demands made upon the catalogue will be similar in kind, and that these demands can be best satisfied by the use of similar means. I give it as an opinion only, that the larger the library the greater will be the advantage of the alphabetical form.

The discussion has been complicated by the introduction of several matters which ought to be excluded, because they apply to both sides.

We may omit, for instance, the claim that the classified catalogue can be issued in sections, and the cost so spread over several years. That is true, but it is true also of the alphabetical catalogue; and in fact two of the largest of British alphabetical catalogues—those of Birmingham and Wigan—have been so issued.

We may disregard too, on the same ground, the question whether the titles are to be bibliographically full, or reduced to the smallest practicable dimensions, and deal only with the order in which they should be arranged.

Then there is the question of annotations in the catalogue, the addition to the entry of the book of explanations, and information which ought to be contained in the title-page. And here I would express in a parenthesis an ardent aspiration that authors would avoid the expending their energy to its last ounce on the body of the book, and would, instead, reserve just so much as will enable them to compose a title-page which will really be a guide to the purpose of their work, and exhibit its intended scope, limitations, and character, so that the evil fashion of truncated and unpunctuated title-pages may pass away and be seen no more. However, while notes of the kind indicated are required, they can be and are used in catalogues of each kind. I refer a little later to the claim that annotations can be more economically introduced in the classified form.

Again, very much has been said of blunders and omissions and excrescences in dictionary catalogues; but all this must be put aside as having no bearing on the subject at issue. No school of catalogues can claim a monopoly of inefficient workers, and no reason has been adduced for supposing that he whose work was perfunctory and careless in compiling a dictionary catalogue would develop into a model of assiduity and accuracy if he were led to undertake a catalogue in classified form. If those who have entered with so much enjoyment into the gentle sport of blunder-hunting in alphabetical catalogues apply themselves to some class-lists, they will find game not less worthy of their powers.

If we are to arrive at a sound conclusion, we must proceed on the line of comparing a good catalogue of the one kind with an equally well-executed one of the other, and not confuse the issue by assaults and reprisals on bad work on either side.

We will then suppose, on the one hand, an alphabetical catalogue, carefully constructed on the lines laid down in Mr. Cutter's rules, although not of necessity conforming to those rules in every particular; and, on the other hand, an equally well-made catalogue in which the entries are arranged in the order of one or other of the available methods of classification, furnished with a full index, which will refer the reader not only to the several classes of literature and their subordinate subject-headings, but also to the names of the authors, and to the titles of such books as are known and quoted by title; and that these two catalogues are of equal rank or grade in the matter of fulness or brevity of entry.

The answer to our question must be sought first in a consideration, in a little detail, of what is required of the catalogue beyond the mere furnishing a list of the books contained in the library. The objects with which readers consult the catalogue have not, I think, been anywhere more clearly or more completely stated than by Mr. Cutter at the forefront of his famous rules, and those who advocate the use of classified catalogues may accept his statement of these requirements of the reader equally with those who think the alphabetical form superior.

There are of course many readers who enter the library and approach the catalogue with what we may, to avoid any appearance of disrespect, call "an open mind." They have half an hour or an hour to spare, and they want something to read—not this thing or that, but something. They open the catalogue and look down its columns or turn over its cards until they find some title which engages their interest. Perhaps visitors of this kind have not the strongest claim for consideration; but their desire, such as it is, is probably more likely to be satisfied in the variety of topics presented to their notice in the alphabetical catalogue than in classified lists in which all the neighbouring entries relate to books on the same kind of subjects.

But the large majority of those who consult the catalogue do so with some definite end in view. To use Mr. Cutter's grouping —one reader desires to find some individual book of which he knows either the author's name, or the title, or the subject with which it deals. Another may wish to see what the library possesses of a given writer's works, or what it possesses on a given subject or in a given kind of literature.

In considering the bearing of these requirements on the question in hand, it is necessary to have regard to the relative frequency with which they occur. In my experience the inquiry which is most frequently made is—What is there in the library on some stated subject? The alphabetical catalogue answers this question under the name of the subject, which is the place first referred to; in the classified catalogue reference must first be made to the index, which guides the reader to the page containing what he wants. But the reader, at least as I know him, does not wish to be referred to some other place; he wants the information "right there," if I may use that phrase in this presence. Following in frequency are those who look for some particular book under the name of its author. Here, again, the alphabetical catalogue answers the question on the first reference. In the classified catalogue reference must, as before, be first made to the index, and the reader may there find a reference to a single page, in which case his second search brings him to his answer; *but* he may also find that there are books by his author on two, or on five, or on ten different pages in the catalogue, and he naturally wonders which he should turn to first. The same situation faces the readers, and they are by no means infrequent, who desire to ascertain what books by a given author are in the library. To illustrate this, I mention one of the latest class-lists which I have seen—a class-list, I would say, well conceived and thoroughly well executed. It is a list of books on the sciences and on the fine and useful arts, and it is furnished with an index to the authors and a second one to the subjects.

I do not trouble you with the names of authors whose works appear on two, or on three, or on four or five pages of the catalogue, but I would ask you to note that the student who wishes to know what the library possesses of Charles Darwin must turn to six different pages; of Professor Tyndall or of R. A. Proctor, to seven places; if he makes the inquiry in relation to the works of our distinguished President, it will cost him an examination of eight separate pages; of Professor Huxley, nine pages; if of J. G. Wood, a list of twelve pages will assuage or stimulate his ardour, according as he is more or less in earnest. Then, in order that the situation may be fully appreciated, it must be remembered that the reference in the index is to a page of the catalogue, and necessitates a careful scanning of each page—a pathetic thought to those who have observed the pain and labour which even the simplest examination of a catalogue entails on many worthy people.

The case of the reader who knows the book he wants by the title only—and this usually applies to books which have titles more or less arbitrary and fanciful—is met in the alphabetical catalogue by the insertion of the title in its alphabetical place. In the classified catalogue it must be sought through the intermediary of the index; again two references instead of one.

There remains for mention the class of consulters who have occasion to inquire what the library contains, not only on specific subjects, but in the large classes to which these specific subjects belong. They desire to know, for instance, what there is not only on, say, baptismal regeneration, but what throughout the whole field of theological learning; not only what books on the camel are available, but what on all divisions of zoology and of natural science. These inquirers are better served by the classified catalogue, no doubt. But it must be observed, first, that this is a demand seldom made; and secondly, that it may be provided for in the alphabetical catalogue by exhibiting a table of such subject-headings as occur in it, in a classified arrangement. Moreover, those who ask this service from the catalogue will generally be persons familiar with books and indexes—persons to whom the consultation of a catalogue of any kind occasions little difficulty.

We must now examine the advantages which the classified form presents, and which are either unattainable, or attainable in an inferior degree, in the alphabetical catalogue.

The advocates of the classified catalogue claim with justice that that arrangement enables the readers to purchase the part of the catalogue that they are interested in, and no more. The advantage is a little reduced in value by the consideration that it may tend to confirm some readers in their exclusive devotion to the literature of fiction; and on general grounds it would seem desirable that everyone should be reminded that there are fields of learning and of literature outside that in which he most delights to labour. Further, to attain this advantage, each class-list must be indexed separately, and that in addition to the index to the entire catalogue.

There is another advantage of the classified catalogue which has not, so far as I have seen, been claimed by its advocates. In libraries where free access to the shelves is permitted, perhaps some convenience would arise from the entries in the catalogue being in most cases in the order in which the books stand on the shelves.

It is claimed that the classified catalogue, by omitting the entries under the authors' names, may be produced at less cost than the alphabetical. This is true, and it is illustrated in the catalogue of the A.L.A. Library, not the least of the many important services rendered to librarianship by the United States. There the same books are catalogued independently by two systems of classification, and on the Cutter plan. The two classed catalogues (without indexes) occupy respectively 108 and 112 pages, the alphabetical one 322 pages. The difference of space occupied is not, however, nearly so great as these figures would appear to show; for, while each of the classified catalogues has its own notation or press-marking only, the alphabetical catalogue is furnished with both, with the result that the line of type devoted to the text is only about two-thirds as long as in the other catalogues. But even allowing for this, and for the absence of indexes in the classed catalogues, it is clear that the last-named form can be printed more cheaply. It is impossible to regard this claim without sympathy. It touches on the painful and pitiful poverty under which many public libraries, especially in our smaller towns, are called on to perform, and do perform, a most important and valuable public duty. But it may be observed that its force is greatest in the case of those libraries where the form of catalogue is of relatively less importance, namely, where the collections are small, and where the catalogue, whatever its form, can be readily examined from end to end.

The claim that explanatory notes can be more economically made in the classed catalogue, as there are no author entries at which they should be inserted, may be mentioned in this connection. The claim is well founded, as was that last named, and it is subject to the same qualification.

I do not dwell on the suggestion that the classed catalogue may be made with less labour to the librarian. I am not prepared to admit that this is so to any appreciable extent, but in any case it is not an argument, I trust, which will have much force with many of us.

Summarising, it would appear that the classed catalogue possesses some advantages—in the main, of economy. On the other hand, the alphabetical catalogue offers what was defined as the test of the best form, namely, the readiest access to the contents of the library.

Of all the readers who consult the catalogue with some definite intention, I am of opinion that, with the alphabetical catalogue, 80 per cent. will find their inquiry answered by the first reference made, and 20 per cent. may find it necessary to make a second reference; whereas, in the case of the classified catalogue, not more than 10 per cent. would be able to go at once to the required entry, and it would be necessary for 90 per cent. to make two or more references before arriving at the information for which they seek.

Thus, after a general survey of the question, which has been of necessity brief, but which I have at least endeavoured to make complete and impartial, I am constrained to say that I find myself confirmed in the opinion that, on a comparison of the respective merits of the classified with those of the alphabetical form of catalogue for use in public libraries, the balance of advantage is largely in favour of the latter form.

F. T. BARRETT.

ON THE AIDS LENT BY PUBLIC BODIES TO THE ART OF PRINTING IN THE EARLY DAYS OF TYPOGRAPHY.

RIEDRICH NIETZSCHE, while treating in the second number of his *Unzeitgemässe Betrachtungen* (Leipzig, 1874) of the advantages and disadvantages of history to life, ascribes to our time a "consuming historic fever," and characterises the historic spirit of the time as a hypertrophic virtue.

This statement certainly does not apply to the efforts of the modern librarian, especially to those of our English and American colleagues, who in this Conference form the preponderating majority. The varied literary demands of the present, the examination and most suitable means of satisfying these demands, indeed, to a certain extent, the investigation and primary support, form the main object of the earnest and successful activity of this large number of professional associates.

So much the sooner may the individual be allowed to glance with retrospective eye at the beginnings of modern books, which gave to libraries, by means of typography, a powerful stimulus, large aims and means; indeed, to glance at an aspect of this subject which to this day has proved conducive to the success of book production. I mean the attitude of the State, or, to speak more in accordance with the disjointed and often still unregulated relations of the fifteenth and sixteenth centuries, of the attitude of secular and ecclesiastic authorities, towards the development of the new art of printing.

How beneficial the opportune intervention of the State can prove has been experienced especially in England and the United States of America by the public library movement. The energetic efforts of the leaders of this movement were from the very beginning directed towards the legal foundation of the establishment of such libraries, which met with success in England in 1850, and at almost the same time in America—first in Boston.

In France also the institution of the similar *bibliothèques communales* rests upon the foundation of a much older law (Decree of 28, I. 1803). In yet another province, which lies very near my theme, did England, not to speak of the isolated and short-lived efforts of certain small States, long take the lead in a legal ordering of relations, that is to say, in the law of 1709 upon copyright. If this was already a full-ripe fruit on the widespreading tree of that protection which the State grants to the book trade, a brief sketch of the beginnings of this protection and of the relations in general between the authorities and printers may not be entirely without interest. Here, as in other provinces, we see that weighty institutions and customs of a later time were even then in part present in the germ; that then already, as later, the same causes were at work, and the same needs were pressing to the same solution. The nature of the material makes it a matter of course that I shall not limit myself strictly to the fifteenth century, but occasionally refer to a later time. Oscar von Hase, the well-known biographer of the Kobergers (2nd ed., Leipzig, 1885) has brought, in the *Archiv für die Gesch. d. deutschen Buchhandels*, Bd. x. (1886) S. 27 ff., documentary evidence in the limited province of the relations of Antonj Koberger to the Council of Nürnberg, to the effect that Koberger experienced, in the most varied directions, the "promotion of the practice of his calling" and "legal protection." I shall of course deny myself here the citation of documentary material; on the other hand, various things will have to be referred to, for the mention of which no occasion was offered by Koberger's relations to his city. Apart from this, however, the survey of the relations of the authorities to printing shall be, in accordance with my theme, as comprehensive as possible.

I. The first and most direct assistance which the authorities bestowed upon the young art of printing consisted in the well-disposed treatment and material support of deserving printers, especially of the prototypographers. The assistance was naturally confined to the narrow limits of the particular place in which the art was practised. In fact, there was at that time practically no central State power in those countries which come chiefly into consideration, Germany and Italy; and especially did the protection of trade and commerce in these lands devolve almost entirely upon the authorities of the cities, among which the German imperial cities, through their powerful and skilful government, were most prominent. France and England were more centralized; hence there, sooner than elsewhere, can the intervention of a greater power of the State be observed.

A good understanding with the authorities and their well-disposed assistance were sought by Gutenberg during his sojourn in Strasburg. For in the year 1434, "in honour of and in affection for the masters and Council of the city of Strasburg," who had interceded with him in behalf of the city of Mainz, he released the town clerk of Mainz, Nicolaus, from arrest and debt, which the latter had incurred to Gutenberg. Then, however, only his first attempts in typography can have been made. The support which he received from the Archbishop of Mainz, Count Adolf of Nassau, in the evening of his life (18th Jan. 1465) we may more definitely ascribe to his great deserts as inventor of the art of printing (cp. J. H. Hessels' *Gutenberg*, p. 114 ff.). In Rome, according to a recent documentary discovery, the first two printers of Italy, Sweynheim and Pannartz, obtained full assent to their far-reaching requests, directed in the year 1472 to Pope Sixtus IV. (cp. Jos. Schlecht in *Festschrift z. 1100 jährigen Jubiläum des dtsch. Campo Santo in Rom*, 1897, S. 207 ff.). We must certainly explain in a similar manner the bestowal of a canonry with benefice upon Breslau's first printer, the *succentor* Caspar Elyan, in whose favour another canon declined it (cp. K. Dziatzko in *Zeitschr. d. Ver. f. Gesch. u. Alt. Schles.* xv. S. 6 ff.). Johann Mentelin of Strasburg received from the Emperor Friedrich III., in the year 1466, a hereditary coat-of-arms (cp. A. v. d. Linde, *Gesch. d. Erfind. d. Buchdr.*, i. S. 98), surely not without recognition of his activity as a printer; and somewhat earlier in the same year his fellow artisan, Heinrich Eggestein, was taken into special guardianship, together with his assistants, through a letter of protection by Friedrich v. d. Pfalz, as Governor of the province of Lower Elsass (cp. Charles Schmidt, *Zur Gesch. d. ältest. Bibl. zu Strasburg*, S. 98 ff.). We are told of similar protection being exercised in 1496 by Bishop Laurence of Würzburg towards Jeorius Reyser (cp. *Archiv f. Gesch. d. deutschen B.H.*, xv. S. 6). In England, Richard Pynson, it is said, had already been appointed court printer by King Henry VIII. In France, the list of important regulations, which served to raise the art of printing, and in the course of the sixteenth century quickly procured French typography the precedence of the productions of other countries, begins with the ordinance of March 1488, of King Charles VIII., which declared 24 *libraires*, 2 *enlumineurs*, 2 *relieurs*, and 2 *écrivains de livres* members of the university, and at the same time, like the scholars, free from taxes. On the other hand, the excellence of their productions in regard to paper, types, and correctness was carefully controlled. Material personal advantages and contributions for the establishment of an artistically and technically complete printing apparatus in connection with the limitation of the number of printers, and strict demands on the excellence of the work, were in fact the means by which the kings of France were able to promote the trade of printing.

There, too, we see the first State printing establishment arise, the model of similar creations in other lands. The number of examples might be greatly increased, even without considering the privileges, which are to be treated of in an especial paragraph.

II. A further advance is made by the attraction of foreign masters when such are lacking at home, or when those who are there are insufficiently qualified. For example, King Charles VII. of France sent, in the year 1458, according to a well-authenticated report (ordonn. of 4th Oct.),

Nicolas Jenson to Mainz, in order to secretly investigate the new art and then introduce it into his own country (cp. *Samml. bibl. Arb.*, ii. p. 41 ff.). Especially do those countries which are more remote from general culture furnish evidence of such interposition of State power. I would call to mind the summons of Jacob Kromberger to Lisbon to print a code of laws for King Manuel in the year 1507-8 (cp. K. Haebler in *Centr. f. Bibl.*, xi. p. 554 f.); likewise the decree according to which foreign Christian printers, who could give evidence of a certain property, were, in case of their taking up their abode in Portugal, to be appointed "knights of the royal household" without incurring the customary obligations.

To print the first Danish Bible Ludwig Dietz was summoned from Rostock (1550) to Copenhagen. In Sweden also the first printers required royal assistance (cp. G. E. Klemming u. J. G. Nordin, *Svensk Boktryck. Hist.*, p. 148 ff.). But also in the countries which took the lead in early printing there is no lack of analogous instances. University cities in particular exerted themselves at an early date to attract competent printers within their walls, as Frankfort-on-the-Oder, Würzburg, and others. In other places ecclesiastical or civil authorities procured suitable skill for the production of separate works which required a special get-up, as, for example, in Regensburg, whither Bishop Heinrich summoned Joh. Sensenschmidt and Joh. Beckenhaub in the year 1485 to print a missal; in Augsburg, whither Erhart Ratdolt was recalled by the bishop in 1486 from Venice; in Nürnberg, where Emperor Maximilian I. caused the *Theuerdank* to be printed in 1517 by Hans Schönsperger of Augsburg; in Königsberg (1519), Berlin (1540), etc. The Roman Curia must also be mentioned here, which made powerful exertions in the sixteenth century, in connection with the counter-reformation, for the establishment of competent printing houses in Rome, and also attracted the celebrated Paulus Manutius under favourable conditions to Rome. The establishment of private printing houses by civil or ecclesiastical rulers, as Frederick II. of Denmark, by French and English kings and princes, by the Bishop Jens Areson in Iceland (1531), and others, falls under the same head.

III. We see the same desire to favour one's own district when the effort is made to retain printing at home as a source of income, and the transference of a printing machine to another place is rendered difficult. Accordingly, as early as 24th Feb. 1468 Dr. Conrad Homery was obliged to give the Archbishop of Mainz, Count Adolf of Nassau, a pledge to use the printing machine formerly among Gutenberg's effects and then belonging to himself (Dr. Homery), only in Mainz, and, in case of its sale, to allow a citizen of Mainz the right of pre-emption (cp. J. H. Hessels, p. 119 f.). In course of time this sort of protection of home industry was given up, since that which was not to be carried away from one place could easily be procured from another.

IV. Of much greater importance, wider extension, and more persistent duration, indeed, of influence even upon the present time, was the effort of the authorities, through the exclusion of foreign printing products, or indirectly through demanding of competition undertakings, to keep for their own district the sale of certain products of printing. Perhaps we can thus explain the production of two editions of the oldest printed letters of indulgence (of 1454-55) which are printed in entirely different types. It still seems to me simplest to suppose with Heinrich Pertz (*Abhandl. Berliner Ak.* 1856, S. 717) that one edition was intended for the archdiocese of Mainz, the other for that of Cologne (cp. *Samml. biblioth. Arb.*, iii. p. 67 ff.).

A similar explanation might be given of the two editions of St. Augustine, *De arte praedicandi*, which were first issued by Joh. Mentelin in Strasburg and then by Joh. Fust in Mainz (cp. J. Schnorrenberg in *Beiträge z. Kenntn. d. Schrift*, etc. *wes.* iii. p. 1 ff.; Dziatzko, p. 5, note), and also, without doubt, of a great part of the numerous pirated editions of other works, of which, however, owing to the remote times, the proof can not be adduced in each instance.

It is well known how actively and effectively in the last century, and even in our own, the authorities of one State promoted with the same motives pirated editions in opposition to another. Under the same head of the protection of home industry belongs the open and covert hostility towards foreign bookdealers, such as the firm of Pet. Schoeffer, for example, had to encounter in 1474-75 in Paris, when their agent, Hermann Stadloe, died there, and the books which were then in his possession, to the value, according to a later estimation, of more than 2425 thaler, were confiscated in accordance with the *droit d'aubaine*, although, as was well known, they were not the man's property. That after prolonged efforts, supported by the German Emperor and the Elector of Mainz, France paid back the money in instalments at the command of Louis XI. to the firm, is an early instance of international action in this province (cp. Fr. Kapp, *Gesch. d. deutsch. B.H.*, p. 71 ff.). Protection of the home book trade against inconvenient foreign competition is to-day the principal motive of the law, which secures in the United States a protection of copyright to those printed productions only which can be proved to have been made in the States themselves or with American printing presses.

V. The rather isolated and occasional instances of local protection which have been considered hitherto, which were favourable to piracy, had also, on the other hand, the apparently opposite result of leading to privilege. The development of this institution in the province of printing, so effective even until our own century, I may assume as known, so that I limit myself to a brief reference to its fundamental lines. It is in each case connected with the definite person of a printer or with a firm, and is limited by the sphere of power of the authority which grants the privilege. It is either general, embracing all the books of a firm; or special, being limited to individual specified works; or even partial, applying to definite categories, as schoolbooks, literary works, Bibles, official decrees, etc. Very rarely does it apply to all times; for the most part, only to definite and not especially long periods. In this way the disadvantages of a partial consumption of literary productions was avoided, and we may observe here a characteristic warning against the modern efforts towards an almost limitless extension of authors' and publishers' rights. At first being of a distinctly individualising tendency, privilege becomes a monopoly when it excludes, to the advantage of the individual, all competitive action on the part of others. In Venice, where in 1469 the exclusive privilege to exercise the art of printing was for the first time foolishly granted to John of Speier, the early death of this man restored freedom of action to the State, fortunately for the State and for this branch of industry. His brother Wendelin did not obtain a renewed monopoly. It soon appeared in large centralised States, like England and France, and no less in smaller territories with a highly developed book trade, like Venice, that the personal element, which is usually connected with privilege, recedes more and more, and the general purpose of publishers' rights comes into more pronounced favour. There was, to be sure, an early though not general or lasting mixture of two factors which counteracted that tendency: the fiscal interest, when privileges were sold by the State, and especially the censorship. Owing to the international character of the industry of printing then as now, privileges were of course fully effective only in those cases in which the work in question could count upon an exclusive or preponderating sale within the limits of the privilege. Such are prints of local or, at most, provincial character, school-books, liturgies of special dioceses,—in which, moreover, the will of the clergy and the recommendation of the authorities could materially support the privilege,—calendars, and other popular writings—on the whole, neither in number nor contents, the main part of literature. In privilege, which is first authenticated both in Italy and Germany at about the same time, towards the end of the fifteenth century (cp. among others Fr. Kapp, p. 37), State protection of publishers and printers found for many centuries its official expression. Apart from the purely personal element which found its expression in the custom of renewing privileges in case of a change either in the proprietorship of a firm or in the person of a ruler, a great disadvantage arose very early in the practice of requesting and granting privileges even for works which had not yet appeared but were only in prospect—a fact which, together with the sale of privileges by the privileged, necessarily crippled the enterprise of other printers and led to material embarrassments. The Republic of Venice, which in the fifteenth century contained in its small territory about as many printing houses as all Germany possessed at the same time, is especially instructive for the earliest history of privilege. The monumental work of Hor. F. Brown, on the Venetian printing presses (London, 1891), makes it possible for us to follow this history step by step. The bestowal of official printing commissions upon certain individual printers, the acquiring of books needed for official purposes from individuals, as well as the official recommendation of individuals, went hand in hand with the privileges and had essentially the same results (cp., for example, O. Hase in *Arch.*, x. p. 28 ff.).

VI. Especially in the territories where the State power had extensive authority and the personal element was gradually lost sight of, did privileges, notwithstanding their inherent faults, contribute greatly to sharpen the sense for the *right* of the publishers to the protection of their interests and to pave the way for the recognition of this right. In the Italian republics, also in the cities of Germany, as well as in England (Stationers' Company reorganised 1554–56), publishers protected themselves against piracy in their own country by means of corporate associations, which came into existence and were supported with the aid of State protection. Before as well as after this time, however, authors sought not infrequently to protect their interests directly by becoming themselves publishers, and obtaining, by means of privileges, the protection of the authorities for their work. The way in which the authors' right, at first, so to speak, included in the publishers' right, developed independently out of the latter, and in fact became the more influential for modern legislation, I have sought to sketch in another place (*Beiträge z. Urheber-Recht. Festgabe* . . . Dresden, 1895, p. 149 ff.). Only, let me here briefly repeat that it was first in Venice, in 1545, as far as we as yet know, that especial mention of the authors was made as requiring protection. The protection, of course, is especially granted to the living author. That in early times a distinction was made between the works of authors who had been long dead, so-called literary public property, and those works which had been recently composed, the latter being protected while only the former were regarded as common property, must not be believed. Numerous works of living authors which were continually pirated and translated contradict this idea. I refer, for example, to Bernh. v. Breydenbach's *Journey to the Holy Land* (Mainz, 1486, in Latin and German, by Erh. Rewick), whose purely personal preface is repeated in all the pirated editions and translations. Only the remark (Bl. 116 ª) that Rewick had carried on the printing in his own house is naturally omitted in the other prints. The repetition of this remark by another printer would not only have been a thoughtless piracy, but, under certain circumstances, an intended deception. In case of the two editions of St. Augustine, *De arte praedicandi* (at Strasburg and Mainz), both of which contain in the preface of the editor the explanation that he had besought Joh. Mentelin, respectively Joh. Fust, to print the work, we must not think of a shameless piracy,—we should rather call it deception,—but of two distinct editions issued in succession by the same editor (cp. Section IV.).

VII. With this chapter another very interesting question is connected, but one which has been hitherto only superficially treated, that of the publishers' and printers' marks. Like the notaries' signets which have been recently (1896) fully discussed by Fried. Leist, and the individual coats-of-arms, these were marks of recognition which, in addition to the signature or even without it, could prove at a glance whose typographical work one saw before him in printed form. They were certainly primarily intended to recommend the books which were thus provided. From this significance of the marks, there developed, under certain circumstances, that of a mark of protection, which prevented foreign undated books being issued — perhaps in retail sales—as productions of the firm which bore the mark. Both of these problems, however, could only be solved by the marks when their imitation by others was both morally and legally inadmissible. This was indeed apparently the case. I know in the fifteenth century, among the countless completely pirated editions, of no example of the imitation of a printers' or publishers' mark, which might have been easily recognised by the varied types. Not until the sixteenth century did the high reputation of the Aldines tempt unauthorised individuals, in their desire for gain, to imitate the Aldine coat-of-arms (anchor with dolphin; cp. A. A. Renouard, *Annal. d. Aldes*, 3rd ed. pp. 70, 72, 317. etc.). This, however, was always regarded as a deceptive act. Paulus Manutius, on the other hand, notwithstanding his own extensive publications, transferred for money, twenty gold scudi per month, the use of his printers' mark to his business friend, Domen. Baza, in Rome (cp. Ed. Fromman, *Aufs. z. Gesch. d. Buch.*, im 16. Jht. 2. Heft, p. 69)—the best proof of the fact that the arbitrary use of a strange mark was not permitted. In the Statutes of the Association of Printers and Booksellers at Milan in 1589, chap. 32, the use of the firm-mark of another establishment was expressly forbidden (cp. Ed. Fromman, p. 153). Similar conditions evidently prevailed, as in case of printers' and publishers' marks, so too in regard to the marks and monograms of artists—for example, the engravers. An interesting instance may confirm this. This is a town record of 2nd Jan. 1512, furnished by G. E. Waldau (*Verm. Beiträge z. Gesch. d. Stadt Nürnberg*, I. 1786, p. 68), and recently reprinted by E. Mummenhoff in the *Archiv f. Gesch. d. deutsch. B.H.'s* (ii. p. 237 ff.). According to this, a stranger who had wood engravings ("Kunstbrief") for sale in Nürnberg, among which some that had Albrecht Dürer's handmark, which had been fraudulently copied, was obliged to remove all these marks, and to offer none of the specified thus for sale. Otherwise, all of these sheets ("brief"), that is to say, surely, those which bore the false mark, were to be confiscated as forgeries ("als ein falsch"). Presumably, the woodcuts as well as the monogram were imitations. The latter was to be unconditionally removed. On the other hand, the sale of the pictures was permitted, in respect to which Dürer probably had no privilege.

VIII. The extensive market which most publications were forced to seek brought printers from the first into countless business relations with the citizens of their own city, with other cities and countries, and gave the book industry an international character such as probably but few callings then possessed. The same reason, that numerous copies had to be set before the cost of the printing was covered, as well as competition, led, moreover, very early to an extensive system of credit among publishers and book agents. Finally, the latter were exposed, while travelling from place to place or establishing themselves in a strange city, to manifold vicissitudes, which involved them in conflicts with the members of foreign communities. All this frequently placed the members of the book trade in a position in which they were obliged to undertake extensive and difficult cases at law, both in their own land and abroad, which they did with the help of their immediately superior authorities.

The willingness to do this, and to promote foreign trade, the providing of a safe conduct through dangerous regions in unsettled times,—all this implies at once a peculiar friendliness on the part of the authorities and a warm interest in the prosperity of the book trade, also the clear recognition of the importance of this prosperity. And yet, notwithstanding the paucity of the sources of our history of those early times, there are numerous instances of such protection on the part of the State authorities. What happened to Peter Schoeffer of Mainz after the death of his agent, Hermann of Stadloe, in Paris, was already mentioned in Section IV. We know that in two instances, 1469 and 1480, the Council of the city of Frankfort-on-the-Main interceded with the Council of Lübeck in behalf of Conrad Henckis and the heirs of Fust, in order that they might receive aid in the collection of sums of money (cp. Fr. Kapp, pp. 759 f. and 762). A dispute between the master printers of Basle and their apprentices (in 1471) had to be settled by the authorities (cp. Fr. Kapp, p. 112); likewise a similar conflict in Paris (1539), and in Lyons (1541), in consequence of which the principles laid down in the royal decree controlled for some time the nature of the relations between the printers and their assistants. Further information on the same subject has been furnished by O. von Hase in connection with the life of Ant. Koberger in the *Archiv*, x. 36 ff.

IX. The reverse side of the well-disposed protection of the authorities of the printer's art in its beginnings is furnished by their supervision, for which they soon found reason in the really, or alleged, dangerous contents of the books and the rapid diffusion which these contents thus obtained. Nor did the attempts to guide and guard the press, having once begun, rest until they found expression in the modern press laws, which received in different countries a varying form. The orthodox circles of the Church in Mainz (1485) and Cologne—that is, the region where the cradle of the new art had stood—made the beginning, and were also, later, as a rule the moving agents, although in the course of time the civil Government also considered itself peculiarly menaced, as, for example, in the peasants' movement of the first decade after the Reformation.

The relations between the authorities and the art of printing, both in respect to aid and supervision, which at first were more accidental and dependent on the attitude of the ruler, became simplified in the course of the centuries, and assumed more and more a legal character. Especially have privilege and censorship disappeared for the most part before the modern principles of freedom in trade and the press, with their imposed limitations. Metternich's plan for a State organisation of the book trade (cp. *Archiv f. Gesch. d. deutsch. B.H's*, i. p. 91 ff.) surely no one would care to undertake, even though one is convinced that in many respects the State can still advantageously influence the development of the book trade. At all events, we librarians, whose life-interest is in books and the printers' productions, have every reason to follow the form of the relations of civil and ecclesiastical authorities towards the exercise of printing in its various aspects with attention and complete sympathy.[1]

C. Dziatzko.

[1] Translated from the German by Miss H. Shute, of Göttingen.

FREEDOM IN PUBLIC LIBRARIES.

HIS is a subject upon which not merely divergent but diametrically opposing views are honestly held and earnestly maintained. Possibly, some of this difference of opinion is due to a failure on the one hand to make clear, and on the other to comprehend, what is meant by free access. We all recognise that there are libraries composed of special collections, not of public interest, or of specimens of early printing or of fine binding, or of books containing fine illustrations, which should be cared for and shown only under such conditions as may ensure their safety. We also know that many public libraries contain collections which should clearly be guarded and shown in the same way. Upon the proper methods of caring for books of special value, both the advocates and opponents of open shelves are agreed. The question is simply whether it is necessary and desirable to exercise practically the same care of the entire library, or whether, as some maintain, it is both possible and desirable to throw open to all qualified users of the library all that part of it which is of interest to the general reader, to pupils of our schools, and to advanced and special students, excepting only such books as require special care, for the reasons already mentioned, or for similar ones.

The question is an important one, involving as it does the plan and arrangement of the library building, the furniture, appliances, and methods. It also brings with it a change in the popular idea of the duties of the librarian, and makes him appear to be, not a mere custodian of the books, but rather a helpful assistant and friendly guide to those who need direction.

A question of such importance deserves careful consideration, from which, as far as possible, all preconceived opinions shall be eliminated and all selfish interests excluded. The sole question should be as to the value of the plan which permits public access, with the limitations I have already mentioned, as compared with the one which prohibits it.

In what I have to say I shall endeavour, as far as is possible for one who is a firm believer in free access, to set forth fairly the relative advantages and disadvantages of each plan.

The principal sources of information upon this subject are the files of the various journals devoted to the work of libraries, and the discussion of it is mostly included within the last few years, as, while freedom of access has been permitted in some smaller libraries for many years, it is only within recent years that it has been introduced in any of the larger libraries.

The two plans may be fairly compared as to their economy, their educational value, and their moral effect, and under each head I shall consider the objections which have been urged.

One of the most important questions of economical administration is that of room; and one of the objections which is urged most strongly against free access is that it takes more room, and is therefore more expensive. There is some force to this objection. It is true that it does require more room to show books in open shelves in alcoves wide enough for public use than in stacks, but not so much more, however, as might appear at first glance—for two or three reasons. First, all libraries issuing books from closed shelves require public delivery-rooms proportioned to the amount of their use. Now, each open alcove is just so much added to the available public space of the library, and lessens the space necessary to reserve for a general public room. Again, as the rare and specially valuable books of the library are to be provided for elsewhere, and shelved on the same plan in libraries permitting free access as in those prohibiting it, we lessen further the amount of additional room required. A still further reduction may be made by shelving compactly in stacks all duplicates which are in surplus during the less busy months, and also such books as are seldom used. For instance, in Italian history, Guicciardini might be represented in the open shelves by a dummy or by a single volume. This is but a single example of what may be done with many books which are only rarely used, and whose absence does not render the collection less valuable to most readers, but, on the contrary, makes it more convenient to examine. A parallel collection convenient of access might thus be established, which could be drawn upon for duplicates, and to which admission might be given readily to the few who wish to exhaust the entire resources of the library upon any particular subject. By thus providing in some suitable way for that part of the library which it is agreed by all should be especially guarded, and by arranging a parallel collection in stacks, or other compact plan of shelving, the amount of extra space required for the open shelves is kept within reasonable bounds, and any serious objection to the plan on this score is removed.

As far as the expense for furniture and appliances, there seems to be no reason for any special difference between the two plans.

The cost of service is the most important consideration. The issue of a book from a library includes getting it from the shelves, charging it, and, when it is returned, crediting and replacing it.

In the open library the time used in getting the book is saved. On the other hand, a certain amount of displacement, due to the examination of the shelves by readers, must be rectified, which may possibly offset this saving. My own observation of one of the large libraries in which free access has been permitted for more than seven years, and in which the disarrangement is readily rectified as the books from the receiving desk are replaced on the shelves, leads me to think that the difficulty from this source is slight, and that the balance of economy of time is in favour of the open-shelf plan as compared even with libraries in which the book borrower is confined strictly to the catalogue for his selection. When, however, libraries with closed shelves endeavour to give their readers some opportunity to examine the books themselves, by carrying a selection to tables in the public room or elsewhere for examination, as many do, there can be no doubt that the open-shelf plan is more economical. I have thus far been speaking of what is absolutely necessary to the issue and return of a book, without taking into account the assistance to readers which is given in most libraries, and which is usually so closely connected with the issue of the books as to render it impossible to make a separate estimate of its cost. The opportunities for thus assisting readers are much greater in the open library, and superior ability, which commands higher pay, is required to do it efficiently.

The value of such service, and the larger amount of it given in the open library, may fairly be taken into consideration in making comparisons of the statistics given in library reports.

The most serious dangers to the library are those of theft, of mutilation, and of careless handling. The mutilation of books from the circulating department, and other misuses of them, occurs when the books are out of the library, and I see no reason why it should be affected by the plan of issue. The possibilities of theft are greater, but the experience of the few large libraries which have adopted the plan shows an inconsiderable loss, and that of books of small value. The great danger to libraries is from the experienced book thief, who slily carries off the rare first edition, or dexterously removes with a wetted string the valuable plates from the folio. The average book of the circulating libraries, labelled and stamped as it is, offers little attraction to the book thief. He cannot turn it into money without great danger of detection, and it has little other value to him. The records of book thieving in libraries show that the greatest thefts have been perpetrated by men of education and address —men who would be able, by plausible statements, to secure special privileges in the library, which, under the plan of restricting access, are denied to the honest mechanic.

The great safety of the open library lies in the appeal which it makes to the honour of those using it. It says in effect, "We trust you, and we believe that you will prove worthy of this confidence." The experience of the largest libraries in which the plan is adopted shows that this appeal is not in vain.

It replaces suspicion by confidence. As Sir Philip Sydney says, "Suspicion is the way to lose that which we do fear to lose." One of the most effective ways of making a thief of an honest man is to treat him as though you thought him a thief.

The open library replaces restricting and annoying rules and regulations by a freedom which is enjoyable to all. It gives to the people the same right in the library, which is their own, as the individual has in his own. This is but simple justice. I question the right of any library board to make any restricting regulation that cannot be clearly proven to be a necessity. It would appear that the rules of some libraries are based upon the assumption that all men are untrustworthy, and that honour and common honesty are non-existent amongst users of libraries.

Is it not better to base our rules upon the nobler assumption that the users of libraries are honest, and only restrict so far as experience proves it necessary? The open library does this, and I have yet to hear of a single instance in which, after a fair trial of open access, under proper conditions, it has proved necessary or advisable to go back to the plan of closed shelves. I know there have been instances of this, but I believe them to be due rather to peculiar circumstances than to any fault of the plan. One instance is the library of one of our largest universities, the use of which was free not only to the students in its classes but to other students. In this the governing board have decided, I understand, for reasons which seem to them sufficient, to close the shelves; the other is that of a large mercantile library, which found it necessary, after a trial of open shelves, to close them on account of losses.

The thing to be noted is that neither of these libraries were used by the people at large. The university library was, from the nature of its collection, only used by students, and the use of the mercantile library was limited by a large fee. Neither was used by the mass of people who are kept outside the bars in most libraries, but rather by those to whom special privileges would be likely to be granted in public libraries which restrict access.

On the other hand, not only many of the smaller libraries, but at least three of the large public libraries, are operating successfully on plans permitting absolutely free access to the shelves to all comers. In one of them the plan has been in operation more than seven years, and in another a little less, but long enough to regard it as fairly past the experimental stage.

One library, which has grown up within a few years, gives an exposition of these free methods on a still larger scale : with fewer books and a smaller income than several others, it is issuing more books for home use than any other library on the Continent. Its success seems to be due to the liberality of its method, and this is giving it a popularity which is likely to secure for it additional public support and the opportunity for still further enlargement.

It is noteworthy that the most conspicuous failure and the most brilliant success of the plan of open shelves have been made in the same large city.

If it be granted that free access in a library is no more expensive, and does not bring any such danger or difficulty as to debar it, there still remains for consideration the question of the advantages of the plan to the educational work of the library, which is the main question, to which all others are subsidiary. Is it true that the library permitting free access to its shelves will do a better educational work than the one which denies this, or is it true, as is claimed by some who advocate the older methods, that the public is better served by means of the catalogue and the intervention of the assistant, than by the privilege of visiting the shelves and selecting from them ? This assertion appears to contain the fallacious assumption that the plan of free access in some way excludes the use of the catalogue and the help of the assistant. Those who make it also seem inconsistent in that, while they lay stress upon the value of the help to be given by the assistant, they take special precautions, by railings, counters, indicators, and other mechanical means, to remove the assistant as far as possible from the inquiring public.

A more exact way of stating the case as between the two methods is, that the open access permits the same use of catalogues and other bibliographical helps, gives opportunity for much more free and valuable help on the part of the assistant, and adds to this the privilege of examining the books on the shelves. In other words, the open-shelf plan includes all the advantages to the reader which the opposite plan can possibly offer, and adds much of inestimable value to them.

The competent assistant can render invaluable assistance to the average inquirer, and can do this with tenfold more effectiveness in the open alcove, in the presence of the books, when the volume required may be handed down directly from the shelves, and may be supplemented by additional volumes by way of illustration, contrast, or collateral information. The view of the subject which may be obtained in this way by the reader is broader and more satisfactory than that by any plan which bars it out and sends an answer to written applications, or answers verbally through an opening in a grating. The advantages of the first plan are so great and apparent that no argument would seem necessary.

In the case of the student and investigator, it seems absolutely indispensable to thorough work that he should have access to books. Even for the younger students, the pupils in our public schools, and for children generally, the advantages of getting directly to the books are very great. In one library of which I know, the assistant in charge of the children's department has placed the stories above and below, and on two shelves carried around the room has gathered a collection of books for young people on almost the entire range of subjects included in the library, and forming a parallel collection. The effect of this mingling of more definitely instructive reading with the stories has been to largely increase their use. The children draw many books when brought to their attention in this way which they would not select from a catalogue.

The opportunity which this plan offers of making prominent and calling attention to the better books has the effect of improving the average quality of the reading. The fiction reader has his attention called to attractive books in other fields, or will have the better novels substituted for the more ephemeral. We all know readers who, if confined to the use of the catalogue, will continue to draw the books of the few lighter novelists with whose names they are familiar. To these the assistant has an opportunity of recommending something better, and leading at least a little way upward.

I need not, however, take your time for further discussion of the educational advantages of the plan.

I have devoted more attention to the economical questions, and possible dangers involved, because I believe that these are the questions upon which there is greater divergence of opinion than upon the question of its advantages.

I have been interested, in looking over the files of the various library journals, to observe that the opposition to the plan of free access comes almost invariably from those who have not tried it, and consists mainly of various apprehensions of difficulties and dangers which it is feared the plan would involve. On the other hand, the warmest advocacy of it comes from those who have tried it and know whereof they speak.

I think I sum up fairly the state of the question in America when I say that ten years ago open access was generally regarded as a thing which was feasible, and on some accounts desirable, in small libraries, but as entirely out of the question in the libraries of the larger towns and cities, and that during that time it has been gradually growing in favour; that it has been adopted successfully by some large and many small libraries; that the authorities of some other libraries regard it with decided favour, and would adopt it if the construction of their buildings admitted of it; that the attitude of still many others towards this question is that of interest and suspended judgment, and that the definitely negative opinion, instead of being general, as it was ten years ago, is now probably in a minority.

In conclusion, let me suggest two things which seem to me to be essential to the fullest success of the free library: first, the books should be clearly and accurately classified on the shelves. A library in which the classification is so broad as to require the constant use of the catalogue will doubtless gain less by opening the shelves than one in which a closer classification renders more readily available the books bearing upon a definite subject.

Second, the shelves should be conveniently arranged for light and access, and all open parts should receive attention from the assistants; and I need hardly say that everything should be done to make the library pleasant and attractive, and to convey the impression of welcome and comfort.

The library which is opened thus freely has greatly enlarged opportunities for usefulness. No longer a mere storehouse for books, it may become an active educational force; it may be indeed, what it has been called by one of our great writers, "The people's university."

Wm. H. Brett.

THE EXPANSIVE CLASSIFICATION.

HERE is a system for classifying books on the shelf, taught in the five library schools of the United States, and used in a number of libraries there, which I believe is entirely unknown in this country. It consists of seven tables of classification of progressive fulness, designed to meet the needs of a library at its successive stages of growth. The first table has few classes and no subdivisions. It is meant for a very small collection of books. The second has more classes and some subdivisions, but retains all the old classes with their previous marks. This is intended for the small collection, when it has swelled so much that it must be broken up into more parts. Now, the books which are put into the new classes must, of course, have new marks; but those in the old ones remain as they are—their marks need no change. In this way we go on, gradually increasing the number of classes and sub-classes, and yet in each transition from the simpler to the more complex scheme preserving all the old notation; so that there is only the absolutely necessary amount of alteration. It is as if an indestructible suit of clothes were made to grow with the growth of the youth who wears them. He would not have to go to a tailor now and then to get a new suit. So the rapidly-growing library does not have to get an entire rearrangement every ten or fifteen years, with entirely new class-marks. Passing through the third, fourth, fifth, and sixth, it comes finally to the seventh, which is full and minute enough for the British Museum, with a capacity of increase that would accommodate the British Museum raised to the tenth power; for there might be an eighth and a ninth and a tenth table, if need be. From this adaptation to growth comes the name *expansive*. It is not a very appropriate name, because all movable location systems, that is, all plans for book arrangement in which the books are not marked by room, alcove, and shelf, but by subject, division of subject, subdivision, and sub-subdivision,—all such, I say, can be made expansive simply by using the first shell of the notation, that is, main classes only, for the smaller libraries; the first and second, that is, class and sub-class, for larger libraries, and so on. But this system is the first in which a series of expanding tables has been actually printed, the first in which the idea was made prominent. Much more characteristic, however, are two features of the notation. The first is not original, the second is. The first is the use of letters for notation, *i.e.* of the twenty-six letters of the alphabet to mark the classes (A being the general classes, polygraphy; B, philosophy and religion; C, the Christian religion; D, ecclesiastical history, and so on), and of a second letter for the sub-classes (Ca being Judaism; Cb, the Bible; Cc, collected works of the Fathers of the Church; Cd, later divines, and so on). This second letter divides each of the twenty-six main classes into twenty-six parts, and then a third letter divides each of these 676 divisions into twenty-six parts, or over 18,000 in all, taking the single-letter, the double-letter, and the triple-letter classes together. This gives, of course, more classes from a smaller base; and, on the other hand, many fewer characters are needed to express the same closeness of classification. For instance, to compare it with the decimal classification, as one uses successively three, four, or five characters, one gets respectively 18 times, 46 times, and 118 times the capacity. The result is, necessarily, much greater elasticity, much greater power to properly express the relations of subjects to one

another and their relations to subordinate subjects, and much more opportunity of making the different portions of the classifications correspond to each other.

I dislike to speak in this abstract fashion. Describing a classification is like describing a statue which is not before the hearers. One glance at the marble itself would be worth pages of elaborate criticism. For this reason I have put bound copies of the printed tables in the Exhibition of Library Appliances, where those who care can see them.

Another good result of this larger base is the greater power of making intercalations of new subjects as they become necessary in the progress of the world; for no classification can ever be complete, since science is never complete. In the main classes, indeed, and their chief divisions, the twenty-six letters are all used; but in the next line, when all the subdivisions that are at present worth making have been made, there are still in many classes letters that can be used hereafter. The other characteristic of which I spoke, the original one, is this: we use figures to mark countries, and letters for all other subjects; so that it is possible to express the local relations of any subject in a perfectly unmistakable way, the letters never being used to signify countries, and the figures never being used for any other subjects but countries. Thus 45 is England wherever it occurs—*e.g.* F being history, F 45 is the history of England; G being geography, G 45 is the geography of England, or travels in England, and so on. This local notation can be used not merely with the main classes, but with every subdivision, no matter how minute, if it is worth dividing by countries, as: K1 45, English law; H1 45, English joint-stock companies; HT 45, English budget; HV 45, English tariff; IG 45, the English poor; IV 45, English schools; IX 45, English universities; JT 45, the English Constitution; JV 45, English politics; JV 45, English administration. Or, to turn to another country and a different order of ideas: X 39, French language; Y 39, French literature; ZV 39, history of French literature; ZV 39, French bibliography; WF 39, French architecture; WP 39, French painting. Wherever one wishes to separate what relates to France from other works on any subject, one has only to add the two figures 39, and the thing is done.

It is true that many libraries do not need such fine division, or need it only here and there. Then they add 39 where they need it, and do not add it where they do not need it. That is all. In the same way, 36 is added for Italy (Italian history, Italian painting), 40 for Spain (travels in Spain, Spanish drama), 47 for Germany (German language, German literature), and so on. No other system has this feature. A notation that uses only letters or **only** figures cannot have it, because, as **the** single kind of characters used must in **that** case mean sometimes countries and sometimes other subjects, there is nothing to show in any particular case whether they mean country or not; whereas, in the expansive classification, as two or three numbers together never mean anything but a country, whenever they occur in a mark one knows at once that the book so marked treats of its subject with special reference to some country; *e.g.*, when one sees N 83, or O 83, or RPF 83, one knows that the mark means something about the United States, 83 being the United States country number. These three marks denote the flora, fauna, and fisheries of the United States.

This local list, as **we call it, by the** two figures from 11 to 99, gives **marks** to the eighty-eight most important countries. The addition of a third figure, and sometimes a fourth figure, enables us to mark all the independent countries of the world. Parts of and places in countries are arranged alphabetically under each.

We are now prepared to comprehend one of the many instances in which the size of our notation base enables us to **lay** out different parts of the classification in such a manner that one part corresponds to another. Y is the class literature; Y 45 would then be English literature; but, in order to have a short mark for the numerous books in a class which is so large in English and American libraries, we use Y alone, marking the general works under literature with the world's mark, 11, therefore Y 11. A German library would of course use Y by itself for German literature, and the full mark Y 45 for English. A French library would use Y for French literature. Z marks the book arts, which include literary history and bibliography. Combine the two and you have ZY, history of English literature. YD is one division of English literature, English drama. ZYD is history of English drama. YP is another division of English literature, **English poetry.** ZYP is history of English poetry. Yғ is English fiction. Zvғ is history of English fiction.

But it sometimes happens that a book treats of a country in many different relations, or it may be that we desire to get together in one place the history, the topography, the art, the educational facilities, the governmental arrangements of a place. This need the local list can supply perfectly. One has only to put the local mark first, the aggregate of such marks forming the locally arranged section of the library. If desired, the books about each country can then be divided by subject by putting the letters after the figures, as : 36 F, Italian history ;[1] 36 W, Italian art, and so on. Then, by simply adding any country mark to Y and to Zv, we have the literature and the literary history of that country. 47 is the German number. In an English library: Y 47, German literature; Zv 47, history of German literature; Y 47D, German drama; Zv 47D, history of German drama; Y 47P, German poetry; Zv 47P, history of German poetry, and so on.

As Zv is literary history, so Zт is bibliography proper. We can transfer all of these divisions to the new class: Zт, English bibliography in general; Zтp, bibliography of English poetry; Zт 47, English bibliography, and so on.

Class Z offers another instance of correspondence. Zw is subject bibliography; it is divided by adding to these two letters the class-mark of the subject, whatever it is, and however small. For example, F being history, 39 France, and E the special letter in the table of French history for the French Revolution,[2] Zwғ is bibliography of history, Zwғ 39 bibliography of French history; and if you have a work on the bibliography of the French Revolution, and think it worth while to separate it from your other bibliographies of French history, the work is Zwғ 39E or Zwғ 393, according as you prefer letters or figures to indicate the subdivisions of French history. Some persons prefer to keep their subject bibliography with the subjects. The expansive notation provides a place for that also. The liberality of choice between different courses is everywhere a very marked characteristic of the system.

The seventh classification was tested before printing by actually classifying 150,000 volumes, and I afterwards found, by careful comparison of one section (social sciences) with the books on the shelves of the British Museum, that a carefully-selected library of that size contains very nearly all the *subjects* that the immense museum has. If I remember right, all my search gave me but one new subject-heading. Medicine was applied to a collection of over 15,000 volumes. Besides this, catalogues were consulted to get suggestions of new topics, and the subjects themselves were studied in books to discover the logical relations of their parts, and to forecast, if possible, their future development.

Philosophy, religion, history, geography, and medicine have been printed, and the social sciences are now in press. The rest was long ago worked out, but is still open to revision. The expansive classification follows the evolutionary idea throughout, in natural history putting the parts of each subject in the order which that theory assigns to their appearance in creation. Its science proceeds from the molecular to the molar, from number and space, through matter and force, to matter and life; its botany going up from cryptogams to phanerogams; its zoology from the protozoa to the primates, ending with anthropology. The book arts follow the history of the book from its production (by authorship, writing, printing, and binding), through its distribution (by publishing and bookselling), to its storage and use in libraries public and private, ending with its description, that is, bibliography, suitably divided into general, national, subject, and selective. Economics, too, have a natural order—population, production, distribution of the things produced, distribution of the returns, property, consumption. Fine arts are grouped into the arts of solid—the landscape gardening, architecture, sculpture, casting; and the arts of the plane—painting, engraving, etc. ; and the mixed arts, being the smaller decorative and semi-industrial arts.

Similar examples of logical, or, if you please, natural arrangement, are : Putting Bible between Judaism—to which the first part, the Old Testament, belongs—and Christianity, whose sacred book forms the second part; putting Church history

---

[1] This use of the local list, which had been only briefly noted in the margin of the paper, was omitted in the reading; and in the discussion Mr. W. G. Lane called attention to the problem and its solution. The statement is included here to make the paper complete.

[2] A double table is provided for French history, one of letters and one of figures, for those who prefer not to mix letters and figures. In the latter, 3 is used instead of E.

between Christian theology and history; putting statistics between geography and economics, since it might have gone in either; putting music between the re-creative arts and the fine arts. There are many such transitions, part of them, at least, novel in classification. They are not merely ingenuities pleasing only to their contriver; they have a certain practical value, since they bring books together which one may wish to use at the same time.

The result of thirty years' library experience would lead me to say to a classifier, Be minute, be minute, be not too minute. Parts of the expanded seventh are worked out to extreme fineness.[1] On the other hand, there are places where, although the scheme gives opportunities for fine work, it counsels, without imposing, broadness. Individual biography, for instance, might be divided according to the professions into groups of engineers, lawyers, warriors, statesmen, etc., or into national groups of Frenchmen, Germans, Englishmen. But many a library—by no means every one—will find it best to put all single biography in one great alphabet, like a biographical dictionary. Artists' lives, because as a class they contain so many reproductions of works of art, are best put with the art books. I will not weary you with other examples, but only call your attention to a principle of some importance: that one should divide when division is easy, and avoid division where it is hard to comprehend the reasons for it, and difficult to see the differences between the separated subjects. Local divisions, it is obvious, are extremely easy to understand, and for the most part easy to make. Even a very small library, therefore, may profitably break up its historical and geographical departments into many subdivisions. Here the local list comes in as a means of doing this neatly and expeditiously. But in such abstract subjects as theology and philosophy, fine division increases the work of the classifier out of all proportion to the very doubtful help which it gives to the user of the library.

The letter part of the notation of this scheme has been objected to. It is urged that the succession of numbers being known to everybody from the earliest youth, is more easily and more quickly grasped by the eye and mind than the less familiar combination of letters when they do not make a word. This is true, but it is of little importance. Nobody has any difficulty at all with one letter or two letters, and three can be taken in at a glance, with scarcely any perceptible hindrance. Now, the marks which can be made with three letters and less amount together to 18,278, which certainly is enough for all but the minutest classing. In fact, the expansive classification reaches the fourth letter only in very minute work; the fifth, though it does occur, is almost unknown.

I have tried to provide a classification at once logical and practical; it is not intended for a classification of knowledge, but of books. I believe, however, that the maker of a scheme for book arrangement is most likely to produce a work of permanent value if he keeps always before his mind a classification of knowledge.

[1] See Greek philosophy BB, Indian religions BZD, the subdivisions to be used with any religion (note after BZY), Bible CB, Apocrypha CBY, Life of Christ CGQ, Papacy DGA, the Huguenots DJ 39x, History of Rome F 35. As a specimen, an unprinted scheme for the arrangement of a large Shakespeare collection is appended.

SCHEME FOR A SHAKESPEARE COLLECTION.
SYNOPSIS.
SA—SM, SHAKESPEARE'S WORKS.

SA—SE	Editions arranged chronologically.
SF	Translations, arranged by languages, and then by translators.
SG, SH	Selections, imitations, tales founded on the plays.
SI—SM	Separate plays and the poems.

SN—SZ, SHAKESPEARIANA.

SN—SU, about the works; SV—SZ, about the man.

SN	General and miscellaneous works, including dictionaries, periodicals, and societies.
SO—SU	Criticism, bibliography, literary history, commentaries, illustration.
SV—SZ	Biography.

For those libraries which use the Cutter-Sanborn order-tables, in which S is followed by figures, not letters.

Y.Sa—Y.Se.	WORKS AND COLLECTED PLAYS.
Y.Sa.	1st folio.
Y.Sad.	1st folio, 1st reprint.
Y.Sae.	1st folio, 2nd reprint.
Y.Sb.	2nd folio.
Y.Sc.	3rd folio.
Y.Sd.	4th folio.
Y.Se.	Later editions arranged chronologically either by Biscoe date-letters or by the full date, *e.g.* Y.Se 1773, an edition published in 1773. Y.Se 1773 B., another edition of 1773 (the editor's initial being B.).
Y.Sf.	TRANSLATIONS, *e.g.* :—
Y.Sffg.	French version by Guizot.
Y.Sfgs.	German version by Schlegel.
	(Translations of single plays go in Y.Si.)
Y.Sg.	SELECTIONS, *e.g.*:—
Y.Sgw.	Selections by Warren.
Y.Sh.	IMITATIONS, TALES founded on the plays, etc., *e.g.*:—
Y.Sh.L	Lamb's Tales from Shakespeare.
Y.Si—Sm.	SEPARATE PLAYS AND THE POEMS. Marked as in the other list, except—
Y.Sj.	Poems.
Y.Sk.	Venus and Adonis.
Y.Sl.	Lucrece.
Y.Sm.	Sonnets.

SHAKESPEARIANA.

Y.Sn.	GENERAL AND MISCELLANEOUS WORKS ABOUT SHAKESPEARE AND HIS WRITINGS.
Y.Sn.5	Dictionaries.
Y.Sn.7	Periodicals.
Y.Sn.8	Societies.
	The society publications are to be distributed when they are independent works.
Y.Sn.9	Collections by several authors.
Y.Sn.A, etc.	General and miscellaneous works arranged by authors.
Y.So.	CRITICISM AND COMMENTARIES.
Y.So.	General criticism or commentaries on the whole works or large parts.
Y.Sp.	Bibliographies.
Y.Sq.	Literary history. (1) The writing.
Y.Sqs.	Authorship.
Y.Sqc.	Sources, Analogues.
Y.Sqd.	Chronology.
Y.Sqf.	Forgeries.
Y.Sr.	Literary history. (2) The performance both in Shakespeare's time and since. The local list may be used.
Y.Ss.	Literary history. (3) The appreciation, *e.g.* "The century of praise," "The Shakespeare cult." The local list may be used.
Y.St.	Literary character.
Y.Stc.	Characters in the plays.
Y.Stl.	Language.
Y.Stt.	Treatment of particular topics, *e.g.* Law, Medicine, Botany.
Y.Su.	Illustrations.
Y.Sua.	Artistic.
Y.Sum.	Musical.
Y.Sv—Sz.	BIOGRAPHIES.
Y.Sv.	Various personal matters, *e.g.* :—
	Autograph .Sva, house .Svh, name .Svn, profession .Svp, religion .Svr, will .Svw. It will be necessary to take care that similar books do not get into .Stt and .Svp or .Svr. Probably it will be best to choose one place to put all the books in.
Y.Sw.	Contemporary or early allusions to Shakespeare (allusions to his *Works* go in Yss) and fictitious or dramatic works in which he is introduced.
Y.Sy.	Iconography.
Y.Sz.	Lives.

CHARLES A. CUTTER.

CLASSIFICATION IN PUBLIC LIBRARIES.

T was with no small misgiving that I consented to come before you to-day and address you on a subject which, as you know, bristles with points. Of all questions which have perplexed, and still perplex, librarians, surely this one of the classification of books, in its different aspects, is the most perplexing, and no one who has followed the treatment it has received during the numerous discussions which have taken place during the last twenty years—to go no further back—can altogether escape at the end a certain feeling of bewilderment, so many and so varied have been the counsellors; and yet, if only you tried to place yourself at their several points of view, you found yourself agreeing with so much advanced by each in turn. But, happily, the last stage of bewilderment—despair and a folding of the hands—has not yet been reached; nor is there any reason why it should be reached by anyone who truly craves for light and solid ground. On the contrary, I am inclined to think that we are very near indeed to that better, brighter state; and in any case, as one who thinks he has himself succeeded in attaining to a clearer view on the subject, I am here to give expression to a few of the ideas which have gradually taken shape in my mind. It may be that they will give help and comfort to some struggling brother who is young, or at least has in his hands the moulding of an institution that is young. For my less fortunate brethren who are wedded to systems of their own creation, or to systems handed on to them, which it is barely possible for them to break away from,—for such my remarks will have, as indeed most remarks aiming at a new and sounder system of shelf-classification must have, a more or less academic and speculative character, interesting as such, but having no immediate and practical bearing. Now, my object is to be practical in the first instance, and, as a proof of this, I will at once say that I have no scheme of shelf-classification of my own to propound, nor do I set myself of purpose to criticise destructively that of anyone else. The time at my command forbids this, even had I the disposition or the ability to attempt any such enterprise. My task is the humbler and more agreeable one of placing before you a few ideas begotten of personal experience and study, which may perhaps be none the less acceptable or profitable because they make no profession of being specially original.

At the outset, then, it may be assumed that every public library must have some form of shelf-classification. As a collection of heterogeneous things which are in constant use and being constantly added to, it must, from its very nature, have its component parts arranged according to some principle or principles of order. The only question is as to what these principles should be, and the consideration of them takes us to the heart of the whole matter. For in dealing with our books for purposes of shelf-arrangement, we have to ask ourselves, Shall we be content to regard only extrinsic qualities in them, or shall we go further and take cognisance of intrinsic qualities also? or, to speak in logical terms, shall we have regard only for those qualities which are mere accidents, or shall we also take into our view those which are of the very essence of the books and are invariable and constituent attributes of them? To the former class belong such features as shape, size, binding, and order of accession; the latter consists of the subject-matter itself of the books, which is ever the same. If we are satisfied that in the one class of features, which are purely external in their character, we have a sufficient means of differentiating the constituents of our collection, then the work of shelf-arrangement is a very simple one indeed, and the burden of life will rest lightly on our shoulders. But I daresay that, common as such a practice may be in small private libraries, whose owners love to see their shelves tidily and prettily arranged, no public librarian would venture to deal with his charge in this easy, unedifying way. Whether he likes it or not, he has to take cognisance of the intrinsic qualities of his books as well as of their extrinsic features, and sooner or later he has, in relation to their subject-matter, to answer the question: Shall I be content to arrange my books in a few, broad, general classes, or shall I proceed further and group the members of each of these large classes in smaller sub-classes, which shall be related to each other in scientific order? In other words, is my arrangement on the shelves to be a broad or a close classification? and, in either case, what is to be my scheme of classification?

Now, in deciding between a broad and a close system of arrangement, a librarian, if he is wise and prudent, will give heed to certain considerations. In particular, he will bethink himself that, though his library may be small to begin with, and may have no representation, or but a scanty one, of many important divisions of knowledge, yet the day will surely come when not only will it contain numerous representatives of all the better-known subjects, but it will also reckon among its volumes not a few which may be of comparatively limited range of subject, but of intrinsically great worth to his particular library. Accordingly, though in the day of small things he may be content, and rightly content, to arrange his library in a few large groups in accordance with generally understood ideas of the divisions of knowledge, and based more upon a consideration of the books actually upon his shelves than upon any philosophical tabulation of human knowledge, yet even then he will do well to remember that soon his stock of books will swell and multiply, and that, too, in some directions more than in others. Having this in view, he will see that his system of classification is such as that he can bend it or break it at various points to suit the varying and pressing needs of his case. Further, if he is wise and prudent, he will have a regard not only to the fact that his collection is growing in size and altering in character, but also to the needs and demands of his readers, which also are ever shaping themselves anew, and becoming more and more defined in character. Thus it may happen that subjects which at first are represented by two or three books, prove to be like grains of mustard seed, which grow into veritable trees of knowledge of a well-defined order. These he will have to recognise, and, though they may cover but a very small section of the great field of knowledge, he ought to dignify them by a careful and special treatment apart. And thus it will come to pass that in course of years the public library, which began as a small thing, broadly classified for the most part, will, by *inevitable pressure of circumstances*, develop into an organisation of very many parts, of which not a few are very minute in size, and the change will have happened in a natural, one might almost say, in an automatic way.

The library which thus expands and adapts itself to its altered conditions will ere long find itself in possession of a system of classification which is not a classification of knowledge, nor is it a classification according to a system devised for some other and perhaps quite different library; but it is such a systematic and orderly arrangement as its immediate practical requirements have determined, and such as the books actually composing it, albeit they are a very small portion of the vast mass which embodies human knowledge and learning, have called for. For such a library happy is the librarian who has not set out by aiming at being strictly philosophical or logical, but has yet kept himself in touch with books and ideas in their scientific relations and with the fluctuations which are ever going on in science and literature.

Close classification, then, in a greater or less degree, must in the long-run be the outcome of the labour of each one of us; and in this we cannot help ourselves, even did we wish to do so. As soon as we begin to act upon the recognition that at some points and for some special purposes it is desirable to bring together those books which are closely alike in their subject or treatment, and to separate out those which are unlike, we are slowly but surely driven to apply the process to an increasing number of subjects, and to apply it at some points in an ever greater degree of minuteness. But the result is only a cause for joy; for not only does it give us librarians a better grip of our resources, but it increases their usefulness manifold to those who have access to them. To many readers it is of the first consequence that they should be able to see and handle on short notice what books a library possesses on some definite subject, and it is equally of consequence to the administration of the library that this should be done with the least expenditure of time and physical energy. For this double service no more convenient way can be found than that which enables us to have books on a special subject ranged side by side on the shelf, with those on related subjects on either hand, and to have these at easy command to place before the reader, or to point to for his personal examination on the shelf. But, some one may say, no system of shelf-classification will reveal the resources of a library as a well-constructed catalogue will reveal them, for many books are composite in their nature, and a book can only be in one place at one time, whereas a title may appear in several places. True, but by having your books classified on the shelves you do not impede in any way the construction or usefulness of your catalogue, you only add to its value. Many readers are unskilled in the use of a complete catalogue, which must often be a complicated catalogue, even though it should be a printed one in book form, and of course their difficulties are immensely increased if they have to deal with a card-catalogue. To such readers the personal examination of a few of the books in the library on a special subject will in most cases be of more help than the scanning of any number of titles in a catalogue. Nor should we forget that in many subjects, especially those which are concerned with concrete sciences, by far the largest proportion of books do treat of limited and well-defined topics, and may therefore be closely classified; and that it would be a mistake and a loss to ignore these, with their eminent facility for classification, just because there are others which it is as evidently difficult or impossible to treat in that way. Many of the latter are such as elude the most skilful cataloguing by classes or subjects, and, so far as they are concerned, the catalogue of no library can ever be a complete guide to its resources in their subject-matter. In respect of them, and for the few thorough students who are pursuing an exhaustive research, the only true and complete guide is the author-catalogue, which is and must ever remain the final and main stay of every librarian. In the course of his reading and investigations such a student gets to know, from books which come into his hands, from bibliographies, from library catalogues, the names of those who have written in book or other form on the subject he is studying; and, having got his references to them, his concern is to ascertain whether these authors are represented in the library to which he has access, and represented by the described works; and this is information which he gets immediately and unerringly from a good author-catalogue.

So far we have been considering only one aspect of our subject—that, namely, which relates to the advisability of arranging the books on our shelves in such a way as that those which are alike shall be brought together and those which are unlike shall be separated. But there is yet another aspect to be considered; and as it is not only one of prime importance, but is also inseparably connected with that just dealt with, we must, before quitting our subject, give it some attention. I refer to the question of the marks which shall be affixed to the individual books as they stand on the shelves, for the purpose of enabling us to get them readily and accurately when we want them, and to return them to their proper places when we are done with them. This is the much-discussed question of notation, which each library tries to solve for itself, unless it adopts one or other of the forms which are associated with the names of Dewey, Cutter, Schwartz, and others. In respect of principle, notation forms divide themselves into two systems—the one being known as the fixed location, the other as the movable or relative location. In the former a number is given to the shelf, indicating that it is such or such shelf in such or such case of shelves in such or such section of the library, and that number is given to every book placed on that shelf with probably some other mark to indicate its particular place on the shelf. In the movable or relative location, on the other hand, the number given to the book has no relation to the shelf or case of shelves on which it is for the time being placed, but is determined solely by the subject of which it treats, or by the literary form in which it is cast. To the fixed location system belongs the merit of requiring but a very small number of signs to indicate the place of any book in the library, for it only requires to be marked with the sign of the case and the number of the shelf in that case, and perhaps also the order on the shelf. But beyond the merit of short and simple notation there is little to be said for the system. In particular, it has the serious, some may think the fatal, objection that in planning out your scheme of shelves, and consequently your notation for the different classes of literature, you must gauge by anticipation the probable rate of growth in the several classes. But experience must have brought it painfully home to most of us how frequently and how speedily our best calculations in this respect have been at fault, some sections overflowing their limits with embarrassing rapidity; others, with an equal embarrassment, growing but slowly, or ceasing altogether to grow. The result is the same in either case—alterations in the original plan of arrangement, much alteration of shelf-marks on the books, and a re-doing of much of our own or our predecessors' work.

It is the distinguishing merit of the movable system, on the other hand, that no such serious trouble as this can arise, and that through all changes and chances the press-mark assigned to a book remains the same, for it was originally determined by an essential feature, namely, by its subject or its form, and, as that cannot change, it stands for all time. A no less distinguishing merit is that it enables us to bring together the books on a particular subject or by a particular author, and to interpolate in its proper place every successive addition to the library, as well as to make fresh class subdivisions if they are desired, and all this without disturbing the existing arrangements or altering the marks of the rest of the books. The convenience of this flexibility and expansiveness is a daily joy, but it is bought at a price—the price, namely, of a form of marking which, in the simplest yet devised, is still somewhat complex and, to the uninitiated, somewhat unintelligible.

This is undoubtedly a disadvantage, but it is a disadvantage of which the effect may easily be exaggerated. My own experience inclines me to think that we may use five or six Arabic figures, if necessary, without causing trouble to either readers or staff. They are easily written and easily read, and have none of the bizarre effect produced by a notation which is composed of a combination of figures and letters.

And now, before I finish, I have just one other remark to offer. It has been my endeavour to show that we are, by the force of circumstances and the operation of natural causes, constrained to go on subdividing the constituents of our libraries, and that it lies to each of us to work out our own classification as determined by those constituents. Does this exclude the hope of our working on a common basis? I think not. On the contrary, when we remember that, though public libraries may differ greatly in size and in the proportion of their component parts, they have a wonderful similarity in their general character and purpose. Then, remembering these things, we may, I think, reasonably hope for the development of some method of classification which shall embrace all the more important subjects in their generally recognised relationships, and find that under this common method each librarian may yet be free to work out the special classification of his own library. For purposes of library comparison, and for its economy of time and thought, such a common scheme would be of priceless value, and the undertaking of it would be a feat that would be worthy of an International Conference.

A. W. ROBERTSON.

LIBRARY WORK IN NEW SOUTH WALES.

OUR conditions of life in this young country are so different from those in the older countries of the world that naturally library work is carried on in a way peculiarly our own, and suited, as we think, to the present needs of the people.

It is not perhaps unnecessary to remind you that the area of New South Wales is about 300,000 square miles, while the population is less than 1,400,000. This sparse population does not tend to encourage the formation of libraries on the system pursued in Great Britain and the United States.

We have no Library Act at present, and therefore the people cannot demand the formation of local libraries out of local funds. The municipal councils have certainly the power to spend a portion of their funds on library purposes, but, generally speaking, the rates are so urgently needed for their own peculiar objects that little can be spared for books.

Libraries are therefore usually started by local committees in connection with schools of arts and mechanics' institutes, and the central Government subsidise such efforts by a capital grant of pound for pound and the annual subscriptions at half that rate. The cost thereby entailed on the central Government varies year by year, but probably averages £10,000 a year. Whenever a municipality determines to form a town library, and has got the approval of the Government to its regulations, a grant of £200 is made from the public funds, solely for the purpose of forming the nucleus of a reference library, and the books are first approved by the Minister for Public Instruction. After this initial grant, these libraries are augmented and supported entirely from local funds.

The number of institutions thus subsidised by the Government comprises 251 country libraries and nearly 100 municipal libraries, which altogether contain approximately 1,000,000 volumes.

In Sydney there are some good libraries, and I am informed by competent authorities that the quantity and quality of reading done in the subscription libraries are both very high. Booksellers in London have also assured me that the Australian colonies generally buy a high class of literature, and that even among the works of fiction those of the classical and literary schools form a wonderfully high percentage.

The Sydney School of Arts is a subscription library containing over 65,000 volumes, the issues consisting largely of fiction. It is a good library of its class, and occupies an analogous position to the subscription library of British cities.

The Sydney University has a good library of about 50,000 volumes, chosen chiefly, of course, for academic purposes. The Royal Society and Linnæan Society have each an excellent scientific library, strong in serial publications best adapted to their special requirements.

There are several very good, well-equipped book clubs, corresponding to your Mudie's, and there are many very good private libraries, chief among which is that of Mr. David Scott Mitchell, M.A., who has got together a unique collection of Australian literature.

The public library of New South Wales is purely a State institution, being under the control of the Minister of Public Instruction and supported by a Parliamentary vote, which amounted to £6970 for last year, but was £10,000 six years ago.

It is controlled by a board of twelve trustees, to whose wise judgment, aided by Mr. R. C. Walker, the late principal librarian, the present high intrinsic value of this national library is largely due.

They are appointed by the Government, and the present president is the Hon. James Norton, LL.D., M.L.C.

Its functions are various, for it embraces a reference library, in which we are trying to get the best Australian collection possible, also a lending branch and a country library branch, which lends boxes of books to country libraries, which thereby get a class of literature that would not otherwise be available to them.

During 1896 our stock of books numbered 116,000 volumes; the number of visits was 415,182, the daily average being 1167.

In the lending branch there are 25,293 volumes. The borrowers during 1896 numbered 6061, and the number of issues was 89,890. Fiction comprises 11.7 per cent. of the total volumes, and 28.3 per cent. of the total issues. We also issued boxes of books to 172 libraries in remote centres, containing 14,208 volumes.

I cannot speak too highly of this branch of our educational work, which is extended to any group of students in lonely country places, and is of great benefit to teachers, clergymen, cultured men and women of various degrees, and students who are striving to improve their minds or to raise themselves out of the narrower environment in which they happen to be placed. We have seventy-four boxes that are constantly equipped for this work, but we also make up special boxes to suit the peculiar needs of any group of students who apply for the library's assistance.

The library staff has other duties to perform, among them being the administration of the Copyright Act, the editing and publishing of the Historical Records of New South Wales,—a very valuable work, of which five large volumes have already been issued,—and all the distributing business connected with the Board of International Exchanges. As chairman of that Board I shall be glad to open communication with any important library which can profitably use our Government publications, and can offer us in exchange any State, historical, or scientific publications that will be of value to any of our Government departments or to our national library.

A few words about our internal administration may not be out of place. Our staff consists entirely of the inferior sex at present, but I believe that our Public Service Commissioners consider our work peculiarly suited for women,—and the experience of librarians in Great Britain and the United States fully supports this view,—so that, when it is necessary to appoint some more juniors, I believe that they will comprise two intelligent, well-educated girls, one of whom may represent the public library of New South Wales at the International Conference which will meet in Sydney about fifty years hence. The junior assistants are chosen by our Public Service Commission after a competitive examination, which ensures the selection of intelligent, well-educated young lads of seventeen years of age.

I hold classes for the junior officers, which I have found invaluable for training these assistants to thoroughly understand our own system of cataloguing and indexing, and to deal intelligently with the public whom we have to serve. We have to deal with all classes of the community, and I have found that the young men who come first into contact with visitors must be far more than messengers: my aim has therefore been to enable them to be of use to the inquirer for information, and thus leave the assistant librarians and myself free for our own special duties. I can speak highly of the good feeling engendered in the younger members of the staff by these classes, and have always the satisfaction of feeling that I have ready to my hand a succession of men well fitted to accept higher duties and responsibilities in our own or any other similar library, and to efficiently fill any vacancy that may arise on our own staff.

The system of cataloguing we have adopted is one that we found best adapted to our conditions.

We have our own printing staff, and the books are catalogued by author-entry in monthly batches, and the printed slips cut up and pasted into two current volumes for the use of the reading-rooms. These different galleys are kept standing till the end of the year, then they are put into alphabetical order, set up in pages, and published as a yearly supplement. At the end of the second year this supplement is combined with the current year's slips, and a two years' supplement is thus available. This process goes on for five years, so that our supplements will not be too frequent, and at the same time always kept up to date.

The author-catalogue comprises the first part of each supplement, and the second consists of a subject-index, in which classes, sub-classes, sections, and subject-headings are given in alphabetical order, and every book is placed under its own appropriate subject-headings.

After the fierce, not to say bloodthirsty, controversy which was waged in your *Library* some months ago on the respective merits of the classified and dictionary systems, I hope that my scalp will be safe when I say that I feel that the dictionary system of classifying or indexing the books is the better suited for our general students, and certainly much better suited for the casual visitor and the average library assistant.

In order to have no confusion among the five men who are more or less engaged upon indexing our library, I have compiled a guide to the library, a copy of which I submit for your criticism. This contains sixty-six rules for cataloguing, in compiling which I freely used, as far as my circumstances demanded, those excellent rules of Mr. Cutter. I have made frequent references to his name to indicate my obligation for the basis of some of my rules, and I now offer him, on behalf of myself, and I believe I can say on behalf of every librarian in Australia, our grateful thanks for the unselfish and invaluable work he has done, in common with other British and American librarians, for library workers throughout the world. His name is frequently invoked in my library, and always with gratitude and respect.

The guide also gives very full details and particular examples for dealing with Government publications from all countries; and here I would venture to express the hope that our large American libraries may some day agree on a common method of nomenclature for their State departments. In one good catalogue you will find a publication placed under United States—Department of War; in another, equally good, you will find the same work under United States—War Department. Surely one of these is the right way. At anyrate, we have adopted one way, and, whether it be always right or not, it shall be always consistent.

Perhaps this guide will be of use to my American fellow-librarians in showing them the recognised sub-headings for Australia in general and each colony in particular. It is just as absurd for a large library to place the publications of the Government departments of New South Wales under the general heading Australia as it would be for us to place the New York State publications under the general heading United States or North America.

In order to practically group together all co-related subjects, we have given in the guide all the subject-headings now used in our index—about 5000—making cross-references from the large general classes to the smaller sub-classes, sections, and allied subject-headings. Thus, under Agriculture, there are cross-references to 43 sub-classes and sections contained in the class Agriculture or closely allied to it, and under each sub-class there are similar cross-references. Each subject-heading is cross-referred to any other that is similar or co-related, and every synonym is given with its appropriate reference.

This guide enables a number of cataloguers to work at the same time on one and the same plan, and consequently our catalogues, whatever their other defects may be, will not be disfigured by the inconsistent class-entries that are so effectual in concealing the contents of a library.

The number of index-entries for each volume averages four to five.

We find it expedient to print index-supplements only twice a year; and these supplements are grouped together each year, as with the author-catalogue, and forms the second part to the latter. A yearly supplement, such as that for 1896, which I submit for your inspection, thus fills about 183 pages of royal quarto, of which 77 pages are occupied with the index, in printing which we use Clarendon type for the headings, and brevier for the entries.

I lately received from America a list of subject-headings for a dictionary-catalogue, which I compared very carefully with my own; and I was gratified to find that we were all working on fairly similar lines, and, if I had received such a list two years ago, might have saved myself many hours of hard work.

After a long visit to Great Britain's national library at the British Museum, I may say that we are working on lines very similar to those of that great institution, and I shall be very proud to continue to build our national library on this grand model.

As delegate from Victoria as well as New South Wales, I should say a few words about the library system of Victoria, the neighbouring colony; but as Mr. E. La T. Armstrong, LL.B., the librarian of the Melbourne Public Library, may possibly write an account of it for publication in your proceedings, I shall content myself by saying that in general principles the library work of the two colonies is identical.

The public library of Melbourne—the State library of Victoria—is a very fine one, both as to its books and its building.

It has adopted the card system of cataloguing, and thus keeps its catalogue up to date in a manner even more prompt, if somewhat less durable, than our own.

To this library's trustees is due the credit of taking the necessary steps to convene a meeting for the purpose of forming an Australian Library Association. This was very successfully formed at Melbourne last year, and the next meeting is fixed to take place at Sydney next Easter.

I shall conclude by expressing the hope that our association will emulate the excellent example of the older associations of Great Britain and America, on whose model it is based, and whose excellent work will ever be of the highest educational value to your distant brother-librarians in Australasia, and an incentive to us to work unselfishly and heartily for the advancement of libraries, which we all deem so important a factor in the higher education of the people.

HENRY C. L. ANDERSON.

THE HISTORY AND CATALOGUING OF THE NATIONAL ART LIBRARY.

THE National Art Library and the museum which it adjoins were founded especially for the use of craftsmen and designers. This end has, however, most unfortunately not been all along kept in view, and I for one regret that the museum did not receive for its title the Museum of Applied Art, or the Industrial Art Museum, or some such title, which would have been a constant reminder that it was not intended to be a place of popular amusement, but an institution designed to help the British craftsman to compete successfully with foreigners.

In July 1890 the keepership of the library became vacant by the death of my dear friend, Mr. Soden Smith, well known to many here present for his archæological knowledge and his extreme urbanity. I was appointed to succeed him. When I entered on my duties, in August 1890, I found that there had never been any rules drawn up for the guidance of cataloguers, beyond that of following their own common-sense. The catalogue in use in the reading-room was in its way a curiosity. It consisted of sixty-three oblong volumes, in which were laid down all the entries in the *Universal Catalogue of Books on Art*, supplemented by MS. titles of books acquired subsequently to the publication of that compilation; so that it was really a catalogue of books in the library and of books relating to art not in the library. As the system of leaving each individual member of the staff to catalogue accessions according to his own ideas could not be allowed to continue, I set to work at once to draw up a set of rules.

All works acquired since the first of September 1890 have been catalogued in accordance with those rules. In order to secure absolute uniformity, every slip was, during four years, revised by me before being sent to the printers. Since the commencement of 1895 I have gradually entrusted more and more of this duty to my able and careful assistant, Mr Palmer.

Since the commencement of 1893 the catalogue of the books acquired each week has been sent to the printers on the Monday following, and a printed proof of this has been, with very few exceptions, posted in the reading-room on the Friday. I believe I am correct in saying that ours is the only library in Europe in which newly-acquired works are so soon made accessible to readers. I should here add that, whereas formerly the titles only of reviews and of the publications of learned societies were entered in the catalogue, now every article relating to art has a separate entry. By this system we not only draw the attention of readers to the existence of these articles, but we are safeguarded from purchasing copies printed apart, which are not only always issued at a relatively higher price, but have to be bound, and take up shelf room. I will mention an example, to show how this works out. The twenty-six volumes of memoirs read at the annual general meetings of the French Departmental Societies of Fine Arts contain from thirty to fifty memoirs each. The volume for 1895 contains fifty-two memoirs. By cataloguing these when the volume came in, we avoid all risk of buying the memoirs separately. The memoirs in the collected one-volume form cost 7s. 6d.; purchased separately, they would cost from £6 to £10. Then we should have to make fifty-two entries instead of one in the inventory, should have fifty-two pamphlets to bind and dust periodically, and the shelf room required would be three times as great.

A general catalogue under the names of authors is an absolute necessity in a library, but such a catalogue, however perfect, is far from supplying all that is needed. It is certain that the value of any library would be immensely increased if properly-classified class-catalogues were available. This is especially the case in a library frequented by craftsmen and artists, who are seldom acquainted with the names of authors of their own country, much less with those of foreign writers. In order to supply this want, I have devised a plan by which we are forming a series of thirty-three classified class-catalogues, enabling students to ascertain in a few minutes what the library contains on any particular branch or subdivision of art. Each main title written for the general or dictionary catalogue is endorsed with the indication of the class-catalogue in which the book or article should be entered, specifying, moreover, the section and subdivision. When the weekly list of accessions has been printed, copies of the slips, with headings transcribed from the endorsements, are at once placed in boxes set apart for them. If a reader wishes to know what books or articles the library contains by any particular author, he has to consult the general catalogue. If, on the other hand, he wants to ascertain what it contains on any particular subject, he will consult the class-catalogue relating to it, and will there find a chronological list of all books and articles on that subject. To the title of each work are appended cross-references to articles or correspondence to which its publication may have given rise, also to reviews which are not mere summaries.

In addition to our weekly catalogues of new publications we print monthly catalogues of works acquired before 1890, and I hope that, in the course of a few years, not only every book but every article relating to any branch of art will be made easily accessible. At the end of last June the card-catalogue commenced by me in September 1890 contained 32,097 entries, the classified class-catalogues over 70,000.

W. H. JAMES WEALE.

REMINISCENCES OF LIBRARY WORK IN LIVERPOOL DURING FORTY YEARS.

T is nearly forty-four years since I issued the first book from one of the two branch lending libraries established in Liverpool in 1853.

That book was Mrs. Shelley's *Frankenstein*.

Everything about that library was modest and unpretentious. It began with one thousand volumes and thirty readers, was located in a schoolroom, and was open during two evenings in the week for two hours. That was the time of tentative work, for it fell to the lot of Manchester and Liverpool, as the pioneers of free libraries in England, to experiment and prove for themselves many things in library economy which other libraries established later have had the benefit of.

The books issued during that first evening numbered seventeen, seven of which were nautical tales by Marryatt and Cooper—a clear proof, you will doubtless say, of literary taste being governed by environment.

One of the volumes issued on that evening, I well remember, was *The Flora of Liverpool*, a book which was responsible for many an ejaculation the reverse of pious among our more youthful readers, who knew nothing of book classification, and whose minds were intent more on tales of adventure and romance than on acquiring a knowledge of plants.

Most of those who asked for and received that useful little book imagined *The Flora of Liverpool* to be a ship, and fondly expected to have the pleasure of reading some thrilling tale of sea life and adventure. In one or two cases Flora was pictured as a local beauty and breaker of hearts.

I need hardly say that that day of small things with us has grown into a day of much larger things, and that in connection with this one branch alone it has been considered desirable to spend some £13,000 in providing fitting accommodation for its many thousands of books and readers.

It seems to me now, that among those who came to our library in those early years of its existence there were proportionately more earnest, persevering, and determined readers than at present.

A desire to remedy deficiencies of early education and to read new books for the sake of what they contained attracted not a few.

During the first year of lending only a little more than half the books issued were novels and romances. In those days we called all tales and stories—except, of course, those in metrical form—novels and romances. We were innocent then of "juveniles" in making up statistics, and we had not learnt the art of bribing readers into taking out a volume of music, history, or philosophy by letting them have a second ticket of membership. All these things have been taught us by a younger school of librarians. Readers of fiction, when disappointed of getting the particular book they wanted, could not be persuaded then, as they can now, into taking a volume of one of the many popular illustrated monthlies, which, though largely devoted to fiction, are not commonly classified under that head.

We had, it is true, *Blackwood*, *Bentley*, *Fraser*, *Sharpe*, the *New Monthly*, and others of similar kind, but none of them, I think, will compare as popular magazines with *Harper*, *Century*, *Pall Mall*, *Strand*, the *Idler*, and others. It will thus be inferred that our 44 or 45 per cent. of books issued other than novels and romances, or prose fiction (as our American friends have taught us to classify them), were books of a somewhat solid character. There was some heroic reading done by the members of the library in its early years. One reader read consecutively the whole of Rollin's *Ancient History*, Alison's *Europe*, Gibbon's *Rome*, and Ranke's *Popes*, and another the *Universal History*, Gibbon, Macaulay, and Lingard. And there were others like them.

Persistent, steady reading like this is now comparatively rare. Magazines, reviews, and journals have to a great extent, particularly with commercial people, superseded the text-book, and the drift of public taste in reading is steadily in their direction. Something of breadth and independence of thought and depth of knowledge may be lost by readers thus confining themselves to the brevity of magazine articles; but it is obvious that if people desire to know something of the many subjects which are always more or less engaging public attention, and if they are closely employed in business, they cannot do more than inform themselves through the medium of magazines and reviews.

Elementary and other schools have undoubtedly raised the level of general education, but, except in the direction of the scientific and literary magazines and reviews, the statistics of public libraries did not indicate this fact.

When I was a junior I knew the book-taste of the majority of the readers frequenting the library to which I belonged, and could always satisfactorily help them when they were disappointed in not getting some particular book they were in quest of. And the help was not all in one direction. I, in turn, had often the benefit of bits of shrewd criticism and bibliographical information from them. It is the benefit I gained in this way that makes me now so indifferent to placing obstacles in the way of librarian and reader coming into personal contact. I fully recognise the merits of the indicator, but it is one of my "obstacles." Of course, if readers would supply us with written opinions of the various books they read (I don't mean on the margins of the pages) and bibliographical tit-bits, the indicator might be dismissed on the charge I have preferred against it; but it is just possible that we might have too much of a good thing, and find ourselves overburdened with such riches. The following piece of criticism, evidently written by a girl, was recently found in one of our books. As the young lady intended her remarks for all readers of the book criticised, it may be not out of place if I read it here. "Dear reader,—Don't you think it is a pity they don't let dear Irene live?—she is the nicest girl in the book. I should have been delighted if she had married Walter. Hilda is too selfish; I don't like her a bit. I like Willie and Aunt Dorothy exceedingly. The Arnison family are too good altogether."

Now, will anyone say after this that the reading of novels is wholly unprofitable? This girl critic despises the selfishness of Hilda, and decidedly objects to her attaining the honourable estate of matrimony in preference to Irene, who has to be content with the love of the gods and die young. Further, she sees in the Arnison family the "unco guid," and despises their hypocrisy accordingly. If our young friend has learnt to despise selfishness and hypocrisy, or only increased her contempt for them, by reading this book, it has done her good.

Librarians have often to find excuses or good and sufficient reasons for what the opponents or lukewarm friends of free libraries call the excessive and disproportionate number of novels circulated, compared with books of a more solid and educational character. Perhaps, therefore, this little piece of girlish criticism may be useful to them. It is this charge of excessive novel-reading which causes us in our annual reports to emphasise any diminution of this class of literature and corresponding increase in the higher classes. Personally I am always ready to do this, for, while I believe in the usefulness of the novel, I think at the same time that the inveterate reader of them would add to his mental bone and sinew if he would vary his reading a little oftener with books of a more thoughtful kind. How to induce such readers to do this is not by any means out of the province of a public librarian.

Looking back again to the youthful days of the branch library to which I belonged, it appears to me that our readers then were much more appreciative of and grateful for their opportunities of borrowing books than they are now. It was then regarded as a boon, now as a right. Our library had not been established very long before some of the readers became wishful to have the opportunity of giving expression to their laudable feelings, and so some of them met together one evening in order to discuss the matter and arrange a suitable occasion. As a public dinner after the orthodox English fashion was not likely to be responded to on account of the expense, a tea-party was resolved upon instead, which came off in due course. A member of our library committee presided, and speeches were delivered which had the appraisement of free libraries and those who administered them as their principal themes. As may be expected, there were rounds of applause. The great event of the evening, however, was the recitation of a poem written for the occasion by a working-man reader, a brushmaker by trade. It was as remarkable a production, both in sentiment and versification, as could be imagined. But versification is nothing when the sentiment it encases is noble and inspiring. When the reciter uttered with marked deliberation and emphasis the line,

"The heart that beats fondest is found in the stays,"

the burst of applause which greeted the sentiment showed unmistakably how deeply it had affected the audience.

It is just forty years since we sought to popularise our lending libraries by circulating vocal and instrumental music. This gave great satisfaction to a number of persons, and the circulation of music has formed a feature of the work of all our libraries ever since. If it is not too late in the day to make the recommendation, I would enjoin all librarians to let the music of the great composers have a place on their shelves and enter into competition for popularity with novels. As an instance of catholicity of taste among lovers of music, we were asked recently by a young woman for *The Gaiety Girl* or *The Messiah*. The introduction of books for the blind, about the same time as we began to circulate music, came as a blessing to an unfortunate class. We published a little list of the books, and, by means of a local society for visiting the blind in their own homes and teaching them to read, we made known to them the books which were at their service in the library. We further suspended the library rules affecting the return of books, and practically permitted the return of them just as weather and opportunity permitted. I remember one of those early blind readers very well, for he made me a confidant and a writer of his love-letters. He has long passed away to where I presume love-letters are not written, otherwise the Braille system would now enable him to write his own, and so keep them inviolate. I felt at times that he suspected I had a twinkle in my eye as he dictated some of his most endearing epithets. He carried a watch, and when he entered the library one of the first things he usually inquired from us was the time of day. He then proceeded to feel the time on the dial of his watch, and adjust its fingers with his own if our time and his did not agree. The long absence from the library of another blind reader led me once to inquire the cause, when he told me that in the winter-time he was prevented a good deal from reading through the cuticle of his finger-tips becoming hard and insensitive through the cold.

It will be seen that a librarian, if, like Barkis, he is "willin'," may make himself very useful in his generation. He will certainly have the opportunities, but it depends upon temperament whether or not he makes use of them. I have already stated that I consider any inducement to readers to vary their reading a little more than many of them do with the more directly instructive in literature is within the sphere of a librarian's duties. It is a delicate thing for a librarian to assume the rôle of mentor, for to attempt giving, unsolicited, the mildest form of advice as to what should or should not be read might be regarded as interference, and so resented.

A librarian actuated with the best intentions in this way, but wanting in a little knowledge of human nature, might easily do more harm than good. Our more illiterate readers often show a preference for borrowing useful books when they are introduced to them and otherwise made acquainted with their existence. Not being accustomed to read the literary reviews or hear new books discussed and criticised, they have no means of knowing what books have been recently published or anything about their contents. Any means, therefore, taken by a librarian to bring readers and books together cannot fail to be an advantage. Some librarians speak favourably of exhibiting a selection of books on the library desk or counter, either in a glass-case, or so that they can be freely handled; and those who advocate open access to the library shelves testify to its effect in increasing the demand for books in the higher classes of literature. This is not the first time I have borne personal testimony to the largely-increased issue of our technical books several years ago, produced by means of a small catalogue or hand-list of them circulated gratuitously in the workshops of Liverpool.

Hand-lists of books on special subjects in our reference library have been printed from time to time and presented gratis to all who applied for them. Many persons have borne testimony to the use these lists have been in revealing to them what books on the several subjects were at their command.

Another way of popularising the public library and making known its contents is to invite, from time to time, the various local literary and scientific societies, and display for their delectation such books as members would regard with the greatest favour and interest.

As a simple inducement to scientific, historical, and geographical reading, the free popular lecture in connection with public libraries deserves to be mentioned on such an occasion as the present. It is well on for forty years since the committee of the Liverpool libraries instituted free lectures, and the unquestionable benefit which has resulted from their delivery has proved the wisdom of their institution and served to establish them as a part of our ordinary library work.

If any librarian is anxious to evolve the scientist and philosopher from the working man, he will have, I think, a better chance of attaining his object through the medium of lectures made attractive and interesting by means of lime-light illustrations, simple experiments, or maps and diagrams, than by supplying him indiscriminately with "dime novels and story weeklies."

It is a fact that old and young of both sexes attend such lectures, and give unmistakable evidence of their appreciation and comprehension of them, who will not read books on the same subjects. To obtain an average of 1200 persons at some forty to fifty lectures every winter is complete evidence of their popularity, and full justification of our administering, so to speak, the pith and marrow of many of our books in this attractive way. That books are referred to by those who have heard our lectures and wish to know something more about the subjects treated of in them, we know with certainty; but even if books are not referred to, it almost goes without saying that none can listen to such lectures without coming away wiser and better.

It is not necessary for me to proceed further in enumerating the directions in which the public library might be made useful, and even a blessing, to a community. Those which I have recorded have stood the test of some forty years, and are likely to bear a still longer test. The librarian whose heart is in his work will never fail to discover new ways of public usefulness, and will, when necessary, adapt the old ways to the ideas and feeling of his day.

PETER COWELL.

PUBLIC LIBRARY ARCHITECTURE FROM THE LIBRARIAN'S STANDPOINT.

IN a short paper, only expected to last fifteen minutes, it is manifestly impossible to go into the details of library architecture, and I can only hope to bring before your notice some few points which seem to me to have received little consideration in many of our more important library buildings.

A librarian naturally considers the question of library architecture from the utilitarian point of view rather than from the artistic. He is chiefly concerned with the internal arrangements of the building, and its adaptability for the proper performance of the work to be carried on within its walls. Of course every building should combine an artistic exterior with a well-arranged plan; but if both cannot be obtained, the librarian would prefer that the plan should be perfect, even if it is at the expense of the elevation.

The first and most important consideration is the provision of a suitable site. This should be central, so as to be easily accessible, and on a main street, so as to be readily seen by strangers and visitors. It should be as quiet as possible, and not have surroundings likely to interfere with the comfort of the readers and the safety of its contents. Above all, it should be large enough not only for present needs, but for the future extension both of shelving for books and accommodation for an increased number of readers. Few architects seem to have realised the rapid growth of our public libraries, and consequently we see in all directions that costly buildings have been erected, which should, in the ordinary course of events, last one hundred years, but which in a decade are found to be too small both for the books and readers.

The idea which the architect has formed of the public library and its work has been founded, insensibly perhaps, on the almost moribund cathedral or college library, with a very limited income and a growth chiefly dependent upon the casual gifts of the few persons interested in it. The stock of the town's library, on the contrary, advances with leaps and bounds, and the larger it is, the more likely is it to attract to itself and absorb smaller collections; and so it needs almost indefinite space for expansion. The rate of growth has been much accelerated during the last few years from the wonderful cheapening of the cost of book production, and the consequent increase of the purchasing power of library incomes.

A few figures taken from a table in my book on *Library Architecture*[1] will illustrate my point. The total stock in 1875 at the central libraries only of Birmingham, Bolton, Cardiff, Glasgow, Leeds, Liverpool, Manchester, and Nottingham, was 276,000 volumes. In twenty years' time, at the end of 1895, the stock was over 800,000, a growth of nearly three times. In 1875 the total issue in the central libraries of these towns was, roughly, one and a half million, but in 1895 the issue had increased to nearly four millions— an increase the more marvellous when it is remembered that branch lending libraries and news-rooms have been opened in the suburbs of most of the towns, to relieve the pressure upon the central establishment. It will be seen, therefore, that in procuring a site for a central library it is most important to obtain a large one, for it will be fatal to the work if the building is only large enough for

[1] "The Library Series," edited by Dr. R. Garnett; vol. ii. *Library Construction and Architecture*, by F. J. Burgoyne, 1897.

present needs and cannot be extended in the near future.

Some of you may think that I have exaggerated the probable rate of growth of new libraries, but examples may be seen in all directions. Here in London, the Battersea Central Library, only erected in 1890, is to be enlarged forthwith. In the provinces the central library at Manchester, opened in 1852, has been removed to new premises, and now has outgrown them, and needs a second removal. Leeds, opened in 1872, Glasgow in 1877, have both outgrown their original buildings, and are now in new buildings, which have also in turn proved too small, while the central libraries of Birmingham, opened in 1866, and Liverpool in 1853, have had to be enlarged by the absorption of adjoining properties, and, in the case of Birmingham, need enlarging a second time.

The internal arrangements or plan of the building will, to a great extent, depend upon local wants. A central library should at least contain rooms for the reading of newspapers, periodicals, magazines, and books, both for adults and children, and a lending library for issuing books for home reading. To these may be added, if funds and space permit, many other useful adjuncts, such as a lecture hall, art gallery, museum, rooms for classes and for the meetings of learned societies, thus making the library the intellectual centre of the life of the town in which it is placed.

The newspaper and magazine rooms are best situated near the entrance, where they are easy of access, for many of the readers will want to use them for but a few minutes daily. They should not be too large—two rooms each 50' x 30' are much less noisy than one 60' x 50', and smaller rooms are generally less draughty and easier to ventilate than larger ones.

The lending department in most of the British libraries is separate from the reference department—the books forming two distinct libraries, with separate numbering and classification; roughly speaking, the cheaper books going into the lending department, and the dearer being reserved for reading upon the premises. In the United States the arrangement seems different; the whole of the books in the library form one collection, and it is allowable to the reader to have any book either for home reading or perusal upon the premises.

The difficulty of printing a complete catalogue of the whole of the books in a library seems to me an objection to the American plan. Our readers are not content with a MS. or card catalogue, which can only be consulted upon the premises; they expect to be able to purchase for sixpence a printed catalogue of the books available for home reading. This they can consult at home, and from it they can make a list, send a messenger for their book, and so save the trouble of a personal visit. Such a catalogue can be reprinted and brought up to date every three or four years, for the growth of the lending department will be comparatively slow, as the new books will take the place of those discarded from being worn out, or as being of but ephemeral interest. It is no hardship to a reader to have to use a card catalogue for the books of reference, for he has to visit the library to use the books.

Before the lending department is planned, the method of issue to be adopted should be considered and settled. If it is decided to have the "open access" system, it will be necessary to provide at least twice as much floor area for the books than will be necessary if the public are not allowed to go to the shelves. A different arrangement of counters and fixtures will also be necessary, and, if an indicator system of issue is adopted, ample counter space for its display, with light on both of its sides, must be provided. The height of the counter will also require careful consideration. Consideration of these matters should prove to library committees the importance of appointing a librarian competent to aid their judgment, before instructions are given to the architect to design a building.

The method of shelving the books should also be determined before preparing plans. It must be decided whether the books are to be arranged in alcoves, or around the walls of the rooms to which the public have access, or whether they shall be shelved in separate stack-rooms. The latter system, of course, is the most economical of space, but in practice it will be found that a combination of both systems will probably be most advantageous. The height of the shelving is now hardly a question for discussion; we are all agreed that high shelving is a mistake, and no book should be placed where it cannot be reached without the aid of a ladder.

The proper lighting of the library is

most important, and the architect should adopt a style which allows high windows with square tops. The windows should be placed as high as possible from the floors, to allow the light to travel readily over the bookcases, newspaper-stands, and other furniture. Double windows are necessary where the street traffic is heavy, and large squares of plate glass are better than small panes or leaded lights. If light can only be obtained from one side of a room, care should be taken to have it of a moderate width, say twenty-five feet, but, if the room is lofty and the windows high in the walls, it may be thirty. In one-storey buildings top lights can be obtained, but they should always be double and have an inner glass ceiling to intercept the direct rays of the sun and prevent draughts in cold weather, caused by the heated air chilling against the outer cold glass and falling back again upon the readers. The great trouble of skylights is the difficulty of keeping them rainproof. This can be minimised by inserting the glass only in the clerestory and not in the slope of the lantern.

The best artificial light for a library is the electric. Where gas is cheap electricity will be a little more expensive, but the saving in other ways compensates for the difference in cost. In none but the largest libraries will it pay to manufacture the light, if it can be purchased from a company at anything below 8d. per Board of Trade unit. If from any cause it is necessary to provide an installation and manufacture the light, the machinery should be placed in a separate detached building away from the library. If it is placed within the main building, the noise and vibration will soon be found to be a nuisance of the first magnitude.

The best kind of gas lighting is some system which conveys all the products of combustion into ventilating shafts and so away from the interior of the building. Probably, the most economical form would be a combination of incandescent burners and ventilators similar to those used in the well-known sun-burner systems.

The heating and ventilation of large buildings is a very wide question. In England most of our libraries are heated by hot water on the low-pressure system, but I notice that in America steam and hot air seem to be the favourite methods. With these it is usual to use a thermostat for regulating the heat, an instrument invented by Dr. Ure about 1830, but which has not come into general use in the land of its birth. I would be glad if some of my auditors from America who have practical experience would give us a few facts as to how it works and as to its reliability. Whatever system of heating is used, it is important that all pipes conveying the heat should be easily accessible, in order that they may be periodically cleansed from dust. Here the librarian is apt to come into collision with the architect, for the latter gentleman generally objects to the look of exposed pipes running round the walls of the rooms, and wants to bury them in trenches and put them out of sight under gratings, where they will collect dirt and dust, and as soon as heated give it off in fine charred particles for consumption by the readers.

All large buildings should have some mechanical method of ventilation, and not trust to the mere opening and closing of windows. A little reflection will show that it is impossible for the same inlets and outlets, which are satisfactory in summer, when the outside air is, say, 20° warmer than the inside, to be also efficacious in winter, when the air inside the building is 30° to 40° warmer than the external. Of the various mechanical methods of ventilation, the system in use in the Aberdeen Public Library seems to be as near perfection as possible. There the air is pumped into the building, in summer being cooled and washed from dust and other impurities by being drawn through a moistened screen of manilla hemp. In winter it is afterwards warmed by passing over steam pipes suitably heated. The air enters the rooms by inlets some six feet high in the walls, and leaves them through grated openings close to the floor, which lead to a large shaft, with exit in the roof. A full description of the working of the system from the pen of our colleague, Mr. Robertson, will be found in vol. vi. of *The Library*.

In reading over this paper I am conscious that I have said nothing new or fresh. It is simply an appeal to architects and committees to see that common-sense is used in the planning of new libraries. But common-sense must be properly informed before it can come to reasonable conclusions; and so I would urge all who intend building, to most fully consider what their prospective wants are likely to be before they either buy a site or give their architect instructions to prepare the plans of their future "Palace of Delight."

FRANK J. BURGOYNE.

LIBRARY ARCHITECTURE FROM THE ARCHITECT'S STANDPOINT.

 VENTURE to address the Conference of Librarians through being moved with some fear that the true character of architectural beauty is in danger of being neglected in the buildings which contain libraries, and that a divorce may be improperly made between an art and a science which are legally, and in no case more fitly, united than in providing a home for the highest and widest embodiments in literature of the poems and romances, as well as of the indexed facts and described sciences, as yet revealed to and discovered by the mind; and inasmuch as the pursuit of architecture herself involves excursions into those delightful concatenations of literature and art, of writing and drawing, of elucidation and illustrations, which constitute both architectural books and an architectural library, I may beg sympathy while hinting, implying, urging, and I hope proving those eloquent artistic convictions which are expressed in didactic arguments so well known to you all, within lettered bindings bearing such legends as *The Seven Lamps of Architecture*, or *The Stones of Venice*—convictions which in idyllic reality colour the visions of all the poets of bliss, and give splendour to the settings of the fictitious characters of romance; and as upon these the public mind founds its ideals and recreates itself, they surely may demand the attention and awaken the interest, if not enthusiasm, of library lovers.

Fear as to the treatment of this aspect of library buildings is not necessarily based upon an assumption that boorish neglect of fine art or mere Philistinism have dictated an abstinence in the employment of either architects or their architectural wares; they are, at all events, sufficiently in evidence in modern libraries to dispel such an idea; but, owing to the considerable attention demanded to the practical working out of a public library, the function of the architect is in some danger of being supposed to consist only of solving the problems of the arrangement of the rooms, so that the work of the librarian and the access of the public may be facilitated with economy and respectability.

The many public libraries of recent years in England illustrate the evolution of an interesting and successful type of plan for buildings of a moderate size, varying naturally with the requirements of site and locality, but always economical, manageable, and useful. There are so many examples of successful planning of this class that no public or private bodies, or architects, are in much need of precedents for their schedule of requirements or arrangements. Upon such matters the librarian is the authority, and the collation of facts and requirements of the working of buildings, with critical estimates upon those already in existence, by such practised authorities as Mr. Greenwood and Mr. Burgoyne, removes difficulty in the provision of data for the architect's work. Without regarding all the problems connected with library planning as completely solved, we can yet well afford now to insert our plea for the higher art, which, accepting the facts of the plan, as arrived at in the best adaptation of the rooms and parts to their respective uses, desires to illuminate the utility of the structure with the impression of the pleasurable exercise of thought by the designer, and, appealing to the onlooker, awaken those sympathies of interest and enjoyment which we express in the admiration of beauty.

Among all classes of public buildings no one so attractively combines opportunities for the proper display of architectural expression as a building that is primarily devoted to what I would venture to describe as intellectual utility,—that has practical service in mental enjoyment and improvement, that is a delightful necessity, and has actual concrete value as well as poetic ideal purpose. Without staying to speak of the varying motives which bring within its walls the readers, for whose use a library is built—as varied as the scope and purport of all its books,—itself a microcosm of the universe, the idea which originates and maintains a public library, as a means of providing an increase of knowledge and pleasure in the lives of the community, is analogous to the vital motive of the great constructive art, which in building builds pleasurably, alike ministering to utility and beauty, in its own prose of use and rhythm of design. Appealing thus to that which is intellectual in man, how consistent should not such a building be with its genius! and, as chief among its many purposes of satisfactory pleasure, minister, by the noble art of design, to the delight of the mind through the eye, perhaps more directly and forcibly, as certainly more simply and widely, without words, in the mysterious impressions of beautiful form which were man's heritage, before even that of literary expression. It is no platitude to assert that the influence exerted by a beautiful library building is of value. It furthers the object for which libraries are founded, and the Philistine (is he to be found?) who would exclude poetry, romance, and philosophy from the library shelves, is no more deserving of blame or pity than he who ignores the influence of art upon man, and disdains the beauty of architecture in the library building.

The existence of such a mood is maybe problematical, and it would be perhaps unpractical to pursue it further, as there are faults and mistakes of another character which render this plea for an earnest consideration of the architectural claims of the library necessary.

If it be granted that library buildings afford a proper opportunity for the display of the higher qualities of architectural design, and possessing a character of their own, should secure its expression in their design, and that this character is not merely utilitarian and commercial, or votive and monumental, but a healthy delight in useful mental effort,—if so much indeed be granted, I fear it must be conceded that the success attending the planning of library arrangements is all that architecture has yet achieved in this field, and that the nobler requirements of the opportunity for fine design have not been satisfactorily fulfilled.

The modern public library has its show front, which fears nothing from comparison with its other municipal rivals for popularity—the baths and washhouses, or local police offices. The council house or vestry hall is perhaps allowed some pre-eminence, as consecrated to the more potent intellectual force of eloquence. But in ornament—and this to most onlookers at public buildings is beauty, architecture, and opulence — the library front is rich. It has the curling gables of town fashion, perhaps the oriels of the suburbs, or the broken and shaped petty pediments of the provinces, the school board *flèche*; each and several and all combined, in contrasting pink and white terra-cotta or stonework, but all front—show front—as histrionic, violent, and effervescent as the illustrated yellow backs of a two-shilling novel, itself an evolution by traceable progression from the penny horrible.

If these buildings were not built so well, if they were but leasehold, or if the ornament were but stucco and gradually paled under coatings of white-lead paint; if they could but afford relief to the distressed ratepayer, by earning rent as advertisement hoardings, say only of book advertisements, they might perhaps pass without any more painful objection than is provoked by the designs on the yellow-backed novel, which, having served their purpose in deluding the purchaser, quickly vanish into mist. But that buildings whose inception and use illustrate the liberal appreciation of arts and learning, which characterise this great Victorian age of ours, should have no other echo or reflection of the higher purposes of art than an ornamental popularity, is an inconsistent anachronism, that it is surely unnecessary to enlarge upon.

It is freely to be admitted that the fault lies more with the designers than with the promoters of library buildings; but a healthy public opinion and spirit must be engendered before a people's art can be affected, and among no branch of the community is it more likely to be favourably received, and influentially attended to, than among librarians. If designs for libraries were judged and adopted, primarily on account of suitability to purpose, and then for real endeavour to produce thoughtful and suitable design, of high purpose and art, we may be sure that the appreciation that would ensue would have a very beneficial effect upon their current architecture.

An instance parallel in many respects may be observed in the history of modern ecclesiastical art, where the Oxford movement, originating in the opinions of Cardinal Newman, and developing a revived interest in pre-reformation doctrine and services in England, infected architecture with a mediæval contagion, the enthusiasm of which is only lately waning, but is leaving behind it throughout the kingdom enduring monuments in the buildings of our cathedrals, churches, and universities, of a Gothic style, owing its vigour and stimulus to contemporary thought and life.

The word "style" in architectural use has, unfortunately, so much lost its true meaning and application, through being applied only to differentiate the forms and details adopted by different races at various times, that it would be vain to attempt another use of it at present. But the word "character" will perhaps serve as well, and then "style" can be reserved for its more accustomed use.

The character of a library building should be expressive of thought in design. There are many buildings in which the idea of free and careless accident is charming,—a small country grange residence, for example, where set purpose in external design would be generally inharmonious with site and locality. A broad picturesqueness of treatment is in that case most desirable, and incidental breaks of roof-line or wall-surface with chimney shafts or dormer windows, suggestive of comfort and ease in the internal arrangement, and of that happy disregard of convention even in dress, which makes country life seem so enjoyable in such summer days as these. A regard for symmetrical purpose, a largeness of proportion and form, simplicity in detail, and great restraint and refinement of moulding and ornament, to indicate the value of expressed study and well-considered and mastered effects, are qualities which may well characterise a public library, avoiding the meritriciousness of features borrowed from domestic buildings, such as oriel windows and ingle nooks. Internally as well as externally such rules and limitations can hold good, and the architect who has the sense of proportion and freedom of hand to guide his knowledge of form will find the passages, halls, rooms, and parts of the building as good material for his skill to play upon, in balancing, adjusting, and designing, as could be wished for. The character of restraint already demanded will govern the employment of ornament. It is hardly a question whether ornament as such—that is, detached and concentrated features and detail—is suitable within library rooms; for is not an ornamental bookcase a waste of thought and art? The concentration of interest is on the titles on the book covers, and, not being unpleasing in their form and variety, the books rob any ornamental features near them of interest and life. In the reading-rooms, more especially, ornament which attracts the eye and creates interest —which it is sure to do if it is good, and if it be bad or weak is irritating and annoying—will really be a hindrance to the usefulness of a room, where quiet for the mind and eye is necessary for reading and reflection. The designer will have enough material in his wall and window spacings, in the ordering of proper bays of light and shade, and perhaps in the opportunity of casing some of the walls with book-shelves, for the exercise of thoughtful design.

The entrance hall and staircase should, however, be regarded as legitimate occasions for imparting more architectural effect and impressiveness to the building; the grouping of the entrances, and the height of the staircase, may all become means to a satisfactory end.

Before passing to the matter of so-called "style," a word generally upon the subject of ornament may not be amiss. It should invariably be not only good, but the best of its kind obtainable. It ceases to be ornamental if, after drawing attention to itself, it proves to be inferior. It should have definite purpose and meaning—that is, its aim ought to be manifestly achieved, it may be to give proportion to a space, to give emphasis to a part, as to the capital of a column, or to a doorway, or to a band in a cornice or frieze; if architectural in nature, having the greatest refinement, and being the most obviously carefully-designed feature in the building. The Ionic volute, or the ornament known as the Greek fret, and the egg and dart enrichment, each would illustrate this point.

And if the ornament is carved, and represents foliage or human and animal forms, the same rule holds, though it may be more difficult to apply. The carving of this class that adorns our smaller public buildings has little or no artistic value. Let the rule, that only the highest and best work is truly ornamental, apply, and nearly all the money that has been expended in the decoration of our modern public libraries is seen to have been wasted. It is a much wiser and better policy to have no ornament at all, and to spend the available money in better material and workmanship, than to fall short of the proper standard of truth and beauty in ornament, by creating a permanent failure. It should be remembered that good figure sculpture in the present day is costly, and cannot be obtained without the assistance of a competent sculptor, and that those accomplished artists whom we have with us, in a small but increasing number, find, happily for themselves, but unfortunately for us, that portraiture is more remunerative than we can make architectural carving; and thus the popular taste for sweets has to satisfy itself with cheap and inferior substitutes for artistic work. Each ornament should be a work of art, expressing the individuality of its artist, and his manifest delight in his work.

A dire parsimony as to ornament, and especially cheap sculpture, among public library commissioners, would have had a healthy effect upon the design of these buildings, and doubtless would have proved a real blessing in disguise, much as some architects would have grumbled thereat.

It is impossible to dictate nowadays the style of architecture to be employed for a public building, though it was not so when the Houses of Parliament, the Government Offices, or the Law Courts were built, as in each of these cases it was expressly stipulated what period the building was to represent. We are in a position of perfect freedom, with every past architecture in a condition of renaissance, and omniscience the demanded acquirement of every architect, as it is the presumed attainment of each philosopher. The requirements of character can be met by the intelligent use of the traditions of the great past, without designing a temple either to poetry or learning. A satisfactory use can be made of the same motives that actuated Greek designers, in the developing and refining of their forms, by a process of elimination, that finds its highest expression in the majestic severity of the Doric order, if employed with insight and affection for the purpose in hand, as well as for the traditions of the past. Similarly, the delightfully romantic Gothic ages supply us with instances of vigour and power in construction, illumined by a charming life in detail, with freedom from conventionality as to proportions or rules, that are lessons instinct with helpfulness and stimulus to the moderns. It is a pleasure to mention how a remarkable American architect, the late H. H. Richardson, has given to the world some instances of very powerful design, based upon Gothic and Romanesque elements rather than features, in some of his library schools of art and museums, and which have acted as examples and precedents for many similar designs in America and here at home.

Libraries of all buildings should, however, be freed from the trammels of a merely archæological architecture. The accidental charms of ancient mediæval buildings, with their old-world associations, of such indefinable though real value, are not to be reproduced in so essentially a modern development of public spirit and progress as a rate-supported library.

The architect of the present day is apt to rely too simply upon precedent, and perhaps is in need of an impetus from without to make him embark upon a natural but original conception of the ideal library. Let him be eclectic as to motives in design, but avoid reproduction and *réchauffé* ornament; the studied architecture of rhythm, which is everything in the design of a Greek temple, is his, as well as the unaffected representation of the plan and meaning of the interior by the exterior, which is so characteristic of Gothic work. The motives are available, the spirit still lives, though the forms are dead.

A passing survey of one of the greatest libraries of the world, itself the work of a master artist, will leave us, in conclusion, with a realisation of artistic dignity and suitability, which perhaps will assist the memory in retaining an ideal of practical value.

The Mediceo-Laurentian Library at Florence was designed for Lorenzo de Medici, by Michael Angelo, in the heyday of the Renaissance of classic learning and arts, during the first quarter of the sixteenth century.

Of its wonderful contents, its unrivalled manuscripts, excelling in value even those of the Vatican, one can only say that the highest effort of architectural skill could scarcely express their preciousness. The "Codex Amiantinus," which is the earliest MS. of the Vulgate; the earliest copy of Virgil; the only MS. of the first five annals of Tacitus; a transcription of the *Divina Commedia*, completed in 1343, twenty-two years after the death of Dante; the *Decameron*, transcribed from the author's autograph by his godson; a copy of Cicero's Epistles from the pen of Petrarch; and a map of the world of 1410, showing the Nile as rising in two great lakes,—these are among the thousands of treasures contained in this building, the character and history of which reflects the genius of the master and the accuracy of his judgment and taste.

The entrance vestibule expresses the sense of dignity and power of which the architect was conscious; he plays with wall and columns as with plastic material, designing and placing his masses, for their purely decorative values of light, shade, and proportion. The cornices and mouldings, the capitals and panels, are each refined and most original in profile, though classic in foundation and proportion. The interior of the apartment itself is rectangular, with a dignified proportion imparted to it, by the order of pilasters that divides the wall-surfaces into bays, and by delicately-adjusted panels around the windows and niches. There is a breadth and subdued power in the design, satisfactory alike to the artist and to the perhaps unconscious reader. Neither is there any lack of wealth of design. The ceiling is of carved woodwork, showing its modelled beams and inlaid panels; the rich lines and forms of decoration being subdued and governed by the square lines of the beams. All was designed by the great architect. The bookcases and stands are very interesting and beautiful; a naturalness of purpose and line governs them, the mouldings are refined and graceful, and the ends have carved panels of great beauty; and withal, conscious of the subdued power of the designer, the effect is most eminently successful, as exhibiting the value of the contents rather than the beauties of the casket.

The ancient college libraries of England before the Renaissance have a picturesqueness and charm of their own, as natural and characteristic—in such instances as Merton College, Oxford, and St. John's, Cambridge—as the unsophisticated beauty of a rural landscape. Sir Christopher Wren's fine library of Trinity College, Cambridge, is a Palladian development of the existing and accepted ideas of arrangement, but contained in an apartment of great stateliness and dignity of scale, well lighted and picturesquely fitted with portrait busts and sculpture—an innovation most strikingly avoided in the great sculptor-architect's library at Florence. Mention can also be made of Wren's smaller charming library building in the cloisters of Lincoln Cathedral, which, by a strange aberration, the Dean and Chapter were recently induced by their architect to remove; but lack of funds happily prevented what lack of wisdom would not have done.

From these a step onwards, through two centuries, to the vast reference-hall of the British Museum two-million library, marks the progress of reading as well as of buildings. This index-room is a noble conception, carried out by Sir Robert Smirke with judgment and success. The vastness of the space is characteristic of the extent of the collection, the circular plan admirable for its special purpose of a reference-index, and the architectural treatment and detail unobtrusive and harmless, but withal not unworthy of so great a whole.

The extension of numerous buildings in the ever-growing subdivision of local public libraries has already met with its approbation for plan and criticism in art. In the general devolution of smaller buildings upon distinct and smaller bodies and individuals, this, though to be regretted, cannot be wondered at; but if the establishment of an architectural ideal by fair criticism, and a wider appreciation of the opportunity afforded in free public libraries for the exercise of the higher qualities of architecture by their designers, is attained, the consideration of this subject by the Conference will have accomplished an object worthy of the occasion and of lasting value to art and life.

BERESFORD PITE.

BOOKS THAT CHILDREN LIKE.

AT a meeting of the New Jersey and Pennsylvania Library Clubs in Atlantic City last April, Mr. Bowker, of the *Library Journal*, made the suggestion that a list of books for children should be printed, with annotations by children themselves. For eight or ten years I have been in the habit of reading book-lists with comments made by boys and girls from twelve to fifteen years old, and afterwards talking over the lists with their young critics. Twice I have asked for letters from children of all the schools in the city where I live, and have received the answers which I shall read you. I wrote to Mr. Bowker that I had material for his annotated list, but before the letter was mailed heard that he had sailed for England. An answer from his office, however, assured me that my paper would in no way conflict with his plans, and he has since expressed his pleasure that the children's opinions had been collected.

The letters are from children of all sorts and conditions—from a boy who has a pony and "prefers books of the equestrian order," and another who has several thousand books at home and does not need the public library, to the children of Russian or Polish emigrants, who read English imperfectly and have no books of their own. I live in a city with a population of from seventy to eighty thousand, made up of descendants of original settlers of English blood, with a later addition of Irish, Germans, Swedes, Danes, Russians, French-Canadians, Italians, and Poles. One child who comes is a bookish boy, the son of a clergyman with a small salary and not much money to spare for books. The next is a Polish Jewess of fourteen, whose teacher sends a note with her, saying that she cannot read English well, and would like a simple and easy book. The third is a little Swede with a liking for books on electricity, and the fourth a girl who cares for nothing except stories about girls of her own age.

These are fair specimens of letters from children whose reading is miscellaneous and not beyond their age :—

"I take books from the library, and I like it very much. I have one card, and it is for stories. I had *Stories for Boys, Little Men, Adventures at Rangley Lakes, Old, old Fairy Tales, The End of the Rainbow,* Grimm's *Fairy Tales, The Three Scouts, Green Fairy Book, The Two Cabin Boys, Children's History Book, Little Smoke, Partners, Chris the Model Maker, At War with Pontiac, Tom Clifton, By Sheer Pluck.* Of all these I like *The Three Scouts,* and in it I like Harry best."

(In some of the schools the children are asked, "What characters in books that you read do you like best, or would you like to have for friends?")

"I like books about ancient history and books about knights, also stories of adventure, and mostly books with a deep plot and mystery about them."

"As a rule, my reading goes in streaks; that is, I will get an Indian story, and will like it so well that I will get half a dozen of the same kind. In the last six months I have read more books on the Civil War and Slavery, and the troubles which the early settlers in the West had with the Indians, than any other kind. I have lately read *Julius Cæsar,* by Shakespeare. I think I like Brutus and Cato best. The books which I do not like the best at first I generally like the best afterwards. I think that you do not enjoy the book which you read so well the first time as the second and third times. I think I like Indian stories the best, and especially Deerfoot in the Ellis books."

The poorer children are, and the fewer books they have at home, the more they love fairy tales. Hawthorne's *Wonder Book* and *Tanglewood Tales* are delightful for children whose vocabulary is large, but the style is too mature for nine-tenths of the children in public schools. Francillon's *Gods and Heroes* is better for them. A writer in *Blackwood* last year defines what he considers the true style of writing for fairy tales: "A style which belongs exclusively to no special period unless it be the first quarter of this century; a style adorned with an occasional touch of grandiloquence, with a fair sprinkling of long words, and with a handsome allowance of idiomatic turns of expression that have now dropped out of common speech." Andrew Lang, the writer says, has adopted his style in the fairy books—Red, Yellow, Green, and Blue, which are among the most popular. The fat *Treasury of Fairy Tales*, with the old-fashioned woodcuts, may sometimes be found nowadays, but is hard to get. There is a simplified abridgment of a part of Lang's *Blue Fairy Book*, in seven little volumes, known as Longman's *Supplementary Readers*, that are the delight of children who do not read very easily. Irish children like Curtin's *Hero Tales of Ireland*. Andersen and Grimm, Irving's *Alhambra* (in the abridged edition), *The Arabian Nights*, Frere's *Old Deccan Days*, if you can get it, Kipling's *Jungle Book*, *Uncle Remus*, for the children who can read the dialect, *Gulliver's Travels* and *Alice in Wonderland*, Alice Corkran's *Down the Snow Stairs*, M'Donald's *Dealings with the Fairies*, Howard Pyle's *Wonder Clock*, Frank Stockton's *Floating Prince* and *Beeman of Orn*, with Kingsley's *Water-Babies*, and Thackeray's *Rose and the Ring*, for the children who enjoy them, as not all the children will, are a very fair beginning for your library of imagination. You will soon find out who the children are who are beginning to love and appreciate the best you can give them, and they are the ones whom you can lead to your own favourites.

The children say of fairy tales—

"I like to read a book over two or three times, for I find something new in it that I did not notice before, and new thoughts appear to me when I read a book the second time. A year or two ago I found, in reading fairy stories, that what seemed to be rather silly corresponded to what was real facts, and what might have happened. My favourite book then of fairy stories was *Wonder Clock*, and I was delighted when I had the book to read over what seemed to be a tenth time, and seemed to be as new as though I had never read it before."

"In the *Adventures of Ulysses*, I liked him best because he always escaped in any time of danger."

"When I used to take books I took *Jack the Giant Killer*. I like Jack the best. He dug a large hole and covered it with trees, and when the giant ran to catch Jack he fell into the hole and was killed. I read the *Wonder Book*, and the story I liked best was the 'Three Golden Apples.'"

"I do not like *Gulliver's Travels*, because I think they are silly."

"I liked *Uncle Remus* because it was funny, and because it told about the Tar Baby. I like the Tar Baby because it was so funny. I liked Uncle Remus because he talked so funny."

"I am much interested in electricity, and have of late been reading books about it," says one boy.

Another writes: "The book 'A.D. 2000' is very interesting. Cobb, who dared trust his life for a hundred years' sleep, had a good deal of courage, and must have been a very smart inventor. The account of the world in 'A.D. 2000' was very good, and some of the things seem not to be impossible. The principle of the pneumatic railroad is already practical on a small scale in the large stores for conveying change, and in New York for conveying messages, and it does not seem impossible to have it on a large scale, or the plan for having stations on the Atlantic Ocean to help shipwrecked people. The method of electing a president would not work very well at the present time, but in time it would not be impossible. The inland sea as told in that book is not at all improbable, and some scientific men say there is danger of such an accident."

I have known many children much interested in *Ants, Bees, and Wasps*, whose author it has been our great pleasure and privilege to meet as President of this Conference.

There are two or three books in story form—Maurice Noel's *Buz, or the Life and Adventures of a Honey Bee*; Marshall Saunders' *Beautiful Joe*; and Anna Sewell's *Black Beauty*—that are great favourites with children. One says—

"*Beautiful Joe*, by Marshall Saunders.

I liked this book because it was about dumb animals. I made a friend with Beautiful Joe. It taught me to be kind to dumb animals."

A child with really scientific tastes soon outgrows the books of elementary science written for children, and spends his pocket-money in a subscription to a scientific journal. Such a boy or girl is ready for the best that the library has for older readers; but for children who need encouragement and can be taught to love stars and flowers and rocks, trace the making of river valleys and cañons in mud-puddles and gullies left by showers, watch for spring birds and collect insects, with the help of simple and interesting books, there are those like Agnes Giberne's *Sun, Moon, and Stars*, Proctor's *Easy Star Lessons*, or Serviss's *Astronomy with an Opera-Glass*, Meadowcroft's *A B C of Electricity*, Jane Andrews' *Stories Mother Nature Told*, Mrs. Herrick's *Earth in Past Ages*, or Charles Kingsley's *Madam How and Lady Why*. This is what one child learned from a book called *Earth, Sea, and Sky* :—

"*Earth, Sea, and Sky* taught me about animal life. In one picture I saw where there was a hungry bear. He lived upon the mountain, and one day the bear came down to get something to eat. He met hundreds of mosquitoes and tried to eat some of them, and there were so many of them they all lit on him and bit him, and the bear died there."

Cochrane's *Wonders of Modern Mechanism* and Hopkins' *Experimental Science* are books that we put into our children's library, and we have had the former carefully analysed, to answer questions about such subjects as the use of Niagara as water-power, the Mont Cenis Tunnel, the Forth Bridge, ice-making, horseless carriages, and many other modern inventions. *Experimental Science* is a book that boys delight in more than in any other of the kind. There are a few others that encourage the use of the hands—*Ways to make and do Things*, *Boys' Useful Pastimes*, Beard's *American Girls' Handy-Book*, *American Boys' Handy-Book and Book of Out-Door Sports*, of which more than one copy is often needed in a library. Then there is a demand for books of games, tableaux, dialogues, "pieces to speak," and suggestions for school-entertainments. It is hard to find books of this class that are not cheap, dull, or silly, but there are a few that are worth putting into libraries, although they are not all well bound. I take a few titles from our own shelves— Camp's *American Football*, Cassell's *Book of In-Door Amusements* (the out-door book is more expensive, and written for English boys), Chadwick's *Sports and Pastimes of American Boys*, Ganthony's *Practical Ventriloquism*, an English book (every boy has aspirations at some time in his life towards being a ventriloquist or a magician), Hale's *Fagots for the Fireside*, *The Book of a Hundred Games*. Some of the best plays for children are in the children's magazines. There are some good little volumes, of Terra-cotta plays by C. M. Prevost, and Half-hour plays by Amabel Jenner, published by Stokes.

Boys say—

"I like sporting books, adventure, and explorers best. I like the African and Alaskan explorers and adventures best."

"I have read a number of the bound volumes of Scribner's, Harper's, and other such magazines, but have been chiefly interested in more practical books. Among them are or were books on printing, machinery, and science. I was also interested in *The Roadway to Wealth, Heroes and Martyrs of Invention*, and *Captains of Industry*."

"The most interesting book I have read was *American Boys' Handy-Book and Book of Sports*. I have tried to make the kites and traps described in the book, and have succeeded in making some."

"I am very fond of books on boats. I have taken the *American Boys' Handy-Book* three or four times, and think it is the best book of the kind I ever read. I took some books on drawing and mechanical operations, but did not read them through."

"The books and stories I like the best are ones that have excitement in them or tell about out-door sports, unless it is a good history story."

We keep on our children's shelves a small collection of poetry—for example, Aytoun's *Lays of the Scottish Cavaliers*, and Macaulay's *Lays of Ancient Rome*; some compilations like Wendell Garrison's *Good-Night Poetry*, Henley's *Lyra Heroica*, Agnes Repplier's *Book of Famous Verse*, and *Our Children's Songs*, published by Harper & Brothers, and edited anonymously. We have Mrs. Lowell's *Posies*, and Patmore's *Children's Garland*; illustrated editions of the *Lady of the Lake, Marmion, The Lay of the Last Minstrel*, Drake's *Culprit Fay*, and a few of Shakespeare's comedies; Christina Rossetti's *Sing-Song*, and Stevenson's *Child's Garden of Verse*. The children are so fond of Longfellow and Whittier, some of whose poems they read in school, that we have some volumes for their especial use.

One little girl says—

"I am very fond of poetry, and Whittier is my favourite poet. I enjoy his *Snowbound* as well as anything."

Another writes, in her imperfect English—

"*Evangeline*, author Longfellow. I did like the book because it told me not to give up and say I can't do such and such a thing. I did make a friend in the book. I made a friend with Evangeline."

A third "liked *Evangeline* because when the British drove the Acadians from their homes Evangeline was separated from Gabriel her husband, and Evangeline had followed Gabriel all around and would not stay with anyone, but she wanted to see Gabriel."

Some of the children have read two or three of Shakespeare's plays in class, and these are their comments :—

"The character I like best in *The Merchant of Venice* was the lady named Portia, who saved a man's life by dressing herself up in men's attire, and disguised herself as a counsellor."

"During this last term of school I have read a few books which I consider very fine. For instance, *The Merchant of Venice*, by Shakespeare, is one of the most interesting books to me in English literature. There arises above all other characters in this book the shrewd, pure, brave, and beautiful form of Portia; next, that of Antonio, who was willing to give his life to save another. There were also the characters of true Bassanio, spry and witty Gratiano, and fierce and just Shylock, the Jew."

"I like Julius Cæsar for his braveness, boldness, kindness, generosity, and nobleness as a consul."

"I have read most of Shakespeare's plays, and think they are lovely. In the *Merchant of Venice* I think Portia is the best character, and in *Hamlet* Polonius. I think the play *A Midsummer Night's Dream* is perfectly lovely."

Most of the children of course read historical stories, but one says—

"I like to read histories better than stories about them." Then he goes on: "For fiction I like stories about life in the country, stories about life at schools better than stories of adventure. I am now reading Miss Alcott's books for about the fourth time, and I become more interested in them the more I read them."

A second says—

"I like Miss Alcott's books the best," but the next writes—

"I read *Little Men*. I did not like this book."

And still another—

"If I was six or eight years old I might like Louise Alcott's or Molly Seawell's stories, but I am a little older. Lately I have been reading *Trilby, Age of Electricity, Cabin in the Clearing, Little Smoke, Log-Cabin to White House*, and a great many other books, but I liked *Age of Electricity* best."

Miss Alcott is unequal, but her best books should be in every library for the wholesomeness of their teaching with regard to work for girls. She has been one of the many inspiring forces that have in the last generation taught girls to regard self-support as honourable.

Cooper's novels please boys and girls. One says, "A book which greatly took my fancy was *The Spy*, by Cooper. The character in this book which greatly interested me was Frances, who would have gladly given everything she possessed in the world to save her brother Walton. Closely beside that of Frances there arises in my mind the character of her lover, Major Dunwoodie, who wants to release her brother, for he knows he is innocent; yet he must be true to his country. There was a strong contrast between Frances and her sister Sarah, who was so foolishly carried away with love."

The testimony of two or three others is—

"I like *The Last of the Mohicans*, because it tells about the adventures of two young girls in the French and Indian war."

"My favourite books are Cooper's works. I like them because they are Indian tales."

"Cooper and Scott describe their characters and scenes beautifully."

The children, ten or twelve years old, in one school, have been reading *A Christmas Carol*. One of the questions which their teacher asked them was, "What characters in the story would you like to have for friends?" They are children from poor homes where English is not spoken.

Their replies are—

"*A Christmas Carol.* The author is Charles Dickens. I liked it because the ghost did Scrooge so much good. I made a friend with the Cratchits because they were poor and happy. It taught me not to be cross."

"I like the *Christmas Carol* because it taught me to be kind and generous."

"*The Christmas Carol*; author, Charles Dickens. I liked it because it was funny. I made friends with Scrooge. It taught me not to be afraid I read it all."

"*Christmas Carol*; author, Charles Dickens. I did like the book. This book taught me not to do mischief—to be good and kind to everyone. I made a friend with Scrooge's nephew."

"*A Christmas Carol*, by Charles Dickens. I read it 20th December. I liked this book. I made a friend of Mr. Fezziwig. I liked him because he tried to make everybody happy. This book taught me to be good. I read it all."

Much has been said in the meetings of the American Library Association both for and against Henty's books, but the general opinion is in favour of them for the historical knowledge that they give to young readers. One of them expresses himself thus: "Of all the books that I have read, I think I like those of Henty best, as they are not just dry history, but a combination of history and adventure in a sort of story form."

Two others have read, besides their Henty stories, several books of history and travel.

"My favourite author is Mr. Henty, who has written books that are both instructive and interesting. He takes for his topics the wars and strifes of olden times. During the last six months I have read *Knight of the White Cross*, a story of the Order of St. John; *Story of the White Hoods* (the butchers of Paris, and the war between Duke Orleans and Burgundy, and the battle at Agincourt); *Young Carthaginian* (Hannibal's invasion of Italy); *In Times of Peril* (mutiny of the sepoys in India); *Condemned as a Nihilist* (escape from the Siberian prisons); *Redskin and Cowboy* (a tale of Western life); and am now reading *Under Drake's Flag*. All of these are written by Henty. I have read also, *Life of Abraham Lincoln*, *Battles for the Union*, *Campaign of General M'Clellan*, *Bushmen of South Africa*, *Discoveries in the Amazon Basin*, *Life of Peter the Great and his Battles*, *Invasion of Napoleon into Russia*, and the early part of the *History of England*. I have also read *Dragon and Raven*, *In Freedom's Cause*, and *Two Thousand Years ago in Italy*."

"On my card for histories I have read *Northern Myths*, *and the Bluejackets of 1812*. This is one of the best books I have read. The most interesting characters in it are Lieutenant Perry, Captain Decatur, and Captain Barry. Besides this, I have read *Starland* and *Two Thousand Years Ago*. On my story card I have read all of Verne's works, and *With Clive in India*, and more of Henty's works. I have read all of Du Chaillu's works, and Stanley's *How I found Livingstone*, and *Down the Congo*. I think this is all I have read."

"Henty is an English writer, but all American boys find much interest in his books."

"I think Henty's books are good, but they are too much alike."

Some of Scott's novels have been read in class this year.

"*Kenilworth* I like better than any other book I have read lately. I am becoming very much interested in Scott's novels, as he describes everything so beautifully. His sketch of the character of Queen Elizabeth and the Earl of Leicester I think is very fine, and he describes life among the English nobility in such a way as to make you imagine that you are amidst the gaieties of the court."

"I like *Ivanhoe*, by Scott, better than any. My favourite characters in this book are Brian de Bois-Guilbert, Rebecca, and Richard. I think, for all his selfishness and jealousy, that Bois-Guilbert had a much stronger character than Ivanhoe. His character shows itself in his love for Rebecca. He would give up what his ambition had hoped for, all for the love of Rebecca. I think it was very noble of him. I also liked Rebecca. I think she had a nobler character than Rowena. I admire her more than ever where she is accused of sorcery. With all Bois-Guilbert's pleadings she remained firm. She would sacrifice her life rather than yield to Guilbert. Richard also was a noble character. I admire him for his courage and bravery. It was very noble of him to forgive his brother John as freely as he did. There are not many who can give good for evil."

"We have read 'Tales of Chivalry,'

which are selections from Sir Walter Scott's *Ivanhoe*. I grew so interested in these parts of *Ivanhoe* that I got the book and read it through."

"I was very much charmed with Rebecca. She was a beautiful person, of a very strong character. She loved all that was right and good."

"I like King Richard, not for his rule as a king, but for his pleasantness as a companion. I think he was a man we would all like to meet. He was a sincere friend to all those he liked, and would do anything for them."

"I like the *Talisman* very much. In fact I like all of Scott's works. I like the *Talisman* because it tells so much about Richard the Lion-hearted and the Crusades. I like it because it is a regular history put in story form, and I like history very much. It has helped me a good deal, for when we were studying English history last year I knew a good deal more than some of the others about the Crusades."

"I do not care much for historical reading, and do not like books by Henty and Ellis. I like Scott in *Lady of the Lake*, and tried to read *Ivanhoe*, but could not get interested in it."

"Some people recommend such ones as Scott's works (all poetry) for boys, but I like one full of adventure."

"I love to read, and have just finished *Rob Roy*, by Scott. I have also read *Kenilworth*, *Marmion*, *Ivanhoe*, and a great many other books written by him."

"I liked *Ivanhoe* because of the good nature and strong mind of Rebecca. And how honourable Rebecca was when Brian de Bois-Guilbert wanted her to run away and not have any trial for the crime the people accused her for. I liked Brutus in *Julius Cæsar* because he was honourable and beloved by all. When he slew Cæsar he did not do it so as to get a place in the State or town, like Cassius did, but because he thought it was right and for the welfare of the people. I liked King Richard in *Ivanhoe* because he was humble, and liked to associate with the common people as well as with the nobility."

"My favourite characters are Ramona and Countess Amy Leicester. I like Ramona because she was so loving and gentle. I liked Countess Amy because she had so many winning ways."

"*Ramona* is one of the most interesting books I ever read. I read it when we were studying about the Indians. Ramona, the heroine, I liked very much. I think she was very brave and patient. I almost hated the Señora. Felipe I liked pretty well, but he was so weak. To use the common phrase, I would say, 'He was tied to his mother's apron strings.'"

"I liked Alessandro, he was such a strong character, and so brave. Reading about him gave me a very different idea of Indians. The priest who visited them I liked because he treated Ramona so kindly."

There are three books which excite children's compassion for the cruelly treated, and have the best influence upon them. These are *Uncle Tom's Cabin*, *Ramona*, and Anna Sewell's *Black Beauty, the Story of a Horse*.

One little girl says, "You will think it very funny that I have not a cross beside *Uncle Tom's Cabin*, but I cannot truly and honestly say I like it very much, because I do not like sad books. I got it for Christmas, and have tried to read it two or three times, but when I get to where Uncle Tom is sold I stop. The other day I made up my mind I would read it, and I did. I am sorry to say that I do not like to read out of a newspaper very well, but my mamma always tells me things that she thinks will interest me. She tells me every morning the news from Greece and Cuba."

Another writes to me that she was so excited over *Uncle Tom's Cabin* that she dreamed she was the kind woman who took Eliza in, and got up in her sleep and opened the house door, saying, "Now she is in."

One "made a friend of Aunt Chloe because she was a nice cook."

Another says, "I like *Uncle Tom's Cabin* because the book tells about slave-life, and makes it seem as if I were there."

"My favourite books are *Uncle Tom's Cabin*, *Christmas Carol*, *The Making of New England*, and *Uncle Remus*. I like *Uncle Tom's Cabin* because it teaches me not to be cruel."

"My favourite books are Andersen's *Fairy Tales*, *The Lamplighter*, Dickens' *Christmas Carol*, Bird's *Christmas Carol*, and *Swiss Family Robinson*. My three favourite characters are the Fezziwigs, because they were so jolly; George Washington, because he tried to help his country; and Eva St. Clare, because she was always trying to help everybody."

"My favourite books are *Tom Sawyer*,

Uncle Tom's Cabin, and Scudder's *American History,* because they are so interesting to read. I like Tom Sawyer because he was so jolly, Uncle Tom because he was so faithful, and Nathan Hale because he was so brave."

"*Uncle Tom's Cabin,* by Harriet B. Stowe. I liked this book very much because it was about slavery. I made a friend with Uncle Tom because he was so faithful. It taught me to dislike slavery."

"*Uncle Tom's Cabin,* by Harriet Beecher Stowe. I liked Mrs. Shelby because she was so sympathetic. I read it all."

"*Uncle Tom's Cabin* I believe I have read fully eight times. It is a book I never tire of, and I think I never will."

One child writes at the end of a long miscellaneous list, "I like the above-named books, because some of them enlighten me in history, others make me feel happy, and the others teach me the different arts of the world."

We cannot measure all children by the exceptional boy of whom Mr. Crunden told us yesterday, or by the other boy of nine, the son of the secretary of the American Library Association, whose list of favourite books is printed in the June number of *Public Libraries.* Sir Walter Scott said, "To write down to children's understanding is a mistake; set them on the scent, and let them puzzle it out," but children who never hear English spoken at home must be considered in buying books for an American library. They are receptive, and often enjoy good literature more than children from better homes, but masterpieces must sometimes be abridged and simplified for them. Do not expect too much of children at first. Out of a hundred such as we have to supply books for, ninety leave school before they can do more than read the daily newspaper, nine can be trained to enjoy the best authors, and one has the true book-hunger that Sir John Lubbock counts as one of his "pleasures of life."

CAROLINE M. HEWINS.

OUR YOUNGEST READERS.

LIBRARY was formerly not much more than a collection of books, to be made use of by a few men of learning, perhaps by very few save the librarian himself. As book knowledge and the use of books became more common, the number of students for whom the library seemed to be designed increased. But it did not for a long time change its essential nature as a workshop for students pure and simple. With the growth of the free public library idea, the feeling became widespread that a collection of books might also well be used as a means for promoting general happiness and well-being.

First, perhaps, by furnishing, through novels and literature, properly so called, entertainment and recreation for the common people; secondly, by furnishing, through books of a popular nature on all kinds of subjects, a means of general education for the adult. The idea that a collection of books might properly be associated with the work in the common schools of the country, schools designed for and patronised by the children of the average citizen, was very slow in growth. It is scarcely twenty years since Mr. Green, of Worcester, Massachusetts, began to talk and write of the work of the free public library in furthering the educational work of the schools proper. And it is only within the last five or six years that librarians generally, even those who are most progressive and are most alive to the possibilities of the public library, have realised that one of the important fields of work for a collection of books, if not the most important field, is the seconding the efforts of the common schools to start the young people of the country on the road to good citizenship.

The issuing of lists of books arranged by grades and by classes, with appropriate annotations or appraisal notes, in all departments of knowledge, for young people—even the very youngest; the spread of the custom of giving to teachers special privileges in the way of carrying from a library large collections of books for use in their schoolrooms; the development of the schoolroom library idea—an idea which involves the placing in every schoolroom in which is a group of forty or fifty children a well-selected group of forty or fifty books adapted to those children; the addition of the library department to the National Educational Association—the largest and perhaps the most influential association of people interested in popular education to be found in the world; the large amount of attention that is paid in the periodical press to the reading of the children,—all these are but indications of the fact that librarians and teachers alike have in the last few years come to realise that even in elementary educational work a collection of books is almost an absolute necessity.

This brief outline of the way in which library and educational work have become intimately related in recent years is perhaps a sufficient demonstration of the duty the librarian is under to adapt his library, to a large extent, to the needs of children and the schools.

Within the past two years careful inquiries have been made in several places in the United States as to the reading habits of children, and in a good many instances these inquiries have extended to the reading habits of the very young. From the data as yet obtained, it is perhaps not safe to make any positive general statements. We can, however, for the purposes of further investigation, and for the purposes of properly directing, in the immediate future, the work of promoting reading among young children, assume that these investigations have demonstrated two or three things:—

First, for example, that average children, whether they come from the homes of well-to-do and fairly well-educated people, or from the homes of the poor and rather illiterate people,—I am speaking now, of course, of the United States in general,—are ready and willing to begin to read by the time they are six and a half or seven years of age.

Second, that the reading habit increases from this time up to about twelve or fourteen years; and that, between the years of eleven and fourteen, children, both boys and girls, are, in their excess of vitality, and in their eagerness for acquisition, and in their half-unconscious desire to touch the life about them at as many points as possible, looking about for things to lay their hands and brains to, and read with great avidity whatever comes in their way.

Third, that during the years from about fourteen to eighteen or nineteen the reading habit loses somewhat in intensity, and gains somewhat in definiteness of direction.

Fourth, that with the child of six or seven, the formation of the reading habit, the subjects he will take an interest in, the class of books he will choose, all depend very largely on the influence of those people who are most closely associated with him, and especially of the teachers. The testimony comes again and again from teachers who have experimented in these matters, that children of six, seven, eight, and nine years of age can be interested in anything in the world if the teacher will but take pains with them, and can be led to read with eagerness about almost any subject in which the teacher herself endeavours earnestly to interest them.

The moral of these few facts is very evident. We must put into the hands of teachers shorthand methods, through appraisal lists largely, of getting acquainted with the best books for the young; and we must extend, as far as possible, the use of these methods among parents. We must make it possible for teachers of children in the very first grades, of children but six, seven, eight, and nine years of age, to put before these little ones the books best adapted to them, and the books which will be most likely to lead them to form the habit of reading.

All this amounts to saying that the free public library, in its educational work, must be, to a very large extent, and to a much greater extent than it has commonly been heretofore, the library for the very young.

J. C. DANA.

THE ORGANISATION OF CO-OPERATIVE WORK AMONG PUBLIC LIBRARIES.

HE possibilities of co-operative library work have been broadly indicated by experiments already tried; the impossibilities have not yet been finally proved, but the obstacles in the way stand quite clearly revealed.

For example, I do not think it can be said that co-operative card cataloguing of current literature has been condemned, on practical or economical grounds, by any experience yet complete; but no satisfactory progress has been made in the contriving of methods for removing the more serious objections to it. How to adjust it to the different ranges of book selection and book purchase in different libraries, without wastefulness, and how to make it prompt enough for most demands, are problems which seem to be far from solution. Nevertheless, there is no warrant for deciding that the solution is impossible, and there is really fair encouragement for hopefulness in the matter.

On other lines of co-operative work the success has been decisive. Critical book selection, for public library guidance, is being systematised by co-operative methods in the United States, and promises to assume the greatest possible importance. Beginning with what is known as the A.L.A. (American Library Association) Catalogue, of 5000 volumes, prepared for the model library exhibited at the Columbian Exposition of 1893 in Chicago, the idea has since developed a continuous undertaking of selective criticism, applied to current literature. The book product of every year is being subjected to sharp examination and sifting, first by the passage of lists from hand to hand, among the members of a considerable jury, for comment and vote-marking, and then, as thus sifted, by discussion at meetings of the library associations, State and national. In this critical, selective work, the librarians have no wish to put trust in their own judgments alone, but are enlisting more and more of help from specialists in every department of literature.

A finer and more perfect expansion has been given to the same idea by Mr. George Iles, of New York, in his plan of a systematic "appraisal of literature" for the guidance of readers. It is a scheme already realised so far as to demonstrate the immeasurable possibilities of educative influence which lie in it. The co-operation contemplated reaches widely out among scholars and men of letters, to bring them into service with the libraries in as great an effort to give light and leading to the public as can well be conceived. The undertakings already carried out by Mr. Iles, at his own cost, in this appraisal of literature, and the larger projects which he has in view, are set forth, I understand, in a paper by himself, to be read at this meeting.

But the field for co-operative work which seems to be peculiar to the libraries, which demands no outside aid, and which has no obvious limit, is comprehensive indexing. By comprehensive indexing I mean the indexing which passes beyond single books, to boldly gather a multitude within the embrace of one alphabetical system. It is wholly modern as a need, wholly modern as a conception, wholly modern as a possibility, on any great scale. The vast multiplication of books in our time—of books more or less necessary to the completeness of increasing human knowledge—has created this new need, and is making it every year more pressing. It is a need that in any former time, if felt at all, would have been the need of a few. The public libraries of this day, which multiply readers and inquiring students even faster than books are multiplied, have made it the want of many. It is for the libraries to satisfy the want they have created, and there is nothing they can do more easily, by co-operative organisation.

Everywhere, in books of all classes, there are topics either suggestively touched or carefully treated which do not lie obviously enough within the bounds of the writer's subject to be readily discovered by any ordinary seeker after light upon them. Lecky's chapters on the causes of the French Revolution, in his *History of England in the Eighteenth Century*, and on industrial history, including slavery, in his *History of Rationalism*; Bryce's chapters on Tammany Hall and on Wall Street, in his *American Commonwealth*; Leslie Stephen's chapter on Political Theories, in his *History of English Thought in the Eighteenth Century*, are instances in point. To make and continuously maintain a subject index or directory to all such out-of-the-way or hidden pieces of information and discussion, is surely one of the greatest services that are waiting to be rendered to the cause of public education. Some steps toward it have already been taken in the A.L.A. *Index to General Literature*, edited by Mr. Fletcher, and published in 1893, with annual continuations since; but they only skirt the field.

When the great *Subject Index to Periodical Literature* was completed, in 1882, by the combined labour of many librarians in England and America, under the editorship of Poole and Fletcher, there seemed to be nothing of its nature too vast to be undertaken in the same mode. And, so far as concerned the labour side of the matter, nothing could offer itself as a project of useful work in this field that would have been discouraging then or since. If we reflect that one hour per week, or ten minutes per working day, given by forty-eight persons united upon the same task, is equivalent to the continuous labour of one person giving eight hours in the day to it, we may reasonably believe that the library staff of Great Britain and America alone might apply, under right conditions, to an undertaking of common interest, what would equal the continuous work of a dozen men and women, and do it so easily that the effort would scarcely be felt.

On the primary labour side of the matter there is nothing to forbid undertakings of any magnitude whatever in useful indexing. The difficulties and obstacles lie on that side of these undertakings which is beyond the reach of volunteer workers. They begin where a question of money has its necessary beginning, and that question rises in advance of the commercial questions of publication and sale. It rises as a question of editorship, for the proper organisation and direction of the co-operative work.

Heretofore, in what has been done, the editorial labour has either been given outright, or it has been dependent for its reward on the chances of commercial profit from the publication; and those chances are slender in the most promising case. If that must continue to be the condition under which such work is done, our co-operative undertakings can never be advanced to the scale which they ought to attain. For the scale as well as the quality of the work depends peculiarly upon the organisation and direction that are editorially given to it. No important undertaking in it can be properly planned and conducted as a casual task, by one who gives night hours and odd moments to it only as he is able to snatch them. The whole attention and whole time of an editor of the first order of ability are none too much for its demands.

As I look at the matter, the results which can easily be attained by a systematic organisation of co-operative work among the libraries of Great Britain and America, if not of the world at large, in the subject-indexing of general literature alone, are so great in importance that the cost of a permanent editorial director for it, salaried with liberality, is an insignificant trifle to pay for them. Among libraries and individuals, are there not enough to be found who will divide the small cost between them? Let it be done, I would suggest, by the formation of a new index society — a subject-index society—more practical and more broadly utilitarian in its aims than the deceased society of that name. A membership of 300 or 400, with an annual membership fee of two guineas, or ten dollars, would provide for the execution of the work, leaving publications to be subscribed for according to their cost, with advantages in price given to members of the society.

I make the suggestion, with little comment of my own, hoping that it may be discussed.   J. N. LARNED.

CO-OPERATION IN A CATALOGUE OF PERIODICAL PUBLICATIONS.

HE subject upon which I have the honour to address you is one of bibliographical as well as practical interest, but it is from the librarian's standpoint, as distinct from that of the bibliographer, that I intend to discuss it. My purpose is to draw attention to the fragmentary and defective condition of the bibliography of periodicals, and to suggest a method of co-operation by which a complete catalogue of serials may be compiled, to the permanent benefit of international bibliography and bibliotheconomy. I venture to hope also that the initial steps to this desirable end may be taken by this Conference. For it appears to me that a meeting of librarians so widely representative as this is, above all things, an opportunity for collective action. I do not depreciate the advantages of discussion and of the interchange of ideas, which constitute the most obvious business of a conference. Librarians as a rule know too little of the stimulus and encouragement derived from personal contact with others of the same calling, and many of the singularities supposed to characterise them as a class, which none of us will admit for a moment, would be cured by mere gregariousness. But, however great the benefits which we as individuals receive from discussion and criticism, there are other important and more lasting results that can be accomplished by united action. An international conference is the highest tribunal of professional opinion that can be called into existence, and its authority may be successfully exercised in a practical sphere where private enterprise or the efforts of a body less influential would fail.

No one who has followed the advances of knowledge in recent years can have failed to notice the growing importance of periodicals, particularly of those devoted to original research The advantages of association for the purpose of enlarging the bounds of science have been long recognised. With that object, academies of science and learned societies were founded, and their meetings were the readiest means of making known discoveries and of submitting theories to the test of expert criticism. The printed reports of the proceedings at these meetings form the nucleus of that periodical literature of science and research which has reached such huge proportions in the present generation. The principle that underlies the existence of technical periodicals is the same as that which led to the foundation of societies. It still is association, to enable individuals to bring their ideas and discoveries before an audience; but the audience has been amplified, from the mere handful of sympathisers that anyone place could assemble, to the whole body of similar specialists in every civilised country. The technical journal is the new vehicle of communication, and to its methods of publication the older academy or society has conformed, issuing bulletins or transactions with the same regularity and with the same object of appealing to a larger public than the audience of active members. With such facilities for publication, it is not surprising to find that every item of original research is now recorded as soon as made, becoming common property and a point of departure for fresh investigations by other workers in the same field. It is also easy to understand that the specialist who intends to keep abreast of the times must have access to all the periodicals in which the observations and discoveries of his fellow-workers are chronicled, that he may know what has already been done, and in what direction he may most profitably employ his energies. Here begins the task of the bibliographer. It is his business to supply the key to the mass of material contained in all the existing journals, and to furnish an inventory of the publications devoted to each department of knowledge. The natural and physical sciences are the subjects in whose service the technical periodical has reached its fullest development, and valuable guides have been furnished the student of science in Scudder's Catalogue of Scientific Serials and the Royal Society's Catalogue of Scientific Papers. But there are other branches of knowledge in which the scientific methods of observation and experiment are also employed, and in which the scientific practice is equally in force of accumulating the records of research in volumes of periodical publications. The student of archæology, or of history, or of philology, is becoming hardly less dependent upon periodicals than the student of chemistry or botany. In short, every department of thought, every branch of science, every business or trade, not excepting our own, has its technical journals, which serve to store up as well as to dispense the information acquired by many workers in the same field.

But, while periodical literature has been growing in extent and importance, bibliographical information about it has been very inadequately provided. The great desideratum, never to be supplied, is a colossal subject-index to the periodicals of the world. By division of labour some steps may be taken to that desirable and impracticable end. The Royal Society propose to begin a subject and author catalogue of the papers contributed to all scientific journals—a huge task, even if, as is reported, it is limited to current issues. Moreover, by the co-operative industry of American librarians, the general reader is already provided with an index to the chief literary and popular magazines in the English language. So, by degrees, an approximation to the ideal index may be reached. But these are tasks for the bibliographer rather than for the librarian. A far more modest requirement, and one that falls properly within the sphere of library economy, is a simple catalogue of the periodical publications of the world,

exclusive of newspapers and literary magazines. Partial lists have been drawn up, limited to certain subjects, or to a single language; but the need, I take it, is for one comprehensive catalogue, classified according to subjects, enabling the librarian or the specialist to ascertain from a single source the extent of the periodical publications in any department or the details of issue in the case of any particular journal. Such a work would, from its comprehensiveness and utility, be worthy to rank with the great national book-catalogues, as part of the indispensable equipment of every library. We have the English Catalogue of Books, the American Catalogue, Lorenz' Catalogue de la Librairie française, the Bücher-Lexicon of Heinsius or of Kayser, and similar repertories for other book-producing countries of Europe. Each of these aims at completeness for the period which it covers, and each is continued and enlarged by supplementary volumes, issued annually or at less frequent intervals, to keep pace with the constant stream of new publications; so that it may fairly be claimed that no book appears that is not recorded in one or another national book-catalogue. Why should we not also be able to claim that no periodical is issued that has not its entry in a similar international catalogue of serials?

Partial lists of periodicals, I have said, do exist, and imperfectly answer to our needs. There are bibliographies, fairly complete, of material on special subjects; there are directories of learned societies; there are national catalogues of current journals, there are also the catalogues of great libraries like the Bibliothèque Nationale or the British Museum, that contain their thousands of periodicals, supplying valuable bibliographical data not easily procured elsewhere. But these sources of information have no relation to one another. Some are large volumes, some are pamphlets, some are but portions of other publications. Few of them are exhaustive even for their own restricted range, and the most perfect will be rendered defective by the lapse of a few years. Moreover, there are not many libraries large and comprehensive enough to have collected all the available catalogues, and, when all are assembled, it will be found that there still remain classes of periodicals unrepresented by any list. I need not dwell longer on inconveniences that each of us has probably felt more or less frequently. What is needed, as much by the smaller as by the larger libraries, is a single publication, superseding the variety with which we now have to deal, exhaustive instead of approximately complete, and continued by supplements at annual or other regular intervals. We should then have a catalogue of periodicals as final and reliable as the great national book-catalogues already mentioned.

Let me particularise a few of the essential, or at any rate the leading, principles to be observed in compiling such a catalogue.

I. First, its scope must be limited to periodicals devoted to science and research. To catalogue the newspapers of the world would hardly be more than a bibliographical amusement. Magazines and literary reviews might also be neglected. They merely reflect the taste of the day, and cater to our entertainment without being serious contributions to knowledge.

II. Secondly, classification by subject should be attempted in some way, either in the arrangement of the catalogue itself or by means of an index. An alphabetical arrangement by title, like that of the Smithsonian Catalogue, or classification by country and place of publication, as in Mr. Scudder's and the British Museum catalogues, is simple and readily intelligible. But the simplicity of either system would seem to be in the interest of the compiler rather than for the enlightenment of those who seek for information. The extent of the periodical literature in any department is a question that often arises, and that is not easily answered with the existing bibliographical guides. A catalogue arranged according to subjects would also admit of satisfactory and logical division into volumes, and the convenience for consultation would be thereby much increased. A title-index and an index of localities would naturally be added.

III. Another, and perhaps the most essential, feature of a satisfactory catalogue of periodicals is, that it should be continued and kept up to date by supplements issued at regular intervals. One of the greatest drawbacks to individual effort in publications of this kind is the isolated character that is necessarily impressed upon them. Being issued spasmodically, so to speak, to meet the requirement of the moment, they fail to maintain the place to which their merit and the industry of their compilers entitle them, chiefly because of the impossibility of providing for revision and re-issue when the accumulation of new material has rendered them obsolete. In course of time a new compiler arises, a new publication is put forth, perhaps on different lines, but with the same fate of premature neglect. The preface to Mr. Scudder's catalogue contains a melancholy recommendation—melancholy because it has been without result—to the effect that a list of additions and emendations should be published in 1880, with decennial supplements thereafter. Nearly twenty years have passed since Mr. Scudder published his catalogue, and no supplement has appeared. The consequence is that, when the next catalogue of scientific serials is issued, all the material so laboriously collected by Mr. Scudder will be re-collected and re-edited, in addition to that which has come into existence since 1876. But supplements at intervals of ten years are not sufficient. Librarians must have information of the latest publications of all kinds. Every year new periodicals are begun and old ones are discontinued, new societies are organised and old ones die. The astonishing growth of periodical literature can only be kept pace with by a system of annual supplements, which should exercise a double function—recording the decease as well as the birth of periodicals and societies. By this means alone can a catalogue, adequate in all other respects, be kept in force perpetually as an authoritative guide, and its value and utility increased instead of diminished with the lapse of years.

In conclusion, let me explain the reason for bringing up the subject before this Conference. The preparation of a catalogue such as I have outlined is a work of considerable magnitude, not so much from the quantity of material involved as on account of the numerous and widely-scattered localities from which information has to be gathered. It is not merely a question of the output of the great publishing centres, London, Paris, Leipzig, New York, etc. The smaller towns in every country have their local societies,— scientific, archæological, and historical,— whose transactions are, as a rule, printed and published in the place where the meetings are held. To obtain accurate and complete accounts of these societies and their publications from every provincial town of the civilised world would be practically impossible for an individual. His name would be unknown to the large majority of those with whom he tried to put himself in communication, the language of his letters might be unfamiliar to them, his very nationality possibly suspect. Information at first hand would therefore be beyond the reach of private enterprise, and the compiler's chief resource would be the partial catalogues already issued, with the addition of such assistance as the largest libraries could render him. Unfortunately, both the catalogues and the libraries have been shown by experience to be untrustworthy guides where absolute completeness is aimed at, and their deficiencies would be too likely to be repeated in the new compilation. Moreover, one feature that I have ventured to call an essential of the catalogue would be absent, viz. the certainty of its continuation by annual supplements. No individual author could supply that guarantee, without which all the labour expended upon the catalogue would in a few years count for nothing. Only co-operation can ensure thoroughness in the collection of information, and nothing but the undying responsibility of an association can provide for the issue of periodical supplements. The Smithsonian Institution, with its correspondents in every part of the world, is able, no doubt, to frame a list of all the existing scientific societies; but there is no great body, enjoying the same advantage of world-wide recognition, to do for history, archæology, and philology what the Smithsonian Institution can do for science. In fact, no specialism is adequate to the task of compiling a catalogue of all periodicals; it is an undertaking coextensive with the whole field of knowledge, and should be the concern of the only class of men making profession of omniscience — librarians. The librarian of a public or of a university library is in touch with the learned of every denomination; he cultivates the friendship of the local geologist and of the local archæologist with perfect impartiality, and both of them look to him for support, intellectual and sometimes financial. None but he, in any town, district, or province, is so likely to be aware of the local associations of specialists and their publications. He is therefore peculiarly fitted to supply the information that is the hardest to gain. In the great cities the publishing trade is sufficiently organised to provide complete lists of the journals that appear there. But the provincial publications are not so easily discovered, and it is through the librarians of municipalities and universities that such material for a catalogue of serials can be collected most easily and most successfully. This Conference represents the librarians of the world, and the influence of its name among them should be at least as great as that of the Royal Society or of the Smithsonian Institution with the men of science. If a committee of this body were appointed for the purpose of compiling an international catalogue of serials, it would speak with the authority of the Conference itself, and letters and circulars issued in its name would command the attention of librarians in every country. By constituting the committee a self-perpetuating body, the publication of supplements would be permanently provided for, and the process of collecting information for them would be the same as for the original catalogue.

A last word on the financial aspect of the question. Bibliographical works that are merely retrospective tend to become more and more obsolete with every year that passes, and consequently the demand falls off and the price goes down. But experience has shown that a serial record of publications, which aims at completeness, has a rising value in the book market. The early volumes are not superseded by the later ones, but the whole forms a single work. The catalogue of periodicals that I have suggested would be a publication of this nature. The annual supplements would refer to the original volume and complete it. In fact, the various portions would depend upon one another in a far more intimate sense than the different volumes of a great book-catalogue. The original catalogue would continue to be consulted for current as well as past issues, until the time when the number of supplements had increased to such an extent as to render it necessary to re-cast the whole publication. Meanwhile the work would remain one and indivisible—a standard catalogue, indispensable to every library of reference. The demand, therefore, for the original volume would not cease until all libraries were supplied, and the commercial success of the undertaking would be reasonably assured.

H. H. LANGTON.

PRINTED CARD-CATALOGUES.

 AM aware, and greatly regret, that my ignorance of the practice of European libraries will make these notes on printed card-catalogues less valuable than they would be if they were prepared by someone of broader experience. Yet I hope that the record of the experiments of a few American libraries in this not unpromising line may be of sufficient interest to justify their presentation.

In the first place, let me say that it is not my intention to compare card-catalogues with other forms of catalogues, nor to treat of points in regard to card-catalogues other than those which are affected directly or indirectly by the use of printed cards, instead of the usual manuscript or typewritten cards. I must pass by, also, the question to what extent printed accession sheets, such as those of the British Museum, the Royal Library at Berlin, and Harvard University, may be considered satisfactory substitutes.

Of American libraries, at least four—the Boston Public, Harvard University, New York Public, and the John Crerar—are now printing all cards added to their catalogues. Many others, while not doing any printing themselves, still make considerable use of printed cards, either as subscribers to the series published by the Publishing Section of the A.L.A., or to one or another of the various card-indexes which have been started within the last few years. These indexes now cover agriculture, botany, zoology, and mathematics; and there are proposed not only co-operation among certain American libraries, but also the far more extensive plans of the International Bureau at Brussels, and of the Royal Society. Under this development in the use of printed cards, the question has become of much wider interest than if it were simply one of the form of the catalogues of isolated libraries.

Returning, however, to this narrower question, the advantages which may be claimed for the printed over the usual manuscript or typewritten cards may be stated briefly as, greater legibility, greater uniformity, greater care almost necessarily taken in preparation, and the possibility of indefinite multiplication without appreciable increase in cost.

It seems unnecessary to do more than mention the first two points—legibility and uniformity. While they may be inconsiderable if the comparison is made with a catalogue written in the best library style, yet it may be said safely that the very large majority of manuscript catalogues are decidedly inferior in these respects to one printed from clean type of good style. A special weight, it seems to me, may be given to such considerations of external form, in the case of libraries which are intended to be ornaments to the city or memorials of their founders. As to the greater care taken by the cataloguers in the preparation of titles which are to be printed, but little needs to be said. It is by no means inconsiderable; but it can be obtained in other ways, as in the preparation of bulletins or printed book-catalogues.

The last advantage mentioned, however,—that of indefinite multiplication,—is so important as to deserve detailed consideration, and its importance increases very greatly with the number of copies used; for, with printed cards, each additional card costs only the cost of the material, while with manuscript or typewritten cards each one costs just as much as the first.

The vital question, then, it seems to me, is whether the circumstances of a library require or allow it to make use of so many copies of its catalogue entries as to justify the extra expense of printing them.

It is surprising to find, when the question is approached from this side, in how many ways these extra copies have been or may be utilised.

In the first place, the number of additional entries, especially under subject-headings, may be increased to any extent desired to secure the maximum of usefulness of the catalogues.

In the second place, the entire catalogue, or such parts of it as may be wanted, may be duplicated for consultation in branches or in the departmental libraries of educational institutions. An experiment along this line is being tried in Chicago by the library which I have the honour to represent. A copy of each printed card-catalogue entry of the John Crerar Library is sent to six institutions in the city or its immediate vicinity. These institutions are the Chicago Public Library, the Newberry Library, the University of Chicago, the Northwestern University, Armour Institute of Technology, and the Field Columbian Museum. It will be seen that they are all institutions whose patrons or teachers and students are likely to use the books of the John Crerar Library. The experiment, which was suggested to me by the plan of an Austrian librarian, has not been on trial long enough to allow judgment to be given, but the welcome given these cards by the authorities of the institutions receiving them, and the requests received from other institutions, give us hope that it will prove successful. It should be said that the cards are sent on condition that they are arranged and stored so as to be accessible to the public. They cannot be considered, therefore, as a free gift, but as one entailing on the recipients some little expense for cases and time necessary for arrangement.

Again, this inexpensive multiplication of our catalogue entries has led us to experiment with a triple form of our card catalogue, giving an alphabetical author, an alphabetical subject, and a classed subject arrangement, which, together with liberal use of additional entries, also made possible by printed cards, we hope will combine all the advantages obtainable in a card-catalogue. Here also, unfortunately, the experiment has not been in operation long enough to warrant the formation of any judgment as to its success. I am confident of it, however, for I agree with Mr. Peddie and the other speakers yesterday, that all three forms of catalogues are required before any library can be considered satisfactorily catalogued. The real question, therefore, is that of the correlation of these forms, and of the ways of presenting each form. It offers a wide field for discussion, but especially should it be remembered that what is the best form of author-catalogue may not be the best form of classed or alphabetical subject-catalogue.

Another use of the extra copies has been brought to the front in the past year by the proposal of the American libraries printing their cards to exchange analytical references, each library agreeing to analyse certain sets of serials. It will be seen that the plan is capable of indefinite expansion, and that it can be made to include books and index work, as well as regular analytical work, as needs or opportunities develop.

In addition to these methods of employing the printed cards, there is the possibility of using the type itself, or electrotypes made from it, for the preparation of lists of accessions, bulletins, classed lists, or, as was done by Columbia University in the case of the Avery Architectural Library, even for the printing of a book-catalogue. At the John Crerar Library the type has been electrotyped in a patent form, which allows the titles to be made up into pages in any desired order.

In this connection it may be of interest to refer to the increasing use of celluloid plates as a substitute for electro plates. These *cellutypes*, as they are called, are not only cheaper and much lighter than electro plates, they are also more durable and less easily damaged. It is not impossible that they will lead to a revival of Mr. Jewett's plan for a central cataloguing bureau which shall furnish material from which each library can print its own catalogue at a minimum expense.

There are, of course, some disadvantages to be set against these many advantages. Here, again, let me remind you that this paper will not deal with those disadvantages which belong to the card system as a system, but only with those which pertain to the printed card in comparison with the manuscript one.

Of these there are two which appear to merit serious consideration, namely, the extra delay in making books available to the public, and second, the increased cost. The time required for the actual printing of the cards can be reduced so as to make any objection on this score untenable. It is rather the extra time needed to complete the title bibliographically, or to perfect the volume or set if any defects are found, or to secure information which could be added afterwards to the written card, that will cause most dissatisfaction with the printing process. It is possible, however, to minimise this, for example, by the use of temporary MS. entries, or by the exposure of new books uncatalogued.

The great and, in many cases, decisive objection is the increased cost. Considerable as this is, it easily may be overestimated, for, as has been said before, it diminishes very rapidly as the number of copies used increases, and may in some cases, therefore, prove to be a positive economy. Still, it is so fundamental a point that it will appear worthy of detailed consideration, even though the details apply only to conditions as they exist in the United States.

The figures which have been given me by the librarians in question are as follows:—

			per title.
Harvard	.	8 copies	. . 20 cents.
Boston .	.	6 ,,	. . 5-10 ,,
New York	.	2 ,,	. . 12 ,,
J.C.L.	.	20 ,,	. . 16 ,,
A.L.A.	.	3 ,,	. . 2½ ,,

The great variations in these figures is caused by the different conditions under which the work is done. Harvard University prints its cards on the college press, and the cost is raised by the fact that a large plant has to be kept ready for occasional heavy demands. The cards of the A.L.A., New York Public Library, and the John Crerar Library are printed by outside printers on a commercial basis, and include all expenses and a fair profit to the printers. Those of the New York Public Library and the John Crerar Library are in very close agreement, and probably represent the minimum attainable in the United States on this basis. The figures furnished by the Boston Public Library are the most interesting as showing what may be looked for under favourable circumstances. Their work is done in the library by library employees, on Mergenthaler linotype machines. By omitting all charges for rent, light, heat, and power, and by supposing that the library can keep two machines constantly at work, there is obtained the lower limit of cost quoted, namely, 5 cents per title. The upper limit, 10 cents, would allow for these omissions and for a much less constant use of the machines. The figures of the American Library Association are interesting as showing the advantages of co-operation.

There is one other element in the additional cost of printed cards, which has been alluded to already, namely, the greater time and care required in their preparation. It is evident that there is a distinct loss of time inevitable when work is done piecemeal, as is necessary to secure prompt current cataloguing, instead of in the better co-ordinated work of revision or of preparation of bulletin material.

On the other hand, in considering the question of cost, it must not be forgotten that, apart from the saving of the time of the library assistants, caused by the many cross-references and analytical cards, there is the positive financial economy where many copies are used, and that this economy often can be obtained by reducing the number of titles. For example, a single card with contents note for a book consisting of a series of articles will give a much cheaper means of analysis than the usual series of analytical cards. Again, the variations of title and editor in the case of any periodical sets can be given more clearly and intelligibly in a single title, which is entered in the card-catalogue as often as is necessary, than on a series of MS. cards, each of which can contain information in regard to a fraction of the set.

A final consideration deserves mention, as it is apt to be passed over in the discussion of the cost of our catalogues. It should not be forgotten that the main cost is in the preparation of the titles, not in their reproduction. Assuming, as I believe is done in the United States, that the preparation of titles will cost, if well done, from 25 to 35 cents each, then the 5 cents paid by the Boston Public Library to put these titles in the most useful and beautiful form cannot but be considered as proportionally a very small matter, while even the highest price paid for the same work is not excessive.

I shall be content if these notes have convinced you that the subject is one having a practical bearing on several lines of library work, and that it is worthy of serious consideration under certain conditions.

I cannot close, however, without expressing my cordial agreement with the remarks of Mr. Lane on the first paper of the Conference, that the real use of these practical methods is to so economise the time of librarian, assistants, and readers, that all may do more work with less drudgery, and my hope that they may succeed in so doing.

C. W. ANDREWS.

LOCAL LIBRARY ASSOCIATIONS IN THE UNITED STATES.

HE organisation which the sixty odd delegates from the United States represent at this Conference is, of course, the American Library Association. That is the only organisation which stands for the federated interests of the libraries of the United States as a whole. But within the past twelve years there have been formed nearly thirty other organisations, which represent federated effort by and in behalf of American libraries, but federated effort within a narrower area. This movement started with the formation on June 18, 1885, of the New York Library Club,—for the City of New York and its immediate vicinity,—which was followed by the formation, in July 1890, of the New York Library Association, the area of whose activities extended to the State at large. The example quickly spread to the west and to the east, so that now, omitting organisations formed for merely temporary purposes and now discontinued or merged, there are in existence twenty-five such local associations.

With us, after a federal association, the next in diminishing constitutional area is a State association. But in the creation of these local library associations formal constitutional requirements have been subordinated to convenience. Of the twenty-five, sixteen are State organisations, four are city organisations, three represent certain districts only of some State, one represents ostensibly two cities, and one at least, the Massachusetts Club, has embraced two States. In fact, however, in most instances, while the area of activity may be local, the area of membership extends to all persons interested.

The objects of organisation are generally stated to be "to promote the library interests" of the State or other area designated. In some cases the constitution expands this into the phrase, "by consultation and co-operation to increase the usefulness and advance the interests of the libraries" included; thus adding purposes more liberally objective, as a project to advance the interests of religion is more liberally objective than one to advance the interests of the Church. The "aim" in view, as stated in the manual of the Chicago Library Club, is so much more explicitly expressed that I venture to quote that statement in full:—

"The Chicago Library Club believes in the broadest possible interpretation of librarianship as a profession, that a wide culture is of equal importance with library technique, and that the opportunities of the librarian should be such as bring him into direct contact with workers in allied lines.

"The club, therefore, will seek co-operation with authorities having in any way to do with the creation of literature and interested in its conservation and use, and will endeavour to establish an acquaintance and friendly relationship with literary workers, especially in Chicago.

"During the coming season, 1895-96, the club will consider the formation of a State Library Association and a State Library Commission, and in its discussions pay particular attention to specialisation in libraries, library architecture, and practical methods of making libraries in cities and vicinity more helpful to the public. Whenever possible and advisable, lectures on these various subjects will be secured from specialists outside of the club. The question of forming a co-operative list of the serials on file in the libraries of Chicago, and of preparing bibliographies on special or local topics, will also be taken up."

There is usually a written constitution; there are the usual four officers—sometimes executive and other committees; the dues are usually but fifty cents, and never exceed one dollar per year; and the expenses are generally confined to postage and minor printing. It is not therefore strange that, although the treasurers are not required to give bond, no instances of malfeasance with respect to funds has yet been reported! The chief responsibility of the executive committee is to determine places and arrange programmes for the various meetings. The place of meeting is constantly shifted, within the general area, with the deliberate purposes: (1) To acquaint the members with the library facilities and conditions of each locality of the larger area; and (2) to stimulate in each such locality in turn the interest of the public in library affairs. The library interests of these more special localities are therefore served by the meetings of these local associations, as those of more prominent places are served by the meetings of the A.L.A. The Nebraska Library Club, for instance, whose leading purpose is "to educate public sentiment," arranges its meetings to coincide with those of the State Teachers' Association.

The number of meetings yearly ranges from one in the case of certain of the clubs, to a maximum of nine in the case of others; and the membership, from 20 in the case of the smallest club (that of Maine), to 356 in the case of the largest (that of Massachusetts). The twenty-five associations and clubs together have an aggregate membership of 1985 persons.

If, therefore, one were to attempt an estimate of the organised effort by and in behalf of the library interests of the United States, one must add to the American Library Association, with its 750 members and its one meeting a year, these twenty-five local associations, with their 1985 members and their aggregate of ninety-two meetings a year.

The need of these local organisations, in addition to the national one, may easily be made intelligible:—

1. The A.L.A. is a national organisation. It stands for an area of 3,000,000 square miles. It must represent the interests of the 7000 libraries of the United States—(*a*) in their relations with federal government; (*b*) in their international relations.

2. The programmes of the A.L.A. must deal with what is common in interest to the libraries of the country as a whole, representing every variety of type.

3. The undertakings of the A.L.A. must be undertakings calculated to render a service in some degree—a service uniform to the hundreds of libraries represented in its membership, and the 7000 in the country at large.

4. The discussions of the A.L.A. at its one annual meeting must be confined in the main to what is theory and generalisation.

In common with the A.L.A., the local associations may discuss the problems of ordinary library economy: Library buildings and equipment, organisation of staff, selection of books, cataloguing, classification, notation, binding, use, access to shelves and other regulations, charging systems, and library statistics. They need not avoid consideration of the treatment to be accorded to pamphlets—that criminal class in literature, whether it is to be dealt with by separate confinement or incarceration in group.

But in nearly all such subjects the local associations will have the advantage over the A.L.A., in that their discussions may *particularise*, by detail and by direct illustration. For instance:—

1. They may study particular libraries —(*a*) by inspection in detail; (*b*) through historical sketches.

2. They may study particular systems and library devices by inspection of these in actual operation.

3. They may induce and arrange specialisation and co-operation between particular libraries within a narrow area, having interests and problems in common, and interdependent constituencies. Specialisation may be in function, or in the purchase of books, convenienced by an interchange of titles. Co-operation may be in the reading of books, in cataloguing, in publication, in service to readers by inter-library loans, in enterprises for mutual protection, *e.g.* as against book thieves. Several of the city clubs have been specially active in securing the compilation of a union list of the periodicals currently taken in the libraries of the vicinity.

The manual issued by the Chicago Library Club has, appended, the description of each of some sixteen public libraries accessible to the constituency represented by the club, and the manual issued by the Library Association of Washington adds to a similar description of sixty-one public libraries of Washington similar information as to twenty-three private collections. The information given covers, in the case of each library, the date of foundation, the location, the hours of opening, the regulations for use, the size, the amount of use, the special strength in the several departments of literature, and the administration.

Such information not merely brings into public and more certain knowledge the library resources of the locality, but serves as an indispensable preliminary to schemes of differentiation and specialisation.

Co-operation as a theory is a matter of principles, easy to determine; the introduction of co-operation as a practical working scheme encounters specially privileged interests, which must be conciliated. In this conciliation the influence of the local associations, exercised directly and personally, is most effective.

4. In the same way they may add to merely theoretic discussion the utilisation of other educational agencies, as schools, museums, reading clubs, working-men's clubs, college settlements.

But these local associations may also, and do, perform services distinct from those possible for the A.L.A.:—

1. They may interest and bring within the circle of organised effort the smaller libraries, which cannot be represented at the A.L.A., and subordinate employees in the larger libraries, who cannot afford the higher dues of the A.L.A. or the expense of attending its distant conferences.

2. The membership being small, the meetings more frequent, an entire programme may be given up to a single department or phase of library work. In this way there may be studied to advantage processes which enter into the manufacture and care of books, and require explanation by experts who may be outsiders, close examination of mechanical appliances or other exhibits, inspection of works, leisure and exemption from other interests.

3. They may stimulate public sentiment in communities too small to be affected by the national association. They may in this way secure the establishment of new libraries—improvement of existing libraries. The State associations have already been influential in the establishment of certain of the seven State library commissions, and in other enterprises involving the extension of State aid to local libraries. For the purpose of stimulating the general sense of the community, it is feasible to introduce into the programmes of the local clubs occasional papers upon the "Value of Libraries," and their "Relation to the Community," upon "How and What to Read," and other such subjects, which, as involving generalisation apt to be platitudinous, ought to be rigidly excluded from the busy annual meeting of the A.L.A.

4. They may make a study of special problems involved in the character of local constituencies. Within the ten years ending 1890 there were introduced into the constituencies of American libraries some five million foreigners. The population of the twenty-eight leading cities of the United States ranges from only 13 per cent. of native whites of native parentage to 55 per cent. of native whites of native parentage. Milwaukee has 87 per cent. of persons foreign born or born of foreign parentage, New York 82 per cent., Chicago 79 per cent., Philadelphia 60 per cent. In New York 30 per cent. of the foreign population are Irish; in Chicago 36 per cent. are Germans; in Minneapolis 56 per cent. are Scandinavians; and the mill cities of Massachusetts and Rhode Island contain a large percentage of French Canadians. It is the duty of a library exercising a public function to help to assimilate this foreign population, and the diversity of the constituent elements introduces problems peculiar to each locality.

More or less peculiar also to each locality, and requiring special treatment, are the various industries which such a library must recognise, study, interest, and assist. The three leading industries of the United States in value of annual product—agriculture ($2\frac{1}{2}$ billion dollars), lumber (587 million dollars), slaughtering and meat-packing—do not seem to present a promising field for the exercise of library activities; but, in the case of iron and steel, machine shops, carpentry, printing and publishing, and others lower on the list, there is certainly opportunity for the introduction of the use of books to good purpose, and even the "reading in our farming communities" has been made a topic upon the programme of one club. At all events, the great diversity of occupation throughout the United States involves a diversity of condition to be studied and locally treated.

5. The local associations may influence in the preservation of local archives.

6. The local associations may, by mutual study and explanation, cultivate a more helpful understanding between libraries and the makers of books on the one side, and libraries and the users of books on the other; for it is possible to introduce into the local programmes, as it is not to the same extent in the national, papers by outsiders not members of the library profession.

7. It is possible to introduce at the meetings of the local associations some practical study of bibliography, together with papers upon bibliothecal history, upon the history of printing and of bookbinding, and upon literary history and criticism pure and simple. In a comparison, recently, of the topics forming the programmes of the L.A.U.K. with those of the A.L.A., a hasty and rough classification showed the following proportions:—

In cataloguing and classification—
  L.A.U.K., 32 papers out of 237.
  A.L.A., 67 out of 271.

On the history of libraries, biography of librarians, description of particular libraries—
  L.A.U.K., 43 papers out of 237.
  A.L.A., 7 out of 271.

On bibliothecal history, on library history, on history of printing—
  L.A.U.K., 34 papers out of 237.
  A.L.A., none out of 271.

The above proportions are significant of the fact that, in its one crowded meeting of the year, the A.L.A. cannot give time to the leisurely discussion of matters purely antiquarian on the one side, nor of subjects purely to the cultivation of the librarian on the other; but, as will appear in the partial list appended of topics which have been discussed at the local associations, it has been found practicable for these smaller organisations at their more frequent and less hurried meetings to enter upon such fields. It seems of great advantage and importance that they should do so; and the result may be to counterbalance a recent tendency to set every vigour towards the purely mechanical in library administration.

Of the utmost practical importance, too, may be the discussion as to books. Principles of selection are all that can advantageously enter into the programme of the A.L.A. It is true that at the last Conference particular books were discussed; but the recorded discussion does not seem to have been detailed nor comprehensive enough, nor does it seem credible that at such meetings there should be leisure in which to make it so. But these smaller groups of librarians, at their more frequent meetings, with the particular character of their several libraries known, with the particular constituency familiar, and with the particular books before them, can discuss the suitability of particular books for particular purposes to really practical result.

Finally, whatever of merely social intercourse may seem desirable at congregations of librarians, may be more appropriately practicable at the meetings of the local than at the meetings of the national association.

For many of the above purposes, even a State organisation is too large. That of Michigan represents an area of over 58,000 square miles—as great as the area of England and Wales. A State association for Texas would represent an area over four times greater still. With reference, therefore, to some of the most valuable services to be performed, and in which effort has already been made, the natural evolution will be the formation of associations within ever-narrowing areas, with the advantageous results of more informal discussion, and more direct, particular, and personal effort and influence—to be summed up in economy of expenditure, through ample knowledge of resources and conditions, through specialisation, and through co-operation.

I append—

1. A schedule of the twenty-five clubs, showing in the case of each the area of its membership, the date of organisation, the number of meetings yearly, and the number of members, and—

2. A partial list of the topics at the various meetings. I have omitted from this list those topics dealing with ordinary library economy, as cataloguing, classification, etc., the oft-repeated topic of libraries and schools, and papers merely historical or descriptive of particular libraries. What are given have been selected to exhibit the range of other topics, and especially to indicate what of the interests above suggested as feasible for the local organisations have actually entered into their programmes.

(These topics have, of course, been mentioned in the *Library Journal* in the reports of the various meetings. My excuse for repeating them here is their significance in group.)

In conclusion, I cannot forbear special emphasis upon one service which has not yet consciously been performed, but which I trust to see developed, as the need for it is certain to develop. The larger portion of the libraries active in these local associations are libraries under municipal control. Dependent upon the favour of the public for funds for their maintenance, they must secure the favour of the public, not merely by making accessible the books they contain, but by conforming their selection of books to the public demand. Here **lies** a peril. For the public is **not a unit,** homogeneous for good literature; **and** **the books** which it demands will include books useless, even books vicious.

Now, the special service in this regard to which I refer as open **to** local associations is to band librarians together **into** an organised insistence upon the proper function of public libraries as *educational institutions*, handling trust funds; to formulate principles accordingly for the **selec**tion of books by its members; and to lend the organised **support** of the association to the rejection **by its** members of any book not falling **within** their province **as** so defined.

HERBERT PUTNAM,
President of the Massachusetts Library Club.

APPENDIX I.

LOCAL LIBRARY ASSOCIATIONS, APRIL 1897.

Name.	Area of Membership.	Date of Organisation.	No. of Meetings Yearly.	Membership.
Central California	San Francisco and 100 miles around.	Feb. 22, 1895	9	60
Chicago	Any person interested.	Dec. 17, 1891	6	110
Colorado	State and all interested.	Dec. 29, 1892	8	45
Connecticut	State.	Feb. 23, 1891	3	97
Illinois	State.	Jan. 23, 1896	2	71
Indiana	State.	Dec. 30, 1891	1	68
Iowa	State.	Nov. 13, 1890	1	30
Maine	State.	Mar. 19, 1891	1	20
Massachusetts	Massachusetts and Rhode Island.	Nov. 13, 1890	4	356
Michigan	State.	Sept. 1, 1891	1	41
Milwaukee (Round Table)	City.	Mar. 7, 1895	12	15
Minnesota	State.	Dec. 29, 1891	1	38
Nebraska	State.	April 22, 1897	As yet but 1	22
New Hampshire	State.	Sept. 11, 1890	2	75
New Jersey	State and all.	Dec. 20, 1890	2	60
New York (City)	City and vicinity.	June 18, 1885	5	157
New York (State)	State.	July 11, 1890	2	84
North Wisconsin (travelling library)	North Wisconsin.	Nov. 14, 1896	At call.	25
Ohio	State.	Feb. 27, 1895	1	125
Pennsylvania	State.	(Phila. Jan. 29, 1892)	7	226
Twin City	St. Paul, Minneapolis.	Feb. 1897	4	25
Vermont	State.	Oct. 17, 1894	5	40
Western Pennsylvania	Western Pa. and adjoining towns.	Sept. 28, 1896	4	40
Washington City	All interested.	June 15, 1894	9	75
Wisconsin	State and all interested.	Feb. 11, 1891	1	80

Total number of associations, 25.
Aggregate number of meetings yearly (see North **Wisconsin**), 92.
Aggregate membership, 1985.

APPENDIX II.

I. Book-printing (by a practical **printer**); **book-binding** (by a practical binder); **book illustration** (by an expert); art illustration (with exhibits); paper and ink (by a **commissioner of public records**); highest **legibility of type**; **size of page**; some bad features of good books; making of a newspaper.

II. Care of maps; keeping a library **clean**; bulletins; delivery stations **vs.** branch libraries; use of costly and rare books; catalogues of portraits and pictures; children's rooms in libraries; the information desk; delivery desk difficulties; what a woman librarian earns; reference **work** of a college library; book thieves; duties of a library to its staff; schoolroom libraries; **district** libraries; ways of advertising a library; **a** "**library institute**" (practical lessons in library **economy**, by a trained teacher from a library **school**); scrap **books**; public documents; "best books" of 1896; how can the character of the reading be improved? how to read and what to read; how far should **reading be controlled in libraries**? **reading for the young**; **rescue from the dime novel habit**; how the **interest of parents in children's reading may be secured**; **place and proper character of fiction in** public libraries; **principles of the selection of** books; the line of exclusion; literature of domestic architecture; **should American literature be especially favoured in our libraries?** specialisation; broad lines on which a reference library should be established and maintained; local collections in public libraries; amateur photography and the public library (by an outsider); collections of photographs of local interest; State laws and publications; travelling libraries of photographs; statistics of reading in grades.

III. **The** relation of the publisher **to** the librarian; book-publishing and book-selling in California (characteristics and vagaries of California printers and publishers; California **magazines**; historical notes on book-selling, **the** import trade, and notes of a random publisher; commercial conditions of the book trade **in California, past** and **present**; **trials of a publisher**; incidents **of the second-hand book trade**; book auctions).

IV. Function **of a public** library; value **of a** public library **to the** community; influence **of** literature upon **the active** life of the time; some of the philanthropic aspects of library work (papers by outsiders engaged in philanthropic work); the library as **a** city missionary; settlement libraries; home and club libraries; parish libraries; railroad libraries; help of libraries **in** training for citizenship; the library and **the** patriotic societies; power of the book; the library and the business man (by an outsider); reading in our farming communities; university extension; library extension; libraries and museums; relation of the library to the higher education (outsider); should mercantile libraries be sustained independently, **or** merged in **public libraries?** library law.

V. The British Museum; libraries and literature of the Orient, India, Ceylon, Tibet; a chat on French libraries; **some** bibliothecal memories; national library of France; history of the libraries of Manchester, England; gleanings **from some** European libraries; **a** whirl through the East; account of the Halliwell-Phillipps library; history of book-binding; the MS. age; books and book-making before the age of printing; early illustration by woodcuts; Plantin press and museum of Antwerp; some of the ancestors of a modern book; John Gutenberg and the early printers; invention of printing—what was it? some of the versions and editions of the Bible; bibliographies; science of books; the literature of libraries—Bibliothekswesen; exhibition and description of fac-similes of renowned books; exhibition and description of issues of the Kelmscott press and publications of the Grolier Club; **a** shelf **of** books; pleasures and regrets of a book collector; books and bookmen; life and works of R. **H.** Barham; books relating to the history of Connecticut; early editions of journals of the Continental Congress; **poets** laureate; Robert Burton; genesis of the **novel**.

THE PUBLIC LIBRARIES OF THE NORTHERN STATES OF EUROPE.

(SWEDEN, NORWAY, DENMARK, AND FINLAND.)

Salmonsens Konversationsleksikon, vol. ii., Köbenhavn, 1894; article "Bibliotek" (by I. B. Halvorsen). *Nordisk Familjebok*, vol. ii., Stockholm, 1878; and supplem. vol. i., Stockholm, 1896. *Minerva, Jahrbuch der gelehrten Welt*, vol. iii., Strassb. 1894 (for the history); latest account in vol. vi., Strassb. 1897.

IT is a characteristic feature of the public libraries of the Northern States of Europe that the scientific libraries and those which are called "people's libraries" are standing much farther apart from each other than in England and the United States of America. While the scientific libraries, with a few exceptions, are State libraries, the people's libraries very often are private institutions though supported by the State or the municipalities. And while the scientific libraries are well off and can bear a comparison with those of foreign nations, the people's libraries are much behindhand, especially in comparison with the libraries of the English-speaking nations. In the scientific libraries every man and woman who can get a guarantee can take out books for home reading; to the reading-room every person is admitted without any formality. The admission to the people's libraries is given to every person, either free or by paying a very small sum.

SWEDEN.

Bernhard Lundstedt: "Notice sur les Bibliothèques Publiques en Suède" (in *Revue internationale des Archives, des Bibliothèques et des Musées*, Paris, 1895). C. M. Carlander: *Svenska bibliotek och ex-libris*, i.-iii., Stockholm, 1889-94. *Aarskatalog för svenska bokhandeln* (an annual catalogue of the Swedish publications of the year).

SCIENTIFIC LIBRARIES.

Kongliga Biblioteket i Stockholm.
(The Royal Library of Stockholm.)

Celsius, M., *Historia Bibliothecæ Regiæ Holmiensis*, Holmiæ, 1751. *Kongl. Bibliotekets Handlingar* (an annual report from 1878).

The history of this library can be traced back to the sixteenth century. It grew very fast, especially in the seventeenth century, by booty obtained from German libraries (Würzburg, Prague, etc.). Great parts of it were, in 1654, brought to Rome by the Queen Christina and incorporated in the library of the Vatican. The remaining parts were greatly increased by the Swedish kings. The library was partly destroyed by fire in 1697, when the royal palace, where it was lodged, was burnt down. It was again lodged in the royal palace from 1768-1877; then it was removed to a new library building. In the last century the library also grew by great donations of books.

The library receives its books by the delivery of all Swedish printed matters ordained by law (since 1661), by purchase (spending *circa* £1890 every year), by exchange, and by donations. It contains more than 335,000 volumes and 11,000 manuscripts, besides several hundred thousands of pamphlets, etc. The Swedish literature forms a special division of the library. There are two catalogues—one alphabetic and one systematic—both of them card-catalogues.

The building is very beautifully situated in the park "Humlegården." It has been constructed exclusively of stone and iron, at a cost of £50,000. It is heated by a system of hot-water pipes, and is lighted by electricity.

The staff consists of a chief librarian,

two librarians, four assistant librarians, and seven extraordinary assistants.

The reading-room has fifty tables, each accommodating several persons.

The library is open from 10 a.m. to 3 p.m.; the reading-room being open during the same hours, and from 5 to 7 p.m.

The library is used by about 30,000 persons every year. In the reading-room 70,000 volumes are used; for home reading *c.* 10,000 volumes are borrowed.

The Royal Library publishes *Sveriges offentliga bibliotek — Stockholm, Upsala, Lund, Göteborg — Accessionskatalog,* an annual systematic inventory of all foreign books acquired by the libraries, stating the library in which each book is placed.

Kongliga Universitets Biblioteket i Upsala.
(The Royal University Library of Upsala.)

Celsius, O.; *Bibliotecæ Upsaliensis Historia, Upsaliæ,* 1745. Annerstedt, C., *Upsala Universitets biblioteks historia till och med* 1702, Stockholm, 1893. C. A[nnerstedt], *Upsala Universitets bibliotek och förslaget till dess omgestaltning,* Upsala, 1887. Annerstedt, C., *Upsala Universitets bibliotek,* 1872–1896, Upsala, 1897 (in *Upsala Universitet,* 1872–1897). Annual reports in *Redogörelse för Kongl. Universitetet i Upsala.*

Founded in the reign of Gustaf Adolph, who presented to it a great part of the Royal Library of Stockholm; it has received large collections of books, which the Swedish kings have brought home as booty in their wars. Since 1707 it has been by law entitled to receive a copy of all Swedish printed matter.

It receives its books in the same way as the Royal Library of Stockholm. It every year spends *c.* £1330 in the purchase of books. It has one catalogue alphabetically arranged, but a systematical catalogue is not available. The Swedish literature forms a separate division of the library. The shelf arrangement is systematical; the place of the book is marked in the alphabetical catalogue. It contains 300,000 volumes and 12,000 manuscripts.

The building, erected in the first half of this century, has lately been very much enlarged.

The staff consists of a librarian, a vice-librarian, three assistants, and four extraordinary assistants.

The library is open every week-day in the two terms (15th Jan.–1st June, 1st Sept.–15th Dec.) from 10 a.m. to 2 p.m., the reading-room at the same time through the whole year. The reading-room is used by 6000 borrowers, who annually consult 60,000 volumes and 4800 manuscripts. For home reading 16,000 volumes are borrowed.

The library published formerly an accession-catalogue, *Upsala Universitets biblioteks accessions-catalog* 1850–1885, Upsala, 1853–86. Since 1886 it has been united with the accession-catalogue published by the Royal Library of Stockholm, and mentioned above.

Kongeliga Universitets Biblioteket, Lund.
(The Royal University Library of Lund.)

Annual Reports in *Lunds Universitets Årsberättelse.*

This was founded in 1666 from the collection of the old library of the cathedral of Lund. Since 1698 it has received a copy of all Swedish printed matter. It has also received large donations of books from Swedish kings, noblemen, and men of science. The yearly purchase of books amounts to *c.* £950. It contains 170,000 volumes and 5000 manuscripts (besides a great collection of pamphlets, etc.).

Two card-catalogues are in existence— one systematical, and one alphabetical. The shelf arrangement follows the systematical catalogue.

The building, the old university building, dates from the fifteenth century. It is to be enlarged this year at a cost of *c.* £9000.

The staff consists of a librarian, a vice-librarian, two assistant librarians, and eight extraordinary assistants.

The library is open at the same hours as the University Library of Upsala; in the vacations, two days in every week. The reading-room has places for thirty-five to forty readers. The library is used by *c.* 9000 readers every year. 26,000 volumes are used in the reading-room. For home reading 9000 volumes are taken out.

From 1853–1885 the library published an accession-catalogue, which since 1886 has been united with the above-mentioned accession-catalogue for all Swedish libraries.

Göteborg Stadsbibliotek.
(The Town Library of Gothenburg.)

Göteborgs musei tjugofemårs-berättelse från 20 December 1861 *till* 20 *December* 1886, Göteborg, 1888 (a report of the Museum of Gothenburg from 1861–86).

The library was founded to replace the libraries of Gothenburg Museum and of

Gothenburg High School, which in 1891 were amalgamated under one administration.

It receives its books by purchase, by donations, and by exchange. The town spends every year *c.* £220 on it; but besides, it receives contributions from the High School and from great legacies.

The library contains more than 60,000 volumes — for the greater part modern literature. The books are shelved in systematic order. It possesses two card-catalogues — one following the shelf arrangement, the other being alphabetic.

A new building is to be erected this year at a cost of £11,000.

There is one librarian, one assistant, and two extraordinary assistants.

The library is open every week-day during four hours. In the reading-room there are twenty-one places. 8500 persons use the library every year. In the reading-room 5500 volumes are used, and 5500 volumes are given out for home reading.

The Libraries of the Royal Grammar Schools ("Allmänna läroverk").

Bidrag til Sveriges officiela statistik. P. Undervisnings-väsendet. 2. *Berättelse om statens elementarläroverk för gossar, Läseåret,* 1876-77.

Each royal grammar school (in all 78) has a library, about which the law ordains that it shall be opened for use to the teachers and pupils of the school and to other persons living in the town and its environs. These libraries are then working, on a smaller scale, in the same way as the great libraries mentioned above. Some of them, especially the grammar school libraries of the episcopal cities, into which the old libraries of the diocese have been incorporated, are of a considerable size. The largest are the libraries of Linköping (80,000 volumes and 1600 manuscripts), of Skara (30,000 volumes and 600 manuscripts), of Strengnäs (25,000 volumes), and of Wexiö (25,000 volumes and 600 manuscripts).

Several scientific institutions have great libraries. In Stockholm the greatest are *Kongliga Vetenskaps-akademiens bibliotek* (the library of the Royal Academy of Science), 70,000 volumes; *Riksdagens bibliotek* (the library of the Parliament), 22,000 volumes; *Kongl. Tekniska Högskolans bibliotek* (the library of the Royal Technical High School), 22,000 volumes.

People's Libraries.

In some of the larger towns the working men's associations have founded libraries.

In Stockholm are *Stockholms Arbetareinstituts Bibliotek* (the library of the Working Men's Institute), and *Stockholms Arbetareforenings Bibliotek* (the library of the Working Men's Association). The first is open every week-day from 6 to 8 p.m., has 2000 volumes, and gives out 3000 volumes to 300 borrowers a year. The second is open twice a week, and contains 2000 volumes.

The Students' Association, "*Verdandi,*" of Upsala, which publishes very cheap scientific booklets, in 1891 founded a library, which contains *c.* 2000 volumes, and gives out *c.* 2000 volumes every year. The association has helped to form twenty-eight people's libraries, by selling books very cheap, and by giving advice in the founding of the library.

In other Swedish towns are older libraries. But from 1850 and the following years many of the towns had libraries which were the property of the municipality. They had from 300 to 3000 volumes. Similar libraries, but smaller, are founded in the villages. They are named "Sockenbibliotek" (libraries of the parish). The Government does not subscribe to the people's libraries. It has been ordained by law that the municipalities are bound to found libraries, and that the inspectors of the public schools shall see that the law is carried into effect. But this law is, in our days, in many places not very much more than a dead letter. It is the teachers of the public schools and the associations of the working men who are the most interested in forming public libraries.

The total of the Swedish people's libraries is *c.* 3000 with 1,000,000 volumes.

NORWAY.

Monrad, S.S., *De bibliothecis Norwegiæ,* Christ. 1777.

Scientific Libraries.

Universitets Biblioteket i Christiania. (The University of Christiania.)

Drolsum, A. C., *Om Universitets Biblioteket,* Christ. 1880 (with a supplem. vol. 1881). *Universitets Bibliotekets Aarbog* (an annual report).

The library, together with the university, was founded in 1811 on 30,000 duplicates from the Great Royal Library in Copenhagen. Since 1851 it has been lodged in the new building of the university. In 1880 it was enlarged and adapted to modern requirements.

Since 1883 it has received copies of all Norwegian printed matter. It spends every year c. £1700 in the purchase of new books. It is divided into a Norwegian and a foreign division, and has an alphabetic and a systematic catalogue.

The staff comprises one chief librarian, two sub-librarians, six amanuenses, and two assistants. The reading-room is open every week-day, 11 a.m. to 3 p.m. and 5 to 8 p.m.; the lending bureau from 12 to 3, and in the vacation (1st July to 15th Aug.) from 1 to 2 p.m. In the reading-room 30,000 persons use 40,000 volumes annually. For home reading 25,000 volumes are borrowed. The library publishes in its annual report, the year-book of the university library mentioned above, an alphabetical catalogue of the Norwegian publications of the year (*Norsk Bogfortegnelse*), which is also published separately.

Other scientific libraries are libraries of some of the royal grammar schools—for instance, *Christiania Cathedralskoles Bibliotek* (the library of the Christiania Cathedral School), 30,000 volumes; and *Trondhjems offentlige Bibliotek* (Trondhjem Public Library), which belongs to the Royal Norwegian Scientific Society.

PEOPLE'S LIBRARIES.

Det Deichmanske Bibliotek i Christiania.

Carl Deichman's *Samlinger. Christiania*, 1790. Moe, B., *Om det Deichmanske Bibliothek.* Christiania, 1839.

Founded 1780 by C. Deichman, it has been augmented by donations from private persons. It is the property of the town, contains 30,000 volumes, spends every year £100 in purchase of books, is open two hours every week-day in the winter months, and two hours twice a week in the summer months. It has a reading-room. 25,000 volumes are borrowed every year.

Bergens offentlige Bibliotek (the Public Library of Bergen) was founded by private donations, and is, since 1872, in the possession of the town. In many respects it is working like the English and American free libraries. It contains 72,000 volumes. A card-catalogue (alphabetically arranged) and a printed class-catalogue are used. The books are arranged in accordance with the class-catalogue. One librarian and three assistant librarians are the staff. The reading-room, which has thirty sitting places, is open every week-day from 12 to 2 p.m. and 5 to 8 p.m.; the lending bureau, 12 to 1 and 5 to 7 p.m. In the reading-room c. 7000 volumes are issued; for home reading 40,000 volumes are borrowed.

In several other towns there are public town libraries, often developed from the libraries of the royal grammar schools. Such libraries are Arendal School public library and museum, and Frederikstad town library, which derives its means chiefly from the "Brændevinssamlag," a company for selling liquor on the Gothenburg system.

The villages in the country often have small libraries; they are subsidised by the State, which every year spends c. £1100 on them. In return the State requires that the library shall be the property of the parish, that the parish shall spend on the library a sum equal to the grant of the State, and that the grant only shall be used in buying books. The libraries each contain several hundreds of volumes.

DENMARK.

Dansk Bogfortegnelse (an alphabetical catalogue, with systematical index, of the publications of the year).

SCIENTIFIC LIBRARIES.

Det store Kongelige Bibliotek i Köbenhavn. (The Great Royal Library, Copenhagen.)

Werlauff, E. C., *Historiske Efterretninger om det store kongelige Bibliothek*, 2 Udg. Kbhvn. 1844. Bruun, C., *Det store kongelige Bibliotheks Stiftelse*, Kbhvn. 1875. Bruun, C., *Det danske Katalog i det store kongelige Bibliothek*, Kbhvn. 1875. Bruun, C., *Til Erindring om Jon Erichsen*, Kbhvn. 1887. Bruun, C., *Paa Hundredaarsdagen efter at det store kongelige Bibliothek, blev erkloeret for at vore et offentligt Bibliothek*, Kbhvn. 15 Nov. 1893. *Aarsberetninger og Meddelelser fra det store kongelige Bibliothek, udg. af Chr. Bruun*, vol. i., 1864, etc. (an annual report). Lange, H. O., *Bemærkninger og Iagttagelser om offentlige Bibliotheker iser om det store kongelige Bibliothek i Kjöbenhavn*, Kbhvn. 1895.

Founded by Frederic III. (1648–1670), it has grown very amply, as well by gifts of books from men of letters as by purchase and other means. It was not open for the public till 1793. It is lodged in a wing of Christiansborg Palace. The greater part of this palace was destroyed by fire in October 1888. The library escaped the danger, but it had been very imminent; and this event, together with the permanent growth of the library, has brought into existence a Library Act of

1897, by which a library building, at a cost of c. £80,000, is planned. This Act also contains provision for a new State library, which is to be founded in Aarhus, Jutland, at a cost of c. £13,000, mainly on duplicates from the Great Royal Library.

The library receives its books — gifts and exchange not included — by purchase (£2000 is spent every year), and by the delivery, ordained by law since 1781, of two copies of all Danish printed matter (from 1697 five copies, in later times three copies, were delivered). The library has 550,000 volumes, of which 20,000 are manuscripts. It is divided into a Danish division (founded 1780) and a foreign division. In both of these the arrangement of the books is by class divisions, very closely worked out. The catalogues are manuscript registers. The shelf arrangement follows that of the catalogue. Some parts of the library have special card-catalogues (music, Danish pictures). Besides, there is a strictly alphabetical catalogue for the use of the staff.

The staff is composed of a chief librarian, two sub-librarians, and eight assistants.

The reading-room is open every weekday from 10 a.m. to 3 p.m, and in the summer months from 5 to 7 p.m. The lending department is open every week-day from 11 a.m. to 2 p.m. The library often lends books to persons not resident in Copenhagen. In the reading-room c. 27,000 volumes are used every year by 9000 borrowers ; c. 12,000 volumes are taken out for home reading.

The library publishes a very important bibliographical work, *Bibliotheca Danica* — a systematical catalogue of the Danish literature from 1482–1830. The first volume of this work was published in 1872.

Köbenhavns Universitets Bibliotek.
(The University Library of Copenhagen.)

Birket Smith, S., *Om Kjöbenhavns Universitetsbibliothek för 1782*, Kbhvn. 1882. Nyerup, R., *Kjöbenhavns Universitets Annaler*, Kbhvn. 1805. Annual reports in *Aarbog for Köbenhavns Universitet*, Kbhvn.

The library can be traced back to 1482. In 1728 it was completely destroyed by a fire, which laid in ashes the church, in the loft of which it was lodged. When re-founded it grew very rapidly, and now contains c. 350,000 volumes, besides a great many pamphlets and c. 5000 manuscripts, among which the Arnamagnæan collection of old Icelandic and old Norwegian manuscripts (catalogued in Kaalund, Kr., *Katalog over den Arnamagnæanske Haandskriftsamling*, B. i. og ii. Kbhvn. 1888 og 1894). It has received large gifts of books from men of letters — for instance, in 1867, *det Classenske Bibliotek*. It spends every year £900 in the purchase of books, and has received, since 1821, one copy of all printed Danish matter. In 1857-60 a new building was erected.

The catalogue arrangement is by class divisions. A card-catalogue, which is destined to replace the old catalogue registers, is being compiled. The shelf arrangement follows the class-catalogue. A strictly alphabetical catalogue exists for the use of the staff only.

The staff consists of a chief librarian, two sub-librarians, three assistant librarians, and three extra assistants.

The reading-room is open every weekday from 11 a.m. to 3 p.m., and in the summer months from 5 to 7 p.m. In the reading-room c. 12,000 readers use 32,000 volumes every year. For home reading c. 23,000 volumes are borrowed.

The summer vacation terms (one month) of the Great Royal Library and the University Library are arranged in such a way that one of them is open when the other is closed.

Every royal grammar school (altogether twelve) has a library containing from ten to thirty thousand volumes. In the episcopal cities of the diocese there are libraries erected for the use of the clergy. Some of them have been connected with the libraries of the royal grammar schools. Most of these libraries are open to the public, but only a few hours in the week. Some of the people's high schools (*i.e.* Askov, in the southern part of Jutland) have libraries.

Other libraries are *Karen Brahes Bibliotek*, in Odense, founded in the last half of the seventeenth century, and containing old Danish and German literature, especially some very rare Danish manuscripts ; *Det kongelige Kunstakademis Bibliotek* (the library of the Royal Academy of Arts) ; *Landbohöjskolens Bibliotek* (the library of the Agricultural College), etc.

PEOPLE'S LIBRARIES.
Köbenhavns Kommunes Folkebiblioteker.
(The People's Libraries of the Municipality of Copenhagen.)

Beretning om Köbenhavns Kommunes Folkebiblioteker (an annual report).

Founded in 1888, it contains seven libraries, of which two have reading-rooms. The town every year spends c. £900 on them. Every borrower pays twopence in the month. The libraries are open on week-days (Wednesday excepted) from 7 to 9 p.m. The printed catalogues are class-lists, but only with a few classes, and alphabetical in each class. The libraries have altogether 25,000 volumes. The borrowers, who for the greater part are artisans and working men, number c. 4300; they borrow every year 290,000 volumes. Other libraries for the people are, in Copenhagen—*Arbejdernes Læseselskabs Bibliotek* (the library of the Reading Society of Working Men), and *Arbejderforeningens Bibliotek* (the library of the Working Men's Association).

Many of the *country towns* have people's libraries, not exceeding a few thousands of volumes. They are, for the greater part, managed by a private committee, and lodged in some board school, supported by contributions from the municipality, from private individuals, and sometimes from savings banks. The catalogues are generally like the catalogues of the people's libraries of Copenhagen; a few of them have a dictionary-catalogue. The borrowers are admitted free, or pay a very small sum (1d. or 2d. a month). The borrowers are, for the greater part, working men and artisans.

The *villages* very often have libraries, which are named *Sognebogsamling* (library of the parish). Of the 1700 country parishes of the kingdom, c. 1100 are said to have libraries. But they are very small, not exceeding a few hundreds of volumes. They very often depend for their existence upon the interest taken by a single person (*e.g.* the teacher), and some of them have been given up for want of interest and money. A few of them have founded a sort of circulating library, by mutual changing of their books. One of the Danish islets has founded a circulating library with a central library, from which book-boxes are sent to the district libraries.

The people's libraries are supported by the State, in two ways. It spends every year £800, which are distributed to the libraries by a committee. It contributes to *Udvalget for Folkeoplysnings Fremme* (the Committee for the Promotion of the Enlightenment of the People), which publishes good and instructive books, that are sold very cheap or presented to small libraries.

FINLAND.

SCIENTIFIC LIBRARIES.

Universitets Bibliokeket i Helsingfors.
(The University Library of Helsingfors.)
Information in the Reports of the University.

The old university library in Aabo, founded 1640, which in 1827 had 40,000 volumes, was destroyed by fire in the same year. 830 volumes, which escaped the fire, together with the library of Calonius, which was given to the town of Helsingfors, formed the stock of a new library, which was established at the university when this was moved from Aabo to Helsingfors.

The library receives a copy of all books printed in Finland, and of all books printed in Russia in other languages than the Russian and the Polish, which books go to the Russian library mentioned below. The library spends every year £1300 in the purchase of books.

It contains 165,000 volumes, besides 7000 pamphlets. The books printed in Finland form a special part of the library. The books are arranged in several divisions according to the subjects, but in these divisions they are arranged by chance. There is one card-catalogue alphabetically arranged, and one following the shelf arrangement. Besides, there are class-catalogues of several parts of the library. Since 1866, printed accession-catalogues have been published every third year (systematical and alphabetical). Just now the Finnish part is under rearrangement.

The staff consists of a librarian, a vice-librarian, three amanuenses, and a varying number of extraordinary amanuenses.

The reading-room has 52 seats for readers. It is open every week-day from 10 a.m. to 3 p.m. and 5 to 9 p.m. (in the summer vacation, only two days from 10 a.m. to 3 p.m.). The loan bureau is open from 12 a.m. to 3 p.m. (in the vacation, only two days a week). 6000 volumes are used in the reading-room every year; for home reading 16,000 volumes are given out.

Rysska Biblioteket (the Russian Library) receives all printed books in the Russian and the Polish languages. It contains 50,000 volumes. Every grammar school (Lyceum) has a library—Aabo, 22,000 volumes; Borgaa, 7000 volumes, etc.

PEOPLE'S LIBRARIES.

Virko, K., *Om Folkbibliotek*, Helsingfors, 1892. Nordmann, P., *Om Bibliotek, Läsesalar och Föredrag för Folket*, Helsingfors, 1889.

Helsingfors Folkbibliotek.
(The People's Library of Helsingfors.)

Annual Reports in the Reports on the Administration of the Town.

The library was founded in 1859 with 517 volumes. It now has more than 18,000 volumes. The town spends every year £1000 on it. The books are arranged in divisions according to subjects, and alphabetically in each division. There are three different catalogues—a stock catalogue, a general catalogue on cards, alphabetically arranged, and a printed systematical catalogue for the use of the public. The building is large and well arranged. It has two reading-rooms—one for newspapers, the other for magazines and books, which cannot be had for home reading. The library is open from 5 to 8 p.m. every week-day; Sundays from 4 to 7 p.m. The reading-rooms are used by 170,000 persons every year. From the loan bureau in 1895, 80,000 volumes were given out (in 1884, 14,000 volumes).

In some other *towns* (Aabo, Wiborg) there are great people's libraries.

In the *country* there were in 1889 606 libraries, with some hundreds of volumes; in 1895 they numbered c. 800 (150 Swedish and the other Finnish). Some of them have reading-rooms.

The movement for people's libraries in later years has been promoted by the *Folkupplysnings sällskapet* (the Association for the Enlightenment of the People) in Helsingfors (secretary, Dr. A. A. Granfeldt), which is working more particularly for the Finnish libraries, and the *Svenska Folkskolans Vänner* (the Friends of the Swedish Primary School; secretary, Dr. P. Nordmann), which has promoted the foundation among the Swedish-speaking population only. The latter society in 1895 founded a special library committee (secretary, Mr. H. Bergroth), which has issued several papers on the organisation and management of public libraries.

ANDREAS SCH. STEENBERG.

"Horsens, Denmark, 10*th July* 1897.

"I have the honour to present to the Committee on Papers and Discussions of the Second International Library Conference a short account of the library resources of the Northern States of Europe, which I have written at the request of the committee. In writing it I have received very kind help from many libraries and librarians. Originally I had founded it on a broader base, but I have been obliged to shorten it for the sake of uniformity. I still hope that it gives a fairly accurate picture of the library resources of the Northern States, and that everyone interested in them may be able to gather some information as to their nature and extent.—Most respectfully,
"ANDREAS SCH. STEENBERG.

"*The Second International Library Conference. The Committee on Papers and Discussions.*"

AN INDICATOR-CATALOGUE CHARGING SYSTEM.

IT is a strange and unaccountable fact that two nations speaking the same language, and with essentially the same laws, manners, and customs, should differ so widely in the manner in which loans to readers of circulating libraries should be recorded. In England, what is known as the "indicator" is, I believe, in some form or other, generally the only system that has found favour, whereas in the United States the "indicator" is practically unknown, the general practice being to depend upon loose slips or cards. A partial explanation of this difference of practice may perhaps be found in the fact that in England the libraries are usually arranged on a broad system of classification, in which books are numbered, in each class, according to the accidental order of their purchase, whereas in the United States the general practice is to have a more or less "close" classification, in which future accessions are interpolated among the books previously added. The English "indicator" system, with fixed pigeon holes, is not of course adapted to such a system of classification, and, even where the partitions are movable, it is with great difficulty that the "indicator" system can be adjusted to the conditions prevalent in the United States.

It has occurred to me that a compromise might be devised which will preserve the salient features of both systems, and which could be applied to American as well as English libraries, and at a comparatively trifling expense, and with more economy of space than is afforded by the usual "indicator."

The method I am about to describe was suggested by a casual remark of my friend, Mr. Charles A. Cutter—who has kindly consented to read this paper—when describing his system of charging in an old number of the *Library Journal*. While he is in nowise responsible for the details of the present plan, I feel that something is due to him for, in a sense, suggesting the original idea. I have therefore concluded that it is no more than right that we should share the credit and the blame equally—that is to say, if the system should be a success, I will take all the credit, whereas, if it should prove a failure, Mr. Cutter is to take all the blame. I am sure nothing could be fairer than that.

I am not acquainted with all the varieties of the "indicator" that the ingenuity of English librarians has evolved; and while I believe my plan to be original (it is certainly original, so far as I am concerned), it may be possible that I have hit upon something that bears a resemblance to some plan already devised, and possibly already in use. If so, I can only comfort myself with the thought that great minds run in the same grooves, and that a presentation of an old difficulty from an American point of view may be of interest, even if it be without value.

After this preliminary and perhaps unnecessary introduction, I will proceed to the description of my plan.

MACHINERY OF THE SYSTEM.

I propose to use two cards or slips—(1) the book card, and (2) the reader's or borrower's card; and (3) some boxes or drawers in which to file the cards or slips.

These cards may be of any size, thickness, quality, or colour that the needs or fancy of any library may suggest as desirable. The only condition I insist upon is, that (1) the book card must have a pocket in which the borrower's card can be slipped into readily, and (2) that the borrower's card be small enough to allow the title of the book, on the book card, to be read easily after the former is slipped into the pocket, and that it be large enough to allow the name of the reader or borrower to be easily read after it is placed in the pocket.

There is to be a separate card for every volume, including every duplicate, in the library. The obverse side is to have a reasonably full title of the book, and the reverse side is to have ruled spaces to stamp each issue.

There is to be a separate card for every reader. The obverse side is to have the name, number, and address of the reader, with such particulars as may be necessary in any individual library to indicate when his card expires, and the reverse side is to have ruled spaces for stamping the date of every book issued.

The samples I submit are merely illustrative of the idea. They are not necessarily for publication, but merely given as an evidence of good faith. They can be altered, of course, to suit the exigencies of each individual library.

Let us suppose that there is a book card for every volume in the library, and a borrower's card for every reader of the library, and the system will be applied as follows:—

The book cards are to be sorted in the order of their shelf numbers, and are to be put in the charge of a special clerk, to whom readers are to go after they have ascertained the number or numbers of the book or books they want. By consulting the assistant or the book cards themselves, readers can learn whether the books they want are *in*. If the book wanted is in, the clerk takes out the card representing it from the general series, and puts the reader's card in the pocket, and hands both to an attendant, who gets the book and stamps the date of issue on *both* cards on the reverse side. These cards are filed in the order of their shelf numbers. If desired, each day's issues can be kept by itself. But in that case it will be necessary to have a slip in each book issued, on which to stamp the date of issue, so that the date, where a given book card is filed, can be instantly ascertained.

Whenever a book is returned the reader's card is returned to him, and he retains it until he draws another book.

Advantages of the System.

(1) There is no writing whatever after the cards are prepared, as the record is kept entirely by stamping the dates of issue.

(2) There is practically a receipt from the reader for every book issued to him, and practically a receipt from the library for every book returned by a reader.

(3) Readers have their cards only when there is no book charged to them, hence the usual objection to readers' cards is reduced to a minimum.

(4) Readers cannot get more than one book at a time.

(5) Readers are sure of getting the books they ask for, because they have to go to the indicator-clerk to find out whether they are in.

(6) The indicator itself can be used as a catalogue.

(7) Readers cannot evade responsibility, as no books will be delivered to them except in exchange for their own cards, and they can prove that they have no books out by simply showing their cards.

(8) Each book card shows how often a book has been used, and each reader's card shows how many times he has drawn books.

(9) It is as easy to figure out fines as in any other system.

(10) The indicator-catalogue — even with 100,000 cards — will take up a comparatively small space compared with the usual English indicators, and it is more satisfactory in its operation, as fairly full titles can be given on the cards, in place of the meagre numbers or brief titles usually provided for in the more popular indicators.

(11) If each day's issues are kept separate, it is easy to send for books overdue.

(12) It is easy to know where any given book is if the book cards are kept in one series, and comparatively easy if they are kept by each day's issue separately; because, if the limit for keeping a book is two weeks, there will be only twelve places to examine in the most extreme case.

Possible Objections.

(1) It will take too much time to consult the indicator.

Answer.—As the majority of the readers in a public library want the most popular books, most of which are usually out, it must save time, on the average, to know that they are *sure* of getting the book they ask for.

Besides, there is no reason why there should not be two, three, or more clerks at the indicator. There might be, for example, one clerk for fiction from A to M, another for fiction from N to Z, and another clerk for the other books, the proportion of clerks being varied, of course, according to circumstances. In any event, one of the great advantages of the system is that the clerks cannot say to the reader that a given book is "out" when in fact it is "in." This difficulty all existing systems in the United States are powerless to overcome.

(2) The reader's card may become separated from the pocket of the book card. If so, there is no way of knowing what book he has.

Answer.—Possible, but not probable. Even if it does happen, there will be a book card without a reader's card, which will connect the two. If there are several such cases, *in the same day*, this identification will not be possible. But in such extreme and unusual cases the reader can be asked to return his book, or the library can wait two weeks, when the matter will probably adjust itself. If none of these plans are satisfactory, the reader's number can be put on the book card opposite the date of issue. This will ensure greater accuracy at the expense of rapidity.

The whole objection could be removed by some simple mechanical device that would prevent the small cards from falling out. At anyrate, the library would be no worse off than in the current systems in vogue in the United States when a wrong book number is put on the reader's card, or a wrong reader's number is put on the book card. In any event, the proposed system shows that a given reader has *a* book, and it is known who the reader is. In systems in which the book card only is kept in the library, the wrong number of the reader on the book card leaves the library entirely at sea as to *who* has the book. So that even here the proposed plan compares favourably with any yet devised, at least in the United States.

(3) The reader's card tells when he got books, but not what books he got.

Answer.—All the charging systems that can't furnish this information are based on the theory that it is unnecessary, hence it cannot be necessary in the present system. If, however, any library should require such information, it could be easily supplied by adding the number of the book opposite every issue stamp on a reader's card. This, however, would hamper speed still further. The reasons why a record of what books each reader has read is useful are: (1) To see if he is making a beneficial use of his privilege. But such knowledge, while theoretically useful, is rarely taken advantage of, even in libraries where the readers' cards are kept in the library; hence it may be dispensed with, unless otherwise essential to the system. (2) If the reader brings in a mutilated or damaged book, other books he has taken out can be examined, and, by similar damage, the guilt can be fastened on him. This is, apparently, a strong point, but if the books are carefully examined when they are returned it loses its force.

(4) It is not possible to tell what book or books a reader has out at a given time, in case he should ask the question.

Answer.—Unless we except subscription libraries, or libraries where a reader can take out as many books as he wants (within limits, of course), libraries ought not to be expected to adjust their systems to the reader's laziness, shiftlessness, or lack of ordinary memory. A reader who takes out one book only should certainly know what book he has out. If he simply wants to know whether he has *a* book out, his possession of his own card will prove that he has, whereas its absence will prove that he has not. Besides, as most all the schemes in existence do not give this information, it certainly cannot be made an objection to the proposed plan. If such information should really be needed in a *public* library, which is a doubtful contingency, the present system cannot give a satisfactory answer.

(5) While the usual objections to the annoyance caused by a reader losing his card are almost removed, still cases of loss of cards may occur.

Answer.—If so, there is no more trouble than in any of the usual systems where the loss of readers' cards occurs frequently. Besides, as the reader's card is small, he can easily put it in his pocket-book; and, at all events, after one experience, he will probably not annoy the library and himself by losing his card again, as the results fall entirely upon himself. Still, if there should be a large percentage of such cases, —that is, large in the *few* cases where readers take their cards home,—it would be an objection to the system, but a lesser objection, in any event, than can be made against any system heretofore devised where readers have possession of their cards.

(6) The indicator-clerk will necessarily pick out some particular duplicate, where the library has duplicates, and the attendant must get that copy and no other. Will this not consume time?

Answer.—Not if the duplicates are numbered 1, 2, 3, 4, etc., or a, b, c, d, etc., or by any other method where they can be arranged consecutively. If they are kept in the same order on the shelves, it will be as easy to pick out a particular duplicate as it is to get a particular edition or a particular volume.

These are all the advantages and disadvantages that occur to me. Doubtless there are others, of both kinds, which will readily suggest themselves to my hearers, especially those who are familiar with the use of "indicators."

Perhaps it may be objected by English librarians that I have been unnecessarily diffuse, and by American librarians that I have been too brief. But our English brethren should remember that, so far as "indicators" are concerned, American libraries are still in the kindergarten class, and that the *modus operandi* of that very useful device is as unfamiliar to American librarians as is, generally speaking, the American card-catalogue to English librarians.

With the hope that the proposed plan may be deemed at least worthy of discussion, the writer submits it to the consideration of the present Conference.

JACOB SCHWARTZ.

A HINT IN CATALOGUING.

T is admitted that no humour is so delicious as unconscious humour. Most of us have seen some tragic actor, whose paroxysmal rant in some supreme crisis has succeeded in making him supremely comical. Indeed, to hold a complimentary ticket and sit in a prominent seat on such an occasion, as was once the writer's experience, and to have your mirth fettered by your obligations as a guest, constitutes what is known in dramatic parlance as a very intense situation. In books there are infinite stores of similar unconscious drollery. In some books the language of the shop or the conventicle intrudes itself grotesquely into poetical environments; in other books wicked straw men are set up and gallantly assaulted by quixotic reformers having a quixotic faith in the vitality of their pet bogies; in others, the stately periods of Gibbon are imitated by some egotist or flatterer narrating the little deeds of his commonplace hero.

How to reveal to the average reader these latent provocatives to mirth is a vast problem for the cataloguer. The indexer of the future who may invent a system by which people in need of relaxation and amusement may select nuggets from this unworked and exhaustless mine of humour will be not only the greatest ornament of his profession, but also one of the chief benefactors of mankind. He will enable us to dispel our gloom at will by turning on a current of laughter, or perhaps even to unfold the wrinkles of care by a continuous smile.

Her collections of books are not the pride of Nova Scotia. The generous beneficence of Nova Scotian testators has not yet embraced the libraries of that province. Our facilities for literary, historical, scientific, artistic, and industrial research lag far behind the other factors of our intellectual progress. And the distinction achieved by various Nova Scotians, in spite of inadequate library equipment, helps to make our people underrate the weight of their handicap. But there is a single bibliographical point in which I flatter myself we are at least up to date, if not even "a little too previous." The Legislative Library of Nova Scotia has taken a pioneer step towards the cataloguing of involuntary humour. And it was this fact alone which emboldened me to accept the honour that was offered me—the high but undue honour of addressing this distinguished assembly of bibliophiles and librarians.

There is a class of publications known too well to librarians, at least to those of the United States and Canada, which illustrates all the phases of unintended drollery. I allude to those biographical dictionaries which are mainly autobiographical. The publishers of these compilations trade successfully upon the vanity of mankind, inviting nonentities to subscribe for a certain number of copies, and send sketches of their lives, adding extra fees if they desire the publication of their portraits. A few real notables, dead and living, are included, and their lives are commonly the sample ones shown by the advance agent to aspiring nobodies, in order to convince them that they will be in distinguished company. The motto of the editors seems to be "De vivis nil nisi bonum," and the only subjects of their strictures are the unsubscribing dead. A favourite maxim of the publishers is that one man's money is as good as another's—and sometimes a very great deal better. For the prig who subscribes also takes upon himself all the trouble of writing his own life; and he is apt to write it in a manner so pleasing to himself that he will exceed his agreement and buy several uncontracted copies, to delight his friends or tantalise his enemies.

A hasty examination of one of these precious publications, which is exclusively Canadian, and has a preface explaining the high ideals of its projectors, showed me a number of refreshing absurdities. It included an Anglican prelate, who had not yet arrived in the Dominion, while it excluded the Anglican metropolitan. It recorded the doings of minor Roman Catholic priests, wholly omitting distinguished archbishops of the same denomination. It had lengthy notices of unknown members of the Dominion and provincial legislatures, and not a word about Sir Richard Cartwright, Mr. Dalton M'Carthy, or Hon. C. H. Tupper. It gave over two columns to the school and college life of a private member of Parliament, and less than two columns to the whole career of Mr. Laurier (then leader of the Dominion Opposition) or of Mr. Fielding (then Premier of Nova Scotia). It omitted more than one principal of a university, and devoted a column and a half to a gentleman whose only named claim to distinction was that "he was formerly principal of the Blank County Academy." Eminent judges were denied, and obscure lawyers were given a place in this delectable publication. Among the happenings recorded was the marriage of a schoolmistress, "a lady," we were told, "of good education and refined taste," to a lawyer, who is characterised as "a man of sound judgment, excellent address, diligent in business, and possessed of an untarnished reputation for integrity." "One son has been born of this union," said the biographer, fitting his style to the historic occasion.

A still smarter business advertisement was worked in by an enterprising physician and druggist, to whose ancestry, progeny, and virtues over three columns are dedicated. "In 188—," according to this charming cyclopædia, "by the death of a professional brother, a valuable drug-stand was put in the market. This he bought and fitted up with all modern improvements, putting a competent man in charge." In addition to this "competent man in charge," the doctor himself, we were told, "has given his profession that close and careful attention which is always necessary to become a model practitioner, and success has abundantly crowned his efforts." "He is a genial companion," we were further informed, "a faithful friend, and self-sacrificing to a degree. It goes without saying that he is beloved even by those who do not agree with his opinions, and by those who do" (*here the affectionate biographer becomes ungrammatical*) "he has their confidence and love to an unlimited extent."

In the field of Canadian letters several such distinguished workers as Goldwin Smith and William Kingsford, the Abbé Casgrain and Louis Frechette, are ignored; while letters to newspapers, and even unpublished manuscripts, are thought worthy of being enumerated among the so-called "works" of certain literary aspirants.

I must accord these biographical or autobiographical dictionaries their due meed of praise for rescuing from oblivion many evidently noble and gifted personages, who have been sadly unappreciated by their generation.

Another merit of these books is that they conclusively prove the doctrine of heredity, for about 99 per cent. of the talented men whose lives they outline are shown to be descended from equally renowned ancestors.

But the chief charm of these delightful works resides in their unconscious humour. Of this I shall give one last sample, from the preface of the very book I have been quoting. "The enterprise," says the altruistic editor, "has been tedious, laborious, and expensive; but if it will supply a record that the country should not let die, if it preserve the memory of worthy men and women whose deeds deserve to be remembered, it surely will have well repaid the time, the anxiety, and the pains that have been expended upon it."

I must ask the pardon of Mr. Cutter and the other lawgivers whose excellent rules for cataloguing I have so often unwittingly transgressed, if I have once sinned against them with premeditation. But I have been presumptuous enough to take a first step in the direction of cataloguing involuntary fun by entering the aforesaid biographical dictionary under the subject-heading of "WIT AND HUMOUR." It may be that, in so entering it in the catalogue of the Legislative Library of Nova Scotia, I may have given it an undue pre-eminence, for I am told that its comic attractions are rivalled, if not excelled, by some kindred publications.

F. BLAKE CROFTON.

THEORETICAL AND PRACTICAL BIBLIOGRAPHY.

N preceding papers read at this Conference very much of what I had intended to say upon theoretical and practical bibliography has been anticipated. My paper will therefore be a short one, and illustrative rather than didactic.

Let me say, first, that I take bibliography in its widest sense as including the making of ordinary book-catalogues, for these are now becoming so full and complete in their descriptions, as well as in the arrangement of their contents—association of books in classes being an additional description—that it is difficult to say where cataloguing ends and bibliography begins. The art of bibliography, too, as evidenced in bibliographies of particular authors, now trenches upon the domain of the literary critic. We have not only the full title-pages, with date, place of publication, size, pagination, and other typographical details, but an infinity of textual details, even to the variations in different editions of the same poem. Some further details than the title of a book are often necessary in the most concise catalogue—a list of the contents of a volume of miscellanies, for example.

The utility of a catalogue is its chief recommendation, and we have had several specimens recently of periodical catalogues which attempt to satisfy the requirements of librarians, booksellers, and general readers, with, I think, only partial success. Perhaps the best-known example in this country is the *English Catalogue*, formerly issued in two parts, now issued as "author" and "index" catalogue combined. Useful as this may be for some purposes—finding the price or publisher of a given work—it is not sufficient for the specialist. Referring to the latest volume for titles of works issued in 1896 upon "Australia" or "Australasia," I find under these headings eleven works only—four novels, two histories, two scientific works, one volume of essays, one of poetry, and a year-book. Surely these do not represent all the literature upon Australia or Australasia published in London during the past year? They do not. Other works kindred to these were published; but that I may discover them it is necessary to search through 224 pages of double columns, when I shall be rewarded with forty or fifty additional titles—provided always that I am acquainted with the subjects or the authors. A stranger would not find half of them. These additional titles thus scattered had not the words "Australia" or "Australasia" upon their title-pages, or, if they appeared in a subsidiary title, the cataloguer has not noticed them. The inclusion of titles under their generic heads would result in the increased circulation of many books; whereas large trade losses result from imperfect cataloguing every year.

Only an analytical or systematic catalogue will answer to the needs of the specialist. Such a catalogue, however, should not be issued too frequently. From long experience I know that the titles in weekly catalogues are not read. Even the monthly *Bookseller*, which contains the most useful classified lists of English books that I know, is issued too often for many readers and some librarians. A quarterly classified list is frequent enough for the generality of readers and for specialists searching for literature more than three months old. I have heard of daily lists of new books, but weekly alphabetical lists and quarterly classified lists, I believe, are all that are necessary.

Upon library catalogues I venture to remark that their utility will consist, first, in their application to the collections they are supposed to represent, and secondly, in the aid they give as works of reference elsewhere. For the latter purpose, the date and place of publication should be given of every separate work, and excerpts or magazine articles should give the name and date of the periodical or transaction from which it is taken. The omission of these last-mentioned details is misleading, and I have often seen works advertised for which never existed in separate form, and therefore cannot be found.

A good catalogue can only be compiled by earnest and enthusiastic labour. It is a mistake to suppose, as many do, that cataloguing is merely mechanical work. No catalogue was ever less useful because the compiler could intelligently abridge or condense a title-page, or because the compiler knew something of the contents of the books catalogued. In addition to such qualifications, the compiler should possess a bird's-eye view of the whole field of knowledge and of the relations and interdependence of books as well as of men, their minds and manner of thinking. One man remembers names of men and places, another remembers subjects and things, the majority of men and women remember neither. The compiler will accordingly endeavour to produce a catalogue which shall help all inquirers. He has also to satisfy his committee, and, as it is more than probable that his financial limits will not allow of his purchasing half the books he needs or those recommended for purchase, he will seek to make the best use of those he has on his shelves. His own memory not being perfect—an encyclopædia is not perfect—he will prepare complete and analytic lists of his collection as it stands, and in doing so will often find that he can supply something better than the work asked for or recommended for purchase. Considering also the valuable time occupied by careful and exact work, and the expense of printing, the prudent librarian or cataloguer will adopt methods with a view to making his work permanent.

Coming to national bibliography, I wish to say that I do not consider it is impracticable, and, as some evidence that it can be accomplished, I respectfully invite attention to a *Bibliography of Australasia and Polynesia*, which has occupied my leisure for many years, the manuscript of which is exhibited in this hall. The work is unfinished, but is sufficiently advanced as to be ready in some sections for the printer. When finished it will contain over thirty thousand titles and references—to all known publications, articles in periodicals, and papers in transactions, in any language—relating to Australia, Tasmania, New Zealand, and other island groups of the Pacific, since the beginning of the sixteenth century. From one-third to one-half of these titles belong to local publications. The titles are grouped under subjects, and arranged in chronological order for convenience of reference. Earlier writers upon every subject thus obtain their rightful precedence, and, on the other hand, the inquirer may see at a glance the latest publication on any subject regarding which he is in search of information. When a date is not printed upon a title-page, the correct year has been ascertained, from internal or external evidence, and inserted in brackets. I have also obtained the names of the real authors of a large number of anonymous and pseudonymous publications. These works will, however, be readily found, as they are catalogued under their respective subjects in the order of their date.

As you will see from the printed prospectus, this bibliography of Australasia is founded primarily upon an extensive library of books, pamphlets, newspapers, and maps, which I have collected during the last thirty years, upon information gathered in the Australian Colonies, and upon searches made in the Record Office, the Colonial Office, the Royal Colonial Institute, the Paris National Library, other Continental libraries, and in the British Museum.

The specimen pages, which I have already printed, and which have been reprinted by the New South Wales Government in the official history of that colony, will show the manner in which I am doing the work. For the rest, as the architect and builder, I point to the work itself, merely adding that I am labouring to produce a historical and bibliographical work of reference, useful to the journalist, the statesman, the statistician, the man of science, the scholar, and the student, as well as to the librarian, the bibliographer, and the bookseller—a work which shall be indispensable in every Australasian collection, and worthy of a place in every important public library in the world.

EDWARD A. PETHERICK.

BIBLIOGRAPHICAL ENDEAVOURS IN AMERICA.

HE wearied **bibliographer,** at work upon **a book** about books, has sometimes **an** overwhelming sense **of the** littleness of human **endeavour.** He feels himself a "second cousin twice removed" from literature, a cube root only in **the** integration of books, a mino· craftsman, **who** makes the key which opens the door to **the vestibule of** "kings' treasuries." **The** scholar, indeed, is disposed to **aver that the bibliographer** often makes **not so much a key as a** burglar's "jemmy," forcing **entry into all** storehouses of knowledge, **which should** be properly approached only by trained skill and patient research. The Scripture text, "Of making many books there is **no** end, and much study is a weariness of **the** flesh," comes home with a realising **sense** indeed to the bibliographer. Perhaps **I** have no right, as chiefly an editor, **a** bibliographer by proxy, to voice **these** complaints; but I am, nevertheless, in **the** better position to recognise that **patient** toil, often done in the dejection I **have** indicated, by the great number **of biblio**graphical scholars, **whose** work, **after all,** is of real and wide **service,** the **more in** these days and in coming days, when even the work of **selection** is beyond the province of any **one** scholar in any one field, and when the bibliographer must be more and **more** depended upon to clear the way for the scholar. It is in this spirit that I shall endeavour to present briefly **to** this company of English and Americans gathered under their common **roof, and of** librarians and bibliographers **from many** sister nations, an index review of American endeavours in bibliography.

In the early years **American** bibliography was largely **a** book-trade matter, and such in good part **it** has continued to be. So early as 1802 an **American com**pany of booksellers was organised, **which** made almost its first business **the publica**tion, in **1804,** of a *Catalogue of all the Books printed in the United States,* which catalogue had the imprint of the " booksellers in Boston." Thereafter there was little outside the book-lists printed periodically in the *Portfolio* and in the *North American Review* until, in 1847, Simeon Ide, of Claremont, N.H., published a *Reference Trade List,* compiled by Alexander V. Blake, which proved the *avant courier* of an important kind of work, though it is scarcely to be classed as bibliography. This publication presented the book-lists of American publishers of the day, printed in the order of publishers, and was the forerunner of the several aggregations of publishers' lists into **one** or more volumes, now to be **found in the** United States, England, **France,** and Italy. The idea was taken **up by** Mr. Howard Challen, who printed **in** 1867 a uniform trade list circular, **into** which publishers' catalogues were combined, which was followed in 1872 by the *Trade Circular Annual,* issued by Frederick Leypoldt. In 1873 Mr. Leypoldt began in its present form the *Publishers' Trade List Annual,* which gave the model for Whitaker's *Reference Catalogue of English Literature,* published successively in 1874, 1875, 1877, 1878, 1880, 1885, 1889, and 1894; for the *Catalogo Collettivo della Libreria Italiana,* doing like service for Italy, first issued in 1878; and for the *Bibliographie Française,* started in France during the year past by . H. Le Soudier.

In the meantime, American bibliographers **in England,** as well as English bibliographers, **were** doing more for American bibliography than the Americans at home. George P. Putnam, the publisher, issued in 1845, while in London, a compilation of *American Facts,* containing a literary **department.** That veteran bibliographer, **Sampson Low,** printed in 1856 his *American Catalogue, or English Guide to American Literature,* purporting to give **works** published in the United States **since 1800,** but containing really books after 1840; Nicholas Trübner published in 1855 his *Bibliographical Guide to American Literature*, and Henry Stevens, of Vermont, printed in 1866 his *Catalogue of the American Books in the Library of the British Museum at Christmas* 1856, supplemented by later bibliographies from his workshop, and by a valuable mass of later entries, now in the possession of his son. It is interesting to note how largely American bibliography during these years had its seat in the mother country.

An enterprising young bookseller, Orvilla A. Roorbach, apprenticed in 1821 to Evert Duyckinck in New York, began, on his removal to Charleston, S.C., "At the sign of the Red Bible," the systematic collection of American book titles, beginning with 1820; and in 1849, being then again in New York with George P. Putnam, he published the first volume of his *Bibliotheca Americana*, including reprints and original American publications from 1820 to 1848 inclusive. This was extended by a supplement published in 1850, both of which were combined in his *Bibliotheca Americana* of 1852, in turn continued by a supplement of 1855, a volume of addenda of 1858, and a volume IV. of 1861. The latter volume was issued by the son of the original compiler, who died in 1861. Roorbach, although his work is most imperfect bibliographically, is entitled to great credit for his personal labours and professional enterprise in making the first real "American Catalogue." His work was complemented in some measure in the periodicals and volumes edited by Charles B. Norton, between 1851 and 1862. With the war, however, the book trade suffered a period of stagnation, but the mantle of Roorbach fell upon a young Irishman named James Kelly, who in 1866 published the first volume of his *American Catalogue*, 1861 to 1865 inclusive, and in 1871 a second volume, bringing the record up to that date.

In 1876, the centennial year, which gave stimulus to many important American enterprises, including the *Library Journal* and the organising meeting of the American Library Association, Frederick Leypoldt, among the foremost of American bibliographers, started the compilation of the original volume of the present *American Catalogue* series. This was confined to books in print and for sale in 1876, and made two huge volumes—one of author and title and one of subject entries—which work has been supplemented by three successive volumes, covering the period 1876–1884, 1884–1890, and 1890–1895; the later ones, with appendixes, giving the publications of the United States, of the several States, and of publishing societies of America—the last containing in the latest volume entries of the issues from nearly 500 such societies, some of them of the first literary or bibliographical importance. This work is the culmination of the trade bibliographical work carried through the office of the *Publishers' Weekly*, beginning with the weekly full-title annotated record, proceeding with the monthly index in the first issue of each month, carried forward in the *Annual American Catalogue*, for which the type has literally been kept standing from week to week till the end of the year, and so on to the great five-yearly volumes. This is perhaps the most comprehensive national bibliography which has been attempted in the book trade.

Work is now going forward upon a volume in this series scheduling the books of the early part of the century not in print in 1876, which, with the volume for 1895–1900, will complete a record of American books of the nineteenth century, and the material for a systematised general catalogue, supplementing that noble achievement, the British Museum printed catalogue, should it be found practicable to print such a comprehensive and costly work. I am glad to note that Dr. Garnett has kindly indicated the willingness of the British Museum authorities to give every facility for completing this material from its rich resources, one of many services, for which I have endeavoured to indicate the gratitude of American bibliographers by inscribing to him the current volume of the *American Catalogue*.

The works of Obadiah Rich, who published his *Bibliotheca Americana Nova*, 1493–1844, in London in 1835 and 1846; of E. G. Allen, who printed a small catalogue of books before 1800 relating to America; and of the two Russell Smiths, whose *Bibliotheca Americana* (really sales catalogues), were published in London in 1849, 1853, 1865, 1871, and 1874, were the predecessors of the very remarkable piece of work initiated by Joseph Sabin, another American veteran, who gave years of his life to the preparations for his *Bibliotheca Americana*, not completed during his lifetime, but continued, under the publishing management of his son. Many of the early volumes had the benefit of the editorship of C. A. Cutter, and the later volumes have been edited by Wilberforce Eames, librarian of the Lenox Library, New York. Mr. Sabin, during his years of bookselling and auction-room experience, collected every title on which he could lay hands, and of his great work one hundred and sixteen parts, carrying the alphabet to "Smith," have already been issued. Whether the work will be ultimately completed through the alphabet, it is not fully possible to say. In this category is to be mentioned also Henry Harrisse's *Bibliotheca Americana*, descriptive of works relating to early America, 1492-1551, published in New York in 1856, with a supplement issued in Paris in 1872.

One of the most interesting of early American publications was the *Bookbuyer's Manual*, published in New York in 1853 by George P. Putnam, which was resumed in 1872, and continued under the title of *Best Reading* in successive volumes, under the general management of his son and worthy successor, George Haven Putnam. These books were intended as select guides to general literature, foreshadowing Sonnenschein's *Best Books*, and since the issue of that more important work it has been found unnecessary to continue the American publication.

Meantime, however, a new class of bibliography has developed in America, based on what Mr. George Iles, its chief promoter, calls the "evaluation" of books. The *Readers' Guide in Economic, Social, and Political Science*, issued, through the Society for Political Education, by Mr. Iles and myself in 1891, was an attempt in this direction; but the best example of it has been found in the so-called "List of Books for Girls and Women and their Clubs," originally planned in other shape by Miss Ellen H. Eve, but issued under the auspices of the American Library Association in 1895, under Mr. Iles' management and chiefly at his cost, Mrs. A. H. Leypoldt being associated in the editorial work. Since the issue of that volume— or, in its small series, volumes—Mr. Iles has also provided for an expansion of a part of the work, the division of fine arts and music, into a very remarkable annotated bibliography of those subjects, prepared respectively by two of the first American scholars in those departments, Mr. Russell Sturgis and Mr. Henry E. Krehbiel. This work, although covering only two specific fields, is an admirable example of the work to which Mr. Iles is most altruistically devoting his time, force, and money. Something of the sort, although not in bibliographical form, had already been done by American scholars in the field of history; but the descriptive notes and comparative annotations planned by Mr. Iles are a distinct development of bibliographical literature proper.

In the library field America has made several bibliographical endeavours worthy of note. The great catalogue of the Boston Athenæum, although now out of date, has been for years a standard in cataloguing. The composite catalogue of the Brooklyn Library, semi-dictionary, semi-classed, compiled by Mr. S. B. Noyes, its first librarian, was for many years used throughout American libraries as a substitute for such a volume as Sonnenschein's work. The Peabody Institute of Baltimore has issued a remarkable catalogue; and there are others beyond possibility of mention. American library bibliography has, however, taken the shape rather of special lists, such as those of the Boston Public, Harvard, Providence, and other libraries, published usually in library bulletins, or of card-catalogues, often with useful notes or annotations as to the value of a book; and this last method has developed into the co-operative card-catalogue promoted by the American Library Association, and published for it by the Library Bureau. The plan of providing co-operatively full-title entries, with annotations for use on library cards, has been under consideration in American library circles for many years, and one attempt was made in the weekly *Title and Slip Registry*, which reprinted the weekly lists from the *Publishers' Weekly* on one side of thin paper, so that the entries might be cut out and pasted on cards of any size. These same titles were also printed for a while on cards; but then, as now, it was difficult to obtain adequate support for such work, and it is still a question whether the cards issued by the A.L.A. Publishing Section, which are subscribed for by less than one hundred libraries, can find a continuous and adequate support.

Within the year past, five of the most important libraries, at the initiative of Dr. John S. Billings, of the New York Public Library, now in process of organisation, have united in the preparation of printed cards for articles in the scientific periodicals, and a plan is under consideration for putting these cards at the service of other libraries through the medium of the Publishing Section.

The Publishing Section of the American Library Association itself is one of the most interesting developments in American bibliographical work. Its purpose is to provide for the printing of bibliographies and other library aids which could not be provided by any one library and would not be issued by any one publisher. Among its distinctive work has been the provision of lists of books for children, such as Sargent's *Reading for the Young* and Miss Hewins' recent little list of *Books for Boys and Girls*. This use of library co-operation may be cordially commended to the associations of other nations, for it has proved one of the best results that the American Library Association can show. Under its auspices, and under the title of the A.L.A. *Index to General Literature*, there has been published an index to essays and the chapters of composite books, edited by Mr. W. I. Fletcher, the associate of Dr. Poole and the chairman of the Publishing Section, which is of international value.

A word should be said of the remarkable work of Dr. Poole himself, known throughout the world as *Poole's Index*, the more remarkable because it was planned and first issued by him while a student in Yale College. This index to periodical literature is perhaps as well known as any single bibliography published. It has been extended in five-yearly supplements by Dr. Poole's associate, Mr. Fletcher, with the co-operation of members of the American Library Association, and is now continued also, as is the A.L.A. *Index to General Literature*, in annual lists, which form part of the *Annual Literary Index*. The monthly and quarterly compilation of this sort had been discontinued with the appearance of the *Annual Literary Index*, but within the year past Mr. W. H. Brett, of Cleveland, has issued from his Cleveland Public Library a "Cumulative Index" to periodical literature of most interesting plan. He uses the linotype to print in January an index to articles in January magazines, in February an index to January and February magazines, and so on, until the December issue covers cumulatively the entries for the whole twelve months, and becomes a record of the year and a permanent volume.

Our National Library, still called the Library of Congress, has not yet taken its proper place, so worthily filled in the mother country by the British Museum, of heading and centralising bibliographical work. The few printed volumes of its catalogue are partial, incomplete, and antiquated, and the physical congestion prevailing until lately has made progress difficult. The *Weekly Register* of copyrights also has not been bibliographically useful. But the National Library is now removing its books to the finest library building in the country, and it is in process of re-organisation, the registry of copyrights being made a distinctive department. This gives the library a remarkable opportunity. For a fee of 50 cents (2s.) additional to a like fee for copyright entry, the register of copyright is obliged to return a record of copyright, and it is the practice of copyright proprietors to pay the double fee and obtain the record in all cases. If, in the new developments, it should be arranged that this record shall take the shape of a printed card for catalogue entry, and if duplicates of such cards could be supplied to subscribing libraries, a great step forward in practical bibliography could be made.

For co-operation, and in this case centralisation, *is* a vital feature in this class, especially of library work. All that can be done once for all and by one for all should be so done. The more "the librarian of the future" is freed from mere record work, the more chance he will have for the useful exercise of his individuality. First *collection*, but foremost *selection*, must be the golden word in the handling of books. So, first *co-operation*, but foremost *individualisation*, must be the golden word in the administration of libraries. The superstition that one book must be catalogued a hundred times in as many libraries to ensure a supply of cataloguers and librarians is unworthy of the day. The printed card, the general bibliography, co-operation helps of all kinds, should liberate the time, the money, and the force of the librarian and his staff for the more vital work of adapting his library to the local and individual needs of the particular community of human beings which it is his duty and his delight to serve.   R. R. BOWKER.

DESCRIPTION OF IMPORTANT LIBRARIES IN MONTREAL, WITH REMARKS UPON DEPARTMENTAL LIBRARIES.

T will be my aim to present to you some information with regard to the libraries of Montreal, and to further allow myself a few words on the subject of departmental libraries or libraries of special subjects, because, for reasons which will appear later, this is a matter of vital interest to at least one of our important libraries, and, so far as I can find, has hardly received the attention which its importance to all universities at least would seem to deserve.

Omitting collections of less than 1000 volumes, Montreal possesses to-day twenty-five libraries, to which the public, or classes of the public, obtain access. This does not include the very valuable archives of St. Mary's (Jesuit) College, and of the Seminary of St. Sulpice.

Of these twenty-five libraries, fourteen contain not less than 5000 volumes each, while the archives are the repositories of many documents of unique interest to the history of the city and the Dominion.

The libraries may be classified as follows :—

	Containing
University or college libraries	130,000 vols.
These consist of those of McGill and her affiliated colleges, about 90,000; and that of the Collège de Montréal, 40,000; with a small collection belonging to the recently established branch of Laval University, and to Bishop's College.	
Free public libraries	40,000 ,,
Law libraries	26,000 ,,
Incorporated Mechanics' Institutions	24,000 ,,
Libraries of various societies and associations, etc.	20,000 ,,
	240,000 vols.

besides the archives of St. Mary's College and the Seminary of St. Sulpice already mentioned.

Fifty years ago, during the political agitation of 1848, the Houses of Parliament in Montreal, which was then the capital of the united provinces of the Canadas, were burned by a mob, and the legislative libraries were destroyed. This act, besides costing the whole country many priceless documents, deprived Montreal of the seat of government as well as of a valuable library. The collections which she now possesses have, in great part, accumulated since that time, and the comparatively unsatisfactory position of libraries in Montreal to-day may, to some extent, be traced to the disturbances of fifty years since.

Recently, however, very fair progress has been made. Within the last five years nearly $400,000 have been bequeathed, or given outright, towards founding or endowing libraries, and, but for an unfortunate incident in connection with the Fraser Institute, the chief free public library of Montreal, a large sum more would now be available for that institution. A library club has been formed, and is doing needed work in the way of acquainting librarians with each other, as well as with the resources and wants of the various institutions with which they are connected. There is increased co-operation between the principal libraries, and a beginning has been made at what will probably soon be a joint-catalogue of the periodical literature in Montreal, both scientific and general, indicating whether a particular set be complete or otherwise, and where it may be found.

Altogether, the position may be said to be one of awakening interest on the part of the public and increased effort on the part of the libraries.

A few words on the history of two of the largest of our libraries may here be of interest.

The Fraser Institute owes its existence to the late Mr. Fraser, of Montreal, who in the year 1870 left property, chiefly real estate, worth about half a million dollars (£110,000), to found and maintain a free library and art gallery for the city of Montreal. Unfortunately, the validity of this will was questioned by an heir-at-law, and, only after years of litigation, and after the capital had been greatly encroached upon, was the matter finally settled in favour of the institute. A building was then leased, a certain number of books got together, and work was begun. The library now owns between 30,000 and 35,000 vols. of excellent quality, and has attracted a collection of German literature belonging to the German Society.

The use of the library is rapidly growing. The number of readers for the last year reached the respectable total of 70,000. In the last few years about $98,000 in subscriptions and bequests have been contributed by various benefactors.

The largest library in Montreal is that of McGill University, and to this I now beg briefly to direct your attention.[1]

The library was founded in 1856, and in 1860 a home was provided for it in the William Molson Hall, erected by the gentleman whose name it bears. The building was planned to accommodate some 20,000 volumes. The space was gradually filled, and the library began to overflow into adjoining rooms. The faculty of medicine was moved to the college grounds, bringing with it the medical books, which have always been housed with the department by which they are chiefly used. In the meantime the affiliated colleges began to draw into close proximity. Each brought its quota of books, which were available for use by the university though controlled directly by the college. With the magnificent gifts extending over the last five years,

which have brought the scientific equipment of the university into merited prominence, there came additional libraries, nominally administered by the library committee of the university, but practically controlled by the department or faculty most interested in them. The books in the central library, though numbering only about 33,000, were usually taken to comprise the entire university library. The large amount of material besides this was hardly available except to students of particular departments. There seems to have been a distinct tendency to disintegrate the central library in favour of department libraries with a central administration. In 1892, however, this policy was modified by Mr. Peter Redpath's timely gift of the fine building in which the library is now established. The books of the departments continue to increase in number, but are confined more strictly than before to working books, while the general library is entrusted with the others. Arrangements have been and are being made with the affiliated colleges, to include their catalogue in that of the general library, and to classify their books on lines parallel, if not identical, with those of the general library.

These steps, when carried out, will make the full library resources of the university available to any reader, and will place some 23,000 volumes at his disposal, besides the 68,000 which the university itself possesses, so that the university library is now, to all intents and purposes, a library of 90,000 volumes.

From what has been said, it will be clear why the question of departmental libraries is, to McGill University at least, an important one. I therefore trust I may be allowed to bring before you now a few observations on this subject. In making these observations, I would remind you that they refer to university or college libraries, and chiefly to conditions which prevail on the west side of the Atlantic.

The term "Departmental Library" as it is here employed is to be distinguished from the so-called class-room library and similar collections. There are books which, in every department of study, are required for constant use, and should always be within reach. The number of such books on a given subject is comparatively small, and these will be dealt with later on.

I refer to collections of at least several hundred, sometimes several thousand

---

[1] May I explain in parenthesis, that McGill University possesses the faculties of arts, law, applied science, medicine, and comparative medicine. There is no theological faculty, but students of the various theological schools may obtain certain privileges in proceeding to the degree of B.A., such as the substitution of Hebrew for a scientific subject. These theological schools are said to be affiliated with the university.

volumes, bearing chiefly upon a single subject, but with more or less fulness upon related subjects, and kept in separate buildings.

Now, no department of science, literature, or art can to-day be said to stand alone. Rather, each is surrounded by and merges, often almost imperceptibly, into a number of others. It is evident, therefore, that if the departmental libraries are to be to any extent self-contained, or capable of being used alone, a large amount of duplication must be the result.

For example, suppose a chemical library be desired. To be fairly complete it must contain, besides the chemical books, which would form its chief part, works on alchemy, on mineralogy, and crystallography, and works on chemical technology, on physics, and on other subjects. A large number of these books will be as important to the physicist as to the chemist. If a musical library is to be formed, there must be works on sound, and also on æsthetics and on the Renaissance; yet the latter will be equally necessary in an architectural library. And so on.

This, then, is the first question that must be settled in regard to the departmental libraries—Is each one to be made fairly complete in itself? If so, the same books must often be obtained for two or even more than two departments. Should this be objected to on the ground of expense,—and large departmental libraries involve many other heavy charges in the way of additional attendance, extra cataloguing, and complexity of management,—then, what departments are to be made complete at the cost of others, and how shall prompt service be attained for those who are working in one of the depleted departments and must visit neighbouring departments to supplement their own?

Moreover, the library of a university is, in its highest and best form, simply a reference library. More than any other, except the great reference libraries themselves, it is liable to be called upon for material and information of the most diverse kind.

It is therefore most important not only that such a library should be kept symmetrical, but that it should have the means of placing its entire resources on a given subject at the disposal of a reader, with a minimum of delay and inconvenience.

How shall symmetry be obtained, though means be never so great, with a constant demand on all sides for the purchase of duplicates? Or, if this be not insisted on, how shall the full resources of the library on a certain point be made promptly available when the books are scattered in different departments?

The objection will doubtless be raised here, that many of the greatest universities, and those with the greatest libraries, have also departmental libraries.

If the collection of books belonging to a university be large and varied, while access to it is restricted and the service slow, the departmental library will undoubtedly appear to be a gain. It renders more books available than were so before, and those, too, the books on the whole most wanted. Half a loaf is better than no bread. But the gain is a costly one to the library, as may be inferred from what has been said, while it tempts the reader to accept what is placed at his hand and go no further. The true course, after all, is in such a case to reform the defective service rather than adopt an expedient to enable it to be continued.

If, however, the chief difficulty arises from a paucity of books and of the means to procure them, then the evils of the situation are all aggravated by the departmental system. If the full resources of a library are insufficient to meet the demands made upon it, what reason is there for depleting them by withdrawing numbers of books, and so placing them that, to use them in conjunction with others, one must vibrate between different buildings? And, if funds are not forthcoming in sufficient amount for the purchase of books, why draw upon them to pay for extra attendance, cataloguing, and duplication? Broadly speaking, this must be the effect of departmental libraries they not only diminish the power to buy, and so retard growth, but they render what the library already has difficult of access to the majority of its readers.

What has thus far been said has reference, it will be observed, to departments in separate buildings. Of course there are cases in which a number of departments are covered by a single roof. Here the force of the objection is lessened, since the inconvenience of getting from one library to another is to some extent removed. The main argument is strengthened, however, since the more nearly the arrangement approximates to that of a general library the less the inconvenience.

In view of all this, I would submit the following suggestion: The difficulty has been that it has generally been thought necessary to make each departmental library complete and self-contained, while it must have appeared, from what has already been urged, that this can never be more than partially accomplished. Why not, then, adopt the opposite course—cut it down to the narrowest limit admissible? There are, as was said some time ago, certain books in every branch of study which are required for constant use, and should always be accessible. They may be defined as "tools," for they are as indispensable as apparatus in the laboratory or tools in the workshop. Let these form the departmental libraries.

Each department should submit to the central administration a list of the "book-tools" which it requires, frequency of use being taken as a guide in making the choice, and the aim being, as stated, to make the special collection not as large but as small as practicable. As a rule, selection will not be difficult. The books chosen should be sent to the department and placed in its charge. They should be removed from the building only under very exceptional circumstances. In this way as many small working libraries as desirable may be formed; and a certain number of duplicates will have to be purchased, though the number will now be well within limits.

If these working libraries be subsidiary to a well-arranged centrally-situated building, with a commodious reading-room, shelved for several thousand volumes, to which access is unrestricted; if the reading-room be kept open as many hours each day as the departmental library would have been; if, further, the building be provided with special rooms which can be employed in cases where unusual freedom and seclusion are desirable, it is submitted that the so-called advantages afforded by the departmental library to the few are off-set by a gain, not for the few, but for every individual reader.

There is no rule without its exception. There may be cases where what has been urged would not apply. If so, these exceptions, I think, only prove the general rule.

Good books are of great use, even taken singly, but to the scholar their power increases enormously with their number. Nowadays every book of value reacts upon so many others, that of two equally well-chosen libraries the worth probably varies, not directly as, but as the square of, the number of their volumes. This being so, it seems little less than a paradox that, when the interdependence of the various sciences and arts is recognised as it never was before, a movement should be countenanced which, by a purely arbitrary process, severs large sections of books from their natural surroundings and makes them available to a certain class only. That such a process hardly satisfies the requirements of reason, is clear; neither, if other conditions are satisfactory, is it needed for purposes of utility.

C. H. GOULD.

LIBRARIES THE PRIMARY FACTOR IN HUMAN EVOLUTION.

T is always pleasing to find that what ought to be true is true. To the librarian, therefore, it is a pleasure if no surprise to learn that, instead of libraries being, as they are sometimes said to be, the flower of civilisation, all human progress is the fruit of libraries. Without stopping for refinements of argument and explanation, it is obvious that human evolution, as distinguished from the evolution of plants and animals, is an evolution in that particular characteristic which distinguishes man from plant and brute. That which makes a man a man and not a brute being "the rational mind" (Cope) or the "process of mental abstraction" (Mivart), the evolution of man as man is consequently an evolution in mind or knowledge. Evolution in mind or knowledge, again, being less an individual than a social process, its chief factor is not so much the effort of the individual as the co-ordinated action of many individuals, and its fundamental characteristic is co-operation in knowledge. Finally, since the only instrument of co-operative knowledge in the more complex stages of knowledge is a collection of books, the library is the fundamental factor in the evolution of mind; and being the only hope for the further progress of man in respect of "(1) the subjugation of nature, (2) the perfection of social machinery, and (3) personal development" (Mackenzie-Giddings), it is in truth the primary factor in human evolution—that factor whose abolishment would bring progress to a standstill and cause degeneration to set in.

If, as Mr. Benjamin Kidd declares, "the evolution which is slowly proceeding in human society is not primarily intellectual but religious"; or, as Mr. Spencer holds, the foundation of human progress is a growth in sympathy rather than a growth in reason; or even if, as Mr. Giddings says, it is a double growth in mind and morality, then, perhaps, libraries are "a primary factor" rather than "the primary factor." But whatever religion, sympathy, and morality may be, they have no substantial existence apart from the rational mind, and whether "a factor" or "the factor," therefore, it is at least true that evolution in knowledge is an indispensable pre-requisite for human evolution, that co-operation in knowledge is the essence of this evolution, and that libraries are the fundamental factor in co-operative knowledge. They are therefore, in this sense at least, the primary factor in human evolution and within the intent of this paper, the aim of which is, first of all, to suggest in what way it is that human progress is affected by libraries, and only secondarily to emphasise the logical result of the analysis as expressed by "the" rather than "a."

The process by which knowledge grows is this: sense impressions are joined together into images; these are again fused together after the analogy of a composite photograph, so that all images of any single object are gathered into one image, which is in turn combined with other similar images into a general concept, and this with other images and concepts into a whole of things observed and reasoned. The fact, however, that every sensation takes time, reduces to narrow limits the number of things which any one man can get through direct knowledge; and, if shut up to his own unaided efforts, no one's total of knowledge would be great. But the process does not stop here. By language, concepts are transferred ready formed from one individual to another, or from many to one; a new synthesis is made, and ideas are built up exactly as if by the individual from his own sense impressions. By extending this process, the results of the labours of all observers, in all lands and all times, on any one thing, are gathered up into one knowledge, which is the essential pre-requisite of some step in human progress. The telephone, e.g., is the accumulated result of the co-operative knowledge of hundreds of practical electricians, each of whose contributions was based on the co-operative labour of thousands of theoretical students of electricity, who in turn depended on the accumulated results of the co-operative labour of multitudes of physicists and mathematicians. The telephone could not exist in its present form except for this bringing together of the work of many, and the only method by which the labours of so many men in many lands and in many ages of the world can be thus accumulated is by recording them in books and bringing the books together. It is, in fact, in this way "that almost the whole of our natural knowledge is practically derived" (Bosanquet). Books thus brought together as a basis for the co-ordination of ideas are of course a library, and the library is therefore the indispensable factor of all evolution in knowledge.

Whether this was the fact in early times or not, it is at least the fact now. Under primitive conditions, it is conceivable that knowledge might be passed from man to man and from father to son by word of mouth; yet it is to be noted that, whether egg from owl or owl from egg, the nations which did make progress in civilisation did make early collections of books; and, further than this, that even the theory of the oral transmission of books before the invention of writing is a testimony to the fact that these formulated results of human experience, gathered up to be joined to the results of individual experience, were the actual instruments of human progress —the priest in this case, with his mind full of books, being really a library. But, however it may have been in a less complex civilisation, it is at least true that now, when our knowledge has become already so complex, the only possibility of further progress lies in this instrument. It is in fact the direct or indirect basis of all legislation, military science, mechanical, industrial, and ethical progress. Every legislator, general, inventor, or moralist rests on accumulated experience, and can get this experience in no other way than through libraries.

The library as here considered may be private or public, composed of a great number of books or a few best books; it is, however, the scientific and not the popular library. The latter plays an important part in human evolution, as a part of the educational machine, but is not to be confused with the collections of books to form a basis for progress in knowledge. The very same library, used both for the general dissemination of knowledge and as the basis of progress in knowledge, is exercising two different functions, the one being indirect and secondary, the other direct and primary. The one multiplies the individuals of a given species; the other unites the favourable variations of many individuals in any one species as material for the creation or evolution of a higher species. The one represents dissemination of knowledge, the other co-ordination; and it is with the latter only that this paper has to do.

There are two or three corollaries or suggestions which come from this statement of human progress as peculiarly the fruit of libraries by virtue of the doctrine of co-ordinate knowledge. (1) As to the philosophy of man: If, as is often said, " mind " exists in animals lower than man, it may not be fanciful to suggest that the distinction between man and brute lies not so much in mind as in that power of co-operation in knowledge whose acme and essence is the library. (2) As to the philosophy of libraries: The germ of the library would certainly seem to lie at that point where human knowledge parts from animal intelligence—the point, that is, where a definitely-formed concept from another mind is placed beside one's own idea for integration, the result being a definite new form including the substance of both. Two formulated ideas set side by side are an embryo library. (3) As to its practical bearing on method: There has been in the past a good deal of discussion as to the value of close classification of books on the shelves. For the dissemination of knowledge the matter is of less importance, but for the co-ordination of knowledge it is all-important. It is evident that the man who would contribute to progress in knowledge should have or get all books of his kind together. It is equally evident that the time saved to such a man by close classification is enormous. A well-classified university library, e.g., may therefore, by reason of its classification, practically contribute annually several lifetimes of individual scientific research to the progress of the race.

ERNEST CUSHING RICHARDSON.

COUNTING AND TIME-RECORDING.

N looking over some old family documents, my attention was recently drawn to a peculiar method by which a number of them expressed the dates. This led me to examine the systems adopted by different nations for recording events, and, as might be expected, prior to the introduction of what are generally known as the Arabic numbers, these systems varied greatly, and, in many cases, were extremely primitive and complicated, especially where the art of writing was unknown or but little practised. Nor need we wonder at this, for, in comparatively recent times, tribes have been found whose knowledge of numbers is so limited that it is difficult to imagine how, except for a very brief period, they could keep count of past events. The faculty of counting, as has been well said, seems to be one of the last to be exercised; and hence we find, even among nations well advanced in civilisation, and with well-developed intellectual powers, their range of using numbers is comparatively restricted. This was particularly noticeable in the case of the ancient Greeks, and has been referred to by Mr. Gladstone. "Homer," for example, "had no definite idea of numbers beyond a very narrow range." He dealt largely in round numbers, and had not infrequently curious roundabout ways of expressing the relative numbers of the combatants. The power of expressing definitely and correctly any considerable number may be considered a good indication of the state of advancement of a people in civilisation. Sir John Bowring's book on *The Decimal System* is full of interesting information in regard to the use of numbers. He shows that the method of employing the fingers, hands, and feet can be traced in the numerals of many of the aboriginal American and Australian tribes, and that, owing to the complex and cumbrous character of their languages, they were prevented from extending their numerical calculations beyond a very limited range; and we can scarcely wonder at this when we are told that one of the tribes on the Amazon broke down when they came to the number 3, which was *paettarrarorincoaroe*. We are also told that some of the Australian tribes could only count as far as 3, and had either to raise their hands to express a greater number or make use of a term signifying multitude.

Dr. Peacock gives a number of similar examples. He states that the Betoi, who formerly dwelt on the banks of the Orinoco, used the word *edojojoi* for 1; for 2 their word was *edoi*, signifying "another"; 3 was expressed by *ibutu*, "beyond"; 4 by *ibutu edojojoi*, "beyond one"; 5 was *rumoscoco*, signifying "hand."

In his *Dacota Grammar*, Dr. S. R. Riggs says that the Dacotas used their fingers in making their calculations, bending down one after another as they proceeded, till they reached 10, when they turn down a little finger to remind them that one ten has been disposed of; and then, commencing again, they go through the same process, till they again reach 10, when down goes another, and so on. When they wish to express 11, they say *wickeemna sanpa wanzidan*, literally "ten more one"; 12 would be *wickeemna sanpa nonpa*, "ten more two," and so on till they reach 19, which is *unma napcinwanka*, signifying "the other nine"; 20 is *wickcemna nonpa*, that is, "ten two" or "ten again"; 21 is *wickeemna nonpa sanpa wanzidan* = (10 × 2) + 1. By them, 1897 would be expressed thus, *kektopawinga opawinga sahdogan sanpa wickeemna nap-*

cinwanka sanpa **sakowin** = 1000 + (100 × 8) + (10 × 9) + 7. It is difficult to imagine how, under these circumstances, this tribe could have any rational system of chronology. We are told that in reckoning time they usually counted their years by winters, and their days by so many nights or sleeps. Their months were counted by moons. It appears they had a strange fancy about the changes of the moon. When it was full, they imagined that a number of mice attacked it, nibbling it gradually away till it disappeared. When the new moon reappeared and again became full, the same nibbling process recommenced. The Kaffirs of South Africa also regulated their time by the moon; and indeed this was the case with most uncivilised nations. They registered it by notches cut in pieces of wood, and their recorded dates, as might be expected, seldom extended beyond one generation, after which they had to make a new departure, commencing with some marked occurrence, such as a great victory achieved over an enemy, or in honour of some renowned chief. It would seem as if the exchequer tallies used in England at one time, and which were abolished by 25 Geo. III., were a survival of this ancient practice of assigning values to these scores or notches. Sometimes, instead of cutting notches, or, as was frequently done, burning the marks on the sticks, they were painted in various colours, were made of different shapes, and these were understood to indicate certain conventional meanings. The same practice was in use among many of the Indian tribes. The Algonkin nation, it is said, very generally preserved their traditions, and events which were of special interest and which were considered worthy of being recorded, by means of marked sticks. The name given to these tally sticks by the Crees and Chippeways was *massinahigan*, which is now used as the word for book, but which, according to Dr. Brinton, originally meant a piece of wood marked with fire, from the verb *masinakisan*, "I burn a mark upon it," thus indicating probably the most primitive system of recording events. The Aztecs of South America, when the Spaniards landed among them, had picture writings for the same purpose, but the Spaniards ruthlessly destroyed these wherever found, looking upon them, we are told, as "symbols of a pestilent superstition," "snares of the Evil One," and so forth, no doubt thinking that in this way they were doing good service to the Church and to religion.[1]

It is greatly to be regretted that these interesting records had not been carefully collected and preserved, as they would doubtless have thrown much light upon the history of those early times. Fortunately, however, a few of these escaped destruction, and are now deposited in several of the European libraries, where they can be examined.

The ancient Peruvians had a curious method of recording events by means of knotting records, or, as they were called, *Quipos*, meaning "cords." 1 was represented by one knot; 2 by inserting the cord through a second time, making a double knot; 3 was represented by what might be called a triple knot; 4 by a kind of loop on the cord; and so the process went on till 100 was reached, when, as may be imagined, the knots became extremely complicated, and must have looked to the uninitiated like a Chinese puzzle. They were of different colours, lengths, and textures, and they are said to be still in use among the shepherds about Lake Titicaca.

Mr. Murdock, in *Notes on Counting and Measuring among the Eskimo* of Point Barrow, says that the Eskimo are not in the habit of using numbers above 5. 6 and all higher numbers are called *anadraktuk*, signifying "many." When they wish to express 6, they can do so by saying "five and one on the next hand"; 7 is "twice on the next"; 9 is expressed by *kodlin oteila*, which is supposed to mean that which is not ten (ten being *kodlin*, signifying "the upper part"), referring to the fingers on the hands. They reckon the year by moons, commencing with the first one after the Elson Bay is frozen over, when the women begin to sew deer-skins. The first is called *Shud-le-wing*, that is, "the time for working or sewing." The third one, which nearly corresponds with December, is called *Kai-wig-win*, that is, "the time for dancing"; and when anything has taken place some years before, they are in the habit of saying *aipani*, which means "in the other" (time being understood). From this it will be seen, as Mr. Murdock justly observes, that the expressions used by them for past time are too vague to make it possible to learn with certainty the date of any event in history.

The Indians in the Canadian North-

[1] See Brantz Mayer in *Amer. Contrib. to Knl.*, vol. ix.

West, prior to their contact with the whites, had no system whatever of recording past events, and hence we have no reliable means of knowing their history in early times.

The Mexicans are said to have kept track of time by means of hieroglyphics. They had only distinct characters for the numbers 1, 20, 400, and 8000, and yet, by a curious process of combination, they were able to express any number. 1 was represented by a small circle, 20 by a standard shaped as a parallelogram, 400 by a feather, and 8000 by a purse, supposed to contain the same number of grains of cocoa. It is said, however, that although the number of units from 1 to 19 was usually represented by so many small circles, they had also other and more direct ways of representing these numbers. By dividing the parallelogram or hieroglyphic for 20 into four squares, and giving each a separate colour, they were able to represent 5, 10, and 15, and by taking half a feather they could express 200. The year 1897 would be thus expressed by them :

By the Assyrians and other Eastern nations which used cuneiform characters, the numbers from 1 to 9 were represented by upright strokes : thus one by |; two by ||; three by |||; four by ▓; five by ▓; and so forth. Ten was expressed by <; eleven by <|; twelve by <||; twenty was <<; fifty was <<<<; one hundred was <⊢; one thousand <⊣. The year 1897 would be thus expressed :

A simple way of using numbers may be seen on the Babylonian inscriptions, where all numbers from 1 to 99 are obtained by the repetition of the vertical arrow-head ᴠ = 1, and a barbed sign < = 10, and when a smaller number is placed to the right of the sign for 100, which is ↳, it is added to it, but, contrary to the usage of the Arabic numbers, when placed to the left, it gives the number of hundreds thus <↳ = 1000, but ∨-< = 110.

Egypt, in ancient times, was a highly intellectual nation, and yet it did not appear to have had a numerical system much, if at all, in advance of other nations. They had symbols for 1, 10, 100, 1000, 10,000, in hieroglyphics, and these when repeated gave the same number so many times more. It is somewhat singular that the hieroglyphic characters were written from left to right, whereas the hieratic or common form of writing was from right to left.

In the hieroglyphic system the units were represented by upright strokes—10 by a character ∩, like an inverted u; 11 was 1∩; 20 ∩∩; 21 1∩∩; 100 was 9, 200 99, and so on. 1000 was ⚑. The year 1897 would thus be expressed Their year was regulated by the seasons, without reference to the changes of the moon. It contained 365 days, divided into 12 months of 30 days each, with 5 supplementary days at the end of the year. According to Dr. Brinton, the Cakchiquels, as well as the Mayas—the ancient inhabitants of Yucatan — and Mexicans did not divide their year into lunar months, as was the case with the hunting tribes. Their year consisted of 20 months of 18 days each, but, as their year was 365 days in length, there was a deficiency of five days in each year, which the Mexicans called by a name signifying "insufficient"; the Mayas called them "days of pain or of peril," and the Cakchiquels "days of evil or days of fault." These were not included in the count of the months.

The Greeks originally expressed their numbers by using the first letters of words : thus ι expressed one, being the initial letter of ἴος—a word which has this meaning; π, five from πέντε; Δ, ten from Δέκα, and so forth. Afterwards, however, the Greek letters of the alphabet came to be used as numerals. The Greek inscriptions, prior to the time of Alexander, were expressed by the initial letters of words, but subsequent to his time their numbers and dates were expressed by letters of the alphabet, as I have stated, used as symbols. 1897 would be αως ζ.

The Roman system of using letters as numerals is well known, and is still in use, where C, the initial letter of centum, represents 100, and M of mille stands for 1000. Instead of these signs, however, older forms were at one time used. Thus a circle divided vertically (Ⓓ) was 1000, and horizontally (⊖) was 100. From the sign for 1000, still shown in print as CIƆ, comes D, the half of the symbol for half the number or 500. The older forms of L are supposed to have been derived from the 100 symbol, giving us 50; and so X, resulting from the cancelling strokes of the ten upright lines, ▓▓ = 10, was divided into two parts, and either V or its variant Λ gives the symbol for five. In later times this Latin system was extended by repeating the symbol for 1000: thus CCIƆƆ was made to represent 10,000, CCCIƆƆƆ 100,000, and so on, and the bisection of these gives us IƆƆ and IƆƆƆ = 5000 and 50,000 respectively. In a *Clavis Homerica* that I have, the date 1604 is CIƆIƆCIV.

In more recent times, as has been said, C was used for 100, being the first letter of centum, and M, written also ₥, was used for 1000, being the initial letter of mille.

The introduction of the Arabic numbers has revolutionised our entire system of computation. A great deal of discussion has been carried on in answering the questions, whence they came, and when they were introduced into Europe. They are now generally supposed to have been of Indian origin, having been invented by the Brahmins in early times. It is probable, however, that they were not introduced into Europe before the tenth or the eleventh century. They were not introduced into England till near the beginning of the seventeenth century, and, what seems strange after their introduction, they were frequently found mixed with Roman numerals, showing that they were only partially understood at that time. Thus we have XXX2 for 32; X4 for 14. We have also 302 and 303 for 32 and 33, from which it is obvious that the signification of the cypher was unknown. We find further changes introduced, such as IV for IIII; IX for VIIII; XL for 40; CD for 400; CM for 900, etc., the smaller number when placed in front being subtracted from the larger one after it.

During the Middle Ages dates were frequently recorded by means of indiction, which consisted of a period of fifteen years, used chiefly by ecclesiastical writers. The introduction of this system of reckoning time has usually been attributed to Constantine the Great. Beginning with indiction 1, it went up to indiction 15, when it commenced again. By counting backward to the commencement of the Christian era, it was found 1 A.D. did not correspond with the first but with the fourth year of an indiction, and hence, to get the position of a year in an indiction, if to any given year of our era 3 be added, and the sum divided by 15, the remainder gives the position of that year. As the commencement of the indiction in different countries varied, there were several kinds in use. Generally, however, they were confined to four. (1) The indiction of Constantinople, calculated from the 1st Sept. A.D. 312. (2) The imperial or Cæsarian one (commonly adopted in England), beginning 24th Sept. 312. (3) The Roman or Pontifical, beginning on Jan. 1st (or Dec. 25, so long as that day was reckoned the first day of the year) A.D. 313. (4) The indiction used in the register of the Parliament of Paris, beginning in October. One of the Greek charters found in Egypt during the latest period of the Byzantine Empire which shows this is given thus: "ἔτους ὀκτωκαιδεκάτου Ἐπειφ̀ κ̄ τρίτης ἰνδ(ικτου)," "the 18th year, the 20th month Epiphi, the 3rd indiction," corresponding to A.D. 600. The transcriber of a work by Gregory Nazianzen, archbishop of Constantinople, closes with a note, giving the name and the date when the MS. was finished, as follows: "μηνὶ μαίῳ ἰνδ. ε̄ ἔτους σφιε, etc.," "in the month of May, indiction 5, in the year 6515," which corresponds with May A.D. 1007. The following is from a Latin charter of Roger, first Norman king of Sicily: "Anno ab incarnatione MC tricessimo indic(tione) VIIII." This was the year 1130, when he erected his countship into a kingdom, and was crowned on Christmas Day of that year.

In a work written by one of the bishops of Toledo in honour of the Virgin, and transcribed by a priest named Gomes, he gives the date 989 thus: D.CCCC.LXXXVIIII. In a receipt signed by Agnes Sorel in acknowledging gifts from Charles VII., we have the date "le xviiime jour d'Avril l'an mil cccc quarante huit," that is, April 18, 1448. The sum received was given thus: "ij^cLxxv livres tournois." On her tomb, after her death, the date is M.CCCC.XL.IX. = 1449.

At this early period we sometimes meet with dates of Arabic numbers: thus we find that Pope Clement VI. presented a Bible to Sainte Chapelle of Bourges, by Robinet d'Etampes, the receipt for which is dated "le 6ᵉ jour de juillet, 1406."[1]

To show some of the various methods of dating documents, the following may be given: 684 = VICLXXXIIII; 1338 = mil trois cens xxxviij. I have already remarked that, for a considerable time after the introduction of the Arabic numerals, they were used conjointly with Roman numerals: thus we have 1547 given MD × 47, and 1558 MID58. On some of the old calendars we have 4 represented

[1] See Sylvestre's *Palæography*, vol. ii

as λ, the upper part of **8**: thus $1^872=$ 1472, and $1^888=1484$. In Mr. Gladstone's visiting-book there **is an entry made by the Archbishop of Sym and** Paros, the date being given thus: I͞η 29 Δεϲϲεμβριαν 1869 / 30 Javragh 1870; **1678 is found in this form,** MDLL, LXVV, VIII / 1600 70 8.

The following is a Saxon date: IcccxxxIII $=1333$. Here ɪ with a dot over it is increased a thousandfold. In the national manuscripts of Scotland there are some curious dates. Here is a Gaelic contract, for example, where 1614 is expressed by mile 6. c. ⩞. 4. x. There are here, as will be seen, two peculiarities in this date. It would appear that the character coming between c and 4 is meant for *and*. Moreover, the position of 4 and **x** is singular, being reversed, and contrary to the usual method of writing **14**, the recognised rule being that when a smaller number is prefixed to a larger one it is subtracted from the larger one.

In commencing **this paper, I stated** that in looking over some old documents that I brought with me when I came **to** Canada I found **a** peculiar method **of** expressing the dates in a number of them. These documents, I may state, consist of charters, receipts, leases of land, bonds, instruments of sasine, etc. Some of them are in Latin, others in Scotch, as then used, which presents many peculiarities in spelling, contractions, and **forms of** letters now obsolete, whose **decipherment, in many cases,** is difficult **to make out.** The **earliest** specimen **of the method referred to in my possession is an instrument** of sasine of date 1640, **expressed** thus, "Jaybj⸳⅋ fourte yeires," where it **will** be seen that the odd years, other than the centuries, **are** written in the usual way. In a document signed by the Earl of Wigton, the date is given "the third day of Julii Jaⱶbiᶜ and three scoir yeirs," that is, 1660. In another document called a *Carta Confirmationis*, also signed by the Earl of Wigton, the year is written 1673, but the body of the document and the date are in Latin. In a receipt I found that "Jaybi⅋ nyntie" and "1691" are used, the former being the year for which the receipt was given, the latter when the money was paid. I might mention that this receipt first afforded a clue to the meaning of these cabalistic-looking **letters,** which at first were a puzzle **to me. In the** two following dates, **1709 and 1710,** given thus, "Jaybjjᶜ⅋ nine," and "Jaybjjᶜ⅋ ten," **there is** a deviation from examples given **above,** where c as well as that peculiar **character ⅋ are both used. The fact seems to** be that at this early period in **Scotland** there was no general established **method** of writing dates. Sometimes they **are given** in Latin, at other times in **Roman** characters, again in Arabic numbers, and very frequently—indeed most frequently—in the manner now under consideration. I have corresponded with a number of gentlemen in regard to the meaning of the first three letters "*Jay*," but I find there is quite a diversity of opinion about them, no two of **them** agreeing in all respects. For **example,** an Edinburgh gentleman, who is considered **an** expert **in** reading old **manuscripts**, says that "**taking** Jajviiᶜ = 1700, the first three letters are a corruption of the original Runic form of M = 1000." Another gentleman suggests that *Jay* may be equal to Iai (sc. anni) = 1000 years. Having written to Dr. Dickson, of the Register House in Edinburgh, who is a recognised authority on matters of this kind, he kindly replied in the following terms: "Your question is one that is very often asked, and yet I do not remember to have seen it explained in any book. Of the explanations you suggest, the second is substantially correct. The number 1000, written jη, was, by a slight change in the form of the η, written jⱶ. Ignorance then interposed and put a dot over the **last** stroke of ⱶ, and closing up the first part of it made the whole jaj. bijᶜ⅋ is simply vijᶜ with an unmeaning terminal flourish (⅋) common in the seventeenth and eighteenth centuries." He further states that these letters are constantly heard used in law offices read phonetically. I might mention that I had sent him several solutions which had been suggested. The second one referred to by him as substantially correct was that *J* stood for I, and *ay*, usually found as *aⱶ* in old script, represents M = 1000. I feel disposed to question the correctness of Dr. Dickson's treatment of the letter *J* in the dates that I have given. I may say that, since hearing from him, I have found other somewhat similar dates which seem to show that *J* stands for I. For example, in a lease I find the date 1774 is given thus: "mvⱶⱶ⅋ and seventy-four." Again, in the oath taken by William and Mary on their acceptance of the throne of Scotland, the document referring to this ends thus: "Signed by

us at Whitehall the eleventh day of May jɑ/bi 8^c four score and nyne years.
   "WILLIAM R.   MARY R."

In the printed form accompanying this, 1689 is thus given, "j^{m}vjc^e," etc. I also find in a document given to the Earl of Murray by Mary Queen of Scots 1565 is written "j^{m}v^{c}lxv."
   "(Signed) MARIE R."

In the Acts of the Parliaments of Charles I. the following are given: "Act in favo'g of Dame Margaret Graham at Edinburgh the ffirst day of ffebruar the ycir of god J^{m}vijc'," and attached to another Act of the "Commiseris of the Comoun burdens" the date is the nynteenth of August J^{m}vjc' fourtie twa yeers." Here obviously m or M represents 1000, and hence the only possible use for the J is that it stands for I; and this view is confirmed by the date mv^{c}ij 8 and seventy-four given above, where the j is omitted. In *The History of Biggar and the House of Fleming* there is a document signed by the "Errl of Athol," Chancellor of Scotland, etc., which concludes as follows: "servit w^t o^r hand in Edinburgh ye zeir of god ye xxvii Oct. Jav 8^e thre scoir auchtene zeirs." Here Jav 8° is used for 1500; but why this is so I am unable to conjecture, unless it be that a mistake has been made in the printing, the y having been left out.

It is worthy of notice that a similar method of expressing dates was at one time in use in Fr. docs. Thus, in the *Jugements et Délibérations du Conseil de la Nouvelle France*, 1675 is thus given: "gbic soixante quinze." I find that on Feb. 1, 1700 = gbiic is found for the last time, and that in all subsequent dates the modern method is used. Here probably g is meant for M, and $b = v$.

Calendars and almanacs came into use in England about the middle of the fifteenth century, and some of the early specimens contained many curious matters, often dealing largely in omens and forecasts of the future.

In one of these we have a "prognostycacyon of Mayster John Thybalt, medycyner and astronomer of the Emperyall Majestie of the year of our Lord God MCCCCCXXXIIJ. (sc. 1533), comprehending the iiij partes of this year, with the constellacions of them that be under the vij planettes, and the revolucions of kyngs, and princes, and of the eclipses and comets."

The date of the reform of the calendar in 1700 is curiously and ingeniously recorded, as shown by Sir John Bowring, where the date is variously indicated by enlarged letters. In one of these chronograms, as they are called, we find Geen *D*erten *CaL*en*D*ers *D*enkzah *L*, that is, DDDCLL (1700), "In remembrance of the reformation of the Calendar."

The following is an example of the same whimsical device from the name of George Villiers, first Duke of Buckingham: GEORG-*IV*s, *DVX*, D*VCk*Inga*M*Iae, the date being $\frac{\text{MDC}}{1600} \frac{\text{XVV}}{20} \frac{\text{VIII}}{8}$ (1628). Here is one in Latin on a medal struck by Gustavus Adolphus: *Ch*ristVs *DVX*; ergotr*IVM*ph*V*s, that is, 100 + 1 + 5 + 500 + 5 + 10 + 1 + 5 + 1000 + 5 = 1632.

A great deal of confusion has arisen from the different systems adopted in dating manuscripts. Sometimes they were dated by the year of indiction, sometimes by the year of the Christian era, sometimes from the commencement of the reign of kings, etc. Another source of confusion arose by commencing the year from different days in different countries, such as the 25th of March, the 25th of December, or 1st January. Without, however, entering more fully into a detailed statement of these, I may state that, to obviate this source of trouble and to regulate the commencement of the year in Britain, an Act of George II., 1751, was passed, making the commencement of the legal year the first day of January. The year 1751, which began on the 25th of March, was brought to a close on the 31st December, but was reduced by eleven days in the month of September, by calling the day after the 2nd the 14th, thus adopting the reformed calendar of Gregory XIII., known as that of the "New Style." Curiously enough, when this took place, we are told that bands of labouring men went round calling out, "Give us back the lost days," supposing that they had been robbed of eleven days. In countries under the Greek Church, such as Russia and Greece, the Julian Calendar, or, as it is called, "Old Style," is still in use, and in some country parts of Scotland, up to a comparatively recent time, the old style was observed.

JOHN THORBURN.

[Note: It has not been found possible to do more than imitate the signs and marks used in old documents, owing to there being no equivalents in modern printing founts.]

THE APPRAISAL OF LITERATURE.

HE American Library Association this year comes of age, and auspiciously marks the event by crossing the Atlantic to exchange counsel and cheer with its British cousin. At such a season a word of retrospect may be in order, carrying with it, as it must, somewhat of forecast.

When the American librarian takes a backward glance as far as '76, and contrasts what he was able to do then with what he can do now, he finds abundant room for gratulation. Every passing year has meant more of usefulness, a corresponding growth of public regard. Toward this happy issue influences of two kinds have impelled him.

The first of these influences was born with the Association itself. In the very act of union there was an inevitable strengthening of hands. At the yearly musters workers from lonely outposts, or from busy centres slow to acknowledge the claims of literature, have been comforted and inspired. They have found how goodly the army in which they were enlisted. Old friendships have been quickened and deepened; new friendships, soon as warm, have been kindled at every gathering. A young man, just across the threshold of his profession, would bring his perplexities with trustees or aldermen to the sympathetic ear of an elder. Forthwith the Hill Difficulty, which had so much dismayed him, would disclose the easiest of curves and gentlest of gradients. At these meetings, too, administrative details, upon which so much of success may turn, have year by year been compared and discussed, until now they emerge as a tolerably clear code of practice. There is substantial agreement to-day as to how our buildings should be constructed, planned, and furnished; how books should be selected, classified, and placed in the hands of the public. Meanwhile, the publication of indexes, bibliographies, and the like, has gone on apace —aids which would never have seen the light without the Association to create them and provide their market. Alliances, already fruitful and big with promise, have united the public library with the public school, the art gallery and the museum. And one State after another wheels into line, to form a chain of library commissions, soon to stretch, let us hope, from Maine to California. How much all this would astonish the old-time librarian who here and there lingered on the stage of '76! A grim warder of alcoves was he, grudgingly dispensing his stores to a favoured few, reluctance in his step, suspicion in his eye. To-day we have no more turnkeys of literature, but bankers rather, whose capital is accumulated in the sole aim that its value be multiplied fifty- or a hundred-fold by the freest using. The librarian's doors stand open; he all but compels us to come in. Little wonder that his hospitality is requited by the heartiest public appreciation. In not a few of our towns and cities the public library is the acknowledged centre of intellectual life, of every movement which stirs the once separated and removed cream of culture back again into the plain people's milk—to enrich their toil, to sweeten their leisure, to lift and widen their outlook. Let a user of libraries, who owes much to librarians, here add his word of thanks to the general chorus.

But forces other than those active within the profession have profoundly stirred the librarian's pulse. They were potent enough two decades ago, to-day they are simply irresistible. They move under the banner of science. It is applied science which has augmented wealth and so diffused education that the ability to write a book

—of some kind or other—is commoner than ever, while the cost of the making falls lower and lower. The first and most evident result, then, of the reign of science is to engulf the librarian in a flood-tide of printed matter, which mounts higher and sweeps faster every twelvemonth. In the United States alone about 80,000 new books or new editions have been published since '76. To pass from quantity to the weightier matter of theme, new books by the thousand deal with subjects barely recognised, or indeed utterly unimagined twenty-one years ago. Consider the recent advances in chemistry, especially in its single department of photography ; bestow a glance at the triumphs of bacteriology, with its new defiance of disease and death. In '76 aluminium was still made into jewellery, to-day electricity gives it to us as kitchenware. The new physics—chemistry, biology, psychology, and the rest—have been won in large measure by new instruments of exquisite ingenuity. These sciences converge in welding a body of scientific method in itself incomparably more powerful as an instrument of exploration than telephone, or spectroscope, or Röntgen bulb. So revolutionary are the victories of science, that literature, to its remotest corner, breathes its ozone, its stimulus to scrupulous exactitude, to unfaltering faithfulness to fact directly observed and patiently interpreted. Accordingly, we to-day find the candour, once rare in biography, steadily growing common. Plain speaking certainly went its full length last year in Hare's *Story of My Life*, Hamerton's autobiography, and Purcell's *Life of Cardinal Manning*. As a shining example of the modern historian, take Francis Parkman. With toil unwearied, and at an outlay only to be met by a private fortune, he gathered the documents upon which his works were based. These documents, open to his critics, are in the library of the Massachusetts Historical Society in Boston. Mr. Parkman visited every town and hamlet which he has described. Frequently in the foreground of his canvas are Indian chiefs and tribes ; wherever their descendants survived, he sought familiar acquaintance with them. Hence he gives us those minor traits of race that are detected only in close and sympathetic scrutiny, together with the traditions, the fringe and tassel of custom, never to be conveyed in second-hand impressions. Whether such a man as Parkman devotes his life to the telescope, the test-tube, or the pen, equally is he the servant of truth.

Turn we for a moment to the novelist, and we shall see him bowing to the new sceptre, for all that his imagination is as chainless as ever. There is Stevenson, in his last days at Samoa, penning his strongest romance, **Weir of Hermiston**, and minded to try Archie Weir on a charge of murder elsewhere than at Edinburgh. But could he do so with truth ? He deemed it incumbent to question a legal friend in far-away Scotland. The response, with its detail of time, court, and place, delighted him ; all was reserved for fullest use. Introducing a fact as a fact, novelists before Stevenson have been careful, but his scrupulous anxiety is quite characteristic of a day when chemists are engaged on analyses true to the fifty-thousandth part, by the help of scales freely turning with a half-millionth of their load. And what does naturalism, that scrofulous offspring of realism, attempt but to tell the truth about the gutter and the sty ? And further, if we refresh ourselves in peering for a moment over the fence that divides letters from art, we shall again see the dominion of the spirit which makes for reality, for immediate impressions, for consent between partners too long at cross purposes. Observe Seymour Haden as he etches a landscape, not from a sketch in the seclusion of his studio, but at the very brookside itself. See Timothy Cole in the presence of the masterpieces of Da Vinci and Raphael, translating their ineffable beauty on the block before him. Note Meissonier as he corrects his drawings of the horse at full gallop with the aid of an eye swifter and surer than his own—that of the instantaneous camera. Listen to Wagner, who, beginning his career when an opera was formed of a libretto and a score that looked askance at each other, gives us at last the music-drama, in which sound echoes sense, in which language and music but interpret and exalt each other.

To return to the library. It is of course in the field of its own literature that the compulsions of science chiefly appear. A little more than a century ago Oliver Goldsmith could indite a *History of Animated Nature*, not because he knew more than his neighbours about animated nature, but because he could re-state the writings of others—themselves perhaps borrowers —with fluent grace. To-day, for the task he assumed so light of heart, how elaborate would be the attack ! First of all would be installed, as editor-in-chief, a naturalist whose mastery of a particular branch of natural history had brought maturity of judgment as to work in other branches. Around him would be assembled a corps of specialists, each a man of wide and thorough familiarity with birds or insects, beasts or fish. Every chapter would be copiously illustrated by the camera. The multitudinous facts of form, colour, and habit would be threaded upon clue-lines of cause and law, while philosophy would redeem, for illustration and instance, every jot and tittle of detail otherwise oppressive through sheer mass and variety. The naturalists of Goldsmith's day looked upon nature as a tableau disposed by the Master long ago, to stand unchanged for ever. The naturalists of our time show us that in truth nature is a drama, of shifting scenes, of personalities mutable to the very core, moulded by forces as coercive now as in the illimitable past. A change of view surely no more significant for science than for its twin phase of reality, literature.

Those historians-in-the-large, the evolutionists, tell us that chief among the faculties of mind which have lifted man from brute are those which flower in language. Golden though the spoken or written word may be, immeasurable harm has been done by its permitted usurpations. Too often the writer, who should first have been an observer, an explorer, a doer, has been but a scribe, putting forth with a scribe's lack of authority the distortions of hearsay, the unavoidable falsities of second- or third-hand impressions. Why does so dreary a desert separate the science of Aristotle from the science of Galileo—a desert across which commentator and disputant flit, one after another, all with empty hands? Simply because Aristotle was followed only in the repetition and discussion of what he had said, not in his direct appeal to fact. Only when nature was probed anew in his own fearless way did the reign of the schoolmen come to an end, did man enter upon his modern comprehension of nature, the new mastery of his fate. We have only to turn the pages of metaphysical abstraction to come upon words that float in a serene detachment from real things, from genuine thoughts, words independent of the solid earth, and useless there. In the juvenile debating clubs of the last generation a favourite question was, "Is the pen mightier than the sword?" Commanders, all the way from Julius Cæsar to General Grant, have demonstrated that the pen is never mightier than when the sword has been laid down that the pen might be taken up. And in other fields than those of war the pen has might only because the chisel or the brush, the scalpel or the lens, has been exchanged for it. To-day, therefore, we find the desk set up in the workshop, the studio, the laboratory, with incalculable profit to literature. The new books of science gain by qualifications, exceptions, sidelights from bafflement and failure, a value incomparably greater than was possible in the recent days which it is no disrespect to call pre-scientific. Thus draws to its term the ancient discord between theory and practice ; theory takes on modification and limit in the face of the complexities which it is the darling vice of language to ignore or over-simplify. Practice, enlightened by generalisation, passes from the rule of thumb to the sway of law. By virtue, too, of a knowledge which comprehends many a distant province of truth, there spring up what Clerk Maxwell happily called the cross-fertilisations of science. The physicist has only to dig deep enough to find that the chemist and himself occupy common ground. Delve from the surface of your sphere to its heart, and your radius at once joins every other. Mark Sir Archibald Geikie, as in his *Geology* he cheerfully lays hands on what the physicist and chemist, the astronomer and meteorologist, might once have regarded as estates exclusively their own. Behold, also, the fruitful reaction of adequate records upon invention and discovery as they march to new victories. Visit Mr. Edison, and you will find his library as generously equipped as his laboratory.

Perhaps in no part of our modern life is the new adjustment of words and deeds more telling than in education. In our best schools, all the way from the kindergarten to the university, books are being gradually withdrawn from work they should never have been allowed to perform. No longer is memorising the printed page the be-all and the end-all of instruction. Anything that should be observed *is* observed ; anything that should be done *is* done, instead of being merely talked or written about. Books come in for reference, for direction, as means of continuous explanation, as sources of knowledge concerning observations, experiments, generalisations far beyond the horizon of the student.

Restricted thus to its rightful sphere, a book rises to a utility, because it has a truth it could not know when the word was a substitute for the act, instead of being its complement.

In those wider spheres of letters whose aim is recreation, charm, inspiration, there is obedience to the same tidal impulses. We have a fiction as true in essence as history; a body of poetry as rightly echoing the perplexities and aspirations of our age as the pages of a cautious analyst may record the commonplaces of trade and treaty. The novelist, the dramatist, the essayist, all the writers who are the servants of beauty, are to-day effectively so in proportion to their allegiance to truth. Thus are the standards of literary criticism heightened and sharpened by that world-movement whose citadel is science, whose conquests are arrayed in provinces of new knowledge, such as no thousand years before our century ever won.

The motto of the American Library Association is, "The best reading for the largest number at the least cost." But how shall we know what part of the enormous mass of modern reading is best, and what other part, while not best, is still useful enough to repay the reader or student? You may tell me that reviewing is a somewhat ancient institution, that from among the criticisms which appear anonymously in such a journal as the *Nation*, of New York, or under signatures in such periodicals as the *American Historical Review* and the *Political Science Quarterly*, there is much to meet our want. But such reviews, good as they are, do not fill the need of the librarian's public; commonly they are too long, too discursive; how shall they be readily found when wanted? What is needed is a brief note of description, criticism, and comparison, written by an acknowledged authority, signed and dated, and placed where the reader cannot help seeing it, both within the lid of the reviewed book itself and on a card next the title card in the catalogue—it being assumed that, according to the practice more and more prevailing in America, a card-catalogue is freely accessible to all. If a book treats of a question in debate, as socialism or bimetallism, fact and opinion should be carefully distinguished, and views of opposed critics might be presented. By this means the inquirer would know which book is best or among the best of its kind; he would be made aware of the defects which mar even the best books; he would learn how one work can gainfully piece out another, and would gather indication of the periodicals or transactions which bring a story of discovery or research down to date. In a final line he might be told where detailed reviews are to be found.

And where shall we find the persons qualified to undertake all this arduous business of appraisal? Chiefly, I think, in the ranks of professional reviewers. Many of these are busy in classrooms, bringing books daily to the severest test of experiment and study. Let them go on writing reviews of customary length for their present employers, and let them also boil down these reviews for us. Wherever necessary, other critics, skilled for the service we require, may lend their aid. Thus shall the seeker and the knower be brought together; thus may everyone who enters a public library have at his elbow competent and trustworthy pilots through the swirling sea of literature. Instruction or recreation may then be pursued with the utmost effect and pleasure, because with the soundest available intelligence. Of course this aid should not be confined to the literature of utility. Why should pleasure in fiction or belles-lettres be flabby when it can so easily be hearty?

Fiction, indeed, in the circulation of some of our libraries rises to a figure exceeding 80 per cent. With this fact in mind, and believing a large part of the fiction to be poor stuff, Mr. Goldwin Smith impugns the whole principle of supporting free libraries out of the public treasury. "People," he says, "have no more right to novels than to theatre tickets out of the public taxes." The point of his objection can be turned only in one way—by seeing to it that only good fiction is placed upon the shelves. Exclusion, courageous and tactful, must be the policy here. Mr. W. M. Stevenson, librarian of the Carnegie Library, Alleghany, Pennsylvania, has dropped from his catalogue a round of novels popular enough but lacking literary merit. To the demand, Why cannot we have what we like, instead of what you think we ought to like? the answer must be, Read Austen, Cooper, Scott, Thackeray, Dickens, Hawthorne, and Stevenson, and you will soon thank us for withholding Mrs. Holmes and Mr. Roe, your appetite for their screeds being irrecoverably lost.

Reading, for all that Dogberry may say, does not come by nature; neither, when the art of reading is acquired, is it spontaneously partnered with power to choose the most gainful and pleasure-giving books. Just as fast as the school educates the public in the intelligent choice of literature, with equal pace will vanish the charge that the public library does aught but public good. There is a difficulty much more serious than that of wishy-washy fiction, with regard to novels of the Satanic school, deliberately produced to contaminate. Against these it is high time that danger signals were set up, so that neither carelessness nor accident may allow their intrusion.

The steps taken in America toward engaging the best available guidance for readers and students in our public libraries are briefly these: About twenty years ago Professor W. G. Sumner, of Yale University, drew up for his classes a short list of works on political economy, with notes. This list, enlarged to an annotated pamphlet of thirty-six pages, was soon after published in New York by the Society for Political Education. The pamphlet was favourably received, and when it passed out of print a widespread demand arose for its reissue in expanded form. Accordingly, the *Reader's Guide in Economic, Social, and Political Literature*—a book of some one hundred and sixty pages—was issued in 1891. In its preparation, the editors, Mr. R. R. Bowker and myself, were assisted by a score of representative American and English specialists. The *Guide* met with a warm reception. Copies of it are to be seen in college libraries, thumbed almost to tatters. To this day it is doing good service in hundreds of editorial offices, classrooms, and public libraries. An appendix to it may appear next year. The next demand for an annotated bibliography came from the clubs of girls and women, which are constantly increasing in number and importance, and are establishing libraries by scores every month. To meet this need, Mrs. Augusta H. Leypoldt, editor of the *Literary News*, New York, and myself edited two years ago, for the American Library Association, *A List of Books for Girls and Women and their Clubs*. This bibliography comprises 2100 titles in the leading branches of literature. Each of its departments was contributed by a man or woman of authority. Although specifically addressed to girls and women, and setting forth especially the books which deal with their livelihoods and home toil, the *List* in the main is as useful to boys and men as to their sisters and mothers. The notes on good literature which chiefly fill it appeal to all readers. Take an example of its usefulness: Wisconsin is an agricultural State, with a population for the most part centred in small towns and villages. The chairman of the State Library Commission, Mr. F. A. Hutchins, writes that the *List* has doubled and quadrupled the purchasing power of the few dollars usually available in forming or extending small libraries. In Milwaukee, much the largest city in the State, the question might be, Which is the best exposition of Browning's *The Ring and the Book*? But what the village of Fox Lake wants to know is, Which are Dickens' six best books, and which are the best editions for six dollars?

Two departments of the *List for Girls and Women* proved particularly helpful—that of fine art, by Mr. Russell Sturgis, and that of music, by Mr. H. E. Krehbiel. Accordingly, these two critics, each a master in his field, were engaged for a fairly full bibliography of Fine Art, about one thousand titles in all. This work, which I edited, also issued by the American Library Association, appeared March 1897, and has thus far met with a gratifying reception. However much we may wish to see notes of appraisal printed on catalogue-cards, it will always be desirable to give book form as well to such notes as those of Mr. Sturgis and Mr. Krehbiel. Only thus can the reader take connected views of his subject, observe the canons of criticism in their broad application, and gather those suggestions which teem from a richly-freighted mind as, in one masterly effort, it passes upon a whole literature, from the first noteworthy volume to the last. The next task of the American Library Association, in the way of appraisal, will probably be a bibliography of American history. A scholar of the highest competence has said that, if possible, he will act as its editor-in-chief, giving his services gratuitously. An attempt will be made to issue its notes in both book and card form. Following this task, we hope to issue a bibliography of applied science: for its departments we are already volunteered the aid of several contributors of mark. What I should like to see would be a series of bibliographics covering with tolerable completeness the whole round of literature, and comprising a selection of about ten thousand works. With these as a basis we might enlist our contributors for the appraisal of every noteworthy book as it leaves the press, distributing the notes on cards. In Boston is an agency of the publishing section of the American Library Association, which selects from current literature and issues title cards for a circle of subscribing libraries,—this with a view to introducing uniformity, and of paying one printer instead of fifty. By adding notes of appraisal in the future, the value of this service could be vastly heightened.

What our publishing section is clearly moving toward is the foundation of a central superintendency (the title Library Bureau is pre-empted), which shall oversee this whole business of appraisal, of entering into relations with the plans, now international in scope, for indexing scientific and other literature, which shall make it easy to establish new libraries on sound lines, and to extend existing libraries with the utmost economy and efficiency. From the work of such a superintendency manifold gain would arise. Throughout America there are constantly appearing annotated lists of works on economics and history, folk-lore and what not. The labour which goes into their production, much of it duplicated, and all of it local, both in origin and utility, might easily be organised for the service of the whole country, with a decided improvement in quality, a saving in time and strength. A systematic effort might also be made to rescue from neglect the great books which, from such causes as the untimely death of their authors or the sheer brunt of advertisement, are overlaid by new and much inferior writing. To a competent hand might be committed, for example, the sifting out all that still retains worth and interest in Bagehot, who was at once an economist, a wit, and a literary critic of distinction. Much that he wrote was for his own day, much remains of the rarest value for our day. What is true of Bagehot is true of Jevons, and of many more. We are not so much concerned about the newest books as about the best. Much might be done also in bestowing upon boys and girls a thorough familiarity with the great classics. Here our hope lies in school libraries, chosen with the most enlightened care. There are, let us say, fifty books which everyone should read between his tenth year and his fifteenth; let us enlist "the concensus of the competent" in drawing up a list of these works, and then, by creating a demand for good and cheap editions, stimulate to the full, not simply acquaintance but intimacy with the masterpieces of all time. A minor service, well worth rendering, is in pointing out which books of the voluminous masters are best worth having. Not more than half Scott's are, and perhaps not so large a fraction of Cooper's. Publishers are interested in supplying complete sets; we desire to see small libraries expend their few dollars for the best choice possible.

No one has gone very far in bibliography without discovering many gaps even in copious literatures. In the *Atlantic Monthly* for June 1893 Mr. Justin Winsor described the Société Franklin of Paris, which acts as a central agency for the libraries of France. It has found that, with an assured sale for its round of libraries, a trained writer and a responsible publisher can be engaged to supply any needed book. This plan avoids the heavy tax for advertising inexorable when a new book lacks an organised circle of buyers. In the ordinary practice of publishing, the odd purchaser here and there, hit through the press, well-nigh costs his weight in ammunition. When the *List for Girls and Women* was being edited, it became clear that, however imperious the voice of science may be upstairs, its echoes in the kitchen are rumblings of the faintest. Scarcely one cook-book in a hundred recognises that cooking is a branch of chemistry, having vital relations as well with physiology and economics. In the colleges where domestic economy is taught, I have been informed that its themes, in their scientific treatment still in the experimental stage, are as yet not crystallised into literature. In this department of household well-being take a singular example of a lack where one would expect repletion. For years the electric light companies have waged war upon the gas interest. One would suppose that the fight would give us many a good pamphlet on the incandescent mantle which multiplies the light from gas, on the multifarious uses of gas for cooking, heating, and manufacturing. Yet not a page on the subject could I find published in America two years ago. Nor could I discover any succinct, connected description of the scores of ingenious devices for relieving household drudgery which attract the eye at every American fair. Nor, so far as I know, is there to this day any brief account of the principles which underlie the judicious care of property—a matter of prime importance, especially to women who may inherit an estate with little qualification for its guardianship. The fact is, publishing is a somewhat haphazard business, and librarians organised for the public behoof can on occasion do something to supply a declared want for a pamphlet or a book. Every twelvemonth sees works on rhetoric, botany, geometry, tumbling from the press by the score; but scarcely ever a book to tell ordinary people an acceptable word about the sciences of food and clothing, shelter and health. Much is said, and truly, about the claims of original research; much, with equal truth, may be said for giving knowledge already acquired the widest diffusion.

Here a word of caution must be spoken. Easy it is to say that a book is needed; it may be impossible to lay hands upon the writer who should give it to the world. Why is there no American work on zoology as sound and good as that on botany by Asa Gray? Because America has no zoologist the size of Asa Gray. Literature lacks a comprehensive work on American forestry; but think of the extent and variety of American forests! So recently has their systematic study been begun, that the first American to be thoroughly trained and equipped for the task is still a young man.

To sum up, on one side stands the great public, encompassed by mountains of books rising ever higher and higher; on the other side stand the critics, who know which of these books are best, which are merely good, or offer here and there a helpful chapter or page. It is plainly time that these critics were judiciously organised by librarians for the aid and comfort of the great public who read or study or may be induced to read or study. The spirit of science has entered the world of letters, but in more than one province of its empire there is sturdy resistance to its sway—an echo is still heard where there should only be a voice. Let every movement that makes for accuracy, sincerity, truth, in literature, be generously and wisely promoted, and in the only possible way—by organisation, with its attendant boons of economy and scope. In these latter days of democracy culture ceases to be the possession of a caste, of a class apart, and works as a leaven throughout the whole mass of the people. To-day workmen and clerks listen to the university lecturer; the great art of the present and the past migrates from the metropolitan museum to the suburban hall; in the concert-room Beethoven and Bach are now appealing to the million instead of the upper ten thousand. So also in the field of literature, the records of the best that has been thought and done in the world grow in volume and value every hour. Speed the day when they may be hospitably proffered to every human soul, the chaff winnowed from the wheat, the gold divided from the clay.

GEORGE ILES.

LIBRARY WORK IN JAMAICA.

N accepting the invitation of the Organising Committee to read a paper before the International Library Conference, I do so with diffidence, for I feel that I can do but little to aid in the important work which will be placed before the meeting. As the committee has left me unfettered as to choice of subject, I have thought I could not do better than say a few words—I much regret that I have to say them by proxy—on library work in Jamaica in general; for, living on a bypath of civilisation, as it were, we in Jamaica must of necessity follow, in the main, the rules laid down in the great centres, modifying them only in so far as our local needs may demand.

The conditions of life in the West Indies are by no means conducive to successful work on the part of the librarian.

In the past, any time that was spared by the sugar-planter or pen-keeper from the making of sugar and rum and the rearing of stock was, for the most part, devoted to political strife with the local administration or the home government, or to amusement of a not highly intellectual character.

In the "great house" of an estate in the so-called palmy days, it was quite the exception to find either a bookcase or pictures. There have, of course, been a few exceptions, but as a rule it was not the planting class which produced Jamaica's few men of letters and book-lovers—*e.g.* Edward Long, the historian, was a judge and Speaker of the House of Assembly, and Bryan Edwards, the historian, was a merchant; but Michael Scott, the author of the ever-green *Tom Cringle's Log*, was, it is true, engaged in agricultural as well as mercantile pursuits. Of men of letters who have visited and written in and of Jamaica, the best known are Sir Hans Sloane; "Peter Pindar"; William Beckford, cousin of the author of *Vathek*; Dr. Wright; Dr. Dancer; William James, the naval historian; "Monk" Lewis and Philip Henry Gosse; but they have only imparted information about Jamaica in England, and have had no influence in forming a taste for literature in the island. Gosse's collaborateur, Richard Hill, a distinguished native of the island, and an ardent student of natural history, laboured also in the cause of literature.

At the beginning of the present century, if we may believe the "gentleman long resident in the West Indies," J. Stewart by name, who published in 1808 *An Account of Jamaica and its Inhabitants*, literature was but little considered in the island.

"Literature," he says, "is little cultivated in Jamaica; nor is reading a very general favourite amusement. There is a circulating library in Kingston, and in one or two other places a paltry attempt at such a thing, these collections of books not being of that choice and miscellaneous nature which they ought to be, but usually composed of a few good novels, mixed with a much larger proportion of those ephemeral ones which are daily springing up, and which are a disgrace to literature and an insult to common-sense."

He further tells us that two attempts at publishing periodicals, intended to diffuse literary taste and promote useful local knowledge, failed, partly by reason of too high a subscription (16 dollars per annum for twelve numbers), and partly because much of the contents was mere transcript from British journals; but he adds, "It is true that the number of subscribers never was good enough to give a fair encouragement to the work." Doubtless the same remarks might be applied with truth to other similar undertakings.

The earliest libraries of any kind in the island were those of the Legislative Council and the House of Assembly, each of which had a collection of books of its own. But they were only intended for the use of members, and the librarians were apparently nothing more than custodians of books. At times the office was held by the sergeant-at-arms, the assistant clerk, or by the messenger. At another time the librarian received £100 per annum, while the messenger received £200.

The library of the Assembly, which may fairly be regarded as the parent of the library of the Institute of Jamaica—for to the former the latter owes a large proportion of its best volumes—consisted chiefly of books treating on law, history, and travel, biography and science, and was intended primarily for the use of the Governor of the island, and all who were connected with the Legislature.

When, in 1872, the seat of government was removed from Spanish Town to Kingston, the library of the House of Assembly was transferred to the new capital, and was first opened as a public library in 1874, in Date Tree Hall, which had been for many years utilised as one of those hostelries—half hotel and half boarding-house—commonly met with in former times in Jamaica. Though it is solid and fairly suitable to the climate as a dwelling-house, it is but ill adapted or adaptable for the purposes of a library; but in it the best that can be done under the circumstances is now being done in the cause of literature.

Other smaller libraries have existed from time to time, but they have lasted only for a comparatively short period, and have exercised no permanent influence on the community.

In 1798 the Kingston Medical Society, which had been instituted four years earlier, had formed a library of sufficient importance to require a librarian. By 1832 the society was apparently defunct, and no traces of its library remain. In 1824 was established, in the parish of St. George, a St. George's Library Society. In 1838 it had seventy-nine members. It existed until 1882, when the books of the society were transferred to the library of the Institute of Jamaica.

In 1836 there was an Athenæum Club formed in Kingston. Attached to it was an extensive library, composed of the most literary, useful, and entertaining works. In 1838 we first find a record of the St. Elizabeth Library, and in 1840 an entry of a St. James's Library Association. In 1850 the old Jamaica Society, which had been founded in 1827 for the cultivation of agriculture and other arts and sciences, ceased to exist, and the property, including the library, was distributed amongst the late contributing members. In its stead was formed, "for the improvement of all classes and the development of the talent which exists—but exists in a latent form—in the island," the Colonial Literary and Reading Society. The then Governor became patron. The annual subscription was at first four shillings a month, but was subsequently reduced to half a crown. In the first four months of its existence 438 volumes were borrowed by readers. The library included copies of *Bohn's Library*, *Murray's Home and Colonial Library*, and the *Family Library*. The society did much useful work for many years, but its existence must have been at times precarious, for at its second half-yearly meeting it discussed and settled a possible division of its property amongst members in the event of its dissolution; and at its third a reference was made to the difficulty experienced in collecting subscriptions. However, in the fourth half-year, with a total of 1105 volumes, no fewer than 1689 books were lent out. At the fifth half-yearly meeting, in May 1852, the committee recorded its opinion that "the society has not only made indubitable and substantial progress, but that, speaking advisedly and in all sincerity, it has attained to such a maturity of age and stability of position as, while they almost preclude positive declension, give ample reason for contemplating the permanent existence of their charge."

After many years of usefulness, however, the society was merged into the Kingston Literary and Reading Society. When this broke up, about the year 1878, the books were distributed amongst its members.

In 1852 the local literary societies existing in the various parishes into which the island is divided had received an addition by the foundation of the St. Catherine Literary Society at Spanish Town; and four years later the Trelawny Literary Society was founded in Falmouth, and the St. Ann's Literary and Reading Society in St. Ann's Bay. In 1867 was founded, through the instrumentality of Sir Francis M'Clintock, who was then commodore of the Jamaica station, the

Port Royal Literary and Mechanics' Institution, which was supported by the Hon. Richard Hill and other men of literary and scientific attainments. Other societies probably existed during the earlier part of the century of which no records are now obtainable.

But in 1869 the only learned societies recorded in the almanac for that year (one of a series dating from 1751 to the present time, in the library of the Institute) were the Royal Society of Arts and Agriculture and the Kingston Literary and Reading Society, both of which were unfortunately waning.

The lesson which one may apparently learn from the history of the few abovementioned of the many societies which have existed in Kingston and in other towns in the island during the eighteenth and nineteenth centuries, is that in a community like that of Jamaica voluntary societies founded at moments of temporary enthusiasm are dependent in great measure on the activity and pecuniary and moral support of a few individuals, and that, so soon as the support is lost, through death or removal, the societies decline. Where the financial conditions are dependent on yearly subscriptions there is no certainty of long life, and, moreover, where the committees of management are self-appointing, there is little likelihood of continuity of policy, without which there can be no permanent success.

Coming from the past to the present, we find that the Institute of Jamaica was founded in 1879 for the encouragement of literature, science, and art, under a board of governors appointed by the Governor, whose duties are to establish and maintain an institution comprising a library, reading-room, and museum; to provide for the reading of papers, the delivery of lectures, and the holding of examinations on subjects connected with literature, science, and art; to award premiums for the application of scientific and artistic methods to local industries; and to provide for the holding of exhibitions illustrative of the industries of Jamaica. The Institute includes, in a new building of its own, a natural history museum, which makes a speciality of collecting examples of local fauna, flora, and geology, the curator of which is in correspondence with many scientists of note throughout the world. But the scientific work of the Institute does not fall within the scope of this paper. In the main building is situated a small art gallery, containing portraits of Jamaica worthies, views of Jamaica scenery, and other objects of local historic interest. On the same (upper) floor are situated a lecture hall (in which meetings are held of members of the Institute and papers are read on literature, science, and art), and the Jamaica and West India Library, which now numbers 1414 volumes. The lower floor is devoted to a reading-room and to the storage of books. The reading-room is open free to the public daily from 11 a.m. to 9 p.m., the ten hours best suited to the community. During the last six years, during which a careful record has been kept, there has been a steady increase in the number of readers—from 11,725 in 1891-92 to 39,573 in 1896-97 The population of the town of Kingston, it may be mentioned, was 46,542 in 1891. So far as records show, the cooler months of the year bring a few more readers than the hotter, but there is no very marked difference. The reading-room is most largely attended in the evening.

All the books in the library are available for reference and perusal in the public reading-room. In addition to this, members of the Institute—by a rule which in 1890 superseded an earlier plan of lending books to any respectable person who deposited £1, the interest on which was manifestly no commensurate return for such loans—have the privilege of borrowing books and periodicals. There are at present, in addition to honorary and corresponding members, about 300 subscribing members, whose subscriptions produce £150 per annum, which makes a useful supplement to a vote of about £2000, which is yearly granted to the Institute by the Legislature, the municipality of Kingston contributing nothing directly to its maintenance. It is essentially an island institute.

The library at present consists of 10,202 volumes, made up as follows:—

Works on Jamaica and West Indies	1,414
Theology	289
Philosophy	219
History	1,396
Biography	1,019
Travels	588
Law, politics, sociology	395
Education	272
Art	1,184
Science and natural history	1,317
Poetry and the drama	294
Linguistics and philology	85
Prose fiction	1,291

Miscellaneous	599
Dictionaries and works of reference	396
Reports of societies	414
	10,202

The 289 members who, during 1896-97, availed themselves of the lending library borrowed 6343 volumes, or an average of 22 apiece. The books were borrowed in the following proportions:—

	per cent.
Theology, philosophy, etc.	1.25
History, biography, travels	8.83
Law, politics, sociology, etc.	1.10
Art, science, natural history	4.89
Poetry and the drama	1.42
Prose fiction	40.20
Miscellaneous	1.70
Periodicals	39.40
West Indies	1.21

from which it will be seen that fiction does not bear so high a proportion to the rest as in many public libraries in England and elsewhere. This is due rather to the fact that the novels in the library bear a smaller proportion to other classes of literature than is commonly the case in public libraries, and also because works which are commonly placed in a reference library are allowed to leave the library, the only exception being made in favour of rare works and works of special value.

So far as fiction is concerned, the "last new novel" is asked for in vain. Good standard novels are added to the library, but the main object kept in view is the procuring of all books obtainable on Jamaica, the best publications on the other West India Islands and the West Indies generally, good works of reference, and as many as possible of the current contributions of the higher branches of literature; while the part of the members' subscriptions available for the purchase of books, which in the aggregate is small, is all that is spent on even the best class of ephemeral books.

For many years the library of the Institute was expected to play the double part of a reference library for the whole island and a popular lending library both for Kingston and the parishes.

Jamaica is somewhat peculiarly situated with regard to library work, on account of the difficulty of travelling and the transmission of parcels, albeit the last few years have seen many and great improvements in this respect.

In most countries it is sufficient to have in every good district a central reference library, containing all the more valuable works, with a lending library of lighter literature.

In Jamaica there are numbers of readers living at considerable distances from Kingston, who desire to consult, for purposes of their occupations, as well as for their intellectual enjoyment, some of the more valuable works in the library. They cannot, in many cases, afford the time to come to town, and they feel it a hardship that the works should not be sent to them. But it would seem that the central, or what one may call the metropolitan, library should have the first consideration; and the risk that a book runs every time that it is sent out of the library by steamer, rail, mail-cart, or mule-back, is too great a one to be lightly undertaken by those who regard the interest of a really solid and useful library in the metropolis of the British West Indies as being of the highest importance.

With respect to means of sending books to places distant from the central library, the first idea that occurs is, of course, that of local branches. In former years branches of the library existed in various towns; but, owing to lack of proper supervision, they resulted in loss of books, and were closed.

During the last few years much consideration has been given by the executive authorities of the library to the question of spreading the advantages of literature to the country districts of the island. A scheme by which boxes of books would be circulated in rural districts—on the lines of the Yorkshire village libraries—was contemplated, but the obvious fact that this, at the best, would only benefit a few isolated readers, and the manifest success during the last few years of the public reading-room in Kingston in attracting the young men of the island, led to the decision to found, if possible, a series of small public reading-rooms, with lending libraries attached, throughout the island.

Last year a branch library, which, it is hoped, may form the first of a series, was opened at Mandeville, a small town in the centre of the island, near the railroad. A sufficient number of books of reference has been furnished, and two sets of books embracing examples of all branches of literature have been lent, and with them book-lists for the use of members. The initial cost of the branch was borne by the Institute, and the local committee is allowed to spend the subscriptions (£20) of its members, who number forty; and it receives in addition a grant to defray the upkeep of the reading-room. It is intended that while the reference books remain, the "sets" of books shall be exchanged from time to time. Judging from the experience gained during the six months of its existence, the Mandeville branch gives every promise of success; the more especially as the one essential feature in these cases, the competent and willing working head, has been found. And a second branch is shortly to be opened at Port Maria, on the north side. The formation of future branches will be dependent on the vote of the Legislature, for it would of necessity be some time before such small libraries—if they have to maintain public reading-rooms—would become self-supporting, even if the books were lent free of charge. Even when some eight or ten of them were founded, it would still leave a very large number of persons living in remote rural districts practically untouched by the influence of literature; but the scheme that is here roughly sketched is all that is possible under existing circumstances. It would be well for Jamaica if she had a few enthusiastic ladies of the type of Miss Verney, of Middle Claydon, for without enthusiasm it is almost impossible to keep alive an interest in library work in small village communities.

One obstacle to the successful working of branches is found in the fact that the local authorities—the fourteen Parochial Boards which govern the local affairs of the fourteen parishes into which the island is divided—pay no heed to the claims of literature. And wherever a desire is evinced for literary advantages, it is at the instigation of private persons —usually the clergy.

For a country with so scattered a population, with many thousands of inhabitants many miles from a town, the best plan would perhaps be that which has been adopted in the small island of Grenada, where country members of the library, on payment of double fees (2s. per quarter), can obtain their books by post, free of extra charge; but this, of course, entails a loss on the post office.

The cost of sending books by mail coach is almost prohibitive. The liberality of the Atlas Steamship Company and the railway company renders their transmission by sea and rail devoid of cost; but that means is, of course, only open to towns near the seaboard and the railway.

So far as the bulk of the population of the island is concerned, it is not a question of providing literature to those who desire it, but rather of creating a desire for books where none exists.

In the old days planters cared nothing for reading, and the slaves were taught anything but to improve their minds. Small wonder is it, therefore, that the community as a whole is unliterary. It is, however, unfortunate that it should be so, for one can imagine no recreation more suitable to a planter who has worked hard in the open air all day than the perusal of a good book. If the clerk who has pored over a ledger from early morn to late afternoon seeks enjoyment in the evening at the billiard-table, one is not surprised; but, as change of occupation is the truest recreation, one would expect the planter and pen-keeper to turn with pleasure to their books after a hard day's toil. Of late years, however, several forces have been at work in improving this state of affairs. The elementary schools of the island, some 930 in number, are undoubtedly producing a generation prone to read—a generation unfit for agriculture in a land dependent on agriculture, the planter and pen-keeper say. But this reproach, even if it be true, has been met by the preparation—under the authority of the Board of Education, and with the approval of well-known scientists possessing local knowledge—of Blackie's *Tropical Readers*, which will tend to produce habits of observance of, and deduction from, incidents in natural life in the island. The volumes of the cheap series of *Colonial Libraries*, issued by various well-known London publishers, and the numberless cheap magazines, find a ready sale; and, last but not least, the press of the island plays an important part in the cause of literature.

A danger in all this is that people are led to "read something," without much caring what it is. As an antidote, a Jamaica branch of the National Home Reading Union was formed last year, which may in time, it is hoped, bear good fruit.

Two things militate against the formation and maintenance of private libraries in Jamaica, as in most other tropical countries. The one is the climatic conditions, and the other is insect life. In some parts of the island, where the rainfall is heavy, books suffer much from the damp, and bookcases with glass doors are essential; but this is not so in the case of the capital, although glass doors are a great protection against dust, which is very prevalent in the plain on which Kingston stands. In damp places books would suffer more from being left open than from the damp arising from cases being closed by glass doors, as Mr. Blades points out is the result in England. For protection against insects, bookcases should be of hard wood, such as mahogany, and the shelves should be of cedar (*cedrela odorata*), the smell of which is unpleasant to insects; for which reason this wood is frequently used by cabinetmakers in the manufacture of wardrobes and cupboards. Cases with glass doors are the best protection; but, if bookcases are closed, they should be inspected periodically. If books are to be left to themselves, they are almost better on open shelves than in closed cases. The worst insect enemy that books have in Jamaica is the bookworm (*anobium*), but its presence is somewhat indicative of neglect and absence of the effect of light. When bookworms are met with in the public library it is usually found that they have been brought in by some book of local interest, purchased from a house where little heed has been paid to the care of books, or in some bookcase which has been longer than usual without its periodical inspection.

Another insect enemy of books is the cockroach (*Periplaneta*). Unlike the bookworm, he never damages the inside of books. He confines his attention to the cover. He appears to be fond of bright colours, especially green. He certainly prefers newly-bound to old books, possibly because the paste is sweeter. Book-loving friends have told me that they have noticed that cockroaches attack the books of some publishers more than those of others. I rather suspect it is that they attack the books of some binders, those that use the sweetest materials, more than those of others. For myself, the books in my private library which have suffered more than any others are the Tennysons, in their original bright green cloth. To those who bind for the tropics I would say, Avoid bright colours, and use poison. The cockroach eats paper and cloth much more readily than he does leather, and, strange to say, the better bound a book is, the more he seems to respect it. But when he does attack a book, he will ruin a side of the cover in a single night. Glass doors are a great protection against the predatory cockroach, though, if left to himself, he will breed behind their shelter. A solution of corrosive sublimate applied to the crevices of bookcases, and, if necessary, to the books themselves, is usually found a sufficient preventive; but the best protection in the case of new books is to have them bound with poisoned paste and glue. All new books bought for the Institute library are thus bound, and all second-hand books that do not need rebinding are washed with the poisoned solution. Some old MS. records, that had to be re-bound in the colony, I had bound with brown paper sides, as I had noticed that all insects respect that material. Another insect found sometimes, but not often, in books is the silver-fish (*Lepisma*), or "fish-moth," as he is called in Jamaica; but, contrary to the experience given by Messrs. L. O. Howard and C. L. Marlath, in their *Principal Household Insects of the United States* (United States Department of Agriculture, Washington, 1896), I have never yet been able to convict him of eating books, although friends have informed me that their experience differs. In any case, however, the fish-moth in Jamaica is not nearly so great a plague as the cockroach. The termite, or white ant, which is such a scourge in some parts of the tropics, does not, so far as my experience goes, interfere with books in Kingston, although in some parts of the island, especially the damper and wooded districts, he does great damage, if books are not frequently inspected. None of the insects touch the wood of the bookcases and their shelves in the library.

The library is lit by electric light, and no harm is done to books by natural heat, so long as they are not left exposed to the actual rays of the sun.

But in spite of insect pests and climatic difficulties, in spite of an unliterary past and a somewhat apathetic present, the future of literature in Jamaica is by no means gloomy; and it may be safely considered as one of the forces of the future in moulding the character of the people of the island.

I have made this paper longer perhaps than the subject demands, but I have felt justified by the belief that much which I have written is true, not of Jamaica alone, but of the whole of the British West India Islands.

FRANK CUNDALL.

EDUCATION AND LIBRARIES OF THE CAPE OF GOOD HOPE.

N answer to the request of your Organising Committee of the approaching International Library Conference "to contribute a paper representing the Colonial side of library work," I regret that it will be impossible for me to be present. To make up for it, however, as far as lies in my power, I have put on paper a few notes, which I trust will not be found devoid of interest.

The colony of the Cape of Good Hope is now two hundred and forty-five years old. It was established in 1652 by the Dutch East India Company as a place of call, or refreshment station, and for nearly five years merely consisted of a commander and a garrison, which, in addition to the discharge of their military duties, were also employed in garden work, in barter expeditions among the neighbouring aboriginals, and in herding such cattle and sheep as were obtained from the Hottentots for the use of the passing vessels.

This system, however, was found unsatisfactory in the long-run, and under certain conditions soldiers and sailors received their discharge, and were allotted portions of land, which they were expected to cultivate properly, and on which, in course of time, they might also breed cattle and sheep to be sold to the Company for the consumption of the garrison, the hospital, and the Company's ships calling here.

The creation of this class, mentioned as freemen, was naturally followed by domestic life, wives and children. Hence not a very long time elapsed before the question arose regarding the education of the young.

Permit me to give you a few examples to show how this momentous subject was grappled with, and the difficulties under which the earliest settlers laboured.

In the Journal of the 30th November 1663 the following is minuted:—

"*Friday, the 30th November 1663.*

"Whereas our new sick-visitor, Ernestus Back, besides his ordinary duties, is daily making every effort to teach the Cape children, both Dutch and Black, to read, as well as catechising them, we have decided to accord him such emoluments as are recorded below—

"Mrs. Blanks shall pay him for each of her children, named Johannes and Johanna, half a rixdollar per month.

"Boomties shall pay the same amount for his daughter Marietje and his two sons, Rynier and Dirk.

"Elbert Diemer likewise an equal sum for his son Dirk.

"Jannetje Ferdinandus, for her son and daughter also half a rixdollar each.

"Jan Reyniersz, for his little daughter Jannetje the same sum.

"This fee to be charged for each freeman's child.

"The two girls Sarah and Maria Rosendaels, as well as a little Hottentot girl (een Hottentoosie) are, however, to be taught *pro Deo.*

"And as the Hon. Company desires that its own as well as other baptized slave children, especially those begotten by European fathers or Christians, shall be taught, and in good time brought to the right knowledge of God, and you have already made a laudable beginning to this end in the case of Amazie, Crisin, Zon, and Basoe, we pray that the Most High may grant His grace and mercy on it.

"(Signed) Z. WAGENAAR."

In 1684 the newly-established village of Stellenbosch, which had asked for a schoolmaster from home, was advised by the

Board of Seventeen (the directors of the Company) to look for one among the men of the passing ships.

On the 15th of July 1685 a code of regulations for the slave school of the Company was promulgated by the Commissioner-General, H. A. van Reede, which required, (1) "That the schoolmaster shall be at his duties from 8 a.m. to 4 p.m. (2) That he shall hear the children's lessons twice. (3) That he shall teach them good Christian conversation and manners, and not permit any evil or vile talk. (4) No other slaves nor any Dutch children shall be allowed in the school. (5) He shall follow them to church every Sunday, and every Wednesday and Saturday, and, according to their apprehension, make them answer the questions in the Heidelberg Catechism or the 'Abridgement' (Kort begrip). (6) The seniors are to be taught to sing the psalms, to write, and daily say their ordinary prayers. (7) No white children are to be accepted. (8) The parents shall take care that the children attend the school regularly, and pay proper respect to all officials encountered in the streets. (9) They shall not neglect their lessons, and are to be punished if they do. (10) They shall appear twice in church on Sundays; and finally, (11) the minister was directed to visit the school twice weekly to see how the children were progressing."

On the 22nd December 1687 Commander Simon van der Stel impressed on his council the great importance of maintaining the schools as "nurseries of all the virtues," especially among these "coarse and rough inhabitants," so that it was decided, in order the more to encourage the children, both free and slave, to present each of them with a prize on Christmas Day, after previous examination by the superintendents (schoolarchs), and, after having given proof of their progress in reading, writing, and ciphering, as well as the Creed; whilst the three first freeborn, of whatever sex they might be, were to receive each a silver pen of the value of a rixdollar, and the next three a similar pen of the value of half a rixdollar. The rest were to receive two skillings in money, whilst everyone, moreover, would be presented with a cake, the size of the latter being in accordance with the child's position in the school. A cake was also given to each slave child for its encouragement, whilst it was further resolved, in the interest of the colony, to exercise the boys from nine to thirteen years old every Saturday afternoon in the use of arms, by means of the drill sergeant on the drill field, to enable them to march under their own banner on New Year's Day, on pain of an arbitrary fine "to be inflicted on their parents, should they be absent without lawful excuse."

On the 6th June 1690 the first infant school for children below seven years of age was established, with Aagjie Keysers as teacher.

On the 3rd April 1700 Governor Willem Adriaan van der Stel informed the political council that, in consequence of the steady growth of the Drakenstein parish, he had felt that also the Dutch portion of the congregation there should be provided with a sick-visitor and schoolmaster, to teach the young reading and writing; and that he had accordingly appointed for the purpose Jacobus de Groot of Haarlem, who was well versed in reading, writing, and the French language.

On the 6th June 1708 the Rev. H. Beck, of Stellenbosch, urged the Government to appoint as permanent teacher at Stellenbosch the soldier Bastiaan Cevaal, at the time on loan to the burgher Jan Mostert. His request was granted, with the proviso that no one else, except pedagogues teaching in private families, would be allowed a similar privilege. The said Cevaal was permitted the use of the church porch for his purpose, and at the same time appointed sexton.

On the 21st August 1714 another code of school regulations was issued in order to secure fit and God-fearing schoolmasters, and to ward off all who would teach otherwise than what the Reformed Church believed.

Every teacher was therefore to be previously examined by the governor and council as to life and doctrine. He was to teach every child as early as possible the Lord's Prayer, the Decalogue, the Creed, the evening and morning prayer, the prayers before and after dinner, and all other ordinary prayers, that it might be imbued with a proper idea of God. Afterwards it was to be taught the Heidelberg Catechism, and to answer its questions in the church; to be exercised in the singing of the psalms, and thus be able to assist in the church singing. At the opening and closing of the school all the children were to say the prayers aloud in turns, and according to circumstances. On church days the teachers were to conduct the children to service, and afterwards examine them in the school on the sermon, speaking to them words of encouragement and admonition, based on the subject discoursed upon, and warning them against all evil, that from their youth they might be imbued with a taste for God's Word, and able, when grown up, to serve God and their country. Boys and girls were not to sit together. All were to be divided into classes. Only such books were to be used as had been approved in Holland. Lessons were to be repeated, and registers of attendance kept. Late comers were to be punished, and the parents visited of those that were absent. The rector and teachers were to frame and hang up a list of the work to be done, the subjects to be treated, as well as the divisions of time, classes, etc. The children were to go home straight from school. All people of position, as well as their own parents, were to be respectfully greeted when met in the streets. Offenders were to be punished. There were to be only two half-holidays weekly, and the children were to be exercised at honest play. The holidays here were to be the same as in Holland. The school fees were to remain as hitherto. The "secunde," minister, and captain of the castle were to act as "schoolarchs" (managers) under the governor and council. The teachers were to sign the same test-form subscribed to by the ministers of the Dutch Reformed Church, with the clause added which embraces the five doctrinal rules of Dordrecht.

Under this ordinance an elementary school was started, which for more than six years was presided over by the Rev. Lambertus Slicher, who had arrived here with the rank of cadet (Adelborst), and afterwards served as minister at the Cape and Drakenstein.

In 1720 the number of scholars had so increased that he was obliged to ask for more desks and benches as well as new ink-pots.

All these laudable though puny efforts to educate the children at the Cape (Cape Town) did not, however, appear to affect those in the country districts, especially those far removed from the centre of government. In 1743 Governor-General Gustaaf Willem van Imhoff, during his stay here, made a journey inland, and with surprise and pain witnessed how little attention was bestowed on public worship, and in what great carelessness and ignorance a large section of the country were living in this respect, caring very little for religion, so that it looked there more like a collection of blind heathens than a colony of Europeans and Christians. He had accordingly consulted the Cape ministers (le Sueur and van Gendt) on the subject, who declared that, though the decline of religion and the non-practice of the same were partly the result of the laziness and want of education of the older residents, they were mainly owing to the fact that the people were scattered about so far from the nearest churches that they had but few opportunities to attend divine service, some being from two to three days' journey from the Stellenbosch and Drakenstein churches, so that they had no opportunity to have themselves and their children instructed in the principles of religion; and that therefore it was of the utmost importance to establish two additional churches in the interior, each provided with an able minister and a clerk (voorlezer). That he intended to act in accordance with this advice, and, moreover, to settle a third sick-comforter in the most distant locality, to open a boarding school in order to meet the excuse of the parents why they did not educate their children.

After consultation, the council decided to establish one church in the "Zwarteland" and the other near the little Berg River, between the "Roode Zand" and the Twenty-four Rivers, provided that the surrounding residents bore all the costs; and to settle a clerk at the so-called "Groot Vader's bosch," to open a boarding school and conduct divine service there every Sunday. And it was further decreed that, as soon as effect had been given to this measure, only such private tutors were to be tolerated as had been properly examined and found fit by the Cape Church Council, as otherwise a door would be opened for all kinds of irregularities among the ignorant congregations.

Notice of this resolution was duly given to the Lords Seventeen.

In 1769 the resolution that all teachers should be properly examined was once more enforced, everyone being required to carry with him a proper certificate, to be produced to the minister in whose parish he desired to work.

On the 2nd September 1779 the first detailed school report was submitted to governor and council. "That on investigation they had found that the complaints of the privileged schoolmasters 'that the numbers of their pupils were considerably decreasing, in consequence of the schools opened by persons not privileged to do so, and that consequently they feared that their schools would finally collapse,' were without any foundation—for, as will appear from the list submitted, every privileged schoolmaster that did his duty had as many children as he could reasonably manage, yea, even more !—and further, that the person of Johan Simon Wedel, against whom the charges are principally levied, as well as other private teachers, mainly confined themselves to the teaching of the French language and various sciences, without interfering with the work of the public schools, which consisted of spelling, reading, writing, and the elements of the Dutch Reformed religion. They also found that the teacher of the slave children was very poorly paid, so that he was compelled to take in hand other work besides to make both ends meet, and that the slave children were often taken away from school to assist in doing light work for the Company before they had been sufficiently instructed, so that they lost more in a month than they had profited in four. They therefore advised that the teacher's salary should be increased, and that arrangements be made by which the slave children are better kept to their lessons. Finally, they requested that, should any improvement in the management of the schools appear to them to be necessary, they might be allowed to make it, and that such regulations may be strictly obeyed.

"On the 13th August 1779 in Cape Town—

The School of Meyer contained—
Boys 37
Girls 34
Slave children . . . 6
Total 77

That of Mellet contained—
Boys 24
Girls 30
Slave children . . . 8
Total 62

That of During contained—
Boys 34
Girls 20
Slave children . . . 2
Total 56

That of Knoop contained—
Boys 49
Girls 62
Slave children . . . 25
Total 136

The School of Joosten contained—
Boys 42
Girls 56
Slave children . . . 17
Total 115

That of Weydeman contained—
Boys 40
Girls 55
Slave children . . . 3
Total 98

That of Redelinghuys contained—
Boys 46
Girls 51
Slave children . . . 5
Total 102

That of Job Jacobse contained—
Boys 18
Girls 16
Slave children . . . 16
Total 50

or a total of 696 children, exclusive of the slave lodge school, in which were instructed of the lodge children 44 and of the burgher slave offspring 40, or a total of 84."

The council adopted this report, and decided henceforth to supply the teacher of the slave school with double rations, and allow him Rds. 3 per month instead of Rds. 2 which he had hitherto received; also to issue instructions that the children were to be kept regularly to their books as long as they attended school, and that from time to time such fresh regulations were to be made as were necessary, and to which the teachers were to submit.

On the 9th April 1782 the governor and council drew up a code of regulations for the licensed schoolmasters of Cape Town, which enacted, "That (1) they were to teach personally, but that the Government would give them assistants approved of by the schoolarchs whenever they had more pupils than they could personally manage. The only holidays were to be the three days succeeding Easter and Whitsunday, the week reckoned from the day preceding Christmas Day until the second New Year. There were also to be holidays during the days of the burgher parade, and finally a holiday on the birthday of the Lord Prince of

Orange and Nassau. Wednesday and Saturday afternoons were likewise to be free, to enable the children to have a moderate exercise. The school hours were to be from 8 to 11 a.m. and 1 to 4 p.m., and careful inquiry was to be made in the case of the absent. The school was to be opened with prayer and closed with prayer and a psalm—everything in an orderly and reverent manner; the children when leaving the school to be admonished to live a moral and virtuous life. The teachers were to provide suitable desks and benches, and keep the boys and girls separate, classifying them according to their abilities. Only such books as have hitherto been in use shall be used; this also applies to catechisation books. They were earnestly to admonish their pupils to fear the Lord, and show all reverence to their parents, those in authority, the ministers, and all who were above them; treat their inferiors in a friendly and unassuming manner, and beware of profaning the name of the Lord and making use of vile and blasphemous language, or in any way insulting anyone. The children were to attend the Sunday services regularly, as well as the lower catechisation classes held in the church on Wednesdays. Each schoolmaster was to take his turn to be present, but the one of the 'Diaconie' (church school) shall always be present with his pupils; the teachers kindly inviting the parents to help them in carrying out this rule. The teachers were to maintain good discipline, praise the industrious and well conducted, and reprimand those who were lazy and irregular, and in case of stubbornness chastise them with the usual domestic instrument of punishment, the birch and ferule (plak), commensurate with their offence and their different natures.

"The teacher may claim fees as follows:—

"(1) For those being taught ciphering and writing, one rixdollar.
"(2) For those being taught spelling and reading, four skillings.
"(3) For those being taught the alphabet, two skillings,

with power to charge less or nothing at all in the case of the poor, it being expected that they will be fully recompensed for this sacrifice by the well-to-do section of the community. For all instruction outside of office hours they may charge extra. Every teacher acting contrary to these rules may expect to be deprived of his office. A copy of the same will be given to every one of them."

In 1788 the chaplain of the Wurtemberg Regiment submitted a very comprehensive educational scheme, regarding which the council decided that, "Bearing in mind the pressing necessity of a good education for the young in a country in which hitherto the opportunities have been wanting, the best course to adopt would be, however much the impossibility of carrying out such an extensive scheme was feared, to lay it before the political commissioners and the ministers forming the board of schoolarchs, for report and advice, in order, as much as possible, to remedy the existing imperfect state of education."

On the 9th July 1790 the governor and council considered a despatch from the directors, dated the 23rd October 1789, regarding the best means of promoting education. They believed that the establishment of public schools in the most thickly-populated centres might meet the want to a very great extent, and that they should be established without burdening the Company with the expense; and further, that it was a matter of such public importance that everyone would contribute according to his means to gain this desirable end. It was decided to refer this also to the schoolarchs for consideration and advice.

On the 12th October following, the latter reported, "That the capital was fairly supplied with such public schools as the directors and the council desired, and that continually every effort had been made to obtain suitable teachers. That, however, as regards the country districts, with the exception of Stellenbosch, which possessed a properly-authorised public school, it was not very practicable to establish schools there, as the homesteads were so distant from each other, so that most of the residents had to obtain private tutors. It was therefore, under these circumstances, necessary to request governor and council to facilitate the obtaining of suitable persons for this purpose from the passing ships, and to suggest that, should it henceforth be necessary to fill the vacancy caused by the retirement or death of a prelector or precentor in the country, to appoint a person who would at the same time be able to discharge the duties of schoolmaster, and who should be bound to act as such and as teacher of a public school, should there be a sufficient number of children in the neighbourhood whose parents might be anxious to make use of the privilege."

This report was unanimously adopted.

During the same year the schoolarchs had also reported on the necessity of establishing a proper French and Latin school, but the departure from South Africa of Governor Cornelius Jacob van de Graaff, who appears to have been the chief promoter of the scheme, left it in abeyance until the 16th of March 1792, when it was once more taken in hand.

The schoolarchs reporting on it refer to the general complaint regarding the very primitive and defective state of education here, many parents being hardly in the position of having their children taught more than reading, writing, and arithmetic, without being able to secure for them an education indispensable to civilised society, and which would enable their offspring to be educated for such positions in life as their desires and abilities might enable them to secure. The only course hitherto open to them was to send their children home at an early age, but the enormous expense which this entailed made it prohibitive to the great majority.

They were therefore agreeably surprised when they found that the public had voluntarily subscribed the sum of nearly sixty thousand guilders as a fund, from the interest of which the projected institute might be supported. They were also sanguine that that sum would soon be considerably augmented.

The money difficulty having been removed, they had sketched a plan on which the institute should be started and continued, and which they wished to be submitted to the directors, with the request that they might approve of it, and appoint such teachers as were selected by the schoolarchs for the school, giving them at the same time a suitable rank, but without any pay attached to the same.

They also desired that administrators of the fund might be appointed, that the money might be returned to the subscribers should the directors not approve of the scheme, and that, as present needs were pressing, the council might permit them, as a temporary measure, to submit to it the names of such persons who were able to teach the elements of the languages named, and appoint them provisionally for the purpose, so that no time need be lost before a reply was received from the directors.

They also requested to be allowed to appoint two or three capable persons in Europe, for the purpose of selecting the required teachers for the final approval of the directors.

They further proposed that the rector, when appointed, should receive the rank of junior merchant (under factor); the conrector that of titular junior merchant; and the French and German master that of bookkeeper.

This gradation they believed would fully answer the purpose.

Finally, they expressed their wish that the fund should be enlarged, and that, as many of the subscribers suggested, the governor should decree that no one should be allowed to make use of the institution before he or she had paid an entrance fee; that a moderate amount might be fixed for the purpose, or that the school fees might be raised in their case; the intention, however, not being to prevent poor and needy children from benefiting from the generosity of the rich, their remarks applying merely to the well-to-do folks, or such people who might send their children hither from other places—for example, from India—to be educated here.

These should certainly be required to contribute to the fund.

In the scheme itself the schoolarchs say that no one at all acquainted with Cape conditions will be unaware of the deep ignorance and the very little refinement in which a large portion of the people found themselves, and that this deplorable state would be considerably minimised if the children were afforded an opportunity for being instructed in the various sciences, as their intellectual powers are naturally very good. This would naturally affect their character, and once more prove the truth of the Roman poet, "that the acquiring of useful knowledge improves the morals, and does not permit man to remain in a savage state."[1]

At present the schools were in such a wretched state that the children were barely taught spelling, reading, writing, and the elements of drawing, to say nothing of singing and religious instruction. The Government, however, was not to be blamed for this, as it had already, as early

---

[1] "Doctrina sed vim promovet insitam,
Rectique cultus pectora roborant;
Utcunque defecere mores,
Indecorant bene nata culpæ."
HORACE.

as the year 1714, endeavoured to mend matters, and, as further appeared from the efforts of Governor-General Baron van Imhoff, in 1743, to prevent irreligion, carelessness, and ignorance, among the country people especially, which led to the resolution of 1769 that no one would be permitted to teach before he had been properly examined by the ministers. Matters, however, had not improved since, and hence the future of this favoured colony looked gloomy indeed, if no change for the better were effected. To bring this desirable change about, the school regulations of the year 1782 were promulgated. The results, however, did not answer expectations. At the present time the progress of the children was as unsatisfactory as before, the cause being the unfitness of the teachers for their work. Never having been trained to the work, hardly one of them could write a decent hand, most of them spelt imperfectly, and could in arithmetic hardly reach the rule of three. But as there were no more eligible subjects, there was no choice. What, therefore, could be expected from the labours of such men? A teacher should be a well-educated and refined man, trained for his work, thoroughly understand spelling, and be able to write a perfect hand, and to sing the psalms in whatever key they might be sung. He should also have sufficient knowledge of music, in order to be able to teach those desirous of learning, to sing the hymns of Lodensteyn and others.

In ciphering he should be able at once to solve the questions in the ordinary little book of Bartjens based on that of Blassière. He should also be no stranger to Italian bookkeeping, for the benefit of those children who might afterwards enter on a mercantile life. It would also be of advantage if he understood the French, English, or any other language; but as all this could hardly be expected from one man, not too much stress would be laid on this. The teacher, however, should be a member of the Dutch Reformed Church, in order to catechise his pupils, at least twice weekly, to prepare them for confirmation. Above all, his conduct should be irreproachable, and an example to his pupils, that he might be able freely to censure them should they misbehave. As long as such schoolmasters were not obtainable, there would be no hope of improvement.

Proper teachers should therefore be obtained from Europe, and not less than three, for the work required; the one to teach reading, writing, singing, ciphering (beyond fractions), and the elements of the Reformed religion.

The second should undertake the higher branches of arithmetic, the French language, geography, the history of the Fatherland, and Italian bookkeeping.

The third should teach the Latin and Greek languages for the benefit of those who might desire to proceed to a European university. But to carry out the latter portion of the programme it would be necessary to have, besides a rector, a conrector, and, if possible, also a preceptor, that the work might not be interrupted by the death of the rector, and that the lower teachers might also be gradually educated for the higher appointments.

The Dutch teacher should therefore have a salary of Rds. 1000, the French one the same amount; the rector of the Latin school 1200 guilders, the conrector 800, and the preceptor 600 guilders.

It would extend this paper beyond reasonable limits were I to mention the suggestions regarding the raising of the fees and other matters financial, all which were carefully weighed by the scholarchs and submitted for consideration: The necessity of securing such rank and emoluments to the teachers as would encourage them to persevere in their work, and to induce other capable men to come out to South Africa to help to further it. The schools were to be well ventilated, and made as convenient as possible for the pupils. Proper examinations were to be held, and prizes awarded to the deserving. Schoolmasters might be trained, and pupil-teachers employed, and the scholars grounded in the elements of religion by attending once a week (those above twelve years old) in the church, to be questioned in the Catechism which the Sunday before had been the subject of the sermon. This would encourage the parents to send their children to church; the diligent ones to sit in the front row, "as, however trivial this arrangement may appear, it causes the greatest emulation." Finally, the scholarchs suggested that, as in Holland, the prizes should be distributed publicly in the church, as the best encouragement for the children.

This report was adopted by the council, the scholarchs being empowered to start the institution as proposed; but beyond the administration of the fund, nothing appears to show that the school was started, the troubles of the year 1795 very likely having prevented any further progress.

In 1804 C. M. Villet and the sworn translator, Benirt de la Motte, were permitted to open a private school for the teaching of the English, French, and Dutch languages. It is therefore evident that the intentions of the council, expressed in 1791, had not been carried out. In the same year the Commissioner-General de Mist published his very exhaustive code of School Regulations, to which, however, the Government had no opportunity to give effect before the second surrender of the Cape to the English, about eighteen months later. Previous to the publication, however, he had requested the Government to appoint a committee to report on the best way to raise a general tax for the support of schools in the capital and country districts. This committee, consisting of the heads of the various departments, suggested as a first step that annually a general collection should be made through the town by the schoolarchs, and further, that the following import duties should be levied for the same purpose:—

On every cask of foreign beer	Rds. 4
On every anker of wine or 40 bottles	Rd. 1
On every adult slave (male or female)	Rds. 5
On every slave (male or female) below twelve years	„ 2½
On all movable property sold, to be paid by the seller	One-half per cent.
On all immovable property, to be paid by the buyer	„
On all new or renewed loans at the Lombard Bank, per mille	Rd. 1
On all emancipated slaves for whom formerly Rds. 50 were paid into the church fund, but which were now to fall to the school only	Rds. 75
On the estate of everyone dying without heirs a voluntary legacy, but never less than	„ 25
On all intestate estates falling to collaterals or strangers the sum of Rds. 25, for each inheritor residing within the colony.	
On everyone residing outside of it	Rds. 50
On every coach used within the town	„ 10
On all horses, exclusive of those of the military and burgher cavalry, four skillings.	
On every owner of twenty slaves, two skillings per head for the first four, four skillings per head for the next eight, and six skillings for the rest per head, and for every additional one above that number	Rd. 1
Members of licensed or private clubs shall pay individually, whether man or woman, one rixdollar annually.	
The landlords of those clubs, lodging-houses and inns, as well as billiard-table keepers	each, Rds. 10
All canteen keepers	„ „ 5
The tax to take effect in 1805.	

No effect, however, was given to this recommendation, for the reason already mentioned, and de Mist's School Regulations remained for a long while a dead letter.

In 1813 Governor Sir John Cradock, by advertisement, also appealed for subscriptions to establish a system of education that would give the required understanding of the Scriptures, and at the same time lay the foundations, among the humble ranks, of civilised, moral, and industrious life. He was sanguine that all would press forward to create a common and extensive fund for the purpose, so that it would not be necessary to direct a general taxation through the several districts commensurate with the expenses of school education within the province.

A Bible and school commission was accordingly appointed, which, according to a proclamation of Lord Charles Somerset four years later, had effected considerable improvement by means of the "seminary, open to all, wherein the first rudiments of education are successfully implanted." As, however, neither the funds hitherto available, nor obtained as voluntary contributions from benevolent individuals, had been sufficient for meeting the unavoidable expense of the said seminary, the governor decided to establish an additional toll at the several outlets of the town on Sundays, and on the side of Green Point during the days of the race weeks, the receipts to be handed over to the school commission. The following tariff was fixed :—

Waggons drawn by six horses
  or more were to pay . 4 skillings.
Waggons drawn by four horses
  and less were to pay . 2 „
Coaches, carriages, etc., drawn
  by four horses . 2 „
Coaches, carriages, etc., drawn
  by two horses . . 1 skilling.
A saddle horse . . 2 stivers.

Ox waggons to pay no toll, as well as officers and others legally exempted from the usual payment. The money to be collected by the Burgher Council at the latter's expense.

The capture of the Cape in 1806 by the English forces had made it almost impossible for the Dutch Reformed Church to obtain ministers from the old mother-country; hence the governor, Lord Charles Somerset, decided to meet the want by the introduction into the colony of a number of ministers of the Established Church of Scotland, who had received instruction in the Dutch language in Holland, as well as "competent and respectable instructors, employed at public expense, and stationed at every principal place throughout the colony, for the purpose of facilitating the acquirement of the English language by all classes of society." The latter having arrived here in 1822, the governor decided that the English language should be exclusively used in all the Courts of the colony from the first day of January 1827, and that after 1825 all documents of the several public offices, the Records of the Court of Justice excepted, were to be drawn up and promulgated in the English language, whilst all documents prepared and issued from the office of the Chief Secretary to the Government were to be in English from and after the first day of January 1823.

On the 25th July 1824 Lord Bathurst authorised the establishment of a classical school at the Cape, to be conducted by a clergyman of the Established Church, a man of first-rate abilities for the purpose, who was to receive £600 per annum for three years, and after that half the amount, as it was supposed that the school would then be so flourishing as to recoup him for the loss of half his previous salary. In both cases he would have a free residence.

On the 20th December of the same year Lord Bathurst informed the governor that the Rev. Mr. Judge had been appointed headmaster of the grammar school.

In 1829 "several persons subscribed certain sums of money, in shares of £10 each, for the purpose of establishing a college or institution for the instruction of young persons in the colony in certain branches of literature and science." The result was the establishment of the "South African College" by ordinance No. 11 of 1837, promulgated by Governor Sir Benjamin D'Urban. It will be superfluous to trace the history of that useful institution, its struggles to make both ends meet, and its final triumph. The good it has done is incalculable. But, fortunately, it was not left to flourish alone; gradually, however slowly, others arose in the peninsula and the country districts, and, whatever the merits of others, the colony has to thank the late superintendent, Sir Langham Dale, that colleges exist in the most important centres of South Africa, and good schools in every village and the great majority of the country homesteads. Of course there is nothing perfect under the sun, and the same may be said of our educational system; but, comparing the present with the past, the difference is as night and day.

After this rapid but imperfect survey of our educational history,—for I have left out much of perhaps equal interest with what I have noted down here,—it will be evident that, with education at such a low ebb, it was impossible to establish a library, or, if one existed, to find many readers to frequent it. Those of a studious inclination were accordingly obliged to form their own private libraries, or small reading clubs, with the object of obtaining as many books as possible for the least amount of money, whilst the East India Company supplied the ministers of religion with a select theological library, and its other servants with books and instruments, such as were individually required by them for the proper discharge of their duties.

Among those at the Cape who loved books, and during the course of their lives succeeded in collecting a considerable number, was Joachim Nicolas von Dessin, secretary to the Orphan Chamber, and a deacon of the Dutch Reformed Church. He made his last will on the 12th July 1761, and it was proved on the 18th September 1761, by S. C. Ronnenkamp, first sworn clerk, at the office of the Secretary of the Council of Policy. He was fifty-seven years old when he died. He appointed the Orphan Masters his executors, left his soul in the hands of Almighty God, his Creator and Saviour, and desired that his dead body should be buried in his own vault in the church.

He left to the Cape Church his whole library, with all the manuscripts, shelves, fittings, etc., all his mathematical and astrological (astronomical) instruments, and his best pictures. The latter were to be selected by the Church Council, or persons properly authorised by them for the purpose—on the absolute condition, however, that the library was under no circumstances to be alienated, as it was intended to be a nucleus of a public library for the colony, and was to be annually further augmented with books of all "faculties," and all kinds of knowledge. And, to prevent the spending of any church funds for the latter purpose, he left the diaconate a legacy of Rds. 1000 (£200), with the interest of which that augmentation was to be met. He also bequeathed to the same Church Council all the books of the Very Reverend and learned Daniel Pels, corrector of the Latin school at Amsterdam, and such other books as might arrive at the Cape after his decease. By this disposition, he believed that he would still be doing some good to the public after his death, and therefore begged the political commissioner, ministers, elders, and deacons, forming the Church Council, to render every assistance in carrying out the terms of his will. Should, however, the Church Council decline to accept the trust, the books, etc., were to go to the Orphan Chamber, to be dealt with as it might deem proper. In the latter case, the Rds. 1000 left to the church would also revert to the Orphan Chamber. . . . To the sergeant at the castle, Benjamin Nöthling, and his wife Johanna Lombard, for having taken care of him during his late illness, as well as for other daily assistance rendered, ƒ. 2000 (Indian valuation, or £166, 13s. 4d.), as well as his vault in the church—No. 27—(date of title deed, 17th Oct. 1752) in which he was to be buried, and which was not to be opened for twenty-five years. After the expiration of that time, the bones of himself, his wife, and daughter were to be collected, placed in one small coffin, and re-deposited in the same vault.

Extract of this will was submitted to the Cape Town Church Council on the 5th October 1761, which decided to accept the library on the conditions mentioned; but, as there existed no suitable building for the safe custody of the collection, to request the governor and councillors to authorise the consistory to build a proper hall for the purpose, and to furnish it with the necessary material on behalf of the Company at invoice price. This request was granted on the 2nd November following. Two days later, the Orphan Masters, as heirs of the late Sieur von Dessin, offered the various curiosities, silver and copper medals and foreign coins, to the Church Council, to be preserved by it, together with the library, which gift that body accepted.

On the 2nd November the Orphan Chamber delivered to the consistory 3856 printed volumes and manuscripts, shelves, fastenings, etc., 4 bookbinders' presses, 2 step-ladders, some mathematical and "astrological" instruments, 32 paintings, Rds. 1000 in cash, some curiosities, consisting of 17 silver medals, 123 divers large coins, 103 medium-sized ditto, 118 small ditto, and some copper coins.

On the 4th January 1762 the consistory received from the Orphan Masters, as heirs of Dessin's estate, and in reply to its letter of the 7th December preceding, Rds. 1000 to assist it in building the hall required for the collection.

On the 14th June following the Church Council considered the advisability of rebuilding the sexton's house, and adding an extra apartment to it, in which to deposit the books. The matter was again referred to on the 6th February 1764, but no conclusion seems to have been arrived at.

On the 7th November 1763 the consistory put out on interest the Rds. 1000 legacy received with the books, etc., and

On the 6th August 1764 appointed the second minister of the Dutch Reformed Church librarian, the first minister having declined the appointment.

On the 1st October following the first regulations for the library were drawn up, and which were briefly as follows:—

(1) The books were to be numbered and catalogued. (2) The library would be open to the general public every Wednesday afternoon, from one to four

o'clock, that all respectable people wishing to visit it might have the opportunity. (3) All persons of quality would be entitled to keep a volume at their house for one month, and those living in the country for three months. (4) Any person damaging a book, to pay its value.

In January 1765 the consistory requested the Government that such books as were bought in Holland for the library might be shipped as Government property, freight and duty free, and to appoint the Amsterdam bookseller, Jan ten Houten, as their agent.

In April 1766 a blank book was opened, in which to mark down all the books presented to the library.

On the 5th January 1765, the interest accruing from the Rds. 1000 having produced $f.452.16$ (Dutch), it was decided to spend that amount on books to be ordered from Holland.

Eighteen months later, the librarian, the Rev. Joh. Fred. Bode, reported that the books had arrived, but had cost $f.757.13$, or $f.304.17$ more than the interest in hand. This deficit the council decided to meet with the interest falling due. This was done on the 2nd January 1769.

On the 7th October 1771 the consistory was informed that a painting had been bought for the collection for Rds. 10.

On the 24th January 1774 the Rev. Mr. Bode reported that there were $f.672$ in hand, and suggested that books for that amount should be obtained from Holland, and the directors of the Company requested to have them conveyed to the Cape, freight and duty free.

On the 2nd October of the following year the books arrived, having cost $f.732.4$.

In September 1777 the librarian reported that he had bought some books very cheaply at a public sale held here.

Three months later it was decided to remit 110 ducatoons to Holland, to pay the bookseller's account, as well as for more books.

The same thing was done in June 1785, when $f.1744$ were remitted to Holland, in payment of books received.

Six months later (2nd Jan. 1786) an additional 200 ducatoons were remitted to Europe for more books, and another 200 on the 4th February 1788.

On the 14th July 1800 a special meeting of the Cape Church Council or Consistory was convened by the political commissioner, Johannes Isaac Rhenius, who communicated to the members the desire of the governor, Sir George Yonge, that the newly-formed Society of Arts and Sciences should hold a general meeting in the building destined for the library. The librarian, however, namely, the Rev. J. P. Serrurier, submitted that the application could not very well be entertained, as, if granted, he would not know what to do with the books, and, moreover, did not wish to be held responsible should any disappear when a crowd of persons was assembled in the hall, to whose misbehaviour no proper attention could be given. On the other hand, should the request be refused, the consistory might expect that the Government would not weigh the reasons adduced by it, but, as was done in the case of the burgher watchhouse, would issue an order; so that, to avoid this, it would be better to grant the request of Mr. Rhenius. The president, however (the Rev. Christiaan Fleck), was of opinion that the council could not comply with the request without at the same time informing the governor of the difficulties in the way. With this the members agreed, likewise bearing in mind that, as the building had been erected from funds of the residents, it did not, according to the capitulation, belong to the properties of the former sovereign, and should therefore be left untouched. All this the political commissioner undertook to communicate to His Excellency.

What the result was I have not found minuted.

On the 6th December 1815 books were again received for the collection from Holland, valued at $f.1000$.

On the 20th March 1818 Governor Lord Charles Somerset issued a proclamation, in the second section of which the standard measure of every wine cask is laid down, and decreed that for the gauge and certificate of each cask passing through the market one rixdollar should be paid to the collector of tithes; the money so received, after deducting the gauger's salary, to be deposited in the Government Bank in the name of the following committee—viz. the Colonial Secretary for the time, the Chief Justice ditto, His Majesty's Fiscal ditto, the senior ministers of the Reformed and Lutheran Churches, and the senior chaplain of the Established Church of England—so as to create a fund for the formation of a public library, to be open to the public under certain regulations to be framed at a later date, and to lay the foundation of a system which shall place the means of knowledge within the reach of the youth of this remote corner of the globe, etc.

On the 28th December 1827 Lieutenant-Governor Sir Richard Bourke repeated the above proclamation, "by virtue of whose provisions a valuable public library had been formed in Cape Town, and which it was desirable to preserve and maintain for the public benefit." Instead of the committee which had hitherto acted, he appointed three trustees to take charge of and make such regulations for the library as to them might seem fit for the preservation of the books, manuscripts, and other things belonging thereto, and for the inspection of the same by the public; the said trustees to be only removable from office by the will of the governor.

This ordinance was repealed by one dated the 3rd February 1830, which mentions that, in consequence of the repeal of the proclamation of the 20th March 1818, "the library had been deprived of those certain means of support which were formerly drawn from the public under the authority of Government; that with the view of preserving that valuable institution from decay, certain persons had entered into a voluntary annual subscription for its support; and that therefore it was expedient that the management and administration of that institution should be vested in a committee of nine persons, to be elected by and out of the said subscribers—the office of trustees being abolished at the same time.

This ordinance, in its turn, was repealed by that of the 25th July 1836, which was intended "to make better and more effectual provision for the management of the said library."

But we must go back to Lord Charles Somerset.

On the 31st July 1818 that governor placed himself in communication with the Church Council, desiring that the Dessinian Collection should be considered as the nucleus of the public library intended to be established, as the flourishing circumstances of the colony permitted the extension; and further, that the new books obtained by the lately-appointed committee should be deposited in the apartment containing the Dessinian Collection.

The consistory did not object to the latter suggestion, if intended as a temporary measure, "care being taken that the Dessinian library be not mixed up with others, and that nothing be broken or altered in the apartment without permission of the consistory; that all expenditure incurred in this respect should be borne by the committee; that mutual arrangements be made that no books were lost or injured; and that, by means of proper conferences, all points be settled that might crop up from time to time." It was also quite prepared to agree, according to von Dessin's will, that his collection should remain a nucleus of a much larger library, be subject to the regulations to be framed for the public library, and under the supervision of the directors of the same; but "it could not forego its right of control over the Dessinian Collection, as an asset of the church, as it had to carry out the terms of the will."

The result was a long correspondence with the governor, who pointed out the great advantage of incorporating the Dessinian Collection into the new one about to be formed, and stated that he had no intention whatever to interfere with the rights of the consistory, but that it would seriously inconvenience the library committee, and cause unnecessary extra expense, if the new collection were only to be temporarily housed in the Dessinian apartment—the second storey of the sexton's house, built expressly for the purpose; that two administrative bodies would cause confusion, and frustrate the objects of the committee; that either the latter should take the complete control over the Dessinian collection, or the Dessinian Collection should be completely severed from the library about to be established, and thus not only cause useless extra expense, but remain for ever incomplete. Nor would the arrangement proposed by him vitiate the terms of the will, as the committee consisted only of persons appointed by virtue of the public offices held by them and representing the corporations to which they belonged; and as the consistory was represented on it by its first minister, the committee might justly be considered as uniting in itself the administration of the Dessinian library originally entrusted to the consistory.

It would not interest the hearer or reader to note all the further arguments adduced on both sides in this lengthy correspondence. Suffice it to say that in the same year (1818) the governor em powered the public library committee to remove the Dessinian Collection, under protest of the consistory, from the apartment specially built for it, and withdrew it from the control of the Church Council. In 1823 the latter complained of this arbitrary proceeding to the commissioners of inquiry, and furnished it with copies of all the correspondence on the subject. The result was the proclamation of Sir Richard Bourke in 1828, already referred to, which altered the administration and *personnel* of the committee of the public library; whilst, by ordinance dated the 3rd February 1830, the administration of the Dessinian Collection once more reverted to the consistory of the Dutch Reformed Church, or a committee appointed by the latter.

The value of this collection has not always been fully appreciated. Rear-Admiral Cornelis de Jong van Rodenburg, who published his *Travels to the Cape of Good Hope* in 1802, and died in 1838, says, on p. 115 of his first volume : "Above the house of the sexton of the Reformed Church there is a public library, the number of whose books is certainly considerable, but the selection might have been better. The majority are in Latin, and those in modern languages are from fifty to a hundred years old. The celebrated Captain Cook, when he was here last, presented the institution with some implements from the South Sea Islands. These and some paintings of little value compose the rest of the contents. The eldest minister, Serrurier, is the superintendent; and, excepting himself and some strangers, I do not believe that this library is frequently visited." A more careful survey, however, will show a far more satisfactory result, the volumes having been classified as follows: Religious literature, 1094; encyclopædias, 899; history, 789; miscellaneous, 495; philology, 306; jurisprudence, 277; geography, 186; physics, 183; philosophy, 161; mathematics, 98; and surgery, 77 volumes. Judging from an article which appeared some time ago in a Dutch paper here, and which is from a trustworthy source, hardly any manuscripts are now to be found in the collection. On the first page of almost every volume the following is read: "Ex libris N. v. Dessin; Ars quæque alit terram;" or again, "Prudentis est caute agere et caute legere." The collection of law works is described by the same hand as almost unequalled as regards Roman-Dutch jurisprudence, which is still the foundation of the South African administration of justice. A rare work in this collection is that of naval laws, known as *Il Consolato del Mare*, or, "The Consulate of the Sea," many of which still hold a place in international law, and show what a height trade and navigation in the Mediterranean had already reached in the early Middle Ages.

The geographical section is simply grand and priceless :—Biographies such as those of Johan van Oldenbarneveldt and William the Silent, the journals of the early Dutch voyagers to India *viâ* the Cape of Good Hope, with their quaint charts of Africa dotted over with lions, elephants, tigers, etc.; the chronicles of Holland, from the time of Adam, printed in 1595 in black letter, with their knights in full armour; the *History of Charles the Fifth*, by Alonzo de Ulloa, printed in 1510; the *History of the Crusades*; the *Life and Deeds of the most celebrated Heroes and Discoverers of New Lands* (1676); *The Life of Loyola*; the *Life of Pope Johanna*; the *History of the Popes*; the *Secret History of Charles and James the Second of England*, etc. etc. All these are but mere specimens to show what the collection contains, and what great value should be attached to it.

When the ordinance No. 71 of 1830 was promulgated, and to which reference has already been made, it contained amongst others the proviso, "That the Dessinian Collection should be kept in a part of the building apart from the public library, under the management of the consistory of the Dutch Reformed Church, which was, however, not to interfere with the management of the public library." This proviso was repeated in ordinance No. 8 of 1836, also mentioned above.

The ordinance No. 71 of 1830 not merely provided for the appointment of a committee of management, but also of a librarian. The fifth who held that office (1832) was the poet Thomas Pringle, who has given us a lively sketch of his experiences in the tenth chapter of his *Narrative of a Residence in South Africa*. He received the magnificent salary of £75 per annum, on which he had to maintain himself and family; but, for valid reasons, he did not enjoy it long. The Cape "Reign of Terror," as he describes it, refused him permission to publish a journal, and thwarted him in many ways, so that he finally decided to resign as Government librarian. But the story of his trials should be read as he wrote it, as no justice can possibly be done to it within the confined limits of this paper.

For many years the public library was housed on the Grand Parade, in one of the wings of the old Exchange building, now broken down to make room for the handsome post-office buildings, now rapidly approaching completion.

Until the year 1862 it had mainly to rely for its maintenance on subscriptions; but for many years after this date it received an annual grant of £600 from the Government, and, according to this year's estimates, it is down for £850, independent of £500 for the purchase of standard works for the reference library, and £200 for lighting and expenses.

On the 21st October 1861 His Excellency Sir George Grey, formerly our governor, presented a valuable number of books and manuscripts to the library, and known as the "Grey Collection." The manuscripts range from the tenth to the seventeenth centuries, and are in the Latin, Italian, Flemish, and other languages. Many of the printed volumes are rare and valuable black-letter editions and early-English printed books. Among the latter is a remarkably fine copy of the *Polychronicon*, printed by Caxton in 1482, and the first edition of the collected works of Shakespeare (1623). It also possesses an unrivalled collection of native literature of South Africa and of New Zealand, which is of considerable interest to the philologist and student.

"A further division of this library is entitled the 'Porter Collection,' presented to the institution by the subscribers to a fund for the purpose of having a life-sized portrait of the Hon. Mr. Porter (attorney-general) painted, to be deposited in the library, as a recognition of the many and valuable services rendered by him to the colony. Mr. Porter having declined to sit for his portrait, the Cape Town subscribers resolved that the amount subscribed by them should be devoted to the purchase of standard works to be placed in the library, and styled the 'Porter Collection.'

"The foundation stone of the present building was laid by His Excellency Sir George Grey on Tuesday the 23rd March 1858. The library hall was inaugurated by His Royal Highness Prince Alfred on the 18th September 1860, who deposited as a first volume a valuable Greek manuscript (*Lectionarium Græcum*) of the tenth century, given for that purpose by His Excellency Sir George Grey. The Prince likewise deposited on the shelf a copy of the *Holy Bible*, Knight's *Shakespeare*, and the *Pictorial History of England*."

The Legislature of the colony has always taken a deep interest in library work. On the 13th July 1854, a fortnight after our first Parliament met, a motion was carried, in the House of Assembly, as follows: "That a select committee be appointed to take into consideration the expediency of Government rendering assistance to the towns and villages of the colony in the establishment of local public libraries, and to bring up a report on the conditions and regulations under which such Government assistance should be afforded."

On the 21st May 1855 a select committee reported to the House as follows: "That having considered the subject referred to them, and having examined several witnesses, they are unanimously of opinion that it is expedient to grant pecuniary assistance to libraries from the public treasury, in all cases where it can be shown that the inhabitants of the place or district desiring such aid have themselves, according to their means, and in a liberal spirit, established such libraries.

"Such assistance was heretofore given to the library in Cape Town, in the shape of a tax upon all wines entering the Cape Town market from any part of the country.

"A grant of land, with a building and £200, has been made to the Grahamstown library.

"A grant of £200 has also been made to the library at Port Elizabeth. The committee find that a sort of promise of aid was held out by the late Secretary to Government to the directors of the Graaff Reinet library, who have expended £1200 and upwards in erecting a suitable building for a library and librarian's quarters, upon a small piece of ground granted by Government.

"Your committee, in following out this recommendation of aid to such as will show a disposition to make efforts themselves, would recommend Graaff Reinet to the favourable consideration of Government as having already complied with the conditions under which that aid is recommended to be granted.

"The committee believe that, by granting such aid to libraries springing up, these useful institutions would soon multiply in the country.

"The committee would recommend that, wherever aid has been granted, or shall be granted, to public libraries, the public, not being subscribers, should have access thereto, under such restrictions, and during certain days and hours of the week, as the directors of such libraries from time to time establish, whereby the books and the property of the library would be safe from damage and destruction, and the institution still in a position to be of that utility to the public for the diffusion of useful knowledge which all founders of institutions of that kind generally contemplate."

This report was adopted, with the result that, according to this year's blue-book on the subject, we have 102 libraries scattered all over the colony, and partly supported by a Government subsidy of twelve thousand six hundred and fifty pounds sterling!

Among the first resolutions carried by both branches of our Legislature in 1854 was one for the creation of a reference library, one for the Legislative Council, and one for the House of Assembly. These libraries remained separate until the year 1885, when both Houses removed under one roof in the spacious building specially erected for their accommodation. A joint-library was then established and placed in my charge. At present it possesses 11,744 volumes, consisting of biographies, letters, speeches, classics (ancient and modern), essays, lectures, geographical, ethnographical, and philological works; works on government, political and social economy, history (constitutional and general), jurisprudence, literature, parliamentary procedure, party writings, polygraphy, practical science, arts and industries, reference works, travels and adventures, and parliamentary papers.

I send you a copy of the *Reports of Public Libraries* for 1896, "Presented to both Houses of Parliament by command of His Excellency the Governor, 1897 (G. '60-97).'" It will afford you such details as may be of interest. I trust that the Congress will be a success, and a further means of creating a more general interest in the establishment and maintenance of libraries all over the world. Much has certainly already been accomplished, but far more still remains to be done. But when we compare the present with the past, in this colony at least, of forty years ago and even less, the progress has been so great that we may hopefully look forward to the future.

H. C. V. LEIBBRANDT.

REGISTRATION OF COLONIAL PUBLICATIONS.

AM sure you will not doubt the sincerity of my regret at being unable to be present at a conference from which a librarian, from Australia particularly, would be certain to gain so much information, and at which he would be afforded an opportunity of realising the mines of literary wealth confined within the walls of the historical institutions in London, which we know so intimately by name. As an Australian librarian, my means of obtaining information on library matters have been limited to the literature of the hour, with which we are of course all familiar, and an occasional visit to the kindred institutions in Melbourne and Sydney. The value of the current literature on library work is of course inestimable; but, notwithstanding the advantages of all the valuable papers in *The Library* and similar publications, and the many excellent works on libraries we now possess, Australian librarians feel the want of interchange of ideas by actual converse with other librarians, and the necessity of personal inspection of kindred institutions whose officers are working on the most modern principles. It is this actual converse with other librarians, this actual inspection of other libraries, which Australians so much desire; but, unfortunately, their wish has few chances of being gratified. The opportunities offered by the Conference of acquiring information upon every subject a librarian should be informed upon, and of personally meeting those distinguished members of the profession whom through their writings we know so well, and for whom we cherish much admiration, present such a fascinating prospect that it is hard for any of us to be obliged to decline an invitation which would mean so much to us.

The chief librarian of the public library of New South Wales has written to inform me that his Government has granted him the necessary leave of absence to attend the Conference. I have received the intimation with delight, and in Mr. Anderson we shall have a worthy and enthusiastic representative. I shall personally await his return with interest, feeling assured he will have much valuable information to give me. A librarian, unlike some members of other professions, has no professional secrets; it is always a great pleasure to him to impart to his fellow-workers all he knows, and to incite to more earnest efforts those less well informed than himself.

Your request that I should write a paper to be read at the Conference has reached me at such a time that it is impossible for me to comply with it, on account of a special pressure of duties in connection with my office. This I greatly regret. I should much like to contribute a paper, not with a vain delusion that I could add to the information of my fellow-librarians in conference assembled, but as an evidence of sympathetic interest regarding several questions of library management.

I hope the subject of the official registration of colonial publications will be discussed. In this colony such a registration is not compulsory, consequently many things are published which never reach the public library of the colony. It is true there is very little matter other than official of any importance published here, and the great bulk of that unimportant matter is issued in pamphlet form. Those pamphlets, however, may have great interest for at least the future descendants of their authors, and they should, if only on that account, be preserved in our national collections. Besides, some of the pamphlets are intrinsically valuable, and without them no collection of South

Australian books would be complete. There certainly should be a record of them somewhere, which would assist in a compilation of a bibliography of the colony, and guide collectors and librarians in their efforts to complete their collections. The work of the Royal Colonial Institute in the direction of improving the conditions for registration of colonial publications has not been, I trust, altogether unattended by success; but Mr. Campbell, in his able book on international bibliography, points out that, so far as South Australia is concerned, a better response to the circular sent to the authorities in that colony might have been expected than was received. I have for many years past endeavoured to secure a copy of all South Australian publications issued, official and private, in pamphlet form or otherwise, but am compelled to admit that I frequently come across publications which, though they are two or three years old, I have not previously heard of; and of course I am forced to think that there must be many which I do not ever come across. Indeed, the fact that in the national collections of Melbourne and Sydney there are many more South Australian publications than are upon the shelves of the public library in Adelaide conclusively proves this to be the case. The machinery for the registration of the different publications of each colony could be provided very simply and inexpensively. In no colony of Australasia is there any great activity in the publishing direction, nor is there likely to be for many years to come. There at present exists in most of the colonies a registrar of patents, copyrights, and trades-marks. In this colony one officer has control of the three, but I am not aware of the systems in other parts of Australasia. To render it compulsory to copyright everything printed for general information not being purely departmental, if official, and with specially enumerated exceptions, if private; to regard the printer—not the writer, who may be only temporarily located in the place; and not the publisher, who in many cases would be the writer—as responsible for such registration; to insist upon a certain number of copies of each publication being deposited when such registration is made,—these would be the three chief features in any Act dealing with the question. I can see no reason why such an Act should not be passed in each colony, and the duties of carrying it out could be undertaken in the office of the registrar of patents, trades-marks, and copyrights, at a very slight, if any, increased expenditure. The number of copies to be deposited should be not fewer than three, and these should be sent to the public library of each colony. Some of the libraries might arrange for an interchange of their copyrighted publications, and this would be one very valuable result of such an arrangement. It is very disappointing to learn that little has been done in the direction of registering works issued. The existing apathy is due to the fact that legislators are not alive to the advertising features involved in a record of the publications issued in the separate colonies, published, say, annually, or at shorter periods if preferred, and distributed all over the world. Librarians are ever eager to add to their collections books bearing upon Australia. The importance of the Australian colonies, and their many still undeveloped industries, lead to the inquiry for new literature upon them in the chief libraries. The circulation of a record of Australian publications, official and private, amongst the leading librarians, would assuredly be very acceptable, and would assist them to provide for the wants of some of their readers. Librarians would further be encouraged to write for official publications, which are usually available for presentation when asked for officially, whereas, without such a record, their existence in some cases might not be suspected. I need not further enlarge upon the possible results of a wider distribution of the literature of the different colonies, for they must be apparent.

I sincerely hope that this second Library Conference may be even more satisfactory than was that of 1877, and that all sections of the community may be able to say that it has conferred a genuine benefit on the cause of science and learning all over the world.

In conclusion, I should like to record my appreciation of the courtesy and liberality which the public library of South Australia has always received from officers of kindred institutions in America. Their energy in every department of scientific research, and their immense resources, make their literature most valuable adjuncts of the different sections in our libraries; while the liberality and courtesy which this library has always received from the authorities in America has been particularly gratifying, and has contributed in no small degree to the enrichment of our collection. In my own search for advice and assistance in library work I have received very greatly-appreciated kindnesses from Mr. Melvil Dewey and other American librarians, and I should be glad, if you have an opportunity, if you would give expression to the sense of gratitude we have in these colonies for the very great consideration we have always received from American librarians and officials generally.

J. R. G. ADAMS.

LIBRARY OF THE UNIVERSITY OF SYDNEY.

THE nucleus of the library consisted of a number of volumes, chiefly ancient classics, originally in the possession of the "Sydney College," which was a college established by a joint-stock association to provide for higher education in New South Wales, but was superseded by the University of Sydney upon its establishment in the year 1850, and the books and scientific apparatus belonging to the college were then transferred to the university.

After the commencement of the university's operations, in the year 1852, grants were from time to time made from the general funds for the establishment of the library, and an excellent selection of standard works was made under the advice of a sub-committee of the Senate, whose chairman was Sir Charles Nicholson, the then vice-provost of the university.

Up to the year 1885 the library was maintained chiefly by similar grants from the general funds of the university, but of smaller amount and by donation.

In the year 1885 the late Thomas Fisher, Esq., of Sydney, bequeathed the sum of £30,000 to the university, "to be applied and expended by the Senate in establishing and maintaining a library for the use of the university, for which purpose they may erect a building and purchase books and do anything that may be thought desirable for effectuating the purposes aforesaid." This handsome bequest enabled the Senate to bestow much more attention upon the library than was previously in their power, and considerable purchases were made to fill the vacancies in many of the teaching departments.

During the past six years the library has increased by purchase and donation at the rate of 3000 volumes per annum, and it now contains more than 45,000 volumes.

The ordinary library grant for the purchase of books is £600, of which about £250 is expended in the purchase of serials, chiefly scientific, special grants for various departments having been made from time to time.

The opportunities of obtaining manuscripts or rare works in Australia are not very frequent, but the university is fortunate in possessing some Hebrew MSS. presented by Sir Charles Nicholson, the complete works of John Gould, Lepsius' *Denkmaeler*, Kingsborough's *Mexican Antiquities*, and others.

The room in the university building originally set apart as a library now proves entirely insufficient for the purpose, and the collection is distributed in a number of different rooms, where many of the books are difficult of access.

An extension of the university buildings is in contemplation, in which it is proposed to make ample provision for the library. It is proposed that the new building should contain a reading-room capable of holding 200 readers; a stack for books with five or six storeys in an adjoining chamber, capable of holding 200,000 books; separate rooms for periodicals and the transactions of learned societies, for Australian books, and for rare books.

It is also proposed to transfer from the main building to a special room to be provided in the new building the Nicholson Museum of Egyptian, Greek, Roman, and Etruscan antiquities, which is unique in the Southern Hemisphere.

The system of cataloguing adopted in the library is the decimal classification of Mr. Melvil Dewey. I have long been of opinion that the time has arrived when there should be more co-operation in cataloguing and classifying than has hitherto been the case. The only way to accomplish this and to create and preserve some uniformity of working is to adopt a system that commends itself to general use. The decimal classification seems to meet this requirement and to answer admirably both for catalogues and readers, and accordingly it was adopted here some four or five years ago. A complete catalogue of the library is gradually being made in accordance with the system.

I hope that the attention of the Conference will be specially directed to this matter of co-operation in cataloguing, and that valuable results will follow its deliberations.

H. E. BARFF.

PUBLIC LIBRARIES IN NEW ZEALAND.

N one important respect New Zealand differs from the neighbouring Australian colonies. In each of the five latter the capital city completely overshadows all other towns. In New Zealand the geographical conditions are such that several towns are of the same order of importance, the capital city, Wellington, being at present, if suburbs are taken into account, the least populous of the four chief cities. This difference is reflected in the public libraries of the colony. The public libraries of Melbourne, Sydney, and Adelaide are State institutions, supported by the taxpayers of the various colonies. In New Zealand there is no State library. Auckland and Wellington have rate-supported libraries; Christchurch has a library supported partly by public endowments and partly by subscriptions; Dunedin has at present only a subscription library, but there is an active agitation proceeding with the object of establishing a free public library.

The largest city in New Zealand is Auckland, which, with its suburbs, had in April 1896 a population of 57,616. It was the first town in New Zealand to possess a free library, and it has been exceptionally fortunate in the matter of gifts. It was opened in September 1880, the new library buildings, including an art gallery, being opened in March 1887. The Costley bequest, amounting to £12,150, produces an income sufficiently great to render a halfpenny library-rate ample for the support of the institution. In addition to this, Sir George Grey presented the library with a valuable collection of about 13,000 volumes and pamphlets, including above 700 manuscripts, 24 incunabula (3 being Caxtons), about 3200 autograph letters, and other valuable items. Sir George Grey has added at various times to this collection. Apart from the Grey Collection, the reference library contains some 10,000 or 11,000 volumes; while there is a lending library of 5000 or 6000 volumes. The latter portion is not free. The Libraries Act as it applies to New Zealand does not provide for free lending libraries; it expressly fixes upon the sum of five shillings, I believe, as the minimum annual subscription to be paid by borrowers. The annual subscription charged at the Auckland Free Library is at present ten shillings; it has recently been increased to this sum from the former amount of six shillings. The number of subscribers, which stood, I believe, at about 1100 or 1200, fell considerably on the change being made. The Auckland Library has been well managed, and the citizens of Auckland are very proud of it.

Wellington, the capital city of New Zealand, had in April 1896, with its suburbs, a population of 41,758, increasing, however, much more rapidly than that of any other city in the colony. Its public library was opened early in 1893. It has been less fortunate in the way of gifts than the Auckland Public Library. The late Mr. W. H. Levin gave £1000, and the citizens raised another £2000, with which the books in the reference library were purchased. One wing of the building is erected, and the overdraft thus incurred is gradually being paid out of current revenue. The library has no endowments, its sole sources of income being a penny rate and the annual subscription of five shillings to the lending library. So valuable, however, is property in Wellington that the rapidly-increasing rate already produces an annual income of £1580. The reference department contains above 9500 volumes, and the lending department above 7000. The number of subscribers to the latter is nearly 900, and is steadily increasing. For some three years the system of filling up a ticket with details concerning the books required was followed in the reference department. No other Australasian library follows this system, which proved so unpopular that it has recently been abolished. Readers now choose their own books, after signing a visitors' book. The change has proved very popular. In Auckland, I believe, readers choose their books without even signing a visitors' book.

Christchurch, with its suburbs, had in April 1896 a population of 51,330. The public library of this city is one of the oldest of the large libraries of the colony, and is supported partly by the income derived from endowments and partly by an annual subscription of ten shillings for borrowing books. It has recently received a bequest from the late Mr. Gammack, which will yield, after certain life interests expire, an income of several hundred pounds annually. The library is under the management of the Board of Governors of Canterbury [University] College. The Christchurch Museum, School of Art, Boys' and Girls' High Schools, and the Lincoln Agricultural College are under the same management. A portion of the income derived from the extensive endowments of this body is devoted to the purposes of the library. As at Auckland and Wellington, the reference library and newspaper rooms are free. The reference library contains above 10,000 volumes, and the lending library about 17,000. The number of subscribers to the latter department is about 1600.

Dunedin, with a population in April 1896, including suburbs, of 47,280, has no public library. It has a subscription library of several hundred members, the annual subscription being one guinea. There is, however, a strong feeling in favour of the establishment of a free public library, which will probably soon be an accomplished fact. The Dunedin Athenæum is chiefly a lending library, its reference department being insignificant in comparison with those of the three libraries already mentioned.

No other town in New Zealand is large enough to support out of rates an important library. Napier, the fifth town in New Zealand, had in April 1896 a population of 9231. Invercargill, Nelson, Wanganui, Palmerston North, and Oamaru, complete the list of towns in this colony with a population of above 5000. All of these towns have subscription libraries, the subscription ranging from ten shillings to twenty-one shillings annually. Some in addition, such as Wanganui, receive subsidies from their respective borough councils, in return for which they provide a free reading-room containing newspapers and periodicals. Much smaller towns also have similar libraries of from 400 or 500 up to 3000 or 4000 volumes, and in boroughs they usually receive a small subsidy from the local governing body. They are well supported as a rule, and supply the wants of readers in the remote country districts. There are no railway station libraries in New Zealand.

The largest library in New Zealand is not a public library in the ordinary sense of the term. This is the General Assembly Library, familiarly known as the Parliamentary Library. It contains about 35,000 volumes, some of them of considerable value. Though primarily intended for the use of members of Parliament, its sphere of usefulness is increased by the plan of lending out books, when Parliament is not in session, to respectable persons whose names have been placed in the "recess list" of borrowers.

It is hoped that these few notes on the libraries of this the remotest of British colonies will be not altogether without interest. At anyrate, they will be sufficient to give some indication of the value and scope of library work in this colony.

THOMAS W. ROWE.

AUCKLAND FREE PUBLIC LIBRARY.

MAY state, by way of introduction, that a mechanics' institute and library were established three years after the foundation of the colony, viz. in 1843, which did good service in their day, and lasted until superseded by the present free public library in 1880.

This, the first, and I may say destined to be the greatest, of public libraries in New Zealand, was opened in September 1880 by Mr. Thos. Peacock, Mayor, with about 5000 volumes, the larger and most valuable portion of which belonged to the Provincial Library, which ceased to exist on the abolition of the province in 1876, and about 1000 volumes belonging to the Mechanics' Institute forming the nucleus of the library. About this time Sir George Grey, K.C.B., whose name is a familiar word in the Colonies—a name for ever to be associated with every good work of progress in New Zealand—in due time promised to donate his library and art collection to the people of this city, which promise he fulfilled in 1887.

The management is in the hands of a committee of the City Council, the Mayor being president, assisted by an advisory committee.

The library is supported by a halfpenny rate, supplemented by the income received from £12,150, a bequest of the late Edward Costley, of Auckland, and the revenue from the circulating branch, opened in 1887. Total income from all sources about £1600 per annum.

The new library was opened by Mayor A. E. T. Devore in March 1887, the foundation stone of which was laid by Mayor W. R. Waddell in 1885. It consists of a handsome building, situate in a central position, on a portion of Albert Park, close to the Auckland University College, Grammar School, Girls' High School, Technical Training School, and the principal State schools of the city. I need hardly say to what extent advantage is taken of the library by the students of these educational institutions.

The Auckland Public Library and Art Gallery to be appreciated should be seen. The library contains the largest and certainly the most valuable collection in the colony, and in many respects the richest of literary treasures this side of the line. In the first place, this is chiefly owing to the munificent gifts of the Right Hon. Sir George Grey, K.C.B., etc., of some 13,000 rare and choice books, about 700 MSS., 3200 autograph letters, etc. etc.; many paintings and water colours, large collection of Maori wood-carvings, greenstone implements, etc.; rare curios from Africa, China, India, and the islands of the Pacific; Maori war-flags and banners, besides many valuable gold Mexican ornaments, and pottery recovered from a tomb near Colon, Central America; a large number of maps, charts, and plans, chiefly relating to the early marine and land surveys of the Colonies; maps of the Indian Mutiny and plans of Maori pas—the collection of a lifetime : secondly, to the late Edward Costley, for the bequest of £12,150: thirdly, to the late J. T. MacKelvie, for his large and very valuable collection of oil and water colour paintings, and other articles of vertu—gold and silver—which now constitutes the MacKelvie Art Gallery, besides his valuable library, composed principally of works of graphic art : fourthly, to Mr. J. M'Cosh Clark, for his gifts of books during his three years' term of mayoralty : and fifthly, to the City Council, for the erection of the library and art gallery, at a cost of £23,000, apart from the new *annexe* containing the MacKelvie Collection. The building also contains the

Elam Free School of Art and the municipal offices.

At present the library contains 33,000 volumes, including 3000 pamphlets, various MSS., about 700 autograph letters, documents, etc. (about 3200), and 450 maps. Every department of literature is represented, special care being taken by Sir George Grey in providing for the wants of those coming from the East and the islands of the Pacific; and European languages—French, German, Italian, Russian, etc.—altogether about 180 languages; early voyages and explorations, mostly in original editions—not a few works relating to the Colonies generally.

There is a large number of mediæval MSS., some being beautifully illuminated in gold and colours. Amongst them is a copy of the Gospels, tenth century; a Lectionarum, eleventh century. Both are written in Greek. A large folio MS. Bible, written in Latin on sheets of vellum, about the thirteenth century, in two volumes, supposed to be the copy from which Gutenberg and Faust set up their type. In the binding of the back of the MS. Sir George Grey found a slip of old paper inserted with a Latin inscription, of which the following is a translation by the present Earl of Stamford, when last in New Zealand, for Sir George Grey: "In the year of Christ 1450, at Mainz, in Germany, John Goudenberg, with two partners, first founded type, arranged and fitted it to a press, to such great amazement of all and to such furtherance of the public advantage, that he wrote on the printing machine, 'It prints in a day as much as scarce can be written in a year.'"

It may be interesting if I subjoin a few details I have been able to obtain from Mr. Curzon's work, an authority on such antiquities, especially as it throws light on MSS. already in the library. In his *Monasteries of the Levant*, p. 106 "The Coptic books were all of them liturgies; one of them, a folio, was ornamented with large illuminations, intended to represent the Virgin and Infant Saviour. It is almost the only specimen of Coptic art that I have ever met with in a book." The Arabic books, as well as the Coptic, consisted of extracts from the New Testament, written on skins or cotton paper. It may be interesting to add that specimens of each of the kinds of MSS. described by Mr. Curzon are now in the library. Page 170, *In the Via Dolorosa*:

"Jerusalem, the Greek Monastery, there is likewise a MS. of the whole Bible; it is a large folio, and is the only one I have ever heard of, with the exception of the one in the British Museum." Since Mr. Curzon thus wrote, another such Bible, a third, has been found in the library of the monastery at Mount Sinai, and there is a fourth one in the Grey Collection, Auckland Library Beside it, in the same case, lies the only MS. of St. Luke's Gospel in the language of the aborigines of the Hunter River, New South Wales, written by the Rev. L. E. Threlkeld. It is beautifully illuminated. A MS. of the New Testament written on sheets of vellum by Thomas à Kempis. A handsomely-illuminated MS. of the statutes from Edward I.—3 to 23—Henry VI., 1445. The Commentaries of Pope Gregory the Great on the Book of Job. This MS. was formerly in the possession of Henry V. Another MS. lately added to the library, a very large vol.— Antiphonal, or Roman Catholic Service Book, written on vellum, original oaken boards, date about 1460. A French MS. translated out of the Latin for Philip le Beau by Jehan de Meun, author of *Roman de la Rose*. The MS. correspondence of Oliver Cromwell's secretary, Sir Philip Meadows, afterwards ambassador to the King of Sweden; and the famous Treaty with the United Protestant Powers, concluded by Richard Cromwell in 1659. The MSS. of Sir Joseph Banks, and a copy of a letter in the handwriting of Captain Cook, dated 1765; besides many African, Maori, and Polynesian manuscripts of great interest.

Amongst the autograph letters are seventeen signatures of Queen Victoria, two of King William IV. (the earliest signature of the Queen is June 26th, 1837); one of Marie Antoinette, being an order on the French Treasury. One letter, dated 26th October 1857, conveys the Queen's thanks to Sir George Grey, governor of Cape Colony, for his action in sending troops from the Cape to the Indian Mutiny.

There are many early printed works of the fifteenth century, amongst which is probably the second book printed with Greek type—*Æsopi Fabulæ*, illuminated (1479); a Bible, the first book printed at Delft (1477); three by Caxton—*Polychronicon* (1482), *Golden Legend* (1483), and Virgil's *Eneydos* (1490); a rare copy of the Polyglot Bible in six volumes (1514–

17). This is probably one of the **earliest** impressions, having the cardinal's hat **in** the centre of the title-page printed **in** black in vol. v., in the others in red, **with the** arms **of** Ximenes at the bottom **of the** title-page. Shakespeare folio editions, 1623 1632 1664, complete with his poems, **which** also contain his portrait; and, last **but not** least, Lopez's *Report of the Kingdom of Congo,* 1597, with maps and plates. **I will now** conclude by saying it is always pleasant **to** know the interest taken in the Auckland Public Library from, starting by such personages as the Earl and Countess **of** Aberdeen, Lord Stanmore, Sir William and Lady Jervois, Lord and Lady Onslow, Lord and Lady Glasgow, the Bishop of Salisbury, H. M. Stanley and Mrs. Stanley, C. W. Holgate, **F. W. Pennefather,** the late J. A. Froude, Baron **von Hübner,** and the late **G. A.** Sala.

EDWARD **SHILLINGTON.**

LIBRARY FACILITIES OF SCIENTIFIC INVESTIGATORS IN MELBOURNE.

HE library equipment of the city of Melbourne and its suburbs is rich and varied. The liberality of the Victorian Government has provided and maintains the Melbourne Public Library; the University and Medical School afford their *alumni* large and valuable collections of books and periodicals; the scientific societies possess important collections, consisting chiefly of the journals of other learned societies and scientific magazines; while the various museums, technical institutes, and the departments of Government are furnished with libraries, generally well stocked with publications relating to the matters which come within their respective provinces. The question I wish to consider is: How far is this mass of material of service to persons engaged in scientific research—a class which seems to merit some exceptional consideration, engaged as its members are in advancing the bounds of natural knowledge?

There are two distinct problems involved —(1) the extent and degree of completeness of the available material—considerations which determine its value to the investigator; (2) its accessibility

(1) Extent and completeness.

It may be taken for granted that the investigator's main requirement is not so much treatises on branches of science, as monographs and original papers dealing with individual problems. These generally, though not always, take one of three forms: they appear either (*a*) in the reports of Government departments; (*b*) in the journals of learned societies, or in special volumes published under the auspices of such societies; or (*c*) in the magazines devoted to special branches of science or to science in general. The value of library equipment to the scientist may therefore be estimated from the amount and variety of this kind of periodical literature.

The scientific publications of Governmental departments are, in most cases, sent to Melbourne. The libraries of the Government offices, the Royal Society of Victoria, the Observatory, the University, and the Melbourne Public Library receive among them a very large amount of such literature. Many publications of this kind are, in fact, sent to more than one of these institutions, so that their availability leaves little to be desired.

Melbourne is rich in journals of those learned societies which—like the Royal Society of London—accept contributions bearing on all branches of science. Nearly all the leading societies and academies of this class exchange publications with the Royal Society of Victoria; while those which do not thus exchange, generally forward their publications to the Public Library, University, or Observatory—in some cases to all three. The Royal Society also exchanges with a large number of smaller societies which concern themselves with general science, and the publications of others are to be found in the public or university libraries. Magazines which deal with general science are taken by all the libraries, to a greater or less degree; most of them are to be found somewhere in Melbourne. The "general science" literature, then, is tolerably complete.

The case with regard to publications dealing with special branches of science is somewhat different.

The astronomical investigator is well cared for. Melbourne is fortunate in the possession of an observatory of the first rank, and in that observatory's library practically all the current astronomical literature of any importance—journals of societies, records of observatories, and magazines—is received. The observatory also receives the principal publications bearing on the sciences of geodesy and meteorology, its collection of the literature of these branches being tolerably complete. Mathematical publications are divided between the Public Library, the University, and the Royal Society. The number both of societies and magazines devoted solely to the advancement of mathematics—pure and applied—is relatively small, and most of the work published by either is to be found on the shelves of one or other of these three institutions. Geographers are well supplied with literature, as might be expected in a new country, where geographical investigation assumes a special importance. Nearly all the important geographical societies exchange their publications either with the Royal Society or with the Victorian branch of the Royal Geographical Society of Australasia—in many cases with both; the Royal Society, moreover, receives a considerable number of geographical magazines.

In other branches of science the worker is too often conscious of his limitations in the matter of information. The chemists and physicists are probably the worst off. True, the proceedings of most of the metropolitan chemical and physical societies of the world, together with a number of the leading magazines, are received by the libraries of the University and Medical School—many of them by other libraries as well. Nevertheless, some important chemical and **physical magazines, to say nothing of the journals of some of** the smaller **chemical societies, are** practically **inaccessible. Naturalists** —including under this **head workers in** the domains of biology, geology, and ethnology—have indeed a rich store of material: all the libraries above mentioned, and a goodly number of others, are in receipt of the publications of societies interested in problems of natural history; most of them also receive a good many magazines, so that the total bulk of the available literature is very large. Unfortunately, the collection in any **one** library is by no means exhaustive; **so** that the unlucky naturalist has generally to wander round to a good many places, in order to collect his information.

As regards *completeness*, it may be said that, in most cases, the series are completed from the period at which their reception commenced; nevertheless, in this respect, Melbourne investigators are at a special disadvantage as compared with those working in older centres of population, inasmuch as the earlier volumes of many serials are not accessible. The expense of procuring "back numbers," even when such are attainable—which is by no means always the case—is **often** prohibitive; **and** though the generosity **of** the Government and of private donors has done much **to** alleviate this disadvantage, it is **not** altogether removed. Apart from this consideration, however, it may be said that the Melbourne stock of scientific periodical literature is much more than respectable; it largely exceeds that to be found in many cities of similar size in Great Britain, and in variety and completeness may be considered well worthy of a metropolitan centre.

(2) Accessibility.

The Public Library stands alone among the larger collections, in that its stores are open, as a matter of right, to every member of the community; but this fact makes little difference to the investigator, seeing that the various Government departments and scientific societies **are at** all times willing to afford him access to the sources of information at their disposal. The great drawback in all cases is the lack of complete published catalogues. The Public Library does, from time to time, issue a catalogue of the periodicals in current receipt, and the societies generally print their exchange lists; but this proceeding would be insufficient, even if it were universal, as these lists take **no** account of publications the receipt **of** which has for any reason ceased, **nor** do they yield information as to the completeness or otherwise **of the sets of serials.** Information **on these heads** can, in general, only **be obtained** by inspection of the full catalogues **at the various libraries; and** it may well happen that **the net result of a** long search may be the **discovery, either** that the desired serial is not **in the library,** or that the particular volume wanted **is** missing from the series. Fortunately, **the** latter result is exceptional, as, in the great majority of cases, the more important series are completed from the date of inception, and others are but seldom required; but it **not** infrequently happens that the earlier **volumes** of a series are not to be found in the same library with the later ones.

To sum up: the scientific investigator in Melbourne can generally—though not always—obtain the information he seeks; in most cases it is ready to his hand, in others the search for it is troublesome. The main difference between his position and that of workers in older centres consists less in the amount of material available than in its comparative lack of accessibility, owing to its distribution over a large number of libraries. It is hoped that steps may ere long be taken to minimise the inconvenience thus caused.

E. F. J. Love.

THE AUSTRALIAN MUSEUM LIBRARY.

HE Australian Museum was founded in the year 1836, and incorporated under trustees in 1853, but the library is of much more recent growth. Not that there were no books in earlier days, but they hardly constituted a library. In 1881 there were about 1000 volumes, now there are over 7000.

The first catalogue was published in 1883. It was compiled by Mr. Thomas Fielding under the supervision of Mr. W. A. Haswell, then acting curator, now professor of biology at the Sydney University. For a few years attempts were made to keep this up to date by annual supplements, but these were discontinued owing to the rapid growth of the library, and an entirely new catalogue has been prepared by the present librarian. As yet this is only in MS., but it is ready for printing when funds and time will permit.

This catalogue when completed will consist of four parts, the first and last of which will contain an account of the whole library, while the second and third will give more detailed accounts of special parts of it.

Part I. An alphabetical list of all the books in the library, arranged mainly under names of authors or institutions.

Part II. A more detailed list of periodical literature, including magazines, proceedings of societies, museum publications, etc., in alphabetical arrangement of publications under their respective countries, with ample cross-references. The geographical order adopted is:—

AUSTRALASIA — General New South Wales, Victoria, Tasmania, South Australia, Western Australia, Queensland, New Zealand, Polynesia.

BRITISH EMPIRE—London, England, Scotland, Ireland, Canada or British America, India, Africa.

UNITED STATES.

EUROPE—France, Belgium and Holland, Germany, Austria, Italy, Switzerland, Spain, Portugal, Sweden, Norway, Denmark, Russia.

ASIA—China, Japan, etc.

Part III. Pamphlets, collected in bound volumes.

Part IV. A general subject-index. This is intended to contain references not only to the titles but to the contents of as many of the books as possible, and will necessarily be the last part to be published. Much consideration has been given to the classification of the books, and all available schemes were studied, including Dewey's decimal classification. None of these was found suitable, as this is a library of limited compass accumulated for a special purpose. The classification adopted is, however, so arranged that it can at any time easily be translated into Dewey's or any other similar system if so desired. It is as follows:—

Class A., ZOOLOGY.—A. O. general; 1, mammalia; 2, birds; 3, reptiles and batrachians; 4, fishes; 5, mollusca; 6, insects; 7, other invertebrata.

Class B., BIOLOGY (other than zoology). — B. 1, botany; 2, anatomy, physiology, and embryology; 3, anthropology, ethnology, and philology.

Class C., GEOLOGY AND PALÆONTOLOGY.—C. 1, geology; 2, palæontology; 3, mineralogy and allied subjects.

Class D., PERIODICALS. — D. 1, museum publications; 2, library catalogues, bibliography, and indexes; 3, exhibition catalogues and literature; 4, magazines; 5, official and parliamentary; 6, reports, proceedings, transactions, etc.

Class E., TOPOGRAPHY.—E. 1, surveys; 2, voyages and travels, Australian and Pacific; 3, Asia and Africa; 4, America; 5, general.

Class F., WORKS OF REFERENCE.—F. 1, encyclopædias; 2, dictionaries; 3, atlases and maps.

Class G., GENERAL SCIENCE.—G. 1, agriculture; 2, physical sciences; 3, aquaria; 4, microscopy; 5, taxidermy and technology; 6, collectors' manuals.

Class H., MISCELLANEOUS.—H. 1, general literature; 2, commerce and colonisation; 3, statistics; 4, Acts of Parliament; 5, rare books; 6, manuscripts.

The books are stored in two rooms, of which the larger has sixty cases and contains the periodical literature, while the smaller with forty cases has the special subjects. As far as funds permit, books are bound uniformly in brown or green half morocco, and they are all marked on the outside with their case and place on shelf. The books are arranged on the shelves somewhat in the same order as the classifications, so that a glance at the shelf-list shows what may be in the library on any given subject. There is no restriction put on the use of the books by the staff of the museum within the institution, and in fact large numbers of books are shelf-marked for cases in the scientific work rooms, besides what are on the shelves in the library.

The museum library at present consists of 7429 volumes under the following main headings:—

PERIODICALS—Including proceedings of societies, museum publications, magazines, etc.

	Publications.	Vols.
British—London	39	1520
England	19	116
Scotland	12	75
Ireland	3	40
India	11	116
Canada	7	84
Australia	72	565
TOTAL	163	2516
United States	57	826
Foreign	102	1668
TOTAL	322	5010

Zoological works	1265
Botanical works	72
Palæontological works	365
Geological works	130
Voyages and travels	370
Dictionaries and encyclopædias	111
Exhibition literature	70
Library catalogues	54
Pamphlets in bound volumes	42
Miscellaneous	50
TOTAL	7429 vols.

The library is strictly for the use of the trustees and the officers of the museum. It is a public library only in the sense that it belongs to a national institution and is maintained by public funds; but it is in practice available to all who may desire to consult it, as no respectable person is refused permission to refer to it, and it is frequently taken advantage of by students and others seeking information. Needless to say, books are not lent out.

The trustees of the Australian Museum are not only accumulating a library for the use of the scientists of Australia, but they also issue publications, which are sold at low prices or given to other institutions in exchange for theirs, and form a very valuable adjunct by means of which many important series are added to the library. The museum publications consist of—

The annual reports of the trustees and their officers, with summaries of museum work.

Catalogues of specimens in the museum and of Australian natural history.

Memoirs, containing accounts of expeditions or description of specimens.

Records, a periodical issued at irregular intervals containing descriptions of new species and details of museum work.

SUTHERLAND SINCLAIR.

THE SECOND INTERNATIONAL LIBRARY CONFERENCE, (1897),

To be held, by the kind permission of

THE CORPORATION OF THE CITY OF LONDON,

IN THE

COUNCIL CHAMBER, GUILDHALL.

On JULY 13th, 14th, 15th, and 16th, 1897.

GENERAL PROGRAMME.

President - The Right Hon. Sir John Lubbock, Bart., M.P., F.R.S.

From 9.30 a.m. to 1 p.m. and from 1.30 p.m. to 3.30 p.m. each day.

Hon. Secretary-General of the Conference:
J. Y. W. MacALISTER.

Hon. Treasurer of the Conference:
HENRY R. TEDDER.

PRESIDENT:

The Rt. Hon. Sir JOHN LUBBOCK, Bart., M.P., F.R.S.

HON. TREASURER:
*Henry R. Tedder, Athenæum, Pall Mall, S.W.

HON. SECRETARY-GENERAL:
*J. Y. W. MacAlister, 20 Hanover Square, W.

ORGANISING COMMITTEE:
Chairman.—Mr. Alderman Harry Rawson.*

T. J. Agar, C.A., Auditor, Lib. Assoc.
John Ballinger, Cardiff P. Lib.
Francis T. Barrett, Glasgow P. Lib.
*James R. Boosé, Libn., Royal Colonial Inst.
*E. M. Borrajo, Guildhall Library.
J. P. Briscoe, Nottingham P. Lib.
*J. D. Brown, Libn., Clerkenwell P. Lib.
*F. J. Burgoyne, Libn., Lambeth P. Lib.
*A. H. Carter, Sub.-Libn., St. Martin's P. Lib.
*Cedric Chivers, Lib. Bureau.
Peter Cowell, Liverpool P. Lib.
W. Crowther, Libn., Derby P. Lib.
H. E. Davidson, American Lib. Bureau.
C. T. Davis, Libn., Wandsworth P. Lib.
R. K. Dent, Libn., Aston P. Lib.
W. E. Doubleday, Libn., Hampstead P. Lib.
*W. R. Douthwaite, Libn., Gray's Inn.
G. Hall Elliott, Libn., Belfast P. Lib.
H. W. Fincham, Commissioner, Clerkenwell P. Lib.
H. T. Folkard, Libn., Wigan P. Lib.
H. W. Fovargue, Hon. Solicitor to L. A.
*Richard Garnett, C.B., LL.D.
Joseph Gilburt, Day's Library.
T. W. Hand, Libn., Oldham P. Lib.
*Miss Hannam, Libn., Obstetrical Society.
Rev. Canon J. Clare Hudson.
G. R. Humphery, Hon. Libn., Deptford Lib.
*L. Inkster, Libn., Battersea P. Lib.

*Herbert Jones, Libn., Kensington P. Lib.
C. V. Kirkby, Libn., Leicester P. Lib.
*J. W. Knapman, Libn. of the Pharmaceutical Society.
T. W. Lyster, Libn., National Lib. of Ireland.
C. Madeley, Libn., Warrington P. Lib.
*Thos. Mason, Libn., St. Martin's P. Lib.
E. Norris Mathews, Libn., Bristol P. Lib.
W. May, Libn., Birkenhead P. Lib.
Hew Morrison, Libn., Edinburgh P. Lib.
J. D. Mullins, Libn., Birmingham P. Lib.
E. W. B. Nicholson, Libn., Bodleian Lib., Oxford.
J. J. Ogle, Libn., Bootle P. Lib.
Frank Pacy, Libn., St. George, Hanover Square, P. Lib.
*A. W. Pollard, British Museum.
*J. H. Quinn, Libn., Chelsea P. Lib.
A. W. Robertson, Libn., Aberdeen P. Lib.
C. E. Scarse, Libn., Birmingham Lib.
E. W. Shackell, Chairman, Cardiff P. Lib.
*Sam. Smith, Libn., Sheffield P. Lib.
Mr. Ald. J. W. Southern, P. Lib. Com., Manchester.
C. W. Sutton, Libn., Manchester P. Lib.
Sam. Timmins, P. Lib. Committee, Birmingham.
*Charles Welch, Guildhall Lib.
Butler Wood, Libn., Bradford P. Lib.
W. H. K. Wright, Borough Libn., Plymouth.

* *The asterisks indicate Members of the Executive Committee and of Sub-Committees.*

N.B.—It will save the time of Correspondents if letters, exclusively on the business of the following Committees, are addressed to their respective Hon. Secretaries.

COMMITTEE ON PAPERS AND DISCUSSIONS
Chairman.—Richard Garnett, C.B., LL.D.
Hon. Secretary.—J. D. Brown, Clerkenwell Public Library, E.C.

RECEPTION COMMITTEE:
Chairman.—Charles Welch.
Hon. Secretary.—E. M. Borrajo, Guildhall, E.C.

EXHIBITION COMMITTEE:
Chairman.—Herbert Jones.
Hon. Secretary.—Thomas Mason, 115 St. Martin's Lane, W.C.

FINANCE COMMITTEE:
Chairman.—Henry R. Tedder.
Hon. Secretary.—J. W. Knapman, 17 Bloomsbury Square, W.C.

NOTES.

Members are earnestly requested at the earliest possible moment to inform the Hon. Secretary of the Reception Committee, Mr. E. M. Borrajo, of their arrival, and supply him, *in writing*, with their London Addresses. It would also facilitate the work of the Reception Committee if they would promptly inform Mr. Borrajo what Entertainments and Visits they propose to take part in.

Tickets for the Conference Dinner must be obtained not later than Tuesday.

It has been decided not to make organised visits to the various Libraries in London, of which a list will be found at the end of this Programme. Members are therefore advised to make their own arrangements for visiting these, as they will be able to do so at much greater advantage, either individually or in small groups.

LATE PAPERS.—A number of papers have been received too late to be included in this Programme, but they will either be printed in the *Transactions* of the Conference, or, with the permission of the Authors, reserved for the Annual Meeting of the Library Association to be held in October next, and will be printed in the *Transactions* of that meeting.

Detailed information as to Entertainments and Visits will be found in the Programme of the Reception Committee, at pp. 224, 225.

PHOTOGRAPH OF THE CONFERENCE.—It is proposed to take a Photograph of the Members of the Conference. Full particulars will be announced at the Morning Session on Wednesday.

TIME TABLE.

Tuesday, July 13th—

10.30 a.m. to 1 p.m.—Opening by the Lord Mayor—President's Address—Papers.
1 p.m.—Luncheon.
1.30 p.m. to 4 p.m.—Second Session—Papers.
4 p.m. to 7 p.m.—Reception at Sion College, Victoria Embankment.
9 p.m. to 11 p.m.—Reception at the Mansion House.

Wednesday, July 14th—

9.30 a.m. to 1 p.m.—Third Session—Papers.
1 p.m.—Luncheon.
1.30 p.m. to 4 p.m.—Fourth Session—Papers.
4 p.m. to 7 p.m.—Marchioness of Bute's Garden Party.
10 p.m. to 12 p.m.—Lady Lubbock's Reception at 2 St. James's Square.

Thursday, July 15th—

9.30 a.m. to 1 p.m.—Fifth Session—Papers.
1 p.m.—Luncheon.
1.30 p.m. to 4 p.m.—Sixth Session—Papers.
4 p.m. to 6 p.m.—Visits to Brook House, Park Lane; Apsley House, Piccadilly (*First Party*); Grosvenor House, Upper Grosvenor St.
8 p.m.—Sir Henry Irving, at the Lyceum.

Friday, July 16th—

9.30 a.m. to 1 p.m.—Seventh Session—Papers.
1 p.m.—Luncheon.
1.30 p.m. to 4 p.m.—Eighth Session—Papers. CLOSE OF CONFERENCE.
4 p.m. to 6 p.m.—Visits to Lambeth Palace; Stafford House, St. James's; Apsley House (*Second Party*).
6.30 p.m.—Conference Dinner at Hotel Cecil.

LIST OF LONDON PUBLIC LIBRARIES

To which visits may be made by Members of the Conference.

These are in addition to the Libraries named in the Programme of the Reception Committee.

The following Libraries are all established under the provisions of the various Public Libraries Acts, and are administered by the Local Boards or Vestries, or by special Boards of Commissioners elected from each district. To those unfamiliar with the local government of the County of London, it may be well to explain that these Libraries are independent of each other. Hours vary from 8, 9, 10, etc., a.m., to 9 and 10 p.m.

NORTH OF THE THAMES.

CHELSEA, Manresa Rd., off King's Rd., S.W. Branch at Kensal Town, Harrow Rd., W. *Librarian:* J. H. QUINN.
CLERKENWELL, Skinner Street, E.C., near Farringdon Road. *Librarian:* J. D. BROWN.
FULHAM, Fulham Road, S.W. Branch at Wandsworth Bridge Road. *Librarian:* FRANKLIN T. BARRETT.
HAMMERSMITH, Ravenscourt Park, W. Branch at Shepherd's Bush, W. *Librarian:* S. MARTIN.
HAMPSTEAD, Priory Road, N.W. Three branches. *Librarian:* W. E. DOUBLEDAY.
HOLBORN, John Street, W.C., near Gray's Inn Road. *Librarian:* H. HAWKES.
KENSINGTON, High Street, W. Branches at Notting Hill, etc. *Librarian:* H. JONES.
POPLAR, High Street, E., near East India Dock Road. Branch at Isle of Dogs. *Librarian:* H. ROWLATT.
ST. GEORGE, HANOVER SQUARE, Buckingham Palace Road, W. Branch at South Audley Street. *Librarian:* F. PACY.
ST. GILES and ST. GEORGE, BLOOMSBURY, High Holborn, W.C. *Librarian:* W. A. TAYLOR.
ST. MARTIN-IN-THE-FIELDS, St. Martin's Lane, W.C., close to Trafalgar Square. *Librarian:* T. MASON.
SHOREDITCH, Kingsland Road, E. Branch at Pitfield Street, E. *Librarian:* W. C. PLANT.
STOKE NEWINGTON, Church Street, N. *Librarian:* G. PREECE.
WESTMINSTER, Great Smith Street, S.W. Branch at Trevor Square, Knightsbridge. *Librarian:* H. E. POOLE.
WHITECHAPEL, High Street, near Aldgate, E. *Librarian:* A. CAWTHORNE.

SOUTH OF THE THAMES.

BATTERSEA, Lavender Hill, S.W., near Clapham Junction. Branches at Lurline Gardens and Lammas Hall. *Librarian:* L. INKSTER.
BERMONDSEY, Spa Road, S.E. *Librarian:* J. FROWDE.
CAMBERWELL, High Street, Peckham, S.E. Branches at Old Kent Road, etc. *Librarian:* E. FOSKETT.
CHRIST CHURCH, Charles Street, Blackfriars Road, S.E. *Librarian:* R. AUSTIN.
CLAPHAM, Clapham Common, S.W. *Librarian:* J. R. WELCH.
LAMBETH, Brixton Oval, S.W. Branches at Kennington, West Norwood, Lower Marsh, Wandsworth Road, etc. *Librarian:* F. J. BURGOYNE.
LEWISHAM, Catford, S.E. *Librarian:* C. W. F. GOSS.
NEWINGTON, Walworth Road, S.E. *Librarian:* R. W. MOULD.
ROTHERHITHE, Lower Road, S.E. *Librarian:* H. A. SHUTTLEWORTH.
ST. SAVIOUR, Southwark Bridge Road, S.E. *Librarian:* H. D. ROBERTS.
STREATHAM, S.W. *Librarian:* T. EVERATT.
WANDSWORTH, S.W. (near High Street). *Librarian:* C. T. DAVIS.

In the immediate neighbourhood of London, the most important Libraries are at Croydon, Ealing, Kingston, Richmond, Tottenham, Willesden, West Ham, Wimbledon, and Walthamstow.

To those Libraries which are not freely accessible to the public, members of the Conference will no doubt obtain admission on making application to the Librarians.

PROGRAMME
OF
PAPERS AND DISCUSSIONS,

With Abstracts of the Contents of Papers.

COMMITTEE ON PAPERS AND DISCUSSIONS.

CHAIRMAN.

RICHARD GARNETT, C.B., LL.D., British Museum.

MEMBERS.

E. M. BORRAJO, Guildhall Library.

L. INKSTER, Public Libraries, Battersea.

HERBERT JONES, Public Libraries, Kensington.

J. W. KNAPMAN, Pharmaceutical Society, Bloomsbury Square.

J. Y. W. MacALISTER, Royal Medical and Chirurgical Society.

T. MASON, Public Library, St. Martin-in-the-Fields.

A. W. POLLARD, British Museum.

H. R. TEDDER, Athenæum, Pall Mall.

C. WELCH, Guildhall Library.

Hon. Secretary of the Committee:
JAMES D. BROWN,
Public Library,
CLERKENWELL, E.C.

All communications relating to Papers and Discussions should be addressed to MR. BROWN.

It is particularly requested that all Papers be handed to the Hon. Secretary of the Papers Committee, to ensure their being read in case of the temporary absence of the Authors, and to secure their appearance in the printed Transactions of the Conference.

ORDER OF PAPERS AND DISCUSSIONS.

Owing to the length of the Programme, discussions must necessarily be limited, and speakers are requested not to occupy more than five minutes with their remarks.

The Papers have been arranged with the view of bringing together all those on kindred subjects, and classifying them according to a systematic scheme.

The Papers will be read as far as possible in the order set forth in this Programme, and any remaining unread at the end of a Session shall be adjourned to the following Session.

Members are particularly requested to keep their seats during the reading of Papers and the discussions thereon.

TUESDAY, JULY 13. First Session, at 10.30 a.m.

Welcome by the RIGHT HON. THE LORD MAYOR to the Members of the Conference, after which the

RIGHT HON. SIR JOHN LUBBOCK, BART., M.P., the President, will deliver the
INAUGURAL ADDRESS.

1.—RICHARD GARNETT, C.B., LL.D., Keeper of the Printed Books, British Museum:—
"**The Introduction of European Printing into the East.**"
(This Paper will be read during the Conversazione on Monday, July 12.)

2.—J. Y. W. MacALISTER, Librarian of the Royal Medical and Chirurgical Society, London; Hon. Secretary of the Library Association:—
"**Some Tendencies of Modern Librarianship.**"

At the beginning of the present reign the average librarian was either a scholar who disdained the practical arts of librarianship, or else an uneducated person (often an old soldier), who owed his position to the selfish generosity of a patron. The scholar knew some of his books, and by their aid wrote others, or gave valuable assistance to scholars working in his own line, but his library was chaos to the ordinary student. The old soldier kept his library tidy, and keenly resented having to disturb his well-drilled files of volumes for the sake of any invading reader.

The pendulum has swung forward—has it not swung too far, and is there not a danger of our losing something worth keeping by ignoring scholarship in our admiration of the modern *soi-disant* practical man, whose ideal of a perfect library is: "Put a ticket in the slot and the book (you don't want) will come out"?

3.—HENRY R. TEDDER, Secretary, Athenæum Club, London; Hon. Treasurer of the Library Association:—

"The Evolution of the Public Library."

A History of Libraries might well form part of the great history of sociological development designed and partly completed by Mr. Herbert Spencer. Brief view of the characteristic features of ancient, mediæval, and modern public libraries. Some curious survivals still to be seen of ancient methods. How does the modern public library differ from earlier examples? Its educational and civilising influences. It is the university of unattached scholars, and the librarian (now recognised as a skilled professional man) is a worker in the cause of intellectual progress. A glimpse at the future.

4.—MELVIL DEWEY, Secretary of the University of the State of New York, and Director of the State Library, Albany, U.S.A.:—

"The Relation of the State to the Public Library."

Plea for an extension of legislation in favour of libraries, on the ground that they are as necessary to the public welfare as are the public schools. Other aspects of the question.

5.—HERBERT JONES, Librarian, Public Libraries, Kensington, London:—

"Public Library Authorities, their Constitution and Powers, as they are and as they should be."

Library authority, varied definitions. Vagueness of the original conception as to this matter in the early Acts. All sorts of conflicting modes of forming and carrying on the authority, and as to numbers, powers, duration of office, etc. Control by other local bodies. Control by the State. Uniformity of constitution of library authority. How it might be arrived at. Great advantages, to the libraries, to the public. Final control by the State through a Government Department.

TUESDAY, JULY 13. Second Session, at 1.30 p.m.

6.—ALDERMAN HARRY RAWSON, Public Libraries Committee, Manchester; President of the Library Association:—

"Duties of Library Committees."

Constitution of Public Library Committees: wholly or partly official; number and proportion of members; comparison of advantages. Duties in regard to librarians and assistants—salaries and hours of work—educational fitness and means of further culture. Attention to lighting, warming, and ventilation. Selection and purchase of books and periodicals. Special provision for boys and girls. Relation of libraries to technical schools. Literary assistance to readers—the question of fines. Improvement of library legislation. Establishment of new libraries and the extension of their usefulness.

NOTE.—*Papers 7, 8, 9, and 9a, being on the same subject, will be dealt with in one discussion.*

7.—CHARLES WELCH, Librarian, Corporation Library, Guildhall, London:—

"The Training of Librarians."

The library as a school, university and college training, the training of the book-mart. Ideal training to combine these three. The problem of the librarian's early education. How can it best be dealt with?

8.—HANNAH P. JAMES, Librarian, Osterhout Free Library, Wilkes-Barré, Pa., U.S.A.:—

"Special Training for Library Work."

Description of the library training schools and classes of the United States.

9.—E. R. N. MATHEWS, Librarian, Public Libraries, Bristol:—

"Female Library Assistants and Competitive Examination."

Introduction of female assistants at Manchester, and afterwards at Bristol, in 1876. Brief résumé of the work at Bristol, and description of the scheme of competitive examinations for appointments. Remarks on the general capacity of young women for the public library service.

9a.—J. J. OGLE, Librarian, Public Library, Bootle:—
"Hindrances to the Training of Efficient Librarians."

WEDNESDAY, JULY 14. Third Session, at 9.30.

10.—F. M. CRUNDEN, Librarian, Public Library, St. Louis, U.S.A.:—
"Books and Text-Books: **the Function of the Library in Education.**"

11.—SIDNEY LEE, Editor of the "Dictionary of National Biography":—
"**National Biography and National Bibliography.**"

> The "Dictionary of National Biography" regarded as a contribution to National Bibliography and as an index to what is memorable in national literature.

12.—A. W. POLLARD, British Museum; Hon. Secretary of the Bibliographical Society:—
"**Relations of Bibliography** and Cataloguing."

> Broadly speaking, the aim of the cataloguer should be such a description of a book in a particular library as will enable a visitor to the library to identify it as the book he wants in the shortest and simplest manner possible. The aim of the bibliographer, on the other hand, should be such a description of a book as will most compactly and conveniently show its relations to other books, either to other copies of the same edition, or to other editions of the same work, or to other works by the same author; or, again, to other works on the same subject; or, lastly, to other books printed by the same printer. The paper will illustrate how the confusion of these two objects may cause needless trouble to everyone who has to use a catalogue, and may, at the same time, lower the standard of bibliographical precision. It will also briefly consider how far bibliographical refinement can be introduced into different kinds of catalogues without injury to their proper usefulness.

13.—F. T. BARRETT, Librarian, Mitchell Library, Glasgow:—
"**The Alphabetical and Classified Forms of Catalogue Compared.**"

> An attempt to estimate the advantages and disadvantages of each form respectively for public library use.

14.—PROFESSOR C. DZIATZKO, University Library, Göttingen, Germany:—
"**On the Aid lent by Public Bodies to the Art of Printing in the Early Days of Typography.**"

WEDNESDAY, JULY 14. Fourth Session, at 1.30.

15.—WM. H. BRETT, Librarian, Public Library, Cleveland, U.S.A.; President of the American Library Association:—
"**Freedom in Public Libraries.**"

> Absolutely free access of all borrowers to the shelves of the public circulating library entirely feasible.
> It is desirable on the score of economy, as it effects a great saving of the time of those using the library.
> It is desirable, as greatly increasing the educational value of the library. It affords facilities for a much more satisfactory selection of books than is possible from a catalogue alone. It broadens the scope of reading, and promotes the use of the better classes of books.
> It is desirable for its moral effect—for its expression of confidence rather than of distrust. The experience of those libraries which are employing this plan shows that this confidence is not misplaced.
> It is consistent with the spirit in which the free library is founded and maintained.

NOTE.—*Papers 16 and 17 will be discussed together.*

16.—CHARLES A. CUTTER, Librarian, Forbes Library, Northampton, Mass., U.S.A.:—
"**A Classification and Notation.**"

> Concise account of the characteristics of the "Expansive Classification" **of books on the shelves,** with remarks on classification in general.

17.—A. W. ROBERTSON, Librarian, Public Library, Aberdeen:—
   "**Classification in Public Libraries.**"

   Necessity of some form of shelf-classification assumed. Though at first the Librarian may be satisfied with a broad general classification, he is gradually driven, by the expansion of his library and the requirements of his readers, to adopt a fuller and closer classification, this last being determined by the books on his shelves and not by any theoretical tabulation of human knowledge. Some good results to librarians and to readers from such increasing application of closeness of shelf-arrangement indicated. The question of a notation an essential part of the problem, and the merits of the fixed and of the movable or relative location discussed; the balance of advantage being shown to lie with the latter, owing to its flexibility and expansiveness. Desirability of having a scheme of classification common to all libraries, such a scheme being an enterprise worthy of an International Conference.

18.—HENRY C. L. ANDERSON, Librarian, Public Library of New South Wales, Sydney:—
   "**Library** Work in New **South** Wales."

19.—W. H. JAMES WEALE, Librarian, National Art Library, South Kensington Museum, London:—
   "**History and Cataloguing of the National Art Library.**"

   Sketch of its history from 1852. Developments—actual contents. Rearrangement and new system of cataloguing introduced in 1890. Its advantages.

THURSDAY, JULY 15. Fifth Session, at 9.30.

The Fifth and Sixth Sessions will be held in the Old Council Chamber at the Guildhall.

20.—PETER COWELL, Librarian, Public Libraries, Liverpool:—
   "**Public Library Work Forty Years** ago.**"

   As exemplified in the work of the Liverpool Public Libraries. Comparison of past and present accommodation. Solid character of books read. Critical readers. Personal contact between librarian and reader desirable. Enthusiasm of readers forty years ago. Circulation of music; its advantages. Books for the blind and the readers thereof. Free lectures as aids to library work.

NOTE.—*Papers 21 and 22, being on the same subject, will be dealt with in one discussion.*

21.—F. J. BURGOYNE, Librarian, Public Libraries, Lambeth, London:—
   "**Public Library Architecture from the Librarian's Standpoint.**"

   The Librarian chiefly concerned with the internal arrangements of library buildings. **The rapid growth of libraries,** and importance of having sites large enough for future extension. The plan. Arrangement of rooms and shelving of books. Systems of issue, lighting, heating, and ventilation.

22.—BERESFORD PITE, F.R.I.B.A., London:—
   "**Library Architecture from the Architect's Standpoint.**"

   The building an extended bookcase with mechanical functions—but more—a good book deserving a good binding. A good collection of books deserves a good building, hence the æsthetic function, similar in contrast to that, say, between a Dictionary of Dates and Ruskin's "Modern Painters." This an overlooked aspect of library architecture. A library building most fitting for the expression of intellectual pleasure in construction and design. Suggestions for such design. Dignity, simplicity, restraint. The fitness or relation of ornament in libraries, *e.g.* in a reading-room or entrance-hall. The use and abuse of decoration. Architectural styles—Philosophic Greek to Romantic Gothic. A possible Eclecticism. Some types. College libraries, club libraries, British Museum Reference. Modern public libraries. An ideal.

NOTE.—*Papers 23 and 24 will be discussed together.*

23.—CAROLINE M. HEWINS, Librarian, Public Library, Hartford, Conn., U.S.A.:—
   "**Books that Children like.**"

24.—J. C. DANA, Librarian, Public Library, Denver, Colorado, U.S.A.:—
   "**Our Youngest Readers.**"

ORDER OF PAPERS AND DISCUSSIONS

THURSDAY, JULY 15. Sixth Session, at 1.30.

NOTE.—*Papers 25, 26, and 27 will be discussed together.*

25.—J. N. LARNED, late Librarian, Buffalo Library, Buffalo, N.Y., U.S.A.:—

"Organisation of Co-operative Work among Public Libraries."

The possibilities of co-operative work among public libraries can be realised only by an organisation that will provide for it a permanent editorial director, adequately salaried, and devoting his whole attention to the work. Probably the best mode in which this may be accomplished is by the formation of a distinct international association for the purpose.

26.—H. H. LANGTON, Librarian, University of Toronto, Canada:—

"Co-operation in the Compilation of a Catalogue of Periodicals."

The increase in number and importance of technical periodicals and of the serials issued by learned societies calls for suitable bibliographical treatment. At present the information obtainable is fragmentary, and scattered among a variety of publications. There is need of a single catalogue, to form a complete international repertory of periodicals, exclusive of newspapers and literary magazines. Provision should also be made for the issue at regular intervals of supplements recording new publications.

The means suggested for compiling the catalogue and ensuring its continuation by supplements is the appointment of an international committee of publication, whose peculiar functions should be to establish communications with the librarians at the provincial centres of every country. By their agency, accurate information could be obtained annually respecting the societies and periodicals of each locality.

27.—C. W. ANDREWS, Librarian, John Crerar Library, Chicago, U.S.A.:—

"Printed Card-Catalogues."

Growth in the use of printed card-catalogues in the United States, their advantages and disadvantages; their cost; and whether or not the advantages overbalance the increased cost.

28.—HERBERT PUTNAM, Librarian, Public Library, Boston, Mass., U.S.A.:—

"Local Library Associations in the United States."

Account of the formation in the United States during the past twelve years of district library associations or clubs for the discussion of local and other matters not specially provided for in the proceedings of the American Library Association. Notices of the work of these associations, and tables giving particulars of their organisation and lists of topics discussed at their meetings.

FRIDAY, JULY 16. Seventh Session, at 9.30.

29.—ANDREAS S. STEENBERG, Horsens, Denmark:—

"Libraries of the Northern States of Europe."

A short history of the scientific and people's libraries of Denmark, Norway, Sweden, and Finland. Description of means of support, methods, public use, and general policy and needs.

30.—JACOB SCHWARTZ, Librarian, Free Library of the General Society of Mechanics, etc., New York, U.S.A.:—

"An Indicator-Catalogue Charging System."

Showing how the generally accepted "Indicator" system of charging in vogue in Britain and the generally accepted "Card" or "Slip" system of charging in vogue in the United States may be combined in a method that preserves the essential features of both systems.

31.—F. BLAKE CROFTON, Librarian, Legislative Library, Halifax, Nova Scotia:—

"A Hint in Cataloguing."

32.—E. A. PETHERICK, London :—

"Theoretical and Practical Bibliography."

Need of librarians, booksellers, and the general reader for something more than "Author," "Index," and "Subject" catalogues, or combinations of these forms. Systematic and analytical catalogues. Compilers should plan and prepare catalogues not too closely to any given form, but rather in accordance (*a*) with the requirements of their readers, (*b*) the character and (*c*) extent of their respective collections, and considering the expense of compilation and printing (*d*) with a view to permanence. Reasons why certain "Author" and "Index" catalogues are insufficient for specialists. Examples of periodical catalogues which are indispensable as works of reference. Examples of complete catalogues of libraries and special collections. British Museum catalogue. Royal Society's catalogue of scientific papers. Bibliography proper. Special bibliographies. National bibliography. A bibliography of Australasia and Polynesia, with plan of the work.

33.—R. R. BOWKER, Publisher, New York :—

"Bibliographical Endeavours in America."

An account of the publication of bibliographical works in America from the earliest to recent times.

FRIDAY, JULY 16. Eighth Session, at 1.30.

34.—C. H. GOULD, Librarian, McGill University, Montreal, Canada :—

"Description of the more important Libraries in Montreal, with some Remarks upon Departmental Libraries."

35.—ERNEST CUSHING RICHARDSON, Librarian, Princeton University, New Jersey, U.S.A. :—

"Libraries the Prime Factor in Human Evolution."

By language, concepts are transferred ready formed from one individual to another, and ideas are built up, exactly as if by the individual from his own sense-impressions. By books, the built-up experiences of former generations and foreign thinkers are also added. Being recorded, they can be gathered and subjected to the co-ordinating activity of the individual. Books thus brought together, as a basis for co-ordination of ideas, are a library. The only possibility of further progress lies in this instrument. The fact of its theoretical aspect suggests that the germ of libraries is to be found at the point where the first idea communicated by another was placed beside the idea or ideas of a conceiver for co-ordination. In its practical aspect the fact points to a fundamental advantage in library administration of arranging like books in close proximity, or what is known as close classification.

36.—JOHN THORBURN, Librarian, Geological Survey of Canada, Ottawa :—

"Counting and Time Recording."

The methods of counting adopted by different nations. The very limited range, in many cases, of the use of numbers, prior to the introduction of the so-called Arabic numbers. The various ways in which dates are given and recorded both in ancient and comparatively modern times. Peculiar method of dating documents practised in Scotland and France up to the beginning of the 19th century.

37.—GEORGE ILES, New York :—

"Expert Appraisal of Literature."

Mr. Iles' Paper has been printed in full by the author, and circulated among the members of the Conference. It describes what has been done by the American Library Association in obtaining from men and women of authority brief notes, descriptive and critical, on books chosen by them. Advocates that such notes be printed and made accessible to the public in card-catalogues and elsewhere.

38.—FRANK CUNDALL, Librarian, Institute of Jamaica, Kingston, Jamaica :—

"Library Work in Jamaica."

Past and present libraries of Jamaica—literary tastes—practical points in the management of libraries in tropical climates, etc.

39.—H. C. V. LEIBBRANDT, Keeper of the Archives of the Cape of Good Hope, and Librarian of the Joint Library of Parliament :—
"Education and Libraries of the Cape of Good Hope."

40.—J. R. G. ADAMS, Public Library of South Australia, Adelaide :—
"Registration of Colonial Publications."

41.—H. E. BARFF :—
"Library of the University of Sydney."

42.—THOMAS W. ROWE :—
"Public Libraries in New Zealand."

43.—EDWARD SHILLINGTON :—
"Auckland Free Public Library."

44.—E. F. J. LOVE :—
"Library Facilities of Scientific Investigators in Melbourne."

45.—SUTHERLAND SINCLAIR :—
"The Australian Museum Library."

Programme

of

Reception Committee

July 12th to 16th, 1897.

CONFERENCE OF LIBRARIANS

MONDAY, JULY 12.

8 p.m.—CONVERSAZIONE in the Guildhall Library, Museum, Art Gallery, and Council Chamber, by invitation of the Reception Committee and the Bibliographical Society. Lecture by Dr. Richard Garnett, C.B., President of the Bibliographical Society. Entertainment by some Members of the Savage Club.

TUESDAY, JULY 13.

10.30 a.m.—WELCOME BY THE RIGHT HON. THE LORD MAYOR TO THE MEMBERS OF THE CONFERENCE, after which the Chair will be taken by the President, the Right Hon. Sir John Lubbock, Bart., who will deliver the Inaugural Address.

1 to 1.30 p.m.—Interval for Luncheon.

1.30 p.m.—AFTERNOON MEETING OF THE CONFERENCE.

4 to 7 p.m.—RECEPTION by the President and Court of Governors at Sion College, Victoria Embankment. Exhibition of Books and Manuscripts.

9 to 11 p.m.—RECEPTION AT THE MANSION HOUSE, by invitation of the Right Hon. the Lord Mayor and Lady Mayoress.

WEDNESDAY, JULY 14.

9.30 a.m.—MORNING MEETING OF THE CONFERENCE.

1 to 1.30 p.m.—Interval for Luncheon.

1.30 p.m.—AFTERNOON MEETING OF THE CONFERENCE.

4 to 7 p.m.—The Most Hon. the Marchioness of Bute will receive the Members at a GARDEN PARTY at St. John's Lodge, Regent's Park.

10 to 12 p.m.—LADY LUBBOCK'S RECEPTION AT 2 ST. JAMES'S SQUARE.

THURSDAY, JULY 15.

9.30 a.m.—MORNING MEETING OF THE CONFERENCE.

1 to 1.30 p.m.—Interval for Luncheon.

1.30 p.m.—AFTERNOON MEETING OF THE CONFERENCE.

4 to 6 p.m.—VISIT TO THE LIBRARY OF BROOK HOUSE, Park Lane, by invitation of the Right Hon. Lord Tweedmouth.

4 to 6 p.m.—VISIT TO APSLEY HOUSE, Piccadilly, by invitation of His Grace the Duke of Wellington. *First Party.*

4 to 6 p.m.—AFTERNOON TEA AT GROSVENOR HOUSE, Upper Grosvenor Street, by invitation of His Grace the Duke of Westminster, K.G.

8 p.m.—SPECIAL PERFORMANCE OF "THE MERCHANT OF VENICE," at the Lyceum Theatre, by invitation of Sir Henry Irving.

FRIDAY, JULY 16.

9.30 a.m.—MORNING MEETING OF THE CONFERENCE.

1 to 1.30 p.m.—Interval for Luncheon.

1.30 p.m.—AFTERNOON MEETING OF THE CONFERENCE.

4 to 6 p.m.—VISIT TO LAMBETH PALACE AND LIBRARY, by invitation of the Most Rev. His Grace the Lord Archbishop of Canterbury. Exhibition of Books and Manuscripts.

4 to 6 p.m.—VISIT TO STAFFORD HOUSE, St. James's, by invitation of His Grace the Duke of Sutherland.

4 to 6 p.m.—VISIT TO APSLEY HOUSE. *Second Party.*

6.30, for 7 p.m.—CONFERENCE DINNER AT THE HOTEL CECIL.

THE LIBRARY OF THE BRITISH MUSEUM will be open to visitors every day in the week between 10 a.m. and 6 p.m. during the Session of the Conference. Dr. Richard Garnett, C.B., Keeper of the Printed Books, has kindly promised to prepare an Exhibition of American Books and Books relating to America, and to receive Members who visit the Museum when he is in the Building.

THE DEPARTMENT OF SCIENCE AND ART will admit Members free to the SOUTH KENSINGTON MUSEUM on any Students' Days, and to the SCIENCE AND ART LIBRARIES when open. Members' Tickets must be shown at the entrance. Mr. W. H. James Weale, F.S.A., Keeper of the National Art Library, will be pleased to receive Members any day, or (by appointment) on Monday, Tuesday, or Saturday evenings.

The MUSEUM and SEARCH ROOMS of the PUBLIC RECORD OFFICE, Chancery Lane, will be open from 10 a.m. to 4 p.m. during each day of the Conference, when Sir H. C. Maxwell Lyte, K.C.B., Deputy Keeper, has kindly promised to afford Members special facilities for their inspection.

The Committees of the undermentioned Clubs have elected Members of the Conference Honorary Members for the week:—

  CITY LIBERAL, Wallbrook.
  JUNIOR ATHENÆUM, 116 Piccadilly.
  NATIONAL LIBERAL, Whitehall Place.
  SAVAGE, Adelphi Terrace.
  ALEXANDRA, 12 Grosvenor Street. (*Ladies' Club.*)

Members availing themselves of this privilege must show their Tickets of Membership to the hall porters whenever they enter the Club-houses.

THE ROYAL BOTANIC SOCIETY OF LONDON will open the Society's Gardens in Regent's Park to Members, during the Conference Week, upon production of their Tickets of Membership.

THE ZOOLOGICAL SOCIETY OF LONDON will open the Society's Gardens in Regent's Park to Members of the Conference, from Sunday July 11 to Saturday July 17, both days inclusive. Members' Tickets must be shown at the gates and the Visitors' Book signed.

Miscellaneous Information.

Cloak Rooms.—A Ladies' Cloak Room is provided in the South Lobby of the Council Chamber, and Cloak Rooms for Gentlemen will be found at the entrance to No. 1 Court, and adjoining the Aldermen's Court Room.

Luncheons and Light Refreshments.—Luncheons and Light Refreshments will be provided by Messrs. Ring & Brymer at a moderate tariff, in the basement of the Council Chamber, Guildhall, from 12 o'clock to the close of the Meeting on each day.

Messengers.—The services of Boy Messengers can be secured at 66 Queen Victoria Street (corner of Queen Street).

Post Office and Telegrams.—Letters can be posted in the Hall, close to the steps leading to the Council Chamber. Other Post Office business, including the despatch of telegrams, can be carried out at 72 Aldermanbury, or at the Wool Exchange, Basinghall Street.

Secretary's Office.—The Honorary Secretary of the Reception Committee (Mr. Edward M. Borrajo) will attend in his office, adjoining the Library, on July 12 (from 10 a.m. to 4 p.m.), and from July 13 to 16 (from 9.30 a.m. to the close of the Meetings), to issue tickets, answer inquiries, etc., in connection with this Programme.

Writing Rooms.—Accommodation for writing, etc., will be provided in the Aldermen's Court Room, and in the Lobby of the Council Chamber.

For a list of London Libraries open to visitors see end of General Programme.

PROCEEDINGS

OF THE

SECOND INTERNATIONAL LIBRARY CONFERENCE.

LONDON, JULY 13, 14, 15, AND 16, 1897.

TUESDAY MORNING, JULY 13th, 1897.

FIRST SESSION.

THE members assembled in the Council Chamber of the Guildhall, which had been kindly placed at their disposition by the Corporation.

The RIGHT HON. THE LORD MAYOR OF LONDON, in welcoming the members of the Conference, said: I believe it should be the custom of Lord Mayors—for I think it is a good custom—that if they have nothing to say they should not take up a long time in speaking at public assemblies. But I have one thing to say to you, and it is a word of welcome—welcome in the name of the Corporation of London, who are delighted to see you here to-day, and will welcome you to this ancient hall and to the City of London. Later on I hope also to see you all at the Mansion House. I am very glad to see that Sir John Lubbock, who is to address you soon, is present to-day, for he will be able to speak to you better than I. The question of public libraries is one in which I take the greatest possible interest. As Chairman of the Public Libraries at Hertford, I believe that the town and the county of Hertford have received undoubted benefit, and I may add my humble testimony to the great interest that is generally taken in the movement. I have been a collector of books all my life, and before I was made a Lord Mayor I occasionally looked inside them. It is all very well to love to collect books, but the collector of books and the reader of books do not always go together. Public libraries are a great boon, and the love of reading is a thing which ought to be inculcated in early youth, or public libraries will lose much of their efficacy. So I think that the two things—collecting books and reading them—should go hand in hand. I am quite aware that in this matter careless reading is to be deprecated, and indiscriminate reading is, I think, the general object. But indiscriminate charity is better than no charity at all, and I believe that indiscriminate reading is better than no reading at all. And now I will retire, for you will shortly have the opportunity of listening to Sir John Lubbock, to whom I now accede the chair.

The PRESIDENT (the Right Hon. Sir John Lubbock, Bart., M.P.).—I am sure that we all hope that the Lord Mayor will remain in the chair a moment or two longer, because I know we would not wish him to depart without passing a vote of thanks to himself and the Corporation for allowing us the use of this hall, which must contribute largely to the success of this Conference. When I had the honour conferred upon me—the honour of being asked to preside over this meeting —I looked back to see what had been said by my eminent predecessors, and I learnt a great deal of information. But the statement of one struck me particularly. This gentleman was delivering an address in Aberdeen, and on that occasion informed his audience that we in London laboured under two serious defects. He said that London, compared with Aberdeen, would be found deficient in opportunities for sight-seeing, and also deficient in hospitality. With all respect to Aberdeen, and without any unkind comparison between London and other cities, I must say that I am surprised to hear anyone say that London is deficient in sight-seeing. I say that there is as much to be seen in London as in any other place. I was also very much surprised to hear that anyone could say that London was deficient in hospitality. But you, ladies and gentlemen, will be able, within the next few days, to judge as to that question. I trust, however, with regard to this latter point, you have already seen enough to satisfy you that there is no such deficiency of hospitality in the City of London. I think that we are very much indebted to the Lord Mayor for his presence here to-day and for the lively interest that he has taken in this Conference. I know that his Lordship has many other pressing engagements to-day, and it is only right that we should try to recompense him for his kindness. I am quite sure that you would not wish him to leave this meeting without expressing our hearty and cordial thanks both to himself and the Corporation for all their kindness.

ALDERMAN HARRY RAWSON (President of the Library Association), in seconding the motion, said: As a member of the Manchester Library Committee, it has been thought fitting that I should second the vote of thanks to the Lord Mayor. Although I should like to say more, I will now content myself by just saying that it gives me great pleasure to second the resolution.

The Chairman put the proposition to the vote, and it was carried unanimously amid cheers.

The LORD MAYOR, replying, said: I am exceedingly indebted to the mover and seconder of this vote of thanks, as well as to you, ladies and gentlemen, for so cordially passing it.

Sir JOHN LUBBOCK then delivered

THE INAUGURAL ADDRESS (see pp. 1–4).

Dr. JUSTIN WINSOR (Harvard University).—I am asked to propose a vote of thanks to our distinguished President for the address which, to my mind at least, was discriminating in an exceptional degree. I have been frequently in the summer time to a small town within sight of the rock upon which the Pilgrim Fathers landed, and there I was accustomed to hear the names of Wapping and Houndsditch—two names which had been brought to that town from this Metropolis. So you see that one may distinguish in this way a link between the New World and London. Nothing strikes a stranger from the other side of the Atlantic in his wanderings through this country more than to see so many names which are familiar to him. I remember a few years ago, in the city of Bath, being introduced to a gentleman whose name was Hallett. I said "Good-day, Mr. Hallett; how do you do? How are your friends in Barnstaple?" Well, he was surprised to find that I knew, but the fact is that the pioneers of that town had borne the name of Hallett across the waters. He stretched his hand out to me, and we then had a talk on international alliance. I shall now request the Right Hon. the Earl of Crawford to second the motion that is before this assembly.

The EARL OF CRAWFORD.—It is my privilege to speak to you after Dr. Winsor, and I will endeavour to be brief, because no words of mine could carry such weight as those falling from the lips of Dr. Winsor. I have to second the request that he has made to you—to accord a cordial vote of thanks to the President of this Conference for his most interesting, able, and discriminating address. But I cannot let Dr. Winsor's remarks pass without saying a word or two about America. It has been my privilege to travel a great deal about the face of the world, and I have been fortunate in meeting a good many people from Columbia across the water. During the whole of my acquaintance with these ladies and gentlemen, it has not been my lot to hear one word in any way expressing dislike to the traditions of Old England. I have, on the other hand, always found a feeling of affection and a feeling that they were true friends of their cousins across the water. I think this is comforting. One reads sometimes in the newspapers about the unfeeling and unsympathetic relations of the people of the United States towards the people of England. I think, however, these statements mean merely the effervescence of nameless writers striving to secure the applause of the moment. I am sure that those wishes do not come from the other continent. I will not just now take up more of your time, but will ask Dr. Winsor to put his motion, the motion to which I so cordially agree.

The proposition was carried amid cheers.

Sir JOHN LUBBOCK.—I am sure I am very grateful to you all for the vote of thanks that has just been passed unanimously. It was with a good deal of hesitation that I accepted the presidency of this Conference, but as a City man and as a man of business I was anxious to show that all of us in the Metropolis take a warm interest in the movement which has brought us together. I have been appointed on a Committee in the House of Commons which meets to-day, and it is my duty to be there as soon as possible. I am glad, however, to have had the opportunity of being present at this assembly for a short time this morning, but must now ask you to excuse me. I understand that Lord Crawford will take the chair, and therefore I feel that you will lose nothing whatever, but gain much by my absence.

The EARL OF CRAWFORD now took the chair, and called upon Mr. J. Y. W. MacAlister (Librarian of the Royal Medical and Chirurgical Society of London, and Hon. Secretary of the Library Association), to read his paper on

"SOME TENDENCIES OF MODERN LIBRARIANSHIP" (see pp. 9–12).

Dr. RICHARD GARNETT, C.B., LL.D.—The subject of Mr. MacAlister's paper seems to offer me a good opportunity to lay before the Conference an advance copy of a publication written by our friend Mr. Ogle, librarian at Bootle. This work treats of the history of free libraries, and gives, I think, one of the best accounts of the development of the movement. Mr. MacAlister said that before the Conference was over we should doubtless hear a good many smooth things; but perhaps such things will not be unwarrantable, as we hope to hear papers of all kinds read by representatives from scientific institutions in almost all parts of the world. We hope that success will attend the Conference in which you, my lord, are taking such a prominent part.

Mr. F. M. CRUNDEN (St. Louis Public Library, Mo., U.S.).—There seems to be no eager competition for the honour of making a few remarks upon the subject of the paper which has just been read. But I venture to rise to express my hearty approval of the whole paper, and particularly of two important points contained in it. The first subject I refer to is that regarding the reading of fiction. I always feel that there is more or less of cant in the general condemnation of fiction. Readers in our library come to me and ask about this question of the reading of fiction. They often deplore the large percentage of works of fiction we have in the library, but hope to find some improvement by and by. Some of these people, however, have been the most eager in coming to get the latest novels. In the case of many of these people their greatest concern is with regard to other people's reading. The other point on which I wish to speak is the one regarding scholarship in the profession. It may be known to many of you that we have a number of training schools in the United States. Now, these schools are not training schools in which students are taught the ordinary subjects, but get the foundation of a librarian's education. No one can be considered efficient without passing an examination which forms a test of library education. Nothing can be more gratifying than to find young men graduating at Harvard and other universities, and adopting librarianship as a profession after a complete course of training, and I think that all this progress augurs a great future for the libraries of America.

Mr. F. T. BARRETT (Mitchell Library, Glasgow). —I should like to put it to Mr. Crunden: Is it a satisfactory thing to find that out of the stores of books, including those on history, sociology, and so on, nine out of ten are works of fiction? I must say that to my mind this state of things is extremely unsatisfactory. The great books of classical writers are not very much read, but outside the field of fiction I think we must recognise a wealth of literature which should be used to a greater extent than 20 per cent.

Mr. HERBERT L. JONES (Public Library, Kensington).—I am sure that we are all very much indebted to Mr. MacAlister for his charming and lucid paper, and I feel sure that he has spoken from the fulness of his heart. Might I say, however, that I believe there is one thing which lies at the root of the whole question, which, perhaps from his kindness, or from a desire not to attack a difficult subject, Mr. MacAlister has not broached in his paper. We talk about improving the libraries, and having better-trained and skilled librarians. But we have not the remotest chance of bringing about this state of things until we confess that the libraries are under-financed, and are inadequately provided-for institutions. Are you going to effect all the improvements with simply a penny rate in a parish where you do not get sufficient to buy a new coal-scuttle for the office?

ALDERMAN MANDLEY (Chairman of the Salford Museum and Libraries).—I will only address myself to one point touched on in this paper: that is the subject of fiction. I myself do not think that the reading of fiction is to be deprecated, but, on the contrary, I think it ought to be encouraged. But, at the same time, I take exception to the immense amount of mental food that some ladies and gentlemen endeavour to swallow but are not able to assimilate.

Sir WILLIAM H. BAILEY (Salford).—I have listened with very great attention and interest to the paper of Mr. MacAlister, and some of the librarians he has described are not yet extinct. It has been my habit for the last few years, in any new town I might visit, to go to the public library and ask to be shown the greatest treasures; and I often come in contact with valuable books. We have ale tasters, inspectors, and medical officers of health, to see that the various traders conduct their business in a proper manner, and that only wholesome articles are supplied to the public. I think that novels should be properly examined before they are placed in our free libraries. Some of them, I think, should be sent to the fire and burnt. We send a man to prison or fine him heavily if he supplies bad meat, and a man in ancient times who sold bad ale was put in the stocks; and yet we sometimes permit nowadays the most abominable novels in our libraries, unfortunately, for young people to read. I have listened with very great pleasure to Mr. MacAlister's paper, but I think it would have been more worthy of him if he had devoted more time to it. I tried to get a copy of it in advance, because I believe that criticism is very useful to him, and he comes out in the end all the better for the criticism.

Mr. W. C. LANE (Boston Athenæum).—There is one thing that Mr. MacAlister has touched upon, but which has not been referred to in the discussion. I refer to the subject of co-operation in our work. This is a subject in which I take very much interest, and in which we have made a good deal of progress in America. Mr. MacAlister expresses the opinion that he fears that any elaborate scheme of co-operation would do away with the skilled librarian. But I believe there is no fear of a wholesale scheme of the kind doing that. Of course there are different needs in different libraries, and a difference in Great Britain and America. We lately started a system in which cards were circulated, and in which this co-operation was to some extent worked out, and it proved fairly successful in our library. Of course it does not do away with the skilled librarian, but it saves a good deal of hard work, and it helps to make more and better use of books he has on hand. The scheme, I may add, is well under way, and with the co-operation of four or five of our libraries.

Mrs. LORD (Kimberley Public Library, South Africa).—I only want to remark that there is a great difference in works of fiction. Fiction is rather a comprehensive term. There is good and there is bad fiction; some is amusing and some is obnoxious.

Mr. W. H. K. WRIGHT (Plymouth Free Public Library).—It has struck me forcibly how this inevitable topic of fiction always crops up at all our meetings. We have discussed it for twenty years, and probably we are now no nearer a satisfactory conclusion than when we started; and perhaps it will be another twenty years before each librarian becomes the censor with regard to the reading of fiction. We have to go lower still, —or perhaps I ought to say higher still,—but we have to look after both books and periodical literature. I might here remark that our newspapers are not entirely free from pernicious influence. If we introduce—as has been done in some libraries—a system of "blacking-out" sporting literature, so also we should take the newspapers and "black-out" many sensational trials, which are most pernicious to young minds. That is my opinion, but I do not think that the librarian should have the option of eliminating from the library, or not admitting to the library, what he believes to be pernicious. The books in a library are for the public service, and the librarian has no right whatever to refuse books which are asked for. But the question of fiction is a much larger one than we can thresh out now. I think we ought to organise a discussion specially upon fiction, and so try to prevent it from cropping up at all our meetings.

Mr. HENRY R. TEDDER (Secretary and Librarian of the Athenæum, London; Hon. Treasurer of the Library Association and of the Conference) read a paper on

"THE EVOLUTION OF THE PUBLIC LIBRARY"
(see pp. 13-18).

Mr. MELVIL DEWEY (Secretary of the University of the State of New York, and Director of the New York State Library, Albany, U.S.A.) addressed the meeting on

"RELATION OF THE STATE TO THE PUBLIC LIBRARY" (see pp. 19-22).

Mr. N. DARNELL DAVIS (British Guiana).—Unless this meeting is a kind of mutual admiration society, I think that many of us must differ from some of the remarks of the last speaker. He described the press as a most poisonous organ; but I do not think that is at all fair to the press with which most of us are acquainted. The good which is done by the press in providing intellectual food for the public is, I think, a matter upon which we should congratulate ourselves. We find here newspapers, which daily not only provide for the readers, but also draw the attention of the readers to the books being issued from the press, which, if they want to read, they may buy—if they, of course, can do so. If it should happen that they have not sufficient money to buy the books, of course they can go and get books from the public library. With regard to the question of providing public libraries, I most fully agree that the movement is a great power for good, and a good library is a sort of lighthouse, and ought to warn the readers from literary dangers. But, at the same time, one might as well desire to keep the Bible out of the hands of people because there are things in it which it is undesirable for them to read, as to want to keep newspapers out of their hands because there may be the report of a case which happens not to be of a desirable character.

Mr. AVERY (Cleveland, Ohio).—As an American, and an old journalist, I think I have a right to say something on behalf of the press. I think, in the first place, there is no need to say anything whatever against the English press. The last speaker did not exactly grasp the meaning of the reader of the paper. The reader used the words "sensational newspapers." With that class of literature we are all too familiar. With newspapers performing the proper functions, proving themselves the greatest lever of the educational engine, we are all in sympathy. While the ordinary sensational papers, however, are generally condemned by the majority both in England and in America, it seems to me that in an Association like this a warning voice should be lifted against this lower class.

Rev. WILLIAM GILLIES (Chairman of the Library Committee, Institute of Jamaica, Kingston, Jamaica).—When referring to the press, I think reference ought to have been made to one of the important facts connected with the press. I do not know anything better calculated to help in the alleviation of suffering humanity, and so well fitted to help the librarian.

TUESDAY AFTERNOON, JULY 13th, 1897.

SECOND SESSION.

MR. HERBERT L. JONES (Public Library, Kensington) read a paper on

"LIBRARY AUTHORITIES: THEIR POWERS AND DUTIES, AS THEY ARE AND AS THEY SHOULD BE" (see pp. 23-26).

ALDERMAN HARRY RAWSON (Manchester, President of the Library Association) read a paper on

"THE DUTIES OF LIBRARY COMMITTEES" (see pp. 27-30).

These papers were both discussed together.

ALDERMAN MANDLEY (Salford).—I should like to say that the institution which I have the honour of representing was, I think, the first, or at least one of the first, to take advantage of the Free Libraries Act. I represent, together with my chief librarian here, a sort of Royal Museum Library Committee; and may tell you that at the beginning that institution was a very small matter, but it has grown to something considerable. In the museum were a lot of costly and valuable exhibits, but, through an evil genius, it became something like a receptacle for lumber and rubbish. People who had things in their houses—things which they did not want—just sent them to our museum. But, on the other hand, we have several costly and valuable exhibits. We have some good plaster casts, a number of paintings—some very good, some only moderately good, and some bad. We have also some good pottery and porcelain exhibits, and antiquities of all sorts, and specimens of industries.

The CHAIRMAN.—I think Alderman Mandley is running rather off the lines of the subject before us. The paper we are discussing is upon the "Duties of Library Committees."

ALDERMAN MANDLEY.—I was simply giving these details as an introduction to my remarks about the work of libraries, and to show that the duty of the Chairman of the Committee is to supervise the literature that is admitted to the library, in conjunction with the librarian. It is the duty of the Chairman of the Library Committee to lend every aid he possibly can to the librarian. With regard to our books, we have tried to make selections dealing with special subjects, and I think that in every library something of the same kind should be done.

Mr. THOMAS KYD (Aberdeen).—It is important that the constitution of a committee should be such as to enable a librarian to do his duties, and we Scotch folk can perhaps give you a wrinkle. The constitution of our Free Libraries in Scotland is for one-half of the Board to be elected by the Town Council, while the other half are citizens who are, to all intents and purposes, life members, and who are elected by the Boards themselves. Mr. Jones has told us that librarians in England differ from one another in many ways. In Scotland this is the case also to some extent, but there is no official standing between the librarian and the Board. He is one of the officers of the Board, and has entire power, subject to the control of the Board. He has practically full control in regard to the selection of books. If you have a good librarian, I think you would do well to leave him a free hand—as far as possible, of course. Our librarian can attend public sales, and, if he chooses, he can spend, say, £20 upon the purchase of new books. He is able to do so, and his conduct is generally approved.

ALDERMAN H. M. GILBERT (Member of Public Library Committee, Southampton).—I have listened with great interest to Mr. Dewey, and I quite agree with him that it is the duty of the State to provide the stream of knowledge, as well as an adequate and constant stream of water. With regard to the water supply, it is seen that there should be absolute power vested in responsible hands, and with regard to the stream of knowledge the same restrictions should be used. I know it is extremely difficult to remove a book from a library after once it has been placed there, but I think we ought to have in our librarians men whom we can trust with the selection of books. I have seen books by some of the first novelists of the day which ought never to be placed in any public library. We must not attach too much importance to the name of the author. I think that the majority of ladies and gentlemen here will agree that the works of some of the most eminent novelists in this country are not fit to place in the hands of pure-minded youths. The Library Committee has indeed a great responsibility, especially in the selection of literature. I think that those who have the control of the libraries ought to go to the library and strike out any books that they think would be likely to contaminate the stream of knowledge. Upon them rests a great responsibility, and I consider that their duties should be discharged with the utmost care.

Mr. CHARLES WELCH (Corporation Library, Guildhall, London) read a paper on

"THE TRAINING OF LIBRARIANS"
(see pp. 31-33).

Miss HANNAH P. JAMES (Osterhout Free Library, Wilkes-Barré, Pa., U.S.A.) read a paper on

"SPECIAL TRAINING FOR LIBRARY WORK"
(see pp. 34-39).

Mr. E. R. N. MATHEWS (Public Library, Bristol) read a paper on

"FEMALE LIBRARY ASSISTANTS AND COMPETITIVE EXAMINATION" (see pp. 40-43).

Mr. J. J. OGLE (Bootle Public Library) read a paper on

"HINDRANCES TO THE TRAINING OF EFFICIENT LIBRARIANS" (see pp. 44-45).

The four papers were dealt with in one discussion.

Mr. MELVIL DEWEY (Albany).—Might I be allowed to say that in my judgment the establishment of training schools would be the best means for getting fully efficient librarians? It is not so much in the ordinary colleges and universities that people can learn what will enable them to become efficient librarians. Then as to the question of salary, my impression is that the way to get more satisfactory salaries is for us to do better work. A good librarian does not merely consider his salary, but works away, heart and soul, to build up a good library. If I were a library trustee, and if I had a librarian who worked so well that he improved the library, I would soon see that his pay was increased. Another matter I should like to mention—I believe it would be a good thing for us to strive to bring our library trustees more into harmony with library work. As in the case of college professors, so also in the case of librarians—these trustees are the native enemies. But the trustee is here, and he is here to stay, and we must therefore deal with him. We must not fight him, but must try to convert him.

ALDERMAN J. W. SOUTHERN (Chairman of the Manchester Public Library Committee).—I have taken great interest in the work of the Library Association for many years, and take an active part in the work; and I suppose Mr. Dewey would place me among the trustees as Chairman of the Manchester Free Public Library. It always gives me great pleasure to come to such conferences as this, and to listen to the experience of those from many places who work under great diversity of conditions. The experience which was recounted by Sir Thomas Baker, many years ago, as to the difficulties in getting assistants having a fair amount of preliminary qualifications and likely to develop into valuable librarians, is just as true now as it was then, and I am not surprised to hear that in America 99 per cent. of those who obtain the diplomas of the Library College there have belonged to the fairer sex. We have now at least four large libraries under the charge of lady librarians. If I were to take a stranger into the Manchester Library, I think it would produce a most favourable impression upon his mind. I should take him to a library in one of the poorest districts of Manchester. In a beautiful structure we should find a library presided over by a lady—a lady who came from what might be termed the lower classes. I might point out that there is always a great demand for the position of assistant librarian, but it is almost impossible to retain even a few names on our books of youths or young men applying for the position. What is the cause of this? I certainly think that the emoluments offered to duly-qualified librarians are not adequate to induce young men to embark upon this line of life. To refer to another important matter, I should like to say I think that those who come to the libraries should find in the librarian one who has a knowledge of books, and one in whom they would be able to find a kindly, ready, and responsive spirit—one who would find for them the information they desire.

Mr. H. R. TEDDER (Secretary and Librarian, Athenæum, London).—I well remember that many years ago, when, I believe, I was the person who first introduced the question of training of librarian assistants, the proposal was not received with great enthusiasm. We had to fight for some years against opposition. The proposal was thought premature and unnecessary. It is therefore a great delight to me to see that now there is not such opposition, but that the idea is approved by everybody. We have been told what the requirements of librarians are, and I think that I might be allowed to say that the prayer of the Scotchman has been vouchsafed, and that God has given us a good conceit of ourselves. But not only should a librarian be fully equipped with technical learning and be a man of business, but above all he should be a lover of books. The love of books and the love of reading are, after all, the chief qualifications of a librarian.

Mr. R. A. PEDDIE (Newcastle).—The paper of Mr. Welch gives us a great deal to think about. We must recognise and admit the point that several speakers have driven home — that the financial condition of public libraries is not as we should like to see it, but we must try to do the best with the conditions which we have. I think that something might be done in the way of getting lectures from prominent people in the labour world, and in trying to start classes to do a work which would have a good effect in the near future. I believe that in America women often do the same work as men, and I consider that if the work is equal the pay should also be equal.

WEDNESDAY MORNING, JULY 14th, 1897.

THIRD SESSION.

R. F. M. CRUNDEN (Public Library, St. Louis, U.S.A.), read a paper on

"BOOKS AND TEXT-BOOKS: THE LIBRARY AS A FACTOR IN EDUCATION" (see pp. 46-54).

The CHAIRMAN (The EARL OF CRAWFORD).— I believe that it will be a very long time before all that Mr. Crunden has prophesied will come to pass. I do not think that it is possible to get such a system as he has suggested to become absolutely universal, and to suit all children. I think that the greater part of it would not be likely to conduce to the true welfare of the child—even to the one he speaks of who had such an extraordinary range of learning at ten years of age. That child, I think also, is an exceptional case. He is certainly not the ordinary child of the British Isles. I do not think it good for a small child to go through such a course of learning, for it would be infinitely better that his body should be developed in the first place.

Mr. SIDNEY LEE (Editor of the *Dictionary of National Biography*) read a paper on

"NATIONAL BIOGRAPHY AND NATIONAL BIBLIOGRAPHY" (see pp. 55-62).

Mr. GEORGE SMITH.—When I came to this meeting, it was in the expectation of being much interested and of receiving great pleasure. I hardly know what I can be expected to say with regard to the *Dictionary of National Biography*, unless it is to state that, during a busy life of more than fifty years, when I have been engaged in more various enterprises than would be generally found in the experience of most commercial men — throughout all my various adventures and works there has been none which has afforded me so much interest and satisfaction as the work connected with the *Dictionary of National Biography*; and at no period has that satisfaction been greater than at the present time, when we may be said to be in sight of our goal. The work may truly be said to have been one of extraordinary labour, and no one who has not been behind the scenes, so to speak, and knows what passes in the editorial room, can know of the difficulties that have been overcome. I need hardly say that the manner in which Mr. Sidney Lee's paper was received, and the personal reference he was good enough to make to myself, have been deeply gratifying.

Mr. N. DARNELL DAVIS.—I should like to be permitted to express my personal indebtedness to both the publisher and editor of the *Dictionary of National Biography*. If this Dictionary is of great value—as it certainly must be—to historical and other students in London, it is true to say that it is doubly valuable to those of us who are not able to get to the British Museum or the Bodleian Library. I look forward to the issue of each new volume of this valuable work, one of the glorious triumphs of the reign of our Queen Victoria. I only hope that Mr. Smith and his co-workers will live long enough to complete the Dictionary, and that they will find it to prove a great success, financially as well as in other ways. We cannot of course imagine that Mr. Smith, who is a prince amongst publishers, should meet with failure, but it seems that no public recognition has yet been made of his great work. I think that the universities and the Government should in some way recognise his services.

Dr. JUSTIN WINSOR. — Might I also be allowed to express my gratification in hearing the paper of Mr. Sidney Lee, and the remarks of Mr. Smith, as well as to say that there is hardly any library in existence of any significance that does not make daily use of the great Dictionary? I might say that in the library of Harvard University we have two copies in constant use. I think that a vote of thanks should be tendered to Mr. Lee and his publisher for carrying forward so stupendous a work.

Mr. H. R. TEDDER.—Might I also add a few words in seconding the resolution? In the first place, because I am one of the humble contributors to the Dictionary, and have had a long relation with the Dictionary from its first inception. I am therefore able to say that I know something of the work, and the extraordinary toil that contributed to build up that great monument. Might I also, as a bibliographer, express my thanks for this help towards a future General Catalogue of English literature? Such an undertaking, if it is ever attempted, will be carried into effect from the impetus given by the *Dictionary of National Biography*. An index would be a very valuable contribution towards the much-needed subject-index to bibliography. As one who has compiled the first classified bibliography of our national dramatist, I should also like to thank Mr. Lee for his article on Shakespeare, one of the longest and best articles in the Dictionary.

Mr. W. SALT BRASSINGTON (Stratford-on-Avon) stated that he was cataloguing the Shakespeare Memorial Library in classified order, on a similar plan.

Mr. F. T. BARRETT (Mitchell Library, Glasgow).—I should like to be permitted to express a hope that an index to the Dictionary will be made. It may seem ungracious to ask anything more, but if an index be provided it will form a great and fitting crown to one of the greatest monuments of our times.

Mr. H. L. JONES.—I am delighted to be able to add my few words to what I believe to be one of the most sincere votes of thanks that any public body ever recorded to those who had successfully carried out a great undertaking. Let me tell Mr. Lee and all those who have been engaged in this great work, that we librarians, joined together for the second time in a National Conference, fully recognise the value of that monumental work.

Mr. SIDNEY LEE.—I have only to thank you for the hearty and kind manner in which you have passed this vote of thanks to Mr. Smith and myself. It is indeed a great encouragement to all of us to hear that our neighbours across the seas, and all those who come from distant lands, have found our work of use and value. I am sure that every suggestion as to an index and so forth will receive the most careful consideration.

Mr. GEORGE SMITH.—The satisfaction which I have already said I derived from the work of the *Dictionary of National Biography* is now added to by the gratification I have received through the compliment which has been given to Mr. Lee and myself.

Mr. A. W. POLLARD (British Museum, Hon. Sec. of the Bibliographical Society) contributed a paper on

"THE RELATIONS OF BIBLIOGRAPHY AND CATALOGUING." This was read by Mr. G. F. BARWICK (*see* pp. 63–66).

Sir FREDERICK YOUNG (Royal Colonial Institute).—I have been much interested in listening to the very interesting paper which has just been read. I think that our catalogues that have been recently published follow out the outlines that have been suggested by the author of this paper, and I think the members of the Conference will agree with me that the model laid down in the paper will prove very valuable indeed for cataloguing in the future.

Mr. L. S. JAST (Peterborough Free Public Library).—There is one point raised by Mr. Pollard which I should like to speak about—I mean his remarks in reference to the usage, in cataloguing, of entering items under the author's pseudonym. Mr. Pollard says that an author's pseudonym is usually better known to the public than the author's real name; but possibly he would think it best to use the pseudonym when it is little known to the public, and the real name when that is better known. The reason why the entry is made under the pseudonym is that the reference may be made quickly and easily. It is often better, of course, to enter under the real name, but I am quite sure that most would be in favour of entering, for instance, not under the name of L. Clemens, but under that of Mark Twain.

Mr. FRANK CAMPBELL (British Museum).—It will always be a pleasure to me to listen to a paper by Mr. Pollard, who has had special opportunities for studying the subject dealt with in his paper to-day, but I take special interest in what he says, on account of being a colleague of his for many years. As Mr. Pollard will know, I have never been able to see eye to eye with the Bibliographical Society, of which he is the Honorary Secretary; but there is no one who has greater admiration than I for the work it performs—as far as it goes. The works it prints are specimens of what Mr. Pollard speaks about—they are the "soul of honour and of honesty." There have been various suggestions made by Mr. Pollard which raise a little antipathy in my mind. These ideas are not confined to himself; they breathe the spirit of many leading librarians in this country. One point which, I think, is of special importance to us, is that there is a clear distinction between the librarian and the bibliographer. To my mind the bibliographer plays a more important part than the librarian, because I do not think that the librarian can be of real service in a library except in proportion as he has a knowledge of the principles which alone render literature of service—the knowledge which makes the hibliographer. The work of the bibliographer must command our admiration, for no one can regard him as a man of pleasure: we must regard him as a man of self-denying power. Mention has been made of scholarship in connection with library work. Of course there is plenty of room for scholarship in this work, but the librarian should never forget that his chief duty is to enable others to become scholars. I will not enter upon the debatable subject of classification. We have, however, in this room, welcome guests from across the water, who have done more in the matter of classification —I may say it without detracting from what the French have done—than perhaps any country has done: certainly more than we have done. The reading public has always been in favour of classified catalogues: that underlies the whole foundation of cataloguing.

Mr. W. H. J. WEALE (National Art Library, South Kensington Museum).—There is one great difficulty when you enter names under the authors' assumed names. Suppose an author has three pseudonyms, and you enter under each, it would scatter about the information which, if entered under the real name, would be easier to get at.

Mr. R. A. PEDDIE (Newcastle-upon-Tyne).—With regard to entering books under the author's assumed name, I might mention that in our library at Newcastle we adopt the name which is best known to the general public. I think that the difficulty regarding several assumed names is thus easily got over. I think Mr. Pollard said that it is not desirable to require the readers to make more than one reference, but, if he always uses the real or assumed name, he must have two references. Does it not contradict what he says previously? But I think that no library can be considered complete without cataloguing under the three heads—under authors' names, according to classification, and also alphabetically.

Mr. COUNCILLOR WELCH (Chairman, Technical

Instruction Committee, Eastbourne).—It is with a great deal of diffidence that I intrude my remarks upon this meeting. I am only the modest Chairman of a committee which last year formed a public library in Eastbourne. I came here to pick up hints and to learn, and during the time I have been here this morning I have derived a great deal of benefit and instruction. With regard to this particular matter, cataloguing, I think it is very important indeed, and that the paper has dealt with it very ably. There is one remark made by Mr. Pollard with which I perfectly concur. He says that, whatever method of cataloguing be used, it should be made perfectly clear to the reader. He also says that a librarian should not follow his own hobbies. As an outsider, I think that the great object in view is to so arrange the catalogues that they may be perfectly clear to the humblest readers.

Dr. JUSTIN WINSOR now took the chair.

Mr. F. T. BARRETT (Mitchell Library, Glasgow) read a paper on

"THE ALPHABETICAL AND CLASSIFIED FORMS OF CATALOGUES COMPARED" (*see* pp. 67-71).

The CHAIRMAN (Dr. Justin Winsor).—It has been my luck, if not my good fortune, to direct two large libraries for the past twenty years,—one at Boston and the other at Harvard University,—and I long ago came to the conclusion that a librarian should adopt that form of cataloguing which best suited his own individuality. If, however, he adopted a class-catalogue, let him also have an author-catalogue; and if he has an author-catalogue, let him also get a class-catalogue. But, besides this, he must also get a proper subject-index.

Mr. DE PUTRON GLIDDON (Montana, U.S.A.). —Although one from the wild and woolly West, I make no apology for what I am going to say. We want to be practical. My idea about libraries is this: The greatest power in the world is thought, and a library ought to be something which helps to direct thought. I was walking along a street in Montana the other day, and I met a man, and said to him, "Have you heard that they are going to have a strike down yonder?" He said, "Come along up the street;" and I went. He said, "We are not going to have a strike." I said, "Why not?" He pointed to the public library, and said, "That has taught us to think." Although I am not a librarian, I am greatly interested in the work of libraries, and I think that the libraries must receive a great deal of assistance from the press, with which I have the honour of being connected. The newspapers know how the librarians can help them, and the libraries may, I am sure, make great use of the press.

Mr. R. A. PEDDIE.—I should like to say that I believe it is owing to the poverty-stricken state of libraries in England that they are unable to adopt full catalogues. With regard to the dictionary system, I think it all depends upon the size of the library whether it be useful or not. The great rule to be followed, I think, is to take the more minute point and put the books under the head, and then refer to the main divisions, giving the headings under which the items may be found.

Mr. C. W. VINCENT (Reform Club Library).—In my opinion, and perhaps in the opinion of a large majority, Dr. Winsor summed up the whole matter when he said there must be classification, and there must be alphabetical cataloguing, as well as a full subject-index. If we cannot have both, then it appears, from a business point of view, we must take that form which makes the books most accessible to the readers; and experience shows that to be the alphabetical system.

A paper contributed by Professor CARL DZIATZKO (University Library, Göttingen, Germany) was partly read by Mr. T. W. LYSTER, National Library of Ireland, Dublin. The subject was—

"ON THE AIDS LENT BY PUBLIC BODIES TO THE ART OF PRINTING IN THE EARLY DAYS OF TYPOGRAPHY" (*see* pp. 72-78).

WEDNESDAY AFTERNOON, JULY 14th, 1897.

FOURTH SESSION.

THE chair was taken by the PRESIDENT (Sir John Lubbock).

Mr. CHARLES A. CUTTER (Forbes Library, Northampton, Massachusetts, U.S.A.) read a paper on

"THE EXPANSIVE CLASSIFICATION"
(see pp. 84-88).

Mr. A. W. ROBERTSON (Public Library, Aberdeen) read a paper on

"CLASSIFICATION IN PUBLIC LIBRARIES"
(see pp. 89-92).

The two above papers were discussed together.

Mr. J. J. OGLE (Bootle).—On this side of the Atlantic, as many of us know, the classification that Mr. Cutter has just described is very little known. It has its merits, and, in view of its natural basis in opposition to an artificial basis, I think it appeals very much and very strongly to the English mind. Mr. Cutter's scheme could be specially fitted for village libraries, while the librarians of larger libraries would find the scheme one that would suit them also. It has a class-index, similar to that referred to by Mr. Dewey, and a type classification is appearing in sections. The section on medicine is really a masterpiece. But while Mr. Cutter's scheme may not be very well known to many in this country, his cataloguing rules are in the hands of every English librarian. When we have all gone home and purchased his system, and studied it, and seen its merits, and thought over the intensely practical remarks of Mr. Cutter, we shall agree that he has achieved a great deal of good.

Mr. F. M. CRUNDEN (St. Louis, U.S.A.).—I remember Mr. Cutter, in his inaugural address as President of Northampton Library Association, dealt with the subject of "Common Sense," and I think that all Mr. Cutter does is based upon that quality. That has always been his guide. Certainly, a most essential thing in any system of classification is capability of expansion. A librarian never knows what a library is going to be. He must go slowly, but he does not want to be encumbered by an elaborate system. Mr. Cutter has provided for all that. There are some things upon which we are all agreed. We all agree, for instance, that we must have classification, and that as the library grows the classification must be closer and closer. As to fixed and relative location, Mr. Robertson made it plain that fixed location is a thing of the past. As to movable location, it is not necessary to have five or six figures, as Mr. Robertson says. In the system referred to by Mr. Robertson it would be necessary for the reader to go and find both the numbers and the letters of any book he required; whereas with us, in our library, he only has to mention the name of a book and gets it. So easily does the system work, that a boy can procure any book in the dark. It is necessary only to have the class mark, and its exact location is determined by the author's name, and the title which everybody knows.

Mr. R. A. PEDDIE (Newcastle-on Tyne).—I should like to point out that in the movable location system there is some difficulty in keeping the books in their right places. I submit that it is almost impossible with the relative location to have a chronological arrangement. Mr. Cutter's is perhaps a more natural system than the figure notation; but I consider, after the experience of last year, that the decimal system, with all its capabilities, works out better than any other system when used for the readers.

Mr. F. T. BARRETT (Glasgow).—My experience appears to be different from that of the last speaker, and what I say relates to libraries of considerable size. In our library we depart largely from orthodox usage. First, we divide the books into three groups—those frequently asked for; those occasionally asked for; and those only asked for perhaps three or four times a year. Those of the first group are arranged in the immediate neighbourhood of the point of service, and the others are put in the other parts of the building. From 70 to 75 per cent. of the books issued come from the first group, and, having these near at hand, a great deal of time is saved. We find that our book service is sometimes only about half a minute per volume, and that the average is one minute. That in a library containing some 120,000 volumes is, I think, very good.

Mr. W. C. LANE (Boston Athenæum).—Of course different libraries have different needs, but I think that, instead of sections of a large library being those of History, Politics, Biography, Geography, Travels, and so on, the first subdivision should be by countries. Then all works relating to England, France, and other places would be found together. When we come to local history this should particularly be the case, and the same is true with regard to small countries. Mr. Cutter uses figures for countries and letters for subjects; it seems possible also that he might use letters for countries and figures for subjects.

Mr. W. H. WESLEY (Royal Astronomical Society, London).—In small libraries I have found it absolutely necessary to adopt a particularly minute subject classification, and, if such a classification were not adopted, the advantages of free access would be almost lost. Those who wish to investigate any particular subject must be able to find the books they want near together. An experience of some twenty years has convinced me most firmly that a subject arrangement is not only necessary, but perfectly feasible. Its adoption is probably illogical, but the system is found to work very satisfactorily. We have arranged our works partly by subjects and partly by author. My endeavour has always been to place the books most frequently required in the most easily accessible places. My library does not look neat, for it is not possible to keep all books of the same size together. We have no systematic arrangement as to size, but, as far as possible, books dealing with the same subject are kept together.

Sir JOHN LUBBOCK again took the chair.

Mr. H. C. L. ANDERSON (Free Public Library, Sydney) read a paper on

"LIBRARY WORK IN NEW SOUTH WALES" (see pp. 93-96).

Mr. J. MACFARLANE (British Museum).—I should like to add a tribute of praise to the work of Mr. Anderson's library. He said, in the outset of his address, that his library possessed a better selection of books on Australia than the British Museum does; but the secret of that is not altogether creditable to Australia. Our friends in other parts—in the Cape, in Canada, for instance—send us their books pretty regularly. May we hope that Australia will follow this good example, for they have not done so in the past?

Mr. J. R. BOOSÉ and Sir JOHN LUBBOCK also spoke.

Mr. F. M. CRUNDEN then occupied the chair.

Mr. W. H. J. WEALE (National Art Library, South Kensington Museum, London) read a paper on

"THE HISTORY AND CATALOGUING OF THE NATIONAL ART LIBRARY" (see pp. 97-98).

THURSDAY MORNING, JULY 15th, 1897.

FIFTH SESSION.

THE EARL OF CRAWFORD took the chair in the absence of the President.

Mr. PETER COWELL (Public Library, Liverpool) read a paper on

"REMINISCENCES OF LIBRARY WORK IN LIVERPOOL DURING FORTY YEARS" (see pp. 99-102).

Mr. F. CURZON (Organising Secretary of the Yorkshire Union of Mechanics' Institutes and Yorkshire Village Libraries).—Might I venture to say a word or two upon a subject referred to in the paper which we have just heard read? I mean the question of village libraries. We are doing an extensive work of this kind up in Yorkshire, and I should like to mention that we find that our best workers are the ladies. These village libraries must always be in existence, however popular, useful, and successful the ordinary public library may be, for the Public Libraries Act can never properly reach these many villages. It would be a very important and a very good thing if other parts of Great Britain, which have remained so long without public libraries, could carry out such an organisation as we have in Yorkshire. We supply some two hundred villages and about fifteen thousand readers with books. This has proved a good thing, and I hope this question will, at some time or other, receive the consideration of the Conference.

Mr. JOHN ELLIOT (Wolverhampton Public Library).—I entirely endorse the remarks of Mr. Cowell with respect to the advantage of giving lectures in connection with libraries. We have had lectures in connection with our library for many years past, and generally these have been largely attended. Many of the lecturers gave addresses on popular authors, and thus have proved the means of drawing the attention of many, who would otherwise have been ignorant upon the subjects, to the works of some of the best authors. Public lectures properly managed are calculated to prove of material help to the people.

Mr. BARRETT, of Glasgow, also addressed the meeting, and Mr. COWELL replied on the discussion.

Mr. F. J. BURGOYNE (Public Libraries, Lambeth, London), read a paper on

"PUBLIC LIBRARY ARCHITECTURE FROM THE LIBRARIAN'S STANDPOINT" (see pp. 103-105).

Mr. F. M. CRUNDEN.—I rise to answer a question of the reader of the last paper as to the use of the thermostat apparatus. We have had it in use at St. Louis ever since we moved into the library building, three years ago. When it is properly looked after, it works satisfactorily. You can regulate the temperature of the room to any degree. The apparatus simply needs care. I might also say that it is automatic. We set the apparatus to the degree of heat we wish to have the room heated, and when it has reached that temperature the steam is automatically shut off, the room, of course, then gradually cooling, until the apparatus is again set to work.

Mr. J. J. OGLE (Bootle).—Might I say a word with regard to another system? I refer to the Sturtevant system. In our own technical school, and also at the Arlington school, this system is used. But, on going into the rooms where this system is adopted, it struck me that the air was very close. In this system the air is admitted by two shafts. First of all it is admitted by one opening, and goes over damp bags, taking in moisture; then the air passes over hot pipes, and so becomes heated. By another shaft cool air is admitted, and, by the arrangement of little taps, you can regulate the amount of cool or warm air admitted. But it is essential in this system to have sealed windows. That seems to me a very dangerous system, and if anything goes wrong with the apparatus you have to break the windows. I should like to hear the experience of any others who have used this system.

Dr. JUSTIN WINSOR (Harvard).—The last speaker asks for the experience of members of the Conference with reference to the heating and ventilating of other libraries. I have had some experience in such matters, and if any member would like to ask me some questions I shall be glad to endeavour to answer them.

Mr. H. R. TEDDER (The Athenæum, Pall Mall).—I should like to ask Dr. Winsor whether he has used the electric fan, and if so, how he found it to work?

Dr. JUSTIN WINSOR.—I have only seen the electric fan used in a few cases. The fact is, my experience with so-called public libraries relates to some twenty years ago; but we have with us two representatives of large public libraries in the United States, and I have no doubt they will give you more information than I am able to.

Mr. F. T. BARRETT (Glasgow).—I should like to ask if Dr. Winsor can tell us whether large pipes with low pressure or small pipes with a high pressure are preferable?

Dr. JUSTIN WINSOR.—I will only say that, as far as my experience goes, small pipes with a high pressure appear to work better.

Mr. F. T. BARRETT.—In one or two cases I have known small pipes under great pressure to produce something like a burnt atmosphere; and that fault, I believe, is not found in pipes of a large diameter heated to a less extent by hot water. I think, therefore, that better results are obtained by the large pipes with a low pressure.

Mr. F. M. CRUNDEN (St. Louis).—I should like to answer Mr. Barrett's question as to large and small pipes, and high and low pressure, as far as my experience will enable me. I have found that small pipes with a high pressure are liable to vitiate the atmosphere.

Mr. RICHARDSON (Newcastle-upon-Tyne).—In the library with which I am connected we have tried both methods—steam and hot water—and we find the hot-water system is much more satisfactory than steam. This system is very much more equable, and seems to make a better atmosphere. A steam-heated room seems stuffy, and is hardly as satisfactory as one heated by water. With regard to lighting by electricity, it may be interesting to some to hear that we produce our own electricity at 1½d. per unit, the usual price in the town being 6d. per unit.

Mr. BARRETT.—What installation do you use, might I ask? 1½d. per unit is something which we shall all like to hear about.

Mr. RICHARDSON.—We use gas; and as in the North of England gas is only about 1s. 10d. per 1000 feet, we are able to produce electricity at a low cost.

Rev. J. E. LUCAS (Chairman, Blackpool Public Library).—I should like to ask if in any libraries where the gas has been exchanged for electricity there is the same difficulty with regard to vitiated air? I have had experiences of places where gas fittings have been taken out and electric fittings put in their place, and we have had the greatest difficulty in ventilating the buildings. I should like to hear the experience of other friends connected with libraries where the electric fan has been adopted. In our library at Blackpool we have an electric fan, and find that it works admirably. We find, however, that it costs 2s. 6d. per hour to work the fan, so we have not been able to use it to a very large extent. We have to pay 6d. per unit for the electricity.

The CHAIRMAN.—I think there must be something wrong with the fan if it costs as much as 2s. 6d. an hour. That would mean that they have about a ten-horse power; and such a power, of course, is not wanted for a small fan.

Mr. D. WATSON (Hawick).—I think that it must be apparent to all, that to use a small pipe and have a great amount of heat is certainly not so good as to have the same amount of heat with larger pipes. With a lower pressure and a larger pipe area the heat is distributed more evenly. Is it not a disadvantage to have an extremely high pressure in a limited space and in a limited time, unless there be some apparatus for distributing the heat?

Mr. H. R. TEDDER.—I had an electric fan in use for a long time—not in a library, but in a kitchen. My experience as to the fan is that it is not of much use unless the windows are constantly closed. We also have a fan in another part of the house, and there, I am bound to say, that theoretically it is perfect; but, practically, we have to fall back on the old system of opening the windows at the top.

The CHAIRMAN.—I think that much depends on where the fan is placed. The usual way is to place the fan in a passage and set it in rapid rotation. That will draw the air from the room at the same time that it puts out the super-heated air. The fresh air has to come in somehow, as best it can. That is why I think the ventilation arrangements by air-shafts are best placed near the floor. I suppose that the best system of ventilation is in the House of Commons. Most days, I think, the ventilation there is found to be very satisfactory. Mr. Richardson said a minute ago that he was able to produce electricity at 1½d. per unit. I think that if anyone could produce electricity at the same price and on a large scale he would soon make a large fortune.

Miss CAROLINE M. HEWINS (Public Library, Hartford, Connecticut, U.S.A.) read a paper on

"BOOKS THAT CHILDREN LIKE."
(see pp. 111–117).

The PRESIDENT (Sir John Lubbock) now took the chair.

Mr. J. C. DANA (Public Library, Denver, Colorado, U.S.A.) contributed a paper, read by Mr. J. J. Ogle, on

"OUR YOUNGEST READERS" (see pp. 118–119).

The two foregoing papers were discussed together.

Sir WILLIAM H. BAILEY (Salford).—Mr. Alderman Harry Rawson, who has just left the room, intended to say a few words about the libraries in Manchester. He, however, left me his notes, and asked me to speak upon the matter for him. I may say, first of all, that in every branch library in Manchester there is a room devoted to children. It is opened on Sunday evenings, and some of the narrow ones in Manchester—Sunday-school teachers and so forth—were afraid that the libraries would rob the Sunday schools. But it was pointed out that the Sunday schools were not conducted in the evening; and at last, by common consent, these rooms were established. They are filled every Sunday night, as well as other nights in the week; and often on winter nights there are as many as 500 or 600. On one occasion I inquired what kind of books were usually asked for by the children, and I was told that there was a great demand for *Robinson Crusoe*, volumes of *Punch*, and fairy tales, and—strange to say—Farrar's *Life of Christ*. Whether they got the idea of reading this book from the Sunday-school teachers or not, I am unable to say. I thought it a very remarkable book for children to read. There is a lady appointed to see that everything is kept in order at the library, and I consider it quite delightful to go on a Sunday night and see the poor children from the slums comfortably treated in the warm, bright, cheerful rooms. It is most delightful for the Library Committee in Manchester to have instituted such a children's room. If we only consider that the intelligent citizen is a unit of civilisation, we shall surely see that it is cheaper when John Bull pays to support such institutions, than would be the case when he spent money on workhouses and jails. The room I refer to is kept open all day, so that the children can go and amuse themselves there, and they are kept out of mischief by getting into the habit of reading. With some instruction from the lady superintendent, the children get on very well, for she suggests the most fitting books for them to read. It would be a very good thing if managers of other libraries would imitate what is done in Manchester, for there the libraries have proved a very great success.

Mr. J. H. QUINN (Public Libraries, Chelsea).—I should like very much to emphasise the remarks of Sir William Bailey with regard to children's rooms in a library. Our library in Chelsea is the only library in the West End which has made special provision for children; and not only has it proved successful, but I might say it has proved too successful. The fact is, that on Sunday evenings children come from surrounding districts—from Battersea, Fulham, and other places. But we think that the Chelsea child should have the first share, and feel it necessary to keep a register and issue tickets, so as to know what children use the books. The amount of reading that is done in this room is surprising, and we look upon this branch as the most successful feature of our work. But it seems strange to me why we should not have a special room for the girls. I might add that we keep the room open from six o'clock in the evening until nine o'clock; but, for some reason or other, the room generally empties, or nearly so, at about eight o'clock. I have wondered whether this is peculiar to London, where we do not keep late hours. Does the same thing occur in Manchester? I should like also to say that I have met the boy that Mr. Crunden referred to. Some little time ago we had a boy at our library who commenced a course of reading on—Egyptology. He devoured anything we had upon the subject, including Budge's *Egyptian Reading Book*.

Mr. F. M. CRUNDEN (St. Louis, U.S.A.).—My theme in the paper I read yesterday was essentially what Miss Hewins and Mr. Dana have insisted upon—namely, the importance of giving children good books to read at an early age. Statistics in America go to show that children become interested in books between the ages of nine and fourteen, but I think we cannot begin too soon. Long before a child is nine years of age, the habit of reading good books must be formed. The essence of my paper lies in the two quotations —"The liking for a good book is of vastly more consequence to a youth than . the ability to work out an equation of four"; and the other quotation from Sir John Lubbock—" It is not so important that every child should be taught, as it is that every child should wish to learn. A boy who leaves school hating his lessons soon forgets what he has been taught; but the one who leaves having a desire for knowledge will soon know more than the other ever knew." I think that Miss Hewins' statistics show the amount of good that can be done with the average child, but to my mind it all depends upon when you begin. I believe in taking the children when they are three or four, or five or six years of age—as soon as you get them in school. Then set them learning, not tasks that worry and disgust them, but let them revel in the regions of the imagination. Miss Hewins has told us what some of the children have said about the books they read, and I ask whether it is not better for them to be taught lessons from such interesting books as those Miss Hewins has mentioned—lessons of justice, kindness, and obedience—than to learn the rules of arithmetic, which may be picked up anywhere?

Mr. C. W. VINCENT (Reform Club).—Some of the remarks to which we have just listened bear so much upon the educational work in London, that you may like to hear what is being done by that much-abused body—the London School Board. The object of the School Board, I may say, is to train and inculcate in the child a desire for learning, and besides this to improve and train the moral side of the child's character. As soon as the child is able to read, suitable books are put into his hands—books of the best authors, the best stories relating to history, geography; and when the child is able to read for itself, the school libraries come into use. Every child is then provided with a certain number of books, and I am only sorry that the number of books is not greater. To say one of our libraries has as many as four hundred books will show, I consider, that it is not nearly enough. But these books, I might mention, are exactly those or similar ones to those referred to by Miss Hewins. Those are the books used in the school libraries, and so well are the books used that they are always out. We have an advantage inasmuch as the schools interchange their volumes at intervals, and so they escape from anything like monotony. I hope to be able to bring before my colleagues what has taken place in this Conference, and through them get public support, so that our library work may be extended and made more useful. Already it has been found in this country that the number of jails has been steadily diminishing. Year after year jails have been shut up, and they have had to centralise the work, so to speak, because there was not enough work for all the warders. All this began with the foundation of the School Board in this country. Of course we have made great mistakes, but we have striven hard, all the time, to make the children worthy citizens of this country. If we introduce party spirit into the work, and bring in troublesome matters, this will cause the fly-wheel to drag and impede our progress. If we increase the use of books for the children we shall increase their wish for learning and their power for learning, and we shall largely and as wonderfully increase the power that education has for the elevation of mankind.

Mr. HERBERT PUTNAM (Boston Public Library, Mass., U.S.A.)—I wish to say a word in appreciation of Mr. Dana's paper, for the possibility of dealing with children in the earlier stages of their career is a most important question. With regard to Miss Hewins' work, every library in the United States should move a vote of thanks to her for what she has done. In Boston, I might say, we have been attempting experiments in the special treatment of children's reading. These experiments, while not being tested by great length of time, are intended to test these three questions — first, whether the books should be placed in open shelves; secondly, whether, if placed in open shelves, the character and standard of the books should not be raised; and thirdly, whether, if a list of books is selected for their special use and placed in open shelves, it is necessary that the list of books should be a very long one. At our central library, and also at the branches, there is now reserved a small selection of books for the children. We have printed a select list of books, of which we propose to multiply copies. That list comprises only 1200 titles, and I doubt whether we shall exceed 1500. With the assumption, which perhaps may not be correct, that 1500 titles will include all the books that a child need reasonably require to read, I think the greatest good is likely to result from such a department of work. A short time before I left home we received a bequest, amounting to £40,000, accompanied by the expression of the desire that it should be devoted chiefly for the benefit of children. In carrying out this work—I say it very heartily—Boston will turn to its Hartford friends for guidance and advice.

Miss K. L. SHARP (Armour Institute, Chicago, U.S.A.).—I should like to say a word with regard to one phase of library work which has not yet been touched upon. I refer to home libraries for children. Our custom is to pack about twenty books in each of a number of small cases, and send them to children in various parts of the district. Besides the supply of books in connection with the home libraries, a good work is also carried on by the library visitors. For a long time home libraries have been started in connection with different library schools, and when once started the work has soon spread to other towns. This kind of work is now being carried on, notably in Boston, New York, and several other cities in the States, and in Chicago it is carried on by the Children's Aid Society. The idea of this work is to get hold of the children before they reach what might be called the "library age"—before they are allowed to use the public library. Then, in order to get the full interest of even the youngest child, we have games and pictures to amuse and instruct them until they are old enough to go to the public libraries. I may say that there is nothing like competition between these home libraries and the public libraries, for as soon as a child is old enough we say to him, "Now you can go to the public library." The books we use are principally of a mixed character we have a little science, a little poetry, a good deal of history, and so on. I should like also to say that the books, on their return, invariably show that they have been used, not misused. The funds for carrying on this work come from voluntary contributions—sometimes small ones; and sometimes large amounts are given—in memory, perhaps, of a child who has died. This work has always gone on most satisfactorily, and has only been limited by the supply of books and the number of visitors. The visitors must always give their services voluntarily, because it is thought that only those could discharge the duties as they ought to be discharged whose hearts are in the work.

Mr. F. T. BARRETT (Glasgow).—I should be much obliged if the lady who has put this interesting work before us would tell us on what principle the homes are selected. There must be thousands of houses, and the work of selection must, I should think, be one of great difficulty.

Miss SHARP.—We found at first that it was a good thing to go to the missions and the Sunday schools, and get the officers there to recommend the children or families to whom we might send the books. Sometimes also a visitor might see a number of children who, she thought, looked as though they needed the books. We usually ask the women of the families if they will allow us to deposit the boxes at their houses, telling them that their children will have the privilege of reading the books, and also asking whether they will look after the other children who come to her house. We have found these women usually take the suggestion very kindly—that the work has invariably had a good effect all round.

Mr. W. H. K. WRIGHT (Free Public Library, Plymouth).—With reference to what has been said about London school libraries, I am told that the head teachers are made responsible for the books supplied to the libraries, and that therefore, if they are lost, the teacher has to make up the deficiency. If this be so, it would not be surprising to find that the teachers did not take very much interest in the work. My chief object, however, in rising is to say that I think that we in England are not doing enough in this direction—in the direction of school libraries. Some of us have been at this work for many years, but too few libraries have adopted such a work. At Plymouth we have been arranging with the School Board for us to supply to each of the schools in the district a certain number of books. The School Board bears the expense of the cases, and the head teachers take charge of the books, appointing someone as librarian, and seeing that the books are circulated. But we not only supply the Board schools, but the Voluntary schools also. We have about 5000 or 6000 volumes in circulation, and the thing works well, in two ways. First of all, the children get the books under the control of the teachers; and secondly, many of the schools being a long way from the central library, the children are saved the trouble of going perhaps several miles to get the books. Of course, when the books get into the houses they are often read by the whole family, and are therefore used probably by tens of thousands. In Norwich, I believe, a special fund has been established for these libraries, and I have no doubt there are many other places also. (A voice, "Leeds.") Yes, I hear that in Leeds also the work is carried on. I mention this matter for the benefit of our American friends specially. We in England are doing our best, not only to give the children good elementary instruction, but also to assist them in getting higher instruction.

Mr. MELVIL DEWEY (Albany).—It seems to me that when we come to this question of the reading of the children we come to the core of the whole matter. Many a child who is able to digest beefsteak is only given gruel. But their instruction should be given in a way that will interest them, and create a desire to know more. Telling a child "you must read this and you must not read that," reminds me of the Sunday-school teacher who said to his scholars, "Little children, love one another—confound you." We must organise some principle of co-operation; we must come together and work together, and with a sufficient amount of time and money we shall be able to accomplish a great work. We have gone to the very heart of the question when we realise this great truth. The child is father of the man.

The PRESIDENT.—This has long been an interesting question to me. More than twenty-five years ago I urged that the teaching of children should not be confined to elementary subjects. I was told, however, by almost everybody, that the children in the elementary schools were too young to be interested in scientific questions. I found great difficulty in altering old conceptions, but at last two things drove away the idea. Matthew Arnold maintained that to teach science to children was out of the question; but he went to Germany, and saw that the children in elementary schools were taught such things, and then his views were different. The other thing that helped people to favour the teaching of science to the children was the act of the London School Board system—for at last they tried to teach elementary science in the schools. At first they had one teacher who took one portion of the children on Mondays, and another portion on Tuesdays, and the good results were found to be very great. In fact it was difficult to keep the children at home, because they became so interested in the science lessons. The lessons were found to be of great use to the children, because they interested them; and I am sure we shall all agree that nothing can be of much use to the children if it does not interest them.

Mr. BERESFORD PITE, F.R.I.B.A. (London), read a paper on

"LIBRARY ARCHITECTURE FROM THE ARCHITECT'S STANDPOINT" (see pp. 106-110).

Sir FREDERICK YOUNG (Royal Colonial Institute, London).—The question that always seems to be a pressing one to me is, Are the books meant for the library, or is the library meant for the books? The greater number of libraries have been built by architects who hold the architectural construction in view rather than the convenience of the readers. But a library ought to be so planned that the books may be displayed, and the room so arranged that the books may be easily accessible. The librarian, I think, should mark out exactly what he requires to make the library as perfect as possible, and then the architect's duty is to put a kind of cover to this plan. Of course the architect starts by making an elaborate façade, so as to attract one's attention. Then as to the lighting arrangements, all such buildings should be lighted from the top, and not from the sides; for, besides not giving such good light, windows at the side of the building interfere with the arrangement of the cases. At the Natural History Museum, South Kensington, for instance, there is one continual growl from the curators, because the lines of cases are so inconveniently placed and broken by the side windows. The mouldings also at the Natural History Museum are so arranged that the showcases become perfectly ridiculous. The mouldings of a room should only be, as it were, an addendum to the room, instead of its essential feature. Where you have a reading-room, of course it is different; but where books and magazines are kept, and you wish them kept so as to economise the space, you must have top lights. This is the only really scientific way of lighting libraries. In regard to ornament, I consider that the books in a library

constitute the ornaments, for there are no better ornaments in the world. But at the Natural History Museum you have the walls covered with nondescript animals—animals certainly not made by the Almighty. These, I consider, have made the place perfectly ridiculous. We have libraries in Manchester, built at an enormous cost, —some perhaps the finest in England, so far as the exterior or structure is concerned,—but I am afraid that some of them, also so very fine, are excessively unsuitable for the true requirements of a library. Of course when we come to big towns and cities the sites for libraries are often very expensive, and so, if we throw away a lot of space on ornament, it is throwing away space that can ill be spared. At the same time, I believe that libraries ought to be on expansive sites, and, as far as possible, in or near the middle of the town or city.

Mr. T. W. LYSTER (National Library of Ireland, Dublin).—I rather think that the last speaker has somewhat misunderstood the drift of Mr. Pite's paper. There is no reason why we should not have artistically-designed libraries. In certain parts of libraries ornamentation may be possible, and we should make them, I think, as beautiful as we can; but, of course, we should not sacrifice the reader's convenience to ornamentation.

Mr. PETER COWELL (Free Public Library, Liverpool).—In my experience I think I have been fortunate, because in the library in Liverpool with which I have been connected we have been wonderfully aided by the architect himself. We laid it down from the first that the library was to have plenty of light, and this was well attained; but as to the question of ventilation, although the architect was anxious to do all he could in this direction, our desires were not fully attained. I do not think that architects really know how to secure proper ventilation in reading-rooms, where there are people all day—perhaps from ten o'clock in the morning until ten o'clock at night. We must have the libraries warm, because many who visit them are ill-fed, and often come in tired and cold. They would feel the inconvenience very keenly if the rooms were not comfortable and warm. We started with gas, and afterwards changed it for the electric light; but the people at once complained when the electric light was put in, because the place was not warm enough. But, returning to the question of architects, I must say that I always found them to work most cordially with me; and I think that if the librarian only goes the right way about it, he, in nine cases out of ten, will be able to get from the architect all that he desires. As to the outside of a library, I see no reason why it should not be made as beautiful as possible.

Mr. MELVIL DEWEY (Albany).—One important matter to consider in the structure of a library is what not to do. Most of the best libraries I know are old buildings, and seem much more useful, as well as comfortable, than buildings that architects have specially designed for libraries. I believe that the solution of the difficulty is to learn from the practical wisdom of the Catholic Church, and make a list of things to be avoided—and the list will be a long one. Then when we have picked out all the things to be avoided, with the residuum we should be able to make a better library than we should be able to do if we started by trying to find out what should be adopted.

Dr. RICHARD GARNETT (Keeper of the Printed

Books, British Museum).—Something has been said about empty shelves, but I am not sure that I do not like to see them, because they show that there is room for new books. When planning the shelves, we should not only study the immediate wants, but provide for the storing of books for almost an indefinite time to come. Every architect, when planning a library, should not only arrange for the present but also for the future.

THURSDAY AFTERNOON, JULY 15th, 1897.

SIXTH SESSION.

MR. MELVIL DEWEY took the chair.

Mr. J. N. LARNED (late Librarian, Buffalo, N.Y., U.S.A.) contributed a paper, read by Mr. W. H. K. Wright (Plymouth), on

"ORGANISATION OF CO-OPERATIVE WORK AMONG PUBLIC LIBRARIES" (see pp. 120-121).

Mr. H. H. LANGTON (University Library, Toronto) read a paper on

"CO-OPERATION IN A CATALOGUE OF PERIODICAL PUBLICATIONS" (see pp. 122-125).

Mr. H. R. TEDDER.—Dr. Lundstedt, the distinguished delegate from the Swedish Government, wishes to present a remarkable book to the Conference, in his own name and in the name of his country. The volume contains the titles of North European periodical literature from 1645 almost to the present day. This great bibliographical work contains a most elaborate and complete account of all the newspapers and periodicals and other works published in Sweden from the earliest times. In it will be found the full titles, number of columns, sizes, and other particulars, with an account of all the editors and publishers connected with the periodical, and also an account of all the pseudonyms used by journalists. This work is in two volumes, and brings the subject down to 1894. The first volume relates to the subject in general, and the second volume to periodicals, etc., published at Stockholm. The third volume, yet to come out, will deal with journals and reviews published in the great provincial localities. I have much pleasure, in the name of Dr. Lundstedt, in presenting this remarkable achievement to the Conference.

The CHAIRMAN.—I am sure that the Conference will greatly appreciate the kindness of Dr. Lundstedt in presenting to them such a valuable work. During the last twenty years many remarkable works have been accomplished, while some of us have been doing perhaps little more than preaching. Personally, I know of no more remarkable work than that of the International Institute of Bibliography at Brussels, and I am sure that the Conference will wish to hear from Paul Otlet, the Secretary-General, something about the work of the Institute. They in Brussels have done what we in Great Britain and America ought to do—they have lashed their waggon to a star; for they are doing their great work under the patronage of the Government. Here is, indeed, an important lesson for us. We must get facts concerning what we have done in different parts of the world, and then, with all the accumulation of material to guide us, we shall only want the courage and faith to go on.

Mr. PAUL OTLET (Secretary-General of the International Institute of Bibliography, Brussels). —I should like to explain to the Conference what we propose to do, and what has been done by the International Institute of Bibliography, for the progress of bibliography on the basis of international co-operation.

This Institute is an international association for the promotion of bibliographical study. Its special object is the promulgation of a method by means of which it may be possible in the future to consider the various parts of individual bibliographical work as parts of a universal bibliography. The method may be thus briefly described. First, a central bureau has been appointed by the Institute to provide that all departments of general and technical literature shall have their bibliographers. This central bureau assumes the task of organising co-operation between the various countries, and will co-operate with any public institution or individual librarian or scholar who will agree to be responsible editors for each part of the Universal Bibliography. The central bureau announces in a periodical list what works are undertaken, in order to avoid duplication. It also publishes a permanent inventory of the works to be analysed. The second point of the method is that the several publications undertaken by the workers are as individual as possible, but are so arranged as to be capable of union in a general collection under the name of *Bibliographia Universalis*. It is also proposed to publish periodically these special bibliographies, and include with them bibliographies of books, of periodicals, and of the transactions of the society. The third important point is that the following rules are applied in each of the various publications:—

The publications are either in book form or in card form. The book-form publications are printed like slips, the back left blank so that they can be cut out and pasted. The cards are the size of those of the library bureau. The International Institute of Bibliography has adopted the well-known decimal system of classification, so that it is possible to translate these classifications into all languages. The International Institute of Bibliography hopes that the application of this method will give to the bibliographical world the co-ordination which is now so much wanted. Their first steps have convinced them that the method has great advantages, and that it is possible to unite many efforts. A *Bibliographia Philosophica* has already been published by the Philosophical Institute of Louvain; a *Bibliographia Sociologica* by the Bureau Sociologique of Brussels; a *Bibliographia Zoologica* and a *Bibliographia Anatomica* by the Concilium Bibliographicum of Zurich—director, M. Field; a *Bibliographia Physiologica* by the Institute of Physiology of Paris—director, M. Richet; a *Bibliographia Astronomica* by the Belgian Astronomical Society; a *Bibliographia Medica Italica*, by one of the most important reviews of Italy, "Il Policlino"; etc. This method enables us to consider the card-catalogues published by the publishing section of the A.L.A. as a branch of this international co-operative work. The methods of the International Institute can be perfected and adapted to the separate wants of individual nations. Therefore we have convoked an International Conference to meet in Brussels the 2nd of August next, and in the name of the Institute I request the members of the International Library Conference to do us the honour of coming to this Conference, and to afford us the assistance of their experience.

Mr. C. W. ANDREWS (John Crerar Library, Chicago, U.S.A.) read a paper on

"PRINTED CARD-CATALOGUES"
(*see* pp. 126-128).

Mr. H. PUTNAM (Boston, Mass.).—I am very glad of this opportunity to direct the attention of the Conference to a small pamphlet. It is a statement of an experience at Boston, in connection with the use of the linotype machine for the printing of cards and catalogues in book form. During the past year and a half we have done all the composing and printing of cards and catalogues in our office by means of a linotype machine. I regard the question as to the practicability of adopting linotype machines for library work as quite beyond dispute, especially if there be a friendly co-operation between the different libraries of a district. If it be possible for us—as it is—to compose press titles, and print eight or ten copies of cards on that title at a cost of 5 to 10 cents, it would also be possible to print thirty cards with an inappreciable increase in the price. So that with the use of linotype we may look forward to a great decrease in the cost of card and catalogue printing.

The CHAIRMAN.—Twenty years ago, one of the great questions which occupied our minds was as to the practicability of printing our cards and catalogues on the library premises. There were some who said it was not likely to come to pass; but the difficulty is solved, and the work has been found to be quite possible.

Mr. R. A. PEDDIE (Newcastle-upon-Tyne).—I should like to ask Mr. Putnam whether the titles can be used and then stored away with a view to their being used again?

Mr. H. PUTNAM.—Yes, it is very easy to store them. We are able to re-group the matter used in the monthly lists for making up the annual lists. It would be possible to store tons and tons within a very narrow compass.

Mr. ANDREWS.—Our printer, I might say, stores the matter and uses it again at what seems to us to be a very inappreciable cost, and the whole work is carried on with comparatively little labour.

Mr. J. J. OGLE (Bootle).—This of course is a financial question, and I have been working out what will be the cost of setting up a catalogue I have to do with. I find that the cost would be '44 of a penny, and for 15,000 copies the cost would be a little under 1 cent per title.

Mr. W. C. LANE (Boston).—I should like to present a copy of the last report of the publishing section of the American Library Association. The experience of the section with regard to printed cards, as referred to by previous speakers, is that the work is fairly successful. We try to do the printing very promptly, including the titles of all the books, leaving out very slight things and very technical things. We have about sixty sets of subscribers, for we only offer to distribute a few sets to each subscriber. The work of selection, however, has been very difficult, and involved a good deal of extra expense. There is a great future for the printed cards and for the work that has been outlined. For printed cards for periodicals there is a still larger field, and this work will be found to be exceedingly easy and inexpensive. The report which I present says something about this, and also about the other work of the publishing section. I hope that in the course of another year the work of printing the cards for articles in periodicals, which can be subscribed for by the libraries, will be well under way.

Mr. G. T. SHAW (Liverpool Athenæum).—If the titles were stored for two or three years, when taken up for use again would their condition be such that they would not require anything which would increase the cost? In a small library, for instance, where they print supplements at the end of five years perhaps, would there not be the cost for repairing the type to consider? If this be the case, the present statistics may be misleading.

Mr. PUTNAM.—We have not yet reached that point, for our work only dates back from two years ago. I do not think, however, that there would be any deterioration of consequence in the type within a few years.

Mr. FRANK CAMPBELL (British Museum).—It was a source of gratification to me to see that the subject of co-operation among libraries was included in the programme of the Conference. I was also gratified to hear the Chairman—so distinguished a librarian—express his views as to libraries being placed in the proper position, namely, under the patronage of Government. I see in all the professions no greater waste of time and energy than is to be found in the library profession. It is not the first time that co-operation in library work has been suggested, as those who follow the subject know. But there is one feature which must strike one, and that is the almost absolute failure to attain our ends. And why is this? It is because we have not sought success in the right direction; the cause of our failure is because there has been among librarians no proper basis for co-operation. Some important points have been raised with regard to classification, and we have had some very good schemes laid before us, namely, those of Mr. Dewey and Mr. Cutter. True, they differ in certain respects, and the very fact that they are each so good is the reason that there has been more discussion upon them. Might I suggest that, as the basis of future registration of literature in the libraries, we should adopt for public class-catalogues the ten general groups which are so well defined?

Mr. R. R. BOWKER (Editor of the *Library Journal*, New York).—I have the misfortune to read to-morrow a paper covering a field which has been pretty well discussed to-day; but I should like to take this opportunity of referring to one question which has been raised. It seems, perhaps, almost useless to expect the copyright difficulty to be solved until there is systematic action all round. But the Library of Congress, I might mention, has now reached a new stage in its development. It has under the law this very year separated the copyright bureaus into separate divisions for carrying on the work, and we hope there will be a re-organisation of the methods at the library, making it a national library and the centre of bibliographical work. The two countries, England and America, are in somewhat different positions as regards the question of copyright. We can indeed claim one or two advantages. Under our copyright laws, the proprietor of a copyright can claim a record of copyright,—which is usually done,—so that he gets from the Library of Congress an acknowledgment that such a book or such a title has been received. In this country there is somewhat of a difficulty, because no such record can be demanded at present by the proprietor. But as to legislation for both countries, we hope that some day the two great national libraries—the British Museum Library and the Library of Congress—may form a record, and thus save the libraries the loss of time and money now sustained, often over the most insignificant books.

Mr. R. A. PEDDIE.—I certainly think that very much might be effected if we co-operated in the matter of printing the cards and catalogues. If we could arrange for a few libraries to have a linotype machine in common, there might, I think, be a great saving.

The CHAIRMAN.—All this seems to confirm what I said on the first day of the Conference.

We need all the good things that have been spoken about, and we must have them. But when we look at the cost of the matter, we see plainly that it is absurd for librarians, underpaid as they often are at present, to do very much. We shall only get a truly satisfactory state of things when we make it clearly understood that the expenses of libraries are just as much Government expenses as those relating to schools or the making of drains. Let us, then, do what we can by co-operation, and we must at the same time agitate for the provision of greater facilities for carrying on our work; and I think our way lies in the direction of national libraries.

Mr. HERBERT PUTNAM (Librarian, Public Library, Boston, U.S.A.) read a paper on

"LOCAL LIBRARY ASSOCIATIONS IN THE UNITED STATES" (see pp. 129-134).

Mr. MADELEY (Warrington Museum).—With regard to local associations, I suppose we have a few in England, but one feels almost afraid to mention our associations in the same breath as those of America. We have such associations, however, and I should like to refer to a curious contrast between our associations and those in the United States. Whereas, in the United States, the discussions upon practical questions are the chief characteristic of the American Library Association, and other less pressing questions are brought forward at the district associations, with us it is quite the other way. Our annual meetings are almost invariably the receptacle of not very important papers upon antiquarian subjects, or of purely local interest; whereas at our district meetings the questions which arise are generally of a highly practical character.

FRIDAY MORNING, JULY 16th, 1897.

SEVENTH SESSION.

THE chair was taken by the EARL OF CRAWFORD.

Mr. ANDREAS S. STEENBERG (Horsens, Denmark) read a paper on

"PUBLIC LIBRARIES OF THE NORTHERN STATES OF EUROPE."
(see pp. 135-141).

Mr. J. J. OGLE (Bootle).—Mr. Steenberg ought not to be allowed to return to his own country without receiving an expression from the Conference of our appreciation of the work which he is accomplishing in Denmark. Two years ago we had the great pleasure and honour of a visit from him, and he then gave us some valuable information which he had made use of in his own country. We are greatly indebted to him for bringing before the Danish people the work that is being done here. Only the other day it was that Mr. Steenberg contributed an illustrated article to one of the magazines of that country, containing photographs of many of the English libraries, and a sort of indication of others, together with a very admirable account, as far as I could judge, of the different libraries which he had visited in certain parts of this country. Mr. Steenberg also sent an article to an illustrated paper, which many of us read to our profit, describing the free libraries of London and the work which has been accomplished since the first International Library Conference, not only in Great Britain but among other English-speaking races. I am sure that we shall give him our hearty congratulations upon the work he has accomplished, and wish him every success and promise him every help we can give him.

Mr. W. H. BRETT (Public Library, Cleveland, U.S.A., President of the American Library Association) contributed a paper, read by Mr. L. S. Jast (Peterborough), on

"FREEDOM IN PUBLIC LIBRARIES."
(see pp. 79-83).

Sir WILLIAM W. BAILEY (Salford).—I have tried to listen with some benevolence to the reading of this paper, but I cannot place myself in sympathy with it. It appears to be entirely in praise of anarchy. I have followed carefully the explanation of the scheme set forth in the paper, but I think there is more to be lost than gained by it. A man knows what he wants if he goes into a library. If he desires to rummage about for things he wants—well, I think it shows that he lacks proper discipline of the mind, and he ought to prepare his chart before he sets sail. Nor can I see that this system would be likely to minimise the work of the library, but I consider that it would reduce the value and culture and position of the library, and place the library in the hands of illiterate persons. In manufacturing districts I have great confidence in the people generally; but to permit the working men to go into a library to upset the shelves and put the books back in the wrong places, to make the place utterly disordered, and render the organisation an utter confusion, is, I think, altogether the wrong way about. I am very sorry to have to object to the contents of this paper. It is the first time, I think, that we have had any objections to speak about in the course of the discussions at this Conference. A little opposition, however, is likely perhaps to somewhat relieve the monotony.

Mr. DARNELL DAVIS (British Guiana).—We ought to recognise that there are libraries and libraries. In the case of many modern circulating libraries there are often many books that are not worth stealing. As to the poor people doing such a thing—why, they cannot afford to do it. Such things are often done by rich people, and, as Mr. Steenberg reminds us, sometimes by royal personages. We all know that the French, a long time ago, when they went to Spain, swept away a lot of the most valuable books of the country; and when another European power forced them to return the stolen property, it was found that the French had carefully taken away the catalogues; therefore there was no check, and the French only gave back what they thought they would. In the British Museum, it is true, we find this system of freedom; but even here it could not be applied throughout, for, even with all their restrictions, there are some thieves who steal the books. But those restrictions prevent many thefts. I would be sorry for another reason if you placed your libraries at the tender mercies of the people. In the colony from which I come we find there is no danger of the people stealing the books, or taking out the plates; but we are troubled with that vice which so many people have of scribbling upon the leaves, and writing all sorts of remarks on the margin. What check can we have, or what fine can we inflict, unless we have some record as to who has been using the books? This matter, however, must be left to each community to manage itself; but to generalise, and say that we should throw open all libraries, is going too far.

Mr. F. H. JONES (Dr. Williams' Library).—The last speaker has answered this question of free or closed libraries, but I venture to go a little further. The Patent Library, where a man knows just what he wants, is exactly an instance of the kind of library in which the shelves are not wisely thrown open to the public. But free public libraries are not generally used by men who wish to pursue some special study, but rather by persons who want something to read. It seems to me that what we want in every library is a large open department, not necessarily throwing open the whole library. We have indeed got this in the British Museum Library itself. With regard to the question of dishonesty of persons in not returning the books—as far as my experience goes, I am sorry to say that the more literary and studious persons appear to be the greatest offenders. We have an open department for the convenience of readers, and they are requested not to replace the books on the shelves, but to put them on a table, and we will put them in their right places. But the people will not do this; they insist upon putting away the books in their wrong places.

Mr. C. MADELEY (Warrington Museum).—Open access is, I consider, pre-eminently an open question. But, unfortunately, it is one that lends itself to the talk of clap-trap, more than perhaps any other question; and that clap-trap talk is not confined to one side. At our library we had open access started about forty years since. The reasons that led us to close the access had nothing to do with practicability of open access, but with the practicability of open access under proper conditions. In fact, the proper conditions are of the essence of this question. Of course a library with shelves, say, 12 feet high is not suitable for open access; but, with proper conditions, open access is, I think, eminently feasible. I would like to recall to the memory of the members of the Association who attended our meeting at Cambridge Mr. Bradshaw's account of the rules of the University Library at Cambridge. He said that the rule was "liberty with discretion," but he found it possible to give liberty to nine-tenths of the readers in such a way that they did not know there were any restrictions. To those who speak of open access but have not tried it, I would say, before they speak against it or make up their minds upon the subject, "Go to Clerkenwell; go and look at a library especially designed for the adoption of open access." They would soon see then the possibility of arranging for the work of open access; they would see a work of which perhaps they had no conception before, and I think they would come away feeling that there certainly was a possibility of making this thing work successfully. Then as to reserving obsolete books, it has this disadvantage: it prevents the real student having the opportunity of glancing over them without loss of time. There must be a strict classification on the shelves, and all books of a class must go together. If one looks back at instances of really serious theft from libraries, he will find that it has generally occurred in libraries which have been most closely guarded; and there does not appear to be any connection between any library's rules and the protection of the books. With regard to the displacement of books on the shelves, we regard that as a matter for the public. If they have open access they must take the consequences of displacement.

ALDERMAN J. W. SOUTHERN (Chairman of the Manchester Free Library Committee).—I may say that I approached the subject with an open mind, and have followed the discussion with a good deal of interest. I have had the opportunity, through the kindness of Mr. Brown, of seeing the Clerkenwell Library, and have seen things there which lead me to consider that there is not much fear of scribbling on the margins of books. But the essential point of the whole matter, I think, is—as has already been remarked—that there are libraries and libraries. This system of open access may be successful under certain conditions, but these are conditions which do not universally exist. In a library I am acquainted with there are 400 or 500 volumes a day used by a working population. You find there probably four-fifths are taken from the shelves between six and nine in the evening. It is at that time that the people come to change their books. If you could imagine 200 or 300 people within that limited period of time having free access to the shelves—well, Sir William Bailey would be right in describing the result as anarchy. With regard to the Patent Department, such open access would certainly be undesirable. Where there are such demands upon a library within such a limited period of time, I think it would be highly inconvenient to have open access; but I do not say that under no circumstances would it be successful, for I understand that it works very successfully at Clerkenwell. On the other hand, I know many libraries which would have to be entirely reconstructed, and where the space would have to be duplicated if people were to go altogether and get the books they desired. Therefore I say that open access is one of those things which we all desire but which is insusceptible of universal adaptation.

Mr. J. T. RADFORD (Mechanics' Institution, Nottingham).—Many who have visited Nottingham know my library, and know the conditions under which we have open access. As I have before stated, the number of books which we have lost annually is very large. We who manage the library did not suggest that the books had been worn out; but we faced the difficulty, and said they must have been stolen during the twelve months. By the conditions under which we worked the library, we were able to show what books were lost. Wherever there is to be open access, the library must be specially designed for the purpose. The shelves must be so arranged that the library may be controlled by the assistants in charge. During the past autumn we have had our library altered, and the whole room can now be controlled from the counter. When we had no control over the readers, the books that we lost were mostly books of fiction, or from the science department, and some of the books which were lost were those that students most usually require to keep—such as standard works on electricity and so forth. I would like Mr. Brown to take stock of his library, and tell us his experience for, say, the past twelve months. But we must wait till the newness of the system has worn off. My opinion, however, is that when the building is properly designed for the purpose of open access it can well be carried out; and I think that the losses likely to occur would not be through the ordinary persons who use the library, but through the educated and plausible persons. These are the persons who would require to be watched most.

Mr. H. PUTNAM (Boston).—I also had the pleasure of visiting Clerkenwell Library, and I certainly hope we may hear from Mr. Brown as to the results of the work there. It seems to me that the architectural construction and the arrangement of shelves at Clerkenwell Library are of a most safe-guarded description. I consider that one of the most important questions in relation to free access is: What sort of books are to be placed before the public? I think that a good deal of discretion is required in this direction, for there is the question of loss, and also that of wear and tear. The librarian should not merely be the guardian of the books in his library, but also the conserver of the books, for something in regard to the library is due to posterity. Then, of course, there is the question of convenience to be considered, and the question as to how best to stimulate a love of reading the more useful books by the general public. I have been associated with a library containing 50,000 volumes, where free access has been tried with success, and I am now associated with one in which there are 700,000 volumes, and here open access has proved pretty successful. In this latter library there are 100,000 books to which free access is given, and in this department our losses were, during the first year, less than 40 volumes. These books were insignificant as regards price, and not such as anyone would be likely to steal deliberately. Then another important point is, that the shelves must be so arranged that the books likely to be required may be placed within as small a space as possible. In the case of libraries, say, of half a million volumes, it is then very necessary to have proper catalogues. But it seems to me that provision for open access must necessarily differ according to circumstances. Some libraries seem to think it necessary to have some attractive books to the front to act as a kind of bait; but my conviction is, that if you let the public approach the books of their own accord, no bait is needed beyond this open access. I do not consider it necessary or wise to put books of a low and questionable nature close at hand, in order to attract the readers. At our library in Boston free access may be had to books of a fairly high order. We have found that the Patent Department may be thrown open, and we have also opened for free access the entire department of fine arts. But it is all a matter of discretion —it is a question of libraries and libraries; while in large libraries it may be a question of departments.

Mr. L. STANLEY JAST (Free Public Library, Peterborough).—The arguments—I use the word in a courteous sense only—used by several speakers this morning who are not in favour of open access have been just of the usual type. We have heard them all before, and I do not think that those who believe in open access are likely to be moved by what they had heard against it this morning. With regard to the remarks of Sir William Bailey, I am quite sure that Sir William would not wish us to take his remarks too seriously. I may say with reference to the arguments about the cost of books which might be stolen, my own opinion is that, taking the worst possible conditions, and supposing the loss to amount to £20, or even £50, in the course of a year, the advantages of open access would be worth the cost. In our own library, where we have not open access (because the library was not built or arranged for the purpose), we have a very close classification on the shelves; and we use the decimal system, and carry it out most satisfactorily in the lending department. Mr. Radford has remarked that at the Clerkenwell Library the assistants were on their honour to make the work successful during the first year; but I think Mr. Brown will tell us that the assistants are on their honour to make it successful every year. If those in a library are not on their honour to make the work successful, then the only thing for the librarian to do would be to resign his position or dismiss his assistants. With reference to what Mr. Putnam said about handing the books on to posterity, the chief duty of the librarian is not to hand the books on to posterity, but to see that good use is made of them in the present. If the books show signs of wear, this is generally also a sign that they have been used; and I do not care two straws if we hand the books on to posterity in such a condition, for I think it will show that we have done our work well in getting the books well used.

Mr. W. E. DOUBLEDAY (Public Library, Hampstead).—I do not think that Mr. Jast has added much to what had already been said, or that his arguments are any better than those used by previous speakers. With regard to the question of open access, a great deal has already been overcome, but there is still a great deal more to be overcome. I see a difficulty, particularly with regard to London libraries which have branch libraries, because it would mean that the staff would have to be enlarged, and this would soon tend to exhaust the library's income. In libraries where there is not much doing during the day, and not very much in the evening, it would be necessary to have an extra assistant to look after the work where there was open access; whereas, with the ordinary indicator, one assistant could do the work. Mr. Brett has said that those who condemn open access are those who have not tried it; but one might just as well say that those who condemn dishonesty are those who have not tried it. I understand that in some places—particularly in Bootle—the open access system is abbreviated, 40 or 50 books only being placed upon the counter for the people to pick up and read. Such books as may be exciting the attention of the public might be used in this way, and, being immediately under the eye of the assistant, it would entail no extra labour.

The CHAIRMAN (the Earl of Crawford).—With regard to this paper, the only thing I have to say about it is concerning what goes on at the British Museum Library. We all know that here there is freedom of access, and not freedom of access. It has already been remarked that the whole question depends upon circumstances, and I entirely agree with that. In the reading-room at the British Museum there is freedom of access to some 20,000 volumes, and anyone may take books from the shelves to the place at which they sit, and when done with the books may leave them there. The readers are not required to return the books to the shelves. This is important, because books put in wrong places are, until discovered and returned to the right places, practically lost to the library. Everybody present will agree that it would be absolutely impossible to allow free access to all the shelves in the British Museum Library. The space is comparatively so small for the myriad of presses that it would be impossible for two persons to examine a press together. I must protest against what Mr. Brett has said about library managers not having the right to make regulations for the use of libraries.

Mr. JAST.—What Mr. Brett said was that he considered no library committee had the right to make regulations for the use of libraries, except such as could be shown to be absolutely necessary.

The CHAIRMAN (continuing).—I think I should go further, and be inclined to give the librarian discretion in the carrying out of the regulations. But I think that full powers should be left in the hands of the governing body.

Mr. JACOB SCHWARTZ (Free Library of the General Society of Mechanics, New York) contributed a paper, read by Mr. C. A. Cutter, on an

"INDICATOR-CATALOGUE CHARGING SYSTEM" (see pp. 142-145).

Mr. THOMAS DUCKWORTH (Public Library, Worcester).—I may mention that this system, which has been so ably explained to us by Mr. Cutter, is not a new system. It is practically the system we use in connection with the open access system. In one place are shown the books which are in, and in another are shown those which are out.

Mr. J. H. QUINN (Chelsea).—I should like to ask Mr. Cutter whether they do not use cards in connection with the catalogues as well as in the charging system? The cards are used in the catalogues of the library, and the charging system also, I think.

Mr. CUTTER.—I understand that is so.

Mr. F. T. BARRETT (Glasgow).—If Mr. Quinn's supposition be right, it would mean that each book would only appear once in the catalogue. With respect to searching for books of a popular character in lending libraries here, I believe that one of the chief difficulties with an indicator arises from the fact that it is necessary to examine perhaps thirty or forty numbers before a suitable book is found.

Mr. CUTTER.—I suppose that the person who wants a book goes first to the indicator-catalogue and finds out whether the work is in before he asks for it, and therefore, of course, would not ask for any he found were not in.

Mr. F. BLAKE CROFTON (Legislative Library, Halifax, Nova Scotia) read a paper entitled

"A HINT IN CATALOGUING" (see pp. 146-147).

Mr. E. A. PETHERICK (London) read a paper on

"THEORETICAL AND PRACTICAL BIBLIOGRAPHY" (see pp. 148-149).

Dr. RICHARD GARNETT (British Museum).—I should like to allude to a subject of national importance, to which this paper provides an opening. I refer to the great importance of the Copyright Act being enforced in the Colonies. It is so very difficult to enforce this Act, and indeed I do not think it will be done except the Colonies see how advisable it is that their books should find their way to England. It is true that a number of the Colonies do give us the benefit of their books, but I think that their number is usually in inverse ratio to their importance. The Cape of Good Hope seems to be the only place from which we receive the books regularly. Canada passed an Act some time ago, from which we expected great things; but so far we have received little else than large selections of Canadian music. But I hope all the Colonies will see the great importance of their affairs being known in England, and do their best by complying with the requirements of the Copyright Act.

Mr. R. R. BOWKER (Editor, *Library Journal*) read a paper on

"BIBLIOGRAPHICAL ENDEAVOURS IN AMERICA" (see pp. 150-153).

Mr. F. T. BARRETT.—I have myself—speaking from an individual point of view—derived so much assistance from works which are the outcome of what Mr. Bowker entitles "Bibliographical Endeavours" that it is impossible for me to allow this opportunity to pass without acknowledgment. There is no department upon which we can look with more satisfaction in the world's history than upon the way in which they in America have devoted their attention to books and reading. As to what Mr. Bowker has said about a cumulative index, the advantages of such a work cannot be overestimated.

FRIDAY AFTERNOON, JULY 16th, 1897.

EIGHTH SESSION

ALDERMAN HARRY RAWSON (Manchester) took the chair.
Mr. C. H. GOULD (McGill University, Montreal, Canada) read a paper entitled

"DESCRIPTION OF IMPORTANT LIBRARIES IN MONTREAL, WITH REMARKS UPON DEPARTMENTAL LIBRARIES" (see pp. 154-157).

Mr. E. CUSHING RICHARDSON (Princeton University, New Jersey) contributed a paper, read by Mr. W. E. Doubleday, on

"LIBRARIES THE PRIMARY FACTOR IN HUMAN EVOLUTION" (see pp. 158-159).

Mr. JOHN THORBURN (Geological Survey of Canada) contributed a paper on

"COUNTING AND TIME RECORDING" (see pp. 160-165).

Mr. GEORGE ILES (New York) contributed a paper, outlined by Mr. C. H. Gould, on

"EXPERT APPRAISAL OF LITERATURE" (see pp. 166-172).

Mr. FRANK CUNDALL (Institute of Jamaica, Kingston, Jamaica) contributed a paper, read by the Rev. William Gillies, on

"LIBRARY WORK IN JAMAICA" (see pp. 173-178).

Mr. DARNELL DAVIS (British Guiana).—I should like, as a "colonial," to make a few remarks upon the paper we have just heard read; and I may say that to a colonial it is exceedingly gratifying to find that we have so many colonials with us to-day. Some years ago, like all lovers of books, I was in the habit of repairing to the haunts of books, or booksellers' shops, and one day I remember talking of books about the Colonies to the shopkeeper. "Oh," said he, "I don't think much of the Colonies. Look at Canada, for instance; they do not seem to buy any books; whereas the Americans are constantly sending orders." This, I think, was a practical remark. Some of our Colonies, when compared with the States, are somewhat behind. It may be worth mentioning that, though we live in an out-of-the-way part of the Empire, we value our librarian. The librarian of our society gets £375 a year, which, I think, compares favourably with salaries generally in England. At the same time, I think that the librarians in England must be regarded as members of a coming profession. Those of us in middle life remember that it is only within the last quarter of a century or so that education has become so general, and the number of readers so multitudinous; and as each generation grows up there will be more and more regard for the librarian. Most of the libraries that have been recently established are larger, I think, than those of former days; and as we get larger libraries and a larger number of readers, the salaries of librarians will increase.

Several papers contributed by Colonial librarians were taken as read. They will be found on pp. 179-208.

VOTES OF THANKS.

Professor COMM. GUIDO BIAGI (Librarian of the Laurentian Library, Florence, and Delegate of the Italian Government).—As delegate from the Italian Government, allow me to manifest my high appreciation of the most important results of this Conference. Allow me also to render our best, our heartfelt thanks, for the kindness with which we have been received by the representatives of this noble Association of the United Kingdom. It is with much pleasure that I have attended the Conference, and I shall look back upon this occasion with great satisfaction. I will close my remarks with the hearty greeting general among this great English people, the founders of liberty, and the ancient friends of Italy, and my greeting shall be in Italian—*Viva la Graziosa Regina*—"Long live the Gracious Queen."

Mr. ANDREAS S. STEENBERG (Denmark).—I should also like to express thanks to this Conference for the kind manner in which we from other countries have been received by our friends of Great Britain—or, I will say, Greater Britain. The representatives of many nations have attended this Conference, and have all been received in the same kind manner; and I am sure we are all grateful for the hospitality we have received, and for all we have been able to learn while attending the meetings.

Dr. B. LUNDSTEDT (Sweden).—I am glad to have had the pleasure of attending this Conference, and beg, on behalf of the Government I have the honour to represent, to thank all those who have extended their kind courtesy to me. I must beg your pardon, ladies and gentlemen, if I speak bad English, but my speech comes from my heart, and I am sure it goes to yours, even though you do not understand every word. (The speaker went on to address the assembly in Swedish, and concluded):—I now propose, in the name of the foreign representatives, our most hearty thanks to your Committee, to the President, and to the members of the Conference.

The CHAIRMAN.—On behalf of the Organising Committee of the Conference, it is with much pleasure that I receive the kind expression of thanks from our friends, the foreign delegates; and I can assure them all that, if it has been a pleasure for them to be here, it has especially been so for us to see them amongst us. Literature knows no distinction of nationality. Before the march of intellect all differences of creed and nationality disappear. I repeat that we are pleased and honoured to have our friends from other lands amongst us, and if we have done anything to render their visit pleasant we are more than gratified. In speaking of the foreign delegates, of course, we do not include our American friends.

Mr. MELVIL DEWEY.—I think that we Americans could not sit still and fail to express our thanks for the kind welcome that has been extended to us here in England. We feel that it has been good for us to be here, and we shall now, I believe, do better work through taking part in the discussions at this Conference, and go home feeling that we are brothers in race with our British friends, labouring together to work out the problems before us. We have, in a comparatively short time, been to many places in England, and everywhere we have received boundless hospitality; and I am sure that I express the feelings of all my American friends when I say that we never received such glorious hospitality as we have received here in London; and some of us, who have not been here before, are sure to come again. Many of those here, who visited London twenty years ago, thought it would be their only visit, but this year found it so easy to come back again. Those who now visit this great city for the first time will, no doubt, find it just as easy to come again; and again I speak for all my American friends when I say that we hope to see our English friends oftener in America. The fact is, it is only a very little farther from London to New York than it is from New York to London. I thought this morning, when we were speaking of the growing freedom of libraries, and free access to the library shelves, that if we looked backward a little it would do us good. The library is a great storehouse, but at first it was only the favoured few who were allowed to use it. Then those who paid a subscription were allowed to come in and use it; then, again, the doors were thrown open and all were allowed to enter. But that was only the beginning. Then came the lending to the favoured few, then to those who paid for the loan of the books—now to all. Now, also, we have libraries extending far and wide, and the larger ones are throwing out branch libraries. But we still go forward, and send books by telephone. We have the home libraries, and still we go on and approach the time when national libraries shall so have spread that by telephoning to one great central library we may be able to expect knowledge of the whole world free of cost. With regard to open access, we can learn practical wisdom from the shopkeeper. Go to him and ask him if he believes in the public having open access to a view of his goods. This open access is another step, and, although it may be long delayed, we are moving in that direction, and the whole work is broadening out in widening circles, as the ripple of the water when a stone is thrown into it. The whole history of the world has been so; we march onward, ever onward and upward. We cannot stand still: we go back if we fail to go forward. But this means labour and effort.

"The heights which great men reached and kept
Were not attained by sudden flight;
But they, while their companions slept,
Were toiling upward in the night."

Again, on behalf of my American friends, I beg to thank our English friends for the hospitality which has been extended to us, and we thank you because you have recognised us as being, as it were, a part of dear old England.

Mr. H. H. LANGTON (Toronto).—As a representative from the Colonies, I should like to convey my own thanks and the thanks of those who also come from the Colonies to our esteemed friends in England for the hospitality which has been accorded to us. Librarians are dealers in words, and are sometimes supposed to deal only in words, but we can go beyond that when occasion requires, and speak from our hearts, and I now wish sincerely to present the thanks of the Colonists here to the other members of the Conference for the most hospitable and courteous reception which has been accorded to us.

ENJIRO YAMAZA (Japan).—As one from a country far distant from this, I should like to say just a word of thanks for the kind reception that has been accorded to me by all the ladies and gentlemen here. After all that has been said by my colleagues, I feel there is very little for me to say for my own sake. I am sorry to say that library work is still in a very primitive condition in Japan, but we are slowly progressing, I think, in the right direction. I need scarcely say that I have profited a great deal by attending this Conference, and I trust that my country will reap great benefit from the proceedings of this Conference.

The CHAIRMAN.—We have to acknowledge our indebtedness for the hospitality received from a great number of friends. Among them are the Lord Mayor of London, the Duke of Westminster, the Duke of Wellington, Lord and Lady Tweedmouth, the Trustees of Sion College, the Marquis and Marchioness of Bute, Sir John and Lady Lubbock, the Duke of Sutherland, and the Archbishop of Canterbury. I propose to say nothing further on this matter beyond just reading out the names of our kind entertainers, but will leave the proposition for Sir William Bailey to second.

Sir WILLIAM H. BAILEY.—It is my privilege to second this vote of thanks, and, in doing so, we from the North of England congratulate you, Mr. Chairman, and all librarians may congratulate you, upon looking so well as you do. Mr. Alderman Rawson is a great deal older than he looks, I may tell the company, and many who come from the North of England will probably be surprised to know that, as I am told, in the early days of free libraries Mr. Rawson was scarcely a young man. It is very gratifying to find such a highly esteemed veteran in the chair at this Conference, and as the President of the Library Association. It must be very gratifying to you, sir, to see public libraries established throughout the country, and to know that their existence is in a great measure due to the labours of yourself and other friends of education. I wish that our expressions of appreciation bore a more equal proportion to our gratitude to those kind friends who have entertained us during this week. I am sure that we who are about to leave London will go away feeling that we have a good stock of pictures in our memories, which we shall look at from time to time with the greatest of pleasure, and that we shall feel we have been well treated during our stay in this great city. We shall leave London full of gratitude and admiration. We shall feel that this Conference has been held with pleasure and profit to ourselves, and I hope to the library movement in this land, in the Colonies, in the United States, and throughout the entire world. In seconding the resolution, I beg to congratulate you, sir, that you have been spared to prove such a useful citizen of Manchester, and that you have shared so much in this noble work.

Mr. ALDERMAN JAMES (Oldham).—On behalf of the Corporation of the Borough of Oldham, I have very great pleasure in supporting the proposition which has just been proposed and seconded. Although Chairman of the Oldham Free Public Library Committee, I am sorry to say that I cannot enter fully into the details of the work, but still I am able to appreciate much of the knowledge that has been set before the Conference. I hope that that knowledge will prove beneficial all round, not only to us in this country, but also to those representatives from other parts of the world.

Mr. R. R. BOWKER (New York).—I am sure that we visitors, and especially we American visitors, consider the hospitality we have received even beyond that large capacity for speech-making which is sometimes attributed to us. The hospitality extended to us has been imperial—imperial as this imperial year. I feel that we of the American party in particular must thank first and especially those who, in the North of England, welcomed us so cordially. But I cannot extend my word of thanks to adequately cover all this most wonderful hospitality which we have received both in the North and here in London. We from America have, I am sure, appreciated most fully the way in which the owners of great houses have opened their doors to us. We feel that we have been welcomed by the British nation, and we ought to recognise, I think, all that that means to us. Once again we thank you with all our hearts. We feel that we are at home here, and are almost sorry to go from this home to our other home. We hope, again and again, to have the pleasure of thanking you for similar hospitality, which we know will ever be extended to us when we visit you.

The CHAIRMAN.—The resolution, ladies and gentlemen, is that the warmest thanks of the Conference be awarded to the Lord Mayor of London, to the noble ladies and gentlemen, and also to the trustees of various institutions which I have named, for the courtesy and hospitality extended to the Conference.

The proposition was carried by acclamation.

The CHAIRMAN.—We also have to thank our President, Sir John Lubbock, and the other gentlemen who have from time to time presided over the meetings of the Conference, and I beg to propose our sincere obligations to them.

The Rev. WM. GILLIES (Jamaica).—I have very great pleasure in seconding the proposal, which, I am sure, will meet with your cordial approbation. The services rendered by our President deserve special notice, and I am sure we all feel, as we felt before we came here, that in Sir John Lubbock we should find the proper head of this great Library Conference. He has contributed to the literature which has tended to the diffusion of elementary science and other branches of knowledge, and his name is so well known that one can go into scarcely any part of the civilised world without hearing of Sir John Lubbock. And then we think of his presence here, and I am sure we all feel that we are under the deepest obligation to him for his great kindness, for the way in which he received us, and for the address with which he opened this Conference. And then our thanks are due to Lord Crawford and the other gentlemen who have presided over these meetings, and to yourself, sir, also. This Conference has given me, I assure you, ladies and gentlemen, a desire to attend another such Conference at an early date, and I hope we shall not have to wait for twenty years before getting it. I think we may hope for it within, say, five years, and when we meet we shall probably be able to record triumphs even greater than those recorded at this Conference, for a great impulse has been given us by these meetings. As has been evidenced by the speeches and papers we have listened to, the cause of library work has become more prominent than upon any former occasion, and we can see that the great advance in civilised countries which has taken place in the way of education is preparing for what you, as librarians, are working for, namely, by united efforts to extend useful knowledge to all parts of the world.

The motion was carried amidst enthusiastic cheers.

Sir JOHN LUBBOCK now came forward, and the whole assembly, rising to their feet, greeted him with prolonged cheering.

Sir JOHN LUBBOCK then said:—I am extremely grateful to you for the resolution which you have just passed. I assure you that it was with some amount of misgiving that I accepted the high and honourable position of President of this Conference, and I am sorry that I have not been able to attend the meetings as much as I hoped to. It unfortunately happened that I had to be sitting on a Committee of the House of Commons, and this rendered it absolutely impossible to attend the meetings as often as I should have liked to do. I feel that I have to join most heartily in supporting the vote of thanks to the other Chairmen who have been good enough to attend in my absence. I will not detain you longer now, as I hope to meet you again this evening, when perhaps I may have the opportunity of addressing you once more. If I do not say much now, it is not because I am not extremely grateful, but I feel I ought not to occupy more of your time at the present moment. In the name of the other gentlemen who have occupied the chair, and on my own behalf, I thank you, ladies and gentlemen, for the vote of thanks which you have so kindly passed.

Taking the chair again, Sir JOHN LUBBOCK continued:—I have now the pleasure of proposing a vote of thanks to Sir Henry Irving for the magnificent entertainment which he was good enough to give us last night, and I am sure you will wish me to join in the acknowledgment the name of Miss Ellen Terry. This is a resolution which will be heartily adopted.

Mr. MACALISTER.—It would be almost impertinent for me to dwell at length upon a motion of this kind, but I might say that the magnificent form of kindness such as Sir Henry Irving has extended to us is a unique thing in the history of conferences. I have had a great deal to do with conferences, and I believe it is perfectly right to say that nothing of the kind has ever been done before.

The proposition was agreed to most heartily.

The CHAIRMAN.—I now have the pleasure of proposing a vote of thanks to the Lord Mayor and the Corporation of London, and I am sure the vote will be carried with acclamation. We are grateful to the Lord Mayor for his presence here at our first meeting, and for the kind reception at the Mansion House, and we are also grateful to the Lord Mayor and to the Corporation of London for allowing us to meet in the Guildhall. We are all the more indebted to him because he has allowed us to come at a time when, perhaps, it was rather inconvenient. I am afraid that we have put them to more inconvenience than perhaps would have been the case at another time, but that makes us all the more grateful to them.

Mr. W. E. A. AXON (Manchester).—It affords me very much pleasure to second this resolution. I am one of a not very large number who look back with very pleasant feelings to the Conference of twenty years ago. Anyone who attended that Conference and this must be greatly struck by the enormous advance that has been made in library work during the past twenty years. It is a great pleasure for us, in coming back to attend the second International Library Conference, to meet under the auspices of the Lord Mayor and the Corporation of London. I cannot think of a better room than this in which to hold a Library Conference. The work of the City of London with regard to all that refers to education has earned the gratitude of all Englishmen, and of all English-speaking persons; therefore it is with peculiar pleasure that I second the vote of thanks.

Sir JOHN MONCKTON (Town Clerk of the City of London).—It will be my duty and great pleasure to convey to the Corporation, at their next meeting, the resolution of thanks so kindly and gracefully proposed and carried. The time was, not long ago, when the Corporation of the City of London grew accustomed to being looked upon as a "close body, regardless of their fellow-men." Whether that was true at the time need not now be discussed,—although I do not think that it was,—but such a gathering as this, I think, furnishes a complete answer to such a charge at the present time. Your meetings this week, I think I may say, so far from being in any way an inconvenience, seem to have enlivened us—to have wakened us up, and a great deal of good, I am sure, will come out of this international gathering. It will be my duty and great pleasure to convey your thanks to the Lord Mayor and Council.

The CHAIRMAN.—Now I have to propose a cordial vote of thanks to the Committee of the Guildhall Library. They have done very much in promoting the success of this Conference, and their officers have shown a kindly desire to render every assistance in their power.

Mr. W. COOLIDGE LANE (Boston), in seconding said :—I count it a privilege indeed to take the humble part of expressing the appreciation of my friends to all those who have been good enough to provide so hospitably for us. We feel under special obligations to the authorities of the Guildhall Library, and also to the staff, for they have taken endless pains that everything should go well with us.

The resolution was carried unanimously.

Mr. CHARLES WELCH (Librarian of the Corporation).—I am sure it has been a great pleasure to the Corporation of London, and also to the Library Committee, to see the members of the Conference here. It was also especially pleasant to me to find that it was possible to get our library in good order before the Conference closed, so that you might be able to see us as we really are. We presented a deplorable appearance until to-day, but now, I think, we are about straight. I am sure I shall be permitted to express the warmest thanks of the Committee for the resolution which has been so kindly passed.

Upon being called upon, Mr. F. M. BORRAJO (Sub-Librarian of the Corporation), said :—I think I shall best consult and conform with your wishes this afternoon by simply asking you to receive my very best thanks.

The Conference then dissolved.

BRIEF ACCOUNT OF THE SOCIAL PROCEEDINGS OF THE CONFERENCE.

By Edward M. Borrajo, Hon. Sec. of the Reception Committee.

THE programme of the Reception Committee commenced on the eve of the Conference with a conversazione at the Guildhall, which, with the adjoining apartments, was placed at the disposal of the committee by the courtesy of the Lord Mayor and the Corporation of the City of London. The Bibliographical Society were associated with the committee as joint-hosts on this occasion, and the proceedings were inaugurated by a lecture, delivered in the council-chamber, by the President of the Society (Dr. Richard Garnett, C.B.) upon "The introduction of European printing into the East," the Earl of Crawford, K.T., in the chair. Upon the motion of Dr. Justin Winsor, a hearty and unanimous vote of thanks was passed to the lecturer. An entertainment by some members of the Savage Club, who had kindly offered their services, followed; in the course of which, amongst others, Mr. Charles Arnold, Mr. Cheeswright, and Mr. Nicholl sang, Mr. Barrett played some flute solos, Mr. Bertram showed card tricks, Mr. Charles Collette recited, Mr. Gribble sketched, and Mr. Ivimey played the pianoforte. Whilst the audience in the council-chamber were enjoying the performances of the Savages, other guests were listening to the concert in the library, where the following programme was rendered by students of the Guildhall School of Music :—

1. Song   "Sing, Sweet Bird" .   *Ganz.*
   Miss JESSIE BRADFORD.
2. Song .   "The Bandolero"   *Leslie Stuart.*
   Mr. B. GRIFFITHS-PERCY.
3. PIANOFORTE SOLO—
   "Caprice Espagnol"   *Moszkowski.*
   Mr. GEO. DOUGLAS BOXALL.
4. Song .   "The Worker" .   *Gounod.*
   Miss MAUDE CLOUGH.
5. Song .   "Home of my Heart" .   *Wallace.*
   Mr. FREDERICK WILLIAMS.
6. Song .   "Killarney" . .   *Balfe.*
   Miss JESSIE BRADFORD.
7. Song .   "The Mighty Deep"   *Jude.*
   Mr. B. GRIFFITHS-PERCY.
8. PIANOFORTE SOLOS—
   (a) "Nocturne" . .   *Chopin.*
   (b) "Irlandaise"   *Francesco Berger.*
   Mr. GEO. DOUGLAS BOXALL.
9. Song .   "When we meet"   *F. H. Cowen.*
   Miss MAUD CLOUGH.
10. Song .   "Tom Bowling" .   *Dibdin.*
    Mr. FREDERICK WILLIAMS.
11. Song .   "Roses" .   *Emil Bach.*
    Miss JESSIE BRADFORD.
12. Song .   "The Soldier's Song"   *Mascheroni.*
    Mr. B. GRIFFITHS-PERCY.
13. Song . . . . —
    Miss MAUD CLOUGH.
14. Song .   "Evening Song"   *Blumenthal.*
    Mr. FREDERICK WILLIAMS.

At the Pianoforte : Miss LOUIE BONHAM.

Many visitors inspected, with much interest, the unique collection of London antiquities in the museum, and the notable loan collection of works of the English school of the Victorian age in the art gallery, where the Blue Viennese Band played the under-mentioned selection of music :—

1. MARCH   "Gigerl"   . *Wagner.*
2. WALTZ .   "Rosen Suden"   . *Strauss.*
3. OVERTURE .   "Orpheus" .   . *Offenbach.*
4. MINUET   .   .   .   *Paderewski.*
5. SELECTION .   "Geisha" .   . *Jones.*
6. INTERMEZZO "Forget-me-not"   *Macbeth.*
7. WALTZ .   "Bonheur Perdu" .   *Gillet.*
8. MARCH   .   "Hungarian" .   *M. Wurm.*

Refreshments were served during the whole evening in the reading-room and at the west end of the library corridor.

On the afternoon of the first day of the Conference (Tuesday July 13) the members were received at Sion College by the President (the Rev. J. H. Rose) and the Court of Governors of that foundation. The reception took place in the library, where an exhibition of some of its more rare and interesting contents had been arranged by the librarian (the Rev. W. H. Milman), assisted by Mr. Henry Guppy. A charming concert was given in the hall, when the following programme of music was performed:—

PART I.

TRIO FOR VIOLIN, VIOLONCELLO, AND PIANO— "Novelleten," Op. 29 . . *Gade.*
(*Allegro—Scherzando—Larghetto con moto—Allegro.*)
Miss ADELINA DINELLI, Mr. BERTRAM LOUD, and Mr. W. R. J. M'LEAN, Mus. B.

SONG . . "My Dreams" . . *Tosti.*
Mr. SAMUEL MASTERS.

SONG . . "A Summer Night" *Goring Thomas.*
Miss LUCIE JOHNSTONE.

VIOLIN SOLOS {(*a*) "Romanzé"} . *Ries.*
{(*b*) "Gavotte"}
Miss ADELINA DINELLI.

VOCAL DUET "Oh! that we two were maying!" *Alice Mary Smith.*
Miss STANLEY LUCAS and Mr. SAMUEL MASTERS.

PART II.

TRIO FOR VIOLIN, VIOLONCELLO, AND PIANO— "Deuxième Trio," Op. 12 . *Fesca.*
(*Adagio—Scherzo.*)
Miss ADELINA DINELLI, Mr. BERTRAM LOUD, and Mr. W. R. J. M'LEAN, Mus. B.

SONGS {(*a*) "Lullaby"} . *Brahms.*
{(*b*) "Snowflakes"} . *Cowen.*
Miss STANLEY LUCAS.

SERENADE "Angels guard thee" . *Godard.*
Mr. SAMUEL MASTERS.

VIOLONCELLO SOLO "Romanzé" . *Karl Matys.*
Mr. BERTRAM LOUD.

VOCAL TRIO . "O Memory" . *Leslie.*
Miss STANLEY LUCAS, Miss LUCIE JOHNSTONE, and Mr. SAMUEL MASTERS.

At the Pianoforte:
Mr. W. R. J. M'LEAN, Mus. B.

The common room and the porch room were devoted to refreshments. A copy of a "Brief account of the library of Sion College," from the pen of the librarian, was given to each guest. In addition to the members of the Conference, many Fellows of the College and their friends were present.

In the evening the Lord Mayor and the Lady Mayoress (Sir George and Lady Faudel-Phillips) welcomed the members of the Conference at the Mansion House. The guests were received on arrival in the saloon, and then passed on into the Egyptian Hall, where Herr Wurm's White Viennese Band played the following programme of music:—

1. MARCH . . "Glocken" . . *Ziehrer.*
2. VALSE . . "Nachtschwärmer" . *Strauss.*
3. OVERTURE "L'Espoir de l'Alsace" *Hermann.*
4. POLKA . . "Wanderlust" . *Fahrbach.*
5. GRAND SELECTION— "Traviata" . *Verdi.*
6. VALSE . "Aux Bords du Alster" *Fetras.*
7. FANTASIE "Round the World" *Conradi.*
8. GALOP . . "Kleine Ursachen" . *Strauss.*

The collection of plate was exhibited here, and traditional civic hospitality was dispensed at two long buffets at either end of the hall. The two pretty drawing-rooms were also thrown open. Among the guests were Lord Crawford, Sir E. Maunde Thompson, Mr. Lecky, M.P.; Sir Henry Howorth, M.P.; Miss Faudel-Phillips, Mrs. Stella Faudel-Phillips, Dr. Garnett, Dr. Justin Winsor, Mr. B. S. Faudel-Phillips, Mr. Lionel Faudel-Phillips, Mr. and Mrs. Philip Henriques, Miss Wingfield, Fraulein Springer, and Miss Marie Corelli.

On Wednesday afternoon the Marchioness of Bute gave a garden party in the grounds of St. John's Lodge, Regent's Park, which was very numerously attended. The Marquis and Marchioness received their guests on the lawn in front of the house. The delightful gardens were looking their best, and the hard-worked members of the Conference enjoyed the relaxation of having nothing to do except listen to the strains of the band of the Scots Guards, amidst such pleasant surroundings. Refreshments were served in a large marquee specially erected for the purpose.

In the evening the President of the Conference and Lady Lubbock gave a reception at their house, 2 St. James's Square, at which practically all the members were present. The "Bijou" orchestra was stationed at the foot of the staircase, and played the following selection of music:—

MENUET . . "Pompadour" . . *Wachs.*
VALSE . . "Meerleuchten" . *Zuhrer.*
AIR DE BALLET "Sylphen Reigen" . *Sabathil.*
VALSE . . "Arc en Ciel" . *Waldteufel.*
AUBADE . . "Pizzicato" . *Schnekead.*
SELECTION . "The Geisha" . . *Jones.*

INTERMEZZO	"Love in Idleness"	.	*Macbeth.*
VALSE	. "Hebe"	.	*Waldteufel.*
RONDE	. "Nuit"	.	*Mariotte.*
SKETCH	. "Darkies' Jubilee"	.	*Turner.*
SELECTION	. "Popular Songs"	.	*Williams.*
CORNET SOLO	"The Plains of Peace"	.	*Barnard.*
VALSE	. "Une Folie de Pesth"	.	*Camillo.*
ROMANCE	. "Frühlings Erwachen"	.	*Bach.*
INTERMEZZO	"Twilight Whispers"		*Laurendeau.*
VALSE	. "Farewell"	.	*Zeller.*
MARCIETTA	"A Petits Pas"	.	*Sudessi.*
SELECTION	. "Tannhauser"	.	*Wagner.*
ROMANCE	. "Simple Aveu"	.	*Thome.*
VALSE	. "Wiener Bonbons"	.	*Strauss.*
MARCH	. "Queen of England"	.	*Pieske.*

Supper was served in the dining-room, and the hospitality of the host and hostess was so much appreciated that the last of the guests did not leave until an advanced hour.

On Thursday afternoon a visit was paid to Brook House, where members were personally received by Lord and Lady Tweedmouth, and entertained at tea. Lord Tweedmouth had kindly arranged an exhibition of books of special interest in his library. Visits were also made to Apsley House by invitation of the Duke of Wellington, and to Grosvenor House by invitation of the Duke of Westminster. Afternoon tea was served at Grosvenor House.

In the evening the members of the Conference were invited by Sir Henry Irving to witness a special performance of Shakespeare's comedy of *The Merchant of Venice* at the Lyceum Theatre. The whole of the stalls and the dress circle were placed at the disposal of the committee, and were filled to their utmost capacity by an enthusiastic and delighted audience. Before the performance commenced, the President, on behalf of the Conference, presented to Miss Ellen Terry a bouquet of orchids, which bore the following inscription: "With the loving greetings of the Librarians of the World to the Queen of Dramatic Art." Sir John and Lady Lubbock occupied a private box on the Grand Tier, and similar accommodation was provided for Mr. Alderman and Mrs. Rawson, and Sir William and Lady Bailey on the Pit Tier. The cast of the play was as follows :—

Shylock	. .	Sir HENRY IRVING.
Bassanio	. .	Mr. F. COOPER.
Duke of Venice	.	Mr. LACY.
Antonio	. .	Mr. MACKLIN.
Prince of Morocco		Mr. TYARS.
Salanio	. .	Mr. FULLER MELLISH.
Salarino	. .	Mr. HARVEY.
Gratiano		Mr. BEN WEBSTER.
Lorenzo		Mr. GORDON CRAIG.
Tubal	.	Mr. ARCHER.
Launcelot Gobbo	.	Mr. S. JOHNSON.
Old Gobbo	.	Mr. REYNOLDS.
Gaoler	.	Mr. GRAHAM.
Leonardo	.	Mr. MARION.
Balthazar	.	Mr. RIVINGTON.
Stephano	.	Mr. BELMORE.
Clerk of the Court		Mr. TABB.
Nerissa	.	Miss MAUD MILTON.
Jessica	. .	Miss EDITH CRAIG.
AND		
Portia	.	Miss ELLEN TERRY.

At the close Sir Henry Irving and Miss Terry were repeatedly summoned before the curtain by the plaudits of an audience eager to testify to their admiration of a superb interpretation of a masterpiece of English literature, as well as to show gratitude for an act of delicate courtesy and great generosity. In reply to calls of "Speech," Sir Henry briefly expressed the gratification which it had given him to play upon so interesting an occasion. A deputation, including Sir John Lubbock, Dr. Justin Winsor, and Mr. Alderman Rawson, waited on Sir Henry Irving in the Green Room to tender their best thanks to him, on behalf of the Conference, for his kindness.

On Friday afternoon a visit was paid to Lambeth Palace, by invitation of the Archbishop of Canterbury, where the party were conducted over the library, the guard-room, the corridor, and the chapel, by Mr. Kershaw, the librarian. Stafford House was also visited, by invitation of the Duke of Sutherland, and a second party visited Apsley House.

In the evening the last item on the programme was reached, when the Conference dinner took place at the Hotel Cecil, under the presidency of Sir John Lubbock. During the dinner the band of the Royal Artillery played the following programme of music :—

MARCH	. "Prodana Nevesta"		*Smetana.*
OVERTURE	. "Esmeralda"	.	*Hermann.*
INTERMEZZO	"Danse des Bacchantes"	.	*Gounod.*
SELECTION	. "The Geisha"	.	*Jones.*
GAVOTTE	. "Windsor Castle"	.	*Gokmer.*
SONG (Cornet Solo)	"Adieu"	.	*Schubert.*
MENUET		.	*Paderewski.*
VALSE,	. "The Queen's Own"	.	*Coote.*
SELECTION	. "Faust"	.	*Gounod.*
GALOP	. "Maraschino"	.	*Lee.*

Conductor : Sergt.-Major W. SUGG.

After dinner the under-mentioned list of toasts was conscientiously gone through ; but, thanks to the brevity of the speakers, the proceedings were not unduly prolonged:—

1. HER MAJESTY THE QUEEN.
   Proposed by the Right Hon. Sir John Lubbock, Bart., M.P., F.R.S.
2. THEIR ROYAL HIGHNESSES THE PRINCE AND PRINCESS OF WALES AND THE OTHER MEMBERS OF THE ROYAL FAMILY.
   Proposed by the Right Hon. Sir John Lubbock, Bart., M.P., F.R.S.
3. THE RT. HON. THE LORD MAYOR AND THE CORPORATION OF THE CITY OF LONDON.
   Proposed by the Right Hon. Sir John Lubbock, Bart., M.P., F.R.S.
   Reply by Charles Welch, Esq.
4. THE LADIES AND GENTLEMEN WHO HAVE ENTERTAINED THE CONFERENCE.
   Proposed by Dr. Richard Garnett, C.B.
   Reply by Bram Stoker, Esq.
5. THE PRESIDENT OF THE CONFERENCE
   Proposed by the Right Hon. the Earl of Crawford, K.T., F.R.S.
   Reply by the Right Hon. Sir John Lubbock, Bart., M.P., F.R.S.
6. THE AMERICAN LIBRARY ASSOCIATION.
   Proposed by Henry R. Tedder, Esq.
   Reply by Melvil Dewey, Esq.
7. THE FOREIGN DELEGATES.
   Proposed by J. Y. W. MacAlister, Esq.
   Reply by Prof. Com. Guido Biagi.
8. THE LIBRARY ASSOCIATION OF THE UNITED KINGDOM.
   Proposed by Dr. Justin Winsor.
   Reply by Mr. Alderman Rawson.
9. THE EXECUTIVE COMMITTEE OF THE CONFERENCE.
   Proposed by Sir William Bailey.
   Reply by E. M. Borrajo, Esq., and Herbert Jones, Esq.
10. THE LADIES.
    Proposed by Frederick M. Crunden, Esq.
    Reply by Miss Hewins and Miss Hannah P. James.

For the design on the menu card, which was much admired, the Reception Committee were indebted to the facile pencil of one of their number, Mr. Herbert Jones. During the whole of the Conference week special facilities were afforded to the members to visit the British Museum Library, the Science and Art Libraries at South Kensington, the Public Record Office, and the gardens of the Zoological and Royal Botanic Societies in Regent's Park; and the committees of the City Liberal, Junior Athenæum, National Liberal, and Savage Clubs elected the members of the Conference honorary members of their several clubs, similar hospitality being extended to the 'lady members by the committee of the Alexandra Club.

CATALOGUE OF THE EXHIBITION OF LIBRARY APPLIANCES HELD IN THE GUILDHALL.

EXHIBITION COMMITTEE.

HERBERT JONES, Kensington Public Libraries (*Chairman*).
F. T. BARRETT, Fulham Public Library.
E. M. BORRAJO, Guildhall Library.
J. D. BROWN, Clerkenwell Public Library.
A. H. CARTER, St. Martin-in-the-Fields Public Library.
C. J. DAVENPORT, British Museum.
W. E. DOUBLEDAY, Hampstead Public Libraries.
H. W. FINCHAM, Commissioner of Clerkenwell Public Library.
RICHARD GARNETT, C.B., LL.D., Keeper of the Printed Books, British Museum.
H. GUPPY, Sion College.
R. W. HEATON, Bishopsgate Institute.
J. W. KNAPMAN, Pharmaceutical Society.
F. W. T. LANGE, St. Bride's Institute.
J. Y. W. MACALISTER, Royal Medical and Chirurgical Society.
FRANK PACY, St. George (Hanover Square) Public Library.
A. W. POLLARD, British Museum.
J. H. QUINN, Chelsea Public Libraries.
SAMUEL SMITH, Sheffield Public Libraries.
ALDERMAN HY. RAWSON, Manchester Public Libraries.
H. R. TEDDER, Athenæum Club, Pall Mall.
CHARLES WELCH, Guildhall Library.
W. H. K. WRIGHT, Plymouth Public Library.
THOMAS MASON, St. Martin-in-the-Fields Public Library (*Hon. Secretary*).

A large collection of Library Plans, Appliances, Catalogues, and Forms, from the Museum of the Library Association, was exhibited on a series of tables and stands on the right of the main entrance to the Guildhall.

OTHER EXHIBITORS.

ADAMS, MAURICE B., F.R.I.B.A., 332 Strand, W.C.—
Plans and Elevations of the Passmore Edwards Libraries at Edmonton, Hammersmith, Shoreditch, St. George's in the East.

ALDRED, T., Librarian, Barrow-in-Furness—
Model of Indicator, invented by the Exhibitor.

ALMACK, EDWARD, 99 Gresham Street, E.C.—
Specimens of Old Binding.

BANTING, J., & SON, 258 King's Road, Chelsea, London, S.W.—
Bindings suitable for Lending Department; Solid Leather Reading Covers; Sanitary Cloth Reading Covers; Readers' Tickets.

BOWRY, W. C., & CO., 28 Dempster Road, Wandsworth, S.W.—
Newspaper Files.

BRISTOL MEDICAL LIBRARY (per L. M. GRIFFITHS, Librarian)—
Photograph of the Library.

CAPETOWN, JOINT LIBRARY OF PARLIAMENT—
  View of Library.

CARDIFF FREE LIBRARIES (per JOHN BALLINGER, Librarian)—
  Public Library Journal of the Cardiff and Penarth Free Public Libraries; View of Central Library, Cardiff.

"CERES" AUTOMATIC LETTER AND CARD FILES (Patentee, T. BOWATER VERNON), 11 Brook Street, W.—
  The "Ceres" Automatic Letter and Card Files, Tables, Desks, etc.

CHELTENHAM PUBLIC LIBRARY (per WILLIAM JONES, Librarian)—
  Cheltenham Public Library, Plans, Catalogues, etc.

CHISWICK ART WORKERS' GUILD (per T. CARR), Bedford Park, Chiswick—
  Specimens of Binding.

COTGREAVE, ALFRED (Librarian, West Ham Public Libraries)—
  Indicators, Library Plans, Catalogues, etc., Racks for Magazines, etc., Automatic and other Steps for Book Presses, Book and Magazine Covers, Newspaper Rods and Clips, Number Labels for Books.

COTTON & COMPANY LIMITED, Victoria Works, Holmes Chapel, Crewe, Cheshire, England—
  Noiseless Chair Pads.

CUTTER, C. A., Forbes Library, Northampton, Mass., U.S.A.—
  Expansive Classification.

DE COVERLEY, ROGER, 6 St. Martin's Court, London, W.C.—
  Specimens of Binding.

DUNDEE FREE PUBLIC LIBRARY (per JOHN MACLAUCHLAN, Librarian)—
  Model of Kennedy Indicator, invented in 1875 by Mr. John Kennedy, of the Dundee Free Library Committee; Model of Book Disinfector used in the Dundee Free Library since 1885; Catalogue, with Annual Supplements, of the Dundee Free Library; Catalogue of the Lochee Branch of the Dundee Free Library.

ELLIOT, JOHN, Librarian, Free Library, Wolverhampton—
  Model of the Original Library Indicator.

FAUX, W., King Square Avenue, Bristol—
  Newspaper Stand.

GARNER, RUSSELL, & COMPANY, 9 Belvoir Street, Leicester—
  Specimens of Bookbinding.

HAMMOND TYPEWRITER.
  Exhibition of the Hammond Typewriter.

IRELAND, NATIONAL LIBRARY OF (per T. W. LYSTER, Librarian)—
  Plans of the New Building, opened August 1890; Photographs by Mr. Robert Welch, of Belfast; Photographs by Mr. Archibald McGoogan, of the Science and Art Museum, Dublin; Supplemental Catalogues, 1874-93, 15 Volumes.

JACKSON, WILLIAM, 18 Back Wynd, Aberdeen—
  Specimens of Bookbinding.

KIDDERMINSTER PUBLIC LIBRARY (per ARCH. SPARKE, Librarian)—
  Ground Plan of the Building; Rules, Catalogues, etc.

LAMBERT, A. W., 11 Sunny Bank, South Norwood, London, S.E.—
  Book Stacks; Charging Systems; Card Catalogues; Newspaper Fastenings; Reading Stands; Periodicals (Indicator) List, etc., and other items.

LIBRARY BUREAU LIMITED (CEDRIC CHIVERS, Manager), 10 Bloomsbury Street, London, W.C.—
  Book Stacks; Card Catalogue Cabinets; Desks; Library Indicator; Library Binding; Choice Bindings; Sundries.

LIBRARY SUPPLY COMPANY, 4 Ave Maria Lane, Paternoster Row, E.C. (W. W. FORTUNE, Manager)—
  Cards and Cabinets for Card Catalogues, Borrowers' Indexes, Application Forms, Museum Catalogues, Desks, Stationery, etc.

LUCY, W., & CO. LIMITED, Eagle Iron Works, Oxford (GEORGE GARDINER, Manager)—
  New System of Overhead Rolling Book Stacks; Stacks fitted with Lambert's Patent Self-adjusting Shelving; American Stacks, patented by "Stikeman."

McGILL UNIVERSITY LIBRARY (per C. H. GOULD, Librarian)—
  Cabinet, showing arrangement of Catalogue; Accession Book (Modified "Library Bureau"); Binding Book; Description of Library Building.

NEW YORK STATE LIBRARY—
  Catalogue Department: Drawers, Cards, etc.; Charging Systems. Shelf Department: Sheets, Records. Library School: Lists, Notes, etc. New York State Library: Reports, etc. New York State Public Libraries Division Publications. New York State Library School: Publications; Dewey's Decimal Classification.

"REVIEW OF REVIEWS" (per Miss HETHERINGTON)—
  "Annual Index to Periodicals."

ROTHERHITHE PUBLIC LIBRARY (per H. A. SHUTTLEWORTH, Librarian)—
  Skeleton Newspaper Holder; "Delivery Station" Application Forms and Registers; New Lettering for Books with Loose Backs; Overdue Circulars.

SACCONI-RICCI, MRS. GIULIA, Biblioteca Marucelliana, Florence—
  Mechanical Binding for Catalogues.

ST. HELENS FREE PUBLIC LIBRARY (per ALFRED LANCASTER, Librarian)—
  View and Plans of the Gamble Institute; Forms for Borrowers, etc.

SANDERSON, T. J. COBDEN, The Doves Bindery, No. 15 Upper Mall, Hammersmith—
  Specimens of Binding.

SCULL, A. S., 17 Redcliffe Street, Bristol—
  The "Bristol" Library Indicator.

SHANNON LIMITED, 14, 15, and 16 Ropemaker Street, London, E.C.—
  Letter Filing Cabinets; Card Indexing Cabinets; Library Desks, etc.

STADERINI, P., Rome—
  Cataloguing Appliances.

TURNER, THOMAS, 44 Holborn Viaduct, E.C.—
Card Index Files; Filing Cabinets; Wernicke Cabinet; Elastic Bookcases.

VOLPRIGNANO, T., 35 Archel Road, London, W.—
Exhibit to show the facility of turning the leaves of a book *one by one*, from end to end, with a single finger. Printed sheets cut in blocks by machinery, and folded and bound in books in the usual way.

WRIGHT, W. H. K., Librarian, Free Public Library, Plymouth—
Model of Catalogue Indicator in use at the Plymouth Free Library; Framed Photographs of L.A.U.K. Groups.

WRIGHT, W. H. K., and FINCHAM, H. W., 172 St. John Street, London, E.C.—
Album containing Book Plates and printed Book Labels belonging to various libraries, and separate exhibits of the Plates of libraries and institutions from various parts of the world.

ZAEHNSDORF, J. W., 144-146 Shaftesbury Avenue, London, W.C.—
Specimens of Binding.

LIST OF (641) MEMBERS OF THE CONFERENCE.

BBATT, Miss, New York, U.S.A.
ABBOTT, T. K. (Librarian), Trinity College, Dublin (*Vice-President*).
ABEL, Sir Frederick A., Bart., K.C.B. (Secretary, Imperial Institute), Kensington (*Vice-President*).
ACLAND, Prof. Sir Henry W., Bart. (Librarian), **Radcliffe** Library, Oxford (*Vice-President*).
ADAMS, J R. G. **(Librarian),** Public Library, Adelaide, **South Australia** (*Vice-President*).
AGAR, Miss E. M. F., care of T. J. Agar, **9** Bucklersbury, E.C.
AGAR, T. J., **9** Bucklersbury, E.C.
AHERN, Miss M. E. (Editor, *Public Libraries*), Library Bureau, Chicago, Ill., U.S.A.
ALDEN, Percy (Chairman of the West Ham Public Libraries), Mansfield **House,** Canning Town, E. (*Vice-President*).
ALDIS, Harry G. (Secretary and Librarian), Philosophical Institution, 4 Queen Street, Edinburgh.
ALDRED, Thomas (Librarian), Public Library, Barrow-in-Furness.
ALLEN, Edward (London Agency for American Libraries), 28 Henrietta Street, Covent Garden, W.C.
ALMACK, Edward, 99 Gresham Street, E.C.
ALMACK, Mrs. **Edward,** 99 Gresham Street, E.C.
AMES, Harriet H. (Librarian), **Hoyt** Library, East Saginaw, Mich., U.S.A.
AMES, Percy W. (Hon. Librarian of the Royal Society of Literature), 20 Hanover Square, W.
ANDERSON, Henry Charles Lennox (Librarian and Secretary, Free Public Library, Sydney; delegated by the Governments of New South Wales and Victoria), 75 Southampton Row, W.C. (*Vice-President*).
ANDERSON, James Maitland (Librarian), University Library, St. Andrews.
ANDERSON, Peter John (Librarian, Aberdeen University Library), University Library, Aberdeen.
ANDERTON, Basil (Librarian), Public **Library,** Newcastle-upon-Tyne.
ANDERTON, Mrs. Basil, Newcastle-upon-Tyne.
ANDREWS, Clement W. (Librarian), The John Crerar Library, Chicago, Ill., U.S.A.
ARMSTRONG, E. L. T. (Librarian), Public Library, Melbourne, Victoria (*Vice-President*).
ARMSTRONG, J. F., 80 North Side, Clapham Common, S.W.
ARROWSMITH, William J. (Librarian), The Edward Pease Public Library, Darlington.
ASHBEE, H. S., Fowlers, Hawkhurst, Kent.
ASHTON, R. (Librarian and Curator), Public Library, Museum, and Art Gallery, Blackburn.
AUMALE, H.R.H. the late Duc d' (*Vice-President*).
AUSTIN, R. (Librarian), Christchurch Public Library, Charles Street, S.E.
AVERY, Miss E. M., Cleveland, O., U.S.A.
AXON, William E. A. (Chairman of the Moss Side Public Library), 47 Derby Street, Moss Side, Manchester (*Vice-President*).

BAER, S. L. (representing **Messrs. Baer &** Co.), Frankfort.
BAGGULEY, W. Hildon (Librarian, Canning Town Branch Library), Public Library, Canning Town, West Ham, E.
BAGGULEY, Mrs. W. H., 104 Balaam Street, Plaistow, E.
BAILEY, Sir William H., Salford Public Library Committee (*Vice-President*).

LIST OF MEMBERS

BAILEY, Lady, Sale Hall, Cheshire.
BAIN, James (Librarian), Public Library, Toronto (*Vice-President*).
BALDWIN, Miss E. G., New York, U.S.A.
BALLINGER, John (Librarian), Public Library, Cardiff (*Vice-President*).
BANTING, G. F., 258 King's Road, Chelsea.
BARFF, H. E. (Librarian), University Library, Sydney, New South Wales (*Vice-President*).
BARKAS, Albert A. (Librarian), Public Library, Richmond, Surrey.
BARKER, Rev. Canon William (Marylebone Public Library Committee), 38 Devonshire Place, W. (*Vice-President*).
BARRETT, Francis T. (Librarian), The Mitchell Library, 21 Miller Street, Glasgow (*Vice-President*).
BARRETT, Franklin T. (Librarian, Fulham Public Library), Fulham Public Libraries, Fulham Road, S.W.
BARTON, Edmund M. (Librarian), American Antiquarian Society, Worcester, Mass., U.S.A.
BARTON, Mrs. Edmund M., Worcester, Mass., U.S.A.
BARWICK, G. F., 20 Regent's Park Road, N.W.
BATSFORD, Herbert (Publisher and Bookseller), 94 High Holborn, W.C.
BATTERSEA PUBLIC LIBRARY, London.
BATTYE, James S. (Librarian), Victoria Public Library, Perth, Western Australia (*Vice-President*).
BEEBY, J. Henry (Chairman of Peterborough Public Library Committee), The Gables, Peterborough.
BEER, William (Librarian, Howard Memorial Library), Howard Memorial Library, New Orleans, Louisiana, U.S.A.
BELINFANTE, L. L. (Assistant Secretary and Librarian), Geological Society, Burlington House, W.
BELJAME, Prof. Alexandre, Université de France, Paris (*Vice-President*).
BELL, George, 95 Upper Street, Islington, N.
BELL, John (Chairman, Wandsworth Public Libraries Committee), 22 Upper Richmond Road, Putney.
BENHAM, Rev. Canon (Manager, London Institution), London Institution, Finsbury Circus, E.C.
BERGROTH, H., 1 Sutherland Place, Bayswater, W.
BESANT, Sir Walter, Frognal End, Hampstead (*Vice-President*).
BIAGI, Prof. Comm. Guido (Librarian of the Laurentian Library; delegate of the Italian Government), Biblioteca Mediceo-Laurenziana, Florence (*Vice-President*).
BIBLIOGRAPHICAL SOCIETY, 20 Hanover Square, W.C.
BIGMORE, Edward C., 4 Trafalgar Square, W.C.
BILLINGS, John S. (Librarian), Public Library, New York, U.S.A. (*Vice-President*).
BIRCH, A. J. (Librarian), Great Western Railway Mechanics' Institution, New Swindon.
BIRTWELL, Mary L., Associated Charities of Cambridge, Cambridge, Mass., U.S.A.
BISCOE, Alice M., U.S.A.
BISCOE, Ellen L., U.S.A.
BISCOE, Lucy W., U.S.A.
BISCOE, Walter S., State Library of New York, U.S.A.
BLACKETT, Spencer C. (Managing Director of Messrs. Kegan, Paul, Trench, Trübner, & Co.), 20 Charing Cross Road, W.C.
BLACKIE, J. Alexander (Publisher), 17 Stanhope Street, Glasgow.
BLACKIE, Walter W., 17 Stanhope Street, Glasgow.
BLACKWOOD, William (Publisher), 45 George Street, Edinburgh (*Vice-President*).
BLADES, EAST, & BLADES, Messrs., 23 Abchurch Lane, E.C.
BLAKEWAY, G. B., care of E. M. Borrajo, The Library, Guildhall, E.C.
BLORE, Charles Christopher, 29 Carlyle Square, S.W.
BOASE, Frederic (Librarian), Incorporated Law Society, Chancery Lane, W.C.
BOLTON, Charles K., Treasurer of American Library Association (Librarian), Public Library, Brookline, Mass., U.S.A. (*Vice-President*).
BOND, Sir Edward A., K.C.B. (late Librarian, British Museum), 64 Prince's Square, W. (*Vice-President*).
BOND, Henry (City Librarian), Public Library, Lincoln.
BOOCOCK, Councillor John (Vice-Chairman of the Southport Library Committee), Sunnyside Hydro., Southport.
BOOSÉ, James R., Royal Colonial Institute, Northumberland Avenue, W.C.
BORRAJO, Edward M. (Senior Sub-Librarian of the Corporation of the City of London), The Library, Guildhall, E.C. (*Hon. Secretary, Reception Committee*).

LIST OF MEMBERS

BOULTON, Frederick George (Commissioner, Clerkenwell Public Library), 75 Goswell Road, Clerkenwell, E.C.
BOWKER, R. R. (Editor of the *Library Journal*, New York) (*Vice-President*).
BRABROOK, E. W., C.B. (Treasurer of the Royal Society of Literature), 28 Abingdon Street, S.W. (*Vice-President*).
BRADSHAW, William (President), Bromley House Library, Nottingham.
BRAMWELL, W. S. (Librarian), Public Library, Preston.
BRASSINGTON, W. Salt (Librarian), Shakespeare Memorial Library, Stratford-on-Avon.
BRETT, William H. (President of the American Library Association), Public Library, Cleveland, Ohio, U.S.A. (*Vice-President*).
BRINKERHOFF, Adelaide, Mansfield, Ohio, U.S.A.
BRISCOE, J. Potter (Librarian), Public Library, Nottingham (*Vice-President*).
BRISCOE, Mrs. J. Potter, care of J. P. Briscoe, Esq., Public Library, Nottingham.
BRITTAIN, Alderman W. H. (Chairman, Sheffield Public Library Committee), Public Library, Sheffield (*Vice-President*).
BRITTAIN, Mrs. W. H., Sheffield.
BROUGH, Bennet H. (Secretary and Librarian), Iron and Steel Institute, 28 Victoria Street, S.W.
BROWN, Edith, Boston, Massachusetts, U.S.A.
BROWN, Dr. Francis H., Boston, Mass., U.S.A.
BROWN, Mrs. Francis H., Boston, Mass., U.S.A.
BROWN, James D. (Librarian), Public Library, Skinner Street, Clerkenwell, E.C. (*Hon. Secretary, Committee on Papers and Discussions*).
BROWN, Joseph, Lancaster House, Upper Dicconson Street, Wigan.
BROWN, Mrs. Joseph, Lancaster House, Upper Dicconson Street, Wigan.
BROWNE, Nina E., American Library Association, Publishing Section, Boston, Mass., U.S.A.
BRUUN, C. W., Royal Library, Copenhagen (*Vice-President*).
BULL, H. W. (Librarian), Public Library, Wimbledon.
BULLEN, A. H. (Publisher), 16 Henrietta Street, Covent Garden, W.C.
BURGOYNE, Frank James (Librarian, Lambeth Public Libraries), The Tate Central Library, Brixton Oval, S.W.
BURRELL, J. Charles (Deputy-Mayor of Hastings, and Chairman of the Brassey Institute), Blacklands, Hastings.
BURRELL, Mrs. J. Charles, Blacklands, Hastings.
BUTCHER, Albert, Belle Grove, Welling, Kent.
BUTLER, W. F., Queen's College, Cork.
BUTT, Arthur N., London Institution, Finsbury Circus, E.C.

CADENHEAD, James F. (Sub-Librarian), Public Library, Aberdeen.
CALVERT, A. E. (Member of the Widnes Corporation Free Library Committee), Widnes Road, Widnes.
CAMERON, Mrs. Malcolm, The Lodge, Yatton, Somerset.
CAMPBELL, Frank (Assistant Librarian, British Museum), British Museum.
CAMPBELL, G. Lamb, 15 Talbot Street, Southport.
CARNEGIE, Andrew, Pittsburg, U.S.A. (Cluny Castle, N.B.) (*Vice-President*).
CART, Rev. Henry, Queen Anne's Mansions, S.W.
CARTER, A. H. (Assistant Librarian), St. Martin's Public Library, London.
CARTER, B. (Librarian), Public Library, Kingston-on-Thames.
CAVE, Rev. Alfred, D.D. (Principal of Hackney College), Hackney College.
CAWTHORNE, A. (Librarian), Public Library, Whitechapel, E.
CHAPMAN, Henry A. (Vice-Chairman, Swansea Public Library Committee), 235 High Street, Swansea.
CHASE, Fredk. A., City Library, Lowell, Mass., U.S.A.
CHIVERS, Cedric (Manager, Library Bureau), 10 Bloomsbury Street, London, W.C.
CHIVERS, Mrs., 10 Bloomsbury Street, W.C.
CHRISTIE, Richard Copley, Ribsden, Bagshot, Surrey (*Vice-President*).
CHRISTIE-MILLER, Wakefield, 21 St. James's Place, S.W.
CLARK, Elizabeth R., University of Nashville, Peabody Normal College, Nashville, Tenn., U.S.A.
CLARK, J. T., Keeper of the Advocates' Library, Edinburgh (*Vice-President*).
CLARKE, Sir Ernest (Secretary of the Royal Agricultural Society of England), 13A Hanover Square, W.
CLIFTON, Alderman George, 48 London Road, Leicester.
COLQUHOUN, James (Treasurer and Sub-Convener of the Library Committee, Glasgow Town Council), 158 St. Vincent Street, Glasgow.

LIST OF MEMBERS

CONANT, Marjory, Boston, Mass., U.S.A.
COPINGER, Miss, The Priory, Manchester.
COPINGER, W. A. (President, Manchester Incorporated Law Library Society), The Priory, Manchester.
CORSAR, David (Donor of the Arbroath Public Library), The Elms, Arbroath (*Vice-President*).
COTGREAVE, Alfred (Librarian), Public Libraries, West Ham, E.
COTTERELL, T. Sturge, The Lodge, Yatton, Somerset.
COWELL, Peter (Librarian), Public Library, Liverpool (*Vice-President*).
COWIE, A. H., St. Oswalds, Claughton, Birkenhead.
COX, Henry Thomas (Librarian), Carlton Club, Pall Mall, S.W.
CRAIG-BROWN, T., Woodburn, Selkirk, N.B.
CRAIGIE, James (Librarian), Public Library, Arbroath.
CRAWFORD, The Right Hon. the Earl of, K.T., Haigh Hall, Wigan (*Vice-President*).
CROFTON, F. Blake (Librarian), Legislative Library, Halifax, Nova Scotia (*Vice-President*).
CROSSLEY, S., 21 Suffolk Street, Pall Mall, S.W.
CROWTHER, W. (Librarian), Public Library, Derby.
CROWTHER, Mrs. W., Derby.
CRUNDEN, Frederick M. (Librarian), Public Library, St. Louis, Mo., U.S.A. (*Vice-President*).
CRUNDEN, Mrs. Frederick M., St. Louis, Mo., U.S.A.
CULLINGWORTH, Charles James, M.D. (President of the Obstetrical Society of London), 14 Manchester Square, W.
CUNDALL, Frank (Librarian), Institute of Jamaica, Kingston, Jamaica (*Vice-President*).
CURRAN, Mrs. Mary H. (Librarian), Bangor Public Library, Bangor, Maine, U.S.A.
CURTIS, Benjamin, Boston, Mass., U.S.A.
CURZON, Frank (Organising Secretary of the Yorkshire Union of Institutes and Yorkshire Village Libraries), Victoria Chambers, Leeds.
CUTTER, Charles Ammi (Librarian, Forbes Library, Northampton, Mass.), Forbes Library, Northampton, Mass., U.S.A. (*Vice-President*).
DALE, Rev. Lawford W. T. (Chairman, Chiswick Public Library Committee), The Vicarage, Chiswick.

DANIEL, Edwin (Librarian), Godshill, Wroxhall, Isle of Wight.
DAVENPORT, Cyril J. H., British Museum, W.C.
DAVIDSON, Herbert E. (First Vice-President of the Boston Library Bureau), 146 Franklin Street, Boston, U.S.A.
DAVIES, Jesse Thomas (Chairman, Wood Green Public Library Committee), Riversdale, Wood Green.
DAVIS, Cecil T. (Librarian), Public Library, Wandsworth, S.W.
DAVIS, Mary L., Pratt Institute Library, Brooklyn, New York.
DAVIS, N. Darnell (British Guiana), Royal Colonial Institute, Northumberland Avenue, W.C.
DAVIS, R. C. (Chairman of the Newington Public Libraries), 7 Falmouth Road, S.E.
DAY, Charles (Day's Library), 96 Mount Street, Grosvenor Square, W.
DEBENHAM, Frank (Marylebone Public Library Committee), 1 Fitzjohn's Avenue, Hampstead, N.W. (*Vice-President*).
DE CELLES, A. D. (Librarian of the Dominion Government of Canada; delegated by the Government of Canada), Houses of Parliament, Ottawa, Canada (*Vice-President*).
DE COVERLEY, R., 6 St. Martin's Court, Charing Cross Road, W.C.
DELISLE, Leopold (Administrator of the Bibliothèque Nationale), Bibliothèque Nationale, Paris (*Vice-President*).
DENT, R. K. (Librarian), Public Library, Aston Manor, near Birmingham.
DEWEY, Melvil (Director, New York State Library; delegated by the United States Government), State Library, Albany, New York, U.S.A. (*Vice-President*).
DONALDSON, S. F. (Librarian), Public Library, Inverness.
DOUBLEDAY, W. E. (Librarian), Hampstead Public Library, 48 Priory Road, N.W.
DOUTHWAITE, D. W., Steward's Office, Gray's Inn, W.C.
DOUTHWAITE, W. R. (Librarian), The Library, Gray's Inn, W.C. (*Vice-President*).
DOWDEN, Prof. Edward (Trustee of the National Library of Ireland), Buonavista, Killiney, Co. Dublin (*Vice-President*).
DOWNING, William (Bookseller), Chaucer's Head Library, Birmingham.
DUCKWORTH, Thomas (Librarian and Secretary), Public Library, Worcester.

LIST OF MEMBERS

DUFFERIN AND AVA, The Most Hon. the Marquess of, K.P., Clandeboye, Belfast (*Vice-President*).
DUFOUR, Th., Bibliothèque de la Ville, Geneva (*Vice-President*).
DUNLOP, Judge J. C., Committee of Public Library, Edinburgh.
DUNN, Mrs. Wm. T., Worcester, Mass., U.S.A.
DURRANT, Kate (Librarian, **Lowestoft** Public Library), Wellington **House**, South Lowestoft.
DZIATZKO, Prof. C., Universitäts-Bibliothek, Göttingen (*Vice-President*).

EAKINS, William George (Librarian of Law Society of Upper Canada), Osgoode Hall, Toronto, Ontario, Canada.
ECKERSLEY, Alderman James (Chairman of the Oldham Public Library Committee), Public Library, Oldham.
EDINBURGH PUBLIC LIBRARY.
EDMOND, John Philip (Librarian to the Earl of Crawford), Haigh Hall, Wigan.
EDWARD, Alfred S., 46 Fountayne Road, Stoke Newington, N.
EDWARDS, J. Passmore, 51 **Bedford** Square, W.C. (*Vice-President*).
ELLIOT, John (Librarian), Public Library, Wolverhampton.
ELLIOTT, G. H. **(Librarian)**, Public Library, Belfast.
ELLIOTT, Mrs. G. H., **Belfast**.
ENJIRO YAMAZA (delegated by the Government of Japan), 8 Sussex Square, Hyde Park, W. (*Vice-President*).
ERDÉLYI PÁL, Dr., X Hedervary-uteza 36, Budapest, Hungary.
EVANS, John Henry (Secretary, Workmen's Institute, Cymmer Colliery), 24 Glyn Street, Cymmer, nr. Porth R.S.O., South Wales.
EVANS, S. W. **(Librarian)**, Incorporated Law **Society of Ireland**, Four Courts, Dublin.
EVERATT, Thomas (Librarian and Clerk, Streatham Library Commissioners), The Tate Public Library, Streatham, S.W.

FAUDEL-PHILLIPS, **Rt.** Hon. **Sir** George (The Lord Mayor of the City of London), Mansion House, E.C. (*Vice-President*).
FETIS, E., Bibliothèque Royale, Brussels (*Vice-President*).
FIELD, Fanny, Avondale, Cincinnati, Ohio, U.S.A.
FIFE, Bailie William (Convener of Library Committee, Glasgow Town Council), 52 **Glassford** Street, Glasgow.

FINCHAM, H. W. (Vice-Chairman, Clerkenwell Public Library Committee), 172 St. John Street, E.C.
FLETCHER, Mary (Librarian of **Girton** College, Cambridge), 9 Stanhope **Street**, Hyde Park Lane, W.
FLINT, Henry, Bridgeman Terrace, Wigan.
FLOWERS, Councillor Robert (Vice-Chairman, Books Committee, Public Library, Newcastle-upon-Tyne), Newcastle-upon-Tyne.
FOLKARD, H. **T.** (Librarian), Public Library, Wigan.
FOLLOWS, Fred. Wm. (Technical Instruction Committee, Manchester), Somerville, Heaton Moor, Stockport, Manchester.
FORBES-ROBERTSON, John (Chairman, St. Giles' Public Library), 22 Bedford Square, W.C.
FORSYTH, Kate **A.,** Public Library, Edinburgh.
FORTESCUE, G. K. (Assistant Keeper of Printed Books), British Museum, W.C.
FOSKETT, Edward (Librarian), Public Library, Camberwell.
FOSTER, W. E. (Librarian, Providence Public Library), Public Library, Providence, R.I., U.S.A. (*Vice-President*).
FOVARGUE, H. W. (Honorary Solicitor **of** the Library Association), **Town** Hall, Eastbourne (*Vice-President*).
FOWLER, Mary, Cornell **University** Library, Ithaca, N.Y., U.S.A.
FRANCIS, Mary, 101 Elm Street, Hartford, Conn., U.S.A.
FRAZER, R. W. (Librarian and Secretary), London Institution, Finsbury Circus, E.C.
FROEHLICH, The Cavaliere, K.C.I. (Italian Consul, Manchester), **30** Faulkener Street, Manchester.
FURNISH, Arthur H. (Librarian), Public Library, York.

GAMBLE, Robert C. (Commissioner, St. Martin and St. Paul's Public Library), 115 St. Martin's Lane, W.C.
GARDINER, George (Representative of Messrs. W. Lucy & Co. Limited), Eagle Ironworks, Oxford.
GARDINER, Miss H. C.
GARNETT, Richard, C.B., Keeper of the Printed Books, British Museum (*Vice-President, and Chairman of Committee on Papers and Discussions*).
GARNETT, William (Secretary to the Technical Education Board of the London County Council), St. Martin's Place, W.C. (*Vice-President*).

LIST OF MEMBERS

GEE, Alderman John, Park View, Wigan.
GEORGE, Henry, 38 West Smithfield, E.C.
GILBERT, Alderman H. M. (representing Southampton Public Library Committee), 26 Above Bar, Southampton.
GILBURT, Joseph (Messrs. Day's Library), 96 Mount Street, W.
GILLIES, Rev William (Chairman of the Library Committee, Institute of Jamaica), 37 Westbourne Road, Sheffield.
GLANFIELD, William Tankerville, 9 Oxberry Avenue, Fulham Road, S.W.
GLIDDON, A. M. de Putron (Delegate of the Butte Public Library, Montana, U.S.A.).
GNOLI, Domenico, Biblioteca Nazionale Centrale, Vittorio Emanuele, Rome (*Vice-President*).
GOLDSMITHS, The Worshipful Company of, Foster Lane, E.C.
GOODFELLOW, J. H. (Southampton Public Library Committee), Public Library, Southampton.
GOODYEAR, Charles (Librarian, Lancashire Independent College), 39 Lincroft Street, Moss Lane East, Manchester.
GOSNELL, R. E. (Librarian), Legislative Assembly Library, Victoria, British Columbia (*Vice-President*).
GOSS, Chas. W. F. (Librarian), Public Library, Lewisham, S.E.
GOULD, C. H. (Librarian), McGill University Library, Montreal, Canada (*Vice-President*).
GOVIER, Albert (Mayor of West Ham), 125 The Grove, Stratford, E.
GRAVES, Robert E. (Assistant Keeper, Department of Printed Books), British Museum, W.C.
GRAY, Albert (Librarian), Public Library, Gosport.
GREEN, John A. (Librarian), Public Library, Moss Side, Manchester.
GREEN, Samuel S. (Librarian), Public Library, Worcester, Massachusetts, U.S.A. (*Vice-President*).
GREENHOUGH, William H. (Librarian and Superintendent), Public Library, Reading.
GREENHOW, J. H. (Member of the Manchester Public Libraries Committee), 46 Princess Street, Manchester.
GREENWOOD, Thomas (Author of *Public Libraries*), Frith Knowl, Elstree, Herts (*Vice-President*).
GREVEL, H. (Publisher), 33 King Street, Covent Garden, W.C.
GREY, Right Hon. Sir George, K.C.B. (*Vice-President*).

GRICE, Henry R., 221 Ebury Street, S.W.
GRIFFITHS, L. M. (Hon. Librarian), Bristol Medical Library, University College, Bristol.
GUILDING, Rev. J. M. (Member of the Reading Public Library, Museum, and Art Gallery), Abbot's Walk, Reading.
GUINNESS, Miss E. M. (Librarian), Royal Holloway College, Egham.
GUPPY, Henry (Assistant Librarian), Sion College, Victoria Embankment, E.C.

HALSBURY, Rt. Hon. Earl (The Lord High Chancellor), 4 Ennismore Gardens, S.W. (*Vice-President*).
HAMILTON, J. C. (Chairman, Preston Public Library Committee), Public Library, Preston.
HAMPSTEAD PUBLIC LIBRARY (represented by Dr. C. W. Ryalls, Chairman of the Hampstead Public Library Committee), 59 Haverstock Hill, N.W.
HAND, Thomas W. (Librarian), Public Libraries, Oldham.
HANNAM, Agnes (Secretary and Librarian, Obstetrical Society; and Assistant Honorary Secretary, Library Association), 20 Hanover Square, W.
HANSON, Alderman Sir Reginald, Bart., M.P., 4 Bryanston Square, S.W. (*Vice-President*).
HARDCASTLE, J. H. (Librarian), Public Library, Eastbourne.
HAWLEY, Mary E., New York State Library, Albany, N.Y., U.S.A.
HAY, The Hon. John (American Ambassador), Carlton House Terrace, S.W. (*Vice-President*).
HAYES, Rutherford P. (Secretary of American Library Association), 675 East Broad Street, Columbus, Ohio, U.S.A. (*Vice-President*).
HAZELL, Rev. James J. (Member of the Bibliographical Society), 41 Brook Green, W.
HEATON, Ronald W. (late Director and Librarian), Bishopsgate Institute, E.C.
HEINEMANN, William (Publisher), 21 Bedford Street, W.C.
HENDERSON, Sir William, 7 Billiter Square, E.C.
HERNE, Frank S. (Secretary and Librarian), Permanent Library, Leicester.
HETHERINGTON, Miss E., 14 Shaftesbury Road, Hammersmith.
HEWINS, Miss Caroline M. (Librarian), Public Library, Hartford, Conn., U.S.A.
HEYWOOD, James (Founder of the Kensington Public Library), 26 Palace Gardens, W. (*Vice-President*).

HILCKEN, G. F. (Librarian), Public Library, Bethnal Green, E.
HILL, B. R. (Librarian), Public Library, Sunderland.
HILL, Frank P. (Librarian), Public Library, Newark, New Jersey, U.S.A. (*Vice-President*).
HILLS, Stuart S. (Librarian), Public Library, Grace Hill, Folkestone.
HILLS, W. J. (Superintendent), Public Library, Bridgeport, Conn., U.S.A.
HOBBES, R. G., 374 Wandsworth Road.
HOBBS, Charles (Commissioner, St. Martin and St. Paul's Public Library), 115 St. Martin's Lane, W.C.
HODGE, G. H. (Chairman of the Chelsea Public Libraries), 19 Tadema Road, Chelsea, S.W.
HOLGATE, Clifford W., The Close, Salisbury.
HOLMES, Richard R. (Queen's Librarian), Windsor Castle (*Vice-President*).
HOPWOOD, O. T. (Librarian), Public Library, Southampton.
HORNBY, James, Swinley House, Wigan.
HORNER, F. W. (Commissioner, St. Martin and St. Paul's Public Library), 115 St. Martin's Lane, W.C.
HOWORTH, Sir Henry H., K.C.I.E., M.P., 30 Collingham Place, S.W. (*Vice-President*).
HUDSON, Baker (Librarian), Public Library, Middlesborough.
HUDSON, Rev. Canon J. Clare (Canon of Lincoln), Thornton Vicarage, Horncastle.
HUGHES, George (Librarian), Public Library, Pontypridd.
HUGHES, William R. (Chairman, Handsworth Public Library), Wood House, Handsworth Wood, Birmingham.
HUISH, Marcus B. (Hon. Librarian, Japan Society), 21 Essex Villas, Phillimore Gardens, Kensington.
HULL, Fanny (Librarian), The Brooklyn Union for Christian Work, Brooklyn, New York, U.S.A.
HULME, E. Wyndham (Librarian of the Patent Office), 53 Lansdowne Road, Notting Hill.
HUMPHERY, George R. (Hon. Secretary of Messrs. Braby's Library and Club), 16 St. Donatt's Road, New Cross, S.E.
HUMPHREYS, Arthur L., 187 Piccadilly, W.
HUNT, Fred. W. (Librarian), Public Library, Devonport.
HUTCHINSON, Alfred J. (Librarian), Public Library, Millom, Cumberland.
HUTCHINSON, Charles Hare (President), The Athenæum, Philadelphia, U.S.A.

INGRAM, Prof. J. K. (late Librarian of Trinity College, Dublin), 38 Upper Mount Street, Dublin (*Vice-President*).
INKSTER, Lawrence (Librarian, Battersea Public Library), Public Library, Lavender Hill, S.W.
IRVING, Emilius, Q.C., Toronto.
IRVING, Sir Henry, 15A Grafton Street, Bond Street, W (*Vice-President*).

JAMES, H. L. (Librarian), Parliament Library, Wellington, New Zealand (*Vice-President*).
JAMES, Hannah P (Librarian), Osterhout Free Library, Wilkes-Barré, Pa., U.S.A. (*Vice-President*).
JAMES, Hugh (Public Accountant), 6 Gorst Road, Wandsworth Common, S.W.
JAST, L. Stanley (Librarian), Public Library, Peterborough.
JENKINSON, Francis J. H. (Librarian), University Library, Cambridge (*Vice-President*).
JENKS, Henry A., Canton, Mass., U.S.A.
JENKS, Rev. Henry F. (Trustee), Canton Public Library, Canton, Mass., U.S.A.
JERVOIS, Edith Y. (Librarian), The Goldsmiths' Institute, New Cross, S.E.
JOHNSON, Alderman Benjamin S. (Chairman, Bootle Public Library Committee), 3 Merton Road, Bootle.
JOHNSON, Alderman G. J. (Birmingham Public Library Committee), 36 Waterloo Street, Birmingham (*Vice-President*).
JOHNSON, James (Commissioner, Clerkenwell Public Library), 50 Baker Street, Lloyd Square, W.C.
JOHNSON, Octavius (Assistant Librarian), University Library, Cambridge.
JOHNSTON, H. E. (Librarian, Gateshead Public Library), Swinburne Street, Gateshead.
JOHNSTON, Thomas (Librarian), Public Libraries, Croydon.
JONES, Evan Penllyn (Librarian), University College of Wales, Aberystwyth, South Wales.
JONES, Francis Henry (Librarian), Dr. Williams' Library, Gordon Square, W.C.
JONES, Gardner M. (Recorder of American Library Association) (Librarian), Public Library, Salem, Mass., U.S.A. (*Vice-President*).
JONES, Mrs. Gardner M., Salem, Mass., U.S.A.
JONES, Herbert L. (Librarian), Public Library, High Street, Kensington, W. (*Chairman, Exhibition Committee*).

JONES, Mary L. (Librarian), University of Nebraska, Lincoln, Neb., U.S.A.
JONES, William (Librarian), Public Library, Cheltenham.
JOSEPH, Gerard A. (Librarian and Secretary), The Museum, Colombo, Ceylon (*Vice-President*).

KAPPEL, A. W. (Librarian), Linnæan Society, Burlington House, W.
KEATING, Geraldine (late Librarian), Rockville, Conn., U.S.A.
KENNING, J. W. (Librarian), Public Library, Rugby.
KETTLE, Bernard (Sub-Librarian), Guildhall Library, E.C.
KINNAIRD, The Right Honourable Lord (Commissioner, St. Martin and St. Paul's Public Library), 115 St. Martin's Lane, W.C.
KIRKBY, C. Vernon (Librarian), Public Library, Leicester.
KIRKBY, Mrs. C. V., 5 Prebend Street, Leicester.
KISTNER, Otto (Representative of F. A. Brockhaus, Leipzig), Schleussigerweg 1A, Leipzig.
KNAPMAN, J. W. (Librarian of the Pharmaceutical Society), 17 Bloomsbury Square, W.C. (*Hon. Secretary, Finance Committee*).
KNIGHT, Henry (Deputy Librarian), The Public Hall, George Street, Croydon.
KNIGHT, T. L. (Chairman), Public Library, East Ham, E.
KNILL, Alderman Sir Stuart, Bart., The Crosslets, The Grove, Blackheath, S.E. (*Vice-President*).
KYD, Mrs., Aberdeen.
KYD, Thomas (Public Library Committee), 74 Queen's Road, Aberdeen.

LA FONTAINE, H. (Director, International Institute of Bibliography, Brussels), Institut International de Bibliographie, Rue de Musée, Brussels (*Vice-President*).
LAING, David (Commissioner, St. Martin and St. Paul's Public Library), 115 St. Martin's Lane, W.C.
LAMBERT, Arthur W., 11 Sunny Bank, South Norwood, S.E.
LANCASTER, Alfred (Librarian), Central Library, The Gamble Institute, St. Helens.
LANCASTER PUBLIC LIBRARY.
LANE, Mrs. C. M., Boston, Mass., U.S.A.
LANE, Lucius P., Boston, Mass., U.S.A.
LANE, W. Coolidge (Librarian), Athenæum, Boston, Mass., U.S.A. (*Vice-President*).
LANGE, F. W. (Librarian of General and Technical Libraries), St. Bride's Foundation Institute, Bride Lane, E.C.
LANGTON, H. H. (Librarian), University of Toronto, Toronto, Canada (*Vice-President*).
LATTER, Charles (Chelsea Public Libraries Committee), Kensal House, Harrow Road, N.W. (*Vice-President*).
LAUDER, James (Secretary), Glasgow Athenæum, St. George's Place, Glasgow.
LAURENCE, H. Walton (Publisher), 16 Henrietta Street, Covent Garden, W.C.
LAW, T G. (Librarian), Signet Library, Edinburgh (*Vice-President*).
LAWRENCE, Hon. P. M. (Judge President, High Court of Griqualand; President, Public Library, Kimberley), Kimberley, South Africa (*Vice-President*).
LAWTON, William F. (Librarian), Public Library, Hull.
LE CRONE, Anna L. (Librarian), Public Library, Champaign, Ill., U.S.A.
LEE, Edward (Chairman of the Guildhall Library Committee), The Library, Guildhall, E.C. (*Vice-President*).
LEE, Sidney, 108 Lexham Gardens, W. (*Vice-President*).
LEE, Venie J., University of Nashville, Peabody Normal College, Nashville, Tenn., U.S.A.
LECKY, W. E. H., M.P., 38 Onslow Gardens, S.W. (*Vice-President*).
LEIBBRANDT, H. C. V. (Librarian of the Library of Parliament, Cape Town), Houses of Parliament, Cape Town, Cape Colony (*Vice-President*).
LEIGH, Charles W E. (Assistant Secretary and Librarian of the Manchester Literary and Philosophical Society), 36 George Street, Manchester.
LEIGH, George H., Moorfield, Swinton, Manchester
LELACHEUR, J. I. (Managing Director, Guille-Allès Library), St. Martin, Guernsey.
LEMCKE, E., U.S.A.
LEMCKE, Mrs. E., U.S.A.
LETTS, Charles (Solicitor), 8 Bartlett's Buildings, E.C.
LEVINSOHN, Henry Raphael (Librarian of the Working Men's College, Great Ormond Street), 16 St. Helen's Place, E.C.
LEWIS, F. S. (Librarian), South African Public Library, Cape Town, Cape Colony (*Vice-President*).
LEWTAS, Miss K. (Librarian), Public Library, Blackpool.
LEWTAS, Miss N., 28 Albert Road, Blackpool.

LIBRARY ASSOCIATION, 20 Hanover Sq., W.C.
LINDSAY, William A., Q.C. (Windsor Herald, Deputy Lieutenant, County Devon), Middle Temple, E.C.
LORD, Mrs. (Librarian), Public Library, Kimberley, South Africa.
LOTON, John J. (Librarian), Public Library, Rathmines, Dublin.
LOVE, E. F. J. (Honorary **Librarian**), Royal Society, Melbourne, **Victoria** (*Vice-President*).
LÖWY, Rev. Dr. A., **15 Acol Road, West** End Lane, N.W.
LUBBOCK, The Right Hon. **Sir John**, Bart., M.P., St. James's Square, **S.W.** (*President of the Conference*).
LUCAS, Rev. J. E. (Chairman, Blackpool Public Library Committee), Public Library, Blackpool.
LUNDSTEDT, Dr. **B.** (delegated by the Swedish Government), Royal Library, Stockholm.
LUZAC, C. G. (Publisher), 46 Great Russell Street, W.C.
LYSTER, T. W. (Librarian), National Library of Ireland, Kildare Street, Dublin (*Vice-President*).

MACALISTER, **Donald, 65 Margravine** Gardens, W.
MACALISTER, George **Ian, 65 Margravine** Gardens, W.
MACALISTER, J. Y. W. (Honorary Secretary of the Library Association and Librarian of the Royal Medical and Chirurgical Society), 20 Hanover Square, W. (*Hon. Secretary-General of Conference*).
MACALISTER, Mrs., 20 Hanover Square, W.
MCCALL, P. J., Dublin.
MCCRORY, Harriette L. (Librarian), State Normal School, Millersville, Pa., U.S.A.
MACDONALD, John M., **3** Lombard Street, E.C.
MACFARLANE, **John, British Museum,** W.C.
MACK, Councillor J. J (Deputy-Chairman, Bootle Public Library Committee), Norfolk House, Breeze Hill, Bootle.
MACLAUCHLAN, John (Librarian), **Albert** Institute, Dundee.
MACLAUCHLAN, Mrs., Albert Institute, Dundee.
MCLEAN, J. Hardie (Representative of Messrs. W. Lucy & Co. Limited), Eagle Ironworks, Oxford.
MACMILLAN, Frederick (Publisher), 29 Bedford Street, Covent Garden, W.C. (*Vice-President*).

MCNICHOLL, Bailie James (Member of the Sandeman Public Library Committee), 22 Kinnoull Street, Perth.
MADELEY, Charles (Librarian **and Curator**), The Museum, Warrington.
MANDLEY, Alderman J. G. de T. (Chairman of the Salford Museum, Libraries, and Parks Committee), Salford.
MANN, Mrs. Frances M. (Librarian), Public Library, Dedham, Mass., U.S.A.
MARSHALL, Edward H. (Librarian, Hastings Corporation Reference Library), The Brassey Institute, Hastings.
MARTIN, Samuel (Librarian), **Public** Library, Hammersmith.
MARTIN, Mrs. Samuel, Public Library, **Hammersmith.**
MASON, **Thomas** (Librarian, St. Martin and St. Paul's Public Library), 115 St. Martin's Lane, W.C. (*Hon. Secretary, Exhibition Committee*).
MATHEWS, E. R. Norris **(Librarian)**, Public Library, Bristol.
MATHEWS, H. J. (Chairman, Brighton Public Library Sub-Committee), 45 Upper Rock Gardens, Brighton.
MATHIESON, F. C., Beechworth, Hampstead Heath, N.W.
MATTHEWS, James **(Librarian)**, Public Library, Dock **Street**, Newport-on-Usk.
MAY, W. (Librarian), Central **Library**, Hamilton Street, Birkenhead.
MAYHEW, A. H. (Library Agent), **8** Shakespeare Road, Herne Hill, S.E.
MEISSNER, Dr. A. L. (Librarian, and Professor of Modern Languages), Queen's College, Belfast.
MERCHANT TAYLORS, The Worshipful Company of, 30 Threadneedle Street, E.C.
MIDLAND RAILWAY INSTITUTE (represented by E. A. Baker), Derby.
MILKAU, Dr. Fritz (Delegate of the German Government), Universitäts-Bibliothek, Dorotheen-Strasse 9, Berlin.
MILL, H. R. (Librarian of the Royal Geographical Society), 1 Savile Row, W.
MILLER, **Arthur W. K.** (Assistant Keeper of Printed **Books**), British Museum, W.C.
MILLWARD, Arthur (Chairman of the Clerkenwell Vestry), 12 Albemarle Street, Clerkenwell, E.C.
MILMAN, Rev. W. H. (Librarian), Sion College, Victoria Embankment, E.C. (*Vice-President*).
MILNER, Alfred (Librarian), Subscription Library, Royal Institution, Hull.

LIST OF MEMBERS

MILSTRA, Joseph, White Lodge, Streatham Common, S.W.
MINTO, John (Librarian), Sandeman Public Library, Perth.
MOCATTA, F. D. (Chairman of Paddington Public Library), 9 Connaught Place, W.
MONFORT, E. M., Mariette, Ohio, U.S.A.
MOON, Z. (Librarian), Public Library, Leyton, E.
MOORE, W. (Librarian), Bromley House Library, Nottingham.
MOORE, Mrs.
MORGAN, Junius S. (Associate Librarian), Princeton University Library, Princeton, N.J., U.S.A.
MORGAN, Thomas (Chairman, Southampton Public Library), Public Library, Southampton.
MORRISON, Hew (Librarian), Public Library, Edinburgh (*Vice-President*).
MOULD, Richard W. (Librarian and Secretary), Public Library, Newington, S.E.
MULLEN, Benjamin H. (Curator and Librarian), Royal Museum and Library, Salford.
MULLINS, J. D. (Librarian), Public Library, Birmingham (*Vice-President*).
MURRAY, John (Publisher), 50 Albemarle Street, W. (*Vice-President*).

NAAKÉ, John T., British Museum, W.C.
NEWMAN, Thomas (Librarian), Atkinson Public Library, Southport.
NEWTON, Henry William (Chairman, Newcastle Public Library Committee), Newcastle-upon-Tyne.
NICHOLSON, E. W. B. (Bodley's Librarian), Bodleian Library, Oxford (*Vice-President*).
NOLAN, Dr. Edward J., Academy of Natural Sciences of Philadelphia, Pa., U.S.A.
NOYES, J. A. (Library, Harvard College), Cambridge, Mass., U.S.A.
NUGENT, Lieut.-Colonel J., Royal St. George Yacht Club, Kingstown, Ireland.

O'DONOVAN, Denis (Librarian), Houses of Parliament, Brisbane, Queensland (*Vice-President*).
OGLE, J. J. (Librarian), Public Library, Bootle.
OMONT, Monsieur H. (Conservateur-Adjoint; delegated by the French Government), Bibliothèque Nationale, Paris.
OTLET, Paul (Secretary-General of the International Institute of Bibliography, Brussels), International Institute of Bibliography, Brussels (*Vice-President*).

OWEN, Henry, 44 Oxford Terrace, Hyde Park, W.

PACY, Frank (Librarian), St. George, Hanover Square, Public Library, 160 Buckingham Palace Road, S.W.
PALMER, G. H. (Assistant Librarian), National Art Gallery, South Kensington Museum, S.W.
PATERSON, W. J. S. (Librarian), Stirling's and Glasgow Public Library, 48 Miller Street, Glasgow.
PEARSON, Howard S., Amberley, Bristol Road, Birmingham.
PEDDIE, Robert Alexander, Library of the Literary and Philosophical Society, Newcastle-upon-Tyne.
PENNOCK, John (Mayor of Birkenhead), Roslyn, Clifton Road, Birkenhead.
PENTLAND, Young J. (Publisher), 38 West Smithfield, E.C.
PERIRA, G. N. Monti, Bibliotheca Nacional, Lisbon (*Vice-President*).
PETHERBRIDGE, Miss, Secretarial Bureau, 9 Strand, W.C.
PETHERICK, Edward, 3 York Gate, Regent's Park, N.W.
PHILLIPS, George Bayne (Librarian), Carnegie Public Library, Ayr.
PHILLIPS, Joseph, 62 Grand Parade, Brighton.
PHILLIPS, Miss M. E. (Librarian), Public Library, Oneonta, N.Y., U.S.A.
PICKLE, R. J., 8 Park View, Wigan.
PICKLES, Councillor Robert, 600 Garnett Terrace, Platt Bridge, near Wigan.
PIERCE, Kate E. (Librarian), Public Library, Kettering.
PINK, John (Librarian), Public Library, Cambridge.
PLANT, William C. (Librarian and Clerk), Public Libraries, Shoreditch.
PLEYTE, C. M. (Director of E. J. Brill's Oriental and Ethnographical Department, Leyden), Leyden.
PLUMMER, Henry (Deputy Chairman, Manchester Public Library Committee), 38 Fountain Street, Manchester.
POLLARD, A. W. (Hon. Sec. of Bibliographical Society), 13 Cheniston Gardens, W.
POPPLEWELL, Alderman John (Chairman, Bradford Public Library), 3 Cowper Place, Bradford.
POTTER, George, 10 Priestwood Mansions, Archway Road, N.
PREECE, George (Librarian and Clerk), Public Library, Stoke Newington, N.
PRESSNELL, George (Librarian), Public Library, Tonbridge.

PROCTER, Foster W. (Commissioner of Chelsea Public Libraries), 25 Elm Park Gardens, S.W.

PROCTOR, Anne J. (Librarian), Public Library, Widnes.

PUSEY, W. H. (Librarian), The Public Hall, George Street, Croydon.

PUTNAM, Herbert (Librarian, Boston Public Library, Mass.; delegated by the United States Government), Boston, U.S.A. (*Vice-President*).

QUARITCH, Bernard, 15 Piccadilly, W.

QUINN, E. (Assistant Librarian), Tate Library, Brixton, S.W.

QUINN, J. Henry (Librarian), Public Libraries, Chelsea, S.W.

QUINTON, John (Librarian), Norfolk and Norwich Library, Norwich.

RADFORD, John T. (Librarian), Mechanics' Institution, Nottingham.

RADFORD, Mrs. John T., 3 Colville Villas, Nottingham.

RAILTON, A. B., 31 Cornford Grove, Bedford Hill, Balham, S.W.

RAILTON, Mrs. A. B., 31 Cornford Grove, Bedford Hill, Balham, S.W.

RAWSON, Alderman Harry (President of the Library Association), Ellesmere Park, Eccles, Manchester (*Vice-President, and Chairman of Organising Committee*).

RAWSON, Mrs., Ellesmere Park, Eccles, Manchester.

REDWAY, George (Publisher), 9 Hart Street, W.C.

REEVES, The Hon. W. P. (delegated by the Government of New Zealand), Westminster Chambers, 13 Victoria Street, S.W.

RHODES, W. E. (Librarian), The Owens College, Manchester.

RICHARDSON, Ernest C. (Librarian), Princeton University Library, Princeton, N.J., U.S.A.

RICHARDSON, Hon. G. F., Public Library, Lowell, Mass., U.S.A.

RICHARDSON, Henry (Librarian), Literary and Philosophical Society, Newcastle-upon-Tyne.

RICKWARD, George (Librarian), Borough Library, Colchester.

RIDDING, C. Mary, 6 Southwold Road, Clapton, N.E.

RIDDLE, Charles (Librarian), Public Library, Bournemouth.

RIVINGTON, Charles R., 74 Elm Park Gardens, S.W.

ROBERTS, H. D. (Librarian, St. Saviour Public Library), 44A Southwark Bridge Road, S.E.

ROBERTSON, A. W. (Librarian), Aberdeen Public Library, Aberdeen, N.B.

ROBERTSON, J. P. (Librarian), Manitoba Legislative Library, Winnipeg.

ROBERTSON, T. S. (Member of the Dundee Public Library Committee), Public Library, Dundee.

ROBINSON, A. B. (Assistant Librarian, Tate Library), Tate Library, Brixton, S.W.

ROBINSON, Christopher, Q.C., Toronto.

ROBSON, William (Commissioner, Clerkenwell Public Library), 40 Myddelton Square, W.C.

ROLLIT, Sir Albert K., M.P., 45 Belgrave Square, S.W. (*Vice-President*).

ROSE, Rev. John H. (President of Sion College; Chairman of Clerkenwell Public Library Commissioners), 16 Claremont Square, N.

ROTHSCHILD, Alfred de, New Court, St. Swithin's Lane, E.C.

ROWE, Thos. W. (Librarian), Public Library, Wellington, N.Z.

RUSSELL of Killowen, Rt. Hon. Lord (Lord Chief Justice of England), 86 Harley Street, W. (*Vice-President*).

RUSSELL, His Honour Judge, Q.C. (Master of Gray's Inn Library), The Library, Gray's Inn, W.C. (*Vice-President*).

RUSSELL, John W. Parberry, 9 Belvoir Street, Leicester.

RUTLAND, Her Grace the Duchess of, Belvoir Castle, Grantham (*Vice-President*).

RYDER, John W. W. (Chairman, Devonport Public Library Committee), 3 Doughty Street, W.C.

RYLANDS, Mrs. John (Founder of the John Rylands Library), Longford Hall, Stretford, Manchester (*Vice-President*).

SARGEANT, Arthur, 42 Long Acre, W.C.

SCARSE, C. E. (Librarian), Birmingham Library, Union Street, Birmingham.

SCHEIB, Frederick G. (Clerkenwell Public Library Committee), 36 Claremont Square, Pentonville, N.

SCOTT-SCOTT, William (Chairman, Camberwell Public Library Committee), 55 St. Mary's Road, S.E.

SEABROOKE, R. Elliott, Public Library, East Ham, E.

SEYMOUR, James (Librarian), Kilburn Public Library, Salisbury Road, N.W.

SHACKELL, E. W. (Chairman, Cardiff Public Libraries Committee), Merlinville, 191 Newport Road, Cardiff.

SHARP, Katherine L. (Librarian), **Armour Institute**, Chicago, Ill., U.S.A.

SHAW, A. Capel (Sub-Librarian), **Public Library**, Birmingham.

SHAW, George T. (Master and **Librarian**), The Athenæum, Liverpool.

SHAW, Sybil, Woburn, Mass., U.S.A.

SHAYLOR, James (representing Messrs. Simpkin, Marshall, Hamilton, Kent, & Co.), **4 Stationers' Hall Court, E.C.**

SHELDON, Helen G., Drexel Institute, Philadelphia, Pa., U.S.A.

SHEPLEY, George F., Q.C., Toronto.

SHILLINGTON, E. (Librarian), **Public Library**, Auckland, N.Z.

SHRIMPTON, R. A. (Librarian), **King's Inns Library**, Dublin.

SHUM, Frederick **(Chairman of the Royal Library Committee), Royal Library, Bath.**

SHUTTLEWORTH, Herbert A. (Librarian), Public Library, Lower Road, Rotherhithe, S.E.

SIMPSON, W. (Librarian), Baillie's Institution Free Reference Library, Glasgow.

SINCLAIR, S., Australian Museum, Sydney, N.S.W.

SMIETON, J. G., Queen's Square **House**, Guildford Street, W.C.

SMITH, Alphæus (Honorary Librarian, Quekett Microscopical Club), 14 Leigham Vale, Streatham, S.W.

SMITH, George (Librarian), Linen **Hall Library**, Belfast.

SMITH, Miss, Linen Hall Library, **Belfast**.

SMITH, George M., 15 Waterloo **Place**, S.W.

SMITH, John (Librarian), Leyland **Public Library**, Hindley.

SMITH, Samuel (City **Librarian, Sheffield**), Central Public Library, **Sheffield**.

SMITH, Dr. Walter G. **(Ex-President of the Royal College of** Physicians, Ireland), **25 Merrion Square**, Dublin.

SOULE, **Charles C.** (Trustee of Brookline Public Library), Public Library, Brookline, Mass., U.S.A.

SOUTHERN, Alderman J. W. (Chairman of the Manchester Public Library Committee), Burnage Lodge, Levenshulme, **Manchester** (*Vice-President*).

SOUTHERN, E. May, Burnage **Lodge**, Levenshulme, Manchester.

SOUTHWORTH, Myra F. (Librarian), Public Library, Brockton, Mass., U.S.A.

SOWERBUTTS, Eli (Secretary, Manchester Geographical Society), 16 St. Mary's Parsonage, Manchester.

SPARKE, Archibald (Librarian), **Public Library**, Kidderminster.

SPECK, Celeste, Public Library, St. Louis, Mo., U.S.A.

SPERRY, Ethel M., Waterbury, **Conn.**, U.S.A.

SPERRY, Helen (Librarian), Carnegie Free Library, Braddock, Pa., U.S.A.

STECHERT, Gustav E., **2 Star Yard**, Carey Street, W.C.

STEENBERG, And. S., **Horsens**, Denmark (*Vice-President*).

STEINER, Dr. Bernard C. **(Librarian), Enoch Pratt Public** Library, Baltimore, U.S.A.

STEPHEN, **Leslie (President of the London Library), 22 Hyde Park Gate**, S.W. (*Vice-President*).

STEVENS, B. F. (Editor of *European Archives relating to America*), 4 Trafalgar Square, W.C. (*Vice-President*).

STEVENS, Henry N., **39** Great Russell Street, W.C.

STEVENSON, W. M. (Librarian), Carnegie Library, Alleghany, Pa., U.S.A.

STRATHCONA AND MOUNT ROYAL, Rt. Hon. Lord, G.C.M.G. (High Commissioner for Canada), 53 Cadogan Square, W.S. (*Vice-President*).

SUTTON, Charles W. (Librarian), Public Library, King **Street**, Manchester (*Vice-President*).

TAIT, Dr. **Lawson, 195** Newhall Street, Birmingham.

TAMAYO Y BAUS, M., Biblioteca Nacional, Madrid (*Vice-President*).

TATE, Henry (Chairman of **the Tate** Public Library, Streatham), **Park Hill**, Streatham Common, S.W.

TAWNEY, C. H. (Librarian, **India Office** Library; delegated by the India **Office**), India Office, Whitehall, S.W.

TAYLOR, L. Acland (Librarian), **The Museum** and Reference Library, **Queen's Road**, Bristol.

TAYLOR, W. A. (Librarian, St. Giles' **Public Library), 198** High Holborn, W.C.

TEDDER, Henry R. (Hon. Treasurer of the Library Association; Secretary and Librarian, Athenæum Club), Athenæum, Pall Mall, S.W. (*Hon. Treasurer of Conference, Vice-President, and Chairman of Finance Committee*).

TEMPANY, T. W. (Chairman, Richmond Public Library), 25 Bedford Row, W.C.

THOMAS, J. J. (Librarian), Law Library, Assize Courts, Small Street, Bristol.

THOMAS, W P. (Secretary to the Park and Dare Workmen's Library Institute), Treorchy R.S.O., Glamorgan.

THOMPSON, Sir Edward Maunde, K.C.B., Principal Librarian, British Museum (*Vice-President*).
THOMPSON, Leonard (Trustee of Woburn Corporation Library, Mass.), 60 Warren Street, Woburn, Mass., U.S.A.
THOMPSON, S. E. (Librarian), Public Library, Swansea.
THONGER, Charles W. (Librarian), Leeds Library, Commercial Street, Leeds.
THORBURN, John (Librarian), Geological Survey of Canada, Ottawa, Canada.
THORNSBY, Frederick (Librarian), **Public** Library, Abingdon, Berks.
THURSTON, Elizabeth P. **(Librarian), Newton** Free Library, **Newton, Mass., U.S.A.**
TIMMINS, Samuel (Birmingham **Public** Library Committee), Hill Cottage, Arley, Coventry (*Vice-President*).
TOOTHILL, Councillor J. S. (Deputy Chairman of the Bradford Public Library), Hazelhurst Road, Bradford.
TREDWAY, Mary, St. Louis, Mo., U.S.A.
TUKE, W. M. (Librarian), Public Library, Saffron Walden.
TURNER, Frederick (Librarian), **Public** Library, Brentford.
TWENEY, C. F. St. Helier (Librarian and Clerk), Putney Public Library, Putney, S.W.

UNWIN, T. Fisher (Publisher), 11 Paternoster Buildings, E.C.
UTLEY, H. M. (Librarian), Public Library, Detroit, Mich., U.S.A. (*Vice-President*).

VAN NAME, Addison (Librarian), Yale University, New Haven, Conn., U.S.A.
VAN VLIET, Jessie, Armour Institute, Chicago, Ill., U.S.A.
VAN ZANDT, M., University of Columbia, U.S.A.
VERNEY, Sir Edmund H., Bart., Claydon House, Winslow, Bucks.
VINCENT, Charles W. (Librarian), Reform Club, Pall Mall, S.W.
VOLPRIGNANO, Prof. P. T., 17 Archel Road, W.

WADE, D. H. (Librarian), Heginbottom Public Library, Ashton-under-Lyne.
WADLEY, William (Senior Sub-Librarian, Kensington Public Libraries), 108 Ladbroke Grove, W.
WALKER, Harriet A., Wellesley College, Wellesley, Mass., U.S.A.
WALKER, Herbert (Librarian), **Public** Library, **Longton**, Staffs.

WALLER, F. W., The Guildhall, Gloucester.
WALPOLE, Sir Horace, K.C.B. (Assistant Under-Secretary of State for India; delegated by the India Office), India Office, Whitehall, S.W.
WALSH, Francis (Librarian), Library of Parliament, Sydney, New South Wales (*Vice-President*).
WARD, Edward J. Keightly, 16 Honor Oak Park, London, S.E.
WARD, Mrs. Mary Keightly (Member of **Board of** Guardians), Shandon, Merton Road, Southsea.
WARD, James (Librarian), Public Library, Leigh, Lancs.
WARD, Mrs. **James**, Avenue **Terrace,** Leigh, Lancs.
WARD, Alderman William (Chairman, Portsmouth Public Library Committee), Shandon, Merton Road, Southsea.
WATERHOUSE, Frederick Herschel (Librarian to the Zoological Society), 27 Ringford Road, Wandsworth, S.W.
WATSON, D. McB. (Member of the Hawick Public Library Committee), Hillside Cottage, Hawick.
WATSON, Col. G., Jersey City, N.Y., U.S.A.
WATTEVILLE, Baron de (late Directeur des Sciences et Lettres, Ministère de l'Instruction Publique), 63 Boulevard Malesherbes, Paris (*Vice-President*).
WAY, Right Hon. S. J. (Chief Justice of South Australia, Delegate of the Adelaide Public Library), (*Vice-President*).
WEALE, W. H. James (Keeper of **the** National Art Library), National **Art** Library, South Kensington, S.W.
WEBSTER, H. A. (Librarian), University Library, Edinburgh.
WEBSTER, J. A., Anthropological Institute, 3 Hanover Square, W.C.
WELCH, Charles (Librarian), Corporation Library, Guildhall, E.C. (*Vice-President, and Chairman, Reception Committee*).
WELCH, Councillor (Chairman of the Eastbourne Technical Instruction Committee), Eversholt, Eastbourne.
WELCH, J. Reed (Librarian and Secretary), Public Library, Clapham, S.W.
WELLBY, Philip S. (Publisher), **9 Hart** Street, W.C.
WESLEY, W. **H.** (Librarian), Royal Astronomical Society, Burlington House, W.
WHEELER, Anne, Albany, N.Y., U.S.A.
WHEELER, Martha T., New York **State** Library, Albany, N.Y., U.S.A.

WHITNEY, James Lyman, Boston Public Library, Boston, Mass., U.S.A.
WHITNEY, Margaret Dwight, Pratt Institute Library School, Brooklyn, New York, U.S.A.
WICKSTEED, Rev. Philip Henry (Chairman of Book Committee), Dr. Williams' Library, Gordon Square, W.C.
WILDMAN, Gertrude, Newton, Mass., U.S.A.
WILDMAN, Linda, Boston Athenæum, Boston, Mass., U.S.A.
WILKINSON, James (Librarian), Public Library, Cork.
WILKINSON, Thomas Read, Vale Bank, Knutsford, Cheshire.
WILLIAMS, John (Head of Artistic Crafts Department, Northampton Institute), Northampton Institute, Clerkenwell, E.C.
WILLIAMSON, George Charles, The Mount, Guildford.
WILMANS, Professor August, Königl. Bibliothek, Berlin (*Vice-President*).
WILSON, Wright (Honorary Librarian of the Archæological Section of the Birmingham and Midland Institute), 85 Edmund Street, Birmingham.
WILSON, W. R. (Superintendent of the Reading Room), British Museum, W.C.
WINDSOR, The Right Hon. Lord, Cardiff (*Vice-President*).
WINKS, Rev. W. E. (Cardiff Public Libraries Committee), Public Libraries, Cardiff.
WINSHIP, George Parker, John Carter Brown Library, Providence, R.I., U.S.A.
WINSOR, Justin (Librarian of Harvard College; delegated by the United States Government), Harvard College, Cambridge, Mass., U.S.A. (*Vice-President*).
WOOD, Butler (Librarian), Public Library, Bradford.
WOOLLCOMBE, Dr. Robert Lloyd, 14 Waterloo Road, Dublin.
WRIGHT, Miss C. R.
WRIGHT, Mrs. Henry, 3 Ambrose Place, Worthing.
WRIGHT, W. H. Kearley (Borough Librarian of Plymouth), Public Library, Plymouth (*Vice-President*).
WRIGHT, Mrs. W. H. K., Plymouth.

YARWOOD, Thomas Y. (Librarian), Brunner Public Libraries and Museums, Northwich.
YOUNG, Sir Frederick, K.C.M.G., Royal Colonial Institute, Northumberland Avenue, W.C.
YOUNG, H.

LIST OF (313) LIBRARIES AND (14) GOVERNMENTS REPRESENTED.

AUSTRALIA.
  Adelaide—Public Library
  Brisbane—Parliament Library.
  Melbourne—Public Library.
  „ Royal Society.
  Perth—Victoria Public Library.
  Sydney—Australia Museum.
  „ Library of Parliament.
  „ Public Library.
  „ University Library.
THE GOVERNMENT OF NEW SOUTH WALES.
THE GOVERNMENT OF SOUTH AUSTRALIA.
THE GOVERNMENT OF VICTORIA.

BELGIUM.
  Brussels—Bibliothèque Royale.
  „ Institut International de Bibliographie.

BRITISH COLUMBIA.
  Victoria—Legislative Assembly Library.

BRITISH GUIANA.

CANADA.
  Halifax (N.S.)—Public Library.
  Montreal—McGill University Library.
  Ottawa—House of Parliament Library.
  „ Geological Survey of Canada.
  Toronto—Law Society of Upper Canada.
  „ Public Library.
  „ University Library.
  Winnipeg—Manitoba Legislative Library.
THE CANADIAN GOVERNMENT.

CEYLON.
  Colombo—The Colombo Museum.

DENMARK.
  Copenhagen — Det Store Kongelige Bibliothek.

FRANCE.
  Paris—Université de France.
  „ Bibliothèque Nationale.
THE FRENCH GOVERNMENT.

GERMANY.
  Berlin—Königl. Bibliothek.
  „ Universitäts-Bibliothek.
  Göttingen—Universitäts-Bibliothek.
THE GERMAN GOVERNMENT.

HUNGARY.
THE HUNGARIAN GOVERNMENT.

INDIA.
THE GOVERNMENT OF INDIA.

ITALY.
  Florence—Biblioteca Mediceo-Laurenziana.
  Rome—Biblioteca Nazionale Centrale.
THE ITALIAN GOVERNMENT.

JAPAN.
THE JAPANESE GOVERNMENT.

NEW ZEALAND.
  Auckland—Public Library.
  Wellington—Parliament Library.
  „ Public Library.
THE GOVERNMENT OF NEW ZEALAND.

PORTUGAL.
  Lisbon—Bibliotheca Nacional.

SOUTH AFRICA.
  Cape Town—Library of Parliament.
  „ South Africa Public Library.
  Kimberley—Public Library.

SPAIN.
  Madrid—Biblioteca Nacional.

LIBRARIES AND GOVERNMENTS REPRESENTED

SWEDEN.
   Stockholm—Kongl. Biblioteket.
   THE SWEDISH GOVERNMENT.

SWITZERLAND.
   Geneva—Bibliothèque de la Ville.

UNITED KINGDOM.
   THE BRITISH GOVERNMENT.
   Aberdeen—Public Library.
      ,,   University Library.
   Aberystwyth—University College of Wales.
   Abingdon—Public Library.
   Arbroath—Public Library.
   Ashton-under-Lyne—Heginbottom Public Library.
   Ayr—Carnegie Public Library.
   Barrow-in-Furness—Public Library.
   Bath—Royal Library.
   Belfast—Linen Hall Library.
      ,,   Public Library.
      ,,   Queen's College.
   Birkenhead—Public Library.
   Birmingham—Aston Manor Public Library.
      ,,   Birmingham Library.
      ,,   Birmingham and Midland Institute.
      ,,   Handsworth Public Library.
      ,,   Public Libraries.
   Blackburn—Public Library.
   Blackpool—Public Library.
   Bootle—Public Library.
   Bournemouth—Public Library.
   Bradford—Public Library.
   Brentford—Public Library.
   Brighton—Public Library.
   Bristol—Bristol Medical Society.
      ,,   Law Library.
      ,,   Museum and Reference Library.
      ,,   Public Library.
   Cambridge—Girton College Library.
      ,,   Public Library.
      ,,   University Library.
   Cardiff—Public Library.
   Cheltenham—Public Library.
   Chiswick—Public Library.
   Colchester—Borough Library.
   Cork—Queen's College.
      ,,   Public Library.
   Croydon—Public Library.
   Cymmer—Workmen's Institute.
   Darlington—Edward Pease Library.
   Derby—Midland Railway Institute.
      ,,   Public Library.
   Devonport—Public Library.

UNITED KINGDOM (*contd.*)—
   Dublin—Incorporated Law Society of Ireland.
      ,,   King's Inn Library.
      ,,   National Library of Ireland.
      ,,   Rathmines Public Library.
      ,,   Royal College of Physicians, Ireland.
      ,,   Trinity College.
   Dundee—Albert Institute.
          Public Library.
   East Ham—Public Library.
   Eastbourne—Public Library.
   Edinburgh—Advocates' Library.
      ,,   Philosophical Institute.
      ,,   Public Library.
      ,,   Signet Library.
      ,,   University Library.
   Egham—Royal Holloway College.
   Folkestone—Public Library.
   Gateshead—Public Library.
   Glasgow—Athenæum.
      ,,   Baillie's Institution.
      ,,   Mitchell Public Library.
      ,,   Stirling's and Glasgow Public Library.
   Gosport—Public Library.
   Guernsey—Guille-Allès Library.
   Hastings—Brassey Institute.
   Hawick—Public Library.
   Hindley—Leyland Public Library.
   Inverness—Public Library.
   Kettering—Public Library.
   Kidderminster—Public Library.
   Kingston-on-Hull—Public Library.
      ,,   Subscription Library, Royal Institution.
   Kingston-on-Thames—Public Library.
   Kingston (*Ireland*)—Royal St. Geo. Yacht Club.
   Lancaster—Public Library.
   Leeds—Yorkshire Union of Institutes and Village Libraries.
   Leicester—Permanent Library.
          Public Library.
   Leigh—Public Library.
   Leyton—Public Library.
   Lincoln—Public Library.
   Liverpool—Athenæum.
      ,,   Public Library.
   London—Anthropological Institute.
      ,,   Athenæum Club.
      ,,   Battersea Public Library.
      ,,   Bethnal Green Public Library.
      ,,   Bibliographical Society.
      ,,   Bishopsgate Institute.
      ,,   Braby's Library and Institute.
      ,,   British Museum.
      ,,   Camberwell Public Library.
      ,,   Carlton Club.

UNITED KINGDOM (contd.)—
London—Chelsea Public Library.
" Christchurch Public Library.
" Clapham Public Library.
" Clerkenwell Public Library.
" Corporation Library (Guildhall).
" Day's Library.
" Dr. Williams' Library.
" Fulham Public Library.
" Geological Society.
" Goldsmiths' Institute.
" Gray's Inn.
" Hackney College.
" Hammersmith Public Library.
" Hampstead Public Library.
" Imperial Institute.
" Incorporated Law Society.
" India Office Library.
" Iron and Steel Institute.
" Japan Society.
" Kensington Public Library.
" Lambeth : Tate Library.
" Lewisham Public Library.
" Library Association.
" Library Bureau.
" Linnæan Society.
" London County Council.
" London Institution.
" London Library.
" Marylebone Public Library.
" Newington Public Library.
" Northampton Institute.
" Obstetrical Society.
" Paddington Public Library.
" Patent Office Library.
" Pharmaceutical Society.
" Putney Public Library.
" Quekett Microscopical Club.
" Reform Club.
" Rotherhithe Public Library.
" Royal Agricultural Society.
" Royal Astronomical Society.
" Royal Colonial Institute.
" Royal Medical and Chirurgical Society.
" Royal Geographical Society.
" Royal Society of Literature.
" St. Bride Foundation Institute.
" **St. George (Hanover Square) Public Library.**
" **St. Giles' Public Library.**
" **St. Martin and St. Paul's Public Library.**
" St. Saviour Public Library.
" Shoreditch Public Library.
" Sion College.
" **South Kensington Museum : National Art Gallery.**

UNITED KINGDOM (contd.)—
London—Stoke Newington Public Library.
" Streatham : Tate Library.
" Wandsworth Public Library.
" Whitechapel Public Library.
" Working Men's Club, Great Ormond Street.
" Zoological Society.
Longton—Public Library.
Lowestoft—Public Library.
Manchester—Incorporated Law Library.
" John Rylands Library.
" Lancashire Independent College.
" Literary and Philosophic Society.
" Manchester Geographical Society.
" Moss Side Public Library.
" Owens College.
" Public Library.
" Technical Instruction Committee.
Middlesborough—Public Library.
Millom—Public Library.
Newcastle-on-Tyne—Literary and Philosophic Society.
" Public Library.
Newport-on-Usk—Public Library.
Northwich—Brunner Public Library.
Norwich—Norfolk and Norwich Library.
Nottingham—Bromley House Library.
" Mechanics' Institution.
" Public Library.
Oldham—Public Library.
Oxford—Bodleian Library.
" Radcliffe Library.
Perth—Sandeman Library.
Peterborough—Public Library.
Plymouth—Public Library.
Pontypridd—Public Library.
Portsmouth—Public Library.
Preston—Public Library.
Reading—Public Library.
Richmond (Surrey)—Public Library.
Rugby—Public Library.
St. Andrews—University Library.
St. Helens—Gamble Institute.
Saffron Walden—Public Library.
Salford—Public Library.
" Royal Museum and Library.
Sheffield—Public Library.
Southampton—Public Library.
Southport—Atkinson Public Library.
Stratford-on-Avon—Shakespeare Memorial Library.
Sunderland—Public Library.
Swansea—Public Library.

LIBRARIES AND GOVERNMENTS REPRESENTED

UNITED KINGDOM (contd.)—
   Swindon, New—Great Western Railway Mechanics' Institution.
   Tonbridge—Public Library.
   Treorchy—Workmen's Library **Institute**.
   Warrington—Museum.
   West Ham—Public Library.
   Widnes—Free Library.
   Wigan—Haigh Hall Library.
       "   Public Library.
   Willesden—Public Library.
   Wimbledon—Public Library.
   Windsor—Queen's Library.
   Wolverhampton—Public Library.
   Wood Green—Public Library.
   Worcester—Public Library.
   Wroxhall (I.W.)—Public Library.
   York—Public Library.

UNITED STATES OF AMERICA.
   Albany (N.Y.)—State Library.
   Alleghany (Pa.)—**Carnegie Library.**
   Baltimore (Md.)—**Enoch Pratt Public Library.**
   Bangor (Maine)—Public Library.
   Boston (Mass.)—American Library Association.
       "   Athenæum.
       "   Library Bureau.
       "   Public Library.
   Braddock (**Pa.**)—Carnegie Free Library.
   Bridgeport (Conn.)—Public Library.
   Brockton (Mass.)—Public Library.
   Brookline (Mass.)—Public Library.
   Brooklyn (N.Y.)—Brooklyn **Union for** Christian **Work.**
               Pratt Institute Lib.
       "
   Butte (Montana)—Public Library.
   Cambridge(Mass.)—AssociatedCharities of Cambridge.
       "   Harvard College Library.
   Canton (Mass.)—Public Library.
   Champaign (Ill.)—Public Library.
   Chicago (Ill.)—Armour Institute.
       "   John Crerar Library.

UNITED STATES OF AMERICA (contd.)—
   Chicago (Ill.)—Library Bureau.
   Cleveland (O.)—Public Library.
   Dedham (Mass.)—Public Library.
   Detroit (Mich.)—Public Library.
   East Saginaw (Mich.)—Hoyt Library.
   Hartford (Conn.)—Public Library.
   Ithaca (N.Y.)—Cornell **University Lib.**
   Jersey City (N.J.)—Public Library.
   Lincoln(Neb.)—University of Nebraska.
   Lowell (Mass.)—City Library.
   Mariette (O.)—Public Library.
   Millersville (Pa.)—State Normal School.
   Nashville (Tenn.) — Peabody Normal College.
   Newark (N.J.)—Public Library.
   New Haven (Conn.)—Yale University Library.
   New Orleans (Lo.)—Howard Memorial Library.
   Newton (Mass.)—Free Library.
   New York (N.Y.)—Public Library.
   Northampton (Mass.)—Forbes Library.
   Oneonta (N.Y.)—Public Library.
   Philadelphia (Pa.)—Academy of Natural Sciences.
       "   Athenæum.
       "   Drexel Institute.
   Princeton (N.J.)—University Library.
   Providence (R.I.)—John Carter Brown Library.
       "   Public Library.
   Rockville (Conn.)—Public Library.
   St. Louis (Mo.)—Public Library.
   Salem (Mass.)—Public Library.
   Washington (Col.)—The University of Columbia.
   Wellesley (Mass.)—Wellesley College.
   Wilkes-Barré (Pa.)—Osterhout Free Library.
   Woburn (Mass.)—Corporation Library.
   Worcester (Mass.)—Amer. Antiq. Soc.
       "   Public Library.
   THE UNITED STATES GOVERNMENT.

WEST INDIES.
   Kingston (Jamaica)—Jamaica Institute.

FINANCIAL STATEMENT.

T will be seen from the appended Account of Receipts and Expenditure that there were 587 subscribing members of the Conference. There were also 54 honorary members, chiefly vice-presidents. The total number was 641. Three hundred and thirteen libraries and fourteen Governments were represented. From the guinea subscriptions of members the sum of £616, 7s. was received. As a large number of American and Colonial library delegates, as well as representatives from the chief libraries of the Continent, were expected to attend the Conference, the Organising Committee felt it their duty to arrange for such hospitalities as foreign visitors might well expect to receive in London. Although the ordinary expenses of the Conference would be fully covered by the guinea subscriptions, the sum thus obtained would not have been sufficient for any entertainment, and it was decided to invite donations towards the anticipated expenses. Donations of more than one guinea were considered as including membership of the Conference. The Reception Fund amounted to £388, 4s., which included the subscriptions (£113, 8s.) of 108 contributors.

As regards expenses, the items of reporting, clerical assistance, advertising, printing, and petty cash amounted to £272, 2s. 4d. The conversazione at the Guildhall and other hospitalities cost £115, 1s. 5d., and the dinner at the Hotel Cecil £86, 8s. 2d. The sum expended on the Exhibition of Library Appliances was £20, 7s. 5d., from which should be deducted the donations of exhibitors (£8, 8s.).

The Account shows a balance in hand of £405, 11s. 8d., and the only expense now to be met is the production of the present volume, a copy of which will be sent to every subscribing member of the Conference. While the cost of printing and binding may be roughly estimated at £200, the expense of distribution cannot be estimated; it will be the duty of the Organising Committee to consider the best method of administering the surplus. A certain sum will also be realised by the sale of a limited number of surplus copies of this volume. A final Balance-sheet will be published in the official organs of the Library Association and of the American Library Association.

The subscription books and all vouchers have been carefully examined by the Honorary Auditor of the Conference (Mr. T. J. Agar), who for many years has been Honorary Auditor of the Library Association. His formal certificate is appended.

HENRY R. TEDDER,
Hon. Treasurer of the Conference.

LIST OF DONATIONS TO RECEPTION FUND.

	£	s.	d.		£	s.	d.
Merchant Taylors Company	31	10	0	F. J. H. Jenkinson, Esq.	5	5	0
Mrs. Rylands	26	5	0	J. M. Macdonald, Esq.	5	5	0
Goldsmiths Company	25	0	0	C. R. Rivington, Esq.	5	5	0
The Bibliographical Society	20	0	0	A. de Rothschild, Esq.	5	5	0
H.R.H. the late Duc d'Aumale	5	5	0	George Murray Smith, Esq.	5	5	0
Sir W. H. Bailey	5	5	0	Lord Strathcona	5	5	0
Messrs. Blades, East, & Blades	5	5	0	Edward Almack, Esq.	5	1	0
Mr. Alderman W. H. Brittain	5	5	0	R. C. Christie, Esq.	5	0	0
F. Debenham, Esq.	5	5	0	F. M. Crunden, Esq.	5	0	0

FINANCIAL STATEMENT

Name	£	s.	d.
Dr. Richard Garnett, C.B.	5	0	0
Sir Reginald Hanson, Bart.	5	0	0
Sir Stuart Knill	5	0	0
C. Latter, Esq.	5	0	0
Mr. Alderman Harry Rawson	5	0	0
Lord Windsor	5	0	0
J. Maclauchlan, Esq.	4	4	0
L. Thompson, Esq.	4	0	0
Sir H. W. Acland, Bart., K.C.B.	3	3	0
G. F. Banting, Esq.	3	3	0
W. Blackwood, Esq.	3	3	0
Sir W. Henderson	3	3	0
Mr. Alderman G. J. Johnson	3	3	0
T. W. Lyster, Esq.	3	3	0
J. Y. W. MacAlister, Esq.	3	3	0
F. C. Mathieson, Esq.	3	3	0
John Murray, Esq.	3	3	0
B. F. Stevens, Esq.	3	3	0
Henry R. Tedder, Esq.	3	3	0
Charles Welch, Esq.	3	3	0
E. Allen, Esq.	2	2	0
Basil Anderton, Esq.	2	2	0
W. E. A. Axon, Esq.	2	2	0
J. Ballinger, Esq.	2	2	0
F. T. Barrett, Esq.	2	2	0
J. H. Beeby, Esq.	2	2	0
Sir Walter Besant	2	2	0
E. C. Bigmore, Esq.	2	2	0
F. Boase, Esq.	2	2	0
Sir E. A. Bond, K.C.B.	2	2	0
Councillor J. Boocock	2	2	0
E. W. Brabrook, Esq., C.B.	2	2	0
A. H. Bullen, Esq.	2	2	0
Rev. H. Cart	2	2	0
Rev. Dr. A. Cave	2	2	0
Cedric Chivers, Esq.	2	2	0
A. Cotgreave, Esq.	2	2	0
Dr. C. J. Cullingworth	2	2	0
H. E. Davidson, Esq.	2	2	0
C. Day, Esq.	2	2	0
Edinburgh Free Library	2	2	0
His Excellency Hon. John Hay	2	2	0
James Heywood, Esq., F.R.S.	2	2	0
Rev. Canon J. Clare Hudson	2	2	0
Herbert Jones, Esq.	2	2	0
O. Johnson, Esq.	2	2	0
C. V. Kirkby, Esq.	2	2	0
A. W. Lambert, Esq.	2	2	0
H. W. Lawrence, Esq.	2	2	0
J. J. Le Lacheur, Esq.	2	2	0
G. H. Leigh, Esq.	2	2	0
Charles Letts, Esq.	2	2	0
H. R. Levinsohn, Esq.	2	2	0
W. Lucy, Esq.	2	2	0
Frederick Macmillan, Esq.	2	2	0
E. R. N. Mathews, Esq.	2	2	0
Rev. W. H. Milman	2	2	0
F. D. Mocatta, Esq.	2	2	0
Colonel Nugent	2	2	0
D. O'Donovan, Esq.	2	2	0
B. Quaritch, Esq.	2	2	0
J. Quinton, Esq.	2	2	0
A. B. Railton, Esq.	2	2	0
A. Smith, Esq.	2	2	0
Mr. Alderman J. H. Southern	2	2	0
Leslie Stephen, Esq.	2	2	0
H. N. Stevens, Esq.	2	2	0
H. Tate, Esq.	2	2	0
Sir E. M. Thompson	2	2	0
T. R. Wilkinson, Esq.	2	2	0
F. S. Lewis, Esq.	2	0	0
George Bell, Esq.	1	11	6
J. R. Boosé, Esq.	1	11	6
E. M. Borrajo, Esq.	1	11	6
A Butcher, Esq.	1	11	6
Frank Cundall, Esq.	1	11	6
R. de Coverley, Esq.	1	11	6
G. R. Humphery, Esq.	1	11	6
J. W. Knapman, Esq.	1	11	6
A. Milner, Esq.	1	11	6
W. Robson, Esq.	1	11	6
W. H. K. Wright, Esq.	1	11	6
T. J. Yarwood, Esq.	1	11	6
Sir Frederick Young	1	11	6
D. H. Wade, Esq.	1	11	0
C. H. Gould, Esq.	1	10	0
E. W. Hulme, Esq.	1	10	0
A. W. Robertson, Esq.	1	5	0
L. S. Jast, Esq.	1	3	6
J. Phillips, Esq.	1	3	6
T. W. Newton, Esq.	0	10	6
F. C. Frye, Esq.	0	10	0

SECOND INTERNATIONAL LIBRARY CONFERENCE, 1897.

RECEIPTS.

GENERAL FUND.
Subscriptions of 587 members (including 108 members referred to below) at £1, 1s. £616 7 0

RECEPTION FUND.
Amount of donations £388 4 0
Less—Subscriptions of 108 members at £1, 1s. (included in General Fund) . . . 113 8 0
. . . . 274 16 0

EXHIBITION FUND.
Amount of donations 8 8 0

. . . . £899 11 0

EXPENDITURE.

GENERAL FUND.
Reporting, clerical and general assistance, and typewriting £106 8 6
Advertising 11 15 6
Printing 127 8 0
Petty Cash: Postage, stationery, travelling, messengers, exchange, etc. etc. . 26 10 4
. . . . . . 272 2 4

RECEPTION FUND.
Conversazione and other Hospitalities—
Printing . . . £9 16 0
Music 19 10 8
Refreshments . . 60 13 9
Incidental Expenses: Attendance, labour, postage, etc. . 25 1 0
. . . . £115 1 5

Dinner at Hotel Cecil—
Hotel Bill . . . £127 14 8
Music 14 14 0
Printing 9 0 0
Other Expenses . . 2 2 0
. . . . 153 10 8
Less—Sum received by tickets sold . 67 2 6
. . . . . . 86 8 2
. . . . . . 201 9 7

EXHIBITION FUND.
General Expenses, including Catalogue of Exhibition and Museum of Library Appliances in the Guildhall . 20 7 5

BALANCE IN HAND 405 11 8

. . . . . . £899 11 0

HENRY R. TEDDER, *Hon. Treasurer.*

AUDITOR'S CERTIFICATE.

I have examined, and compared with the items, the Treasurer's books and vouchers, the foregoing Account of Receipts and Expenditure, and find the same correct. I have verified the Balance in hand with the amount standing to the credit in the banking account of the Conference.

T. J. AGAR, *Hon. Auditor.*

INDEX.

ABERDEEN PUBLIC LIBRARY: System of Ventilation, 105.
Acts relating to Public Libraries, see Public Libraries and the Acts.
Adams, J. R. G., on the Registration of Colonial Publications (Paper), 194.
Administration of the Acts, see **Public Libraries Acts**.
Afghan Campaigns, 57, **58.**
Africa:
  Early Printed Books, 7-8.
  Public Libraries in S. Africa, 1.
  Education and Libraries of the Cape of Good Hope, by H. C. V. Leibbrandt (Paper), 179.
Albany (New York) Library School, 34-37, 39, 42.
Alcott, Miss, Works of, **114.**
Aldine Press, 76.
Alexander, Bishop, 14.
Alexandria: Early Libraries, **14, 17.**
Algonkin Indians, 161.
Alleghany, Pennsylvania: **Carnegie** Library, 169.
Allen, E. G., Publisher, 151.
Allibone's "Dictionary of **English** Literature," 60, 61.
"American Boys' Handy-Book," 113.
"American Catalogue" of James Kelly, 151.
"American Catalogue" **of F. Leypoldt,** 151.
"American Catalogue" **of Sampson Low,** 150.
"American Facts," 150.
American Historical Review, 169.
American Journal of Sociology, 50.
American Library Association:
  Organisation, 130.
  Programmes, 132.
  Publishing Section, 153.
  Bibliographies issued by the A.L.A., 152, 170.
The A.L.A. **Library Catalogue, 70-71, 120.**
A.L.A. Index to General Literature, 121, 153.
A.L.A. Card-Catalogue, 128, 152.
Poole's Index to Periodical Literature, 121, 153.
American Library Work **(see also American Library Association** above):
  Copyright in America, 243.
  Government Publications, 3.
  Public Libraries, 1, 27, 72.
  New York State Libraries' Department, 22.
  Travelling Libraries, 22.
  Libraries for Children, see Juvenile Libraries.
  Library Associations, etc., 17.
  Local Library Associations in the United States, by Herbert Putnam (Paper), 129; Discussion, 243.
  Special Training for Library Work, by Miss H. P. James (Paper), 34; Discussion, 231-2.
  Library Schools, 34, 42.
  Summer Schools, 38-39.
  Bibliographical Endeavours in America, by R. R. Bowker (Paper), **150;** Discussion, 246.

American Library Work—*contd.*
  Printed Card-Catalogues, by C. W. Andrews (Paper), 126; Discussion, 242-3.
  The Organisation of Co-operative Work among Public Libraries, by J. N. Larned (Paper), 130.
  George Iles's Bibliographical Work, 130, 152, 166, 170.
  Brooklyn Library Catalogue, 68, 152.
  Peabody Institute Catalogue, 152.
  Cutter's Rules, 69, 95.
  Cutter's Dictionary Catalogue, 67-70.
  The Expansive Classification, by C. A. Cutter (Paper), 84; Discussion, 235-6.
  Dewey Classification, 197, 241.
  Open Access at Boston, 245.
  Philadelphia Library Company, 17.
  Amherst College Summer School, 38.
  Anderson, Henry C. L., on Library Work in New South Wales (Paper), 93; Discussion, 236.
  Andrews, C. W., on Printed Card-Catalogues (Paper), 126; Discussion, 242-3.
  "A.D. 2000," 112.
  "Annual American **Catalogue**" of F. Leypoldt, 151.
Anti-Jacobin, 67.
Antiochus the Great, **14.**
Antonio, Nicolas, 7, 8.
Appliances, see Library Appliances.
Arabic Numbers, Origin of, 163.
Architecture of Public Libraries:
  Public Library Architecture from the Librarian's Standpoint, by F. J. Burgoyne (Paper), 103; Discussion, 236-7, 240-1.
  Public Library Architecture from the Architect's Standpoint, by Beresford Pite (Paper), 106; Discussion, 240-1.
Arcson, Bishop J., 74.
Aristotle, Book-Collector, 13.
Armarium and Armarius, 15.
Armour Institute (Chicago) Library, 127.
Armour Institute **(Chicago) Library** Class, 38, 39.
Armstrong, E. La T., Librarian, 95.
Art:
  The History and Cataloguing of the National Art Library, by W. H. J. Weale (Paper), 97.
  Russell Sturgis's "Catalogue of Works on the Fine Arts," 152, 170.
Ascham, Roger, and Lady Jane Grey, 3.
Assistants, see **under Librarians.**
Assyria:
  Ancient Libraries, 13.
  Use of Numbers, 162.
"At the Sign of the Red Bible," 151.
Athens, Ancient:
  Care of State Documents, 13.
  Libraries, 13-14, 17.
Atkinson, Prof., 53.
Atlantic Monthly, 171.
Auckland Public Library, 199.
  Paper by Edw. Shillington, 201.
Augustine, St., Bishop of Hippo, Book-Collector, **14.**

Augustine's (St.) "**De Arte Praedicandi,**" 74, 76.
Augustinians and Libraries, 15.
Augustus and Public Libraries, 14.
Australasia (see also Australia, New Zealand, Tasmania):
  Bibliography of Australasia, 148.
  "Bibliography of Australasia and Polynesia," 149.
Australia:
  Early Printing, 8.
  The Registration **of Colonial Publications,** by J. R. G. Adams (Paper), 194.
  Public Libraries, 1.
  Library Work in New South Wales, by H. C. L. Anderson (Paper), 93; Discussion, 236.
  Sydney Libraries, 93.
  Sydney Public Library, 8.
  New South Wales Public **Library,** 93-95.
  The Library **of the University of** Sydney, by H. E. Barff (Paper), 197.
  Victoria's Library System, 95.
  Library Facilities of Scientific Investigators in Melbourne, by E. F. J. Love (Paper), 204.
  The Australian Museum Library, by Sutherland Sinclair (Paper), 207.
Austria: Public Libraries, 17.
Author-Catalogues: Pseudonyms, 63, 233.
Authority or Commissioners, see under **Public Libraries Acts.**
Avery Architectural Library, 127.
Avery, Mr., on Newspapers, 230.
Axon, W. E. A., on the Conference, 250.
Aztecs of S. America, 161.

BABYLONIAN USE OF **NUMBERS,** 162.
Bacon-Shakespeare Controversy, 56.
Bailey, Sir William H.,
  On the Choice of Fiction, 229.
  On Children's Libraries at **Manchester,** 237.
  On the Conference, 248.
Baker, Sir Thomas, on Women Assistants, 40, 231.
Barff, H. E., on the Library of the University of Sydney (Paper), 197.
Barnwell Priory Library, 15.
Barrett, F. T., (Glasgow),
  On the Alphabetical and Classified Forms of Catalogues compared (Paper), 67; Discussion, 234.
  On Classification in Libraries, 235.
  On the Reading of Fiction, 229.
  On the "Dictionary of National Biography," 233.
  On American Bibliographical Work, 246.
  On Heating, etc., 237.
  On the Indicator, 246.
Batavia and the Art of Printing, 7.
Bathurst, Lord, and Education at the Cape, 187.
Bayeux Monastic Bookcase, 15.
Baza, Domen., Printer, 76.
Beaconsfield, Lord, quoted, 8.

36

Beck, Rev. H., and Education at the Cape, 189.
Beckenhaub, J., Printer, 74.
Beckford, William, 173.
Belgium: Public Libraries, 17.
Benedictine Libraries, 15, 16.
Bergen Public Library, 138.
"Best Books" of W. S. Sonnenschein, 152.
"Best Reading" of G. H. Putnam, 152.
Betoi of the Orinoco, 162.
Biagi, Prof. Comm. Guido, on the Conference, 247.
"Bibliographer's Manual," by W. T. Lowndes, 60, 61.
"Bibliographia Anatomica," 242.
"Bibliographia Astronomica," 242.
"Bibliographia Medica Italica," 242.
"Bibliographia Philosophica," 242.
"Bibliographia Physiologica," 242.
"Bibliographia Sociologica," 242.
"Bibliographia Zoologica," 242.
"Bibliographical Guide to American Literature," 151.
Bibliographical Society, 17.
"Bibliographie Française" of H. Le Soudier, 150.
Bibliography (see also Cataloguing, Classification):
 The Relations of Bibliography and Cataloguing, by A. W. Pollard (Paper), 63; Discussion, 233-4.
 Theoretical and Practical Bibliography, by E. A. Petherick (Paper), 148; Discussion, 246.
 National Biography and National Bibliography, by Sidney Lee (Paper), 55; Discussion, 232-3.
 Bibliographical Endeavours in America, by R. R. Bowker (Paper), 150; Discussion, 246.
 The International Institute of Bibliography at Brussels, 241.
 Robert Watt's "Bibliotheca Britannica," 60, 61.
 W. T. Lowndes's "Bibliographer's Manual," 60, 61.
 Allibone's "Dictionary of English Literature," 60, 61.
 The British Museum Catalogue, 61, 151.
 G. K. Fortescue's Subject - Catalogues, 57.
 Colonial Publications, see Colonial Literature.
 Children's Books, see Juvenile Libraries.
 Special Subjects, see Art, Music, Science, Shakespeare, Scott (Sir Walter), Raleigh (Sir Walter).
 Bibliography of Periodicals, see under Periodicals.
 Classified Catalogues, see Classification.
"Bibliotheca Americana" of Henry Harrisse, 152.
"Bibliotheca Americana" of O. A. Roorbach, 151.
"Bibliotheca Americana" of Joseph Sabin, 151-2.
"Bibliotheca Americana" of Russell Smith, 151.
"Bibliotheca Britannica," by Robert Watt, 60, 61.
"Bibliotheca Americana Nova" of Obadiah Rich, 151.
Billings, Dr. John S., 113.
Biography: National Biography and National Bibliography, by Sidney Lee (Paper), 55; Discussion, and Vote of Thanks, 232-3.
Birmingham Proprietary Library, 17.
Birmingham Public Library: Shakespeare Books, 55.
Blackpool Public Library: Ventilation, 237.
Blackwood's Magazine quoted, 112.
Blake's (Alexander V.) "Reference Trade List," 150.
Blind, Books for, 101.
Bode, Rev. J. F., Librarian at the Cape, 189.

Bodleian Library, 8, 17.
Bohn, Henry George, and Lowndes's "Manual," 60.
Bonifacius, Joannes, 6.
"Bookbuyer's Manual" of G. P. Putnam, 152.
Bookcases of Mediæval Libraries, 15.
Bookplates: The Ex-Libris Society, 17.
Books (see also Bibliography, Cataloguing, Classification, Typography, Literature, etc.):
 Definition of a Book, 2.
 Titles, 2.
 Educational Value of Books, see Libraries.
Books of Public Libraries (see also Fiction, Periodicals, Music, etc.):
 Selection of Books, 19-22, 28.
 Children's Books, see Juvenile Libraries.
"Books for Boys and Girls," by Miss Hewins, 153.
Bookseller referred to, 28, 148.
Booksellers' Libraries of 18th Century, 17.
Bookworm in Jamaica, 178.
Bosanquet, Bernard, quoted, 159.
Boston Athenæum Catalogue, 152.
Boston Public Library:
 Card-Catalogue, 128.
 Open Access, 215.
 Shakespeare Collection, 55.
 Children's Books, 238-9.
Bourke, Sir Richard, and Libraries at the Cape, 190, 191.
Bowker, R. R.,
 On Bibliographical Endeavours in America (Paper), 150; Discussion, 246.
 On Copyright in the United States and in England, 242.
 On Children's Books, 111.
 On the Conference, 249.
Bowring's (Sir John) "Decimal System," 162, 165.
Brassington, W. Salt, 233.
Breton, Nicholas, 61.
Brett, William H., on Freedom in Public Libraries (Paper), 79; Discussion, 243-6; "Cumulative Index to Periodical Literature," 153.
Breydenbach, B. von, 76.
Brinton, Dr., 162, 164.
Bristol Public Library: Female Library Assistants and Competitive Examination, by E. R. Norris Mathews (Paper), 40; Discussion, 231-2.
British Museum Library:
 Reference Hall, 110.
 Number of Volumes, 2.
 Early Printed Books, 6-8.
 General Catalogue, 61, 151.
 G. K. Fortescue's Subject - Catalogues, 57.
 Shakespeare Books, 55.
Brooklyn Library: S. B. Noyes's Catalogue, 68, 152.
Brooklyn: Pratt Institute Library School, 37, 39.
Brown, H. F., 75.
Bryce's (James) "American Commonwealth," 121.
Buffalo Meeting of the A.L.A., 35.
Burgoyne, Frank J., on Library Architecture from the Librarian's Standpoint (Paper), 103; Discussion, 236-7, 249.
Bury, Richard de, 15, 16.
Byron, Lord, and His Friends, 57.

CÆSAR AND PUBLIC LIBRARIES, 14.
Caine, T. Hall, quoted, 42.
Cakchiquels of Yucatan, 162.
Cambridge: University and College Libraries, 16, 110.
Camoens referred to, 6.
Campbell, Frank,
 Quoted, 2, 195.
 On the Bibliographer and the Librarian, 233.
 On National Libraries, etc., 242.

Canada:
 Public Libraries, 1.
 Important Libraries in Montreal, by C. H. Gould (Paper), 154.
 Legislative Library of Nova Scotia, 146.
Canary Ids.: Early Printing, 8.
Canterbury Monastic Library, 15.
Cape Colony, see under Africa.
Card-Catalogues, see under Cataloguing.
Cardigan, Lord, 57.
Carlyle, Thomas, quoted, 50.
Carthage Libraries, 14.
Carthusians and Libraries, 15.
"Catalogo Collettivo della Libreria Italiana," 150.
"Catalogue of American Books in the British Museum, 1856," 151.
"Catalogue of Books printed in the United States," 150.
Cataloguing (see also Bibliography, Classification):
 The Relations of Bibliography and Cataloguing, by A. W. Pollard (Paper), 63; Discussion, 233-4.
 The Alphabetical and Classified Forms of Catalogues compared, by F. T. Barrett (Paper), 67; Discussion, 234.
 Classification, see Classification.
 Bibliographies and Catalogues of Special Subjects, see Bibliography, Classification, Art, Music, Science, Periodicals, Colonial Literature, Juvenile Libraries, etc.
 The A.L.A. Card-Catalogue, 128, 152.
 The A.L.A. Library Catalogue, 20-1, 120.
 Printed Card-Catalogues, by C. W. Andrews (Paper), 126; Discussion, 242-3.
 The Linotype for the Printing of Catalogues, etc., 153, 242.
 Cutter's Rules, 69, 95.
 Cutter's Dictionary-Catalogue, 67-70.
 A Hint in Cataloguing, by F. Blake Crofton, 146.
 Pseudonyms in Catalogues, 63, 233.
 Brooklyn Library Catalogue, 68, 152.
 Peabody Institute Catalogue, 152.
 Catalogue of the New South Wales Public Library, 94-95.
 An Indicator-Catalogue Charging System, by Jacob Schwartz (Paper), 142; Discussion, 246.
Cathedral Libraries, 14-16.
Catholic Church and Libraries, 14-16.
Cesena Library, 16.
Chained Books, 16, 34.
Challen, Howard, Publisher, 150.
Charge of the Light Brigade, 57.
Charging: An Indicator - Catalogue Charging System, by Jacob Schwartz (Paper), 142; Discussion, 246.
Charles VII. of France and the Early Printers, 73.
Charles VIII. of France and the Early Printers, 73.
Chelsea Public Library: Children's Library, 238.
Chicago Libraries, 38, 127.
Chicago Library Club, 129, 130.
Children's Books, see Juvenile Libraries.
China and the Art of Printing, 5-7.
Chippeway Indians, 161.
Christchurch, N.Z., Public Library, 199, 200.
Christian Literature in Libraries, 14-16.
Christiania Libraries, 137, 138.
Church and Monastic Libraries (see also Vatican):
 Early Libraries, 14-15.
 Benedictine and other Monastic Libraries, 15-16.
Circulating Libraries of 18th Century, 17.
Cirta Library, 15.
Cistercians and Libraries, 15.

Cistercian Monastic Library, 15.
City Poets, 57.
Clairvaux Monastic Library, 15.
Clark's (J. M'Cosh) Gift to Auckland, 201.
Clark's (J. Willis) "Libraries in the Mediæval and Renaissance Periods" referred to, 16.
Classification (see also Bibliography):
  The Alphabetical and Classified Form of Catalogues compared, by F. T. Barrett (Paper), 67; Discussion, 234.
  Classification in Public Libraries, by A. W. Robertson (Paper) 89; Discussion, 235-6.
  The Expansive Classification, by C. A. Cutter (Paper), 84; Discussion, 235-6.
  Dewey Classification, 197, 241.
  Classification in the Bibliographies of the "Dictionary of National Biography," 56.
  Special Subjects and Bibliographies, see Bibliography, Colonial Literature, Juvenile Libraries, Art, Music, Science, Scott (Sir Walter), Raleigh (Sir Walter), Shakespeare.
Clerkenwell Public **Library:** Open Access, 244, 245.
Cluniacs and Libraries, 15.
Colden, Richard, quoted, 30.
Cochrane's "Wonders of Modern Mechanism," 113.
Cockroach, Enemy of Books, **178.**
Cole, Timothy, Engraver, 167.
College and University Libraries, see Universities.
Colonial Libraries, see Africa, Australia, Canada, Jamaica, New Zealand.
"Colonial Libraries" Series, **177.**
Colonial Literature (see also Australasia, etc.):
  The Registration of Colonial Publications, 3.
  The Registration of Colonial Publications, by J. R. G. Adams (Paper), 194.
  The Colonies and Copyright, 246.
  Literature in the Colonies, 247.
Columbia College (New York) Library School, 34-35.
Committee or Authority, see under Public Libraries Acts.
Congressional Library, **Washington,** 153.
Constable & Co., and Watt's "Bibliotheca Britannica," 60.
Constantine the Great, 14, 163.
Constantinople: Early Library, 15.
Cook, Captain, Relics of, 191.
Cooper's (James Fenimore) **Works,** 114.
Co-operation in **Library** Work, 10, 153, 229.
  The Organisation of Co-operative Work among Public Libraries, by J. N. Larned (Paper), **120;** Discussion, 242-3.
  Co-operation in a Catalogue of Periodicals, by H. H. Langton (Paper), 122; Discussion, 242-3.
Cope, Prof. E. D., quoted, 158.
Copenhagen Libraries, 138-140.
Copyright:
  Copyright, Law of 1709, 72.
  Copyright in England and America, 243.
  Copyright in the Colonies, 246.
  Copyright Act in New South Wales, 94.
Cordier, Henri, 7.
Costley (Edward) Bequest to Auckland, 199, 201.
Counting and Time-Recording, by John Thorburn (Paper), 160.
Cowell, Peter,
  On Library Work in Liverpool during Forty Years (Paper), 99; Discussion, 236.
  On Library Architecture, 240.
Cradock, Sir John, and Education at the Cape, 186.

Crawford, Earl of,
  Seconded Vote of Thanks to Sir John Lubbock, 228.
  Chairman, 228, 236.
  On the Early Education of the Child, 238.
  On Ventilation, 237.
  On Open Access, 246.
Cree Indians, 162.
Crerar (John) Library, **Chicago,** 197-8.
Crimean War, 57.
Crofton, F. Blake, **on Cataloguing:** in Eliot, 146.
Crunden, Frederick M.,
  Chairman, 236.
  On Books and Text-Books; the Library as a Factor in Education (Paper), 46; Discussion, 232.
  On the Early Training of Children, 238.
  On the Reading of **Fiction, 228.**
  On Scholarship **among Librarians,** 229.
  On the Cutter Classification, 235.
  On the Thermostat Apparatus, 236.
  On Heating, **237.**
Cruz (Estevão da) "Life of St. Peter," 6.
Cundall, Frank, on Library Work in Jamaica (Paper), 173; Discussion, 247.
Curran, J. P., quoted, 47-48.
Curtis, George William, quoted, 53.
Curzon, F., on the Yorkshire Village Libraries, 236.
Curzon's (Hon. G. N.) "Monasteries of the Levant" quoted, 202.
Cutter, Miss Mary S., 39.
Cutter, C. A., 152.
  On the Expansive Classification (Paper), 84; Discussion, 235-6.
  Cutter's Rules, 69, 95.
  Cutter Dictionary-Catalogue, 67-70.

DACOTAS AND THE USE OF NUMBERS, 160.
Daily News referred to, 29.
Dale, Sir Langham, and **Education at the Cape,** 187.
Damascus, Pope, 15.
Dana, J. C., on Our Youngest Readers (Paper), 118; Discussion, 237-40.
Dancer, Dr., 173.
Darwin, Charles, 46.
Darwin, Dr. Erasmus, 67.
Davis, N. Darnell,
  On the Newspaper Press, 230.
  On the "Dictionary of National Biography," 232.
  On Open Access, 245.
  On Literature in the Colonies, 247.
Dawson, Sir J. W., quoted, 13.
Decimal **Classification of** Melvil Dewey, 197, 241.
"Decimal System," Book, by Sir John Bowring, 160, 165.
Deichman Library, 138.
Denmark:
  Early Printing, 74.
  Public Libraries, 138, 243.
Denver Public Library **Training** Class, 38.
Dessin, Joachim Nicolas von, Book-Collector, 189-190.
Deutsche Rundschau referred to, 47.
Devore, A. E. T., Auckland, 201.
Dewey, Melvil,
  Chairman, 241.
  On the Relation of the State to **the** Public Library (Paper), 19; Discussion, 229-30.
  On Library Training Schools, etc., 231.
  On Children's Reading, 239.
  On the Structure of the Library, 240.
  On the International Institute of Bibliography at Brussels, 241.
  On the Printing of Catalogues, 242.
  On National Libraries, 243.
  On the Conference, 248.
  Library School at Albany, 34-37, 39, 40.
Dewey Classification, 197, 241.

Dickens [?] quoted, 112, 115.
Dickson, Dr., Edinburgh, 169.
  "Dictionary of English Literature," by Allibone, 60, 61.
  "Dictionary of National Biography," by Sidney Lee (Paper), 55; Discussion, and Vote of Thanks, 231-3.
Diderot quoted, 47.
Dietz, Ludwig, Printer, 74.
Dominion and Public Libraries, 14.
Donnelly's "Cryptogram," 56.
Doubleday, W. E.,
  On Open Access, 246.
  On the Classified Catalogue, 67.
Drexel Institute (Philadelphia) Library Class, 37-38, 39.
Duckworth, Thomas, on Open Access, 246.
Dunedin, N.Z., Libraries, 199, 200.
Dürer, Albrecht, 77.
Durban Monastic Library, 15.
Dziatzko, Prof. C., on the Aids lent by Public Bodies to the Art of Printing in the Early Days of Typography (Paper), 72.

EAMES, WILBERFORCE, Librarian, 152.
"Earth, Sea, and **Sky,"** 113.
Ebert, Librarian, 17.
Ecclesiastical Libraries, 14-16.
Edinburgh: Booksellers' Libraries, 17.
Edinburgh Review referred to, 29.
Edison, Thomas A., 168.
Education and Libraries of the Cape of Good Hope, by H. C. V. Leibrandt (Paper), 179.
Educational Aims of Public Libraries.
Edwards, Bryan, Historian, 173.
Edwards, Edward, Librarian, 17.
Eggestein, Heinrich, Printer, 73.
Egypt, Ancient:
  The Art of Printing, 5.
  Early Libraries, 13-14, 17.
  Use of Numbers, 162.
Electric Fan, 237.
Electric Light, **237.**
Eliot, President C. W., quoted, 48, 50.
Eliot, George:
  "Romola" quoted, 22.
  George Eliot in the Catalogue, 63.
Elliot, John, on Lectures on Books, 236.
Elyan, Caspar, Printer, 73.
"English Catalogue of Books," 148.
Enjiro Yamada on the Conference, 248.
Escurial Library, 16.
Eskimo Use of Numbers, 161.
Euphorion of Chalcis, Librarian, 14.
Eve, Miss Ellen H., 152.
Ewart (William) Act of 1850, 1, 17, 27, 72.
Ex Libris Society, 17.
Exhibition of Library Appliances, etc., 255.
Expansive Classification, see under Classification.

FAIRY TALES, 112.
Faudel-Phillips, Sir George:
  His Welcome to the Members of the Conference, 227.
  Votes of Thanks to, 227, 249.
Fiction in Public Libraries, 2, 11, 100, 169, 228, 229, 231.
Field Columbian Museum, 127.
Fielding, Thomas, 61, 207.
Finance in connection with **Public** Libraries:
  The Penny Limit, 29-30, 45.
  Income-Tax: The Manchester Case, 29-30.
Salaries of Librarians, 45.
Financial Statement (International Conference), 229.
Finland Public Libraries, 140.
Fish-Moth in Jamaica, 178.
Fisher, Thomas, Sydney, 197.
Fleay's "Biographical Chronicle of the English Drama," 56.
Fleck, Rev. Christiaan, of the Cape, 189.

INDEX

Fletcher, W. I., 38, 121, 153.
"Flora of Liverpool," 99.
Florence: The Laurentian **Library**, 16, 109.
Foreign Libraries, see France, Italy, Germany, Norway, Sweden, Denmark, Finland.
Fortescue's (G. K.) Subject-Catalogues, 57.
Fountains Monastic **Library**, 15.
France:
  Early Printing, 73.
  French Incunabula, 65.
  Société Franklin of Paris, 171.
  Public Libraries, 17.
  Provincial Libraries **of** 18th Century, 17.
  Library at St. Germain-des-Prés, 16.
  The Library of the Sorbonne, 16.
  The Bibliothèque Mazarine, 16, 17.
  Bibliothèques Communales, 72.
Franklin and the Philadelphia Library Company, 17.
Franklin's Theory of Education, 50.
Fraser Institute, Montreal, 154, 155.
Frederick II. of Denmark and the Early Printers, 74.
Frederick III., Emperor of Germany, and the Early Printers, 73.
Freedom (Open Access) in Libraries, see Open Access.
Froman, F., 76.
Fuller's "Worthies," 56.
Funchal: Early Printing, 7-8.
Fust, J., 74, 76, 77.

GAMA, VASCO DA, 5.
Gammack's (Mr.) Bequest to Christchurch, N.Z., 200.
Garnett, Dr. Richard,
  On the Introduction of European Printing into the East (Paper), 5.
  On the Conference, 228.
  On Bookshelves, 241.
Gas and Electric Light, 237.
Gasquet's (Dom) "The Old English Bible" referred to, 15.
Geikie, Sir Archibald, 168.
Gellius, Aulus, 13.
Germany,
  Early Printing, 72-77.
  Public Libraries, 17.
Giddings, Mackenzie, quoted, 158.
Gilbert, Alderman H. M., on the Selection of Books, 231.
Gillies, Rev. Wm.,
  On the Newspaper Press, 230.
  On Sir John Lubbock and the Conference, 249.
Gladstone, W. E., 46, 59.
Glasgow (Mitchell) Library: Arrangement of Books, 235.
Gliddon, A. M. de Putron, **on** Libraries, 234.
Goa: Early Printing, 6.
Goldsmith's (Oliver) "Animated Nature," 167.
Gosse, Philip **Henry**, 173.
Gothenburg Town Library, 136.
Gould, C. H., **on Important Libraries in** Montreal **(Paper),** 154.
Government Publications, 2.
Governments represented at the Conference, 273.
Graaff, Governor Cornelius Jacob van de, and Education at the Cape, 184.
Grahamstown Library, S. Africa, 192.
Grand's (G. F.) "Memoirs of a Gentleman," 8.
Gray, Asa, 172.
Greece, Ancient:
  Care of State Documents, 13.
  Early Libraries, 13-14, 17.
  The Use of Numbers by the Ancient Greeks, 160, 162.
Green, Mr., Worcester, Mass., 118.
Grenada Library, 177.
Grey, Sir George, 3; "Grey (Sir George) Collection" in the Public Library, Capetown, 192; "Grey (Sir George) Collection" at Auckland, 199, 201, 202.
Grey, Lady Jane, and Roger Ascham, 3.
Gutenberg **Printer, 73.**

HADEN, SEYMOUR, **Etcher**, 167.
Haebler, K., 74.
Hain's "Repertorium," 65.
Hamerton's (P. G.) "Autobiography," 167.
Hare's (Augustus **J. C.**) "**Story of** My Life," 167.
Harris, Dr. Wm. T., quoted, 50.
Harrison, Robert, 45.
Harrisse's (Henry) "Bibliotheca Americana," 152.
Harvard University Library: Card-Catalogue, 128.
Hase, Oscar von, 72, 76, 77.
Haswell, W. A., 207.
Hawthorne's "Wonder Book," etc., 112.
Heating of Libraries, 105, 236-7.
Heinrich, Bishop, 74.
Helsingfors Libraries, 140-141.
Henckis, **Conrad**, 77.
Henry VIII. and the Early Printers, 73.
Henty's (G. A.) Works, 115.
Hereford Cathedral Chained Books, 34.
Hessels, J. H., 73, 74.
Hewins, Miss Caroline M., on Books That Children Like (**Paper**), 111; Discussion, 237-40; "Books for Boys and Girls," 153.
Hill, Richard, 173, 175.
Hippo Library, 14.
Home Libraries for Children in America, 239.
Homery, Dr. Conrad, Printer, 74.
Hopkins's "Experimental Science," 113.
Horace quoted, 184.
Horology Literature, 57.
Horta's (Garcia da) "Dialogues **on** Indian Samples and Drugs," 6.
Howe, Wm., Bushranger of Tasmania, 8.
Hughes's (Judge) "Tom Brown's Schooldays" quoted, 47.
Hutchins, F. A., 170.
Huxley, Prof., 20.

ICELAND: Early Printing, 74.
Ide, Simeon, Publisher, 150.
Iles, George, 120, 152, 170.
  On the Appraisal of Literature (Paper), 160.
Iles (G.) and R. R. Bowker's "Reader's Guide in Economic, Social, and Political Science, 152, 170.
Illinois State Library School, 38.
Imhoff, Governor-General Gustaaf Willem van, and Education at the Cape, 181, 185.
Inaugural Address, by Sir John Lubbock, 1; Discussion, and Vote **of** Thanks, 228.
Income Tax: The **Manchester Case**, 29-30.
Index Society, 17.
Indexing:
  The **Index Society**, 17.
  Indexing on a Co-operative Plan, 120-121.
  Classified **Index of the London** Library, 3.
  The "A.L.A. **Index to General** Literature," 121, 153.
  Poole's "Index to **Periodical Literature**," 121, 153.
  W. H. Brett's "**Cumulative Index** to Periodical **Literature**," 153.
India
  Government Publications, 3.
  The Art of Printing, 5-6.
  The Indian Mutiny, 57.
Indians of America and the Use of Numbers, 160-1.
Indicator-Catalogue Charging System, by Jacob Schwartz (Paper), 142; Discussion, 246.
Insect Enemies of Books, 178.
International Conference:
  Inaugural Address, by Sir John Lubbock, 1; Vote of Thanks, 228.
  Programme, 209-226.
  Proceedings, 227-254.
  Financial Statement, 279.

Irving, Sir Henry, 249, 253.
Isham, Sir Charles, and His Library, 39.
Italy:
  Early Printing, 73-77.
  Ecclesiastical Libraries, 15.
  The Vatican Library, 14.
  Public Libraries, 17.
  The Laurentian Library, **Florence**, 16, 109.
  Cesena Library, 16.

"JACK THE GIANT-KILLER," 112.
Jacobite Rebellions, 57.
Jamaica Library Work, by F. Cundall (Paper), 173; Discussion, 247.
Jamaica, Institute of, 175.
James, Alderman, on the Conference, 249.
James, Miss Hannah P., on Special Training for **Library Work (Paper)**, 34; Discussion, 231-2.
James, Miss M. S. R., on Women Librarians, 42.
James, William, Naval Historian, 173.
Japan and the Art of Printing, 7.
Jast, L. Stanley,
  On the Pseudonym in the Catalogue, 233.
  On Open Access, 245.
Jenner, Annabel, 113.
Jenson, Nicolas, 74.
Johnson, Dr. Samuel, and **His Disciples**, 57.
Jones, F. H., on **Open Access**, 244.
Jones, Herbert,
  On Library **Authorities: Their Powers and Duties (Paper)**, 23; Discussion, 230-1.
  On the Financial **Condition of** Libraries, 229.
  On the "**Dictionary of National Biography**," 233.
Jordan, Poet, 57.
Judge, Rev. Mr., **Teacher at the** Cape, 187.
Julian and Public Libraries, 14.
Juvenile Libraries, Children's Books:
  Books That Children Like, by Miss C. M. Hewins (Paper), 111; Discussion, 237-40.
  Our Youngest Readers, by J. C. Dana (Paper), 118; Discussion, 237-40.
  Children's Libraries at Manchester, 237.
  Children's Library at Chelsea, 238.
  Work of the London School Board, 238, 239, 240.
  Other School Libraries, 239.
  Home Libraries in America, 239.
  Other Work in America, 238, 239.

KAPP, F., 75.
Keble on National Apostacy, 59.
Kelly's (James) "American Catalogue," 151.
Kidd, Benjamin, quoted, 158.
Kingston (Jamaica) Libraries, 174.
Kirkstall Monastic Library, 15.
Klemming, G. E., 74.
Koberger, Antonij, 72, 75.
Korea and the Art of Printing, 5.
Krehbiel's (Henry E.) "Catalogue of Works on Music," 152, 170.
Kroeger, Miss Alice B., 37.
Kromberger, Jacob, Printer, 74.
Kyd, Thomas, on the Library Committee in Scotland, 231.

LAMB'S "Tales from Shakespeare," 48.
Lanciani's (R.) "Ancient Rome" referred to, 15.
Lane, W. Coolidge,
  On Co-operation in Library Work, 229.
  On the Cutter Classification, 235.
  On Printed Card-Catalogues, 242.
  On the Conference, 250.
Lang's (Andrew) Fairy Books, 112.
Langton, H. H.,
  On Co-operation in a Catalogue of Periodicals (Paper), 122; Discussion, 247-9.
  On the Conference, 248.

INDEX

Larned, Prof. J. N., 38.
  On the Organisation of Co-operative Work among Public Libraries (Paper), 120; Discussion, 242-3.
Laurence, Bishop, of Würzburg, 73.
Laurentian Library, Florence, 16, 109.
Law Libraries in 17th Century, 17.
Lelo's (Archbishop Gaspar de) "Spiritual Compendium of the Christian Life," 6.
Lecky's (W. E. H.) "England in the Eighteenth Century" and "History of Rationalism," 121.
Lectures in Public Libraries, 102, 236.
Lee, Ann, 52.
Lee, Sidney, on National Biography and National Bibliography (Paper), 55; Discussion, 239-3.
Leeds: School Libraries, 239.
Leeds Proprietary Library, 17.
Leibbrandt, H. C. V., on Education and Libraries of the Cape of Good Hope (Paper), 179.
Leist, F., 76.
Le Soudier, H., and the "Bibliographie Française," 150.
Levin's (W. H.) Gift to Wellington, N.Z., 199.
Lewis, "Monk," 173.
Leypoldt, Mrs. A. H., 152, 170.
Leypoldt, Frederick, Publisher, 150, 151.
Librarians and Assistants:
  Development of the Librarian, 17.
  Some Tendencies of Modern Librarianship, by J. V. W. MacAlister (Paper), 9; Discussion, 228-9.
  The Librarian of the Future, 18, 22.
  The Society of Public Librarians, 17.
  Salaries of Librarians, 45.
  The Library Assistants' Association, 17, 40.
  The Training of Librarians, by Charles Welch (Paper), 31; Discussion, 231-2.
  Hindrances to the Training of Efficient Librarians, by J. J. Ogle (Paper), 44; Discussion, 231-2.
  Special Training for Library Work, by Miss H. P. James (Paper), 34; Discussion, 231-2.
  Female Library Assistants and Competitive Examination, by E. R. Norris Mathews (Paper), 40; Discussion, 231-2.
  Women in Library Work, 18, 27, 231.
  Library Schools in America, 34, 42.
  Summer Schools in America, 38-39.
  Summer School of the Library Association, 27, 40.
Libraries:
  The Evolution of the Library, by H. R. Tedder (Paper), 13.
  Books and Text-Books: The Library as a Factor in Education, by F. M. Crunden (Paper), 46; Discussion, 232.
  The Relation of the State to the Public Library, by Melvil Dewey (Paper), 19; Discussion, 229-30.
  Libraries the Primary Factor in Human Evolution, by E. C. Richardson (Paper), 158.
  Children's Books, see Juvenile Libraries.
Libraries represented at the Conference, 273-4.
Libraries Abroad, see France, Germany, Italy, Norway, Sweden, Denmark, Finland.
Libraries under the Acts, see Public Libraries.
Libraries in the Colonies, see Africa, Australia, Canada, Jamaica, New Zealand.
Libraries in the United States, see American Library Work.
Library, 194.
"Library Age," 19.
Library Appliances, Library Work:
  Exhibition of Appliances, etc., 255.
  Bookcases in Mediæval Libraries, 15.

Library Appliances, etc.—contd.
  An Indicator-Catalogue Charging System, by Jacob Schwartz (Paper), 142; Discussion, 246.
  Freedom in Public Libraries, by W. H. Brett (Paper), 79; Discussion, 243-6.
  Library Architecture, see Architecture.
  Co-operation in Library Work, see Co-operation.
  Catalogues, see Cataloguing, Classification, Bibliography, etc.
  Books, Fiction, Newspapers, Periodicals, see Books, Fiction, Newspapers, Periodicals.
  Lectures, 102, 236.
  Library Work at Liverpool during Forty Years, by Peter Cowell (Paper), 99; Discussion, 236.
Library Assistants' Association, 17.
Library Association, 17, 29.
  Programmes, 132.
Library Association of America, see American Library Association.
Library Association of the Mersey District, 17.
Library Association of the Midlands, 17
Library Associations, Local, in the United States, by H. Putnam (Paper), 119; Discussion, 243.
Library Journal, 151.
Lighting of Libraries, 104, 237.
Lincoln Cathedral Library, 110.
Linde, A. v. d., 73.
Linotype Printing for Catalogues, etc., 153, 242.
"List of Books for Girls and Women," 152, 170.
Literature (see also Books, Bibliography, Cataloguing, Colonial Literature, etc. etc.):
  The Appraisal of Literature, by George Iles (Paper), 166.
  The Educational Aims of Libraries, see Libraries.
Liverpool Flora, 99.
Liverpool Proprietary Library, 17.
Liverpool Public Library:
  Reminiscences of Library Work in Liverpool during Forty Years, by Peter Cowell (Paper), 99; Discussion, 236.
  The Library Building, 240.
Local Government Board Act of 1894, 25.
Local Library Associations in the United States, by Herbert Putnam (Paper), 129; Discussion, 243.
London:
  Early Circulating Libraries, 17.
  Public Libraries Act, 2, 17.
London City Poets, 57.
London Library: Classified Index, 3.
Long, Edward, Historian, 173.
Longfellow's Poems, 48, 114.
Lord, Mrs., on Works of Fiction, 229.
Lord Mayor's Show, 57.
Los Angeles Library Classes, 38.
Louis XI. of France and the Book Trade, 75.
Love, E. F. J., on the Library Facilities of Scientific Investigators in Melbourne (Paper), 204.
Low, Sampson, Publisher, 150.
Lowell, James Russell, referred to, 46, 48.
Lowndes's (W. T.) "Bibliographer's Manual," 69, 61.
Lubbock, Sir John, 46, 70, 112, 117, President, 235, 237.
  Proposed Vote of Thanks to the Lord Mayor and Corporation, 227.
  Quoted, 49.
  On Library Progress: Inaugural Address, 1; Vote of Thanks, 228.
  On the Library Work of the London School Board, 240.
  On the Conference, 249.
Lucas, Rev. J. E., on Gas and Electricity, 237.
Lucullus, Book-Collector, 14.
Lund Royal University Library, 136.
Lundstedt, Dr. B., on the Conference, 247.

Lumisden's (Dr.) "History of Scottish Periodicals and Newspapers," 241.
Lyster, T. W., on Library Architecture, 240.

MacALISTER, J. Y. W.,
  On Some Tendencies of Modern Librarianship (Paper), 9; Discussion, 228-9.
  Seconded Vote of Thanks to Sir Henry Irving and Miss Ellen Terry, 247.
Macaulay, Lord, quoted, 47.
Macedo, Antonio, 7.
Macfarlane, J., on Australian Publications, 236.
McGill University Library, Montreal, 155.
MacKelvie (J. T.), Art Gallery, Auckland, 201.
Mackenzie, Prof. John S., quoted, 51.
Madeira : Printing at Funchal, 7-8.
Madeley, Charles,
  On Local Library Associations in England, 243.
  On Open Access, 244.
Magliabecchi, 17.
Maine Library Association, 130.
Maine State College Library Class, 38.
Manchester Public Libraries, 29-30.
  Women Librarians and Assistants, 27, 40, 231.
  Children's Libraries, 237.
Mandley, Alderman,
  On the Reading of Fiction, 229.
  On the Duties of Library Committees, 230.
Manila : Early Printing, 7.
Manuel, King of Portugal, and the Early Printers, 74.
Manutius, Paulus, Printer, 74, 76.
Marvell, Andrew, 61.
Massachusetts Historical Society, 167.
Massachusetts Library Club, 129, 130.
Mathews, E. R. Norris, on Female Library Assistants and Competitive Examination (Paper), 40 ; Discussion, 231-2.
Mauritius : Early Printing, 8.
Maximilian I., Emperor, 74.
Maxwell, Clerk, 168.
Mayas of Yucatan, 162.
Mayer, Brantz, 161.
Mazarin Library, Paris, 16, 17.
Meaux in Holderness Monastic Library, 15.
Mechanics' Institutions, 17.
Medina, José T., 6, 7.
Meissonier, Artist, 167.
Melbourne, see under Australia.
Members of the Conference, 259.
Mendicant Friars and Libraries, 15.
Mentelin, Johann, Printer, 73, 74, 76.
Mersey District Library Association, 17.
Merton College Library, 16, 110.
Metternich and the Book Trade, 78.
Mexican Time-Recording, 162.
Michigan Library Association, 132.
Middleton, Thomas, Poet, 57.
Midland Library Association, 17.
Miller, Patrick, and Steam Navigation, 57.
Mitra, Commissioner-General de, and Education at the Cape, 186.
Mitchell, David Scott, Library of, 93.
Mitchell's (Dr.) "The Orbs of Heaven," 2.
Mivart, Prof. St. George, quoted, 158.
Molson, William, Montreal, 155.
Monastic and Church Libraries, 14-16.
Monckton, Sir John, on the Conference, 250.
Montagu, Mrs. Elizabeth, Bluestocking, 57.
Montreal Libraries, by C. H. Gould (Paper), 154.
Mudge, Thomas, Watchmaker, 57.
Muggleton Sect, 57.
Mummenhoff, E., 77.
Munday, Poet, 57.
Murdoch, William, and Coal Gas Lighting, 57.
Murdoch's "Counting and Measuring among the Eskimo," 163.

Museums Association, 17.
Music in Public Libraries, 101.
Henry E. Krehbiel's "Catalogue of Works on Music," 152, 170.

NAMUR, Librarian, 17.
Nassau, Count Adolf of, and Gutenberg, 73, 74.
Nation of New York, 169.
National Art Library: History and Cataloguing of the Library, by W. H. J. Weale (Paper), 97.
National Home Reading Union referred to, 9, 177.
Natural History Museum: Building, 240.
Nebraska Library Club, 130.
Netley Monastic Library, 15.
New South Wales, *see under* Australia.
New York Library Club, 129.
New York Library Association, 129.
New York Public Library: Card-Catalogue, 128.
New York State Libraries Department, 22.
New York State Library School at Albany, 34-37, 39, 42.
New York State Summer School, 38.
New Zealand:
Public Libraries, 1.
Public Libraries in New Zealand, by Thomas W. Rowe (Paper), 199.
Auckland Free Public Library, by Edw. Shillington (Paper), 201.
Newberry Library, Chicago, 127.
Newcastle-on-Tyne Literary and Philosophical Society's Library: Heating, etc., 237.
Newman, Cardinal, 58, 59.
Newspapers in Libraries, 19-20, 28-29, 229, 230.
Nicholson, Sir Charles, Sydney, 197.
Nietzsche, Friedrich, quoted, 79.
Nolan, Capt., and the Charge of the Light Brigade, 57.
Nordin, J. G., 74.
North, Lord, and the American Colonies, 48.
North American Review Book Lists, 150.
"Northern Myths," 115.
Northwestern University Library, 127.
Norton, Charles B., 151.
Norton, Prof. Charles Eliot, quoted, 59.
Norton, Dr. James, 94.
Norway: Public Libraries, 137.
Norwich: School Libraries, 239.
Nottingham Mechanics' Institution: Open Access, 245.
Nova Scotia, Legislative Library of, 146.
Novels, *see* Fiction.
Noyes's (S. B.) Catalogue of the Brooklyn Library, 68, 152.
Nürnberg, Council of, and Antonj Koberger, 72.

OGLE, J. J.,
On Hindrances to the Training of Efficient Librarians (Paper), 44; Discussion, 231-2.
"The Free Library," 228.
On the Cutter Classification, 235.
On the Sturtevant System of Ventilation, 236.
On the Printing of Catalogues, 242.
On Mr. Steenberg, 243.
Open Access, 18.
Freedom in Public Libraries, by W. H. Brett (Paper), 79; Discussion, 243-6.
An Indicator-Catalogue Charging System, by Jacob Schwartz (Paper), 142; Discussion, 246.
"Orbs of Heaven," by Dr. Mitchell, 2.
O'Kelly, Max, in the Catalogue, 63.
Otlet, Paul, on the International Institute of Bibliography at Brussels, 241.
Ouida in the Catalogue, 63.
Owens College, Manchester, 28.

Oxford:
Bodleian Library, 8, 17.
College Libraries, 16, 110.
Oxford Movement, 59.

PACCONIO, FRANCISCO, referred to, 5.
Palmer, G. H., 97.
Panizzi, Sir A., referred to, 9, 17.
Pannartz, Printer, 73.
Paris:
Library at St. Germain-des-Prés, 16.
Sorbonne Library, 16.
The Bibliothèque Mazarine, 16, 17.
Parkhurst, Dr., quoted, 51.
Parkman, Francis, Historian, 167.
Pattison, Mark, quoted, 12.
Paulus, Aemilius, Book-Collector, 14.
Peabody Institute (Baltimore) Catalogue, 152.
Peacock, Dr., 160.
Peacock, Thomas, Auckland, 201.
Peacock, Thomas Love, 61.
Peddie, R. A.,
On the Financial Condition of Libraries, etc., 232.
On the Pseudonym in the Catalogue, 233.
On the Form of Catalogue, 234.
On Classification, 235.
On Co-operation in the Printing of Catalogues, 243.
Peignot, Librarian, 17.
Pellechet's (Mlle.) Catalogue of French Incunabula, 65.
Peh, Very Rev. Daniel, 188.
Penny Rate, 29-30, 45.
Pergamus: Early Libraries, 14.
Periodicals:
Selection of Periodicals, 28-29.
Periodicals in the Liverpool Public Library, 99-99.
Co-operation in a Catalogue of Periodicals, by H. H. Langton (Paper), 122; Discussion, 242-3.
Poole's "Index to Periodical Literature," 121, 153.
W. H. Brett's "Cumulative Index to Periodical Literature," 153.
Persia and the Art of Printing, 6.
Pertz, Heinrich, 74.
Peruvian "Quipos," 161.
Petherbridge, Miss, on the American Library School, 41.
Petherick, Edward A., on Theoretical and Practical Bibliography (Paper), 148; Discussion, 246.
Petzholdt, Librarian, 17.
Philadelphia: Drexel Institute Library Class, 37-38, 39.
Philadelphia Library Company, 17.
Philippine Ids.: Printing at Manila, 7.
Phillips, Wendell, quoted, 46.
Photius, 15.
Pilgrim Fathers, 57.
"Pindar, Peter," 173.
Pisistratus, Book-Collector, 13.
Pite, Beresford, on Library Architecture from the Architect's Standpoint (Paper), 106; Discussion, 240-1.
Plummer, Miss Mary Wright, 37.
Plymouth: School Libraries, 239.
Poe's (E. A.) "Goldbug," 49.
Political Science Quarterly, 169.
Pollard, Alfred W., on the Relations of Bibliography and Cataloguing (Paper), 63; Discussion, 233-4.
Polfio, Asinius, and Libraries, 14.
"Polynesia, Bibliography of," 149.
Poole's "Index to Periodical Literature," 121, 153.
Port Elizabeth Library, S. Africa, 192.
"Porter Collection" in the Public Library, Capetown, 192.
Portfolio Book Lists, 150.
Portugal: Early Printing, 74.
Portuguese Introduction of Printing into India, 5-6.
Pratt Institute (Brooklyn) Library School, 37, 39.
Premonstratensians and Libraries, 15.
Presidential Address, by Sir John Lubbock, 1; Discussion, and Vote of Thanks, 228.
Prevost, C. M., 213.
Priests as Librarians, 17.

Pringle, Thomas, Librarian at the Cape, 191.
Printing, *see* Typography.
Printing of Catalogues, *see under* Cataloguing.
Proceedings of the Conference, 227-250.
Proprietary Libraries, 17.
Pseudonyms in the Catalogue, 63, 233.
Public Librarians, Society of, 17.
Public Libraries:
General Statistics, 1.
The Evolution of the Public Library, by H. R. Tedder (Paper), 11.
The Educational Aim of Libraries, *see* Libraries.
Library Appliances, Library Work, *see* Library Appliances, etc.
Librarians and Assistants, *see* Librarians.
Public Libraries under the Acts:
Ewart Act of 1850, 1, 17, 27, 72.
Adoptions of the Act, 1.
Adoptions in London, 1, 17.
Library Authorities: Their Powers and Duties, by Herbert Jones (Paper), 23; Discussion, 230-1.
The Duties of Library Committees, by Alderman H. Rawson (Paper), 27; Discussion, 230-1.
The Penny Rate, 29-30, 45.
Income Tax Case at Manchester, 29-30.
Publisher's Circular referred to, 28.
"Publishers' Trade List Annual," 150.
Publishers' Weekly, 152.
Purcell's (E. S.) "Cardinal Manning," 167.
Putnam's (George Haven) "Best Reading," 152.
Putnam, George P., Publisher of "American Facts," 150; Roorbach's "Bibliotheca Americana," 151; and the "Bookbuyer's Manual," 152.
Putnam, Herbert,
On Local Library Associations in the United States (Paper), 129; Discussion, 243.
On Children's Reading, 238-9.
On the Printing of Catalogues by the Linotype Machine, 242.
On Open Access, 245.
Pynson, Richard, Printer, 73.

QUARE, DANIEL, Watchmaker, 57.
Quarterly Review referred to, 8, 29.
Quinn, J. H.,
On Children's Libraries, 238.
On the Use of Cards with Open Access, 246.

RADFORD, J. T., on Open Access, 245.
Raglan, Lord, 57.
Rainier, Archduke, 5.
Raleigh (Sir Walter) Bibliography, 56.
Rameses 1, and Libraries, 13, 18.
"Ramona," 116.
Ramsay, Allan, Poet, 17, 57.
Ratdolt, Erhart, 74.
Rate levied, 29-30, 45.
Rawson, Alderman Harry,
Seconded Vote of Thanks to the Lord Mayor, 228.
Chairman, 247.
On the Duties of Library Committees (Paper), 27; Discussion, 230-1.
On the Foreign Delegates, 247.
"Reader's Guide in Economic, Social, and Political Science," by G. Iles and R. R. Bowker, 152, 170.
"Reading for the Young," by Sargent, 153.
Redpath, Peter, Montreal, 155.
Reede, Commander-General H. A. van, and Education at the Cape, 180.
"Reference Catalogue of English Literature," 150.
"Reference Trade List" (of Books), by A. V. Blake, 150.
Registration of Colonial Publications, *see* Colonial Literature.
Rein, Dr., 47.
Reinet (Graaff) Library, S. Africa, 192.

INDEX

Kenouard, A. A., 76.
Rewick, E., 76.
Reyser, Joorius, Printer, 74.
Rhenius, Johannes Isaac, of the Cape, 169.
Rich's (Obadinh) "Bibliotheca Americana Nova," 151.
Richardson, Ernest Cushing, on Libraries the Primary Factor in Human Evolution (Paper), 158.
Richardson, Henry, on Heating, etc., 237.
Richardson, H. H., American Architect, 107.
Richardson, Miss, on Women Librarians, 42.
Riggs's (Dr. S. R.) "Dacota Grammar," 160.
Robertson, A. W., on Classification in Public Libraries (Paper), 69; Discussion, 235–6.
Rodenburg, Rear-Adm. Cornelis de Jong van, quoted, 191.
Rome, Ancient:
  Care of State Documents, 13.
  Early Libraries, 14, 15, 17.
  The Roman Use of Numbers, 162–3.
Rome, Modern:
  Early Printing, 73, 74.
  Early Ecclesiastical Libraries, 15.
  The Vatican Library, 14.
Rosebach's (O. A.) "Bibliotheca Americana," 151.
Rowe, Thomas W., on Public Libraries in New Zealand (Paper), 199.
Royal Astronomical Society's Library: Classification, 235.
Royal Colonial Institute and the Registration of Colonial Publications, 3.
Royal Society's Catalogue of Scientific Papers, 3, 123.

SABIN'S (JOSEPH) "Bibliotheca Americana," 151–2.
Sacheverell, Henry, 59.
St. Germain-des-Prés Library, 16.
St. John's College (Cambridge) Library, 16, 110.
St. Mary's College Library, Montreal, 154.
St. Sulpice Seminary Library, Montreal, 154.
Saintsbury's (G.) "Calendar of the Paper of the East India Company" referred to, 6.
Sanctos, Ribeiro dos, 6.
Sande, Eduardus de, 6, 7.
Sandeman Sect, 57.
Sargent's "Reading for the Young," 153.
Sargent's "Standard Speaker," 47.
Satow, Sir Ernest Mason, and Printing in Japan, 7.
Saunders's (Marshall) "Beautiful Joe," 112.
Schlecht, Jos., 73.
Schmidt, Charles, 73.
Schnorrenberg, J., 74.
Schoeffer, Peter, 74, 77.
Schoesperger, Hans, Printer, 74.
School Libraries in Sweden, 137.
Schwartz, Jacob, on an Indicator-Catalogue Charging System (Paper), 142; Discussion, 246.
Science:
  Catalogue of Scientific Papers compiled by the Royal Society, 3, 123.
  Scudder's Catalogue of Scientific Serials, 123, 124.
  Bibliographies of Special Subjects, 247.
  Library Facilities of Scientific Investigators in Melbourne, by E. F. J. Love (Paper), 204.
  The Australian Museum Library, by Sutherland Sinclair (Paper), 207.
  Scientific Libraries in Sweden, 135; Norway, 137; Denmark, 138; Finland, 140.
Scipio at Carthage, 13.
Scotland: The Constitution of Library Committees, 231.
Scott, Michael, 173.

Scott, Thomas, and his Biblical Commentaries, 58.
Scott, Sir Walter,
  Quoted, 117.
  His Works, 48, 52, 115–6.
  Scott Bibliography, 56.
Scudder's "Catalogue of Scientific Serials," 123, 124.
Sennenschmidt, J., Printer, 74.
Serrurier, Rev. J. P., Librarian at the Cape, 169, 191.
Settle, Elkanah, Poet, 59.
Shakers, 57.
Shakespeare Bibliography, 55, 65, 87–8.
Shakespeare Memorial Library, 233.
Shakespeare's Plays, 111, 114, 116.
Sharp, Miss Katharine L., 38.
  On Home Libraries for Children in America, 239.
Shaw, G. T., on the Linotype for the Printing of Catalogues, 247.
Shelley's (Mrs.) "Frankenstein," 99.
Shillington, Edward, on Auckland Public Library (Paper), 201.
Simon, Jules, quoted, 46.
Sinclair, Sutherland, on the Australian Museum Library (Paper), 207.
Sixtus IV., Pope, and the Early Printers, 73.
Sixtus V., Pope, and the Vatican Library, 14.
Slicher, Rev. I., of the Cape, 181.
Sloane, Sir Hans, 173.
Small, Prof. Albion W., quoted, 50.
Smirke, Sir Robert, 110.
Smith, George, Publisher of the "Dictionary of National Biography," 55, 67, 232, 233.
Smith, Prof. Goldwin, quoted, 160.
Smith's (Russell) "Bibliotheca Americana," 151.
Smith, Soden, 97.
Smith, Sydney, 46.
Smithsonian Institution, 124, 125.
Social Proceedings of the Conference, 251.
Société Franklin of Paris, 171.
Somerset, Lord Charles, and Education and Libraries at the Cape, 186, 187, 189, 190.
Sonnenschein's (Wm. Swan) Bibliographies, etc., 57, 58.
  "Best Books," 152.
Sorbonne Library, 16.
Sorel, Agnes, 163.
Southern, Alderman J. W.,
  On Librarians, 231.
  On Open Access, 244.
Spain: The Escurial Library, 16.
Speier, John and Wendelin of, Printers, 73.
Spencer, Herbert, quoted, 13, 47, 52, 53, 158.
Stadloe, Hermann, 74, 77.
Steenberg, A. C.,
  On the Public Libraries of the Northern States of Europe (Paper), 135; Discussion, 243.
  On the Conference, 97.
Stel, Commander Simon van der, and Education at the Cape, 180.
Stel, Governor Willem Adriaan van der, and Education at the Cape, 180.
Stephen, Leslie, 60; "English Thought in the Eighteenth Century," 121.
Stevens, Henry, Publisher, 151.
Stevenson's (Robert Louis) "Weir of Hermiston," 169.
Stevenson, W. M., Librarian, 169.
Stewart's (J.) "Jamaica" quoted, 173.
Stockholm Libraries, 135, 137.
Stockholm Royal Library, 135.
Stowe's (Mrs.) "Uncle Tom's Cabin," 116–117.
Strabo referred to, 13.
Sturgis's (Russell) "Catalogue of Works on the Fine Arts," 152, 170.
Sturtevant System, 236.
Subject-Catalogues, see Bibliography, etc.
Subscription Libraries: Philadelphia Library Company, 17.
Success, Definition of, 46.
Suidas referred to, 14.
Sulla, Book-Collector, 14.

Sully, James, quoted, 9.
Summer Schools, see under Education.
Sumner, Prof. W. G., 170.
Sweden:
  Early Printing, 74.
  Public Libraries, 135.
Sweynheim, Printer, 73.
Sydney, Sir Philip, quoted, 8.
Sydney, see under Australia.
Sydney Gazette 1803, 8.
Sylvestre's "Palæography," 163.

TALLIES AND NOTCHES, 161.
Tamil Books printed in India, 6.
Tasmania: Early Printing, 8.
Taxation of Public Libraries, see under Finance.
Technical Education, 17, 19.
Tedder, Henry R.,
  On the Evolution of the Public Library (Paper), 13.
  Shakespeare Bibliography, 56.
  On the Training of Librarians, 231.
  On the "Dictionary of National Biography," 232.
  On the Electric Fan, 237.
  On Dr. Lundstedt's History of Periodicals, 241.
  Financial Statement as Treasurer, 227.
Terry, Miss Ellen, 249, 251.
Theodolus and Public Libraries, 14.
Thermostat Apparatus, 105, 236.
Thomason's Collection of 17th Century Tracts, 61.
Thorburn, John, on Counting and Time-Recording (Paper), 160.
Thring, Edward, quoted, 51.
Tiberius and Public Libraries, 14.
Time-Recording and Counting, by John Thorburn (Paper), 160.
Times referred to, 99.
Tintern Monastic Library, 15.
"Title and Slip Registry" (of Books), 152.
Titles of Books, 2.
"Trade Circular Annual," 150.
Traill, H. D., quoted, 3.
Training of Librarians, see under Librarians.
Travelling Libraries in America, 22.
Travelling Libraries in New South Wales, 94.
Trinity College Library, 16.
"Tropical Readers" Series, 177.
Trübner, Nicholas, Publisher, 151.
Typography:
  On the Aids lent by Public Bodies to the Art of Printing in the Early Days of Typography, by C. Driatzko (Paper), 72.
  Introduction of European Printing into the East, by Dr. R Garnett (Paper), 5.
  Early Printed Books at the Capetown Public Library, 188–192.
  Early Printed Books in the Auckland Public Library, 199, 201–202.
  Cataloguing of Early Printed Books, 64–65.
  Hain's "Repertorium," 64.
  Printing of Catalogues, see under Cataloguing.

ULMAN LIBRARY, 14.
"Uncle Remus," 112.
"Uncle Tom's Cabin," 116–117.
United States Libraries, etc., see American Library Work.
University and College Libraries:
  Early Libraries, 16–17, 110.
  Cambridge: St. John's, etc., 16, 110.
  Oxford: Merton College, 16, 110.
  McGill University Library, Montreal, 155.
  Sydney University Library, by H. E. Barff (Paper), 197.
  University Libraries in Sweden, Norway, Denmark, Finland, 136–140.
Upsala Royal University Library, 136.
d'Urban, Sir Benjamin, and Education at the Cape, 189.
Ure's (Dr.) Thermostat, 105, 236.

INDEX

VALIGNANUS, ALEXANDER, 6.
Varro, 14.
Vatican Library, 14.
Venice: Early Printing, 75-76.
Ventilation of Libraries, 105, 237.
Vera, Juan de, Printer, 7.
Verney, Miss, of Middle Claydon, 177.
Victoria, see under Australia.
Village Libraries in Yorkshire, 236.
Vincent, C. W.,
  On the Catalogue, 234.
  On the Libraries of the London School Board, 238.

WADDELL, W. R., Auckland, 201.
Wagenaar, Z., and Education at the Cape, 179.
Wagner's Music-Dramas, 167.
Waldan, G. E., 77.
Wales : Welsh History, 57.
Walker, R. C., Librarian, 93.
Walworth, E. H., on English National Archives, 2.
Warner, Charles **Dudley**, **quoted**, 52.
Washington Library Association, 130-131.

Watson, D., on Heating, 237.
Watt's (Robert) "Bibliotheca Britannica," 60, 61.
Watts, Librarian and Scholar, 17.
Weale, W. H. James,
  On the History and Cataloguing of the National Art Library (Paper), 97.
  On the Pseudonym in the **Catalogue**, 233.
Welch, Councillor, on Cataloguing, 233.
Welch, Charles,
  On the Training of Librarians (Paper), 31 ; Discussion, 231-2.
  On the Conference, 250.
Wellington, N.Z., Public **Library**, 199-200.
Wesley, W. **H.**, **on Classification, 235.**
Westminster **Cathedral Library, 16.**
Westminster **Public Library referred** to, 1.
White Ant in Jamaica, 178.
Whittier's Poems, 114.
Winsor, Dr. Justin,
  Proposed Vote of Thanks **to Sir** John Lubbock, 228.
  Chairman, 234.

Winsor, Dr. Justin—contd.
  On the Société Franklin of Paris, 171.
  On the "Dictionary of National Biography," 232.
  On the Catalogue, 234.
  On Heating and Ventilation, 237.
Wisconsin University Summer School, 38.
Wolverhampton Public Library : Lectures, 236.
Women Librarians, see under Librarians.
Wotton quoted, 52.
Wren, Sir Christopher, **16, 110.**
Wright, W. H. K.,
  On Fiction in Libraries, 229.
  On School Libraries, 239.
Wright, Dr., **173.**

YONGE, SIR **GEORGE**, Governor at the Cape, 189.
Yorkshire Village Libraries, 236.
Young, Sir Frederick,
  On Cataloguing, 233.
  On Library Architecture, 240.
Youngest Readers, see Juvenile Libraries.
Yucatan Time-Recording, 162.

E. H.

PRINTED BY MORRISON AND GIBB LIMITED, EDINBURGH.

www.ingramcontent.com/pod-product-compliance
Lightning Source LLC
Chambersburg PA
CBHW032048230426
43672CB00009B/1518